Lexique juridique des lois fédérales

Legal Glossary of Federal Statutes

P9-EDZ-908

Bulletin de terminologie 192

Terminology Bulletin 192

Projet conjoint / Joint Project

SECRÉTARIAT D'ÉTAT DU CANADA

MINISTÈRE DE LA JUSTICE DU CANADA

DEPARTMENT OF THE SECRETARY OF STATE OF CANADA

DEPARTMENT OF JUSTICE CANADA

Données de catalogage avant publication (Canada)

Vedette principale au titre:

Lexique juridique des lois fédérales = Legal glossary of federal statutes.

(Bulletin de terminologie = Terminology bulletin ; 192)
Texte en français et en anglais.
Publié par le Bureau de la traduction, Direction de la terminologie et des services linguistiques.
ISBN: 0-660-54823-2

1. Canada. Lois révisées du Canada (1985)--Termes. 2. Droit--Canada--Termes. 3. Anglais (Langue)--Dictionnaires français. 4. Français (Langue)--Dictionnaires anglais. I. Canada. Secrétariat d'État du Canada. II. Canada. Ministère de la justice. III. Canada. Bureau de la traduction. Direction de la terminologie et des services linguistiques. IV. Titre: Legal glossary of federal statutes. V. Coll.: Bulletin de terminologie (Canada. Bureau de la traduction. Direction de la terminologie et des services linguistiques) ; 192.

KE184.L49   1989   348.71'003
C89-099414-5F

Canadian Cataloguing in Publication Data

Main entry under title:

Lexique juridique des lois fédérales = Legal glossary of federal statutes.

(Bulletin de terminologie = Terminology bulletin ; 192)
Text in English and French.
Issued by the Translation Bureau, Terminology and Linguistic Services Directorate.
ISBN: 0-660-54823-2

1. Canada. Revised statutes of Canada, 1985--Terms and phrases. 2. Law--Canada--Terms and phrases. 3. English language--Dictionaries--French. 4. French language--Dictionaries--English. I. Canada. Dept. of Secretary of State of Canada. II. Canada. Dept. of Justice. III. Canada. Translation Bureau. Terminology and Linguistic Services Directorate. IV. Title: Legal glossary of federal statutes. V. Series: Bulletin de terminologie (Canada. Translation Bureau. Terminology and Linguistic Services Directorate) ; 192.

KE184.L49   1989   348.71'003
C89-099414-5E

REF.

61,498

Table des matières

Table of Contents

Avant-propos

Déjà partenaires dans la normalisation de la common law en français, la Direction de la terminologie et des services linguistiques et le ministère fédéral de la Justice s'associent de nouveau pour préparer le **Lexique juridique des lois fédérales** qu'ils présentent aux juristes canadiens.

L'évolution qu'a connue la rédaction législative depuis quelques années a entraîné des modifications importantes dans le style et la terminologie des lois fédérales. Les Lois révisées du Canada (1985) ne sont plus libellées comme les Statuts révisés du Canada (1970).

Je suis convaincu que le présent lexique constituera une source de référence indispensable aux magistrats, juristes, traducteurs et à tous ceux qui doivent consulter les deux versions - anglaise et française - des lois fédérales. Je remercie et je fécilite tous ceux qui y ont collaboré.

Foreword

As was the case for the standardization of the common law in French, the Terminology and Linguistic Services Directorate and the Federal Department of Justice have once again combined their efforts in producing the **Legal Glossary of Federal Statutes** which they are now pleased to present to the Canadian legal community.

The evolution which took place in legislative drafting over the past few years has brought many significant changes in the wording and terminology of the federal statutes. In this respect, the Revised Statutes of Canada of 1985 differ greatly from the Revised Statutes of 1970.

I personally believe this glossary will prove to be invaluable as a reference tool for judges, jurists, translators and all those who need statutes. I wish to congratulate and thank all those who participated in the development of this publication.

Le sous-secrétaire d'État adjoint
(Langues officielles et Traduction),

Alain Landry
Assistant Under Secretary of State
(Official Languages and Translation)

Introduction

Le **Lexique juridique des lois fédérales** contient les termes juridiques relevés dans les Lois révisées du Canada (1985) ainsi que dans les quatre premiers suppléments. Au total, près de 20 000 pages de textes de lois ont été dépouillées.

Le présent lexique comprend principalement des termes et expressions qui sont porteurs d'une notion juridique. Nous avons écarté à dessein les termes techniques qui relevaient d'autres domaines que le droit. Dans certains cas, il nous a été difficile de trancher; nous avons donc inclus des termes techniques laissant à l'usager le soin de tirer ses propres conclusions.

Le dépouillement des textes de lois a été confié à sept avocats, et leur travail a été révisé par un jurilinguiste expérimenté. Une équipe qui avait déjà travaillé à la publication d'un lexique similaire portant sur des lois provinciales, a été chargée du traitement informatique des données.

Nous espérons que ce lexique saura répondre aux besoins des juristes canadiens, quel que soit leur domaine de spécialité.

Nous invitons le lecteur à communiquer ses observations à l'adresse suivante :

Direction de la terminologie et des
    services linguistiques
Secrétariat d'État du Canada
Ottawa (Ontario)
K1A 0M5

Introduction

The **Legal Glossary of Federal Statutes** comprises the legal terms contained in the Revised Statutes of Canada (1985) and in the first four supplements thereto. Altogether, nearly 20 000 pages of federal legislation were scanned for this project.

This glossary lists mainly terms and expressions relating to legal concepts. Technical terms pertaining to fields other than law have been for the most part excluded. However, in some cases, the distinction was slurry which resulted in some technical terms being included in the glossary, leaving users to draw their own conclusions.

The scanning of the federal statutes was performed by seven lawyers and their product was revised by an experienced jurilinguist. A team that previously developed a similar glossary based on provincial legislation was responsible for the processing of the terminological data.

We hope this glossary will meet the needs of the Canadian jurists whatever their specialty.

Any comments on the **Glossary** should be forwarded to the following address:

Terminology and Linguistic
    Services Branch
Department of the Secretary of
    State of Canada
Ottawa, Ontario
K1A 0M5

Avec la participation de / With the participation of

Dépouillement des lois / Scanning of statutes

David Bolger, avocat / lawyer
Lise Croteau-Coderre, avocate / lawyer
Florence Fortin, avocate / lawyer
Julie Gagnon-Gravelle, avocate / lawyer
Geneviève Parent, avocate / lawyer
Lyne Pelletier, avocate / lawyer
François Ramsay, avocat / lawyer

Révision et coordination / Revision and Coordination

Normand Bélair, jurilinguiste / jurilinguist

Traitement informatique des données / Processing of the Terminological Data

Université d'Ottawa / University of Ottawa

Andrée Duchesne
Chef, Section de terminologie juridique / Chief, Legal Terminology Section
Direction de la terminologie et des services linguistiques / Terminology
  Directorate and Linguistic Services
Secrétariat d'État du Canada / Department of the Secretary of State of
  Canada

Dans le cadre du Programme national de l'administration de la justice dans
  les deux langues officielles / Within the framework of the National Program
  for the Integration of the two Official Languages in the Administration of
  Justice

Me Réjean Patry, coordonnateur / coordinator
Programme national de l'administration de la justice dans les deux langues
  officielles / National Program for the Integration of the two Official
  Languages in the Administration of Justice
Ministère de la Justice du Canada / Department of Justice Canada.

Guide d'utilisation

Les entrées sont classées dans l'ordre alphabétique des termes ou du premier mot des expressions :

Exemples : term
         term of year
         terms and conditions

Le lexique ne tient pas compte des occurrences. Ainsi lorsque l'équivalent français pour un terme ou une expression est le même dans plusieurs textes, une seule source est indiquée.

Index français-anglais

L'index français-anglais vise principalement à faciliter le repérage des entrées anglaises à partir des termes français. Il ne se pose pas comme un outil de traduction vers l'anglais des termes français.

Parenthèses

Nous avons utilisé les parenthèses pour signaler un contexte d'utilisation.

Exemple : shareholder (of a
          company)

Renvois

Tous les termes et expressions ont été repérés dans les Lois révisées du Canada (1985). La mention "R.S.C. 1985" n'apparaît donc qu'une fois au haut de chaque page.

Pour ce qui est de la terminologie du Code criminel, le chapitre C-46 est l'unique source mentionnée même si nous avons tenu compte des modifications apportées dans le premier supplément.

User's Guide

Single-word entries are listed in alphabetical order, followed by multiple-word entries beginning with the same word, in word-by-word order:

Examples: term
         term of year
         terms and conditions

The frequency of French equivalents has not been taken into account for this glossary. Consequently only one source is mentioned even though the same French equivalent of a term or expression may be used in numerous texts.

French-English Index

The index is designed to facilitate consultation of English entries when the French term is known. It is not intended as a tool for translating French terms into English.

Parentheses

Parentheses are used to indicate a usage context.

Example: shareholder (of a
          company)

Cross-references

All the terms and expressions have been drawn from the Revised Statutes of Canada of 1985, and the first four supplements thereto. Therefore, the abbreviation "R.S.C. 1985" appears only once at the top of each page.

Regarding the terminology of the Criminal Code, chapter C-46 is the sole source indicated even though we have taken into account the amendments appearing in the first supplement.

a

abandon/to
 (an appeal)   abandonner
  c. C-46, s. 695(2)
 (rights)   délaisser
  c. B-3, s. 81(2)
 abandon or expose/to   abandonner ou exposer
  c. C-46, s. 214
abandonment
 taking or abandonment (of   prise de possession ou cession
 property)
  c. C-25, s. 11(1)
abate/to
 (a proceeding)   devenir caduc
  c. B-3, s. 213
 (fees)   réduire
  c. B-3, s. 197(7)
abatement
 (of a petition)   annulation
  c. C-39, s. 81
abduction   enlèvement
  c. C-46, s. 7(3)
 child abduction   enlèvement d'enfant
  c. 4 (2nd Supp.), s. 10(1)
 kidnapping, hostage taking and   enlèvement, prise d'otage et rapt
 abduction
  c. C-46, s. 279
abet/to
 abet any person to commit an   encourager
 offence/to
  c. C-46, s. 21(1)(c)
 aid, consent, abet or procure the   aider, assister, conseiller ou amener
 commission of an offence/to   quelqu'un à commettre une
         infraction
  c. C-39, s. 57
ability   faculté
  c. A-14, s. 2
ABN Bank Canada   Banque ABN du Canada
  c. B-1, Schedule II
abode
 at his latest or usual place of   à sa dernière ou habituelle
 abode   résidence
  c. C-46, s. 509(2)
aboriginal
 aboriginal peoples of Canada   peuples autochtones du Canada
  Constitutional Act, 1982,
   Schedule B, s. 35(1)
abortion   avortement
  c. C-46, s. 163(2)(c)
abrogate/to
 (a provision)   abroger
  c. B-3, s. 72(1)
 abrogate or derogate (from a   porter atteinte
 rule)
  c. C-3, s. 22(3)
abscond/to
 (an accused)   s'esquiver
  c. C-46, s. 475(1)
 (from Canada)   s'évader
  c. B-3, s. 168(1)(a)

(witness)
    c. C-46, s. 704(1)   s'esquiver

absence
  unavoidable absence   cas d'absence forcée
    c. L-2, s. 190(h)

absentee
  deserter or absentee without   déserteur ou absent sans
  leave (from the Canadian   permission
  Forces)
    c. C-46, s. 420(1)

absolute
  absolute discharge   libération inconditionnelle
    c. Y-1, s. 36(2)
  absolute jurisdiction   juridiction absolue
    c. C-46, s. 536(1)
  absolute privilege   immunité absolue
    c. C-44, s. 234
  absolute title   titre définitif de propriété
    c. B-1, s. 185(1)

absolutely
  (to terminate)   définitivement
    c. C-25, s. 12(1)(a)
  either absolutely or subject to   soit absolument, soit sous réserve
  such exceptions   des exceptions
    c. A-2, s. 8(1)(f)

abstract
  abstract of title   extrait de titre
    c. C-46, s. 385(1)
  extract or abstract (of a report)   extrait ou résumé
    c. P-1, s. 9

academic
  academic year   année scolaire
    c. C-28, Schedule 5(1)

accede/to
  (to the Convention)   accéder
    c. C-42, Schedule II, Article
    25

accelerate/to
  accelerate death/to   hâter la mort
    c. C-46, s. 226

acceptance
  (of a bill or note)   acceptation
    c. B-4, s. 6(2)(b)
  acceptance for honour under   acceptation par intervention
  protest
    c. B-4, s. 151(1)
  general or qualified acceptance   acceptation générale ou restreinte
  (of a bill)
    c. B-4, s. 37(1)
  unqualified acceptance   acceptation pure et simple
    c. B-4, s. 82(1)

accepting
  making, accepting, discounting   création, acceptation, escompte ou
  or endorsing of a bill of   endossement d'une lettre de
  exchange, cheque, draft or   change, d'un chèque, d'une traite
  promissary note   ou d'un billet à ordre
    c. C-46, s. 362(1)(c)(vi)
  party accepting (a bill)   accepteur
    c. B-4, s. 39(1)(a)

acception
  (of a bill)   accepteur (d'une lettre de change)
    c. B-4, s. 128

acceptor
    (of a bill)   accepteur
        c. B-4, s. 145(e)
    (of an offer)   acceptant
        c. B-1, s. 110(6)(b)

access
    (to children)   accès
        c. C-3, s. 16(1)
    access right (to a child)   droit d'accès
        c. 4 (2nd Supp.), s. 2
    access to information   accès aux documents
        c. A-1, s. 2(1)
    free and unimpeded access   libre accès
        c. C-25, s. 14
    full and equal access (to courts)   universalité d'accès
        c. 31 (4th Supp.), s. preamble
    request for access   demande de communication
        c. A-1, s. 3
    right of access to or visitation (of   droit d'accès ou de visite
    a child)
        c. 4 (2nd Supp.), s. 2

accessibility
    (of health care insurance plan)   accessibilité
        c. C-6, s. 7(e)

accession
    (to a convention)   adhésion
        c. C-26, Schedule I, Article
        38(1)
    (to the Convention)   accession
        c. C-42, Schedule II, Article
        25

accessory
    accessory after the fact   complice après le fait
        c. C-46, s. 23(1)

acclamation   élection par acclamation
    c. C-24, s. 17(3)(g)

accommodated
    party accommodated (by a bill)   bénéficiaire de la complaisance
        c. B-4, s. 138(3)

accommodation
    private accommodation   logement privé
        c. C-46, s. 431

accomodation
    food, lodging or other   aliments, logement ou autres
    accomodation (at an inn)   commodités
        c. C-46, s. 364(1)
    housing accomodation of the   facilités de logement de type foyer
    hostel or dormitory type   ou pension
        c. N-11, s. 9(3)(a)(ii)

accordance
    in accordance with (an Act)   aux termes de
        c. A-10, s. 13(3)

according to   conformément à
    c. A-11, s. 21(1)
    according to the practice of the   conformément à la procédure
    court (Supreme Court)   devant la Cour
        c. S-26, s. 63

account   compte
    c. F-11, s. 7(1)(c)
    account receivable   compte-client
        c. B-1, s. 193(1)
    banking account   compte de banque
        c. B-3, s. 6(2)

book of account — livre de comptabilité
  c. B-3, s. 200(1)(a)
contributed surplus account — compte surplus d'apport
  c. B-1, s. 120(2)
in the name or on the account of another person — au nom ou pour le compte d'une autre personne
  c. C-46, s. 374(a)
on account of insanity — pour cause d'aliénation mentale
  c. C-46, s. 614(1)
  c. Y-1, s. 13(1)(b)
paid-in capital account — compte capital versé
  c. B-1, s. 120(1)
pay account — compte de solde
  c. C-17, s. 53(1)
render the final account/to (liquidation) — faire une reddition de comptes définitive
  c. C-44, s. 217(o)

Account
Superannuation Account — compte de pension de retraite
  c. C-17, s. 2(1)

account/to
(revenues) — comptabiliser
  c. F-11, s. 7(1)(c)

account for/to — être responsable de
  c. B-1, s. 174(2)(b)
(money received) — rendre compte
  c. F-11, s. 76(1)(b)
(property) — rendre compte
  c. B-3, s. 120(4)

accountable — redevable
  c. B-1, s. 172(4)(b)
  c. C-50, s. 20 — comptable
(for a sum) — responsable
  c. F-11, s. 78
hold accountable/to — tenir comptable
  c. C-44, s. 242(2)
to be ultimately accountable to Parliament — être responsable en dernier ressort devant le Parlement
  c. F-11, s. 88
ultimately accountable/to be (to Parliament) — responsable en fin de compte
  c. S-22, s. 2(1)
ultimately accountable/to be (to Parliament) — être tenu de rendre compte
  c. 31 (4th Supp.), s. preamble

accounted for
(benefit) — comptabilisé
  c. C-8, s. 89(1)(d)

accounting — comptabilité
  c. F-11, s. 10(c)
accounting policies — conventions comptables
  c. A-17, s. 6
generally accepted accounting principles — principes comptables généralement reconnus
  c. F-11, s. 132(2)(a)(i)
to provide for the repayment of accounting for and recovery of (accountable advances) — prévoir le remboursement, la justification et le recouvrement
  c. F-11, s. 38(1)(b)

accounts
books and accounts — livres et comptes
  c. A-5, s. 7

to keep detailed accounts
 c. C-44, s. 104(2)
    tenir une comptabilité détaillée

accounts of Canada
 c. A-13, s. 32
 c. C-17, s. 4(2)
    comptes du Canada

accredited hospital
 c. C-46, s. 287(6)
    hôpital accrédité

accretion to the value
 c. A-13, s. 30
    plus-value

accrue/to
 (a liability)
  c. B-1, s. 278(1)
    arriver à échéance
 accrue and fall due/to (interest)
  c. C-41, s. 34
    échoir et devenir exigible

accrued
 (interest)
  c. C-8, s. 110(7)
    couru
 accrued dividends
  c. C-44, s. 173(1)(g)
    dividendes accumulés
 accrued or accruing (liabilities)
  c. C-8, s. 3(2)
    nés ou à naître
 interest accrued
  c. C-30, Schedule, Article III, 2
    intérêts échus

accruing due
 debt accruing due
  c. B-3, s. 2
    dette à échoir

accruing due obligation
 c. B-3, s. 2
    obligation à échoir

accumulated
 accumulated dividends
  c. C-44, s. 27(2)
    dividendes cumulatifs

accuracy
 c. C-20, s. 14(1)
    exactitude
 attest the accuracy of the information/to
  c. F-11, s. 152(3)
    attester l'exactitude des renseignements

accused
 c. C-46, s. 493
    prévenu

acknowledge/to
 acknowledge a recognizance of bail, a confession of judgment, a consent to judgment/to
    reconnaître un engagement de caution, une confession de jugement, un consentement à jugement
  c. C-46, s. 405

acknowledgement
    reconnaissance
 c. C-44, s. 49(1)
 c. B-1, s. 98(2)
    avertissement
 c. C-20, s. 7(1)
    attestation
 receipt for or acknowledgement of property
    reçu ou récépissé de biens
  c. C-46, s. 388(a)
 written acknowledgement or confession
    aveux écrits
  c. F-11, s. 77

acquiescence
    approbation
 c. B-1, s. 160
 c. C-44, s. 147
 consent or acquiescence
    consentement ou acquiescement
  c. C-42, s. 4(2)

acquire/to
 (a share)
    souscrire
  c. B-1, s. 122(1)

(citizenship)
 c. C-29, s. 3(1)(c) — obtenir par acquisition
(possession)
 c. B-1, s. 97(1)(a) — prendre possession
acquire and dispose/to
 c. B-7, s. 2(ii) — acquérir et disposer de
acquire or incur a right or obligation/to
 c. A-16, s. 3(2) — assumer un droit ou une obligation
acquire or incur a right or an obligation/to
 c. C-12, s. 11(4) — assumer un droit ou une obligation
acquire, hold or dispose of or otherwise deal with shares/to
 c. A-14, s. 4(1)(a) — acquérir, détenir ou céder des actions, ou effectuer toute autre opération à leur égard
acquisition of majority control
 c. L-12, s. 51(1)b) — prise de contrôle majoritaire
acquit/to
(an accused)
 c. C-46, s. 570(2) — acquitter
acquittal
 c. C-46, s. 610(3) — acquittement
act
 c. A-12, s. 7(2) — acte
act, matter or thing
 c. A-2, s. 14(1)(a) — acte ou chose
commit an act or omission/to
 c. C-46, s. 7(1) — commettre une action ou omission
commit an act or omission/to
 c. C-46, s. 7(3)(d) — commettre un acte
act/to
act as an agent/to
 c. C-40, s. 33(3) — agir à titre de mandataire
act fraudulently or dishonestly/to
 c. C-44, s. 229(2)(d) — commettre des actes frauduleux ou malhonnêtes
act in good faith/to
 c. C-46, s. 32(3)(a) — agir de bonne foi
act for the time being/to
(as chairman)
 c. C-12, s. 6(3) — assurer l'intérim
act of God
 c. C-24, s. 52(4) — cas de force majeure
 c. C-27, Schedule, Article IV, 2(d) — acte de Dieu
Act of Parliament
 c. A-1, s. 4(1) — loi fédérale
act on/to
(a by-law)
 c. B-1, s. 43(3) — mettre à exécution
act on behalf/to
 c. A-1, s. 61 — agir au nom de
acting
acting chief justice
 c. C-46, s. 680(1)
 c. S-26, s. 30(1)(b) — juge en chef suppléant
acting Chairman
 c. C-19, s. 10(5) — président suppléant
acting President
 c. A-13, s. 24 — président intérimaire
Deputy Governor or Acting Governor (of the Bank of Canada)
 c. C-24, s. 8(2)(b) — sous-gouverneur ou gouverneur par intérim

action
    c. A-12, s. 6(3) — mesure
    c. B-1, s. 80 — procès
    c. C-26, Schedule II — action en recouvrement
    action for damages — action en responsabilité
      c. C-26, Schedule I, Article 24(1)
    action for money had and received — action en recouvrement de sommes reçues
      c. S-26, s. 67
    action in personam — action personnelle
      c. F-7, s. 43(4)
    action in rem — action réelle
      c. F-7, s. 43(7)
    action to enforce a claim — action en recouvrement
      c. C-26, s. 3
    action to recover (damages) — action en recouvrement
      c. N-7, s. 87(3)
    administrative action — poursuite administrative
      c. B-1, s. 23(2)
    bring or take an action, suit or other legal proceedings/to — ester en justice
      c. A-16, s. 3(2)
    civil, criminal or administrative action or proceeding — poursuite civile, pénale ou administrative
      c. C-44, s. 124(1)
    criminal action — poursuite pénale
      c. B-1, s. 23(2)
    derivative action — action indirecte
      c. C-44, s. 124(2)
    derivative action — action oblique
      c. C-44, s. 239(1)
    direct an action/to — ordonner une mesure
      c. A-12, s. 6(3)
    enemy action or counteraction against the enemy — opération de l'ennemi ou contre-opération
      c. C-31, s. 48
    penal action — action pénale
      c. C-45, s. 27
    representative action — action en justice collective
      c. C-44, s. 226(5)
    taking of action — prise des mesures
      c. A-12, s. 6(2)(a)

active service
    (army) — service en campagne
      c. C-17, s. 6(b)(ii)(C)

activity
    sexual activity — comportement sexuel
      c. C-46, s. 276(1)

actual
    actual and peaceable possession (of real property) — possession effective et paisible
      c. C-46, s. 72(1)
    actual loss or damage — perte ou dommage véritables
      c. C-46, s. 737(2)(e)
    actual physical possession — possession matérielle
      c. C-25, s. 13
    actual possession — possession réelle
      c. B-1, s. 187(2)(a)
    actual producer — producteur-exploitant
      c. C-24, s. 2(1)
    actual, implied or apparent authority — autorisation réelle, implicite ou apparente
      c. B-1, s. 75(2)

actual, visible and continued possession
    c. B-1, s. 2(1)(a)
possession réelle, publique et continue

to have something in actual possession or custody (of another person)
    c. C-46, s. 4(3)(a)(i)
avoir une chose en la possession ou garde réelle (d'une autre personne)

with actual knowledge and consent
    c. C-39, s. 57
avec connaissance et consentement véritables

actuarial report
    c. C-17, s. 55(1)(a)
rapport actuariel

ad hoc
ad hoc judge
    c. S-26, s. 30(1)
juge suppléant

ad testificandum
subpoena ad testificandum or duces tecum
    c. C-39, s. 25
bref d'assignation à témoigner ou à produire des pièces

add/to
(to an account)
    c. C-44, s. 26(8)
porter au crédit

add a party to a proceeding/to
    c. L-2, s. 16(0)
mettre une autre partie en cause

add as a party/to
    c. C-44, s. 226(5)(a)
mettre en cause

addition
in addition to or in lieu of any other punishment
    c. C-46, s. 718(1)
en sus ou au lieu de toute autre peine

Additional Protocol
    c. C-26, s. 2(3)
protocole additionnel

additive
fuel and additive
    c. C-32, s. 15(2)
combustible et additif

address
address of the prosecutor by way of summing up
    c. C-46, s. 646
exposé du poursuivant par voie de résumé

on address of the Senate
    c. S-26, s. 9(1)
sur adresse du Sénat

address for service
    c. C-44, s. 82(1)
adresse aux fins de signification

adduce/to
adduce evidence/to
    c. C-46, s. 276(2)(a)
produire une preuve

adduce evidence/to
    c. Y-1, s. 58(2)
produire des preuves

adherence
(to Convention)
    c. C-42, s. 65
adhésion

instrument of adherence
    c. C-26, Schedule III
instrument d'adhésion

adhesion
(to clauses)
    c. C-42, Schedule II, Article 25
adhésion

adjacent
adjacent property
    c. N-7, s. 113
biens-fonds adjacents

adjacent to
(waters)
    c. C-25, s. 9(1)(b)
contigu

adjourn/to   ajourner
     c. B-6, s. 27(1)
     (a meeting)   ajourner
       c. C-36, s. 7
     adjourn the court/to   ajourner le tribunal
       c. C-46, s. 474
     adjourn the proceedings/to   ajourner l'affaire
       c. Y-1, s. 9(10)(a)
adjournment
     (a meeting)   ajournement
       c. B-1, s. 63(4)
     adjournment or remand   ajournement ou renvoi
       c. C-46, s. 485(1)
adjudication   décision
     c. C-46, s. 608
     c. Y-1, s. 6
     c. C-46, s. 100(11)(a)   jugement
     c. Y-1, s. 13(7)
     (of grievances)   arbitrage
       c. C-23, s. 8(2)
     consideration and adjudication   étude et décision
     (claim for compensation)
       c. C-31, s. 21(1)
     make an adjudication/to   rendre une décision
       c. C-46, s. 555(2)
     memorandum of adjudication   procès-verbal de décision
       c. C-46, s. 570(3)
     statement of adjudication   énonciation de la décision
       c. C-46, s. 778(a)
adjudicative
     adjudicative function   fonction judiciaire
       c. 31 (4th Supp.), s. 16(2)
     adjudicative function   fonction judiciaire ou quasi-judiciaire
       c. A-1, s. 21(2)(a)
adjudicator   arbitre
     c. P-35, s. 2
     c. T-7, s. 2
adjust/to
     (a sum)   réajuster
       c. C-24, s. 35
     (an account)   rectifier
       c. C-24, s. 39(1)(a)
adjustment
     adjustment program   programme d'adaptation
       c. L-2, s. 221(1)
     adjustment year   année de rajustement
       c. P-1, s. 55(3)(b)(i)
     compromise, adjustment or   compromis, transaction ou
     settlement (of a charge or   règlement
     complaint)
       c. F-11, s. 80(f)
Adjutant-General   adjudant général
     c. C-31, s. 16(b)
administer/to
     (a statutory declaration)   recevoir (une déclaration)
       c. C-12, s. 19(e)
     (an oath)   faire prêter (serment)
       c. A-2, s. 10(3)
     (narcotic)   administrer
       c. N-1, s. 2
     administer a program/to   gérer un programme
       c. A-13, s. 4(a)

administer, take, swear, make or affirm/to (oath)
　c. S-26, s. 81(2)　　souscrire

expand, administer and dispose/to (of the money)
　c. C-13, s. 6(3)　　employer, gérer et aliéner

administration
(of an Act)
　c. A-12, s. 15(1)(c)(ii)　　application
　c. C-8, s. 2(1)
(of contracts)
　c. C-10, s. 11(d)　　mise en oeuvre
(of the Act)
　c. C-42, s. 50　　administration

administration and enforcement (of this Act)
　c. A-7, s. 15(1)　　contrôle d'application

administration of the laws of Canada
　c. S-26, s. 3　　application du droit canadien

administration or enforcement of the Act
　c. C-10, s. 17　　application de la présente loi

in the administration or enforcement of the law
　c. C-46, s. 25(1)　　dans l'application ou l'exécution de la loi

proper administration of justice
　c. C-12, s. 34(1)　　bonne administration de la justice

public administration
　c. C-6, s. 7(a)　　gestion publique

administrative
administrative expenses
　c. A-5, s. 10　　dépenses d'ordre administratif

administrator
　c. C-40, s. 106(1)　　administrateur séquestre

trustee, guardian, committee, curator, tutor, executor, administrator or representative of a deceased person
　c. B-1, s. 75(2)　　fiduciaire, tuteur, curateur, exécuteur ou administrateur de succession

admiralty
court of admiralty
　c. F-7, s. 3　　tribunal d'amirauté

Admiralty
Admiralty appeal
　c. S-26, s. 31(1)　　appel en matière maritime

admissible
　c. A-1, s. 36(1)(c)　　admissible

admissible in evidence
　c. P-2, s. 29　　admissible en justice

admission
admission, confession or statement (of accused)
　c. C-46, s. 542(1)　　aveu, confession ou déclaration

to collect as fare, toll, ticket or admission
　c. C-46, s. 392(a)(i)　　percevoir un prix de passage, un péage, un billet ou un droit d'entrée

written admission
　c. B-3, s. 42(1)(f)　　aveu par écrit

admit/to
(in evidence)
　c. A-12, s. 21(3)　　recevoir (en preuve)

administration

(the loss)
    c. C-26, Schedule I, Article
      13(3)

adopted child
    c. C-46, s. 214

adopter
    c. C-26, Schedule II

adoption
    connected by blood relationship,
    marriage or adoption/to be
      c. B-3, s. 4(2)(a)

adult
    c. Y-1, s. 2(1)

adulterate/to
    (food)
      c. F-27, s. 4(/d/)

advance
    c. C-14, s. 11(1)(b)
    c. B-1, s. 52(1)
    accountable advance
      c. F-11, s. 38(1)(a)
    make an advance/to
      c. B-1, s. 174(2)(f)

advance payment
    (of assistance)
      c. A-15, s. 3(3)

advantage
    loan, reward, advantage or
    benefit (to an official)
      c. C-46, s. 121(1)(c)(ii)
    work for the general advantage
    of Canada
      c. C-24, s. 2(1)

adventure
    c. C-8, s. 2(1)

adverse
    adverse claim
      c. C-44, s. 206(4)
    adverse claim
      c. B-1, s. 75(2)
      c. C-44, s. 48(2)
    adverse party
      c. S-26, s. 88
    adverse person
      c. B-1, s. 75(2)
      c. C-44, s. 48(2)
    draw an inference adverse (to
    the accused)
      c. C-46, s. 475(2)
    party adverse
      c. C-39, s. 20(1)

advertise
    c. C-38, s. 2

advice
    investment advice
      c. L-12, s. 116(1)

advisability
    (of negotiating)
      c. C-3, s. 9(2)

advisable
    advisable advance
      c. B-3, s. 31(1)

reconnaître

enfant adoptif

celui qui l'a adopté

être uni par les liens du sang, du
    mariage ou de l'adoption

adulte

falsifier

avance

avance de fonds
avance comptable

consentir une avance de fonds

avance (sur les subventions)

prêt, récompense, avantage ou
    bénéfice

ouvrage à l'avantage général du
    Canada

spéculation

avis d'opposition

opposition

partie adverse

opposant

tirer une conclusion défavorable

partie adverse

publicité ou annonce

conseil en matière de placements

opportunité

avance opportune

necessary or advisable
    c. A-2, s. 18(1)(q)   souhaitable

advise/to
(the Minister)   conseiller
    c. A-2, s. 17

adviser   expert
    c. C-11, s. 16(3)
professional adviser   expert
    c. C-2, s. 7

advisory
administrative, research,   fonctions étatiques
supervisory, advisory or   d'administration, de recherche, de
regulatory functions of a   contrôle, de conseil ou de
governmental nature   réglementation
    c. F-11, s. 3(1)(a)
advisory body   organisme consultatif
    c. B-2, s. 10(4)(b)
advisory committee   comité consultatif
    c. A-13, s. 25
consultative and advisory   comité consultatif
committee
    c. L-2, s. 138

Advisory Committee on   Comité consultatif du travail pénal
Penitentiary Industry
    c. P-5, s. 32(1)

advocacy
advocacy, protest or dissent   défense d'une cause, protestation ou
                                   manifestation d'un désaccord
    c. C-23, s. 2

advocate
(in Quebec)   avocat
    c. C-46, s. 183
barrister or advocate   avocat
    c. S-26, s. 5
barrister-at-law or advocate   avocat
    c. C-39, s. 88
    c. C-45, s. 3(e)
barrister, advocate, and counsel   avocats
    c. S-26, s. 22

advocate/to
advocate or promote genocide/to   préconiser ou fomenter le génocide
    c. C-46, s. 318(1)
teach or advocate (the use of   enseigner ou préconiser
force)/to
    c. C-46, s. 59(4)(a)

Aerospace Industries   Association des Industries
Association of Canada   Aérospatiales du Canada
    c. C-18, Schedule

affairs   affaires
    c. B-6, s. 22(d)
(of corporation)   affaires internes
    c. B-1, s. 2(1)
internal affairs (of Board)   fonctionnement interne
    c. N-7, s. 8(d)
public affairs   affaires publiques
    c. C-46, s. 310(a)
to manage the business and   gérer les affaires tant commerciales
affairs (of a corporation)   qu'internes
    c. C-44, s. 104(2)

affect/to   toucher
    c. C-20, s. 27
    c. B-5, s. 3   porter atteinte à

(a right) c. C-19, s. 9(2)	atteindre un droit
(by a mortgage or hypothec) c. B-1, s. 185(1)	grever
(persons in Canada) c. C-32, s. 23(3)(a)	toucher

(the validity)
   c. C-26, Schedule I, Article
    3(2)
	affecter

(the validity of the proceedings) c. Y-1, s. 9(8)	vicier
affect prejudicially/to c. C-42, s. 27(4)(b)	porter préjudice à
affected	
affected person c. C-10, s. 43(1)	personne visée
property injuriously affected c. A-2, s. 8(10)	bien lésé
affection	
injurious affection c. F-7, s. 17(2)(c)	trouble de jouissance
affiant	
affiant or declarant c. C-46, s. 138(c)	auteur d'un affidavit ou d'une déclaration solennelle
affidavit	affidavit

c. B-1, s. 78(7)(c)
   c. C-8, s. 106(5)
   c. C-46, s. 118	

receive evidence on affidavit/to c. L-2, s. 16(1)	accepter par voie d'affidavit un témoignage
take or receive affidavit/to c. P-5, s. 9(2)	recevoir des affidavits
verify by affidavit/to c. S-26, s. 38	certifier par affidavit
affidavits	
commissioner authorised to take and receive affidavits c. S-26, s. 82(a)	commissaire habilité à recevoir les affidavits
commissioner for taking affidavits c. B-2, s. 16	commissaire aux serments
affiliate	personne morale appartenant à un groupe
c. B-1, s. 2(1)	
(corporations) c. C-44, s. 2(1)	groupe
non-bank affiliate c. B-1, s. 28(8)(b)	établissement non bancaire appartenant à un groupe
affiliated/to be c. C-34, s. 39(4)(c)	être affilié
affiliation order c. B-3, s. 178(1)(c)	ordonnance d'attribution de paternité
affirm/to	
(a decision) c. A-7, s. 10(2)	confirmer
(an appointment) c. B-3, s. 61(2)	confirmer
administer, take, swear, make or affirm/to (oath) c. S-26, s. 81(2)	souscrire

affirm a conviction/to c. C-46, s. 691(1)	confirmer une condamnation
affirmance (of judgment) c. S-26, s. 73(2)	confirmation
affirmation administer a solemn affirmation/to c. L-2, s. 16(6)	recevoir une affirmation solennelle
declaration or affirmation c. C-8, s. 106(5)	déclaration ou affirmation solennelle
affirmative affirmative vote (of shareholder) c. L-12, s. 35(3)a)	vote positif
affirmative action affirmative action program Constitutional Act, 1982, Schedule B, s. 6(4)	programme de promotion sociale
affix/to affix or impress/to (an official seal onto a document) c. C-42, s. 58(1)	apposer
attach or affix/to (seal) c. Y-1, s. 63	apposer
against appeal against sentence c. C-46, s. 822(6)	appel d'une sentence
age retirement age c. C-17, s. 2(1)	âge de la retraite
agencies departments and agencies (of the Government of Canada) c. A-3, s. 8	autorités fédérales
agency c. A-13, s. 4(b)	organisme
(of a provincial government) c. A-3, s. 3	organisme
(of government) c. B-1, s. 2(1)	agence
(office of the Bank of Canada) c. B-1, s. 178(5)	agence
agency association c. L-12, s. 68(1)	association mandataire
appropriate agency c. B-1, s. 178(5)	agence appropriée
approved instalment credit agency c. N-11, s. 2	organisme agréé de crédit à tempérament
board or agency (of the Government of Canada) c. A-9, s. 4	organisme fédéral
department or agency c. Y-1, s. 40(2)(d)	ministère ou organisme
establish a branch or an agency/to c. B-2, s. 4(2)	ouvrir un bureau régional ou local
private agency c. A-13, s. 4(b)	organisme privé
public agency c. A-13, s. 4(b)	organisme public

public housing agency c. N-11, s. 6(2)(d)	agence de logement public
public housing agency c. N-11, s. 78	organisme de logement public
selling agency c. A-5, s. 2	organisme de vente
agent c. C-46, s. 185(1)	mandataire
(of an accused) c. A-12, s. 20(1)	mandataire (d'un accusé)
agent and principal c. C-46, s. 426(4)	agent et commettant
agent corporation c. F-11, s. 83	être de connivence ou de collusion
agent or employee (of Her Majesty) c. B-1, s. 8(1)	mandataire ou agent
any officer, director or agent (of a corporation) c. A-4, s. 5(2)	dirigeant, administrateur ou mandataire
as owner, landlord, lessor, tenant, occupier or agent (of common gaming house) c. C-46, s. 201(2)(b)	en qualité de possesseur, propriétaire, locateur, locataire, occupant ou agent
as principal or agent c. C-46, s. 386	en qualité de commettant ou d'agent
as principal or as agent c. C-40, s. 87(1)	à titre de commettant ou de mandataire
bargaining agent c. L-2, s. 3(1)	agent négociateur
cleaning agent c. C-11, s. 19	agent de nettoyage
collecting agent (mutual fund) c. B-1, s. 191(4)	agent de recouvrement
department, board, commission or agent c. C-46, s. 376(c)	ministère, office, bureau, conseil, commission, agent ou mandataire
factor or agent c. C-46, s. 325	facteur ou agent
selling agent (mutual fund) c. B-1, s. 191(4)	agent de placement
solicitor or agent c. C-46, s. 385(1)	procureur ou agent
to plead by counsel or agent c. C-46, s. 620	plaider par avocat ou représentant
aggravated aggravated or mitigated by a plea/to be (guilt) c. C-46, s. 612(3)	être aggravé ou atténué par le plaidoyer
aggravation circumstances of aggravation c. C-46, s. 610(1)	circonstances aggravantes
aggregate c. C-8, s. 13(3)(b)	total
aggregate fair market value c. C-20, s. 2(1)	total de la juste valeur marchande
aggregate of property c. B-3, s. 2	totalité des biens
aggregating (Consumer Price Index) c. P-1, s. 55(4)(c)(i)	regroupement

aggressive
    pattern of persistent aggressive
    behaviour   répétition continuelle d'actes
        c. C-46, s. 753(a)(ii)   d'agression

aggrieve/to   léser
        c. B-3, s. 37

aggrieved
    person aggrieved   personne lésée
        c. C-46, s. 194(1)

aggrieved/to be   subir un préjudice
        c. B-1, s. 65(8)

agreement   accord
        c. B-7, s. 2
        c. A-2, s. 18(1)(f)   convention
        c. A-5, s. 2   entente
        c. C-26, Schedule I, Article   stipulation
          1(1)
    agreement for sale   convention de vente
        c. C-24, s. 27(2)
    agreement for sale   convention de vente
        c. C-7, s. 2
    agreement for sale of land   promesse ou contrat de vente d'un
                     immeuble
        c. B-3, s. 218(2)(c)
    agreement of purchase and sale   contrat d'achat ou de vente
    (of securities)
        c. B-1, s. 151(2)
    agreement to assign (mortgages)   promesse de cession
        c. C-7, s. 27(1)(b)(i)
    amalgation agreement   accord de fusion
        c. L-12, s. 102(1)
    clause, covenant or agreement   clause, convention, accord
    (in a contract of carriage)
        c. C-27, Schedule, Article III,
          8
    enter into an agreement/to   conclure un accord
        c. A-13, s. 4(c)
    half-interest agreement   contrat d'intérêt à demi
        c. C-19, s. 23(3)(d)
    international agreement or   entente ou convention
    convention   internationale
        c. A-2, s. 18(1)(h)
    lease agreement   contrat de location
        c. B-1, s. 193(1)(c)(ii)
    partnership agreement   contrat de société de personnes
        c. C-44, s. 77(7)
    purchase agreement   engagement d'achat
        c. B-1, s. 208(7)(e)
    resale agreement   engagement de revente
        c. B-1, s. 208(7)(e)
    trust agreement   contrat de fiducie
        c. C-44, s. 77(7)
    underwriting agreement   contrat de souscription
        c. B-1, s. 168(1)

**Agreement for an International
Bank for Reconstruction and
Development**   accord relatif à la Banque
                    internationale pour la
                    reconstruction et le
                    développement
        c. C-41, s. 11(1)(a)(iii)

agricultural equipment   installations agricoles
        c. B-1, s. 2(1)
        c. B-1, s. 2(1)   matériel agricole immobilier

agricultural implements   instruments agricoles
     c. B-1, s. 2(1)
     c. B-1, s. 2(1)   matériel agricole mobilier
Agricultural Products Board   Office des produits agricoles
     c. A-1, Schedule I
aid
     aid, consent, abet or procure the   aider, assister, conseiller ou amener
     commission of an offence/to   quelqu'un à commettre une
         infraction
     c. C-39, s. 57
     legal aid or assistance program   service d'aide juridique ou
         d'assistance juridique
     c. Y-1, s. 11(4)(a)
     to be present as an aid, second,   assister en qualité d'aide, second,
     surgeon, umpire, backer or   médecin, arbitre, soutien ou
     reporter   reporter
     c. C-46, s. 83(1)(c)
aid/to
     aid or assist a person to make a   aider ou assister une personne à
     disposition of anything/to   disposer d'une chose
     c. C-46, s. 389(1)(b)
air
     air carrier   transporteur aérien
     c. A-2, s. 12
air contaminant   contaminant
     c. C-32, s. 2
     c. C-32, s. 2   contaminant atmosphérique
air gun
     firearm, air gun or air pistol   arme à feu, fusil à vent ou pistolet à
         vent
     c. C-46, s. 244
air navigation
     air navigation facility used in   installation utilisée pour la
     international air navigation   navigation aérienne
         internationale
     c. C-46, s. 7(8)
air pistol
     firearm, air gun or air pistol   arme à feu, fusil à vent ou pistolet à
         vent
     c. C-46, s. 244
air pollution   pollution atmosphérique
     c. C-32, s. 2
air raid precautions worker   engagé de la défense passive
     c. C-31, s. 30
air traffic control recording   enregistrement contrôle
     c. C-12, s. 36(1)
air waybill   lettre de transport aérien
     c. C-26, Schedule I, Article
     5(1)
aircraft   aéronef
     c. C-12, s. 2
     aircraft in flight   aéronef en vol
     c. C-46, s. 7(1)(b)
alarm/to
     alarm or annoy/to (a person)   alarmer ou ennuyer
     c. C-46, s. 372(2)
alcohol
     concentration of alcohol (in   alcoolémie
     blood)
     c. C-46, s. 256(1)
alien
     (juror)   étranger
     c. C-46, s. 638(1)(d)

alienate/to   aliéner
    c. B-1, s. 189(2)(a)
    alienate or part with the   aliéner un bien ou s'en dessaisir
    property/to
    c. C-46, s. 390
alimony   pension alimentaire
    c. B-3, s. 178(1)(b)
all
    all or part (of the property)   tout ou partie
    c. C-44, s. 224(1)(b)
    all or substantially all (property)   totalité ou quasi-totalité
    c. C-44, s. 224(1)(a)
allegation
    averment or allegation of   expression technique ou allégation
    matters   de choses
    c. C-46, s. 581(2)(a)
allege/to   imputer
    c. A-12, s. 25(2)
    c. B-6, s. 25(2)   alléguer
    (a fact)   exposer
    c. C-34, s. 41(2)
    allege in the indictment/to   alléguer dans l'acte d'accusation
    c. C-46, s. 356(2)
alleged
    (breach)   prétendu
    c. C-44, s. 242(1)
    (contravention)   imputé
    c. B-9, s. 15(3)
    (offence)   imputé
    c. C-24, s. 71(1)
    (person) alleged to have   à qui une infraction est imputée
    committed an offence
    c. Y-1, s. 4(1)
    alleged breach (of a regulation)   prétendue violation
    c. A-2, s. 8(1)(o)
    alleged contravention   infraction présumée
    c. C-23, s. 19(2)(a)
    alleged offence   infraction dont on allègue la
        perpétration
    c. C-34, s. 20(1)(b)
    alleged offence   infraction présumée
    c. C-46, s. 568
    contravention or alleged   contravention
    contravention
    c. 31 (4th Supp.), s. 89
    for any contravention or alleged   pour violation, effective ou
    contravention of law   prétendue, de la loi
    c. F-11, s. 80(f)
    the truth of the matters charged   la vérité des matières imputées
    in an alleged libel   dans son prétendu libelle
    c. C-46, s. 612(1)
alleviate/to
    (hardship)   remédier
    c. C-29, s. 5(4)
allied
    country allied with the United   pays allié aux Nations Unies
    Nations
    c. C-31, s. 56(1)(d)(i)
    defence of Canada or any state   défense du Canada ou d'États alliés
    allied or associated with Canada   ou associés avec le Canada
    c. A-1, s. 15(2)
allocate/to
    (money)   répartir
    c. C-25, s. 11(3)

allotment
allotment of shares (association)   attribution des parts
   c. C-40, s. 3(1)
allotment of stock   répartition des actions
   c. L-12, s. 29(1)a)
allow/to
allow an appeal/to   faire droit à un appel
   c. C-3, s. 21(5)(b)
allow the appeal/to   admettre l'appel
   c. C-46, s. 112(11)(b)
allowance   remise
   c. C-34, s. 51(1)
   c. C-2, s. 6(1)   indemnité
   c. F-11, s. 68(5)   allocation
consolidate with due allowance   consolider en réservant une
for minority interest/to   provision convenable pour la
      participation minoritaire
   c. C-41, s. 11(1)(e)(ii)
detention allowance   allocation de détention
   c. C-31, s. 13(1)
representational allowance   frais de représentation
   c. J-1, s. 27(6)
sessional allowance   indemnité annuelle de session
   c. P-1, s. 55(1)
alone
tried alone/to be   subir son procès séparément
   c. C-46, s. 636
alter
alter or interfere/to (with seized   modifier l'état
property)
   c. F-27, s. 24(2)
alter/to
(a notice)   modifier
   c. C-44, s. 264
(a security)   modifier
   c. B-1, s. 85(2)
alter or interfere/to (with fuel   modifier l'état de
seized)
   c. C-32, s. 27(4)
alter, deface or remove/to (a   modifier, maquiller ou effacer
serial number on a firearm)
   c. C-46, s. 104(3)(a)
to alter a genuine document in   altérer, en quelque partie
any material part   matérielle, un document
      authentique
   c. C-46, s. 366(2)(a)
alteration
erasure, alteration or   rature, altération ou interlinéation
interlineation on election   dans un document d'élection
document
   c. C-46, s. 377(1)(d)
alternate
alternate director   administrateur suppléant
   c. C-21, s. 9(1)(b)
alternate proxyholder   fondé de pouvoir suppléant
   c. C-44, s. 148(1)
alternative measures   mesures de rechange
   c. Y-1, s. 2(1)
amalgamate/to   fusionner
   c. B-1, s. 116(2)(b)
(corporations)   fusionner
   c. C-44, s. 181

amalgamated

amalgamated association
c. C-40, s. 129(1)

association née de la fusion

amalgamated body corporate
c. C-44, s. 26(4)

personne morale issue de la fusion

amalgamated body corporate

c. B-1, s. 261(1)(e)

société financière à naître de la fusion

amalgamated company
c. L-12, s. 102(1)

nouvelle société

amalgamated company

c. C-19, s. 23(6)

compagnie qui fait l'objet de la fusion

amalgamating

amalgamating body corporate
c. C-44, s. 26(3)(b)

personne morale fusionnante

amalgamating corporation
c. B-1, s. 257(2)(d)

personne morale absorbée

amalgamation

amalgamation agreement
c. C-44, s. 182(2)

convention de fusion

amalgamation agreement
c. C-40, s. 64(4)(a)
c. L-12, s. 102(1)

accord de fusion

amalgamation or reconstruction
c. C-40, s. 125(5)

fusion ou reconstitution

articles of amalgamation
c. C-44, s. 184(2)(b)(ii)

statuts de fusion

certificate of incorporation,
continuation, amendment or
amalgamation
c. C-40, s. 5

certificat de constitution en
personne morale, de continuation,
de modification ou de fusion

horizontal short-form
amalgamation
c. C-44, s. 182(1)(b)

fusion horizontale simplifiée

vertical short-form
amalgamation
c. C-44, s. 184(2)

fusion verticale simplifiée

amateur

amateur sport
c. C-34, s. 6(2)

sport amateur

ambient air
c. C-32, s. 2

air ambiant

amenable/to be

amenable to justice/to be
c. C-46, s. 592

être traduit en justice

amend/to

amend a by-law/to
c. B-1, s. 43(3)

modifier un règlement administratif

amendment
c. B-1, s. 152(2)

notice modificative

certificate of amendment
c. C-44, s. 13(1)

certificat modificateur

certificate of incorporation,
continuation, amendment or
amalgamation
c. C-40, s. 5

certificat de constitution en
personne morale, de continuation,
de modification ou de fusion

consequential amendment (to
Acts)
c. 31 (4th Supp.), s. 99

modification corrélative

related amendment (to Acts)
c. 31 (4th Supp.)

modification connexe

amends
willingness to make amends | désir de réparer le tort
c. Y-1, s. 14(2)(c)(i)
amortization | amortissement
c. B-7, s. 2(a)
c. F-11, s. 18(5)
amortized
amortized value (of a | valeur amortie d'un titre rachetable
redeemable security)
c. L-12, s. 78(1)
amortized value | valeur amortie
c. B-1, Schedule X, Section 8
amount
amount of traffic | intensité de la circulation
c. C-46, s. 249(1)(a)
negative or positive amount | résultat déficitaire ou bénéficiaire
c. C-52, s. 20(3)
amplify/to
(a report) | développer
c. P-35, s. 87(4)
analyst | analyste
c. A-7, s. 2
ancillary
ancillary or incidental power | pouvoir auxiliaire ou accessoire
c. C-40, s. 16(a)
reasonably ancillary business | activité commerciale suffisamment
reliée
c. C-41, s. 12(1)(e)
Andrew Mercer Reformatory | maison de correction Andrew
Mercer
c. P-20, s. 12(1)
angle
limit, boundary or angle of a | limite ou angle d'une concession,
concession, range, lot or parcel | d'un rang, d'un lot ou d'un lopin
of land | de terre
c. C-46, s. 443(1)(b)
animal
injure any animal or bird/to | estropier un animal ou un oiseau
c. C-46, s. 373(1)(c)
animate
animate or inanimate (thing) | animé ou inanimé
c. C-46, s. 322(1)
annoy/to
alarm or annoy/to (a person) | alarmer ou ennuyer
c. C-46, s. 372(2)
annual statement | état annuel
c. F-11, s. 49
annuity | annuité
c. C-17, s. 4(1)
deferred annuity | annuité différée
c. C-17, s. 10
immediate annuity | annuité immédiate
c. C-17, s. 10
original annuity | annuité originaire
c. C-17, s. 41(1)
annul/to
(an order) | annuler (un décret)
c. A-15, s. 5(4)
annulment
(of a remarriage) | annulation de mariage
c. C-17, s. 27
answer
full answer and defence | réplique et défense complètes
c. N-1, s. 8(2)

antedated/to be
(a bill)
    c. B-4, s. 26(d)   être antidaté
antique firearm
    c. C-46, s. 84(1)   arme à feu historique
apparel
    fish, tackle, rigging, apparel,   poissons, agrès, apparaux,
    furniture, stores and cargo   garnitures, équipement, matériel,
                                    approvisionnements et cargaison
    c. C-33, s. 2
apparent
    actual, implied or apparent   autorisation réelle, implicite ou
    authority   apparente
    c. B-1, s. 75(2)
    apparent condition   état apparent
    c. C-26, Schedule I, Article
    8(j)
    defect apparent on the face   vice de forme apparent à sa face
    thereof   même
    c. C-46, s. 601(1)
appeal   appel
    c. A-11, s. 15(1)
    appeal against a sentence   recours formé contre une sentence
    c. N-1, s. 25(4)
    appeal from order or judgment appel d'ordonnance ou de jugement
    c. N-1, s. 17(5)
    bring an appeal/to   interjeter un appel
    c. S-26, s. 2(1)
    bring an appeal/to   interjeter appel
    c. A-11, s. 15(1)
appeal/to
    (to the Supreme Court)   se pourvoir (devant la Cour)
    c. S-26, s. 65(2)
appealed
    court appealed from   tribunal dont il est interjeté appel
    c. C-36, s. 14(2)
    court appealed to   tribunal saisi de l'appel
    c. C-36, s. 14(2)
    decision being appealed   décision faisant l'objet de l'appel
    c. C-36, s. 14(2)
    judgment appealed from   jugement attaqué
    c. S-26, s. 65(1)(c)
appear/to   comparaître
    c. A-12, s. 22(2)
    appear and be heard in person comparaître en personne ou par
    or by counsel/to   ministère d'avocat
    c. C-44, s. 124(6)
    appear at and be present during être présent et demeurer présent
    proceedings/to (accused)   lors des procédures
    c. C-46, s. 7(5.1)(a)
    notice to appear   avis de comparaître
    c. Y-1, s. 23(8)
    promise to appear   promesse de comparaître
    c. C-46, s. 493
appearance
    (of witnesses)   comparution
    c. A-7, s. 8(4)
    appearance notice   citation à comparaître
    c. C-46, s. 493
    enforce the appearance/to   contraindre à comparaître
    c. C-23, s. 50(a)
    false appearance (of active   apparence fausse
    public trading)
    c. C-46, s. 382

appellate
   appellate civil jurisdiction   juridiction d'appel en matière civile
     c. S-26, s. 35
   appellate criminal jurisdiction   juridiction d'appel en matière
                                         pénale
     c. S-26, s. 35
   exclusive ultimate appellate   juridiction suprême en matière
   civil jurisdiction   d'appel au civil
     c. S-26, s. 52
applicable
   made applicable generally/to   être d'application générale
   (a regulation)
     c. L-2, s. 136(2)
   made applicable particularly to   être applicable à un comité
   a committee/to be (a regulation)   particulier
     c. L-2, s. 136(2)
applicant   requérant
     c. A-2, s. 18(1)(h)
     c. C-8, s. 2(1)
     c. C-20, s. 2(1)   demandeur
     c. C-44, s. 215(1)
     c. C-47, s. 4(6)
     c. N-1, s. 15(2)
   applicant for incorporation   fondateur
     c. B-1, s. 26(2)
   applicant for the order   celui qui demande l'ordonnance
     c. C-46, s. 527(1)(d)
application   demande
     c. C-8, s. 11(4)
   (money)   imputation
     c. B-1, s. 206(2)
   application for leave to appeal   demande d'autorisation d'appel
     c. C-46, s. 678(2)
     c. F-7, s. 16(1)
   application to purchase (land)   offre d'achat
     c. T-7, s. 25
   ex parte application   demande ex parte
     c. C-34, s. 11(1)
   extension of the application (of   extension du champ d'application
   the Act)
     c. C-24, s. 47(3)
   on application (to the Governor   sur demande
   in Council)
     c. A-2, s. 21(4)
   on its own motion or on the   d'office ou à la demande de
   application (of a person)   quelqu'un
     c. Y-1, s. 13(1)(e)
   on summary application   sur demande sommaire
     c. C-46, s. 490(15)
apply/to
   (excess money to a deficit)   appliquer
     c. A-5, s. 3(2)
   (to court)   s'adresser (au tribunal)
     c. B-3, s. 37
   apply to a court/to   saisir un tribunal
     c. C-44, s. 190(16)
apply force/to
   (to a person)   employer la force
     c. C-46, s. 265(1)a)
appoint/to   nommer
     c. A-1, s. 3
   (a provincial parole board)   instituer
     c. P-20, s. 7(2)

appellate

(members) c. A-3, s. 9(1)	désigner
appoint and employ/to c. A-16, s. 8(b)	recruter
appoint counsel/to c. Y-1, s. 11(5)	désigner un avocat
appointed	
person appointed (by a Minister) c. A-11, s. 11(1)	délégué
person appointed by the Minister c. A-11, s. 20(1)	personne nommée par le ministre
appointment c. C-17, s. 2(1)	emploi
c. B-3, s. 166	convocation
(under the government) c. C-46, s. 118	fonction
(Board) c. A-13, s. 10	nomination
evidence of appointment or incumbency c. B-1, s. 104(4)	preuve de la nomination ou du mandat
power of appointment c. F-11, s. 7(2)	pouvoir de nomination
purport to sell an appointment/to c. C-46, s. 124(a)	prétendre vendre une nomination
will, codicil or other testamentary writing or appointment c. C-46, s. 2	testament, codicille ou autre écrit ou disposition testamentaire
apportion/to	
(money) c. C-3, s. 15(7)(b)	répartir
(royalties) c. C-42, s. 29(6)	répartir
appraisal c. B-3, s. 52(1)	évaluation
appraised	
appraised value of the land c. N-11, s. 2	valeur estimative du terrain
appraiser c. C-44, s. 206(18)(d)	estimateur-expert
c. F-11, s. 115(3)(b)	estimateur
appraising	
method of appraising c. C-7, s. 26(a)	méthode d'évaluation
apprehend/to	
(a person) c. A-11, s. 21(1)	appréhender
(an offender) c. A-11, s. 42(2)	arrêter
apprehended	
apprehended loss c. C-27, Schedule, Article III	perte présumée
danger to be apprehended c. C-46, s. 32(4)	danger à craindre
apprehension	
apprehension and recommitment(of the inmate) c. P-2, s. 16(2)	arrestation et réincarcération
apprenticeship c. C-8, s. 2(1)	apprentissage

contract of service or apprenticeship c. C-42, s. 13(3)	contrat de louage de service ou d'apprentissage
appropriate	
(official or public body) c. C-44, s. 188(1)	compétent
appropriate authority c. B-1, s. 122(2)(g)	autorités compétentes
appropriate chief justice c. C-46, s. 745(6)	juge en chef compétent
appropriate for collective baigaining/to be c. L-2, s. 27(1)	être habile à négocier collectivement
appropriate Minister c. F-11, s. 83(1)	ministre de tutelle
appropriate/to	
(funds) c. A-3, s. 6	affecter
(moneys) c. A-8, s. 15(1)	affecter
appropriate moneys/to c. C-25, s. 32	affecter des crédits
appropriation c. B-1, s. 215(3)(c)	provision
c. F-11, s. 2	crédit
appropriation act c. F-11, s. 29(2)	loi de crédits
charge expenditures against appropriation/to c. F-11, s. 28	imputer les dépenses sur les crédits
payable out of the appropriation c. B-3, s. 6(1)	payable sur les crédits affectés
approval	
(of the Governor in Council) c. A-8, s. 6(1) c. B-8, s. 5(2)	assentiment
(of the Governor in Council) c. A-16, s. 9	agrément
(of the Governor in Council) c. B-1, s. 7(2)	autorisation
(of the Governor in Council) c. B-1, s. 12(4)	approbation
(of the Minister) c. A-16, s. 8(c)	agrément (du ministre)
grant approval/to c. B-1, s. 114(8)(b)	autoriser
submit for the approval/to (a plan) c. C-25, s. 17(1)	soumettre pour approbation
approve/to	
(an accountant's nomination) c. A-5, s. 7	agréer
approved	
approved container c. C-46, s. 254(1)	contenant approuvé
approved hospital c. C-46, s. 287(6)	hôpital approuvé
approved instrument c. C-46, s. 254(1)	alcootest approuvé
approved screening device c. C-46, s. 254(1)	appareil de détection approuvé
arbitrate/to	
arbitrate and decide on the matter/to c. B-6, s. 32(3)	arbitrer et régler le différend

appropriate

arbitration
  (of a dispute)
    c. C-23, s. 9(1)(a)   arbitrage
  arbitration board
    c. L-2, s. 3(1)   conseil d'arbitrage
arbitrator
  arbitrator or umpire
    c. C-46, s. 118   arbitre ou tiers-arbitre
architectural work of art
  (copyright)
    c. C-42, s. 2   oeuvre d'art architecturale
arctic waters
    c. A-12, s. 2   eaux arctiques
area
    c. C-11, s. 9   zone
  designated area (by an Act)
    c. A-5, s. 2   région désignée
arise/to
  (matter of complaint)
    c. A-7, s. 23   prendre naissance
arm's length
  transaction at arm's length
    c. B-3, s. 3(1)   transaction à distance
arrangement
    c. B-1, s. 110(2)   accord
    c. A-5, s. 2   arrangement
  corrupt arrangement   arrangement entaché de corruption
    c. C-39, s. 79
  scheme of arrangement
    c. B-3, s. 2   accommodement
array
  challenge the array/to (of jurors)
    c. C-46, s. 629(2)   récuser le tableau des jurés
arrears
    c. N-11, s. 12(3)(a)   arrérages
  amount in arrears
    c. C-17, s. 11(1)   montant d'arriéré
  in arrears/to be
    c. 4 (2nd Supp.), s. 16(a)(i)   être en retard dans les versements
  in arrears/to be
    c. B-3, s. 69(2)(b)   être en souffrance
arrest
    c. C-46, s. 28(2)(a)   arrestation
  arrest, detention or sale (of
  goods)   saisie, détention ou vente
    c. C-50, s. 14
arresting officer
  arresting officer or officer in
  charge   agent qui a procédé à l'arrestation
    c. Y-1, s. 11(2)   ou fonctionnaire responsable
arson
    c. C-46, s. 433(1)   crime d'incendie
articles
  (of incorporation)
    c. C-44, s. 2(1)   statuts
  articles of association
    c. C-40, s. 3(1)   statuts constitutifs
  articles of continuance (of a
  corporation)   clauses de prorogation
    c. F-11, s. 83(1)
  articles of incorporation   statuts constitutifs
    c. C-44, s. 2(1)

articles of revival (of a
corporation)
    c. F-11, s. 83(1)

clauses régissant la reconstitution

artifice
by a threat or an artifice or by
collusion with a person

au moyen d'une menace ou d'un
artifice ou de collusion avec une
personne

    c. C-46, s. 350(b)(i)

artistic
literary, scientific or artistic
domain
    c. C-42, s. 2

domaine littéraire, scientifique et
artistique

artistic work
(copyright)
    c. C-42, s. 2

oeuvre artistique

as soon as practicable
forthwith or as soon as
practicable
    c. C-46, s. 254(3)

immédiatement ou dès que possible

ascertain/to
    c. F-27, s. 34(1)(b)

acquérir la certitude

(a quantity)
    c. C-11, s. 15(2)(a)

établir

(an amount)
    c. C-26, s. 2(6)

fixer

ascertainable
fixed or ascertainable amount
    c. C-46, s. 347(2)

somme déterminée ou déterminable

Asia-Pacific Foundation

Fondation Asie-Pacifique du
Canada

    c. A-13, s. 1

Asian Development Bank
    c. B-1, s. 190(5)(a)(iii)

Banque asiatique de développement

    c. C-41, s. 11(1)(a)(vii)

Banque de développement asiatique
voies de fait

assault
    c. C-46, s. 265(1)
aggravated sexual assault
    c. C-46, s. 265(2)

agressions sexuelles graves

self-defence against unprovoked
assault
    c. C-46, s. 34(1)

légitime défense contre une attaque
sans provocation

assault/to
(an inspector)
    c. L-9, s. 29(/b/)

attaquer

assault/to (a person)

se livrer à des voies de faits (sur
une personne)

    c. C-46, s. 343(c)
commit an assault/to
    c. C-46, s. 77(a)

se livrer à des voies de fait

assay
assay, test or valuation
    c. C-46, s. 396(1)(a)

essai, épreuve ou évaluation

assembling
(of a conference)
    c. C-26, Schedule I, Article
    41

réunion

assembly
unlawful assembly
    c. C-46, s. 63(1)

attroupement illégal

Assembly of First Nations
    c. C-18, Schedule

Assemblée des premières nations

assent
(of an Act)
    c. I-23, s. 5(3)

sanction

assent/to
(to a proposal)
c. B-3, s. 53 — approuver

assert/to
(a claim)
c. B-1, s. 107(1) — faire valoir (un droit)

assert the ineffectiveness/to
(of an endorsement)
c. C-44, s. 68(1)(b) — opposer l'invalidité

assertion
c. C-46, s. 133 — assertion

assertion of fact, opinion, belief or knowledge
c. C-46, s. 118 — assertion de fait, opinion, croyance ou connaissance

introductory assertion
c. C-46, s. 584(2) — affirmation préliminaire

oral, written or recorded assertion
c. C-12, s. 37(a) — relation verbale, écrite ou enregistrée

assess/to
(a tax)
c. B-1, s. 308(2) — établir (une cotisation)

assess or levy/to (municipal taxes)
c. B-3, s. 136(1)(e) — établir ou percevoir

assessment
c. B-7, s. 4 — prélèvement

notice of assessment
c. C-8, s. 22(2) — avis d'évaluation

on the basis of a security assessment
c. F-11, s. 9(1) — en raison d'une évaluation de sécurité

security assessment
c. C-23, s. 2 — évaluation de sécurité

assessor
c. A-11, s. 15(1) — évaluateur
c. F-7, s. 46(1)(ix) — assesseur
(Admiralty cases)
c. S-26, s. 31(1) — assesseur

assets
assets and liabilities
c. A-2, s. 18(1)(d) — actif et passif

assets and liabilities (of Canada)
c. F-11, s. 64(2)(a)(ii) — ressources et charges

assets of the estate
c. C-8, s. 23(4) — masse des biens

retention of assets
c. C-44, s. 217h) — rétention d'éléments d'actif

statement of assets and liabilities
c. F-11, s. 25(2) — état des ressources et des charges

take control of the assets/to
c. L-12, s. 83(2)c) — prendre le contrôle de l'actif

assign
c. B-6, s. 8(2) — ayant droit

assign/to
(a benefit)
c. C-17, s. 70 — céder

assign an interest/to
c. B-1, s. 212(1) — céder un droit

assignable
c. F-11, s. 67(a) — cessible

assignment
(of a security) cession
 c. B-1, s. 92(3)
(of powers) délégation
 c. C-13, s. 22(d)
assignment by way of security cession en garantie
 c. B-3, s. 94(4)
assignment or grant (of an cession ou concession
interest)
 c. C-42, s. 13(4)
assignment or transfer (of a cession ou transfert
security)
 c. C-44, s. 65(3)
conveyance, assignment and acte de transfert, acte de cession et
assurance assurance
 c. B-1, s. 273(4)
copy of the assignment copie de l'acte de cession
 c. F-11, s. 69(1)
gift, conveyance, assignment, don, transport, cession, vente,
sale, transfer or delivery of transfert ou remise de biens
property
 c. C-46, s. 392(a)(i)
make an assignment/to effectuer une cession
 c. B-1, s. 178(7)(a)
assignor cédant
 c. F-11, s. 68(2)
assigns
successors and assigns héritiers et ayants cause
 c. C-30, Schedule Article I(e)
assist/to
(a person) prêter assistance (à une personne)
 c. C-23, s. 24(b)
aid or assist a person to make a aider ou assister une personne à
disposition of anything/to disposer d'une chose
 c. C-46, s. 389(1)(b)
lawfully assist/to (a peace prêter légalement main-forte
officer)
 c. C-46, s. 31(1)
assistance
guidance and assistance conseils et assistance
 c. Y-1, s. 3(1)(c)
legal aid or assistance program service d'aide juridique ou
  d'assistance juridique
 c. Y-1, s. 11(4)(a)
reasonable assistance aide nécessaire
 c. C-20, s. 16(1)
reasonable assistance assistance raisonnable
 c. C-20, s. 15(3)
Assistant Clerk of the Privy greffier adjoint du Conseil privé
Council for Canada pour le Canada
 c. B-1, s. 275(3)
Assistant Comptroller General contrôleur général adjoint du
of Canada Canada
 c. F-11, s. 158
Assistant Information commissaire adjoint à l'information
Commissioner
 c. A-1, s. 56(1)
associate
(corporations) liens
 c. C-44, s. 2(1)
senior associate chief justice, juge en chef associé, juge en chef
associate chief justice, adjoint, juge surnuméraire, juge
supernumerary judge, chief principal et juge junior
judge, senior judge and junior
judge

assignment   **29**

c. J-1, s. 2, "judge"
Associate Chief Justice
(of the Federal Court)   juge en chef adjoint
c. A-1, s. 52(1)
Associate Parliamentary   bibliothécaire parlementaire associé
Librarian
c. C-10, s. 35(2)(c)
associated
associated or related, federal   entreprises fédérales associées ou
works   connexes
c. L-2, s. 255(1)
connected or associated/to be (a   avoir des rapports ou des liens
business)
c. B-1, s. 310(6)(a)
country associated with the   pays associé aux Nations Unies
United Nations
c. C-31, s. 56(1)(d)(i)
defence of Canada or any state   défense du Canada ou d'États alliés
allied or associated with Canada   ou associés avec le Canada
c. A-1, s. 15(2)
associates
associates of the non-resident   associés du non-résident
c. L-12, s. 49(1)
associates of the resident   associés du résident
c. B-1, s. 113(1)
association   association
c. A-13, s. 3(b)
c. A-14, s. 2
association or lawful   association ou alliance légitime
combination of workmen or   d'ouvriers ou d'employés
employees
c. C-46, s. 425(a)
Association of Universities and   Association des Universités et
Colleges of Canada   Collèges du Canada
c. C-18, Schedule
assumed/to be   être réputé
c. C-25, s. 12(2)
assumed name   nom d'emprunt
c. B-4, s. 131(1)
assumption
(of liability)   prise en charge (des obligations)
c. B-1, s. 270(2)
assurance
conveyance, assignment and   acte de transfert, acte de cession et
assurance   assurance
c. B-1, s. 273(4)
give reasonable assurance/to   donner des assurances suffisantes
c. B-1, s. 103(1)(b)
reasonable assurance   garanties suffisantes
c. C-44, s. 76(1)d)
astray
cattle found astray   bestiaux trouvés errants
c. C-46, s. 338(1)(a)
at large/to be
(on his undertaking or   être en liberté (sur sa promesse ou
recognizance)   son engagement)
c. C-46, s. 145(2)
athletic board   commission athlétique
c. C-46, s. 83(2)
Atlantic Council of Canada   Conseil Atlantique du Canada
c. C-18, Schedule
Atlantic Ferrying Organization   Atlantic Ferrying Organization
c. C-31, s. 52

Atlantic Fisheries	secteur des pêches de l'Atlantique
c. A-14, s. 2	
Atlantic Pilotage Authority	Administration de pilotage de l'Atlantique
c. A-1, Schedule I	
c. F-11, Schedule III, Part I	
Atomic Energy Control Board	Commission de contrôle de l'énergie atomique
c. A-1, Schedule I	
c. C-12, Schedule	
c. F-11, Schedule II	
Atomic Energy of Canada Limited	Energie atomique du Canada, Limitée
c. F-11, Schedule III, Part I	
attach/to	saisir
c. C-8, s. 65(1)	
(conditions to a licence)	joindre
c. A-2, s. 21(9)	
attach or affix/to (seal)	apposer
c. Y-1, s. 63	
attached or seconded/to be	
(employee)	affecté ou détaché
c. C-23, s. 2	
attachment	saisie-arrêt
c. B-7, Schedule II, Article VII, Section 3	
c. S-26, s. 96(2)	contrainte par corps
c. 4 (2nd Supp.), s. 23	
attachment and garnishment	saisie et saisie-arrêt
c. B-3, s. 70(1)	
execution or attachment	exécution ou saisie-arrêt
c. B-3, s. 73(2)	
attainment of its objects	réalisation de sa mission
c. C-25, s. 16(1)(d)	
attempt	
(to commit an offence)	tentative
c. C-46, s. 24(2)	
attend/to	
summon to attend/to	assigner à comparaître
c. C-34, s. 19(6)	
attendance	comparution
c. C-46, s. 347(6)	
c. Y-1, s. 7(4)	
(before the court)	présence
c. C-46, s. 699(1)	
school attendance and performance record and the employment record	assiduité et résultats scolaires, et antécédents professionnels
c. Y-1, s. 14(2)(c)(vii)	
secure the attendance/to (of a witness)	garantir la comparution
c. C-46, s. 550(1)	
attest/to	
attest the accuracy of the information/to	attester l'exactitude des renseignements
c. F-11, s. 152(3)	
sign, certify, attest or execute/to	signer, certifier, attester ou établir
c. A-2, s. 27(1)(c)	
attorney	mandataire
c. B-1, s. 161(2)	
c. C-44, s. 148(2)	
attorney or solicitor	procureur
c. S-26, s. 23	

attorney or solicitor
   c. S-26, s. 69(1)
                 avocat

trustee, banker, merchant,
attorney, factor, broker or other
agent
   c. C-46, s. 491.1(3)(a)
                 fiduciaire, banquier, marchand, fondé de pouvoir, courtier ou autre mandataire

Attorney General of Canada
   c. A-1, s. 63(2)
                 procureur général du Canada

attorney-at-law
attorney-at-law or solicitor
   c. C-39, s. 88
                 avocat ou procureur

attributable
properly attributable (sum)
   c. F-11, s. 20(2)
                 régulièrement imputable

auction
public auction
   c. B-1, s. 177(6)
                 enchères publiques

sale by auction
   c. B-1, s. 184(c)
                 vente aux enchères

audit/to
(accounts)
   c. C-12, s. 14
                 examiner

(books and accounts)
   c. A-5, s. 7
                 apurer

audited statement
(of its accounts)
   c. B-7, Schedule I, Article
     XII, Section 7(a)
                 état vérifié (de ses comptes)

auditor
   c. A-13, s. 35
                 vérificateur

Auditor General of Canada
   c. A-17, s. 2
                 vérificateur général du Canada

authentic
in notarial or authentic form
   c. L-12, s. 42(1)c)
                 suivant la forme notariée ou authentique

authenticate/to
   c. C-46, s. 540(3)(b)
                 authentiquer

(a copy)
   c. C-44, s. 51(7)(b)
                 certifier authentique

authenticated
(a copy)
   c. B-1, s. 78(7)(b)
                 certifié authentique

(deposition)
   c. C-39, s. 24
                 authentiqué

certified or authenticated copy
   c. C-37, s. 7(3)
                 copie certifiée ou authentifiée

authenticating
(a trustee, registrar or transfer
agent)
   c. B-1, s. 84(a)

authoritative
equally authoritative/to be
(versions of an Act)
   Constitutional Act, 1982,
     Schedule B, s. 57
                 avoir également force de loi

authorities
prison authorities
   c. C-46, s. 231(4)(c)
                 autorités de la prison

authority
   c. A-12, s. 28(1)
                 autorité

   c. A-11, s. 40
                 autorisation

(of a judge) c. S-26, s. 30(3)	habilitation
(of a person) c. C-44, s. 51(3)	qualité
(of Governor in Council) c. A-4, s. 4(1)	autorisation
(person or organization) c. A-3, s. 5(a)	autorité
authority of a public department c. C-46, s. 305(b)	autorité d'un ministère public
authority to sign c. C-44, s. 77(1)(a)	compétence
by or by the authority of c. A-2, s. 27(1)(b)	par la personne ou sous son autorité
exercice of authority c. C-46, s. 265(3)(d)	exercice de l'autorité
fact-finding authority c. C-12, s. 2	mission de constatation
general authority c. C-46, s. 303(2)	autorisation générale
have authority to act/to c. B-2, s. 8(1)	être investi des pouvoirs
high authority c. C-42, Schedule II, Article 21	haute autorité
judicial authority c. C-46, s. 305(a)	pouvoir judiciaire
lawful authority (of the government) c. C-46, s. 2	autorité légitime
legislative authority c. C-8, s. 4(3)	autorité législative
person in authority c. A-12, s. 14(2)	responsable
person in authority c. C-46, s. 43	personne exerçant l'autorité
public authority c. C-44, s. 160(4)(b)	administration publique
taxing authority c. N-11, s. 92(6)	autorité fiscale
terminate an authority/to c. L-2, s. 113	mettre fin à un mandat
under the authority c. C-19, s. 18(3)	sous le régime de
under the authority of (a sovereign power) c. A-12, s. 12(2)(a)	sous l'autorité de
under the authority of a licence c. C-15, s. 12(1)(d)	autorisé par permis
authorization document of authorization c. A-2, s. 27(2)	document d'autorisation
authorize/to c. A-11, s. 3(q)	autoriser
(a shareholder) c. B-1, s. 68(4)	mandater
(by resolution) c. B-1, s. 68(2)	accréditer
(under the law) c. A-6, s. 2(1)	habiliter
authorize in writing/to c. F-11, s. 33(1)	donner une délégation écrite

authorize to perform/to
c. A-1, s. 59(1)
subdéléguer

authorize in writing/to
c. F-11, s. 33(1)
donner une délégation écrite

authorize to perform/to
(duties)
c. A-1, s. 59(1)
déléguer

authorized
authorized agent
c. F-11, s. 2
agent agréé

authorized capital
c. B-1, s. 2(2)(b)
capital social autorisé

authorized search
c. A-2, s. 7(14)
fouille autorisée

duly authorized in writing (as legal representative)
c. C-42, s. 2
régulièrement constitué par mandat écrit

person authorized by the Minister
c. A-11, s. 20(1)
personne autorisée par le ministre

authorized agent
c. F-11, s. 2
agent agréé

authorship
(of a work)
c. C-42, Schedule III, Article 6
paternité (d'une oeuvre)

work of joint authorship
c. C-42, s. 2
oeuvre créée en collaboration

automated teller machine
c. C-46, s. 321
guichet automatique

automobile master key
c. C-46, s. 353(5)
passe-partout d'automobile

autrefois acquit
c. C-46, s. 607(1)(a)
autrefois acquit

autrefois convict
c. C-46, s. 607(1)(b)
autrefois convict

availability of community services and facilities
c. Y-1, s. 14(2)(c)(v)
existence de services communautaires et installations

available
recourse available
c. C-17, s. 9(4)
recours accessible

avails
to live on the avails of prostitution
c. C-46, s. 212(1)(j)
vivre des produits de la prostitution

average
(price)
c. A-5, s. 5(2)(a)
moyen

general average
c. C-27, Schedule, Article IV, 6
avarie commune

Average Maximum Pensionable Earnings
c. C-17, s. 15(3)
moyenne des maximums des gains ouvrant droit à pension

average monthly pensionable earnings
c. C-8, s. 2(1)
moyenne mensuelle des gains ouvrant droit à pension

average secondary reserve
c. B-2, s. 19
réserve secondaire moyenne

averment
averment or allegation of matters
c. C-46, s. 581(2)(a)
expression technique ou allégation de choses

avoidance
    for the avoidance of doubt   pour plus de sûreté
        c. C-26, s. 5
    repudiation or avoidance   désaveu
        c. B-1, s. 78(5)
        c. C-44, s. 51(5)
award
    (of board of arbitration)   sentence arbitrale
        c. B-6, s. 35(2)
    arbitral award   décision arbitrale
        c. P-35, s. 2
award/to
    (a contract)   adjuger (un contrat)
        c. C-9, s. 12(2)
    (costs)   adjuger
        c. B-3, s. 197(2)
    (money or costs)   adjuger
        c. F-7, s. 57(1)
award costs/to   accorder les frais et dépens
        c. A-1, s. 53(2)
aware/to become   avoir connaissance
        c. A-7, s. 8(1)

b

back/to
    (a warrant)   contresigner
        c. F-32, s. 3(1)
backer
    to be present as an aid, second,   assister en qualité d'aide, second,
    surgeon, umpire, backer or   médecin, arbitre, soutien ou
    reporter   reporter
        c. C-46, s. 83(1)(c)
background
    (of a person)   antécédents
        c. Y-1, s. 16(2)b)
bad debt   créance irrécouvrable
        c. B-1, s. 308(1)
badge
    military medal, ribbon, badge or   médaille, ruban, insigne ou chevron
    chevron   militaire
        c. C-46, s. 419(b)
bag
    bag, sack or other container or   sac ou autre contenant ou
    covering, (for mail)   couverture
        c. C-46, s. 356(1)(a)(ii)
baggage check   bulletin de bagages
        c. C-26, Schedule I, Article
          4(1)
bail   cautionnement
        c. C-46, s. 482(3)(c)
    bail bond   cautionnement en matière pénale
        c. B-3, s. 178(1)(q)
bailee   dépositaire
        c. B-1, s. 102
        c. C-44, s. 75
    bailee of things under seizure   dépositaire de choses frappées de
           saisie
        c. C-46, s. 324

bailiff   huissier
     c. B-3, s. 2
     c. C-9, s. 46(4)
     police officer, police constable,   officier de police, agent de police ou
     bailiff or constable   hussier
       c. C-46, s. 2
bailment   gage
     c. C-37, s. 8
baiting
     (of animals)   harcèlement
       c. C-46, s. 446(4)
balance   reliquat
     c. B-3, s. 112
     (amount)   solde
       c. B-1, s. 32(3)
     (of a bill)   surplus
       c. B-4, s. 111(3)
     balance of payments   balance des paiements
       c. B-7, Schedule I, Article I,
         (V)
     balance of the term (of office)   reste du mandat
       c. B-2, s. 28(3)
     balance remaining in its account   solde créditeur
       c. C-24, s. 33(2)
     balance sheet   bilan
       c. C-43, s. 5(2)(a)
     credit balance   solde créditeur
       c. B-1, s. 201(2)
     on a balance of probabilities   selon la prépondérance des
         probabilités
       c. Y-1, s. 4(4)(a)
     operating balance   solde d'opérations courantes
       c. B-1, Schedule X, Section 5
ballot   bulletin de vote
     c. L-2, s. 16(i)(ii)
     c. B-1, s. 69(1)   scrutin secret
     c. C-44, s. 141(1)
     ballot box   urne
       c. L-2, s. 16(i)(ii)
ballots
     method of casting ballots   mode de scrutin
       c. P-35, s. 36(3)(b)
     method of casting ballots   mode de dépouillement
       c. P-35, s. 36(3)(b)
bank   banque
     c. B-1, s. 2(1)
     c. C-46, s. 2
     bank note, bank bill and bank   billet de banque, papier de banque
     post bill   et effet postal de banque
       c. C-46, s. 2
     international regional bank   banque régionale internationale
       c. B-1, s. 190(5)(a)(iii)
Bank for International   Banque des règlements
Settlements   internationaux
     c. B-2, s. 18(m)
Bank Hapoalim (Canada)   Banque Hapoalim (Canada)
     c. B-1, Schedule II
Bank Leumi le-Israel (Canada)   Banque Leumi le-Israel (Canada)
     c. B-1, Schedule II
bank note
     bank note, bank bill and bank   billet de banque, papier de banque
     post bill   et effet postal de banque
       c. C-46, s. 2

blank bank note	blanc de billet de banque
c. C-46, s. 448	
forged blank bank note	faux blanc de billet de banque
c. C-46, s. 448	
Bank of America Canada	Banque d'Amérique du Canada
c. B-1, Schedule II	
Bank of Canada	Banque du Canada
c. A-1, s. 70(2)	
bank service corporation	société de service bancaire
c. B-1, s. 193(1)	
banker	
trustee, banker, merchant, attorney, factor, broker or other agent	fiduciaire, banque, marchand, fondé de pouvoir, courtier ou autre mandataire
c. C-46, s. 491.1(3)(a)	
banking	opérations bancaires
c. B-1, s. 28(1)	
banking business	opération bancaire
c. B-2, s. 18(o)	
business of banking	opérations bancaires
c. C-40, s. 6(f)	
bankrupt	failli
c. B-1, s. 35(1)(d)	
state of being bankrupt	état de faillite
c. B-3, s. 2	
bankrupt/to be	être en faillite
c. B-3, s. 50(2)(a)	
bankruptcy	
act of bankruptcy	acte de faillite
c. B-3, s. 2	
c. C-36, s. 5.2	
trustee in bankruptcy	syndic de faillite
c. C-44, s. 51(2)(c)	
Banque Nationale de Paris (Canada)	Banque Nationale de Paris (Canada)
c. B-1, Schedule II	
bar	
natural bar (harbour)	barre naturelle
c. C-46, s. 440	
bar/to	faire obstacle
c. B-1, s. 209(5)	
(a right)	interdire
c. C-44, s. 157(3)	
(a subsequent indictment)	constituer une fin de non-recevoir
c. C-46, s. 610(1)	
Barclays Bank of Canada	Banque Barclays du Canada
c. B-1, Schedule II	
bareboat charter	contrat d'affrètement coque nue
c. C-31, s. 6	
bargain	marché
c. C-40, s. 33(1)	
bargain price	prix d'occasion
c. C-34, s. 57(1)	
bargaining	
bargaining agent	agent négociateur
c. L-2, s. 3(1)	
bargaining unit	unité de négociation
c. L-2, s. 3(1)	
barrister	barrister
c. C-46, s. 183	
barrister or advocate	avocat
c. S-26, s. 5	

barrister, advocate, and counsel c. S-26, s. 22	avocats
counsel, barrister or solicitor c. C-46, s. 2	avocat ou procureur
barrister-at-law	
barrister-at-law or advocate c. C-39, s. 88 c. C-45, s. 3(e)	avocat
barrister, solicitor, lawyer or advocate c. C-3, s. 9(1)	avocat
barter/to c. C-46, s. 206(1)(b)	troquer
(a firearm) c. C-46, s. 94	échanger
base loan c. N-11, s. 64	prêt de base
base price c. A-8, s. 2(1)	prix de base
basic	
basic benefit c. C-17, s. 60(1)	prestation de base
basic exemption c. C-8, s. 2(1)	exemption de base
basic list c. C-44, s. 21(3)	liste principale
basic list (of shareholders) c. B-1, s. 156(3)	liste principale
basic number of contributory months c. C-8, s. 42(1)	nombre de base des mois cotisables
basis	
inquire into the basis or substance of a decision/to c. P-35, s. 97(6)	discuter le fondement ou la substance d'une décision
on a confidential basis c. 4 (2nd Supp.), s. 13	à titre confidentiel
on the basis of a security assessment c. F-11, s. 9(1)	en raison d'une évaluation de sécurité
bear/to	
bear (the cost)/to c. C-46, s. 723(2)(iii)	supporter
bearer	
(of a security) c. C-44, s. 48(2)	porteur
in bearer form or in registered form (security) c. B-1, s. 75(2)	valeur mobilière au porteur ou valeur mobilière nominative
securities to bearer c. C-40, s. 96(1)	valeurs payables au porteur
becoming due	
existing or future debt due or becoming due by the Crown c. F-11, s. 66	créance existante ou future échue ou à échoir sur Sa Majesté
behaviour	
good behaviour (of an accused) c. C-46, s. 737(2)	bonne conduite
illegal behaviour c. Y-1, s. 3(1)(b)	conduite illicite
offence involving traitorous or treasonable behaviour c. C-17, s. 18(4)(d)	infraction pour conduite assimilable à la trahison

pattern of repetitive behaviour
    c. C-46, s. 753(a)(i)
répétition d'actes

belief
on the information and belief
    c. C-46, s. 196(4)
sur la foi de renseignements tenus pour véridiques

to the best of their knowledge and belief
    c. C-45, s. 5
au mieux de leur connaissance et croyance

believe/to
(on reasonable grounds)
    c. C-10, s. 43(1)
soupçonner (avec des motifs raisonnables)

belongings
personal belongings
    c. P-5, s. 37(2)
effets personnels

beneficial
beneficial interest
    c. C-44, s. 2(1)c)
droit du véritable propriétaire

beneficial interest
    c. C-44, s. 2(1)
propriété effective

beneficial use (in lands)
    c. T-7, s. 3(2)
jouissance

beneficial ownership
    c. C-46, s. 379
propriété bénéficiaire

beneficially
own beneficially/to
    c. C-44, s. 2(1)a)
avoir la propriété effective

beneficially owned
    c. C-16, s. 10(2)(b)

beneficiary
    c. C-17, s. 26(d)(i)
bénéficiaire

(of a trust)
    c. C-20, s. 4(d)
bénéficiaire

benefit
    c. C-8, s. 2(1)
prestation

    c. C-17, s. 4(1)
    c. C-26, s. 2(5)
réparation

benefit of an exception
    c. C-27, Schedule, Article IV, 2(q)
bénéfice d'une exception

for the public benefit
    c. C-46, s. 309
pour le bien public

for the use or benefit of
    c. B-1, s. 110(7)
à l'usage ou au profit de

loan, reward, advantage or benefit (to an official)
    c. C-46, s. 121(1)(c)(ii)
prêt, récompense, avantage ou bénéfice

payment, consideration, gratuity or benefit
    c. A-2, s. 12
paiement, contrepartie, gratification ou profit

public benefit
    c. C-46, s. 319(3)(c)
intérêt public

benefit/to
(a person)
    c. A-5, s. 4(4)
profiter (à une personne)

benefits
(as an employee)
    c. A-8, s. 6(2)
avantages

benevolent
for a normal, social or benevolent purpose
    c. C-46, s. 176(2)
pour un objet moral ou social ou à des fins de bienfaisance

for charitable or benevolent objects
    c. C-41, s. 10(1)(g)
    à des fins de charité ou de bienfaisance

bequest
    c. A-13, s. 4(j)
    legs

acquire by gift, bequest or otherwise/to (securities)
    c. A-13, s. 4(j)
    acquérir par don, legs ou autre mode de libéralités

bereavement

bereavement leave
    c. L-2, s. 210(2)
    congé de décès

Bertillon Signaletic System
    c. I-1, s. 2(1)(a)
    bertillonnage

beset/to

beset and watch/to (a place)
    c. C-46, s. 423(1)(f)
    cerner et surveiller

best interests

(of the child)
    c. C-3, s. 16(8)
    intérêt

in the best interests (of a young person)
    c. Y-1, s. 10(1)
    dans l'intérêt

to be in the best interests of the administration of justice
    c. C-46, s. 186(1)(a)
    servir au mieux l'administration de la justice

with a view to the best interests of the corporation
    c. F-11, s. 115(1)(a)
    au mieux des intérêts de la société

bestiality
    c. C-46, s. 160
    bestialité

bet
    c. C-46, s. 197(1)
    pari

private bet
    c. C-46, s. 204(1)(b)
    pari privé

betting
    c. C-46, s. 553(c)(iii)
    pari ou gageure

book-making, pool-selling or betting
    c. C-46, s. 201(2)(e)
    bookmaking, vente d'une mise collective ou pari

beyond

act beyond one's jurisdiction/to
    c. F-7, s. 28(1)(a)
    outrepasser sa compétence

bid
    c. B-1, s. 309(2)(c)
    soumission

    c. B-3, s. 33(2)
    offre

call or request for bids or tenders
    c. C-34, s. 47(1)(a)
    appel ou demande d'offres ou de soumissions

share-for-share bid
    c. C-44, s. 200
    offre d'achat avec échange d'actions

bid/to
    c. B-3, s. 129(2)
    enchérir

bid-rigging
    c. C-34, s. 47(1)
    truquage des offres

bidder
    c. B-1, s. 184(c)
    enchérisseur

bidder or tenderer
    c. C-34, s. 47(2)
    enchérisseur ou soumissionnaire

false bidder
    c. B-3, s. 86(4)
    fol enchérisseur

bidding

false bidding
    c. B-3, s. 86(4)
    folle enchère

bigamy
    c. C-46, s. 290(i)

bigamie

bilateral
    bilateral discussion
      c. C-6, s. 14(2)(b)

discussion bilatérale

Bilingual Districts Advisory Board
    c. A-1, Schedule I

Conseil consultatif des districts bilingues

bill
    accommodation bill
      c. B-4, s. 138(3)

lettre de complaisance

    bank note, bank bill and bank post bill
      c. C-46, s. 2

billet de banque, papier de banque et effet postal de banque

    bill of costs
      c. B-3, s. 70(2)

mémoire d'honoraires

    bill of exchange
      c. B-1, s. 173(1)(c)

lettre de change

    bill of indictment
      c. C-46, s. 576(2)

projet d'acte d'accusation

    bill of lading
      c. A-7, s. 16(1)(c)

connaissement

    bill of lading
      c. C-24, s. 25(2)(a)

lettre de voiture

    consumer bill
      c. B-4, s. 189(1)

lettre de consommation

    debenture, deed, bond, bill, note, warrant, order or other security for money
      c. C-46, s. 2

débenture, titre, obligation, billet, lettre, mandat, ordre ou autre garantie d'argent

    inland bill
      c. B-4, s. 24(1)

lettre intérieure

    making, accepting, discounting or endorsing of a bill of exchange, cheque, draft or promissary note
      c. C-46, s. 362(1)(c)(vi)

création, acceptation, escompte ou endossement d'une lettre de change, d'un chèque, d'une traite ou d'un billet à ordre

    private bill
      c. S-26, s. 54

projet de loi d'intérêt privé

bill of lading
    c. A-7, s. 16(1)(c)
    c. B-1, s. 2(1)
    c. B-5, s. 2

connaissement

    c. C-24, s. 25(2)(a)

lettre de voiture

    bill of lading, cargo manifest, shipping order, way-bill and switching order
      c. T-19, s. 2

connaissement, manifeste, ordre d'expédition, feuille de route et bulletin de manoeuvre

bill of sale
    c. B-3, s. 72(2)

acte de vente

bind/to
    c. B-3, s. 101(3)

lier

    bind in law/to
      c. C-46, s. 366(4)

lier légalement

binding
    binding arbitration
      c. C-6, s. 12(2)(b)

arbitrage obligatoire

    final and binding (decision)
      c. C-8, s. 29(1)

définitif et obligatoire

    final and binding/to be (a decision)
      c. P-35, s. 96(3)

être final et obligatoire

bird
    animal or bird that is the
    property of any person
      c. C-46, s. 264.1
    injure any animal or bird/to
      c. C-46, s. 373(1)(c)

animal ou oiseau qui est la
    propriété de quelqu'un

estropier un animal ou un oiseau

blackout
    c. C-31, s. 40

obscurcissement

blame or liability
    c. C-12, s. 8(2)

faute ou responsabilité

blank
    blank cartridge
      c. C-46, s. 84(1)
    endorsement in blank
      c. B-4, s. 66(2)

cartouche à blanc

endossement en blanc

blasphemous libel
    c. C-46, s. 296(1)

libelle blasphématoire

blood relationship
    connected by blood relationship,
    marriage or adoption/to be
      c. B-3, s. 4(2)(a)

être uni par les liens du sang, du
    mariage ou de l'adoption

blood test
    c. L-9, s. 42(1)

épreuve de sang

board
    (of the Government of Canada)
      c. A-9, s. 4
    board of directors
      c. C-44, s. 2(1)
    board of inquiry
      c. A-2, s. 10(1)
    board or agency (of the
    Government of Canada)
      c. A-9, s. 4
    conciliation board
      c. L-2, s. 3(1)
    department, board, commission
    or agent
      c. C-46, s. 376(c)
    joint board
      c. C-11, s. 5 in fine
    local advisory board
      c. L-12, s. 27

organisme fédéral

conseil d'administration

commission d'enquête

organisme fédéral

commission de conciliation

ministère, office, bureau, conseil,
    commission, agent ou mandataire

office mixte

comité consultatif local

board of governors
    board of governors, management
    or directors, or the trustees,
    commission or other person

      c. C-46, s. 287(6)

conseil des gouverneurs, conseil de
    direction, conseil d'administration
    ou fiduciaire, commission ou autre
    personne

**Board of Trustees of the Queen
Elizabeth II Canadian Fund to
Aid in Research on the Diseases
of Children**
    c. A-1, Schedule I

Conseil de fiducie du Fonds
    canadien de recherches de la
    Reine Elizabeth II sur les
    maladies de l'enfance

boarding
    lodging, boarding or eating
    house
      c. C-46, s. 364(1)

hôtel garni, maison de pension ou
    restaurant

bodily harm
    bodily harm or damage to
    property
      c. C-46, s. 80(b)
    grievious bodily harm
      c. C-46, s. 25(3)

blessure corporelle ou dommage à la
    propriété

lésion corporelle grave

body   organisme
    c. A-1, s. 3
    collegial body   organe collégial
      c. C-46, s. 2
    municipal or public body   corps municipal ou public
      c. B-1, s. 109(1)(a)
body corporate   personne morale
    c. A-10, s. 6(1)(g)
    c. A-14, s. 2
    c. B-1, s. 2(1)
    c. C-44, s. 2(1)
    c. B-1, s. 254   société financière
    c. C-30, Schedule Article V,   société
      1(d)
    company or other body corporate   aucun équivalent
      c. F-11, s. 83(1)(b)
    company, body corporate,   compagnie, personne morale,
    unincorporated body or society   organisme non constitué en
         personne morale ou société
      c. C-46, s. 328(e)
body politic and corporate   personne morale
    c. B-1, s. 4
    c. L-12, s. 102(8)
bona fide
    bona fide proposed nominee   candidat sérieux
      c. B-1, s. 161(3)
    bona fide purchaser   acheteur de bonne foi
      c. C-44, s. 72(1)
    bona fide purchaser for   acheteur de bonne foi pour
    adequate valuable consideration   contrepartie valable et suffisante
      c. B-3, s. 75
    bona fide purchaser for valuable   acquéreur de bonne foi à titre
    consideration without notice   onéreux, et qui n'a reçu aucun
         avis
      c. C-46, s. 206(6)
    bona fide reason   raison valable
      c. C-46, s. 110(3)
bond   cautionnement
    c. A-12, s. 8(1)
    c. L-12, s. 43(1)   bon
    bind by bond/to (parties in a   s'obliger par cautionnement
    case)
      c. B-6, s. 32(3)
    bond, debenture, note or other   obligation, débenture, billet ou
    evidence of indebtedness   autre preuve de créance
      c. C-44, s. 2(1)
    debenture, deed, bond, bill, note,   débenture, titre, obligation, billet,
    warrant, order or other security   lettre, mandat, ordre ou autre
    for money   garantie d'argent
      c. C-46, s. 2
    guaranty bond   cautionnement
      c. B-3, s. 5(3)(c)
    indemnity bond   cautionnement
      c. A-12, s. 8(1)
      c. B-1, s. 105(2)(b)
      c. C-44, s. 78(2)b)
    post a bond/to   garantir par un cautionnement
      c. A-7, s. 13(f)
    security by bond   cautionnement sous forme de lettre
         de garantie
      c. B-3, s. 16(1)
    to provide a security or fidelity   fournir une sûreté ou une
    bond   assurance-responsabilité
      c. C-44, s. 223(4)

bonding
  (of employees)   cautionnement à fournir
    c. L-12, s. 62(4)

book
  (of the Board)   document comptable
    c. F-11, s. 9(1)
  stock book   registre des actions
    c. L-12, s. 11(1)

book debt   créance comptable
    c. B-3, s. 30(1)(a)

book value   valeur comptable
    c. C-43, s. 3(1) in fine

book-keeping   tenue de livres
    c. C-40, s. 6(2)(b)

book-making
  book-making, pool-selling or   bookmaking, vente d'une mise
  betting   collective ou pari
    c. C-46, s. 201(2)(e)

books
  books and accounts   livres et comptes
    c. A-5, s. 7

boom
  lumber, timber, log, float, boom,   bois de construction, de service ou
  dam or slide   en grume, radeau, barrage
          flottant, digue ou glissoir
    c. C-46, s. 433(1)(i)
  slide, dam, pier or boom   glissoir, digue, jetée ou barrage
          flottant
    c. T-7, s. 19(a)

boom chain
  boomchain, chain line and   chaîne d'estacade, chaîne, ligne et
  shackle   lien
    c. C-46, s. 339(6)
  timber mark or boom chain   marque de bois ou marque de
  brand   chaîne d'estacade
    c. C-46, s. 339(4)

borough
  chief magistrate of a city,   premier magistrat d'une
  borough or town corporate   municipalité, ville ou autre
          agglomération
    c. S-26, s. 82(/c/)

borrow/to
  borrow amounts/to   contracter des emprunts
    c. C-9, s. 51
  borrow money/to   contracter un emprunt
    c. C-44, s. 189(1)(a)

borrower   emprunteur
    c. B-1, s. 58(2)(a)

bottomry
  bottomry or respondentia   prêt à la grosse
    c. F-7, s. 22(2)(c)

bound
  bound form register   registre en volumes reliés
    c. F-11, s. 60(2)

boundary
  boundary line of land   ligne de démarcation de terrains
    c. C-46, s. 442
  boundary mark   borne
    c. C-46, s. 443(1)(b)
  international boundary   frontière internationale
    c. C-11, s. 2(1)
  international or provincial   frontière ou limite internationale ou
  boundary   provinciale
    c. C-46, s. 443(1)(a)

limit, boundary or angle of a concession, range, lot or parcel of land c. C-46, s. 443(1)(b)	limite ou angle d'une concession, d'un rang, d'un lot ou d'un lopin de terre
Boxing Day c. L-2, s. 193(2)	lendemain de Noël
branch	
(of a bank) c. B-1, s. 2(1)	succursale
(of a trade union) c. L-2, s. 3(1)	subdivision
branch office c. C-14, s. 5	bureau
branch securities register c. B-1, s. 77(2)	registre local
establish a branch or an agency/to c. B-2, s. 4(2)	ouvrir un bureau régional ou local
head of the branch of government c. C-46, s. 121(1)(b)	chef de la division du gouvernement
branch office c. C-14, s. 5	bureau
branch securities register c. B-1, s. 77(2)	registre local
brand	
brand or mark (on cattle) c. C-46, s. 338(1)(b)(i)	marque ou empreinte
mark, brand, seal, wrapper or design c. C-46, s. 376(3)	marque, signe, sceau, enveloppe ou dessin
brand-mark c. A-7, s. 21	marque distinctive
breach c. B-1, s. 96(4)	manquement
(of a duty) c. C-44, s. 242(1)	inexécution
alleged breach (of a regulation) c. A-2, s. 8(1)(o)	prétendue violation
breach of a fiduciary duty c. C-44, s. 75	violation d'une obligation de représentant
breach of discipline c. F-11, s. 11(2)(f)	manquement à la discipline
breach of duty or malfeasance c. C-46, s. 723(2)(ii)	abus de fonction ou prévarication
breach of faith c. B-4, s. 55(2)	abus de confiance
breach of the peace c. C-46, s. 30	violation de la paix
breach of trust c. B-3, s. 173(1)(k)	abus frauduleux de confiance
breach of trust c. C-46, s. 122	abus frauduleux de confiance
breach of trust or confidence c. C-42, s. 63	abus de confiance
break c. C-46, s. 321	effraction
break/to	
break a contract/to c. C-46, s. 422(2)	violer un contrat
break a prison/to c. C-46, s. 144(a)	commettre un bris de prison

break the public peace/to   violer la paix publique
    c. C-46, s. 49(a)
break into/to
    forcibly break into or forcibly   accomplir une effraction ou
    enter the dwelling-house/to   s'introduire de force dans une
        maison d'habitation
    c. C-46, s. 40
break open/to
    door, window, etc.   forcer l'entrée du lieu
        perquisitionné et y fracturer tout
        objet s'y trouvent
    c. N-1, s. 14
break out/to
    break out of a place/to   sortir d'un endroit
    c. C-46, s. 348(1)(c)
breakdown
    breakdown of marriage   échec du mariage
    c. C-3, s. 8(1)
breaking
    safe-breaking   effraction de coffres-forts
    c. C-46, s. 351(1)
breaking and entering   introduction par effraction
    c. C-46, s. 348
breaking open
    order the breaking open of a   ordonner que soit forcé un
    building/to   immeuble
    c. B-3, s. 189(1)
bribe   pot-de-vin
    c. C-46, s. 139(3)(a)
bring/to
    (proceedings)   intenter
    c. A-2, s. 8(11)
    bring an action/to   engager une action
    c. C-44, s. 226(4)
    bring, defend or take part in any   ester en justice, lors de toute
    action or proceeding/to   procédure
    c. C-44, s. 222(1)(b)
bringing
    on the bringing of (a certificate)   dès la production
    c. P-1, s. 7(3)
broadcast   émission
    c. C-46, s. 539(1)
    c. Y-1, s. 17(1)   presse parlée
broadcasting   radiodiffusion
    c. C-22, s. 2
broadening
    broadening the base of the   diversification de l'économie
    economy
    c. C-25, s. 17(1)
broker
    (livestock)   courtier
    c. L-9, s. 31
    (securities)   courtier
    c. C-44, s. 48(2)
    c. C-46, s. 383(1)(b)
    broker or dealer (in securities)   agent de change ou courtier en
        valeurs
    c. B-1, s. 15(c)(iv)
    correspondent broker   correspondant (courtier)
    c. B-1, s. 98(1)(b)
    securities broker or dealer   courtier ou négociant en valeurs
        mobilières
    c. C-44, s. 147

selling broker | courtier vendeur
   c. B-1, s. 98(1)(a)
   c. C-44, s. 71(1)(a)

brokerage | courtage
   c. C-40, s. 30(3)
  for a brokerage fee | en contrepartie de droits de courtage
   c. L-9, s. 31.

BT Bank of Canada | Banque BT du Canada
   c. B-1, Schedule II

budget
  operating budget | budget de fonctionnement
   c. F-11, s. 123

buffer stocks
  international buffer stocks of primary products | stocks régulateurs internationaux de produits primaires
   c. B-7, Schedule I, Article XXX(c)(ii)

buggery | sodomie
   c. C-46, s. 160

builder | constructeur
   c. N-11, s. 2

building
  building or place | lieux
   c. C-38, s. 15(5)
  building or structure | bâtiment ou construction
   c. C-46, s. 2
  building society | société de prêt à la construction
   c. N-11, s. 2

buoy
  to make fast a boat to a signal, buoy or other sea-mark | amarrer un bateau à un signal, une bouée ou un autre amer
   c. C-46, s. 439(1)

Bureau of Pensions Advocates | Bureau de services juridiques des pensions
   c. A-1, Schedule I

burial
  burial of a dead human body | inhumation d'un cadavre humain
   c. C-46, s. 182(a)

burial ground | cimetière
   c. T-7, s. 23(1b1)

business | entreprise commerciale
   c. B-7, Schedule II, Article III, Section 4
   c. B-1, s. 34 | affaires commerciales
   c. C-8, s. 2(1) | entreprise
  business activities | exploitation commerciale
   c. C-20, s. 2(1)
  business combination | regroupement d'entreprises
   c. B-1, s. 172(3)
  business day | jour ouvrable
   c. B-4, s. 6(2)(a)
  business day (of a company) | jours de travail
   c. L-12, s. 52
  business of the meeting | questions à l'ordre du jour
   c. C-44, s. 143(3)(c)
  business practice | pratique commerciale
   c. C-46, s. 362(5)
  carry on business/to | traiter des affaires
   c. C-41, s. 54(1)(b)
  chief place of business | principal lieu d'affaires
   c. C-41, s. 35(2)

chief place of business (of a company)   principal établissement
    c. L-12, s. 45(4)

do business/to   exercer des opérations
    c. B-6, s. 3(2)

during usual business hours   pendant les heures normales d'ouverture
    c. C-44, s. 138(4)(a)

federal work, undertaking or business   entreprises fédérales
    c. L-2, s. 2

in the ordinary course of business   dans le cours ordinaire des affaires
    c. C-46, s. 2

on public business   en service commandé
    c. P-1, s. 33(1)(c)

place of business   établissement commercial
    c. C-42, s. 10

place of business   établissement
    c. C-20, s. 14(1)

principal place of business   établissement principal
    c. C-38, s. 10(b)(i)

proper conduct of business   bon fonctionnement
    c. P-2, s. 11(2)

reasonable business hours   heures ordinaires d'affaires
    c. C-41, s. 35(2)

regular business hours of the office   heures normales d'ouverture du bureau
    c. L-12, s. 7(8)

to manage the business and affairs (of a corporation)   gérer les affaires tant commerciales qu'internes
    c. C-44, s. 104(2)

transact business/to (at a meeting)   délibérer
    c. C-44, s. 114(3)

transaction of business   conclusion d'affaires
    c. C-46, s. 121(1)(a)(iii)

Business Council on National Issues   Conseil d'entreprises questions d'intérêt national
    c. C-18, Schedule

by law   légalement
    c. A-12, s. 7(2)

by virtue of
(a provision of an Act)   en vertu de
    c. C-8, s. 77

(a section)   sur le fondement de
    c. C-50, s. 10

(a subsection)   aux termes de
    c. B-1, s. 110(5)

by way of compensation   à titre de compensation
    c. A-15, s. 4(1)

by-law
(of a corporation)   règlement administratif
    c. C-44, s. 6(2)

ordinary by-law   règlement administratif ordinaire
    c. C-40, s. 3(1)

by-laws
(of a corporation)   statuts
    c. B-1, s. 178(5)(a)

charter, constitution or by-laws (of a trade union)   charte, statuts et règlements administratifs
    c. L-2, s. 29(3)

C

caisse populaire — caisse populaire
   c. C-34, s. 50(3)
  credit union or caisse populaire — caisse populaire
   c. C-40, s. 6(1)(h)
  credit union or caisse populaire — caisse populaire ou credit union
   c. C-46, s. 347(2)
calculated
  reasonably calculated — concerté en vue de
   c. C-44, s. 147b)
calendar year — année civile
   c. A-4, s. 6
call — option d'achat
   c. B-1, s. 168(1)
  (of shares) — appel
   c. C-40, s. 57(2)
  (securities) — option d'achat
   c. C-44, s. 2(1)
  call or put (in respect of a share) — option d'achat ou de vente
   c. C-44, s. 131(1)
  day, call and short (loan) — au jour le jour, à vue ou à court terme
   c. B-1, Schedule X, Section 12(a)
call/to
  (a meeting) — convoquer
   c. C-44, s. 111(2)
call in/to
  (coins) — retirer
   c. C-52, s. 9(1)(d)
  call in and demand/to (shares) — demander et exiger
   c. C-40, s. 57(1)
call in question/to — contester
   c. C-8, s. 41(6)
calling
  calling of meeting — convocation de réunion
   c. C-7, s. 10(3)(a)
  lawful profession or calling — profession ou occupation légitime
   c. C-46, s. 179(1)(a)
camp
  community, residential centre, group home, child care institution, or forest or wilderness camp — centre résidentiel local, foyer collectif, établissement d'aide à l'enfance, camp forestier ou camp de pleine nature
   c. Y-1, s. 20(7)
Canada Council — Conseil des Arts du Canada
   c. A-1, Schedule I
   c. C-2, s. 2
Canada Day — fête du Canada
   c. L-2, s. 193(2)
Canada Deposit Insurance Corporation — Société d'assurance-dépôts du Canada
   c. A-1, Schedule I
   c. B-1, s. 251(1)
   c. C-44, s. 206(7)
Canada Development Investment Corporation — Corporation d'investissements au développement du Canada
   c. F-11, Schedule III, Part II
Canada Employment and Immigration Advisory Council — Conseil consultatif canadien de l'emploi et de l'immigration
   c. C-4, s. 2

Canada Employment and Immigration Commission c. A-1, Schedule I c. F-11, Schedule II	Commission de l'emploi et de l'immigration du Canada
Canada Gazette c. A-12, s. 11(2)	Gazette du Canada
Canada Grain Act c. B-1, s. 180(2)(e)	Loi sur les grains du Canada
Canada Harbour Place Corporation c. F-11, Schedule III, Part I	Corporation Place du Havre Canada Inc.
Canada Labour Code c. A-1, Schedule II	Code canadien du travail
Canada Labour Relations Board c. A-1, Schedule I	Conseil canadien des relations de travail
Canada Lands Company Limited c. F-11, Schedule III, Part I	Société immobilière du Canada, Limitée
Canada Mortgage and Housing Corporation c. F-11, Schedule III, Part I	Société canadienne d'hypothèques et de logement
Canada Pension Plan c. A-1, Schedule II c. C-8, s. 1	Régime de pensions du Canada
Canada Pension Plan Advisory Committee c. C-8, s. 116(1)	comité consultatif du régime de pension du Canada
Canada Plan Investment Fund c. C-8, s. 108(4)	Fonds de placement du régime de pension du Canada
Canada Ports Corporation c. A-1, Schedule I	Société canadienne des ports
Canada Post Corporation c. A-10, s. 2(1) c. C-46, s. 356(1)(a)(iii) c. F-11, Schedule III, Part I	Société canadienne des postes
Canada-Arab Federation c. C-18, Schedule	Fédération Canada-Arabe
Canadian Advisory Council on the Status of Women c. A-1, Schedule I	Conseil consultatif canadien de la situation de la femme
Canadian Army Active c. C-17, s. 2(1)	Armée active canadienne
Canadian Army Special Force c. C-17, s. 6(b)(ii)(d)	Contingent spécial de l'armée canadienne
Canadian Arsenals Limited c. F-11, Schedule III, Part I	Les Arsenaux canadiens Limitée
Canadian Association for the Club of Rome c. C-18, Schedule	Canadian Association for the Club of Rome
Canadian Association of University Teachers c. C-18, Schedule	Association canadienne des professeurs d'université
Canadian Aviation Safety Board c. A-1, Schedule I	Bureau canadien de la sécurité aérienne
Canadian Broadcasting Corporation c. B-9, s. 2 c. F-11, s. 85(1)	Société Radio-Canada

Canadian Centre for Arms Control and Disarmament
c. C-18, Schedule
Canadian Centre for Occupational Health and Safety
c. A-1, Schedule I
c. F-11, Schedule II
Canadian Chamber of Commerce
c. C-18, Schedule
Canadian Coalition for Peace Through Strength Inc.
c. C-18, Schedule
Canadian Commercial Bank
c. B-1, Schedule I
Canadian Commercial Corporation
c. A-1, Schedule I
c. C-14, s. 2
c. F-11, Schedule III, Part I
Canadian Commission for UNESCO
c. C-18, Schedule
Canadian Conference of Catholic Bishops
c. C-18, Schedule
Canadian Council of Churches
c. C-18, Schedule
Canadian Council of International Cooperation
c. C-18, Schedule
Canadian Council on Hospital Accreditation
c. C-46, s. 287(6)
Canadian Cultural Property Export Control List

c. C-51, s. 2
Canadian Cultural Property Export Review Board

c. A-1, Schedule I
c. C-51, s. 2
Canadian Dairy Commission
c. A-1, Schedule I
c. C-15, s. 2
c. F-11, Schedule III, Part I
Canadian Dairy Commission Account
c. C-15, s. 15(1)
Canadian Depository for Securities Limited
c. B-1, s. 174(9)
Canadian Disarmament Information Service
c. C-18, Schedule
Canadian dollar
c. F-11, s. 48(2)
Canadian Export Association

c. C-18, Schedule
Canadian Federation of Agriculture
c. C-18, Schedule

Centre canadien pour le contrôle des armements et le désarmement

Centre canadien d'hygiène et de sécurité au travail

Chambre de commerce du Canada

Canadian Coalition for Peace Through Strength Inc.

Banque Commerciale du Canada

Corporation commerciale canadienne

Commission UNESCO Canadienne

Conférence des évêques catholiques du Canada

Conseil Canadien des Églises

Conseil Canadien pour la Coopération Internationale

Conseil canadien d'accréditation des hôpitaux

Nomenclature des biens culturels canadiens à l'exportation contrôlée

Commission canadienne d'examen des exportations de biens culturels

Commission canadienne du lait

compte de la Commission canadienne du lait

Caisse canadienne de dépôt de valeurs Limitée

Canadian Disarmament Information Service

monnaie canadienne

Association canadienne d'exportation

Fédération canadienne de l'agriculture

Canadian Federation of
Independent Business
    c. C-18, Schedule
Canadian Federation of
Students
    c. C-18, Schedule
Canadian Federation of
Vietnamese Associations
    c. C-18, Schedule
Canadian Film Development
Corporation

    c. F-11, s. 85(1)
Canadian Forces
    c. C-17, s. 2(1)
Canadian Government
Railways
    c. C-19, s. 2
Canadian Government
Specifications Board
    c. A-1, Schedule I
Canadian Grain Commission
    c. A-1, Schedule I
Canadian health care policy
    c. C-6, s. 3
Canadian Heritage
Preservation Endowment
Account
    c. C-51, s. 36(1)
Canadian Human Rights
Commission
    c. A-1, Schedule I
Canadian Imperial Bank of
Commerce
    c. B-1, Schedule I
Canadian Import Tribunal
    c. A-1, Schedule I
Canadian Institute for
International Peace and
Security
    c. A-1, Schedule I
    c. C-18, s. 2
Canadian Institute for Strategic
Studies
    c. C-18, Schedule
Canadian Institute of
International Affairs
    c. C-18, Schedule
Canadian International
Development Agency
    c. A-1, Schedule I
Canadian Jewish Congress
    c. C-18, Schedule
Canadian Judicial Council
    c. J-1, s. 2
Canadian Labour Congress
    c. C-18, Schedule
Canadian Lebanese League
    c. C-18, Schedule
Canadian Legion War Services
Inc.
    c. C-31, s. 16

Canadian Federation of
Independent Business

Fédération Canadienne des
Étudiants

Canadian Federation of Vietnamese
Associations

Société de développement de
l'industrie cinématographique
canadienne

Forces canadiennes

Chemins de fer du gouvernement
canadien

Office des normes du gouvernement
canadien

Commission canadienne des grains

politique canadienne de la santé

Compte des dotations pour la
conservation du patrimoine
national

Commission canadienne des droits
de la personne

Banque Canadienne Impériale de
Commerce

Tribunal canadien des importations

Institut canadien pour la paix et la
sécurité mondiales

Institut des études stratégiques du
Canada

Institut canadien des affaires
internationales

Agence canadienne de
développement international

Congrès juif canadien

Conseil canadien de la magistrature

Congrès du Travail du Canada

Canadian Lebanese League

Canadian Legion War Services Inc.

Canadian lessee	locataire canadien
c. C-53, s. 2(1)	
Canadian Livestock Feed Board	Office canadien des provendes
c. A-1, Schedule I	
c. F-11, Schedule III, Part I	
Canadian Manufacturers' Association	Association des manufacturiers canadiens
c. C-18, Schedule	
Canadian National Railway	Chemins de fer nationaux du Canada
c. C-19, s. 2	
Canadian National Railway Company	Compagnie des chemins de fer nationaux du Canada
c. A-10, s. 15(1)(a)	
Canadian Nationals Act	Loi des ressortissants du Canada
c. C-31, s. 6	
Canadian Ownership and Control Determination Act	Loi sur la détermination de la participation et du contrôle canadiens
c. A-1, Schedule II	
Canadian Patents and Development Limited	Société canadienne des brevets et d'exploitation Limitée
c. F-11, Schedule III, Part I	
Canadian Payments Association	Association canadienne des paiements
c. B-1, s. 174(9)	
Canadian Peace Research and Education Association	Canadian Peace Research and Education Association
c. C-18, Schedule	
Canadian Penitentiary Service	Service canadien des pénitenciers
c. P-5, s. 2	
Canadian Pension Commission	Commission canadienne des pensions
c. A-1, Schedule I	
c. C-31, s. 2(1)	
Canadian Polish Congress	Canadian Polish Congress
c. C-18, Schedule	
Canadian Ports Corporation	Société canadienne des ports
c. F-11, Schedule III, Part II	
Canadian Pugwash Group	Canadian Pugwash Group
c. C-18, Schedule	
Canadian Radio-television and Telecommunications Commission	Conseil de la radiodiffusion et des télécommunications canadiennes
c. A-1, Schedule I	
Canadian Red Cross Society	Société canadienne de la Croix-Rouge
c. C-31, s. 48	
Canadian salt water fisherman	pêcheur canadien en eau salée
c. C-31, s. 6	
Canadian Saltfish Corporation	Office canadien du poisson salé
c. F-11, Schedule III, Part I	
Canadian Security Intelligence Service	Service canadien du renseignement de sécurité
c. C-46, s. 193(2)(f)	
Canadian Sports Pool Corporation	Société canadienne des paris sportifs
c. F-11, Schedule III, Part I	
Canadian Student Pugwash Group	Pugwash étudiant du Canada
c. C-18, Schedule	
Canadian Teachers Federation	Fédération canadienne des Enseignants
c. C-18, Schedule	

Canadian Transport Commission
  c. A-1, Schedule I
Commission canadienne des transports

Canadian Unity Information Office
  c. A-1, Schedule I
Centre d'information sur l'unité canadienne

Canadian Wheat Board
  c. C-24, s. 2(1)
Commission canadienne du blé

  c. C-48, s. 13(1)
Commission canadienne du blé Canagrex

Canagrex
  c. F-11, Schedule III, Part I

cancel/to
  (a decision)
    c. A-7, s. 10(2)
annuler

cancellation
  (of a debt)
    c. A-10, s. 14(2)
annulation

  (of a licence)
    c. L-9, s. 33(/d/)
révocation

Cannabis sativa/L.
  c. N-1, s. 2
Cannabis sativa/L.

capabilities
  c. C-23, s. 16(1)
moyens

capacities
  c. A-10, s. 11
pouvoirs

capacity
  capacity of a natural person
    c. A-13, s. 4
capacité d'une personne physique

  capacity, rights, powers and privileges of a natural person
    c. C-10, s. 16(1)
capacité d'une personne physique

  have the capacity/to
    c. A-13, s. 6
posséder la capacité

  in any capacity
    c. C-46, s. 167(2)
en n'importe quelle qualité

  in his official capacity
    c. C-46, s. 119(1)(a)iii)
en sa qualité officielle

  in the capacity of a legal representative
    c. C-44, s. 32(1)
en qualité de mandataire

  lack of capacity
    c. C-40, s. 28(1)
défaut de capacité

  legal capacity
    c. B-1, s. 96(1)(c)
    c. C-44, s. 69(1)c)
capacité juridique

  private person of full age and capacity
    c. C-50, s. 3
personne physique majeure et capable

  public officer in his capacity as such
    c. F-11, s. 159(1)
fonctionnaire public ès qualités

  to have capacity (to dispose or to deal with)
    c. B-3, s. 71(2)
être habile

  to have capacity (to dispose or to deal with)
    c. B-3, s. 71(2)
être habile

  to have capacity to contract
    c. C-46, s. 748(3)
avoir qualité pour passer un contrat

Cape Breton Development Corporation
  c. F-11, Schedule III, Part I
Société de développement de Cap-Breton

capital

capital account
  c. C-19, s. 39

compte de capital

capital budget
  c. C-41, s. 100(3)
  c. F-11, s. 102(2)(c)

budget d'investissement

capital expenditure program

programme de dépenses en
  immobilisations

  c. C-9, s. 57(2)

capital project
  c. C-9, s. 57(1)(e)

projet d'investissement

capital requirements
  c. C-41, s. 100(3)

besoins de capital

capital stock
  c. B-1, s. 2(1)

capital social

capital stock
  c. A-2, s. 20

capital-actions

capital transfers
  c. B-7, Schedule I, Article VI,
    Section 1

transferts de capitaux

issued capital
  c. B-1, s. 29(1)

capital souscrit

paid-in capital account
  c. B-1, s. 120(1)

compte capital versé

working capital
  c. C-9, s. 52(1)

fonds de roulement

capitalization
  c. A-2, s. 18(1)(d)

capitalisation

capitalized value
  c. C-17, s. 7(1)(j)

valeur capitalisée

carbon

carbon, photographic or other
copy (of a document)

copie au carbone, copie
  photographique ou autre copie

  c. C-34, s. 69(1)

card

payment card
  c. B-1, s. 173(1)(k)

carte de paiement

care

care and supervision (of
children)

entretien et surveillance

  c. Y-1, s. 3(1)(h)

care, diligence and skill of a
reasonably prudent trustee

soin, diligence et compétence d'un
  bon fiduciaire

  c. C-44, s. 91b)

care, supervision and control (of
a person)

soins, surveillance et contrôle

  c. C-46, s. 2

have under his care and
control/to

avoir sous ses soins ou son contrôle

  c. C-46, s. 79

reasonable care
  c. A-1, s. 74

diligence nécessaire

reasonable care and skill
  c. C-46, s. 45(a)

soins et habileté raisonnables

to be under a legal duty to have
and to use reasonable
knowledge, skill and care

être légalement tenu d'apporter une
  connaissance, une habilité et des
  soins raisonnables

  c. C-46, s. 216

to have the care or control of a
vehicle

avoir la garde ou le contrôle d'un
  véhicule

  c. C-46, s. 253

carelessly
  c. A-7, s. 19(1)(a)

par négligence

cargo
cargo, stores and tackle of a vessel wrecked, stranded or in distress
c. C-46, s. 2

cargaison, approvisionnement, agrès et apparaux d'un navire naufragé, échoué ou en détresse

cargo manifest
bill of lading, cargo manifest, shipping order, way-bill and switching order
c. T-19, s. 2

connaissement, manifeste, ordre d'expédition, feuille de route et bulletin de manoeuvre

Caribbean Development Bank

c. B-1, s. 190(5)(a)(iii)

Banque de développement des Antilles

carriage
(of agricultural products)
c. A-7, s. 5(2)

transport

carrier
air carrier
c. A-2, s. 12

transporteur aérien

common carrier
c. C-46, s. 422(1)(e)

voiturier public

keeper of a warehouse, factor, agent or carrier
c. C-46, s. 389(1)(a)

gardien d'un entrepôt, facteur, agent ou voiturier

carry on a business/to
c. C-44, s. 174(1)b)i)

exercer une activité commerciale

carry on an activity/to
c. A-13, s. 5

exercer une activité

carry on business/to
c. B-6, s. 3(1)

poursuivre des opérations

carry out/to
(a program)
c. C-11, s. 11(2)(c)

réaliser

establish, maintain and carry out/to (security measures)
c. A-2, s. 7(4)

prendre et exercer

carrying out
(of services)
c. A-2, s. 4(g)

exécution

case
(in court)
c. S-26, s. 30(5)

cause

before the close of the case of the prosecution
c. C-46, s. 615(5)(a)

avant que la poursuite n'ait terminé son exposé

specific case or particular matter
c. A-4, s. 4(2)

cas bien précis ou spécifiques

cased
coin cased with gold
c. C-46, s. 448

pièce doublée d'or

cash
c. B-1, Schedule XI
c. L-12, s. 75(6)(a)(i)(A)

encaisse

numéraire

(of a company)
c. L-12, s. 60(10)

espèces en caisse

cash contribution
c. C-6, s. 2

contribution pécuniaire

cash on hand
c. L-12, s. 72(4)a)

fonds en caisse

cash on hand and on deposit
c. C-41, s. 50(a)

espèces en caisse ou en dépôt

cash resources   liquidités
    c. B-1, Schedule XI
cash termination allowance   allocation de cessation en espèces
    c. C-17, s. 10
cash/to
    (a cheque)   encaisser
       c. F-11, s. 159(1)
    cash or negotiate/to (a cheque)   encaisser ou négocier (un chèque)
       c. B-2, s. 24(3)
casting vote   voix prépondérante
    c. B-6, s. 30(2)
    c. C-41, s. 20(3)
casual   fortuit
    c. C-8, s. 6(2)(b)
    casual expense   dépense imprévue
       c. P-1, s. 77
category
    occupational category   catégorie professionnelle
       c. P-35, s. 2
cattle
    cattle found astray   bestiaux trouvés errants
       c. C-46, s. 338(1)(a)
    horses, cattle, sheep, swine   chevaux, bovins, ovins, porcins
       c. L-9, s. 10
cause
    dismissal for just cause   congédiement justifié
       c. L-2, s. 230(1)
    good and sufficient cause   cause valable et suffisante
       c. C-34, s. 65(2)
    original cause   cause en première instance
       c. S-26, s. 65(1)
    reasonable cause   motif raisonnable
       c. B-1, s. 136(6)
       c. C-44, s. 20(6)
cause/to
    cause bodily harm/to   infliger des lésions corporelles
       c. C-46, s. 267(1)b)
cause of action   cause d'action
    c. B-1, s. 23(2)
    c. C-19, s. 44(3)
    c. C-50, s. 22(3)(c)   fait générateur
    c. F-7, s. 39(1)
    c. C-46, s. 724(2)   fait générateur de litige
    c. F-7, s. 22(3)   droit d'action
caution
    caution, caveat or memorial   mise en garde, avertissement ou
                          bordereau
       c. B-1, s. 177(8)(b)
    caveat or caution (in respect of   mise en garde ou avis
    land)
       c. B-3, s. 74(3)
caveat
    caution, caveat or memorial   mise en garde, avertissement ou
                          bordereau
       c. B-1, s. 177(8)(b)
    caveat or caution (in respect of   mise en garde ou avis
    land)
       c. B-3, s. 74(3)
cease/to
    cease to be an employee/to   perdre le statut d'employé
       c. L-2, s. 3(2)
    cease to exist/to (a corporation)   être dissous
       c. B-1, s. 154(b)

cease to have effect être périmé
   c. A-8, s. 11(2)
ceiling
  (for quantities or values) plafond
   c. A-8, s. 14(a)
celebration
  (of marriage) célébration
   c. C-3, s. 8(2)(b)
census recensement
   c. C-2, s. 15(2)(b)
center-fire
  rim-fire or center-fire munition à percution annulaire ou
  ammunition centrale
   c. C-46, s. 84(1)
central cooperative credit société coopérative de crédit
society centrale
   c. B-1, s. 2(1)
   c. C-21, s. 2(1)
central securities register registre central
   c. B-1, s. 77(2)
Centre québécois de relations Centre québécois de relations
internationales internationales
   c. C-18, Schedule
ceremonial procedure cérémonial
   c. C-29, s. 27(g)
certain
  sum certain somme déterminée
   c. C-24, s. 32(1)(b)
certificate certificat
   c. A-11, s. 7(1)
  baptismal certificate certificat de baptême
   c. Y-1, s. 57(2)(a)
  birth certificate certificat de naissance
   c. Y-1, s. 57(2)(a)
  certificate of amendment certificat modificateur
   c. C-44, s. 13(1)
  certificate of citizenship certificat de citoyenneté
   c. C-29, s. 2(1)
  certificate of continuance certificat de prorogation
  (corporation)
   c. C-44, s. 268(8)
  certificate of his designation certificat attestant sa qualité
  (inspector)
   c. C-32, s. 30(2)
  certificate of insurance certificat d'assurance
   c. A-2, s. 18(1)(j)
  certificate of judgment certificat de jugement
   c. S-26, s. 51
  certificate of naturalization certificat de naturalisation
   c. C-46, s. 58(2)
  certificate of title certificat de titre
   c. T-7, s. 9(1)
  duplicate instrument, memorial, double de tout instrument,
  certificate or document in mémoire, certificat concernant
  respect to registration of titles l'enregistrement de titres
   c. C-46, s. 2
  non-interest bearing certificate certificat ne portant pas intérêt
   c. F-11, s. 2
  parole certificate certificat de libération
   conditionnelle
   c. P-2, s. 18
  security certificate certificat de valeur mobilière
   c. C-44, s. 48(2)

share certificate c. B-1, s. 9(6)	certificat d'action
certification	
(of aircraft) c. A-2, s. 8(1)(b)	certification
(of bargaining unit) c. L-2, s. 24	accréditation
certified	
(by a Minister) c. C-8, s. 11(1)	reconnu
certified copy c. A-2, s. 27(1)(b)	copie certifiée
certified non-Canadian ship c. C-31, s. 6	navire non canadien certifié
certified translation of the judgment c. C-30, Schedule, Article VI, 4(b)	traduction certifiée conforme du jugement
certified under his hand and official seal c. S-26, s. 82(/b/)	authentifié, signé et revêtu de son cachet officiel
copy purporting to be certified c. A-4, s. 5(3)	copie censée certifiée conforme
notarially certified (copies of mortgages) c. C-19, s. 33	visé par notaire
certify/to	
(a certificate) c. L-2, s. 164(2)(a)	attester
(a cheque) c. C-21, s. 31(2)(a)	viser
(a copy) c. A-11, s. 6	certifier
sign, certify, attest or execute/to c. A-2, s. 27(1)(c)	signer, certifier, attester ou établir
certiorari c. A-7, s. 12 c. C-46, s. 482(3)(c)	certiorari
cessation	
(of work) c. L-2, s. 3(1)	arrêt de travail
chair	
leave the chair/to (of the Senate) c. P-1, s. 17	abandonner la présidence
chairman	
(of the board) c. C-44, s. 126(1)(a)	président du conseil d'administration
challenge/to	
(an election or an appointment) c. B-1, s. 74(2)(a)	contester
challenge the array/to (of jurors) c. C-46, s. 629(2)	récuser le tableau des jurés
chambers	
in chambers (court) c. B-3, s. 183(1)	en chambre
judge in chambers c. S-26, s. 71(1)	juge siégeant en chambre
judge sitting in chambers c. C-46, s. 834(2)	juge siégeant en chambre
jurisdiction of a judge sitting in chambers c. S-26, s. 18	juridiction d'un juge en chambre

sitting in chambers (judge of the court)   siègeant en chambre
    c. C-46, s. 482(3)(b)

chance

game of chance or skill   jeu de hasard ou d'adresse
    c. C-34, s. 59(1)

chancery

master in chancery   conseiller maître en chancellerie
    c. C-39, s. 22(1)

character

(of the accused)   réputation
    c. C-46, s. 737(1)

evidence of character and repute   preuve de moralité ou de réputation
    c. C-46, s. 757

official character (of a person)   qualité officielle
    c. C-23, s. 11

official character (of a person)   caractère officiel
    c. A-2, s. 27(2)

original character (of a work)   caractère original
    c. C-42, s. 2

person of known immoral character   personne reconnue de mauvaises moeurs
    c. C-46, s. 212(1)(b)

previously chaste character   moeurs antérieurement chastes
    c. C-46, s. 153(2)(a)

without proof of the signature or official character of the person (by whom the certificate purports to be signed)   sans qu'il soit nécessaire de prouver l'authenticité de la signature ni la qualité officielle du signataire
    c. C-46, s. 136(2.1)

charge   commission
    c. B-7, Schedule I, Article V, Section 8(a)(i)

    c. C-37, s. 8   servitude

(for aircraft)   taxe
    c. A-2, s. 5

(for treatment of waste)   redevance
    c. C-11, s. 17(2)(a)

(in court)   frais
    c. F-11, s. 119(2)

(on land)   servitude foncière
    c. B-3, s. 219(2)(c)

charge expenditures against appropriation/to   imputer les dépenses sur les crédits
    c. F-11, s. 28

charge or surcharge   taxe ou surtaxe
    c. A-10, s. 2(1)

charge to the jury   exposé du juge au jury
    c. C-46, s. 682(2)

charge, encumbrance or restriction (of a share)   charge ou restriction
    c. B-1, s. 9(2)

charge, mortgage, hypothecate, cede and transfer, pledge or otherwise create a security interest/to   consentir une sûreté, notamment par hypothèque, cession, transfert ou gage
    c. A-10, s. 18(c)

costs, charges and expenses   frais judiciaires et extrajudiciaires
    c. L-12, s. 43(3)

first charge   charge de premier rang
    c. N-11, s. 29(3)

have the charge, management or control/to (person)   avoir compétence ou pleine autorité
    c. C-32, s. 2

in charge of/to be (baggage)   être sous la garde de
    c. C-26, Schedule I, Article
    18(2)
interest in or charge on property   droit grevant des biens
    c. C-44, s. 2(1)
lawful charge   imputation régulière
    c. F-11, s. 33(3)(a)
overdraft charge   frais pour découvert de compte
    c. C-46, s. 347(2)
person in charge of (a place)   responsable
    c. F-27, s. 22(2)
statutory charge   sûreté prévue par des textes
    législatifs

    c. L-12, s. 61(1)e)
subsequent charge   inculpation subséquente
    c. C-46, s. 736(3)(c)
to have lawful charge (of a   avoir la charge légale
person)
    c. C-46, s. 280(1)
trial of the charge   audition du procès
    c. C-46, s. 556(2)(a)
trial of the charge   procès sur l'inculpation
    c. C-46, s. 525(3)
charge/to   inculper
    c. C-9, s. 22(3)
    c. Y-1, s. 18
(a share)   grever (une action)
    c. A-14, s. 4(1)(b)
(against an account)   porter au débit
    c. C-24, s. 38
(for costs)   imputer
    c. A-3, s. 5(e)
(to expenditures)   imputer (aux dépenses)
    c. C-16, s. 20(b)
charge a toll/to   facturer une taxe
    c. A-15, s. 3(2)
charge the charges/to   facturer les frais
    c. A-15, s. 3(2)
charge, hypothecate, mortgage   créer des charges, hypothèques ou
or pledge/to   nantissements
    c. C-41, s. 10(2)(a)
secure by mortgage, charge or   garantir au moyen d'une
pledge/to   hypothèque, d'une charge ou d'un
    nantissement
    c. C-40, s. 90(1)(e)
charge card
credit or charge card   carte de crédit
    c. B-1, s. 173(1)(k)
charged
(to an account)   imputé (sur un compte)
    c. A-13, s. 32
charged to the Consolidated   débité au Trésor
Revenue Fund
    c. C-17, s. 55(3)
the truth of the matters charged   la vérité des matières imputées
in an alleged libel   dans un prétendu libelle
    c. C-46, s. 612(1)
charges   frais
    c. A-3, s. 5(e)
borrower's charges   frais à la charge des emprunteurs
    c. N-11, s. 2
charge the charges/to   facturer les frais
    c. A-15, s. 3(2)

cost and charges
   c. C-9, s. 46(1)
                            frais

costs and charges
   c. C-46, s. 809(5)
                            frais et charges

costs and charges to be taxed
   c. C-46, s. 779(1)
                            frais et dépens à taxer

make the charges/to
   c. A-15, s. 3(2)
                            réclamer les frais

operating and income charges
                            frais de fonctionnement et frais
   c. C-10, s. 31
                            imputables sur le revenu

charging
charging of losses against
appropriations
                            imputation des pertes sur les
   c. F-11, s. 80(f)
                            crédits

charitable
charitable corporation
                            société de bienfaisance doté de la
   c. L-12, s. 61(1)d)
                            personnalité morale

charitable corporation
   c. N-11, s. 87
                            association de bienfaisance

charitable or religious
organization
                            organisme de charité ou organisme
   c. C-46, s. 207(1)(b)
                            religieux

charitable organization
   c. C-40, s. 123(2)
                            organisme de bienfaisance

charitable organization
   c. A-13, s. 29
                            oeuvre de charité

for charitable or benevolent
objects
                            à des fins de charité ou de
   c. C-41, s. 10(1)(g)
                            bienfaisance

religious, educational or
charitable object
                            entreprise religieuse, éducative ou
   c. C-42, s. 27(3)
                            charitable

charity
registered charity
   c. C-13, s. 24
                            organisme de charité enregistré
   c. L-2, s. 70(4)

charter
(of a bank)
   c. B-1, s. 4
                            statuts

(of a corporation)
   c. B-1, s. 178(5)(a)
                            charte
   c. C-44, s. 268(1)

charter, constitution or by-laws
(of a trade union)
                            charte, statuts et règlements
   c. L-2, s. 29(3)
                            administratifs

charter/to
(ship)
   c. C-19, s. 28
                            noliser

charter by-law
   c. C-40, s. 3(1)
                            règlement administratif homologué

charterer
   c. C-27, Schedule, Article
     I(/a/)
                            affréteur
   c. C-31, s. 6

charterparty
   c. F-7, s. 22(1)(i)
                            charte-partie

chaste character
previously chaste character
                            moeurs antérieurement chastes
   c. C-46, s. 153(2)(a)

chattel
                            bien meuble
   c. C-25, s. 14
   c. F-7, s. 2

chattel mortgage c. N-11, s. 20(1)(e)	hypothèque sur des biens meubles
deemed to be a chattel/to be c. C-46, s. 4(1)	être censé un bien meuble
chattel mortgage c. B-3, s. 72(2)	nantissement

chattel personal
   title to or interest in a chattel
   personal
   c. C-46, s. 2
	titre à un bien ou droit mobilier ou
	   à un intérêt dans ce bien ou droit

chattels c. B-3, s. 230(3)	biens meubles
goods and chattels, lands and tenements c. C-46, s. 773(1)	biens, effets, terrains et bâtiments

chattels real
   delivery of possession of real
   property or chattels real
   c. S-26, s. 65(1)(c)
	livraison de biens-fonds ou de biens
	   personnels immobiliers

cheating
   cheating at play
   c. C-46, s. 553(c)(v)
	tricher au jeu

check-off
   compulsory check-off (union
   dues)
   c. L-2, s. 70(1)
	précompte obligatoire des
	   cotisations

cheque c. B-4, s. 6(3)	chèque
cancelled cheque c. B-3, s. 6(2)	chèque annulé
crossed cheque c. B-4, s. 7	chèque barré
the making, accepting, discounting or endorsing of a bill of exchange, cheque, draft or promissory note c. C-46, s. 362(1)(c)(vi)	création, acceptation, escompte ou endossement d'une lettre de change, d'un chèque, d'une traite ou d'un billet à ordre

chevron
   military medal, ribbon, badge or
   chevron
   c. C-46, s. 419(b)
	médaille, ruban, insigne ou chevron
	   militaire

chicks c. L-9, s. 42(1)	poussins

chief
   chief agent
   c. L-12, s. 72(2)a)
	principal mandataire

chief place of business (of a company) c. L-12, s. 45(4)	principal établissement
chief accountant c. B-1, s. 47(1)(a)	chef comptable

**Chief Actuary of the
Department of Insurance**
   c. C-8, s. 111(1)(b)
	actuaire en chef du ministère des
	   Assurances

chief executive officer
   c. A-7, s. 7(5)
   c. P-2, s. 11
	premier dirigeant

chief general manager c. B-1, s. 47(1)(a)	premier directeur général
Chief Government Whip c. P-1, s. 62(c)	whip en chef du gouvernement

Chief Justice
   (of the Federal Court)
   c. A-1, s. 55(2)
	juge en chef

chief of the Defence Staff
    c. C-23, s. 29(b)
    chef d'état-major de la défense

Chief of the Defense Staff
    c. C-17, s. 60(1)
    chef d'état-major de la défense

chief officer of customs
    c. A-11, s. 33(3)
    préposé en chef des douanes

Chief petty officer in the Royal Canadian Navy
    c. C-17, s. 60(1)
    premier maître de la Marine royale du Canada

chief place of business
    (of a company)
    c. C-36, s. 9(1)
    principal bureau d'affaires

chief provincial firearms officer
    c. C-46, s. 84(1)
    chef provincial des préposés aux armes à feu

Chief Statistician of Canada
    c. B-3, s. 28(1)
    c. C-8, s. 18(5)(b)
    c. C-34, s. 70(2)(a)
    statisticien en chef du Canada

child
    c. Y-1, s. 2(1)
    enfant

    child of tender years
    c. C-46, s. 118
    enfant en bas âge

    child of the marriage
    c. C-3, s. 2(1)
    enfant à charge

child care institution
    community, residential centre, group home, child care institution, or forest or wilderness camp
    c. Y-1, s. 20(7)
    centre résidentiel local, foyer collectif, établissement d'aide à l'enfance, camp forestier ou camp de pleine nature

Chinese Canadian National Council
    c. C-18, Schedule
    Chinese Canadian National Council

choke/to
    choke, suffocate or strangle another person/to
    c. C-46, s. 246(a)
    étouffer, suffoquer ou étrangler une autre personne

chose in action
    c. C-46, s. 385(1)
    c. F-11, s. 66
    droit incorporel

Christmas Day
    c. L-2, s. 193(2)
    jour de Noël

cinematograph
    (copyright)
    c. C-42, s. 2
    oeuvre cinématographique

circuit
    (court)
    c. J-1, s. 35(1)
    circuit

circular
    dissident's proxy circular
    c. B-1, s. 65(5)(d)
    c. C-44, s. 137(5)(d)
    circulaire dissidente sollicitant des procurations

    management proxy circular
    c. B-1, s. 41(3)
    circulaire de sollicitation de procurations envoyée par la direction

    securities exchange take-over bid circular
    c. C-44, s. 2(7)(a)
    circulaire d'offre d'achat en bourse visant à la mainmise

circulate/to
    circulate a prospectus/to
    c. C-46, s. 400(1)
    mettre en circulation un prospectus

circumstances
  history and circumstances (of a   antécédents et situation
  prisoner)
    c. C-46, s. 761(2)
Citibank Canada   Citibanque Canada
    c. B-1, Schedule II
citizen   citoyen
    c. A-1, s. 4(1)(a)
  Canadian citizen   citoyen canadien
    c. A-1, s. 4(1)(/a/)
citizenship
  certificate of citizenship   certificat de citoyenneté
    c. C-29, s. 2(1)
  citizenship judge   juge de la citoyenneté
    c. C-29, s. 2(1)
city
  chief magistrate of a city,   premier magistrat d'une
  borough or town corporate   municipalité, ville ou autre
    agglomération
    c. S-26, s. 82(/c/)
civil
  civil action ou suit   action au civil
    c. P-35, s. 108
civil action   poursuite civile
    c. B-1, s. 23(2)
    c. C-39, s. 46   action au civil
civil aircraft   aéronef civil
    c. C-46, s. 78(2)
civil aviation   aviation civile
    c. A-2, s. 16
civil process   acte de procédure en matière civile
    c. B-1, s. 178(5)(b)
civil right of action   droit d'action au civil
    c. C-34, s. 62
civilian   civil
    c. C-31, s. 56(1)
Civilian member of Overseas   membre civil du personnel navigant
Air Crew   (outre-mer)
    c. C-31, s. 52
claim   réclamation
    c. A-12, s. 6(4)
    c. B-1, s. 51(6)   créance
    c. B-2, s. 23(c)
    c. C-21, s. 31(2)
  (against Her Majesty)   réclamation
    c. C-46, s. 121(1)(a)(iv)
  (to compensation)   droit à indemnisation
    c. A-11, s. 10
  action to enforce a claim   action en recouvrement
    c. C-26, s. 3
  adverse claim   avis d'opposition
    c. C-44, s. 206(4)
  claim an interest/to   revendiquer un droit
    c. N-1, s. 17(1)
  claim between subjects   action relevant du droit privé
    c. C-9, s. 59(1)
  claim to be collected   créance
    c. C-44, s. 63(3)
  contingent claim   créance conditionnelle
    c. B-7, Schedule II, Article
    VI, Section 5(d)
  contingent claim   créance éventuelle
    c. B-7, Schedule II, Article
    VI, Section 5(c)

debt, obligation or claim c. F-11, s. 25(1)	créance
legality of claim c. L-12, s. 43(1)	légimité des prétentions
to have an interest in a mining claim c. C-46, s. 395(1)	avoir un intérêt dans un claim minier
claim/to c. B-1, s. 80(d)	invoquer un droit
c. C-25, s. 13	prétendre
(ownership) c. B-1, s. 74(2)(d)	prétendre
(under a section) c. C-44, s. 190(3)	se prévaloir
claim of right under a claim of right c. C-46, s. 39(1)	en vertu d'un droit invoqué
claimant c. C-44, s. 190(25)(b)	créancier
c. C-44, s. 216(3)(c) c. C-46, s. 194(4)	réclamant
c. F-7, s. 36	demandeur
(of compensation) c. A-2, s. 8(10)	réclamant
claims rights, interests, claims and demands c. C-9, s. 43(5)	droits et créances
clandestine clandestine or deceptive activities c. C-23, s. 2	activités de nature clandestine ou trompeuse
class (of shares) c. B-1, s. 2(1)	catégorie d'actions
(of traffic) c. A-15, s. 5(1)	catégorie (de trafic)
variety, grade or class (of grain) c. C-24, s. 48(1)	variété, grade ou classe
classification classification and form of licences c. A-2, s. 18(1)(a)	classification et forme des permis
classification of positions c. F-11, s. 10(2)(c)	classification des postes
occupational classification c. L-2, s. 212(3)(b)	catégorie professionnelle
classify/to (a position) c. P-35, s. 7	classifier
(persons into group) c. A-6, s. 2(2)(a)	classer
clause (of an Act) c. A-11, s. 3(k)	disposition
clause, covenant or agreement (in a contract of carriage) c. C-27, Schedule, Article III, 8.	clause, convention, accord
clear clear day c. C-50, s. 25	jour franc

clear of all encumbrances (a title)
c. N-11, s. 12(1)(b)
libre de toute charge

clear title (to lands)
c. N-14, s. 3(2)(a)
titre incontestable

free and clear (of a charge)
c. B-1, s. 9(2)
libre

clearance
c. B-1, s. 98(1)(b)
compensation

(of a sale)
c. C-44, s. 71(1)b)
compensation

effect a clearance/to
c. B-1, s. 98(1)(b)
effectuer une compensation

grant a clearance/to (to a vessel)
c. C-9, s. 42(4)
accorder un congé

security clearance
c. C-23, s. 42(1)
habilitation de securité

security clearance
c. Y-1, s. 40(3)(j)
habilitation sécuritaire

clearing
clearing arrangement
c. B-7, Schedule I, Article VIII, Section 5(a)(xii)
accord de clearing

clearing arrangement
c. C-21, s. 18(1)(d)
accord de compensation

clemency
c. P-2, s. 26
recours en grâce

clergyman
clergyman or minister
membre du clergé ou ministre du culte
c. C-46, s. 176(1)(a)

clerk
(of the court)
c. S-26, s. 38
greffier

clerk of the court
c. C-46, s. 2
greffier du tribunal

clerk of the Crown
c. C-39, s. 22(1)
greffier de la Couronne

clerk or clerk of the court
c. C-39, s. 2(1)
greffier ou greffier du tribunal

clerk, servant or officer
c. B-3, s. 10(3)
commis, préposé ou dirigeant

officer, clerk or employee
c. A-4, s. 3(7)
effectifs

registrar or clerk (of the Court of appeal)
c. C-46, s. 673
registraire ou greffier

solicitor's clerk
c. B-3, s. 113(2)
clerc d'avocat

Clerk
(of the Senate or House)
c. P-1, s. 7(1)(a)
greffier

Clerk of the Privy Council
c. C-10, s. 20(4)
greffier du Conseil privé

clerks
officers, clerks and employees
c. A-2, s. 25
fonctionnaires, commis et préposés

officers, clerks and employees
c. A-4, s. 3(7)
personnel

close
(of a meeting)
c. C-44, s. 106(5)
clôture

at the close of business
    c. C-44, s. 134(3)(a)(i)
before the close of the case of the
prosecution
    c. C-46, s. 615(5)(a)

co-op share
    c. C-40, s. 3(1)
coal division
    c. C-25, s. 2
Coalition of First Nations
    c. C-18, Schedule
coastal waters of Canada
    c. C-46, s. 339(6)
coasting trade
    c. C-53, s. 9(1)
cockpit
    c. C-46, s. 447(1)
cockpit voice recording
    c. C-12, s. 32
codicil
    will, codicil or other
    testamentary writing or
    appointment
    c. C-46, s. 2
cognizance
    c. A-12, s. 22(1)
cohabit/to
    c. C-8, s. 55(2)
cohabitation
    continued cohabitation (of
    spouses)
    c. C-3, s. 8(2)(b)(ii)
coin
    coin or token-operated device

    c. C-46, s. 454(b)
    current coin
    c. C-52, s. 12
    subsidiary coin
    c. C-52, s. 2
coin-operated
    coin-operated or currency
    exchange device
    c. C-46, s. 351(2)
coinage
    c. A-1, s. 18(/d/)(i)
collateral
    collateral mortgage
    c. B-1, s. 176(1)
    collateral security
    c. C-40, s. 93(2)
    collateral security
    c. L-12, s. 61(3)(a)i)
    original or collateral agreement
    or arrangement
    c. C-46, s. 347(2)
    person holding stock as
    collateral security
    c. L-12, s. 41(4)
    security as collateral
    c. L-12, s. 61(9)

à l'heure de fermeture des bureaux

avant que la poursuite n'ait terminé
    son exposé

part sociale

division des charbonnages

Coalition of First Nations

eaux côtières du Canada

cabotage

arène pour les combats de coqs

enregistrement pilotage

testament, codicille ou autre écrit
    ou disposition testamentaire

compétence

cohabiter

maintien de la cohabitation

appareil automatique fonctionnant
    au moyen d'une pièce de monnaie
    ou d'un jeton

pièce ayant cours légal

pièce de monnaie divisionnaire

appareil à sous ou distributeur
    automatique de monnaie

monnayage

hypothèque subsidiaire

garantie subsidiaire

bien donné en garantie

convention initiale ou annexe

gagiste d'actions nanties

sureté supplémentaire

collateral security	sûreté accessoire
c. C-7, s. 27(3)	
collect/to	
(data)	recueillir
c. C-11, s. 7	
(information)	recueillir
c. C-23, s. 12	
(payment)	percevoir
c. A-2, s. 12	
collect one's property/to	recouvrer ses biens
c. B-1, s. 287(7)(c)	
fix, impose and collect/to (levies or charges)	instituer et percevoir
c. A-6, s. 2(2)(a)	
collectable	
(taxes)	recouvrable
c. C-41, s. 11(1)(a)(iv)	
collection	
(of a cheque)	encaissement
c. B-4, s. 168(b)	
(of information)	collecte
c. C-23, s. 16(1)	
(of taxes)	perception
c. B-1, s. 103(1)(d)	
agent for collection (of a cheque)	encaisseur
c. B-4, s. 172(1)	
for collection or for surrender	pour recouvrement ou pour remise
c. B-1, s. 88(1)(a)	
recovery or collection of any debt or obligation due or payable	recouvrement d'une créance
c. F-11, s. 156(a)	
collective agreement	convention collective
c. L-2, s. 3(1)	
collective work	recueil
c. C-42, s. 2	
collegial body	organe collégial
c. C-46, s. 2	
collision	
action for collision	action pour collision
c. F-7, s. 2	
collude/to	
connive at or collude in (the commission of an offence)	être de connivence ou de collusion
c. F-11, s. 80(a)(ii)	
conspire or collude/to (to defraud)	participer à une entente délictueuse ou collusoire
c. F-11, s. 80(b)	
collusion	collusion
c. 3 (2nd Supp.), s. 11(4)	
by a threat or an artifice or by collusion with a person	au moyen d'une menace ou d'un artifice ou de collusion avec une personne
c. C-46, s. 350(b)(i)	
colour	
under colour of pretended authority	sous le prétexte d'une prétendue autorisation
c. C-46, s. 146(c)	
colour of right	
fraudulently and without colour of right	frauduleusement et sans apparence de droit
c. C-46, s. 322(1)	
without colour of right	sans apparence de droit
c. C-46, s. 72(2)	

combination
  alone or in combination with others   seul ou en liaison avec d'autres
    c. C-46, s. 422(1)
  association or lawful combination of workmen or employees   association ou alliance légitime d'ouvriers ou d'employés
    c. C-46, s. 425(a)
  business combination   regroupement d'entreprises
    c. B-1, s. 168(4)
  conspiracy, combination, agreement or arrangement   complot, association d'intérêts, accord ou arrangement
    c. C-34, s. 21(3)
combine   coalition
    c. C-37, s. 4(c)
combine/to
  (with another person)   se coaliser
    c. C-34, s. 45(1)
combined
  consolidated or in combined form (financial statement)   sous forme consolidée ou cumulée
    c. C-44, s. 160(5)(a)
come into force/to   entrer en vigueur
    c. A-2, s. 28(1)
    c. Y-1, s. 20(2)   être exécutoire
command
  lawful command   ordre légitime
    c. C-17, s. 18(4)(c)
commence/to
  (an action)   intenter
    c. F-7, s. 43(3)
  (prosecution)   intenter
    c. A-2, s. 26
commencement
  (an action or proceeding)   introduction
    c. B-1, s. 159(2)
  formal commencement   préambule formel
    c. C-46, s. 590(3)
commerce
  trade or commerce   commerce
    c. C-46, s. 379
commercial
  commercial air service   service aérien commercial
    c. A-2, s. 12
  commercial establishment   établissement commercial
    c. P-1, s. 80(1)(c)
  reasonable commercial standards   normes commerciales raisonnables
    c. C-44, s. 75
comminatory
  (clause of a contract)   comminatoire
    c. F-7, s. 37
commission
  (appointment)   commission
    c. A-9, s. 2(1)
  (of an offence)   perpétration
    c. C-11, s. 33
  (payment)   commission
    c. B-1, s. 33(3)
  (to take evidence)   commission rogatoire
    c. A-1, s. 54(1)
  civil or military commission   commission civile ou militaire
    c. C-46, s. 118

commission of terrorist acts	perpétration d'actes de terrorisme
c. A-1, s. 15(2)(c)	
commission under the Great Seal	commission sous le sceau
c. A-17, s. 3(1)	
empower by commission/to	habiliter par commission
c. S-26, s. 81(1)	
joint commission	commission mixte
c. C-11, s. 5 in fine	
on commission (for taking evidence)	commission rogatoire
c. F-7, s. 53(1)	
secret commission	commission secrète
c. C-46, s. 426	
commission merchant	
(livestock)	commissionnaire
c. L-9, s. 10	
commissioner	
commissioner authorised to take and receive affidavits	commissaire habilité à recevoir les affidavits
c. S-26, s. 82(a)	
commissioner for administering oaths in the Supreme Court of Canada	commissaire aux serments auprès de la Cour suprême du Canada
c. S-26, s. 81(3)	
commissioner for oaths	commissaire aux serments
c. C-7, s. 13(2)	
commissioner for taking affidavits	commissaire aux serments
c. A-16, s. 19(1)	
c. B-2, s. 16	
c. B-6, s. 7(1)	
conciliation commissioner	commissaire-conciliateur
c. L-2, s. 3(1)	
Commissioner of Patents	commissaire aux brevets
c. C-42, s. 47	
Commissioner of Corrections	commissaire aux services correctionnels
c. P-5, s. 2	
commit/to	
commit an act or omission/to	commettre une action ou omission
c. C-46, s. 7(1)	
commit to stand trial/to (an accused)	renvoyer pour subir son procès
c. C-46, s. 478(4)	
commit waste/to	
(on property)	dégrader
c. S-26, s. 65(1)(/c/)	
commitment	engagement
c. A-2, s. 19	
(to prison)	incarcération
c. B-3, s. 189(2)	
financial commitment	engagement financier
c. F-11, s. 7(1)(c)	
committal	
order of committal	ordonnance de placement
c. Y-1, s. 24(2)	
warrant of committal	mandat d'incarcération
c. C-46, s. 718(7)	
warrant of committal	mandat de dépôt
c. C-46, s. 734	
committal to custody	envoi sous garde
c. Y-1, Schedule, Form 7	

committee
    c. C-17, s. 36(2)
  committee of directors
    c. F-11, s. 110(1)
  committee of directors (of
  corporation)
    c. C-44, s. 115(1)
  executive committee
    c. C-40, s. 69(5)
  executive committee
    c. L-12, s. 24(2)
  executive committee(of the
  Board)
    c. P-2, s. 3(3)
  trustee, guardian, committee,
  curator, tutor, executor,
  administrator or representative
  of a deceased person
    c. B-1, s. 75(2)
    c. C-44, s. 48(2)
  youth justice committee
    c. Y-1, s. 69

commodities
    c. C-14, s. 9(1)(b)(i)

commodity
    c. A-15, s. 5(1)
  agricultural commodity
    c. A-8, s. 2(1)

common bawdy-house
    c. C-46, s. 197(1)

common betting-house
    c. C-46, s. 197(1)

common gaming house
    c. C-46, s. 197(1)

common intention
    c. C-46, s. 21(2)

common jail
  penitentiary, common jail,
  public or reformatory prison,
  lock-up, guard-room

    c. C-46, s. 2

common law
  at common law
    c. C-42, Schedule II
  common law of England
    c. B-4, s. 9
  offence at common law
    c. C-46, s. 9(a)
  principles of common law
    c. C-46, s. 8(3)

common nuisance
    c. C-46, s. 180(2)

commonly known/to be
  (name)
    c. C-42, s. 34(4)(b)

commotion
  riot and civil commotion
    c. C-27, Schedule, Article IV,
    2

communicate/to
    c. C-20, s. 18(2)
    c. C-42, s. 3(1)(f)

curateur

comité d'administration

comité du conseil d'administration

comité exécutif

comité de direction

bureau

fiduciaire, tuteur, curateur,
exécuteur ou administrateur de
succession

comité de la justice pour la jeunesse

denrées

marchandise

produit agricole

maison de débauche

maison de pari

maison de jeu

intention commune

pénitencier, prison commune,
prison publique, maison de
correction, poste de police ou corps
de garde

d'après la common law

common law d'Angleterre

infraction en common law

principes de la common law

nuisance publique

être généralement connu

émeute ou trouble civil

divulguer

transmettre

communicate an information/to
c. A-16, Schedule I, Article 19
communities
English and French linguistic minority communities
c. 31 (4th Supp.), s. 84
community
community, residential centre, group home, child care institution, or forest or wilderness camp
c. Y-1, s. 20(7)
master plan of community development and land utilization
c. N-11, s. 2
community service

c. Y-1, s. 20(1)(g)
commute/to
(sentence)
c. P-2, s. 8(2)
company
c. C-44, s. 2(1)
amalgamated company
c. L-12, s. 102(1)
company acquired
c. A-16, s. 2
company incorporated
c. A-16, s. 2
company or corporation

c. A-16, s. 20(2)
company or other body corporate
c. F-11, s. 83(1)(b)
company or other legal person
c. C-30, Schedule, Article II, 2(d)(v)
company, body corporate, unincorporated body or society

c. C-46, s. 328(e)
debtor company
c. C-36, s. 2
federal company
c. C-44, s. 4
incorporated company

c. C-41, s. 5(1)
insurance company
c. C-7, s. 2
c. C-44, s. 3(2)(b)
joint stock company
c. C-41, s. 43
loan company
c. C-7, s. 2
c. C-21, s. 2(1)
c. C-44, s. 3(2)(d)
private company
c. C-44, s. 49(12)
society or company
c. B-6, s. 45(a)

communiquer un renseignement

minorités francophones et anglophones

centre résidentiel local, foyer collectif, établissement d'aide à l'enfance, camp forestier ou camp de pleine nature

plan directeur de développement local et d'occupation du sol

travail bénévole au profit de la collectivité

commuer

compagnie

nouvelle société

personne morale acquise

personne morale constituée

personne morale, y compris une compagnie

aucun équivalent

société ou autre personne morale

compagnie, personne morale, organisme non constitué en personne morale ou société

compagnie débitrice

personne morale de régime fédéral

compagnie constituée en personne morale

compagnie d'assurance

compagnie par actions

société de prêt

compagnie privée

société ou compagnie

trust company c. C-44, s. 3(2)(c)	société fiduciaire
trust company c. C-7, s. 2 c. C-21, s. 2(1)	société de fiducie
comparative financial statements c. C-44, s. 155(1)(a)	états financiers comparatifs
compassionate ground c. C-29, s. 5(3)	raison d'ordre humanitaire
compel/to	
(a court) c. B-1, s. 125(9)	ordonner
(a person) c. C-12, s. 19(e)	contraindre
(to testify) c. B-3, s. 164(3)	contraindre
compellable	
competent and compellable witness c. C-46, s. 112(10)	témoin habile à témoigner et contraignable
competent or compellable (to be) c. C-3, s. 10(4)	être apte ou contraignable
compelling	
compelling the appearance c. C-46, s. 738(5)	comparution forcée
compensate/to	
(loss) c. C-10, s. 22(3)	indemniser
compensation	indemnisation
c. A-11, s. 10	
c. A-10, s. 12(1)(c) c. A-11, s. 10	indemnité
c. B-1, s. 203(2)	rétribution
c. B-1, s. 293(4) c. C-44, s. 222(4)	indemnité compensatoire
(for performance of duties) c. P-35, s. 2	rétribution
by way of compensation c. A-15, s. 4(1)	à titre de compensation
by way of compensation c. Y-1, s. 20(1)(c)	à titre d'indemnité
by way of satisfaction or compensation c. C-46, s. 725(1)	comme réparation ou dédommagement
compensation for higher cost of living c. J-1, s. 27(2)	indemnité de vie chère
order for compensation or for restitution (of property) c. C-46, s. 689(1)	ordonnance d'indemnisation ou de restitution
payment in full of compensation or damages c. C-46, s. 722(4)	paiement intégral de l'indemnité ou des dommages-intérêts
payment of compensation c. A-15, s. 4(2)	paiement de compensation
compete/to c. A-15, s. 6(1)	concurrencer
competence	
(of a court) c. A-2, s. 8(6)	ressort
competent	
competent and compellable witness c. C-46, s. 112(10)	témoin habile à témoigner et contraignable

competent or compellable (to be)   être apte ou contraignable
    c. C-3, s. 10(4)
to be competent (to act)   avoir qualité
    c. B-3, s. 106(1)
competing purchasers   acheteurs concurrents
    c. C-34, s. 51(2)
competition
public competition   adjudication publique
    c. P-1, s. 14(4)(b)
competitive
competitive or qualifying   examen de concours ou d'aptitudes
examination
    c. C-46, s. 404
competitive position   compétitivité
    c. A-1, s. 20(6)
complainant   plaignant
    c. C-46, s. 2
complained of
act or omission complained of   le fait reproché - acte ou omission
    c. A-6, s. 4(2)
complaint   protestation
    c. C-26, Schedule I, Article
    26(1)
    c. C-46, s. 785   plainte
investigate a complaint/to   faire enquête sur une plainte
    c. A-1, s. 30(1)
make a complaint/to   déposer une plainte
    c. A-1, s. 9(1)(c)
receive a complaint/to   recevoir une plainte
    c. A-1, s. 30(1)
recent complaint   plainte spontanée
    c. C-46, s. 275
complete
(defence)   péremptoire
    c. B-1, s. 82(3)
become complete/to (an   devenir parfait
acceptance)
    c. B-4, s. 38
complete defence   moyen de défense péremptoire
    c. C-44, s. 55(3)
the offence is complete   l'infraction est consommée
    c. C-46, s. 358
completely
control substantially or   contrôler pour une grande part ou
completely/to (business)   complètement
    c. C-34, s. 2
completeness
(of information submitted)   intégralité
    c. C-20, s. 14(1)
completion
(of a contract)   exécution
    c. P-1, s. 40(b)
before the completion of the   avant que l'achat soit complété
purchase
    c. C-46, s. 385(1)
date of completion (of a project)   date d'achèvement
    c. N-11, s. 81(2)(c)
on completion (of an   à l'issue
investigation)
    c. C-23, s. 52(1)(a)
on completion and execution   une fois rempli et signé (formulaire)
(form)
    c. C-44, s. 147

compliance — exécution
    c. A-7, s. 11(1)
    (with a directive) — application
      c. A-10, s. 12(1)(a)
    (with an Act) — observation
      c. P-35, s. 21(1)
    (with conditions) — observation
      c. C-44, s. 87(b)
    (with directions) — exécution
      c. L-2, s. 128(3)
    consent deemed a compliance — consentement vaut observation
      c. S-26, s. 65(2)
    date for compliance (to an order or decision) — date d'exécution
      c. L-2, s. 66(1)
    in compliance with — conformément à
      c. B-1, s. 105(3)(b)
    in substantial compliance — d'une façon qui respecte les conditions essentielles
      c. C-20, s. 10(4)
    monitor the compliance/to (with policies) — suivre l'observation
      c. C-23, s. 30(2)(a)
    to be sufficient compliance with the law — être considéré comme légal
      c. P-5, s. 15(1)

complicity
    innocent of any complicity/to be — ne pas être coupable de complicité
      c. N-1, s. 17(4)(a)

comply/to
    (with a regulation) — respecter
      c. P-35, s. 23(1)(d)

composition — concordat
    c. B-3, s. 2

compound/to
    compound or conceal an indictable offence/to — composer avec un acte criminel ou le cacher
      c. C-46, s. 141

comprehensive
    comprehensive (review) — complet
      c. C-23, s. 56(1)
    comprehensive pension plan — régime général de pension
      c. C-8, s. introduction

comprehensiveness
    (of health care insurance plan) — intégralité
      c. C-6, s. 7(b)

compromise — transaction
    c. B-1, s. 289(h)
    compromise or arrangement (bankruptcy) — transaction ou arrangement
      c. C-36, s. 3(b)
    compromise, adjustment or settlement (of a charge or complaint) — compromis, transaction ou règlement
      c. F-11, s. 80(f)
    payment, satisfaction or compromise (of claims) — paiement, règlement ou transaction
      c. C-44, s. 217(h)

compromise a debt/to — transiger sur une dette
    c. B-3, s. 30(1)(h)

comptroller — contrôleur
    c. C-40, s. 3(1)

Comptroller General of Canada   contrôleur général du Canada
    c. F-11, s. 6(3)
compulsion
    compulsion by threats   contrainte par menaces
      c. C-46, s. 17
    compulsion of spouse   contrainte du conjoint
      c. C-46, s. 18
compulsory
    compulsory borrowing   emprunt forcé
      c. C-40, s. 89
    compulsory licence (copyright)   licence obligatoire
      c. C-42, s. 9(1)
compute/to
    (the average wholesale price)   calculer
      c. A-5, s. 3(1)
computer
    computer program   programme d'ordinateur
      c. C-46, s. 342 1 (2)
    computer service   service d'ordinateur
      c. C-46, s. 342.1(2)
    computer system   ordinateur
      c. C-46, s. 342(2)
conceal/to
    compound or conceal an   composer avec un acte criminel ou
    indictable offence/to   le cacher
      c. C-46, s. 141
    conceal, withhold or   dissimuler, retenir ou détourner
    misappropriate (property)/to
      c. C-44, s. 222(3)
    harbour or conceal a deserter or   receler ou cacher un déserteur ou
    absentee/to   un absent
      c. C-46, s. 54
    knowingly conceal a material   dissimuler intentionnellement un
    circumstance/to   fait essentiel
      c. C-29, s. 10(1)
concealing
    concealing dead body (of a child)   suppression de part
      c. C-46, s. 243
concealment
    without secrecy or attempt at   ouvertement ou sans tentative de
    concealment   dissimulation
      c. C-46, s. 322(3)
concentration
    concentration of alcohol (in   alcoolémie
    blood)
      c. C-46, s. 256(1)
    maximum concentration within   concentration maximale des
    the ranges   niveaux
      c. C-32, s. 2
concern
    concern in the nature of trade   affaire d'un caractère commercial
      c. C-8, s. 2(91)
    public concern   intérêt public
      c. B-9, s. 3(d)
concert
    jointly or in concert   conjointement ou de concert
      c. C-44, s. 194(a)
concession   concession
      c. B-9, s. 30(1)(j)
      c. C-46, s. 207(1)(c)
    limit, boundary or angle of a   limite ou angle d'une concession,
    concession, range, lot or parcel   d'un rang, d'un lot ou d'un lopin
    of land   de terre
      c. C-46, s. 443(1)(b)

conciliation
    c. C-6, s. 12(2)(a)   conciliation
    conciliation board   commission de conciliation
        c. L-2, s. 3(1)
    conciliation commissioner   commissaire-conciliateur
        c. L-2, s. 3(1)
    conciliation officer   conciliateur
        c. L-2, s. 3(1)
conclude/to
    (a proceeding)   mener à terme
        c. C-34, s. 33(6)
    (an agreement)   conclure
        c. C-42, Schedule II, Article
          10
conclusion
    conclusion of the contract   conclusion du contrat
        c. C-26, Schedule I, Article
          11(1)
    final conclusion of a proceeding   issue des poursuites
        c. C-11, s. 23(4)(b)
    final conclusion of the   issue de la poursuite
    proceedings
        c. N-1, s. 15(3)(b)
conclusive
    (a decision)   sans appel
        c. B-3, s. 194
    be admitted in evidence as   faire foi en justice, de façon
    conclusive proof/to   concluante
        c. C-9, s. 39(3)
    conclusive evidence   preuve concluante
        c. C-39, s. 5(2)
        c. C-46, s. 316(3)
    conclusive evidence   preuve péremptoire
        c. S-26, s. 30(3)
    conclusive evidence/to be   faire foi de son contenu
        c. C-26, s. 2(3)
    conclusive judgment   jugement ayant l'autorité de la
                              chose jugée
        c. C-30, Schedule, Article
          VIII
    conclusive of the matters stated   faire péremptoirement foi de son
    therein/to be   contenu
        c. C-29, s. 20(5)
    final and conclusive (a decision)   définitif et sans appel
        c. A-7, s. 12
        c. B-9, s. 16
        c. C-36, s. 15(5)
    final and conclusive judgment   arrêt définitif et sans appel
    (Supreme Court)
        c. S-26, s. 52
conclusive/to be
    conclusive proof/to be   faire foi de son contenu d'une
    (certificate)   manière irréfragable
        c. C-44, s. 256(2)
conclusively
    conclusively presumed/to be   être irréfutablement présumé
        c. L-2, s. 258(3)
concur/to
    (in a report)   donner son agrément
        c. C-18, s. 25(c)
concurrence
    (of a majority of judges)   accord
        c. Y-1, s. 68(1)

written concurrence (of the Commission) c. C-34, s. 16(1)	assentiment écrit
concurrent	
concurrent jurisdiction c. F-7, s. 17(4)	compétence concurrente
concurrent jurisdiction (of courts) c. C-42, s. 37	juridiction concurrente
concurrently	
serve concurrently or consecutively a term of imprisonment/to c. C-46, s. 149(1)	purger concurremment ou consécutivement une peine d'emprisonnement
to serve concurrently (sentence) c. P-2, s. 14(1)(b)	purger concurremment
try concurrently/to (offences) c. L-2, s. 161	instruire concurremment
condemnation c. C-51, s. 51	condamnation
condition	
(prescribed by regulation) c. A-1, s. 8(1)	condition réglementaire
financial condition c. C-46, s. 362(1)(c)	situation financière
condition precedent c. C-44, s. 161(2)(b)iii	condition préalable
conditional	
(delivery) c. B-1, s. 82(4)	sous condition
conditional sale c. C-41, s. 11(1)(d)(ii)	vente sous condition
conditional sale agreement c. B-1, s. 173(1)(e)	contrat de vente conditionnelle
conditionally	
release from custody conditionally/to c. C-46, s. 503(2)	mettre en liberté conditionnelle
conditioner	
water conditioner c. C-11, s. 19	conditionneur d'eau
condominium	
condominium unit c. N-11, s. 2	unité en copropriété
condonation	
condonation or connivance c. C-3, s. 11(1)(c)	pardon ou connivence
conducive c. 31 (4th Supp.), s. 36(1)(c)(i)	propice
conduct	
(of business) c. C-10, s. 12	exercice d'activités
(public conduct (libel)) c. C-46, s. 310(a)	conduite publique
conduct and discipline (of employees) c. C-23, s. 8(2)	conduite et discipline
conduct of proceedings c. P-2, s. 6	déroulement des travaux
control the conduct of the action/to c. C-44, s. 240(a)	assurer la conduite de l'action

criminal conduct — conduite criminelle
    c. Y-1, s. 3(1)(b)
duty and conduct (of officers) — responsabilité professionnelle et morale
    c. C-25, s. 28(d)
improper conduct — conduite répréhensible
    c. C-31, s. 32
past conduct — conduite antérieure
    c. C-3, s. 16(9)
proper conduct (of business of the Board) — exécution
    c. A-4, s. 3(7)
proper conduct (of business) — bonne marche
    c. C-21, s. 6(1)4
proper conduct of business — bon fonctionnement
    c. P-2, s. 11(2)
vexatious conduct — conduite vexatoire
    c. C-39, s. 73(1)(a)

conduct/to
    (a defence) — conduire
      c. C-46, s. 615(1)
    (an inquiry) — conduire
      c. C-45, s. 11(1)
    conduct his defence/to — mener sa défense
      c. C-46, s. 537(3)
    conduct or manage any scheme, contrivance or operation/to — conduire ou administrer un plan, un arrangement ou une opération
      c. C-46, s. 206(1)(d)
    institute and conduct/to (a prosecution) — entamer et diriger
      c. C-34, s. 73(1)

Confederation of National Trade Unions — Confédération des syndicats nationaux
    c. C-18, Schedule

confer/to
    (powers) — attribuer
      c. A-2, s. 10(3)
    (powers or duties) — conférer
      c. A-8, s. 2(2)

conference
    (of judges) — conférence
      c. S-26, s. 30(5)
    pre-hearing conference — conférence préparatoire
      c. C-46, s. 625.1(1)

Conference of Defence Associations — Congrès des Associations de la Défense
    c. C-18, Schedule

confession
    admission, confession or statement (of accused) — aveu, confession ou déclaration
      c. C-46, s. 542(1)
    written acknowledgement or confession — aveux écrits
      c. F-11, s. 77

confession of judgment
    to aknowledge a recognizance of bail, a confession of judgment, a consent to judgment — reconnaître un engagement de caution, une confession de jugement, un consentement à jugement

      c. C-46, s. 405

confidence — renseignements confidentiels
    c. C-23, s. 31(2)

R.S.C. 1985

breach of trust or confidence | abus de confiance
c. C-42, s. 63
confidential basis
on a confidential basis | à titre confidentiel
c. C-12, s. 28(2)
confidential capacity
employed in a confidential | occuper un poste de confiance
capacity/to be
c. L-2, s. 3(1)
confine/to
confine, imprison or forcibly | séquestrer, emprisonner ou saisir
seize another person/to | de force une autre personne
c. C-46, s. 279(2)
confinement | incarcération
c. N-1, s. 26(2)
place of confinement | lieu de détention
c. P-2, s. 19(1)
c. P-20, s. 2
confirm/to
(an act) | entériner
c. C-44, s. 100(d)
confirm a by-law/to | confirmer un règlement
administratif
c. B-1, s. 43(3)
confirm or reverse/to (an act or a | confirmer ou infirmer
decision)
c. B-3, s. 37
confirmation
(of purchase) | confirmation
c. B-1, s. 97(1)(c)
confiscation | confiscation
c. B-7, Schedule I, Article IX,
Section 4
conflict
conflict between sections of an | dispositions incompatibles
Act
c. C-22, s. 14(3)
conflict/to | être en contradiction
c. C-26, Schedule I, Article
33
conflict of interest | conflit d'intérêts
c. B-1, s. 134(1)
c. C-44, s. 83(1)
conflicting
(instructions) | contradictoire
c. C-44, s. 152(2)
conflicting interest | situation de conflit
c. C-12, s. 23(2)
conjugal rights | droits conjugaux
c. C-46, s. 290
restitution of conjugal rights | restitution de droits conjugaux
c. C-46, s. 166(1)(b)
conjugal union | union conjugale
c. C-46, s. 293(1)(a)(ii)
conjunction
in conjunction with an | corrélativement à une demande
application
c. C-46, s. 106(3)
conjuration
witchcraft, sorcery, | magie, sorcellerie, enchantement ou
enchantment or conjuration | conjuration
c. C-46, s. 365(a)

connected
connected by blood relationship, marriage or adoption/to be
c. B-3, s. 4(2)(a)

être uni par les liens du sang, du mariage ou de l'adoption

connected or associated/to be (a business)
c. B-1, s. 310(6)(a)

avoir des rapports ou des liens

most substantially connected/to be (in a province)
c. C-3, s. 6(1)

avoir ses principales attaches

connection
in connection with
c. C-44, s. 217

à l'occasion de

substantial connection (with Canada)
c. C-29, s. 8(/b/)

liens manifestes (avec le Canada)

connivance
condonation or connivance
c. C-3, s. 11(1)(c)

pardon ou connivence

sanction or connivance
c. C-39, s. 55(a)

assentiment ou connivence

connive/to
connive at or collude in (the commission of an offence)
c. F-11, s. 80(a)(ii)

être de connivence ou de collusion

consecutively
sentence served consecutively
c. C-46, s. 85(2)

sentence purgée consécutivement

serve concurrently or consecutively a term of imprisonment/to
c. C-46, s. 149(1)

purger concurremment ou consécutivement une peine d'emprisonnement

consent
c. A-12, s. 20(1)

consentement

c. B-1, s. 16(1)(c)

autorisation

(board of directors)
c. B-1, s. 174(11)(b)

consentement

consent or acquiescence
c. C-42, s. 4(2)

consentement ou acquiescement

mutual consent
c. F-7, s. 37

consentement mutuel

with the knowledge and consent
c. C-46, s. 4(3)(b)

au su et avec le consentement

without his knowledge or consent
c. A-2, s. 22(3)

sans sa connaissance ou son consentement

consent/to
c. B-1, s. 55(1)

acquiescer

(to disclosure)
c. A-1, s. 13(2)(a)

consentir

aid, consent, abet or procure the commission of an offence/to

aider, assister, conseiller ou amener quelqu'un à commettre une infraction

c. C-39, s. 57

consent to judgment
to aknowledge a recognizance of bail, a confession of judgment, a consent to judgment

reconnaître un engagement de caution, une confession de jugement, un consentement à jugement

c. C-46, s. 405

consequence
consequence of the endorsement
c. B-5, s. 3(d)

conséquence de l'endossement

consequences
    legal consequences   sanction
        c. C-42, Schedule II, Article 9
consequential
    consequential amendment   modification corrélative
        c. 3 (2nd Supp.), s. 28
conservatory measure   mesure conservatoire
        c. B-3, s. 46(2)
consider/to
    (a complaint)   étudier
        c. L-2, s. 134(a)
    (evidence)   tenir compte
        c. A-7, s. 10(2)
    consider, draft and prepare for   étudier, rédiger et préparer
    approval/to (regulations)
        c. A-2, s. 4(l)
consideration   apport
        c. B-1, s. 119(1)
        c. C-44, s. 25(1)
        c. B-1, s. 2(2)(b)(i)   contrepartie
        c. C-44, s. 25(3)
        c. C-44, s. 197(d)   prix
    (of an application)   examen
        c. A-2, s. 21(4)
    (of grievances)   étude
        c. C-23, s. 8(2)
    consideration and adjudication   étude et décision
    (claim for compensation)
        c. C-31, s. 21(1)
    corrupt consideration   compensation vénale
        c. C-46, s. 139(3)(c)
    fact or consideration   fait ou considération
        c. B-6, s. 6(1)(e)
    for a consideration   moyennant une contrepartie
        c. C-25, s. 9(2)(b)
    for valuable consideration   à titre onéreux
        c. B-1, s. 145
    for valuable consideration   en contrepartie d'une cause ou
                            d'une considération valable
        c. B-5, s. 4
    for valuable consideration   contre rémunération
        c. C-42, s. 13(2)
    nominal consideration   somme symbolique
        c. T-7, s. 23(1c1)
    payment, consideration, gratuity paiement, contrepartie,
    or benefit   gratification ou profit
        c. A-2, s. 12
    usurious consideration   cause usuraire
        c. B-4, s. 58
    valuable consideration   contrepartie valable
        c. B-3, s. 158(g)
        c. C-46, s. 119(1)(a)iii) in fine
consignee   consignataire
        c. B-5, s. 2
        c. C-26, s. 2(1)
        c. C-46, s. 389(1)(a)
        c. C-26, Schedule I, Article   destinataire
          6(2)
consignment
    (bill of lading)   consignation
        c. B-5, s. 2
    (of agricultural products)   consignation
        c. A-7, s. 14

selling consignment vente par voie de consignation
 c. C-34, s. 38
consignor consignateur
 c. C-26, s. 2(1)
 c. L-9, s. 11(c)
 c. C-26, Schedule I, Article expéditeur
  5(1)
consistent with
 (a section) en conformité avec
 c. A-10, s. 12(1)
consolidate/to
 (a debt) consolider
 c. A-10, s. 17(1)
 (proceedings) joindre
 c. B-3, s. 43(4)
 consolidate accounts/to consolider des comptes
 c. C-44, s. 157(1)
 consolidate with due allowance consolider en réservant une
 for minority interest/to provision convenable pour la
   participation minoritaire
 c. C-41, s. 11(1)(e)(ii)
consolidated
 consolidated index (of répertoire général
 regulations)
 c. S-22, s. 14(1)
 consolidated or in combined sous forme consolidée ou cumulée
 form (financial statement)
 c. C-44, s. 160(5)(a)
 consolidated report on the rapport global des activités
 businesses and activities (of
 corporations)
 c. F-11, s. 151(1)
 consolidated return of assets relevé consolidé de l'actif et du
 and liabilities passif
 c. B-1, Schedule X
Consolidated Revenue Fund Trésor
 c. F-11, s. 2
consolidation unification
 c. A-2, s. 18(1)(e)
 (of a debt) consolidation
 c. A-10, s. 17(2)
 (of shares) regroupement
 c. B-1, s. 45(1)(a)
 c. C-44, s. 49(17)(a)
 consolidation accounting method technique comptable de
   consolidation
 c. B-1, s. 216(1)(a)
 consolidation or amalgamation réunion ou fusion
 (of companies)
 c. C-19, s. 2
 revision or consolidation (of révision ou codification
 regulations)
 c. S-22, s. 15(1)
 split or consolidation (of shares) fonctionnement ou regroupement
 c. B-1, s. 123(6)
consolidation or amalgamation
 (of companies) réunion ou fusion
 c. C-19, s. 2
consortium
 consortium of lenders consortium de financement
 c. B-1, s. 215(6)(c)(iii)
 consortium or syndicate of consortium ou syndicat de
 financing financement
 c. B-1, s. 190(8)

conspicuous
    post up in a conspicuous part/to (of an aircraft)   afficher dans quelque partie bien en vue
        c. C-46, s. 208(3)
conspicuously   ostensiblement
        c. C-44, s. 49(8)
conspiracy   complot
        c. C-46, s. 465(1)
conspire/to   comploter
        c. A-11, s. 47(1)
    conspire or collude/to (to defraud)   participer à une entente délictueuse ou collusoire
        c. F-11, s. 80(b)
    conspire to commit/to   conspirer pour commettre
        c. C-46, s. 46(2)(c)
constable   agent de police
        c. C-39, s. 44(3)
        c. T-7, s. 20(3)
    police constable   agent de police
        c. L-2, s. 3(1)
    police officer or constable   agent de police
        c. C-34, s. 12(5)
    police officer or police constable   officier ou agent de police
        c. C-46, s. 84(3)
    police officer, police constable, bailiff or constable   officier de police, agent de police ou huissier
        c. C-46, s. 2
    private constable   agent de police privé
        c. L-2, s. 3(1)
    special constable   gendarme spécial
        c. C-31, s. 22
    special constable   gendarme auxiliaire
        c. P-35, s. 2
constating
    constating instrument   acte constitutif
        c. C-21, s. 2(1)
constituant   électeur
        c. C-10, s. 35(3)
constitute/to
    (a meeting)   tenir (une réunion)
        c. C-44, s. 114(8)
    (a quorum)   constituer
        c. A-7, s. 7(8)
    constitute a place/to   déclarer un lieu
        c. A-11, s. 30
constitution
    charter, constitution or by-laws (of a trade union)   charte, statuts et règlements administratifs
        c. L-2, s. 29(3)
constitutionally
    constitutionally established system of government   régime de gouvernement constitutionnellement établi
        c. C-23, s. 2
constrain/to   imposer une restriction
        c. C-44, s. 174(1)
    constrain an issue/to (of shares)   limiter une émission
        c. B-1, s. 25(1)
constrained
    constrained share   action faisant l'objet de restrictions
        c. C-44, s. 46(2)
constraint   restriction
        c. B-1, s. 70(2)(f)
        c. C-44, s. 174(2)

constructive
    express, implied or constructive
    trust
        c. L-12, s. 89(1)
                fiducie explicite, implicite ou
                   judiciaire

constructive possession
    transfer of constructive
    possession
        c. B-4, s. 2
                transfert de possession présumée

constructive trust
        c. B-1, s. 206(1)
                fiducie judiciaire

construe/to
        c. B-1, s. 113(3)
        c. C-28, Schedule 9(2)(b)
                interpréter

consul
    consul, vice-consul, acting
    consul, pro-consul or consular
    agent of Her Majesty
        c. S-26, s. 82(e)
                consul ou tout autre agent
                   consulaire de Sa Majesté

consular agent
    consul, vice-consul, acting
    consul, pro-consul or consular
    agent of Her Majesty
        c. S-26, s. 82(e)
                consul ou tout autre agent
                   consulaire de Sa Majesté

consultant
        c. C-10, s. 12
                expert

consultation
    determine by consultation/to
        c. C-32, s. 23(4)(b)
                établir en consultation

consultative
    consultative and advisory
    committee
        c. L-2, s. 138
                comité consultatif

Consumer Price Index
        c. C-8, s. 2(1)
        c. C-28, Schedule, 9(1)(b)
        c. P-1, s. 55(3)(b)(ii)
                indice des prix à la consommation

consumer purchase
        c. B-4, s. 188
                achat de consommation

contact
    sexual contact
        c. C-46, s. 276(1)(b)
                rapports sexuels

container
        c. C-38, s. 2
                contenant
        c. T-19, s. 2
                conteneur
    approved container
        c. C-46, s. 254(1)
                contenant approuvé
    bag, sack or other container or
    covering, (for mail)
        c. C-46, s. 356(1)(a)(ii)
                sac ou autre contenant ou
                   couverture

containment
    secure containment or restraint
        c. Y-1, s. 24(11)
                placement ou internement
                   sécuritaires

contemplate/to
    (a payment)
        c. C-17, s. 50(f)
                envisager

contempt
        c. C-34, s. 19(3)
                désobéissance
    contempt of court
        c. B-1, s. 303(10)
                outrage au tribunal
    contempt of court
        c. B-3, s. 192(3)
                résistance au tribunal

contempt of court committed in the face of the court
   c. C-46, s. 10(1)
criminal contempt of court

   c. P-2, s. 2
to expose a person to hatred, contempt or ridicule
   c. C-46, s. 298
contention
   c. C-42, s. 23(1)
continental margin
outer edge of the continental margin
   c. C-53, s. 2(1)
continental shelf
   c. C-53, s. 2(1)
contingency
   c. C-46, s. 197(1)
(of a bank)
   c. B-1, s. 215(3)(c)
contingency reserve
   c. L-12, s. 67(2)
contingent
contingent expenses
   c. P-1, s. 54
direct and contingent liabilities
   c. F-11, s. 63(2)
future or contingent (obligation)
   c. B-1, s. 289(h)
immediate, contingent or otherwise (interest)
   c. C-34, s. 2
unliquidated, future or contingent claim
   c. C-44, s. 216(3)(c)
continuance
articles of continuance
   c. C-44, s. 187(2)
articles of continuance (of a corporation)
   c. F-11, s. 83(1)
incorporation, amendment, amalgamation, continuance, reorganization, arrangement, dissolution or revival

   c. C-44, s. 2(1)
continuation
certificate of incorporation, continuation, amendment or amalgamation
   c. C-40, s. 5
continuation or repetition of offence
   c. C-34, s. 34(1)(b)
instrument of continuation (of an association)
   c. C-40, s. 10(3)
continuation or resumption
(of cohabitation)
   c. C-3, s. 11(3)

outrage au tribunal commis en présence du tribunal

outrage au tribunal en matière pénale

exposer quelqu'un à la haine, au mépris ou au ridicule

représentation

rebord externe de la marge continentale

plateau continental

contingence, éventualité

éventualité

réserve pour risques généraux

dépenses imprévues

charges directes ou éventuelles

futur ou éventuel

actuel, éventuel ou autre

créance non liquidée, future ou éventuelle

clauses de prorogation

clauses de prorogation

clauses réglementant la constitution ainsi que toute modification, fusion, prorogation, réorganisation, dissolution, reconstitution ou tout arrangement

certificat de constitution en personne morale, de continuation, de modification ou de fusion

continuation ou répétition d'une infraction

acte de maintien en existence

maintien ou reprise

continue/to
  (a company)   continuer une compagnie
    c. C-19, s. 2
  (a corporation)   maintenir une personne morale
    c. A-10, s. 3
  (an injunction)   proroger
    c. C-34, s. 33(5)(a)
  (Parliament)   continuer à fonctionner
    c. P-1, s. 2
  continue as a corporation/to   proroger en société
    c. C-44, s. 3(1)
  continue in office/to   poursuivre son mandat
    c. 31 (4th Supp.), s. 108
  continue or discontinue   poursuivre ou interrompre
  (proceedings)
    c. C-44, s. 217(n)(i)
  continue/to (an order)   proroger
    c. L-2, s. 93(2)(a)
continued
  actual, visible and continued   possession réelle, publique et
  possession   continue
    c. B-1, s. 2(1)(a)
continuing
  forbid the doing or continuing of interdire l'accomplissement ou la
  any act/to   continuation de tout acte
    c. A-2, s. 14(2)(b)
  of continuing effect (summons)   à effet continu
    c. 4 (2nd Supp.), s. 30
continuous
  to commit to continuous custody placer sous garde de façon continue
    c. Y-1, s. 24(12)
contraband   objets détenus illégalement
    c. P-5, s. 35(4)
contraceptive device   moyen anticonceptionnel
    c. F-27, s. 2
contract   disposition contractuelle
    c. A-12, s. 2
    c. A-14, s. 2   contrat
    c. A-17, s. 15(2)   marché
    c. F-11, s. 66
    c. B-5, s. 2   convention
  contract of carriage   contrat de transport
    c. C-27, Schedule, Article I(b)
  contract of purchase   contrat d'acquisition
    c. C-44, s. 71(2)
  contract of service or   contrat de louage de service ou
  apprenticeship   d'apprentissage
    c. C-42, s. 13(3)
  enter into a contract/to   conclure un contrat
    c. A-13, s. 4(c)
  make a contract/to   conclure un contrat
    c. B-1, s. 53(6)
  service contract   contrat de service
    c. C-40, s. 77(1)
  simple contract   contrat simple
    c. B-4, s. 52(1)(a)
  to have capacity to contract   avoir qualité pour passer un contrat
    c. C-46, s. 748(3)
  usurious contract   contrat usuraire
    c. B-4, s. 58
contract/to   contracter
    c. B-7, Schedule I, Article IX,
      Section 2(i)

contract a liability, a debt/to   contracter une obligation, une dette
    c. B-1, s. 180(1)(b)
contract marriage/to   contracter mariage
    c. C-46, s. 290(3)
contractor
    dependent contractor   entrepreneur
      c. L-2, s. 3(1)
contractual arrangement   arrangement contractuel
    c. B-1, s. 269(1)(a)
contrary
    contrary evidence   témoignage contraire
      c. C-46, s. 136(1)
    evidence to the contrary   preuve contraire
      c. A-7, s. 21
      c. A-11, s. 7(2)
contravene/to   enfreindre
    c. B-1, s. 136(6)
contravention
    (of a by-law)   violation
      c. C-9, s. 40
    (of a regulation)   infraction
      c. A-2, s. 18(1)(o)(i)
    (of a section)   contravention
      c. A-12, s. 7(4)
    (of any Act of Parliament)   violation
      c. C-46, s. 2
    contravention notice   avis de contravention
      c. C-24, s. 72(1)
    for any contravention or alleged   pour violation, effective ou
    contravention of law   prétendue, de la loi
      c. F-11, s. 80(f)
    in contravention of   en violation de
      c. B-1, s. 110(15)
    in contravention of   contrairement à
      c. C-42, s. 2
    to bear responsability for their   assumer la responsabilité de leur
    contravention   délit
      c. Y-1, s. 3(1)(a)
contribute/to
    (to a pension plan)   cotiser
      c. L-2, s. 235(2)(b)
contributing
    contributing factors and causes   causes et autres facteurs en jeu
    (of an accident or incident)
      c. A-2, s. 10(1)
contribution   contribution
    c. A-13, s. 33
    c. C-8, s. 2(1)   cotisation
    to be entitled to contribution   répéter les parts des autres
    from other directors   administrateurs
      c. C-44, s. 118(3)
contributor   cotisant
    c. C-8, s. 2(1)
    (to superannuation)   contributeur
      c. C-17, s. 2(1)
contributory   contributeur
    c. C-40, s. 127(3)
    (of a company)   contributeur
      c. C-36, s. 6(b)
    contributory period   période cotisable
      c. C-8, s. 2(1)
    contributory salary and wages   traitement et salaire cotisables
      c. C-8, s. 2(1)

contributory self-employed
earnings
   c. C-8, s. 2(1)

gains cotisables provenant du
travail qu'une personne exécute
pour son propre compte

contrivance
   c. C-42, s. 5(3)

organe

conduct or manage any scheme,
contrivance or operation/to
   c. C-46, s. 206(1)(d)

conduire ou administrer un plan, un
arrangement ou une opération

control
   c. A-17, s. 9(b)
   c. C-8, s. 42(1)

contrôle

surveillance

(of a harbour)
   c. C-9, s. 39(1)

régie

(of an air carrier)
   c. A-2, s. 18(1)(e)

contrôle

(of documents)
   c. A-7, s. 8(4)(a)

garde

(of property)
   c. B-1, s. 189(2)

garde

acquisition of majority control
   c. L-12, s. 51(1)(b)

prise de contrôle majoritaire

administration, management
and control
   c. A-10, s. 11(a)

administration, gestion et
surveillance

be in possession or control/to (of
premises or things)
   c. C-34, s. 12(2)

être en possession ou avoir le
contrôle

care, supervision and control (of
a person)
   c. C-46, s. 2

soins, surveillance et contrôle

control and management (of the
Service)
   c. C-23, s. 6(1)

gestion

control status
   c. C-20, s. 2(1)

état de contrôle

custody or control (of a child)
   c. C-46, s. 214

garde ou contrôle

custody, control or distribution
(of a thing)
   c. C-17, s. 18(4)(c)

garde ou distribution

exercise control or direction/to
(over votes)
   c. C-44, s. 126(1)

exercer le contrôle et avoir la haute
main

have the charge, management or
control/to (person)
   c. C-32, s. 2

avoir compétence ou pleine autorité

have the control of a child/to

   c. C-17, s. 28

être investi de l'autorité sur un
enfant

have under his care and
control/to
   c. C-46, s. 79

avoir sous ses soins ou son contrôle

in one's possession or control
(moneys)
   c. C-24, s. 8(1)

en sa possession ou sous sa
responsabilité

in the possession of or under the
control of (a person)
   c. C-51, s. 22(2)

en la possession ou sous l'autorité
de qqn

internal control and audit
   c. F-11, s. 31(3)

contrôle et vérification internes

jurisdiction over or control
   c. C-9, s. 33

compétence ou pouvoir de contrôle

lawfully under its control/to be
   c. B-6, s. 23 — être légalement sous sa direction

management and control (of a penitentiary)
   c. P-5, s. 16(1) — gestion et contrôle

person having control or direction over an employee
   c. L-2, s. 126(3) — supérieur hiérarchique

person ostensibly in control of the place or premises
   c. C-46, s. 487.1(7) — personne apparemment responsable des lieux

supervision, discipline and control (of young persons)
   c. Y-1, s. 3(1)(e) — surveillance, discipline et encadrement

take control of the assets/to
   c. L-12, s. 83(2)(c) — prendre le contrôle de l'actif

take into one's custody or control/to
   c. B-1, s. 292(c) — prendre sous sa garde et sous son contrôle

to have the care or control of a vehicle
   c. C-46, s. 253 — avoir la garde ou le contrôle d'un véhicule

Canadian ownership or control (of shares)
   c. C-44, s. 174(1)(c) — participation ou contrôle canadien

control/to

(a corporation)
   c. B-1, s. 35(1)(j) — contrôler

(shares)
   c. C-44, s. 2(1)(a) — avoir le contrôle

control and regulate/to (air navigation)
   c. A-2, s. 8(1) — contrôler et régler

control or manage assets/to
   c. B-1, s. 173(4) — contrôler ou gérer un actif

control substantially or completely/to (business)
   c. C-34, s. 2 — contrôler pour une grande part ou complètement

control the conduct of the action/to
   c. C-44, s. 240(a) — assurer la conduite de l'action

control status

(Canadian ownership)
   c. C-20, s. 2(1) — état de contrôle

controlled

controlled drug
   c. F-27, s. 38 — drogue contrôlée

controlled/to be

(a corporation)
   c. B-1, s. 2(2)(e) — être sous le contrôle

(premises)
   c. L-2, s. 109(1) — être placé sous la responsabilité de quelqu'un

controlling

controlling instrument
   c. C-44, s. 65(10) — acte qui habilite

controversy

   c. B-1, s. 74(1) — différend

(between parties to an appeal)
   c. S-26, s. 48(1) — contestation

determine a controversy/to (at election of director)
   c. C-44, s. 145(1) — trancher un différend

matter in controversy litige
  c. C-50, s. 22(1)
convenience
  for convenience of reference only pour la seule commodité de la
    consultation
  c. C-46, s. 3
  public convenience and necessity commodité et besoins du public
    c. A-2, s. 21(10)
conveniently commodément
  c. C-46, s. 509(2)
convention
  international agreement or entente ou convention
  convention internationale
    c. A-2, s. 18(1)(h)
Convention on the means of Convention concernant les mesures
prohibiting and preventing the à prendre pour interdire et
illicit import, export and empêcher l'importation,
transfer of ownership of l'exportation et le transfert de
cultural property propriété illicite des biens
  culturels
  c. C-51, s. 38
conversion détournement
  c. B-1, s. 102
  (of a security) détournement
    c. C-44, s. 75
  (securities) conversion
    c. C-44, s. 2(6)(a)
  conversion of the property (of usurpation du droit de propriété
  copyrighted material)
    c. C-42, s. 38
  conversion privileges privilèges de conversion
    c. B-1, s. 123(2)
  cost of conversion (housing) coût de transformation
    c. N-11, s. 2
  taking or conversion of anything prise ou détournement d'une chose
  (fraudulent)
    c. C-46, s. 322(3)
convert/to
  (a corporation) transformer
    c. B-1, s. 119(2)(d)
  (an endorsement) convertir
    c. B-4, s. 66(5)
  convert into money/to (a réaliser en numéraire
  property)
    c. C-44, s. 227(1)
convertibility convertibilité
    c. B-7, Schedule I, Article
      VIII, Section 4(b)(i)
convertible
  (securities) convertible
    c. C-44, s. 2(1)a)
  convertible share action convertible
    c. C-44, s. 26(5)
convey/to
  (agricultural products) acheminer
    c. A-7, s. 14
  send or convey/to expédier
    c. A-7, s. 4
conveyance
  (of prisoner) transfèrement
    c. C-46, s. 527(3)
  conveyance, assignment and acte de transfert, acte de cession et
  assurance assurance
    c. B-1, s. 273(4)

conveyance, assignment,
transfer and assurance
    c. C-41, s. 10(2)(c)
execution of a conveyance

    c. S-26, s. 65(1)(b)
gift, conveyance, assignment,
sale, transfer or delivery of
property
    c. C-46, s. 392(a)(i)
mail conveyance
    c. C-46, s. 345

conveying
sending or conveying (of
agricultural products)
    c. A-7, s. 5(1)

convict/to
    c. B-1, s. 162(4)
    c. C-8, s. 103(2)

conviction
affirm a conviction/to
    c. C-46, s. 691(1)
on conviction
    c. C-8, s. 103(2)
on conviction or indictment
    c. C-15, s. 20(1)(b)
on summary conviction
    c. C-15, s. 20(1)(a)
previous conviction

    c. C-46, s. 360(2)
cooperative
    c. A-14, s. 2
cooperative association
    c. C-40, s. 3(1)
cooperative basis
    c. C-40, s. 3(1)
cooperative credit association
    c. C-40, s. 6(g)
cooperative enterprises
    c. C-40, s. 6(2)(b)
cooperative organisation
    c. C-21, s. 2(1)
cooperative organization
    c. B-1, s. 2(1)
cooperative society
    c. B-3, s. 2
local cooperative credit society
    c. B-1, s. 2(1)
coordinate/to
(programs)
    c. A-3, s. 7(2)
copies
copies of, or make extracts
from/to (records)
    c. F-27, s. 23(1)(c)
copies or extracts (of books)
    c. A-7, s. 16(1)(c)
copy
    c. B-9, s. 15(4)
    c. B-9, s. 9(3)
(of a document)
    c. C-26, Schedule I, Article
    36

transport, cession, transfert et
constitution de droits

souscription d'un acte translatif de
propriété

don, transport, cession, vente,
transfert ou remise de biens

transport du courrier

transport

déclarer coupable

confirmer une condamnation

sur déclaration de culpabilité

par mise en accusation

par procédure sommaire

déclaration antérieure de
culpabilité

coopérative

association coopérative

principe coopératif

association coopérative de crédit

entreprises coopératives

coopérative

coopérative

société coopérative

société coopérative de crédit locale

coordonner

faire la reproduction totale partielle

reproduction

exemplaire

copie
exemplaire

true copy
  c. A-2, s. 27(1)
true copy (of a notice)
  c. L-2, s. 164(2)(b)
copyright
  c. C-42, s. 3(1)
Copyright Appeal Board

  c. C-42, s. 67(2)
Copyright Office
  c. C-42, s. 46
Corp.
  (corporation)

  c. C-44, s. 10(1)
corporal
  corporal punishment
    c. P-20, s. 10(2)(a)
corporate
  corporate affairs
    c. F-11, s. 88
  corporate existence
    c. C-44, s. 211(6)
  corporate plan
    c. F-11, s. 122(1)
  corporate seal (of an association)
    c. C-40, s. 13(o)
  trademark, trade-name or
  corporate name

    c. B-1, s. 16(1)(c)
corporation
    c. B-1, s. 2(1)
    c. C-44, s. 2(1)
    c. C-44, s. 2(1)
  charitable corporation

    c. L-12, s. 61(1)(d)
  charitable corporation
    c. N-11, s. 87
  corporation of a city
    c. C-46, s. 2
  departmental corporation
    c. F-11, s. 2
  distributing corporation
    c. C-44, s. 21(1)
  financial corporation
    c. B-1, s. 254
  incorporate, form or organize a
  corporation/to
    c. B-1, s. 109(1)(b)
  municipal corporation
    c. C-41, s. 10(1)(a)(ii)
  non-profit corporation
    c. N-11, s. 2
  offeree corporation
    c. C-44, s. 194
  philanthropic corporation

    c. L-12, s. 61(1)(d)
  school corporation
    c. C-41, s. 11(1)(a)(iv)
    c. L-12, s. 61(1)a)vi)

copie conforme

copie certifiée conforme

droit d'auteur

Commission d'appel du droit
  d'auteur

Bureau du droit d'auteur

S.A.R.F. (société par actions de
  régime fédéral)

châtiment corporel

activités des sociétés

personnalité morale

plan d'entreprise

sceau de l'association

marque de commerce, nom
  commercial ou dénomination
  sociale

personne morale

société
société par actions
société de bienfaisance dotée de la
  personnalité morale

association de bienfaisance

personne morale d'une ville

établissement public

société qui fait appel au public

société de crédit

constituer, former ou établir une
  personne morale

municipalité

association personnalisée

société pollicitée

organisme humanitaire doté de la
  personnalité morale

administration scolaire

Canadian corporation c. B-1, s. 190(1)	société canadienne
Crown corporation c. Y-1, s. 36(3)(b)	société d'État
Corporation (Corp.)	Société par actions de régime fédéral (S.A.R.F.)
c. C-44, s. 10(1)	
corporeal	
property of any kind, whether real or personal or corporeal or incorporeal c. F-7, s. 2	biens de toute nature, meubles ou immeubles, corporels ou incorporels
real or personal corporeal property c. C-46, s. 428	bien corporel immeuble ou meuble
correct/to	
(a sentence) c. C-46, s. 777(2)(a)	corriger
to correct a substantial wrong or miscarriage of justice c. C-3, s. 21(6)	réparer un dommage important ou remédier à une erreur judiciaire
correctional	
provincial correctional facility c. Y-1, s. 24(14)	centre correctionnel provincial
treatment or correctional ressources c. Y-1, s. 16(4)(d)	moyens de traitement ou de réadaptation
correctness	
(of copy) c. P-1, s. 8(1)	conformité
corroboration	
(evidence) c. C-46, s. 47(3)	corroboration
corrupt	
corrupt arrangement c. C-39, s. 79	arrangement entaché de corruption
corrupt consideration c. C-46, s. 139(3)(c)	compensation vénale
corrupt means c. C-46, s. 139(3)(a)	moyens de corruption
corrupt or illegal practice c. C-45, s. 3(a)	manoeuvre frauduleuse ou illégale
corrupt practices c. C-39, s. 2(1)	manoeuvres frauduleuses
corruptly	dans un but de corruption
c. B-1, s. 313(1)(a)	
c. C-46, s. 119(1)a)	par corruption
cost	au prix coûtant
at cost c. B-1, Schedule X, Section 10	
cost of borrowing c. B-1, s. 202(2)	coût d'emprunt
costs, charges and expenses c. L-12, s. 43(3)	frais judiciaires et extrajudiciaires
legal cost (of acquisition) c. N-11, s. 12(2)(e)	frais légaux
proportion of the cost (of a project) c. A-3, s. 5(b)	contribution
costs	frais et dépens
c. C-9, s. 59(3) c. L-12, s. 45(5) c. A-1, s. 11(1)(b)	frais

c. A-11, s. 33(3)
c. A-12, s. 6(1)(c)
award costs/to (supreme court)   adjuger des frais
c. C-36, s. 15(2)
costs and charges   frais et charges
c. C-46, s. 809(5)
costs and charges to be taxed   frais et dépens à taxer
c. C-46, s. 779(1)
costs and expenses   indemniser des frais et dépenses
c. B-3, s. 11(2)
costs of and incidental (to   les frais et dépens
proceedings)
c. A-1, s. 53(1)
deposit of security for costs   dépôt d'un cautionnement
c. S-26, s. 64
fees and costs (to be taxed)   honoraires et frais
c. S-26, s. 97(1)(d)
indemnify against all costs,   indemniser des frais et dépenses
charges and expenses/to
c. C-44, s. 124(1)
operate at cost (an enterprise)   couvrir ses frais
c. C-40, s. 3(1)
sign judgment for costs/to   demander la taxation
c. S-26, s. 69(2)
tariff of fees and costs   tarif d'honoraires
c. C-50, s. 35(a)
with costs   avec dépens
c. A-12, s. 16(3)
council
(of trade unions)   regroupement
c. L-2, s. 16(e)(i)
council of trade unions   regroupement de syndicats
c. L-2, s. 32(1)
Council of employee   regroupement d'organisations
organisation   syndicales
c. P-35, s. 2
Council of National Ethno-   Council of National Ethno-Cultural
Cultural Organizations of   Organizations of Canada
Canada
c. C-18, Schedule
counsel   avocat
c. C-8, s. 86(2)
c. C-39, s. 22(2)
c. C-46, s. 518(1)(d)
c. Y-1, s. 4(1)(d)
appear and be heard in person   comparaître en personne ou par
or by counsel/to   ministère d'avocat
c. C-44, s. 124(6)
appoint counsel/to   nommer un avocat
c. C-34, s. 15
barrister, advocate and counsel   avocats
c. S-26, s. 22
by counsel   par l'intermédiaire d'un avocat
c. C-23, s. 48(2)
by counsel (to appear)   par ministère d'avocat
c. B-1, s. 56(6)
counsel, barrister or solicitor   avocat ou procureur
c. C-46, s. 2
general counsel   chef du contentieux
c. B-1, s. 168(1)(a)
legal counsel   conseiller juridique
c. B-1, s. 138(b)(i)

solicitor or counsel c. C-50, s. 29(1)	conseil
to plead by counsel or agent c. C-46, s. 620	plaider par avocat ou représentant
counsel/to	
counsel or procure/to (a person to be a party to an offence) c. C-46, s. 22(1)	conseiller ou inciter
counselling	
investment counselling c. B-1, s. 174(1)	conseil de placements
marriage counselling or guidance facilities c. C-3, s. 9(1)(b)	services de consultation ou d'orientation matrimoniales
count	
information, presentment and count (indictment) c. C-46, s. 2	dénonciation, déclaration d'un acte d'accusation émise par le grand jury et chef d'accusation
separate count c. C-46, s. 611(2)	chef d'accusation séparé
count/to	
(votes) c. L-2, s. 16(i)(ii)	dépouiller
counter-claim c. B-4, s. 2 c. F-7, s. 43(5)	demande reconventionnelle
counteraction	
enemy action or counteraction against the enemy c. C-31, s. 48	opération de l'ennemi ou contre- opération
countercharge c. C-46, s. 166(1)(b)(ii)	contre-accusation
counterclaim c. C-50, s. 22(1)	demande reconventionnelle
counterclaimant c. C-30, Schedule Article V, 1(6)	demandeur reconventionnel
counterfeit coin c. C-52, s. 10	fausse pièce de monnaie
counterfeit money c. C-46, s. 448	monnaie contrefaite
countermand/to	
(payment) c. B-4, s. 106(e)	contremander (le paiement)
countermand of payment	
(of a cheque) c. B-4, s. 167(a)	annulation de l'ordre de paiement
county town	
county town of the county c. J-1, s. 35(1)	chef-lieu du comté
coupon	
interest coupon c. F-11, s. 60(1)(c)	coupon d'intérêt
course	
in the course of duty c. A-2, s. 9(1)	dans l'exécution de ses fonctions
in the course of employment c. C-42, s. 13(3)	dans l'exercice d'un emploi
normal course of trade c. A-7, s. 8(1)	cours normal des affaires
ordinary course of one's duties c. B-1, s. 84(b)	cadre normal de ses fonctions

ordinary course of the trade	cours ordinaire du commerce
c. C-46, s. 400(1)(c)	
course of education or instruction	cours d'éducation ou d'instruction
c. C-28, Schedule 8	
course of study	
full-time course of study	cours d'études à plein temps
c. C-28, Schedule 7	
court	tribunal
c. A-12, s. 25(1)	
c. B-1, s. 2(1)	
c. A-12, s. 25(1)	juge
c. A-1, s. 3	cour
additional court	tribunal additionnel
c. S-26, s. 3	
court appealed from	juridiction inférieure
c. S-26, s. 2(1)	
court house	palais de justice
c. C-39, s. 9(2)	
court of criminal jurisdiction	cour de juridiction criminelle
c. C-46, s. 2	
court of justice	tribunal judiciaire
c. C-46, s. 118	
court of law	tribunal
c. A-1, s. 36(1)(c)	
court of law	tribunal judiciaire
c. C-46, s. 369(c)	
court of record	cour d'archives
c. A-7, s. 8(3)	
court room	salle d'audience
c. C-39, s. 87	
c. C-46, s. 486(1)	
district court	cour de district
c. C-50, s. 21(1)(b)	
general court of appeal	cour générale d'appel
c. S-26, s. 3	
highest court of final resort in a province	plus haut tribunal de dernier ressort dans une province
c. S-26, s. 2(2)	
pending in any court (action)	pendante devant un tribunal
c. C-45, s. 27	
rules of court	règles de cour
c. C-46, s. 482(1)	
summary conviction court	cour des poursuites sommaires
c. C-46, s. 669.2(1)(b)	
summary conviction court	cour de poursuite sommaire
c. C-46, s. 785	
superior court of record	cour supérieure d'archives
c. A-1, s. 36(1)(a)	
courtroom	salle d'audience
c. C-46, s. 649	
covenant	
(in a contract)	engagement
c. F-7, s. 37	
(in a mortgage)	engagement découlant d'une hypothèque
c. B-3, s. 218(2)(c)	
clause, covenant or agreement (in a contract of carriage)	clause, convention, accord
c. C-27, Schedule, Article III, 8	
covenant to insure	convention d'assurer
c. C-19, s. 34(1)(a)	

covenant/to
 c. B-1, Schedule VIII
         s'engager à

covering
 bag, sack or other container or
 covering (for mail)
         sac ou autre contenant ou
          couverture
  c. C-46, s. 356(1)(a)(ii)

covert
 covert unlawful acts
         actions cachées et illicites
  c. C-23, s. 2

crafty science
 occult or crafty science
         science occulte ou magique
  c. C-46, s. 365(c)

creation
 creation of reserves
         création de réserves
  c. A-6, s. 2(2)(b)

credible
 credible and trustworthy
         utile et digne de foi
  c. A-7, s. 8(4)(c)
 credible or trustworthy
 (evidence)
         plausible ou digne de foi
  c. C-46, s. 518(1)(e)

credit
         crédit
  c. B-1, s. 202(2)
 deposit to the credit/to
         porter au crédit
  c. C-14, s. 12(2)
 grant or extension of credit
         couverture ou extension d'un crédit
  c. C-46, s. 362(1)(c)(iv)
 to the credit
         à son actif
  c. P-2, s. 25(2)(d)

credit/to
 (an amount)
         porter au crédit
  c. C-17, s. 55(3)

credit advanced
         capital prêté
  c. C-46, s. 347(2)

credit agency
 approved instalment credit
 agency
         organisme agréé de crédit à
          tempérament
  c. C-7, s. 23(c)

credit card
         carte de crédit
  c. C-46, s. 321

**Crédit Commercial de France
(Canada)**
         Crédit Commercial de France
          (Canada)
  c. B-1, Schedule II

Crédit Lyonnais Canada
         Crédit Lyonnais Canada
  c. B-1, Schedule II

credit society
 local cooperative credit society
         société coopérative de crédit locale
  c. C-21, s. 2(1)

Crédit Suisse Canada
         Crédit Suisse Canada
  c. B-1, Schedule II

credit union
         caisse de crédit
  c. C-34, s. 50(3)
  c. C-24, s. 2(1)
  c. C-7, s. 2
         caisse populaire
  c. N-11, s. 2
 credit union or caisse populaire
         caisse de crédit ou caisse populaire
  c. C-40, s. 6(1)(h)
 credit union or caisse populaire
         caisse populaire ou credit union
  c. C-46, s. 347(2)
 credit union or other cooperative
 organization
         caisse populaire ou autre
          coopérative
  c. C-41, s. 10(1)(h)

crediting
  (of interests)   inscription au crédit
    c. C-40, s. 3(1)(d)
creditor   créditeur
    c. B-7, Schedule II, Article
      VI, Section 5(c)
    c. C-10, s. 39(1)
  judgment creditor   créancier en vertu d'un jugement
    c. C-41, s. 48
  secured creditor   créancier garanti
    c. C-36, s. 2
    c. C-44, s. 94
  unsecured creditor   créancier chirographaire
    c. C-36, s. 2
credits
  earn credits/to   accumuler des crédits
    c. C-46, s. 718.1(1)
crew
  (of aircraft)   équipage
    c. C-46, s. 7(9)
crime comic   histoire illustrée de crime
    c. C-46, s. 163(7)
criminal
  criminal proceedings   poursuites pénales
    c. C-20, s. 18(1)
  criminal record   dossier ou relevé relatif à des
                                                 affaires pénales
    c. C-47, s. 6(2)
Criminal Code   Code criminel
    c. C-46, s. 1
criminal interest rate   usure
    c. C-46, s. 183
criminal law
  administration of criminal law   administration du droit criminel
    c. C-46, s. 120(a)
criminal means
  use of criminal means   emploi de moyens criminels
    c. A-1, s. 15(2)(d)
criminal rate   taux criminel
    c. C-46, s. 347(2)
criminate/to   incriminer
    c. B-3, s. 10(5)
    c. C-34, s. 22(2)
    c. C-44, s. 233   entraîner une inculpation
criteria   critère
    c. C-11, s. 18(1)(d)
    c. C-6, s. 15(1)   condition
crop   récolte
    c. C-48, s. 2
  crop year   campagne agricole
    c. C-24, s. 24(1)(c)
    c. C-49, s. 2(1)
Crop Reinsurance Fund   caisse de réassurance-récolte
    c. C-48, s. 6(1)
**crops growing or produced on   récoltes sur pied ou produites à la
the farm**   ferme
    c. B-1, s. 2(2)(a)(i)
cross-examination   contre-interrogatoire
    c. A-12, s. 21(2)
cross-examine/to   contre-interroger
    c. C-46, s. 540(1)(a)
crossing
  (of a cheque)   barrement (chèque)
    c. B-4, s. 168(1)

Crown
    c. C-50, s. 2
    c. F-11, s. 72
   minister of the Crown
    c. F-11, s. 2
   Crown corporation
    c. Y-1, s. 36(3)(b)
Crown Assets Disposal
Corporation
    c. A-1, Schedule I
cruelty
   cruelty to animals
    c. C-46, s. 446
crustaceans
   shellfish, crustaceans and
   marine animals
    c. C-33, s. 2
culpable
   culpable homicide
    c. C-46, s. 742(a.1)
   culpable neglect
    c. B-3, s. 173(1)(e)
cultivated land
    c. C-48, s. 13(1)
cultivation
   (of marihuana)
    c. N-1, s. 20(a)
cumulative
   cumulative dividends
    c. C-44, s. 21(2)
   cumulative voting
    c. C-44, s. 107
curative treatment
   (alcoholic)
    c. C-46, s. 255(5)
curator
    c. B-1, s. 278(1)
    c. B-8, s. 14(a)
   guardian, curator, committee,
   executor, administrator or other
   legal representative

    c. C-8, s. 2(1)
   trustee, guardian, committee,
   curator, tutor, executor,
   administrator or representative
   of a deceased person
    c. B-1, s. 75(2)
    c. C-44, s. 48(2)
   tutor, curator, guardian or
   trustee
    c. L-12, s. 41(3)
curb market
   stock exchange, curb market or
   other market
    c. C-46, s. 382
cure/to
   (a defect)
    c. C-46, s. 601(1)
currency
    c. A-1, s. 18(d)(i)
    c. A-1, s. 18(d)(v)
    c. C-26, Schedule II

État

Sa Majesté
ministre

société d'État

Corporation de disposition des biens
  de la Couronne

cruauté envers les animaux

mollusques, crustacés et animaux
  marins

homicide coupable

négligence coupable

terre cultivée

culture

dividendes cumulatifs

vote cumulatif

cure de désintoxication

curateur

tuteur, curateur à la personne ou
  aux biens, conseil judiciaire,
  exécuteur testamentaire ou autre
  représentant légal

fiduciaire, tuteur, curateur,
  exécuteur ou administrateur de
  succession

tuteur, curateur ou fiduciaire

bourse de valeurs, curb market ou
  autre bourse

remédier

monnaie

devises
unité monétaire

(of a country)   devise
    c. F-11, s. 48(1)
coin-operated or currency   appareil à sous ou distributeur
exchange device   automatique de monnaie
    c. C-46, s. 351(2)
currency of Canada   monnaie canadienne
    c. F-11, s. 63(3)
national currency   monnaie nationale
    c. C-26, Schedule II
current   courant
    c. C-46, s. 448
current coin   pièce ayant cours légal
    c. C-52, s. 12
current liability   passif à court terme
    c. L-12, s. 61(1)(h)
curtilage
(of a dwelling-house)   enceinte
    c. C-46, s. 2
custodial
custodial disposition   décision comportant la garde
    c. Y-1, s. 20(6)
custodian   gardien
    c. B-1, s. 181
custodian or depository (of   gardien ou dépositaire
money)
    c. C-46, s. 204(1)(a)
custody   garde
    c. A-12, s. 23(2)
    c. A-17, s. 9(b)
    c. C-44, s. 206(7)
(of an accused)   détention
    c. C-46, s. 478(3)(b) in fine
(of public property)   garde (des biens publics)
    c. F-11, s. 62
custody for treatment   détention aux fins de traitement
    c. N-1, s. 25(2)
custody or control (of a child)   garde ou contrôle
    c. C-46, s. 214
custody order   ordonnance de garde
    c. C-3, s. 2(1)
deliver into the custody of/to   confier à la garde de
    c. A-12, s. 23(2)
detention in custody   mise en détention
    c. Y-1, s. 7(2)
lawful custody   garde légale
    c. C-46, s. 145(1)(a)
open custody   garde en milieu ouvert
    c. C-46, s. 733(3)
    c. Y-1, s. 24(1)
order of committal to   ordonnance de placement sous
intermittent custody   garde discontinue
    c. Y-1, s. 24(13)
place of custody   lieu de garde
    c. C-46, s. 733(3)
protective custody (of a sheriff)   garde
    c. B-3, s. 160
remand to custody/to   ordonner l'envoie en détention
    c. N-1, s. 24
secure custody   garde en milieu fermé
    c. C-46, s. 733(3)
    c. Y-1, s. 24(1)
take into one's custody or   prendre sous sa garde et sous son
control/to   contrôle
    c. B-1, s. 292(c)

to commit to continuous custody c. Y-1, s. 24(12)	placer sous garde de façon continue

to have something in actual
possession or custody (of
another person)
  c. C-46, s. 4(3)(a)i)
	avoir une chose en la possession ou
	  garde réelle (d'une autre
	  personne)

custom c. L-2, s. 168(1)	usages

customary
  legal or customary right
	droit découlant de la loi ou de la
	  coutume

c. 31 (4th Supp.), s. 83(1)	

customs
  officer of customs
  c. A-11, s. 33(1)
	douanier

d

Dai-Tchi Kangyo Bank (Canada) c. B-1, Schedule II	Banque Dai-Tchi Kangyo (Canada)

daily
  daily allowance
  c. P-35, s. 2
	allocation journalière

dam
  lumber, timber, log, float, boom,
  dam or slide
	bois de construction, de service ou
	  en grume, radeau, barrage
	  flottant, digue ou glissoir

c. C-46, s. 433(1)(i)
  slide, dam, pier or boom
	glissoir, digue, jetée ou barrage
	  flottant

c. T-7, s. 19(a)	

damage
  c. A-12, s. 6(1)(c)
  c. F-7, s. 22(2)(c)
	dommage

(to baggage)
  c. C-26, Schedule I, Article
  26(2)
	avarie

actual damage c. C-27, Schedule, Article III	dommage certain

bodily harm or damage to
property
  c. C-46, s. 80(b)
	blessure corporelle ou dommage à la
	  propriété

claim for damage	réclamation pour dommages- intérêts

c. B-3, s. 145
  severe psychological damage
  c. C-46, s. 752
	dommages psychologiques graves

damage/to
  (agricultural product)
  c. A-7, s. 19(1)(a)
	endommager

damaged
  damaged security
  c. F-11, s. 60(1)(c)
	titre détérioré

damages
  c. B-1, s. 99(1)
  c. C-9, s. 46(2)
  c. C-44, s. 72(1)
  c. F-7, s. 2
	dommages-intérêts

action for damages
  c. C-26, Schedule I, Article
  24(1)
	action en responsabilité

damages awarded on the appeal
  c. S-26, s. 65(1)(d)
damages, payment, compensation of indemnity
  c. B-1, s. 249
payment in full of compensation or damages
  c. C-46, s. 722(4)
punitive damages
  c. C-46, s. 194(1)
  c. C-50, s. 17(1)

data
data processing, storage or retrieval of data

  c. C-46, s. 342.1(2)

day
business day
  c. B-4, s. 77(a)
day, call and short (loan)

  c. B-1, Schedule X, Section 12(a)
from day to day
  c. C-46, s. 527(1)(c)

day loan
  c. B-1, s. 208(7)(e)

daylight
daylight hours
  c. P-2, s. 21(4)

days of grace
  c. B-2, s. 18(g)
  c. B-4, s. 41

de novo
trial de novo
  c. C-46, s. 822(4)

deal/to
(with a grevance)
  c. L-2, s. 97(4)(b)(i)

deal at arm's length/to
  c. C-44, s. 26(3)(a)(i)

deal in/to
(a security)
  c. C-44, s. 48(2)(b)
deal in and discount/to (a bill of exchange)
  c. B-1, s. 173(1)(c)
deal in goods, wares and merchandise/to
  c. B-1, s. 174(2)(a)
have in one's possession, use or deal in any other way with/to (a credit card)
  c. C-46, s. 342(1)(c)
otherwise deal in/to
  c. A-8, s. 12(1)(d)

deal with/to
  c. A-11, s. 3(k)
(property)
  c. C-44, s. 97
deal with matters/to
  c. C-44, s. 114(5)

dommages-intérêts adjugés à l'issue de l'appel

remboursements, dommages-intérêts, indemnisations

paiement intégral de l'indemnité ou des dommages intérêts

dommages-intérêts punitifs

traitement des données, mémorisation, recouvrement ou relevé des données

jour ouvrable

au jour le jour, à vue ou à court terme

de jour en jour

prêt au jour le jour

temps diurne

délai de grâce

procès de novo

statuer

ne pas avoir de lien de dépendance

négocier

négocier et escompter

faire le commerce de produits, de denrées ou de marchandises

disposer notamment en l'ayant en sa possession ou en l'utilisant

faire l'objet d'autres opérations

prendre une mesure

gérer

régler des questions

deal with the accused in the manner authorised by law/to
  c. C-46, s. 570(1)
dispose of or deal with/to
  c. C-46, s. 461(2)
dispose of or deal with/to
  c. C-46, s. 199(3)
dispose of or otherwise deal with/to (property)
  c. B-3, s. 71(2)
deal with the proceeds/to
  c. C-46, s. 772
dealer
  c. A-7, s. 14
  c. C-38, s. 2
  (livestock)
  c. L-9, s. 10
broker or dealer (in securities)

  c. B-1, s. 15(c)(iv)
securities broker or dealer

  c. C-44, s. 147
dealing
business of dealing in securities
  c. C-34, s. 5(1)
fair dealing (with a work)
  c. C-42, s. 27(2)(a)
dealings
  c. C-46, s. 121(1)(b)
dealings and transactions (of the bankrupt)
  c. B-3, s. 10(1)
debates
in any debates and other proceedings (of Parliament)
  c. 31 (4th Supp.), s. 4(1)
debenture
bank debenture
  c. B-1, s. 46(4)(c)
bond, debenture, note or other evidence of indebtedness
  c. C-44, s. 2(1)
debenture stock
  c. C-46, s. 206(8)(c)
debenture stock
  c. L-12, s. 44(1)(j)
debenture, deed, bond, bill, note, warrant, order or other security for money
  c. C-46, s. 2
ordinary debenture debt

  c. L-12, s. 74(2)
outstanding debenture

  c. C-43, s. 4(1)(k)
perpetual debenture
  c. C-40, s. 91
debit/to
  (an account)
  c. B-4, s. 16(3)(a)

traiter le prévenu de la manière autorisée par la loi

disposer ou traiter

disposer de

céder ou aliéner

traiter le produit

marchand

fournisseur
négociant

agent de change ou courtier en valeurs

courtier ou négociant en valeurs mobilières

commerce de valeurs

utilisation équitable

relations d'affaires

négociations et transactions

dans les débats et travaux

débenture bancaire

obligation, débenture, billet ou autre preuve de créance

stock-obligation

débentures-actions

débenture, titre, obligation, billet, lettre, mandat, ordre ou autre garantie d'argent

dette de la société au titre de ses débentures ordinaires

débenture émise mais non remboursée

débenture perpétuelle

inscrire au débit

debit balance
  c. C-17, s. 53(1)
reliquat débiteur

debt
  c. B-1, s. 159(4)
créance
  c. C-44, s. 2(1)
dette
  bad and doubtful debt
créance irrécouvrable ou douteuse
  c. B-2, s. 27
  c. C-7, s. 29(2)
  debt due (to Her Majesty)
créance
  c. 4 (2nd Supp.), s. 59
  debt obligation
titre de créance
  c. A-10, s. 6(1)(g)
  c. C-10, s. 27
  c. C-44, s. 2(1)
  debt or equity interest
droits de créance ou actions
  c. A-2, s. 21(3)
  debt or obligation due
créance
  c. F-11, s. 25(1)
  debt, obligation or claim (by someone)
créance
  c. F-11, s. 25(3)
  deposit debt
dette au titre des dépôts
  c. L-12, s. 74(3)
  ordinary debenture debt
dette de la société au titre de ses débentures ordinaires
  c. L-12, s. 74(2)
  public debt
dette publique
  c. F-11, s. 18(2)

debt due
  (to Her Majesty)
créance
  c. 4 (2nd Supp.), s. 59

debt, obligation or claim
  (by someone)
créance
  c. F-11, s. 25(3)

debtor
débiteur
  c. B-1, s. 90(4)
  c. C-44, s. 63(4)
  judgment debtor
débiteur
  c. 4 (2nd Supp.), s. 45
  judgment debtor
débiteur par jugement
  c. C-46, s. 771(3)

deceit
  by deceit, falsehood or other fraudulent means
par supercherie, mensonge ou autre moyen dolosif
  c. C-46, s. 380(1)

decency
  public decency or order
décence ou ordre public
  c. C-46, s. 174(2)

deception
supercherie
  c. C-46, s. 222(5)(c)

deceptive
  clandestine or deceptive activities
activités de nature clandestine ou trompeuse
  c. C-23, s. 2
  false or deceptive statement
déclaration fausse ou trompeuse
  c. A-8, s. 16(1)(b)

deceptively
  deceptively misdescriptive (a name)
description fausse et trompeuse
  c. B-1, s. 16(1)(b)

decide/to
  arbitrate and decide on the matter/to
arbitrer et régler le différend
  c. B-6, s. 32(3)

decision
 c. A-1, s. 2(1)
 judgment, rule, order, decision,
 decree, decretal order, or
 sentence
  c. S-26, s. 2(1)
declarant
 c. C-29, s. 25(1)
 affiant or declarant

  c. C-46, s. 138(c)
declaration
 c. A-11, s. 6
 (of interest)
  c. C-44, s. 120(6)
 declaration of interest
  c. B-1, s. 53(6)
 declaration or affirmation

  c. C-8, s. 106(5)
 deliver a declaration/to
  c. A-11, s. 23
 solemn declaration
  c. C-46, s. 133
declaratory
 declaratory order
  c. C-40, s. 80(1)
 grant declaratory relief/to
  c. F-7, s. 18(a)
declare/to
 c. A-11, s. 6
declared
 value declared
  c. C-26, Schedule I, Article
  4(3)(g)
declaring
 entitled to an order declaring/to
 be
  c. N-1, s. 17(4)
decline/to
 c. C-46, s. 567(a)
decree
 judgment, rule, order, decision,
 decree, decretal order, or
 sentence
  c. S-26, s. 2(1)
decree absolute of divorce
 c. C-8, s. 55(1)
decretal order
 judgment, rule, order, decision,
 decree, decretal order, or
 sentence
  c. S-26, s. 2(1)
deduct/to
 (a reduction)
  c. C-44, s. 38(2)
 (an amount)
  c. C-44, s. 39(1)
 (from an amount)
  c. C-24, s. 33(1)
deduction
 c. C-24, s. 48(1)

décision

décision

déclarant

auteur d'un affidavit ou d'une
 déclaration solennelle

procès-verbal

divulgation

déclaration d'intérêt

déclaration ou affirmation
 solennelle

dresser un procès-verbal

déclaration solennelle

ordonnance déclaratoire

rendre un jugement déclaratoire

déclarer

valeur déclarée

avoir droit à l'obtention d'une
 ordonnance déclaratoire

refuser

décision

jugement irrévocable de divorce

décision

porter au débit

débiter

prélever

prélèvement

to recover by deduction or set-off against garnishable moneys

recouvrer, par déduction ou compensation de sommes saisissables

    c. 4 (2nd Supp.), s. 59

deed

debenture, deed, bond, bill, note, warrant, order or other security for money

débenture, titre, obligation, billet, lettre, mandat, ordre ou autre garantie d'argent

    c. C-46, s. 2

deed of sale

acte de vente

    c. C-37, s. 7(1)

deed of trust

acte de fiducie

    c. C-19, s. 34(1)

deed or indenture

acte

    c. B-1, s. 133(1)

deed, indenture or other instrument, including any supplement or amendment thereto

instrument ainsi que tout acte additif ou modificatif

    c. C-44, s. 82(1)

trust deed

acte de fiducie

    c. C-36, s. 2

    c. N-7, s. 29(3)(b)

deeds

registrar of deeds

directeur de l'Enregistrement

    c. N-7, s. 2

deem/to

estimer

    c. A-12, s. 11(1)

    c. A-16, s. 8(b)

    c. A-11, s. 16

juger

    c. A-17, s. 9(b)

    c. A-6, s. 4(2)

réputer

    c. C-23, s. 9(2)

présumer

(advisable)

juger

    c. C-14, s. 10(1)(b)

(appropriate)

estimer

    c. C-14, s. 3(2)

(expedient)

sembler

    c. C-14, s. 10(1)

(necessary)

estimer

    c. A-3, s. 9(1)

deemed

présumé

    c. A-12, s. 27(2)

consent deemed a compliance

consentement vaut observation

    c. S-26, s. 65(2)

person deemed not to be guilty

personne réputée innocente

    c. C-46, s. 6(1)(a)

deemed/to be

faire foi

    c. A-11, s. 7(2)

    c. C-24, s. 25(2)(a)

être assimilé à

    c. C-44, s. 2(2)(b)

être réputé

(to be wages)

être assimilé à

    c. L-2, s. 186

deemed to be a chattel/to be

être censé un bien meuble

    c. C-46, s. 4(1)

deemed to have notice/to be (of an adverse claim)

être réputé avisé (de l'existence d'opposition)

    c. C-44, s. 53(c)

deface/to

(a coin)

dégrader

    c. C-46, s. 456(a)

alter, deface or remove/to (a serial number on a firearm)

modifier, maquiller ou effacer

    c. C-46, s. 104(3)(a)

cut, break or deface/to (coins)
   c. C-52, s. 10
defalcation
  fraud, embezzlement,
  misappropriation or defalcation
   c. B-3, s. 178(1)(d)
defamatory
  defamatory matter
   c. C-46, s. 611(2)
defamatory libel
   c. C-46, s. 297
default
   c. B-1, s. 131
   c. C-44, s. 45(1)
   c. B-5, s. 4
   c. C-6, s. 15(1)(a)
   c. C-46, s. 770(1)
   c. C-8, s. 40(1)(d)
   c. L-12, s. 109
   c. L-12, s. 47(3)
  default of payment (of an
  instalment)
   c. B-4, s. 27(1)(c)
  employer in default to pay
   c. B-3, s. 68(6)
  event of default
   c. B-1, s. 133(1)
  failure or default
   c. B-7, Schedule I, Article
    XIII, Section 3
  in default of payment
   c. C-46, s. 717(3)
  in default of payment
   c. C-46, s. 717(4)(b)
  loan in default
   c. C-41, s. 57(6)
defaulter
   c. C-46, s. 722(5)
defeat/to
  (creditors)
   c. B-3, s. 42(1)(g)
  obstruct, pervert or defeat the
  course of justice/to
   c. C-46, s. 139(1)
defect
   c. B-1, s. 80(c)
   c. B-4, s. 17(1)
   c. B-1, s. 83
   c. C-40, s. 69(5)
  (in a ship)
   c. F-7, s. 22(2)(g)
  (in issue of security)
   c. C-44, s. 56
  defect apparent on the face of
  the information
   c. C-46, s. 548(3)
  defect apparent on the face
  thereof
   c. C-46, s. 601(1)
  defect of form
   c. C-34, s. 3
  defect of form or irregularity in
  procedure
   c. C-46, s. 189(3)(b)

couper, briser ou défigurer

fraude, détournement, concussion
  ou abus de confiance

matière diffamatoire

libelle diffamatoire

faute

manquement

omission

inobservation
défaut de paiement

employeur défaillant de payer

cas de défaut

faillite ou carence

à défaut de paiement

faute de paiement

prêt en souffrance

personne défaillante

frustrer

entraver, détourner ou contrecarrer
  le cours de la justice

vice

défaut
irrégularité
vice de construction

défaut

vice de forme apparent à la face
  même de la dénonciation

vice de forme apparent à sa face
  même

vice de forme

vice de forme ou de procédure

defalcation

inherent defect   vice propre
    c. C-26, Schedule III
inherent defect   vice caché
    c. C-27, Schedule, Article IV,
      2(m)
irregularity or defect in the   irrégularité ou défaut dans la
substance or form (of a warrant)   substance ou la forme
    c. C-46, s. 546(a)
latent defect   vice caché
    c. C-27, Schedule, Article IV,
      2

defective
    (a receipt)   défectueux
      c. B-1, s. 147(2)
    defective stores   approvisionnements défectueux
      c. C-46, s. 418(1)
defective/to be
    (a title to a bill)   être défectueux
      c. B-4, s. 138(2)
defence   moyen de défense
    c. B-4, s. 14
    complete defence   moyen de défense péremptoire
      c. B-1, s. 82(3)
    conduct his defence/to   mener sa défense
      c. C-46, s. 537(3)
    full answer and defence   réplique et défense complètes
      c. N-1, s. 8(2)
Defence Construction (1951)   Construction de défense (1951)
Limited   Limitée
    c. A-1, Schedule I
    c. F-11, Schedule III, Part I
defend/to
    (an action or a legal proceeding)   contester
      c. B-3, s. 30(1)(d)
    bring, defend or take part (in an   ester en justice
    action)
      c. B-1, s. 293(1)(b)
    bring, defend or take part in any   ester en justice, lors de toute
    action or proceeding/to   procédure
      c. C-44, s. 222(1)(b)
    defend an action/to   présenter une défense à une action
      c. C-44, s. 239(2)(c)
defense   moyen de défense
    c. C-44, s. 124(3)(a)
deferred
    (stock)   différé
      c. L-12, s. 35(2)
    deferred delivery permit   permis de livraison différée
      c. C-24, s. 32(4)
    deferred profit sharing plan   régime de participation différée aux
       bénéfices
      c. L-12, s. 114(1)
deficiency   découvert
    c. B-1, s. 214
    payment of a deficiency (arising   paiement du déficit
    on a sale)
      c. S-26, s. 65(1)(c)
    to pay the deficiency   payer la différence
      c. S-26, s. 65(1)(c)
defilement   déflorement
    c. C-46, s. 170(b)
definite
    definite period   délai ferme
      c. C-34, s. 33(5)(a)

defraud/to   frauder
    c. F-11, s. 80(b)
    (creditors)   frauder
      c. B-3, s. 42(1)(g)
    (the public)   frustrer
      c. C-46, s. 553(a)(iii)
    with intent to defraud   avec une intention de fraude
      c. C-44, s. 229(2)(a)
degree
    (of participation)   degré
      c. C-20, s. 21(1)(a)
    degree or kind of punishment   degré ou genre de peine
      c. C-46, s. 717(1)
delay
    unreasonable delay   délai anormal
      c. C-46, s. 525(3)
delay/to
    (a proceeding)   ajourner
      c. F-11, s. 23(4)(b)
    (creditors)   retarder
      c. B-3, s. 42(1)(g)
delegate
    (of the Attorney General)   délégué
      c. Y-1, s. 4(1)(a)
    delegate system of voting   système de vote par délégation
      c. C-40, s. 3(2)
delete/to   retrancher
    c. C-20, s. 2(2)(a)
delict
    delict and quasi-delict   délit et quasi-délit
      c. C-50, s. 2
delinquency
    delinquency under (the Act)   délit tombant sous le coup de (la loi)
      c. Y-1, s. 24(4)(b)
    finding of delinquency   déclaration de culpabilité pour acte
                           de délinquance
      c. Y-1, s. 14(2)(c)(iii)
    offence of delinquency   infraction de délinquance
      c. Y-1, s. 45(8)
deliver/to
    (a lecture)   débiter
      c. C-42, s. 3(1)
    (a security)   livrer
      c. C-44, s. 52(1)(a)
    (narcotic)   livrer
      c. N-1, s. 2
    deliver a notice/to   délivrer un avis
      c. A-11, s. 25(1)
    deliver a person/to (to a peace   livrer une personne
    officer)
      c. C-46, s. 503(1)
    deliver personally/to (order)   remettre en mains propres
      c. Y-1, s. 10(2)
    duty to deliver   obligation de livrer
      c. B-1, s. 98(1)(a)
    send or deliver/to (securities)   envoyer ou remettre
      c. C-44, s. 2(1)
delivery   livraison ou remise
    c. C-44, s. 48(2)
    (lecture)   débit
      c. C-42, s. 2
    (of a security)   livraison
      c. C-44, s. 60(1)

(transfer of possession)
    c. B-1, s. 75(2)
  livraison ou remise

acceptance completed by delivery
    c. B-4, s. 2
  acceptation complétée par livraison

by endorsement or delivery (document)
    c. C-46, s. 2
  par endossement ou livraison

conditional delivery (of a security)
    c. B-1, s. 82(4)
  livraison sous condition

delivery of judgment
    c. S-26, s. 27(1)
  prononcé

delivery of possession of real property or chattels real
    c. S-26, s. 65(1)(c)
  livraison de biens-fonds ou de biens personnels immobiliers

delivery or demand delivery (option)
    c. B-1, s. 168(1)
  tradition ou transfert

delivery permit
    c. C-24, s. 2(1)
  carnet de livraison

delivery point
    c. C-24, s. 24(1)(d)
  point de livraison

endorsement completed by delivery
    c. B-4, s. 2
  endossement conplété par livraison

gift, conveyance, assignment, sale, transfer or delivery of property
    c. C-46, s. 392(a)(i)
  don, transport, cession, vente, transfert ou remise de biens

non-delivery (of a security)
    c. B-1, s. 82(4)
  absence de livraison

oral rendition or delivery (of judgment)
    c. 31 (4th Supp.), s. 20(3)
  prononcé

take delivery/to (of a security)
    c. B-1, s. 75(2)
  prendre livraison

to take or receive by transfer or delivery (a negotiable instrument)
    c. C-46, s. 491.1(3)(b)(iii)
  transférer

transferable by delivery (securities)
    c. C-44, s. 2(1)
  négociable par tradition ou transfert

delusion
    c. C-46, s. 16(3)
  idée délirante

demand
    c. C-8, s. 25(2)
  demande formelle

    c. C-46, s. 258(5)
  ordre

delivery or demand delivery (option)
    c. B-1, s. 168(1)
  tradition ou transfert

demand deposit
    c. B-1, s. 208(8)(c)
  dépôt à vue

demand of the plaintiff
    c. C-50, s. 22(1)
  demande du plaignant

demand, seizure or detention
    c. C-10, s. 40(3)
  revendication, saisie ou rétention

on the demand of
    c. C-44, s. 85(2)
  sur demande de

payable on demand (a bill or note)
    c. B-4, s. 6(2)(b)
  payable sur demande

demand/to
  call in and demand/to (shares)   demander et exiger
    c. C-40, s. 57(1)
  demand notice/to   mettre en demeure
    c. C-20, s. 6(2)
demands
  rights, interests, claims and   droits et créances
  demands
    c. C-9, s. 43(5)
demise
  demise of the Crown   dévolution de la Couronne
    c. I-23, s. 46(1)
    c. P-1, s. 2
demonstration project   projet pilote
    c. C-32, s. 4(1)(d)
demote/to
  dismiss, demote, transfer (an   faire l'objet d'un renvoi, d'une
  individual)   rétrogradation ou d'une mutation
    c. C-23, s. 42(1)
denominated
  (securities)   libellé
    c. C-52, s. 17(2)(d)(i)
denomination
  (money)   dénomination
    c. C-46, s. 448
denominational
  denominational, separate or   écoles séparées et autres écoles
  dissentient schools   confessionnelles
    Constitutional Act, 1982,
    Schedule B, s. 29
denounce/to
  (a convention)   dénoncer
    c. C-26, Schedule I, Article
    39(1)
denunciation
  (international agreement)   dénonciation
    c. C-42, Schedule II, Article
    29
deny/to
  (a challenge)   repousser
    c. C-46, s. 639(3)
department   ministère
    c. A-1, s. 3
departmental corporation   établissement public
    c. F-11, s. 2
departments
  departments and agencies (of   autorités fédérales
  the Government of Canada)
    c. A-3, s. 8
departure
  place of departure   point de départ
    c. C-26, Schedule I, Article
    1(2)
dependent
  dependent contractor   entrepreneur
    c. L-2, s. 3(1)
  dependent/to be   être à la charge
    c. C-17, s. 2(2)
depict pictorially/to   représenter au moyen
                              d'illustrations
    c. C-46, s. 163(7)
depiction
  depiction or symbol (on product)   description ou symbole
    c. C-38, s. 7(2)(a)

deponent	déposant
c. C-34, s. 13(2)	
deportation order	mesure d'expulsion
c. C-29, s. 2(2)(c)	
deposit	
deposit account	compte de dépôt
c. B-2, s. 18(b)	
deposit certificate	certificat de dépôt
c. F-11, s. 2	
deposit debt	dette au titre des dépôts
c. L-12, s. 74(3)	
deposit liabilities	passif-dépôt
c. B-1, s. 176(2)	
c. B-2, s. 19	
deposit to ensure the doing of any act or thing	cautionnement en garantie d'exécution d'un acte ou d'une chose
c. F-11, s. 20(1)	
money deposit	dépôt de fonds
c. L-12, s. 72(1)	
required deposit balance	dépôt de garantie
c. C-46, s. 347(2)	
deposit/to	
pledge or deposit as security/to	mettre en gage ou déposer en garantie
c. C-46, s. 322(b)	
deposit with/to	
deposit with him/to (a sum of money)	déposer entre ses mains
c. C-46, s. 550(3)(b)	
deposition	
take down a deposition in writing/to	prendre une déposition par écrit
c. C-46, s. 540(2)(a)	
depositor	titulaire du compte
c. B-1, s. 211(1)(a)	
c. C-46, s. 362(5)	déposant
c. L-12, s. 74(3)	
depository	dépositaire
c. B-2, s. 18(m)	
c. L-12, s. 72(4)(a)	
c. C-41, s. 50(a)	caisse de dépôts
c. B-7, s. 6	dépositaire
custodian or depository (of money)	gardien ou dépositaire
c. C-46, s. 204(1)(a)	
depreciation	dépréciation
c. B-7, Schedule I, Article I(iii)	
(of value)	dépréciation
c. B-1, s. 308(1)	
accumulated depreciation	amortissement accumulé
c. B-1, s. 200(b)	
depreciation in assets	dépréciation de l'actif
c. C-7, s. 29(2)	
deprive of a right/to	priver d'un droit
c. B-1, s. 63(2)	
deputed/to be	
(a person)	être délégué
c. C-34, s. 27	
deputy	
(of the Attorney General)	substitut légitime
c. C-46, s. 2	

deputy head of a department   administrateur général de
    ministère
    c. A-1, s. 55(1)
deputy judge   juge suppléant
    c. F-7, s. 10(1)
deputy magistrate   magistrat adjoint
    c. C-46, s. 552
lawful deputy (of a mayor)   adjoint légitime
    c. C-46, s. 67
mayor, warden, reeve, sheriff,   maire, président de conseil de
deputy sheriff, sheriff's officer   comté, préfet, shérif, shérif
and   adjoint, officier de shérif et juge
    de paix
    c. C-46, s. 2
warden, deputy warden,   directeur, sous-directeur,
instructor, keeper, jailer, guard,   instructeur, gardien, geôlier,
or other officer or permanent   garde ou tout autre fonctionnaire
employee of a prison (peace   ou employé permanent d'une
officer)   prison
    c. C-46, s. 2

Deputy Government Whip   whip suppléant du gouvernement
    c. P-1, s. 62(d)
Deputy Governor
Deputy Governor or Acting   sous-gouverneur ou gouverneur par
Governor (of the Bank of   intérim
Canada)
    c. C-24, s. 8(2)(b)
Deputy Registrar
(of the Supreme court)   registraire adjoint
    c. S-26, s. 12(1)
Deputy Registrar General   sous-registraire général
    c. C-47, Schedule, s. 4
derivative
derivative action   action indirecte
    c. C-44, s. 124(2)
derivative action   action oblique
    c. C-44, s. 239(1)
derogate/to
abrogate or derogate (from a   porter atteinte
rule)
    c. C-3, s. 22(3)
descent
devolve by descent, limitation or   échoir par voie de transmission ou
marriage/to   pour cause de prescription, ou par
    mariage
    c. P-1, s. 40(b)
describe/to
(in an Act)   définir
    c. A-7, s. 7(6)
desert/to
(a child)   abandonner
    c. C-29, s. 4(1)
deserter
deserter or absentee without   déserteur ou absent sans
leave (from the Canadian   permission
Forces)
    c. C-46, s. 420(1)
to harbour or conceal a deserter   receler ou cacher un déserteur ou
or absentee   un absent
    c. C-46, s. 54
desertion
offence of desertion   infraction de désertion
    c. C-17, s. 18(4)(e)

design
  mark, brand, seal, wrapper or
  design
    c. C-46, s. 376(3)

marque, signe, sceau, enveloppe ou
dessin

designate/to
  (acricultural products)
    c. A-4, s. 2

classer

  (as a bank)
    c. C-24, s. 2(1)

agréer

  (as chairman)
    c. A-4, s. 3(2)

désigner

  (as Minister)
    c. A-3, s. 2

charger

designated
  designated area
    c. C-24, s. 2(1)

région désignée

  designated employer (public
  service)
    c. P-35, s. 2

fonctionnaire désigné

  designated goods
    c. C-53, s. 2(1)

biens désignés

  designated Minister
    c. A-1, s. 3

ministre désigné

designated employer
  (public service)
    c. P-35, s. 2

fonctionnaire désigné

designating number
  (of a corporation)
    c. C-44, s. 11(2)

numéro matricule

designation
  (of shares)
    c. C-44, s. 6(1)(c)ii)

désignation

  collective or descriptive
  designation
    c. C-19, s. 13

désignation collective ou descriptive

designedly
    c. F-11, s. 80(c)

intentionnellement

desirable
  desirable in the interests of the
  safety (of the applicant)
    c. C-46, s. 112(5)

souhaitable pour la sécurité

destination
  place of destination
    c. C-26, Schedule I, Article
    1(2)

point de destination

destitute
  to be in destitute or necessitous
  circumstances
    c. C-46, s. 215(2)(a)(i)

se trouver dans le dénuement ou
dans le besoin

destructive
  poison or other destructive or
  noxious thing (Criminal Code)
    c. C-46, s. 245

poison ou autre substance
destructive ou délétère

detailed accounts
  to keep detailed accounts
    c. C-44, s. 104(2)

tenir une comptabilité détaillée

detain/to
  (a vessel)
    c. C-9, s. 43(3)

retenir

  detain in custody/to
    c. A-11, s. 21(2)

détenir

detainer
  forcible entry and detainer

    c. C-46, s. 73

prise de possession et de détention
par la force

detection
  (of offences)   dépistage
    c. C-46, s. 195(3)(b)
detention
  (of things seized)   rétention
    c. C-46, s. 490(1)(a)
  demand, seizure or detention   revendication, saisie ou rétention
    c. C-10, s. 40(3)
  detention in custody   mise en détention
    c. Y-1, s. 7(2)
  Sentence of detention   peine de détention
    c. C-46, s. 753(b)
deteriorate/to
  (in quality)   altérer
    c. A-7, s. 19(1)(b)(i)
determination
  determination of a dispute   règlement d'un litige
    c. C-44, s. 145(2)(a)
  determination of appeal   décision de l'appel
    c. C-46, s. 679(1)
  determination of guilt   détermination de culpabilité
    c. C-46, s. 736(3)(a)
  determination of policy   fixation d'orientations générales
    c. S-22, s. 2(1)
  summary determination   décision sommaire
    c. C-46, s. 685
determine/to   juger
    c. A-1, s. 45
  determine a controversy/to (at   trancher un différend
  election of director)
    c. C-44, s. 145(1)
  determine a substantive right/to   statuer au fond sur un droit
    c. S-26, s. 2(1)
  determine or dissolve/to   interrompre ou dissoudre
  (Parliament)
    c. P-1, s. 2
  hear and determine an   entendre et statuer sur une
  application/to   demande
    c. C-46, s. 754(1)
  hear and determine/to (a   instruire
  complaint)
    c. L-2, s. 98(1)
  hear and determine/to (a   instruire
  complaint)
    c. L-2, s. 98(1)
  hear and determine/to (actions)   instruire et juger
    c. C-42, s. 37
  hear and determine/to (by the   entendre et décider
  court)
    c. C-46, s. 754(2)
  hear and determine/to   connaître de
  (questions of law)
    c. A-7, s. 12
  hear, try and determine a   connaître d'une plainte
  complaint/to
    c. L-2, s. 160
  hear, try and determine/to (by a   instruire et juger
  magistrate)
    c. A-7, s. 23
  hear, try or determine/to (a   connaître de
  complaint)
    c. C-32, s. 40

settle and to determine/to (by a judge)
   c. B-1, s. 32(4) — statuer

determine sentence to be imposed/to
   c. C-46, s. 721(3) — fixer la sentence à imposer

detriment
  to result in serious and unwarranted detriment
   c. S-22, s. 20(d)(iii) — être la cause de préjudice grave et injustifié

detrimental
   c. C-23, s. 2
   c. C-44, s. 156 — préjudiciable
  commercially detrimental information
   c. F-11, s. 153(1) — renseignements commerciaux nuisibles

detrimental/to be
  (to the operation of an establishment)
   c. L-2, s. 175(1)(a)(i) — causer préjudice

develop/to
  (a plan)
   c. C-11, s. 15(2)(c) — mettre au point
  develop closer ties/to
   c. A-13, s. 3 — resserrer les liens

Development and Peace
   c. C-18, Schedule — Organisation catholique canadienne pour le développement et la paix

deviation
  (at sea)
   c. C-27, Schedule, Article IV, 2 — déroutement

device
   c. F-27, s. 2 — instrument

devolution
  devolution by law
   c. C-29, s. 38(e) — dévolution légale

devolve/to
  (interest)
   c. C-42, s. 14(1) — être dévolu
  (ownership)
   c. B-1, s. 78(3) — être dévolu
  devolve by descent, limitation or marriage/to
   c. P-1, s. 40(b) — échoir par voie de transmission ou pour cause de prescription, ou par mariage

difference
  (in price)
   c. A-5, s. 4(3) — désaccord
  (relating to the collective agreement)
   c. L-2, s. 3(1) — désaccord

differences
  final settlement of differences (disputes)
   c. C-46, s. 422(2)(b) — règlement définitif des différends

digging
  mine, quarry or digging
   c. C-46, s. 333 — mine, carrière ou fouille

diligence
  care, diligence and skill of a reasonably prudent trustee
   c. C-44, s. 91(b) — soin, diligence et compétence d'un bon fiduciaire

exercice all due diligence/to   prendre les mesures nécessaires
    c. C-15, s. 20(3)
exercise good faith and   agir de bonne foi et avec une
reasonable diligence/to   diligence raisonnable
    c. C-44, s. 81(1)(a)
lack of diligence   manque de diligence
    c. C-46, s. 603(6)(iii)
reasonable diligence   diligence raisonable
    c. C-46, s. 188(2)
reasonable diligence   diligence normale
    c. L-2, s. 40(2)(a)
diligently   avec diligence
    c. C-44, s. 239(2)(a)
diminish/to
impair, diminish or lighten   affaiblir, diminuer ou alléger
(coin)/to
    c. C-46, s. 455(a)
direct
direct and contingent liabilities   charges directes ou éventuelles
    c. F-11, s. 63(2)
direct/to   ordonner
    c. C-46, s. 737(1)(a)
    c. F-27, s. 27(3)   prescrire
(a person to observe a   enjoindre
prohibition)
    c. P-35, s. 23(2)
(payement)   enjoindre
    c. B-3, s. 68(3)
(that a vote be taken)   ordonner
    c. P-35, s. 36(2)
direct a verdict of not guilty/to   ordonner que soit enregistré un
    verdict de non-culpabilité
    c. C-46, s. 316(2)
direct, supervise and   diriger, contrôler et coordonner
coordinate/to (a program)
    c. C-11, s. 5 in fine
direct equity percentage
(Canadian ownership)   pourcentage de participation directe
    c. C-20, s. 2(1)
direct for cause/to   ordonner pour cause
    c. C-34, s. 12(4)
direction
(made by the Commission)   instruction
    c. A-2, s. 14(1)(a)
(of a Act)   prescription
    c. C-46, s. 643(3)
(of the court)   instruction
    c. B-3, s. 16(2)
(of the Commission)   instruction
    c. B-9, s. 13(1)(a)
(Commission may issue)   directive
    c. A-2, s. 14(1)(b)
act under the direction/to   agir sous l'autorité de
    c. A-1, s. 61
direction and management (of   conduite
business)
    c. C-21, s. 16(2)
exercise control or direction/to   exercer le contrôle et avoir la haute
(over votes)   main
    c. C-44, s. 126(1)
general or special direction   instruction générale ou particulière
    c. A-16, s. 7

give a direction or make a reference/to (Minister of Justice)
c. C-46, s. 679(7)

prendre une ordonnance ou faire un renvoi

have management and direction/to (of a department)
c. C-37, s. 2(3)

assurer la direction et la gestion

have supervision over and direction of/to (activities and staff)
c. A-13, s. 17

assurer la direction et contrôler la gestion

on the direction of the Governor in Council
c. A-12, s. 6(2)(a)

sur l'ordre du gouverneur en conseil

under the direction (of a department)
c. A-2, s. 9(1)

sous la direction

directions
(of the Minister)
c. A-2, s. 16

instructions

give directions/to (judge)
c. C-46, s. 525(9)

donner les instructions

directive
(from a Minister)
c. B-9, s. 8(4)

instruction

director
c. C-44, s. 2(1)

administrateur

any officer, director or agent (of a corporation)
c. A-4, s. 5(2)

dirigeant, administrateur ou mandataire

executive director (of the Corporation)
c. C-16, s. 12(1)

directeur général (de la Société)

managing director (of corporation)
c. C-44, s. 126(1)(a)

administrateur délégué

managing director (of corporation)
c. C-44, s. 115(1)

administrateur-gérant

Director of Investigation and Research
c. C-34, s. 2

directeur des enquêtes et recherches

Director of Soldier Settlement

Directeur de l'établissement de soldats

c. A-1, Schedule I
disability
disability pension
c. C-8, s. 12(1)(b)

pension d'invalidité

mental disability
c. C-8, s. 42(2)(a)
c. Y-1, s. 13(1)(e)

invalidité mentale

physical disability
c. C-8, s. 42(2)(a)

invalidité physique

physical or mental illness or disorder, psychological disorder, emotional disturbance, learning disability or mental retardation

maladie ou dérèglement d'ordre physique ou mental, dérèglement d'ordre psychologique, troubles émotionnels, troubles d'apprentissage ou déficience mentale

c. Y-1, s. 13(1)(e)
disabled
c. C-8, s. 2(1)
c. C-17, s. 2(1)

invalide

disadvantaged person personne défavorisée
 c. N-11, s. 59(1)
disallow/to
 (a claim) rejeter
  c. B-3, s. 125
 (an act or order) rejeter
  c. B-8, s. 13
disallowance
 (of a toll) annulation
  c. A-2, s. 18(1)(m)(i)
disburse/to
 (an amount) prélever
  c. B-1, s. 32(3)
disbursement débours
  c. F-7, s. 22(2)(p)
 (of cash) décaissement
  c. C-41, s. 73(1)(a)
disbursements
 accounts of receipts and comptes de recettes et de débours et
 disbursements and final états définitifs
 statements
  c. B-3, s. 5(3)(g)
 legal fees and disbursements honoraires légaux et déboursés
  c. C-44, s. 242(2)
disbursing
 person disbursing public money ordonnateur de fonds publics
  c. F-11, s. 9(1)
discharge quittance
  c. B-1, s. 206(2)
 (of bankrupt) libération
  c. B-3, s. 41(1)
 absolute and conditional libération inconditionnelle et sous
 discharge condition
  c. C-47, s. 2(3)
 absolute discharge libération inconditionnelle
  c. Y-1, s. 36(2)
 absolute order of discharge ordonnance de libération absolue
  c. B-3, s. 172(1)
 application for discharge of a demande de libération d'un failli
 bankrupt
  c. B-3, s. 28(1)(d)
 final discharge (of a prisoner) élargissement définitif
  c. P-20, s. 12(b)
 provide for the discharge of its constituer une provision pour
 oblibations/to honorer ses obligations
  c. C-44, s. 217
 release, receipt, discharge or décharge, reçu, quittance ou autre
 other instrument evidencing instrument constatant le
 payment of money paiement de deniers
  c. C-46, s. 2
 valid and binding discharge libération valide
  c. C-40, s. 51(2)
discharge/to
 (a bankrupt) libérer (un failli)
  c. B-3, s. 29(1)
 (a bill) acquitter
  c. B-4, s. 138(1)
 (a constable) licencier
  c. C-9, s. 22(5)
 (a liability) libérer
  c. C-8, s. 37
 (a person) renvoyer
  c. L-2, s. 256(1)(c)

(a person)
c. L-2, s. 155(1)(c) — congédier

(a prisoner)
c. C-46, s. 527(5)(b) — libérer

(the liability)
c. C-8, s. 37 — éteindre

discharge a duty/to
c. B-1, s. 103(1)(c) — s'acquitter d'une obligation

discharge a liability/to
c. C-44, s. 210(3)(b) — effectuer le règlement d'une dette

discharge an obligation/to
c. C-44, s. 211(7)c) — honorer une obligation

discharge an obligation/to
c. C-46, s. 767 — se libérer d'une obligation

discharge from any further obligation/to
c. Y-1, s. 32(7)(b) — délier pour l'avenir de toute obligation

discharge the accused/to
c. C-46, s. 316(2) — libérer le prévenu

pay or discharge a valuable security/to
c. C-46, s. 491.1(3)(b)(ii) — payer ou rembourser des valeurs

release and discharge a security/to
c. F-11, s. 81(a)(ii) — donner quittance et mainlevée d'une garantie

discharged inmate
c. P-5, s. 34(2) — libéré

disciplinary
disciplinary offence
c. P-5, s. 26 — mauvaise conduite

disciplinary court
c. P-5, s. 26 — tribunal disciplinaire

discipline
conduct and discipline (of employees)
c. C-23, s. 8(2) — conduite et discipline

good order and discipline (on a vessel)
c. C-46, s. 44 — bon ordre et discipline (à bord d'un navire)

disclaim/to
(a lease)
c. B-3, s. 30(1)(k) — désavouer

disclose/to
(information)
c. C-23, s. 18(1) — communiquer

(the property or funds of an estate)
c. B-3, s. 6(3) — déclarer

disclose an interest/to
c. C-44, s. 120(1) — divulguer un intérêt

disclosure
c. A-1, s. 2(1) — communication

c. A-1, s. 14 — divulgation

(of a record) — communication
c. C-42, s. 27(2)(i)

(of an intercepted communication)
c. C-23, s. 25(a) — révélation

(of interest)
c. C-44, s. 120(2) — divulgation

(of name and identify)
c. L-2, s. 260 — révélation

disclosure and production (of a contract)
    c. C-34, s. 11(1)

révélation et production

disclosure necessarily incidental
    c. C-46, s. 193(2)(d)

divulgation nécessairement accessoire

discontinuance

discontinuance of a function
    c. L-2, s. 240(3)(a)

suppression d'un poste

discontinuance of proceedings
    c. S-26, s. 69

désistement

discontinuation

(of production)
    c. C-25, s. 17(1)

arrêt

discontinue/to

(a proceeding)
    c. F-11, s. 23(4)(b)

abandonner une action

(an action)
    c. C-44, s. 239(2)(c)

mettre fin (à une action)

(proceedings)
    c. S-26, s. 69(1)

se désister

continue or discontinue/to (proceedings)
    c. C-44, s. 217(n)(i)

poursuivre ou interrompre

discontinue an operation/to
    c. C-32, s. 18(1)

cesser une exploitation

discount
    c. C-24, s. 35

réfaction

(on a sale)
    c. F-11, s. 48(3)(c)

escompte

issue at a discount (debenture)
    c. C-40, s. 93(8)

émission au-dessous du pair

make a discount/to
    c. C-24, s. 35

appliquer une réfaction

discount/to

(bill of exchange)
    c. B-2, s. 23(f)

escompter

deal in and discount/to (a bill of exchange)
    c. B-1, s. 173(1)(c)

négocier et escompter

discounting

the making, accepting, discounting or endorsing of a bill of exchange, cheque, draft or promissary note
    c. C-46, s. 362(1)(c)(vi)

création, acceptation, escompte ou endossement d'une lettre de change, d'un chèque, d'une traite ou d'un billet à ordre

discovery

examination for discovery
    c. F-7, s. 46(1)(a)(i)

interrogatoire au préalable

production or discovery (of a cockpit voice recording)
    c. C-12, s. 34(1)

production ou examen

discretion

(of a judge)
    c. L-2, s. 163(2)

pouvoir discrétionnaire

(of a Minister)
    c. B-1, s. 28(6)(b)

choix

(of the inspector)
    c. C-11, s. 22(2)

appréciation

(of the Court)
    c. S-26, s. 62(3)

à l'appréciation (de la Cour)

at the discretion of (someone)
    c. P-20, s. 6(4)

à l'appréciation de (quelqu'un)

in its discretion c. C-36, s. 7	à sa discrétion
in its discretion c. C-44, s. 190(21)	
in its discretion c. B-7, Schedule I, Article V, Section 4	discrétionnairement
in its sole discretion (of the Board) c. P-35, s. 42(3)	à son appréciation
in one's sole discretion c. C-24, s. 32(3)	à sa seule appréciation
judicial discretion c. S-26, s. 42(1)	pouvoir judiciaire discrétionnaire
discretionary power c. A-1, s. 21(2)(a)	pouvoir discrétionnaire
discriminate/to	
(against a person) c. L-2, s. 155(1)(c)	faire preuve de discrimination
(against a person) c. L-2, s. 256(1)(c)	désavantager
(against a person) c. P-35, s. 8(2)(a)	faire des distinctions injustes
(between persons) c. C-29, s. 35(3)(c)	établir une distinction
disctrict	
bankruptcy district c. B-3, s. 12(2)	district de faillite
disguise c. C-46, s. 351(2)	déguisement
disgusting object c. C-46, s. 163(2)(b)	objet révoltant
dishonestly	
act fraudulently or dishonestly/to c. C-44, s. 229(2)(d)	commettre des actes frauduleux ou malhonnêtes
dishonour	
evidence of presentation and dishonour c. B-4, s. 10	preuve de la présentation et du défaut d'acceptation
notice of dishonour c. B-4, s. 96	avis de refus
disloyalty	
insubordination, disloyalty, mutiny or refusal of duty c. C-46, s. 62(1)(c)	insubordination, déloyauté, mutinerie ou refus de servir
dismiss/to	
(a constable) c. C-9, s. 22(5)	destituer
(an appeal) c. S-26, s. 43(2)(b)	rejeter
(an employee) c. F-11, s. 13(1)	destituer
(complaint) c. A-7, s. 8(5)(a)	rejeter
dismiss an action/to c. C-44, s. 242(1)	rejeter une action
dismiss the appeal/to c. C-46, s. 112(11)(a)	rejeter l'appel
dismissal c. B-7, Schedule I, Article XII, Section 4(b)	révocation

(public servant) — destitution
  c. P-35, s. 8(2)(c)
dismissal for just cause — congédiement justifié
  c. L-2, s. 230(1)
dismissal with disgrace — destitution ignominieuse
  c. C-17, s. 18(4)(a)
move the Court for dismissal of the appeal/to — demander le rejet de l'appel à la Cour
  c. S-26, s. 71(1)

disobedience
  punishment for disobedience — peine pour défaut de se conformer
    c. C-34, s. 19(1)

disobey/to
  disobey a lawful order/to — désobéir à une ordonnance légale
    c. C-46, s. 127(1)

disorder
  mental disorder — déséquilibre mental
    c. C-46, s. 106(4)(b)
    c. Y-1, s. 13(1)(e)
  physical or mental illness or disorder, psychological disorder, emotional disturbance, learning disability or mental retardation — maladie ou dérèglement d'ordre physique ou mental, dérèglement d'ordre psychologique, troubles émotionnels, troubles d'apprentissage ou déficience mentale
    c. Y-1, s. 13(1)(e)

disorderly house — maison de désordre
  c. C-46, s. 197(1)

disparities
  equalization and regional disparities — péréquation et inégalités régionales
    Constitutional Act, 1982, Schedule B, s. 36

dispatch
  reasonable dispatch — diligence raisonnable
    c. C-46, s. 90(3)
  with all due dispatch — le plus rapidement possible
    c. C-8, s. 115(2)
  with all due dispatch — avec toute la diligence voulue
    c. C-8, s. 27(5)
  with all reasonable dispatch — avec toute la célérité raisonnable
    c. C-46, s. 50(1)(b)

dispatching — répartition du travail
  c. L-2, s. 69(1)

dispense/to
  (with the notice) — passer outre
    c. Y-1, s. 9(10)(b)

dispensed with
  unless notice has been dispensed with — sauf dispensation
    c. Y-1, s. 9(9)(b)

displace/to
  (an employee) — supplanter
    c. L-2, s. 230(2)

display
  handling, secure storage and display (of firearms) — manipulation, entreposage et mise en montre
    c. C-46, s. 116(b)

displayed
  article offered or displayed for sale — article mis en vente ou exposé pour la vente
    c. C-34, s. 52(2)(a)

disposal
(of shares)   aliénation
   c. B-1, s. 122(5)
(of shares)   vente
   c. B-1, s. 122(6)
disposal or realization (of a   aliénation ou réalisation
security)
   c. N-11, s. 47(f)(i)
sale or disposal   cession
   c. L-12, s. 100(2)
dispose/to   aliéner
   c. A-11, s. 3(q)
(a security)   aliéner
   c. B-1, s. 102
(of a complaint)   trancher
   c. L-12, s. 134(a)
(of the shares)   se dessaisir
   c. L-12, s. 101(2)
absolutely dispose of/to (an   se départir entièrement de
interest)
   c. C-22, s. 5(2)
acquire, hold, sell or otherwise   acquérir, détenir ou aliéner
dispose of/to (real property)
   c. A-13, s. 4(i)
buy, sell, lease, construct or   acquérir - notamment par achat ou
otherwise acquire, dispose of   location - vendre, construire,
and maintain and operate/to   aliéner, entretenir et exploiter
   c. A-10, s. 6(1)(b)
dispose by gift or settlement/to   aliéner par donation ou disposition
                                                       en fiducie
   c. B-3, s. 158(g)
dispose of a mortgage, an   céder une hypothèque, un privilège,
hypothec, a lien, a charge/to   une sûreté
   c. C-25, s. 23(1)(d)
dispose of a weapon/to (to   disposer d'une arme
surrender)
   c. C-46, s. 112(6)
dispose of or deal with/to (a   disposer ou traiter (d'une chose
thing seized)   saisie)
   c. C-46, s. 461(2)
dispose of or destroy   fixer l'usage qui sera fait des
documents/to   documents ou les détruire
   c. C-44, s. 217(h)(i)
dispose of or otherwise deal   céder ou aliéner
with/to (property)
   c. B-3, s. 71(2)
expend, administer and   employer, gérer et aliéner
dispose/to (of the money)
   c. C-13, s. 6(3)
sell or otherwise dispose of all or vendre ou d'une façon générale,
substantially all of the assets/to   céder la totalité ou la quasi-
                                                       totalité des actifs
   c. F-11, s. 90(2)
settle and dispose of/to (of an   régler et disposer de
appeal, an objection, an
application
   c. B-3, s. 41(4)
disposition   décision
   c. Y-1, s. 2(1)
(of an investment)   réalisation
   c. C-2, s. 17(2)
(of articles seized)   destination
   c. A-7, s. 18(4)(b)

(of assets)   affectation
    c. B-1, s. 279(1)
(of grain)   écoulement
    c. C-24, s. 6(b)
(of property)   emploi (des biens)
    c. B-3, s. 10(1)
acquisition or disposition (of a   acquisition ou aliénation
right)
    c. C-44, s. 126(2)(e)
aid or assist a person to make a   aider ou assister une personne à
disposition of anything/to   disposer d'une chose
    c. C-46, s. 389(1)(b)
disposition of appeal   jugement sur appel
    c. C-46, s. 759(3)
disposition of property   aliénation de biens
    c. C-46, s. 331
disposition on review   décision en matière d'examen
    c. Y-1, Schedule, Form 7
final disposition (of the   adjudication définitive
application or action)
    c. C-44, s. 242(2)
final disposition of the   décision finale sur la demande
application
    c. C-46, s. 109(7)
make a disposition/to   rendre une décision
    c. C-46, s. 523(1)(b)(ii)
dispute   litige
    c. B-1, s. 74(2)(a)
(in respect of collective   différend
agreement)
    c. L-2, s. 3(1)
determination of a dispute   règlement d'un litige
    c. C-44, s. 145(2)(a)
dispute/to
(a statement)   contester
    c. B-3, s. 170(6)
disputed
(appointment)   litigieux
    c. C-44, s. 145(2)(b)
disputes
settlement of industrial disputes   règlement de conflits industriels
    c. C-46, s. 422(2)(b)
disqualification   incapacité
    c. Y-1, s. 36(2)
(from driving)   interdiction
    c. C-46, s. 259(5)
(of a judge)   inhabilité à siéger
    c. S-26, s. 30(1)
disqualification, incapacity or   inhabilité, incapacité ou décès
death (of a candidate)
    c. B-1, s. 36(9)
disqualified
driving while disqualified   conduite pendant interdiction
    c. C-46, s. 553(c)(vii)
disqualified/to be
disqualified from being a   être déchu de son mandat
member/to be (of the Senate)
    c. P-1, s. 41(2)
disregard
wanton or reckless disregard   insouciance déréglée ou téméraire
    c. C-46, s. 219(1)
disregard/to
(a requirement)   ne pas tenir compte
    c. L-2, s. 29(3)

dissatisfied
person dissatisfied (with a decision)
c. C-36, s. 13 — personne mécontente

dissent
(of director)
c. C-44, s. 123(1)(a) — dissidence
advocacy, protest or dissent
c. C-23, s. 2 — défense d'une cause, protestation ou manifestation d'un désaccord
express a dissent/to
c. B-4, s. 82(2) — signifier son opposition
grounds of dissent
c. C-46, s. 677 — motif de dissidence
notice of dissent
c. C-44, s. 190(25)(a) — avis de dissidence
notice of dissent (in a meeting)
c. F-11, s. 111(1) — avis de désaccord
right to dissent
c. C-44, s. 190(5) — droit à la dissidence

dissent/to
c. C-44, s. 190(3) — faire valoir sa dissidence
(from a proposal)
c. B-3, s. 53 — désapprouver

dissentient
denominational, separate or dissentient schools
Constitutional Act, 1982, Schedule B, s. 29 — écoles séparées et autres écoles confessionnelles

dissolution
c. F-11, s. 60(1)(b)(i) — déclaration de cessation de commerce
dissolution of marriage
c. C-46, s. 166(1)(b) — dissolution de mariage
order of prohibition or dissolution (against a monopoly)
c. C-34, s. 34(3) — ordonnance d'interdiction ou de dissolution
voluntary dissolution
c. B-1, s. 287(1) — dissolution volontaire

dissolve/to
(a corporation)
c. F-11, s. 6(a) — dissoudre
(a merger or a monopoly)
c. C-34, s. 34(1)(b) — dissoudre
determine or dissolve/to (Parliament)
c. P-1, s. 2 — interrompre ou dissoudre

distinguishing mark
c. C-46, s. 417(3) — marque distinctive

distress
cargo, stores and tackle of a vessel wrecked, stranded or in distress
c. C-46, s. 2 — cargaison, approvisionnement, agrès et apparaux d'un navire naufragé, échoué ou en détresse
distress or seizure
c. C-46, s. 271(1)(c)(i) — saisie
lawful distress or seizure
c. C-46, s. 129(c) — saisie légale

distribute/to
c. N-1, s. 2 — distribuer
(securities)
c. B-1, s. 145 — mettre en circulation

distributing
  distributing bank — banque ayant fait appel au public
    c. B-1, s. 168(1)
  distributing corporation — société qui fait appel au public
    c. C-44, s. 21(1)
distribution
  (of a circular) — diffusion
    c. C-44, s. 205(3)(a)
  (of an amount) — répartition
    c. B-1, s. 32(3)
  (of securities) — mise en circulation
    c. B-1, s. 154(c)(iv)
  (of Canada Gazette) — diffusion
    c. S-22, s. 13(1)
  custody, control or distribution — garde ou distribution
  (of a thing)
    c. C-17, s. 18(4)(c)
  distribution to the public (a — émission publique
  security)
    c. C-44, s. 126(1)
  distribution to the public — souscription publique
  (securities)
    c. C-44, s. 2(6)
  initial distribution (of shares) — première émission
    c. B-1, s. 148(2)
  liquidation distribution — partage consécutif à la liquidation
    c. B-1, s. 62(1)(f)
  primary distribution (of a — distribution primaire
  security)
    c. C-34, s. 5(1)
  public distribution (of shares) — émission publique
    c. B-1, s. 110(9)
  secondary distribution (of a — distribution secondaire
  security)
    c. C-34, s. 5(1)
district — circonscription
    c. A-11, s. 44
  electoral district — circonscription électorale
    c. C-24, s. 17(3)(b)
  judicial centre or district town — centre ou chef-lieu de la circonscription
    c. J-1, s. 35(1)
  mining, land or timber district — minier, agricole ou district forestier
    c. T-7, s. 23(g)
  provisional judicial district — district judiciaire provisoire
    c. C-46, s. 480(1)
District Court of Ontario — cour de district de l'Ontario
    c. J-1, s. 11(1)
disturb/to
  disturb the peace and quiet/to — troubler la paix et la tranquillité
  (of occupants)
    c. C-46, s. 175(1)(d)
  disturb the peace — troubler tumultueusement la paix
  tumultuously/to
    c. C-46, s. 63(1)(b)
disturbance
  cause a disturbance/to — faire du tapage
    c. C-46, s. 175(1)(a)
  physical or mental illness or — maladie ou dérèglement d'ordre physique ou mental, dérèglement d'ordre psychologique, troubles émotionnels, troubles d'apprentissage ou déficience mentale
  disorder, psychological disorder,
  emotional disturbance, learning
  disability or mental retardation

    c. Y-1, s. 13(1)(e)

disturbed
 to be disturbed (balance of the   être déséquilibré
 mind)
  c. C-46, s. 537(b)(iv)
divert/to
 (amounts)   distraire
  c. C-17, s. 36(1)
divest oneself/to
 (of a share)   se départir
  c. B-1, s. 110(15)
divested/to be
 (of an interest)   perdre un droit
  c. C-44, s. 46(3)
divide/to
 (a class of shares)   diviser
  c. C-44, s. 173(1)(i)
 divide a count/to   diviser un chef d'accusation
  c. C-46, s. 590(2)
 divide in its existing form/to   partager en nature
  c. B-3, s. 30(1)(j)
dividend
 declare a dividend/to   déclarer un dividende
  c. C-44, s. 24(3)(b)
 dividend sheet   bordereau de dividendes
  c. B-3, s. 28(1)(c)
 stock dividend   dividende en actions
  c. B-1, s. 154(c)(i)
dividends
 accrued dividends   dividendes accumulés
  c. C-44, s. 173(1)(g)
 accumulated dividends   dividendes cumulatifs
  c. C-44, s. 27(2)
 cumulative dividends   dividendes cumulatifs
  c. C-44, s. 176(1)(c)(i)
divisible
 (a count in an indictment)   divisible
  c. C-46, s. 662(1)
 (an instrument)   divisible
  c. C-44, s. 48(2)(c)
division
 (a class of shares)   subdivision
  c. B-1, s. 2(1)
 (of business)   fractionnement
  c. C-44, s. 192(1)(d)
 bankruptcy division   division de faillite
  c. B-3, s. 12(1)
 division of profit   répartition des bénéfices
  c. L-12, s. 35(2)
 judicial division   division judiciaire
  c. A-2, s. 8(6)
 judicial division   circonscription judiciaire
  c. C-46, s. 2
 territorial division   circonscription territoriale
  c. C-46, s. 465(5)
divorce
 divorce proceeding   action en divorce
  c. C-3, s. 2(1)
divulge/to
 (a name)   communiquer
  c. L-2, s. 146(4)(a)
document   titre
  c. C-26, Schedule I, Article
  5(1)

document of authorization
  c. A-2, s. 27(2)

document d'autorisation

document of title
  c. C-27, s. 4

document

document of title
  c. C-27, Schedule, Article I(b)

document formant titre

document of title to goods or
lands
  c. C-46, s. 340(a)

titre de marchandises ou de biens-
fonds

document purporting to be
certified
  c. A-2, s. 27(1)

document donné comme étant
certifié

original document
  c. A-2, s. 27(1)(a)

pièce originale

production of a document
  c. A-11, s. 7(1)

production d'un document

doing
doing of anything
  c. A-2, s. 8(1)(j)

exécution de toute chose

forbid the doing or continuing of
any act/to
  c. A-2, s. 14(2)(b)

interdire l'accomplissement ou la
continuation de tout acte

domain
literary, scientific or artistic
domain
  c. C-42, s. 2

domaine littéraire, scientifique ou
artistique

public domain
  c. C-42, Schedule II, Article
  18

domaine public

domestic
domestic assets
  c. B-1, s. 174(2)(e)

actif national

domestic laws
  c. C-42, Schedule III, Article
  7

droit interne

domestic legislation
  c. C-42, Schedule II, Article 2

législation intérieure

domicile
(of an association)
  c. C-40, s. 35(1)

domicile

domiciled/to be
  c. C-42, s. 4(5)

être domicilié

dominate/to
(a trade union)
  c. L-2, s. 25(1)

dominer

Dominical year
  c. I-23, s. 37(1)(c)

millésime

Dominion Coal Board
  c. C-25, s. 12(1)(b)

Office fédéral du charbon

Donner Canadian Foundation
  c. C-18, Schedule

Donner Canadian Foundation

door-to-door
door-to-door delivery of the mail
  c. C-46, s. 476(e)

livraison à domicile du courrier

in-store, door-to-door or
telephone selling
  c. C-34, s. 52(2)(d)

opération de vente en magasin, par
démarchage ou par téléphone

doorway
doorway or passage-way (in
dwelling-house)
  c. C-46, s. 2

baie de porte ou passage

dormitory
housing accomodation of the
hostel or dormitory type
  c. N-11, s. 9(3)(a)(ii)

facilités de logement de type foyer
ou pension

doing

doubt
    raise beyond reasonable doubt a
    presumption/to
       c. C-17, s. 37

créer une présomption hors de tout
    doute raisonnable

doubtful debt
       c. B-1, s. 308(1)

créance douteuse

draft
       c. B-1, s. 90(3)

traite

    making, accepting, discounting
    or endorsing of a bill of
    exchange, cheque, draft or
    promissary note
       c. C-46, s. 362(1)(c)(vi)

création, acceptation, escompte ou
    endossement d'une lettre de
    change, d'un chèque, d'une traite
    ou d'un billet à ordre

    sight draft
       c. B-4, s. 162

traite à vue

    to collect a draft or other claim

recouvrer une créance, notamment
    une traite

       c. C-44, s. 63(3)

draft/to
    consider, draft and prepare for
    approval/to (regulations)
       c. A-2, s. 4(f)

étudier, rédiger et préparer

    draft legislation
       c. A-1, s. 69(1)(f)

avant-projet de loi

draftmanship
    form and draftmanship (of
    regulations)
       c. S-22, s. 3(2)(d)

présentation et rédaction

dramatic work
       c. C-42, s. 2

oeuvre dramatique

draw
    draw an inference adverse (to
    the accused)
       c. C-46, s. 475(2)

tirer une conclusion défavorable

draw/to
    (a bill of exchange)
       c. C-46, s. 362(5)

tirer

    (a bill of exchange)
       c. B-1, s. 188

tirer (une lettre de change)

    make, execute, draw, sign,
    accept or endorse a document/to
       c. C-46, s. 374(a)

faire, souscrire, rédiger, signer,
    accepter ou endosser un document

draw in a set/to
    (a bill)
       c. B-4, s. 157

tirer en plusieurs exemplaires

draw on/to
    (from a financial institution)
       c. C-21, s. 2(1)

tirer

draw up/to
    (a document)
       c. C-26, Schedule I, Article
       36

rédiger

drawback
    drawback or penalty
       c. F-7, s. 37

retenue ou pénalité

drawee
       c. B-4, s. 6(3)

tiré

    (of a cheque)
       c. C-21, s. 31(5)

tiré

drawer
    (of a bill)
       c. B-1, s. 188
       c. B-4, s. 33

tireur

drawing
  drawing right   droit de tirage
    c. B-7, Schedule I, Article III,
      Section 1
  party drawing (a bill)   tireur
    c. B-4, s. 39(1)(a)
  special drawing rights (for   droits de tirage spéciaux
  currency)
    c. C-52, s. 17(2)
drilled to the use of arms/to be   s'exercer au maniement des armes
    c. C-46, s. 70(1)
drover
  (livestock)   commerçant
    c. L-9, s. 10
drug
  controlled drug   drogue contrôlée
    c. F-27, s. 38
  restricted drug   drogue d'usage restreint
    c. F-27, s. 46
drunkenness
  habitual drunkenness   ivrognerie habituelle
    c. C-46, s. 172(1)
duces tecum
  subpoena ad testificandum or   bref d'assignation à témoigner ou à
  duces tecum   produire des pièces
    c. C-39, s. 25
due
  become due/to   devenir exigible
    c. C-17, s. 9(4)
  become due/to (an amount of   à échoir
  money)
    c. F-11, s. 68(1)(a)
  debt due   dette échue
    c. B-3, s. 2
  due and payable (payment)   exigible
    c. B-1, s. 129(3)
  due and unpaid (amount)   exigible et impayé
    c. C-41, s. 46
  due date   délai imparti
    c. B-7, Schedule I, Article V,
      Section 7(g)
  due obligation   obligation échue
    c. B-3, s. 2
  due obligation   obligation échue
    c. B-3, s. 2
  existing or future debt due or   créance existante ou future échue
  becoming due by the Crown   ou à échoir sur Sa Majesté
    c. F-11, s. 66
  recovery or collection of any debt recouvrement d'une créance
  or obligation due or payable
    c. F-11, s. 156(a)
  secure the due performance/to   garantir la bonne exécution
  (of contracts)
    c. F-11, s. 41(1)(b)
  sum due or payable   somme due
    c. F-11, s. 155(4)
duel
  fight a duel/to   se battre en duel
    c. C-46, s. 71(a)
dues   cotisations
    c. C-21, s. 6(1)(b)
duly   régulièrement
    c. B-1, s. 21(d)

duly authorized
    c. C-24, s. 20(3)
régulièrement autorisé

duly authorized in writing (as legal representative)
    c. C-42, s. 2
régulièrement constitué par mandat écrit

duly certified copy
    c. C-26, Schedule I, Article 36
copie certifiée conforme

duplicate
    c. C-24, s. 65(3)
double

duplicate instrument, memorial, certificate or document in respect to registration of titles
    c. C-46, s. 2
double de tout instrument, mémoire, certificat concernant l'enregistrement de titres

duplicate originals
    c. C-44, s. 262(2)(a)
duplicata

in duplicate
    c. C-26, Schedule I, Article 4(1)
en deux exemplaires

to sign in duplicate
    c. C-46, s. 501(3)
signer en double exemplaire

duration
(of the agreement)
    c. A-8, s. 13(2)(d)
durée

during good behaviour
    c. C-12, s. 5(3)
à titre inamovible

dust
gold in dust, solution or otherwise
    c. C-46, s. 451
or en poudre, en solution ou sous d'autres formes

duties
    c. A-12, s. 19(2)(c)
fonctions

(of the Council)
    c. C-4, s. 8(1)
mission

duties and functions
    c. A-12, s. 16
fonctions

duties and taxes (paid under federal customs)
    c. C-53, s. 3(2)
droits et taxes

duties or tolls
    c. C-10, s. 42(1)
droits ou taxes

functions and duties (of the Commission)
    c. A-2, s. 15
attributions

powers, duties and functions
    c. C-4, s. 7
compétence

duty
    c. A-11, s. 45
obligation

(imposed by law)
    c. C-46, s. 219(2)
devoir

admit free of duty/to
    c. C-34, s. 31
admettre en franchise

duty and conduct (of officers)
    c. C-25, s. 28(d)
responsabilité professionnelle et morale

place of duty
    c. C-17, s. 18(4)(f)
poste

power, duty and function (of the Auditor General)
    c. A-17, s. 15(3)
responsabilité, pouvoir et fonction

public duty
    c. C-46, s. 118
fonction publique

under a legal duty/to be   être dans l'obligation légale
    c. C-46, s. 79
dwelling
    multiple-family dwelling   habitation multifamiliale
      c. N-11, s. 2
    one-familly dwelling   maison unifamiliale
      c. N-11, s. 2
dwelling house   maison d'habitation
    c. C-46, s. 2
dwelling-place
    private dwelling-place   local d'habitation
      c. C-11, s. 26(1)(a)

e

earlier
    earlier redemption   remboursement anticipé
      c. L-12, s. 71(2)(e)
earn/to
    earn credits/to   accumuler des crédits
      c. C-46, s. 718.1(1)
earned
    statutory and earned remission   réduction de peine légale ou méritée
      c. P-2, s. 25(2)
earnings
    retained earnings   bénéfices non répartis
      c. B-1, s. 129(4)
    surplus earnings   surplus de bénéfices
      c. N-11, s. 30(3)(e)
    unadjusted pensionable   gains non ajustés ouvrant droit à
    earnings   pension
      c. C-8, s. 2(1)
easement   servitude
    c. B-3, s. 2
    c. T-7, s. 2
    easement, servitude and all   servitudes ou autres droits de
    other interests in real property   nature immobilière
      c. T-7, s. 2
eating house
    lodging, boarding or eating   hôtel garni, maison de pension ou
    house   restaurant
      c. C-46, s. 364(1)
Economic Council of Canada   Conseil économique du Canada
    c. A-1, Schedule I
    c. F-11, Schedule II
economic lifetime
    economic lifetime of the   durée économique des améliorations
    improvement
      c. L-12, s. 114(2)
edible
    edible and potable (product)   comestible et potable
      c. C-38, s. 8
editor
    law report editor   arrêtiste
      c. F-7, s. 58(2)
educational
    educational institution   établissement d'enseignement
      c. C-28, Schedule 2
    religious, educational or   entreprise religieuse, éducative ou
    charitable object   charitable
      c. C-42, s. 27(3)

effect

   cease to have force or effect/to (a subsection)   cesser de s'appliquer
     c. B-1, s. 113(2)

   force or effect (of an agreement)   effet
     c. A-3, s. 6

   have effect/to   être opérant
     c. C-9, s. 30

   have effect/to   être exécutoire
     c. C-26, s. 2(5)

   have full force and effect/to (act)   être pleinement exécutoire et effectif
     c. C-36, s. 8

   have no effect/to (order)   devenir inopérant (décret)
     c. A-15, s. 5(5)

   have no force or effect/to   être inopérant
     c. B-1, s. 263(3)

   legal effect prejudicial to the person   conséquence juridique préjudiciable à l'intéressé
     c. F-11, s. 23(8)

   legal effect/to have (order)   être valide
     c. C-3, s. 20(2)

   legal effect/to have (order)   être exécutoire
     c. C-3, s. 18(2)

   of no force or effect/to be (a term)   être réputé non écrit
     c. C-24, s. 51(2)

effective   exécutoire
     c. C-8, s. 55(2)(b)

   (security)   valable
     c. B-1, s. 178(1)(e)

   become effective/to   prendre effet
     c. B-1, s. 39(2)
     c. C-44, s. 164(2)

   become effective/to   devenir opérant
     c. C-44, s. 245(1)

   effective against   opposable à
     c. B-1, s. 97(4)

   effective and rightful transfer   régularité et caractère effectif du transfert
     c. C-44, s. 63(2)a)

   effective annual rate of interest   taux d'intérêt annuel effectif
     c. C-46, s. 347(2)

   effective date (of a regulation)   date d'entrée en vigueur
     c. C-12, s. 42(3)

   effective/to be   prendre effet
     c. C-44, s. 103(3)

effectiveness   validité
     c. B-1, s. 95(1)(b)

effectual

   (deed)   efficace
     c. B-3, s. 75

   effectual/to be (an instrument)   produire un effet
     c. B-4, s. 31(1)

   fair and effectual trial   instruction équitable et efficace
     c. C-39, s. 9(2)(a)

effluent discharge

   effluent discharge fee prescribed   redevance de pollution réglementaire
     c. C-11, s. 15(4)(c)

ejusdem generis   du même ordre
     c. S-26, s. 53(2)

elect/to
 (to accept compensation)   décider
  c. A-2, s. 9(2)
 (to be tried by a jury)   choisir
  c. C-46, s. 472
 elect a member/to   choisir un membre
  c. A-13, s. 14
elected
 duly returned or elected/to be   être dument élu
  c. P-1, s. 30(2)
election   option
  c. C-17, s. 8(4)
  c. C-8, s. 11(2)   choix
election document
 erasure, alteration or   rature, altération ou interlinéation
 interlineation on election   dans un document d'élection
 document
  c. C-46, s. 377(1)(d)
elective   par choix
  c. C-17, s. 60(1)
elective service   service accompagné d'options
  c. C-17, s. 6(b)
electro-magnetic, acoustic,   dispositif électromagnétique,
mechanical or other device   acoustique, mécanique ou autre
  c. C-46, s. 183
elevator   silo
  c. C-24, s. 2(1)
eligible
 eligible contribution recipient   bénéficiaire admissible
  c. N-11, s. 95(1)
 eligible to be re-appointed/to be   pouvoir recevoir un nouveau
             mandat
  c. A-7, s. 7(3)
eligible plan   plan admissible
  c. C-24, s. 53(1)
elimination
 (of a term or condition of   suppression
 employment)
  c. P-35, s. 57(2)(a)
embezzlement
 fraud, embezzlement,   fraude, détournement, concussion
 misappropriation or defalcation   ou abus de confiance
  c. B-3, s. 178(1)(d)
embody/to
 (a stipulation)   renfermer
  c. C-42, Schedule II, Article
  20
 (within a licence)   formuler
  c. C-42, s. 25(1)
emergency
 meet an emergency/to   faire face à un état d'urgence
  c. C-32, s. 22(3)
emission
 emission standards (air quality)   normes d'émission
  c. C-32, s. 21(1)
 rate of emission   taux d'émission
  c. C-32, s. 21(3)(a)(i)
emolument   émoluments
  c. B-3, s. 201(2)
 hold office of emolument/to   remplir des fonctions rétribuées
  c. S-26, s. 7
 salary, remuneration or other   traitement, rémunération ou autres
 emolument   émoluments
  c. C-19, s. 8(1)

emoluments
    fees or emoluments   salaire ou émolument
        c. C-42, s. 68(3)
empanelling
    empanelling of the jury   constitution du jury
        c. C-46, s. 670(a)
employ/to   engager
        c. C-21, s. 6(1)(c)
    (a person)   employer
        c. A-2, s. 9(1)
    (a solicitor)   employer un avocat
        c. B-3, s. 30(1)(e)
    (personnel)   engager
        c. A-8, s. 6(1)
employed
    employed in the public service of   faire partie de l'administration
    Canada/to be   publique fédérale
        c. A-7, s. 7(10)
    person employed by the Minister   délégué du ministre
        c. A-11, s. 43(2)
employee   salarié
        c. C-43, s. 2(1)
    (in the Public Service)   fonctionnaire
        c. A-16, s. 12
    (of a government institution)   employé
        c. A-1, s. 18(c)
    (of the Corporation)   membre du personnel
        c. A-10, s. 24
    officer, clerk or employee   effectifs
        c. A-4, s. 3(7)
    redundant employee   surnuméraire
        c. L-2, s. 211
    seasonal or temporary employee   saisonnier ou employé temporaire
        c. L-2, s. 190(f)
employee of/to be   être au service de
        c. C-29, s. 3(2)(a)
employee organization   organisation syndicale
        c. P-35, s. 2
employees
    employees of the Government of   fonctionnaires fédéraux canadiens
    Canada
        c. A-1, s. 15(2)(f)
    officers and employees   personnel
        c. C-11, s. 16(2)
    officers, clerks and employees   fonctionnaires, commis et préposés
        c. A-2, s. 25
    officers, clerks and employees   personnel
        c. A-4, s. 3(7)
employment
    continuous employment   période d'emploi ininterrompu
        c. L-2, s. 183
    employment or engagement   emploi
        c. A-13, s. 26(d)
    in the employment of/to be   être employé
        c. C-42, s. 13(3)
    multi-employer employment   travail au service de plusieurs
                              employeurs
        c. L-2, s. 203
    position or employment in a   poste ou emploi dans un ministère
    public department   public
        c. C-46, s. 118
    public employment   emploi public
        c. C-46, s. 748(1)

year of employment c. L-2, s. 183	année de service
empower/to	investir du pouvoir
c. C-24, s. 29(1)	
c. C-24, s. 46(f)	conférer un pouvoir
c. C-44, s. 51(a)	donner le pouvoir
empower by commission/to c. S-26, s. 81(1)	habiliter par commission
empowered c. B-1, s. 42(5)	habilité
enable/to	
(a section) c. B-4, s. 46(2)	habiliter
enact/to	
(a law) c. C-8, s. 85	édicter
enact a by-law/to c. B-1, s. 43(2)	prendre un règlement
enacting	
enacting clause (of an Act) c. I-23, s. 4(1)	formule d'édiction
enactment	
(Act or regulation) c. I-23, s. 2(1)	texte
enactment of Parliament c. C-17, s. 2(1)	disposition édictée par le Parlement
enchantment	
witchcraft, sorcery, enchantment or conjuration c. C-46, s. 365(a)	magie, sorcellerie, enchantement ou conjuration
enclosure	
pen or enclosure (for animals) c. C-46, s. 348(3)(d)	parc ou enclos
encumbered	
in the form of assets pledged or encumbered to secure a guarantee c. C-44, s. 44(1)(d)	par mise en gage de biens ou constitution de charges sur des biens en vue d'obtenir une caution
encumbrance c. B-1, s. 184(b) c. C-25, s. 10(2)	charge
encumbrance on the title c. C-46, s. 385(1)(a)	charge sur le titre
encumbrancer c. B-1, s. 184(b)	créancier détenteur d'une charge
encumbrances	
free from any and all encumbrances c. C-25, s. 10(2)	libre de toute charge
End the Arms Race c. C-18, Schedule	End the Arms Race
endanger/to	
(health) c. C-32, s. 2	mettre en danger
endangered	
claim endangered c. B-2, s. 23(c)	créance compromise
endorse/to	
(a share certificate) c. B-1, s. 66(2)(b)(i)	endosser
(a warrant) c. C-46, s. 487(2)	viser

(an order)
    c. C-46, s. 260(2)
(an order)

    c. Y-1, s. 23(5)
(on an Act)
    c. I-23, s. 5(1)
make, execute, draw, sign,
accept or endorse a document/to
    c. C-46, s. 374(a)

endorsed
endorsed copy
    c. C-46, s. 109(7)
endorsed in blank (a security)
    c. C-44, s. 48(2)

endorsee
    c. B-4, s. 14
    c. B-5, s. 2
holder or endorsee (of a receipt)
    c. C-46, s. 390

endorsement
    c. B-1, s. 75(2)
(on a warrant)
    c. C-46, s. 487(4)
by endorsement or delivery
(document)
    c. C-46, s. 2
cancellation of endorsement
    c. C-24, s. 55(2)
endorsement completed by
delivery
    c. B-4, s. 2
endorsement on the face
    c. C-19, s. 42
endorsement to bearer
    c. C-44, s. 65(5)
make an endorsement/to (in a
permit)
    c. C-24, s. 55(1)
necessary endorsement
    c. C-44, s. 64
restrictive endorsement
    c. B-4, s. 67(3)
special endorsement
    c. B-4, s. 66(3)
special endorsement
    c. B-1, s. 92(1)(a)
    c. C-44, s. 65(1)a)
written or stamped signature of
an official to the endorsement of
the duplicate summary
    c. C-40, s. 118(4)

endorser
    c. B-1, s. 96(1)
    c. C-44, s. 65(8)

endorsing
party endorsing (a bill)
    c. B-4, s. 39(1)(a)
the making, accepting,
discounting or endorsing of a bill
of exchange, cheque, draft or
promissary note
    c. C-46, s. 362(1)(c)(vi)

---

signer

apposer sa signature (sur
l'ordonnance)

inscrire

faire, souscrire, rédiger, signer,
accepter ou endosser un document

copie visée

endossé en blanc

endossataire

détenteur ou endossataire

endossement

visa

par endossement ou livraison

annulation de l'inscription

endossement complété par livraison

mention au recto

endossement au porteur

porter une mention

endossement obligatoire

endossement restrictif

endossement spécial

endossement nominatif

signature manuscrite ou griffe d'un
fonctionnaire, apposée sous la
mention faite sur le double

endosseur

endosseur

création, acceptation, escompte ou
endossement d'une lettre de
change, d'un chèque, d'une traite
ou d'un billet à ordre

Endowment Fund   Caisse de dotation
    c. C-2, s. 13
ends
    ends of justice   fins de la justice
      c. C-46, s. 527(1)(e)
Energy Supplies Allocation   Office de répartition des
Board   approvisionnements d'énergie
    c. A-1, Schedule I
enforce/to   rendre exécutoire
    c. B-3, s. 16(4)
    (a decision of a judge)   exécuter
      c. C-46, s. 680(2)
    (an Act)   exercer des pouvoirs de police dans
                    le cadre d'une loi
    c. C-33, s. 2
    (rights)   assurer l'exercice (de droits)
      c. C-42, s. 5(2)
    enforce payment/to (of a bill) exiger le paiement
      c. B-4, s. 144(2)
    enforce the appearance   contraindre à comparaître
      c. C-23, s. 50(a)
enforce a liability/to   poursuivre l'exécution d'une
                    obligation
    c. B-1, s. 209(3)
enforceable
    (judgment)   exécutoire
      c. C-46, s. 194(3)
    (security interest)   réalisable
      c. C-44, s. 82(1)(a)
    recoverable or enforceable (in recouvrable ou exécutoire
    civil proceedings)
      c. C-46, s. 724(1)
enforced
    after payment made or enforced après le paiement volontaire ou par
    by process or execution   voie d'exécution forcée
      c. F-11, s. 23(3)(b)
enforcement
    (of an act)   application
      c. A-1, s. 16(4)(a)
      c. C-11, s. 18(1)(e)
    (of orders)   exécution
      c. A-7, s. 8(4)
    administration and enforcement contrôle d'application
    (of an Act)
      c. A-7, s. 15(1)
    enforcement or realization (of a recouvrement ou réalisation
    security)
      c. C-24, s. 52(3)
    in the administration or   dans l'application ou l'exécution de
    enforcement of the law   la loi
      c. C-46, s. 25(1)
    institution and enforcement (of établissement et application
    laws, rules)
      c. A-2, s. 8(1)(i)
    provincial enforcement service autorité provinciale
      c. C-3, s. 2
engage in/to
    (a trade or business/to)   se livrer (à un commerce ou à une
                    industrie)
    c. B-1, s. 174(2)(a)
    (an undertaking)   participer à
      c. C-22, s. 5(1)(a)

(prostitution) c. C-46, s. 213(1)	se livrer (à la prostitution)
(the performance of duties) c. A-7, s. 7(9)(a)	exercer
engage in/to (trade or business)	s'engager dans (un commerce ou une entreprise)
c. B-3, s. 139	

engagement

employment and engagement c. A-13, s. 26(d)	emploi
intermediate engagement c. C-17, s. 2(1)	engagement de durée intermédiaire
short engagement c. C-17, s. 2(1)	engagement de courte durée

engraving
    c. C-42, s. 2 — gravure

facsimile of signature printed from engraving c. F-11, s. 50(2)	griffe dont l'empreinte reproduit la signature autographe

enhancement

enhancement in value c. C-25, s. 12(1)(b)	plus-value

enhancement of the multicultural heritage
    Constitutional Act, 1982,
    Schedule B, s. 27
	valorisation du patrimoine multiculturel

preservation and enhancement (of languages) c. 31 (4th Supp.), s. 83(2)	maintien et valorisation

enjoin/to
    c. B-1, s. 303(5)(a) — enjoindre

(a person from continuing an action) c. L-2, s. 163(1)	interdire

enjoy/to

(land) c. C-19, s. 29	avoir à sa disposition

enjoyment

enjoyment and exercise (of a right) c. C-42, Schedule II, Article 4	jouissance et exercice
exercice of any right or enjoyment of any interest c. C-34, s. 2	exercice d'un droit ou jouissance d'un intérêt

enlistment

(in the Canadian Forces) c. C-46, s. 421(1)	enrôlement

enrolment

(in the Canadian Forces) c. C-46, s. 421(1)	enrôlement

enter/to

(a transaction) c. C-44, s. 31(2)	conclure (une opération)
(an order) c. L-2, s. 163(2)	enregistrer
(dwelling-house) c. N-1, s. 12	pénétrer
(premises) c. N-14, s. 8(2)(b)	visiter
enter a plea/to c. C-46, s. 606(2)	inscrire un plaidoyer
enter as a judgment/to c. C-46, s. 725(2)	faire enregistrer comme jugement

enter in the minutes/to   consigner au procès-verbal
     c. C-44, s. 120(1)
enter lawfully/to   procéder légalement à la visite de
     c. C-32, s. 31(2)
enter on duties/to   entrer en fonctions
     c. B-2, s. 16
enter the premises/to   pénétrer dans un local
     c. C-34, s. 12(1)
enter into/to
     (a contract)   conclure
         c. A-2, s. 23
     (an agreement)   conclure
         c. A-3, s. 3
     (contract)   contracter
         c. A-8, s. 4(2)
     enter into a security/to   contracter une garantie
         c. C-46, s. 401(1)(d)
     enter into an agreement/to   passer un accord
         c. Y-1, s. 70
entering
     (of premises)   visite
         c. A-2, s. 8(1)(l)
enterprise
     energy enterprise   entreprise énergétique
         c. C-20, s. 18(1)(d)
entertain/to
     (proceedings)   connaître de
         c. C-50, s. 21(3)
entertainment
     immoral, indecent or obscene   représentation, spectacle ou
     performance, entertainment or   divertissement immoral, indécent
     representation   ou obscène
         c. C-46, s. 167(2)
entice away/to
     (a person)   entraîner
         c. C-46, s. 281
entitle/to   donner droit à
     c. B-1, s. 177(12)
entitled   habile
     c. B-1, s. 2(1)
     entitled to vote (shareholders)   fondé à voter
         c. C-44, s. 163(3)
     notice entitled in the Court and   avis portant le sceau de la Cour et
     in the cause   l'intitulé de la cause
         c. S-26, s. 69(1)
entitled/to be   être habile à
     c. C-44, s. 2(1)
     (person)   avoir qualité
         c. B-1, s. 45(7)
entitled as of right/to be   avoir le droit absolu
     c. C-23, s. 48(2)
entitled to/to become   acquérir des droits sur
     c. C-24, s. 29(2)
entitlement   conséquence juridique
     c. P-5, s. 31
entity   entité
     c. C-20, s. 16(7)
     legal entity   personne morale
         c. B-7, Schedule II, Article
         IV, Section 8(iv)
entrusted with/to be
     to be entrusted with the receipt,   être chargé de la réception, garde
     custody or management (of   ou gestion
     revenue funds)
         c. C-46, s. 399

entry
  (into a register) — inscription
    c. C-42, s. 49
  book entry — inscription dans un registre
    c. A-2, s. 27(1)
  entry in an account — inscription à un compte
    c. C-46, s. 332(2)
  entry of causes — mise au rôle
    c. S-26, s. 79(1)
  entry of the transfer — inscription du transfert
    c. L-12, s. 47(1)(b)
  false entry (in a statement or an accounting) — fausse inscription
    c. B-3, s. 198(d)
  forcible entry — prise de possession par la force
    c. C-46, s. 72(1)
  forcible entry and detainer — prise de possession et détention par la force
    c. C-46, s. 73

environment
  personal and family history and present environment — antécédents et situation actuelle (de l'adolescent et de sa famille)
    c. Y-1, s. 2(2)

equality
  equality of status (of official languages) — égalité de statut
    c. 31 (4th Supp.), s. 38(1)(e)
  in case of an equality of votes — en cas de partage
    c. C-41, s. 20(3)

equality status
  to have equality of status and equal rights and privileges (of official languages) — avoir un statut et des droits et privilèges égaux
    c. 31 (4th Supp.), s. preamble

equalization
  equalization and regional disparities — péréquation et inégalités régionales
    Constitutional Act, 1982, Schedule B, s. 36

equalization fund — fonds de péréquation
    c. C-24, s. 39(1)

equalization or adjustment
  (of moneys) — répartition ou péréquation
    c. A-6, s. 2(2)(b)

equipment
  agricultural equipment — installations agricoles
    c. B-1, s. 2(1)
  agricultural equipment — matériel agricole immobilier
    c. B-1, s. 2(1)
  equipment issue (of securities) — émission gagée sur le matériel
    c. C-19, s. 32
  forestry equipment — matériel sylvicole immobilier
    c. B-1, s. 2(1)
  plant or equipment — usine ou matériel
    c. C-41, s. 11(1)(b)(ii)

equipment trust certificate — certificat garanti par du matériel
    c. B-1, s. 2(1)
    c. C-19, s. 41(1) — certificat gagé sur le matériel

equitable
  legal and equitable estate — droits de propriété en droit et en equity
    c. B-3, s. 84

equities
 c. C-40, s. 45(b)
 c. F-11, s. 68(3)
equity
 (of a shareholder)
  c. B-1, s. 215(3)(d)
 court of equity
  c. F-7, s. 3
 court of law and equity
  c. S-26, s. 3
 debt or equity interest
  c. A-2, s. 21(3)
 equity accounting method

  c. B-1, s. 216(1)
 equity of security
  c. B-1, s. 190(1)
 equity security
  c. B-1, s. 193(1)
 equity share
  c. L-12, s. 64(4)
 formal equity
  c. C-20, s. 2(1)
 in equity or otherwise (contract)
  c. B-3, s. 4(3)(c)
 informal equity
  c. C-20, s. 2(1)
 jurisdiction at law and equity
  c. B-3, s. 183(1)
 proceeding in equity
  c. S-26, s. 42(1)
 shareholders' equity
  c. B-1, s. 242(5)
equivalent
 fair equivalent (of a money
 consideration)
  c. C-44, s. 25(4)
 fair equivalent (of the money)
  c. C-44, s. 24(3)c)
erasure
 erasure, alteration or
 interlineation on election
 document
  c. C-46, s. 377(1)(d)
escape
  c. C-46, s. 149(3)
 escape by flight
  c. C-46, s. 25(4)
escape/to
  c. C-46, s. 23(1)
escort
 absence with escort for
 humanitarian and rehabilitative
 reasons
  c. C-46, s. 747(2)
 temporary absence without
 escort
  c. P-2, s. 13
espionage
  c. A-1, s. 15(2)(a)
  c. C-23, s. 2
establish/to
 (a board)
  c. A-4, s. 2
  c. A-7, s. 7(1)

avoirs

droits

avoir

tribunal d'équité

tribunal de droit et d'équité

droits de créance ou actions

méthode de comptabilisation à la
 valeur de consolidation

action

action ordinaire

action assortie du droit de vote

participation ordinaire

en équité ou autrement

participation non ordinaire

compétence en droit et en équité

procédure en équité

avoir des actionnaires

juste équivalence

juste valeur

rature, altération ou interlinéation
 dans un document d'élection

évasion

fuite

s'échapper

sortie sous surveillance pour des
 raisons humanitaires ou en vue de
 la réadaptation

permission de sortir sans
 surveillance

espionnage

constituer

equities

(a claim)	établir (le bien-fondé d'une demande)
c. C-44, s. 226(5)	
(a department)	constituer
c. A-9, s. 2(1)	
(a signature)	prouver
c. B-1, s. 80(c)	
(an account)	ouvrir (un compte)
c. C-15, s. 15(1)	
(committees)	constituer
c. A-3, s. 9(1)	
establish to the satisfaction of the magistrate/to	prouver à la satisfaction du magistrat
c. C-46, s. 112(12)	
establish, maintain and carry out/to (security measures)	prendre et exercer
c. A-2, s. 7(4)	
establish, maintain and operate/to (facilities)	constituer et exploiter
c. A-13, s. 4(f)	
establishment	
(of a board of adjudication)	institution
c. P-35, s. 95(1)	
(of a corporation)	constitution
c. C-9, s. 24(1)	
(of committees)	création (de comités)
c. C-10, s. 11(b)	
commercial establishment	établissement commercial
c. P-1, s. 80(1)(c)	
establishment, operation, maintenance and administration (of public works)	mise sur pied, exploitation, entretien et gestion d'ouvrages
c. N-14, s. 7(1)(v)	
industrial establishment	établissement
c. L-2, s. 166	
estate	actif
c. B-1, s. 173(1)(b)	
c. T-7, s. 9(5)	droits
(bankruptcy)	biens
c. C-8, s. 23(4)	
(of a deceased)	succession
c. C-8, s. 44(1)(c)	
(of an insolvent member)	patrimoine
c. C-21, s. 31(2)	
estate or interest (in hydrocarbons or minerals)	droit de propriété ou droit de jouissance
c. B-1, s. 177(1)(c)	
freehold real estate	immeuble détenu en propriété libre et perpétuelle
c. L-12, s. 2	
legal and equitable estate	droits de propriété en droit et en equity
c. B-3, s. 84	
personal estate	bien meuble
c. L-12, s. 31	
personal estate	bien personnel
c. C-40, s. 48	
service estate	succession militaire
c. C-17, s. 53(1)	
trust or estate	fiducie ou succession
c. C-44, s. 2(1)(c)	
estimate	prévision budgétaire
c. F-11, s. 7(1)(c)	

(of sums)   état estimatif
    c. P-1, s. 51(1)
estimate/to
  (an amount)   estimer
    c. A-5, s. 2
estimated
  estimated revenue   recettes estimatives
    c. B-2, s. 5(2)
  estimated saving   montant estimatif de l'économie
    c. A-15, s. 5(2)
evade/to
  (compliance with the Act)   se soustraire (à l'application)
    c. C-8, s. 44(4)(d)
  (payment)   éluder
    c. C-8, s. 41(4)(b)
  evade service/to   se soustraire à la signification
    c. C-46, s. 698(1)
evaluate/to
  (activities and organization of   procéder à l'examen
  Foundation)
    c. A-13, s. 37
event
  follow the event/to (costs)   suivre le sort du principal
    c. 31 (4th Supp.), s. 81(1)
event of default   cas de défaut
    c. C-44, s. 82(1)
evidence   élément de preuve
    c. A-1, s. 36(1)(c)
    c. C-38, s. 15(2)   pièce à conviction
    c. C-46, s. 118   témoignage ou déposition
  admissible in evidence   admissible en preuve
    c. A-12, s. 21(1)
  admissible in evidence   admissible en justice
    c. P-2, s. 29
  conclusive evidence   preuve concluante
    c. C-39, s. 5(2)
    c. C-40, s. 4
    c. C-46, s. 316(3)
  conclusive evidence   preuve péremptoire
    c. S-26, s. 30(3)
  conclusive evidence/to be   constituer une preuve concluante
    c. B-5, s. 4
  contradictory evidence   témoignage contradictoire
    c. C-12, s. 40
  contrary evidence   témoignage contraire
    c. C-46, s. 136(1)
  evidence of appointment or   preuve de la nomination ou du
  incumbency   mandat
    c. C-44, s. 77(4)
  evidence of character and repute   preuve de moralité ou de réputation
    c. C-46, s. 757
  evidence of indebtedness   titre de créance
    c. L-12, s. 61(1)(b)
  evidence of sexual reputation   preuve de réputation sexuelle
    c. C-46, s. 277
  evidence of/to be   faire foi
    c. P-2, s. 29
  evidence supporting an opinion   éléments de preuve à l'appui d'une
                     opinion
    c. C-34, s. 9(2)(c)
  evidence to the contrary   preuve contraire
    c. A-7, s. 21
    c. C-11, s. 37(1)

fresh evidence — preuve nouvelle
   c. C-46, s. 784(3)
give evidence on oath/to — déposer sous serment
   c. C-44, s. 230(1)(g)
give evidence under oath/to — témoigner sous la foi du serment
   c. C-12, s. 19(e)
give evidence/to — témoigner
   c. C-44, s. 233
give evidence/to — déposer en justice
   c. C-8, s. 104(6)
give oral or written evidence/to — déposer verbalement ou par écrit
   c. A-1, s. 36(1)(a)
in the absence of evidence to the contrary — en l'absence de preuve contraire
   c. Y-1, s. 2(1)
law of evidence — droit de la preuve
   c. C-23, s. 39(2)
material evidence — preuve pertinente
   c. Y-1, s. 59
material evidence — preuve substantielle
   c. C-46, s. 698(1)
oral evidence — témoignage oral
   c. Y-1, s. 62(1)
take evidence/to — recueillir des témoignages
   c. C-46, s. 118

evidence/to — indiquer
   c. A-12, s. 12(3)(a)
   c. C-44, s. 158(1) — attester
   (a security) — attester l'existence
   c. B-1, s. 75(4)(a)
   (an indebtedness) — constater
   c. B-1, s. 2(1)
evidence/to be — faire foi du contenu
   c. A-11, s. 6
   c. A-11, s. 6 — constituer la preuve
   c. A-11, s. 8 — faire foi
   c. B-6, s. 7(2)
   c. C-24, s. 20(3)
evidence of indebtedness
   bond, debenture, note or other evidence of indebtedness — obligation, débenture, billet ou autre preuve de créance
   c. C-44, s. 2(1)
evidence of obligations — titres d'obligations
   c. B-3, s. 60(4)
evidenced
   evidenced in writing/to be — être constaté par écrit
   c. C-17, s. 8(1)
evil
   injury, pain or other evil — sévices ou autres maux
   c. C-46, s. 753(b)
evolution — développement
   c. C-21, s. 5
ex officio
   ex officio director — administrateur de droit
   c. F-11, s. 102(9)
   ex officio director — administrateur nommé d'office
   c. F-11, s. 83(2)(b)
ex parte — ex parte
   c. A-12, s. 22(2)
   c. A-1, s. 47(1) — en l'absence d'une partie
   ex parte application — demande ex parte
   c. B-3, s. 10(2)
   c. C-44, s. 229(5)

exact/to
  (a penalty)   imposer
    c. C-34, s. 39(1)
examination
  (of witnesses)   interrogatoire
    c. A-7, s. 8(4)
  examination or investigation   examen ou recherches
    c. B-1, s. 139(b)
  examination or investigation   examen et enquêtes
    c. B-1, s. 139(c)
  explanatory examination   interrogatoire explicatif
    c. C-39, s. 20(2)
examine/to   interroger
    c. A-17, s. 13(4)
examiner   examinateur
    c. A-2, s. 18(1)(p)
    c. F-11, s. 120
    c. C-39, s. 20(1)   commissaire-enquêteur
  fingerprint examiner   préposé aux empreintes digitales
    c. C-46, s. 667(1)(a)(iii)
  special examiner   commissaire-enquêteur spécial
    c. C-39, s. 22(1)
exceed/to
  (his jurisdiction)   outrepasser
    c. C-46, s. 783
excepted employment   emploi excepté
    c. C-8, s. 2(1)
exception   dispense
    c. B-1, s. 155(1)(c)
exceptions
  saving all just exceptions   sous réserve de toute objection
                          valable
    c. S-26, s. 91(2)
excess
  (of the assets)   excédent
    c. L-12, s. 62(2)(b)(i)
  excess of jurisdiction   excès de compétence
    c. C-46, s. 830(1)(b)
  process issued without   acte judiciaire délivré sans
  jurisdiction or in excess of   juridiction ou au-delà de la
  jurisdiction   juridiction
    c. C-46, s. 25(2)
excessive
  excessive force   force excessive
    c. C-46, s. 26
exchange   marché boursier
    c. B-1, s. 98(1)
    c. C-44, s. 71(1)
  (securities)   échange
    c. C-44, s. 2(6)(b)
  exchange contract   contrat de change
    c. B-7, Schedule I, Article
    VII, Section 2(b)
  exchange market   marché des changes
    c. B-7, Schedule I, Article V,
    Section 3(d)
  exchange regulation   réglementation de change
    c. B-7, Schedule I, Article
    VIII, Section 4(b)(iii)
  exchange transaction   opération de change
    c. B-7, Schedule I, Article
    VIII, Section 6

foreign exchange   devise étrangère
    c. B-7, Schedule II, Article
      IV, Section 3(c)
livestock exchange   halle aux animaux de ferme
    c. L-9, s. 10
rate of exchange   taux de change
    c. B-4, s. 27(1)(d)
    c. B-7, s. 11
rate of exchange   taux d'échange
    c. B-1, s. 132(7)
securities exchange or market   bourse ou marché de valeurs
          mobilières
    c. C-44, s. 48(2)(b)
stock exchange   bourse de valeurs mobilières
    c. B-1, s. 98(3)
Exchange Fund Account   Compte du fonds des changes
    c. C-52, s. 17(1)
exchangeable
(shares)   échangeable
    c. B-1, s. 76(12)(b)
exchequer acquittance
order, exchequer acquittance or   ordre, quittance de l'échiquier ou
other security   autre valeur
    c. C-46, s. 2
exchequer bill   bon du Trésor
    c. C-46, s. 321
exchequer bill paper   papier de bons du trésor
    c. C-46, s. 321
exclude/to
(from a provision)   exempter de l'application
    c. C-24, s. 28(h)
exclude an employee from the   soustraire un employé à
application/to (of a section)   l'application
    c. L-2, s. 129
exclusive
exclusive dealing   exclusivité
    c. C-34, s. 39(1)
exclusive right   droit exclusif
    c. C-44, s. 109(2)
sole and exclusive jurisdiction   compétence exclusive
    c. A-7, s. 12
excuse   excuse
    c. A-11, s. 40
justification or excuse for an act   justification ou excuse d'un acte
    c. C-46, s. 8(3)
reasonable excuse   excuse valable
    c. C-50, s. 12(2)(b)
excuse/to
(from presentment)   dispenser
    c. B-4, s. 80(b)
excused
excused from answering/to be   être dispensé de répondre
    c. B-3, s. 10(5)
excused from giving evidence/to   être dispensé de témoigner
be
    c. C-34, s. 22(2)
execute/to
(a form)   signer
    c. B-1, s. 160
(an agreement)   signer
    c. P-35, s. 58(1)(b)
(an instrument)   signer
    c. C-44, s. 23

make, execute, draw, sign, accept or endorse a document/to
c. C-46, s. 374(a)
faire, souscrire, rédiger, signer, accepter ou endosser un document

sign, certify, attest or execute/to
c. A-2, s. 27(1)(c)
signer, certifier, attester ou établir

execute and perform a duty/to
c. A-16, Schedule I
remplir une fonction

execution
(against Crown)
c. C-50, s. 30(1)
exécution par voie de contrainte

(an Act)
c. A-11, s. 3(t)
application

(of a trust)
c. B-1, s. 206(1)
exécution

(of an order)
c. A-11, s. 42(1)
exécution

after payment made or enforced by process or execution
c. F-11, s. 23(3)(b)
après le paiement volontaire ou par voie d'exécution forcée

date and place of execution (of a waybill)
c. C-26, Schedule I, Article 8(a)
lieu où le document a été créé et la date à laquelle il a été établi

execution of a conveyance

c. S-26, s. 65(1)(b)
souscription d'un acte translatif de propriété

execution of process
c. C-46, s. 683(4)
exécution d'un acte judiciaire

execution or attachment
c. B-3, s. 73(2)
exécution ou saisie-arrêt

in the lawful execution of a process against lands or goods

c. C-46, s. 270(1)(b)
dans l'exécution légale d'un acte judiciaire contre des terres ou des effets

liable to execution/to be (property)
c. F-7, s. 56(3)
saisissable

on completion and execution (form)
c. C-44, s. 147
une fois rempli et signé (formulaire)

sale under execution
c. B-1, s. 184(a)
vente sur exécution

sale under execution
c. N-7, s. 114(1)(a)
vente en justice

sell under execution/to
c. T-19, s. 15(7)
vendre par exécution forcée

sell under execution/to
c. A-12, s. 25(4)(b)
vendre en justice

writ of execution
c. B-3, s. 230(3)
mandat d'exécution

executive
chief executive officer
c. I-23, s. 35(1)
fonctionnaire de premier rang

executive board (of a union)
c. C-43, s. 13(3)
bureau de direction

executive board (of the Centre)
c. C-13, s. 14(1)
bureau

executive committee
c. C-40, s. 69(5)
comité exécutif

executive committee
c. B-2, s. 8(1)
comité de direction

executive committee
c. C-9, s. 19(2)(a)
c. L-12, s. 24(2)
comité de direction

executive committee 　　c. A-13, s. 25	comité directeur
executive committee (of association) 　　c. C-41, s. 19(2)	comité exécutif
executive committee (of the Board) 　　c. P-2, s. 3(3)	bureau
executive committee (of Board) 　　c. A-10, s. 11	bureau du conseil
executive director 　　c. C-18, s. 3	administrateur délégué
senior executive officer 　　c. C-43, s. 13(5)	premier dirigeant
to exercise a regulative, administrative or executive jurisdiction 　　c. S-26, s. 2(1)	exercer des pouvoirs réglementaires, administratifs ou exécutifs

executive committee
(of association) 　　c. C-41, s. 19(2)	comité exécutif
(of Board) 　　c. A-10, s. 11	bureau du conseil

executor
trustee, guardian, committee, curator, tutor, executor, administrator or representative of a deceased person 　　c. B-1, s. 75(2)	fiduciaire, tuteur, curateur, exécuteur ou administrateur de succession

exempt/to
c. C-8, s. 6(2)(h) 　　c. B-1, s. 2(3)	dispenser
(from operation) 　　c. A-11, s. 3(k)	accorder une dispense soustraire à

exempt/to be
(from execution or seizure) 　　c. B-3, s. 67(b)	être exempt

exempt a person/to
(from personal liability) 　　c. B-4, s. 51(1)	dégager une personne (de sa responsabilité personnelle)

exempt from seizure
(security) 　　c. B-1, s. 173(1)(d)(i)	insaisissable

exempt from the application/to
(of a section) 　　c. B-1, s. 145(b)	dispenser de l'application

exempt offer
c. C-44, s. 194	offre franche

exemption
exemption order 　　c. C-44, s. 127(8)	rapport de dispense
exemption period (customs) 　　c. C-53, s. 6(5)	période d'exemption
refuse to grant exemption/to 　　c. C-44, s. 246(c)	refuser la dispense

exercice of the right
(to access) 　　c. A-1, s. 5(1)(b)	exercice du droit

exercisable
(option) 　　c. B-1, s. 168(1) 　　c. C-44, s. 194(b)	susceptible d'exercice

exercisable option (to purchase shares)
 c. C-44, s. 2(1)(a)
  option

exercisable option or right
 c. C-44, s. 126(1)(b)
  option ou droit susceptible d'exercice

exhaust/to
(the reviews or appeals)
 c. C-29, s. 2(2)(c)(i)
  épuiser

exhibit
 c. C-46, s. 520(7)(b)
  pièce

exhibition
agricultural fair or exhibition
 c. C-46, s. 207(1)
  foire ou exposition agricole

expose or exhibit indecent exhibition/to
 c. C-46, s. 175(1)(b)
  étaler ou exposer des choses indécentes

existence
come into existence/to (a corporation)
 c. C-44, s. 9
  exister

existing
(cause of action)
 c. B-1, s. 23(2)
  déjà né

existing licence
 c. A-2, s. 21(3)
  permis déjà délivré

existing or proposed (proceeding)
 c. C-46, s. 137
  existant ou projeté

existing or prospective oil well
 c. C-46, s. 396(1)(a)
  puits de pétrole existant ou en perspective

exonerate/to
(from liability)
 c. B-3, s. 101(3)
  libérer

exonerate himself/to
 c. B-5, s. 4
  dégager sa responsabilité

exonerate partly or wholly from liability/to
 c. C-26, Schedule I, Article 21
  atténuer ou écarter la responsabilité

expectancy
mediately or immediately, in possession, or expectancy
 c. C-29, s. 38(e)
  directement ou par intermédiaire, pour jouissance immédiate ou ultérieure

expectant on
(interest)
 c. C-42, s. 14(1)
  en expectative

expedient
 c. C-42, s. 62(1)
  opportun

expedite/to
(the hearing)
 c. C-46, s. 679(10)
  hâter l'audition

expedite the proceedings/to
 c. C-46, s. 526
  hâter le déroulement des procédures

expend/to
expend, administer and dispose/to (of the money)
 c. C-13, s. 6(3)
  employer, gérer et aliéner

expenditure
 c. A-2, s. 18(1)(d)
  dépense

expense
administrative expense — frais d'administration
  c. B-7, Schedule I, Section 5(i)
costs, charges and expenses — frais judiciaires et extrajudiciaires
  c. L-12, s. 43(3)
expense of administration — dépense d'administration
  c. B-7, Schedule I, Article V, Section 12(h)(i)
operating expense — dépense de fonctionnement
  c. C-11, s. 12(1)(c)
operating expense (of a corporation) — frais d'exploitation
  c. N-11, s. 30(3)(c)

expenses — dépenses
  c. A-12, s. 6(1)(c)
(in court) — dépens
  c. F-11, s. 119(2)
administrative expenses — dépenses d'ordre administratif
  c. A-5, s. 10
fees and expenses of transmission (of a case) — droits et frais de transmission
  c. S-26, s. 63
incorporation expenses — frais de constitution
  c. B-1, s. 30(1)
operating expenses — dépenses d'exploitation
  c. C-14, s. 11(4)
organization expenses — frais d'établissement
  c. B-1, s. 30(1)
travel and living expenses — frais de déplacement et autres
  c. A-7, s. 7(9)(b)

expert
expert examiner — expert-vérificateur
  c. C-51, s. 2
expert witness — expert appelé comme témoin
  c. C-46, s. 755(4)
expiditiously
as informally and expiditiously as — avec aussi peu de formalisme et autant de célérité
  c. C-51, s. 28
expiration
(of time) — expiration (du délai)
  c. A-1, s. 37(2)
explanatory
explanatory examination — interrogatoire explicatif
  c. C-39, s. 20(2)
explosive substance — substance explosive
  c. C-46, s. 2
offensive weapon or explosive substance — arme offensive ou substance explosive
  c. C-46, s. 78(1)
explosive-driven rivet
firing stud cartridge, explosive-driven rivet or similar industrial ammunition — cartouche d'ancrage, rivet explosif ou autre munition industrielle
  c. C-46, s. 84(1)
export
interprovincial and export trade — marchés interprovincial et international
  c. A-6, s. 2(1)
Export Development Corporation — Société pour l'expansion des exportations
  c. F-11, Schedule III, Part I

Export Finance Corporation of Canada Ltd.
    c. B-1, s. 193(5)(b)

Export Finance Corporation of Canada Ltd.

expose/to
    abandon or expose/to
        c. C-46, s. 214

abandonner ou exposer

express
    express contract
        c. C-8, s. 2(1)

contrat exprès

    express trust
        c. B-1, s. 206(1)

fiducie expresse

    express, implied or constructive trust
        c. L-12, s. 89(1)

fiducie explicite, implicite ou judiciaire

extend/to
    (a period)
        c. B-1, s. 9(9)

proroger (la période)

    (the right)
        c. A-1, s. 4(2)

étendre (le droit)

    extend the time limit/to
        c. A-1, s. 9(1)

proroger le délai

extended
    extended coverage
        c. C-48, s. 9(1)

garantie supplémentaire

    extended health care services
        c. C-6, s. 2

services complémentaires de santé

extension
    (of period)
        c. B-1, s. 9(9)

prorogation

    extension of the application (of the Act)
        c. C-24, s. 47(3)

extension du champ d'application

    extension of time
        c. C-46, s. 678(2)
        c. S-26, s. 59(2)

prorogation de délai

    extension of time
        c. B-3, s. 2

atermoiement

    grant or extension of credit
        c. C-46, s. 362(1)(c)(iv)

couverture ou extension d'un crédit

    notice of extension
        c. A-1, s. 9(1)(c)

avis de prorogation de délai

    unreasonable extension (time limits)
        c. A-1, s. 30(1)(c)

prorogation abusive

extinction
    extinction of liabilities
        c. C-52, s. 20(2)(ii)

extinction de dettes

extinguish/to
    extinguish or reduce/to (a liability)
        c. C-44, s. 37

supprimer ou limiter (une obligation)

extort a consent/to
    c. C-46, s. 162(2)b)(i)

extorquer un consentement

extra-billing
    c. C-6, s. 2

surfacturation

extra-judicial proceedings
    c. A-1, s. 36(3)

procédures extrajudiciaires

extract
    (of a document)
        c. C-23, s. 21(3)(b)

extrait

    extract or abstract (of a report)
        c. P-1, s. 9

extrait ou résumé

to issue a certified copy of, extract from or certificate in respect of a register, record or document
   c. C-46, s. 378(a)

émettre une copie ou un extrait d'un registre, dossier ou document, ou un certificat relatif, attestés conformes

extracts
copies of, or make extracts from/to (records)
   c. F-27, s. 23(1)(c)

faire la reproduction totale partielle

copies or extracts (of books)
   c. A-7, s. 16(1)(c)

reproduction

extradition
warrant of extradition
   c. C-37, s. 7(1)

mandat d'extradition

f

fabricate/to
(evidence)
   c. C-46, s. 137

fabriquer

fabrique
   c. C-41, s. 11(1)(a)(viii)
   c. L-12, s. 60(1)a)(xi)

fabrique

face
(contempt of court) whether or not committed in the face of the court
   c. Y-1, s. 47(2)

au cours de ses audiences ou en dehors de ses audiences

contempt of court committed in the face of the court
   c. C-46, s. 10(1)

outrage au tribunal commis en présence du tribunal

defect apparent on the face of the information
   c. C-46, s. 548(3)

vice de forme apparent à la face même de la dénonciation

defect apparent on the face thereof
   c. C-46, s. 601(1)

vice de forme apparent à sa face même

on its face
   c. C-46, s. 487.1(11)

face value
(of a coin)
   c. B-1, s. 208(1)(a)

valeur nominale

(of a debenture)
   c. C-43, s. 4(1)(k)

valeur nominale

facilities
(for simultaneous interpretation)
   c. 31 (4th Supp.), s. 15(2)

services

facilities to be made available
   c. 31 (4th Supp.), s. 4(2)

pourvoir

marriage counselling or guidance facilities
   c. C-3, s. 9(1)(b)

services de consultation ou d'orientation matrimoniales

offices or facilities (of federal institutions)
   c. 31 (4th Supp.), s. 29

bureaux

facility
   c. F-11, s. 19

installation

air navigation facility used in international air navigation
   c. C-46, s. 7(8)

installation utilisée pour la navigation aérienne internationale

privately owned facility
   c. C-11, s. 15(4)(f)
station du secteur privé

provincial correctional facility
   c. Y-1, s. 24(14)
centre correctionnel provincial

telecommunication facility or service
   c. C-46, s. 327(1)
installations ou service en matière de télécommunication

waste treatment facility
   c. C-11, s. 15(4)(f)
station de traitement

facsimile

(of a signature)
   c. C-19, s. 41(2)
fac-similé

facsimile of signature printed from engraving
   c. F-11, s. 50(2)
griffe dont l'empreinte reproduit la signature autographe

fact

fact or consideration
   c. B-6, s. 6(1)(e)
fait ou considération

in law or in fact
   c. C-46, s. 150
en droit ou de fait

in law or in fact
   c. Y-1, s. 2(1)
en droit ou en fait

legally or in fact
   c. C-43, s. 2(3)(c)
de droit ou de fait

matter of fact or knowledge
   c. C-46, s. 136(1)
question de fait ou de connaissance

fact-finding

fact-finding authority
   c. C-12, s. 2
mission de constatation

factor

factor or agent
   c. C-46, s. 325
facteur ou agent

keeper of a warehouse, factor, agent or carrier
   c. C-46, s. 389(1)(a)
gardien d'un entrepôt, facteur, agent ou voiturier

trustee, banker, merchant, attorney, factor, broker or other agent
   c. C-46, s. 491.1(3)(a)
fiduciaire, banquier, marchand, fondé de pouvoir, courtier ou autre mandataire

factoring

factoring corporation
   c. B-1, s. 193(1)
société d'affacturage

facts of the case

set out the facts of the case/to
   c. C-46, s. 527(1)(d)
exposer les faits de l'espèce

fail/to

fail to comply/to (with a condition)
   c. A-2, s. 21(12)
contrevenir

fail to do/to (something)
   c. A-2, s. 14(1)(a)
omettre d'accomplir

failure
   c. B-1, s. 103(2)
défaut

(to keep books)
   c. C-46, s. 400(2)(b)
omission

(to perform)
   c. B-1, s. 245(2)
carence

failure in a duty
   c. C-27, Schedule, Article III, 8
manquement à un devoir

failure or default
   c. B-7, Schedule I, Article XIII, Section 3
faillite ou carence

failure to comply	inobservation
c. C-40, s. 93(9)	
failure to comply (with a decision)	inexécution
c. A-7, s. 13(c)	
failure to comply (with a regulation)	défaut de se conformer
c. A-2, s. 18(1)(o)(i)	
failure to meet (standards)	inobservation
c. A-7, s. 8(1)	
failure to stop (at the scene of accident)	défaut d'arrêter
c. C-46, s. 252(1)	
failure to stop	
(at the scene of accident)	défaut d'arrêter
c. C-46, s. 252(1)	
fair	
fair and reasonable	juste et raisonnable
c. A-5, s. 4(1)	
c. A-10, s. 14(2)	
fair relationship	juste rapport
c. A-8, s. 7(1)(b)	
full, fair and plain (disclosure)	complet, exact et clair
c. B-1, s. 148(1)	
full, fair and plain (disclosure)	sincère et complet
c. B-1, s. 149(2)	
reasonable and fair (contract)	équitable
c. C-44, s. 120(7)	
fair comment	
(libel)	commentaire honnête et loyal
c. C-46, s. 307(1)	
fair market value	juste valeur marchande
c. C-25, s. 12 (1)	
fair report	
fair report of the proceedings (of the Senate)	compte rendu loyal des délibérations
c. C-46, s. 307(1)	
fair value	juste valeur
c. B-1, s. 295(3)(a)	
fairly	sincèrement
c. B-1, s. 219(2)	
fairness	équité
c. C-51, s. 28	
faith	
in good faith	de bonne foi
c. B-1, s. 54(1)(a)	
faithfully	
faithfully, impartially and to the best of one's abilities	avec fidélité, impartialité et dans toute la mesure de ses moyens
c. C-23, Schedule	
fall	
rise or fall in price of stocks	hausse ou baisse des actions
c. C-46, s. 383(1)	
fall due/to	
accrue and fall due/to (interest)	échoir et devenir exigible
c. C-41, s. 34	
false	
false document	faux document
c. C-46, s. 321	
false or deceptive statement	déclaration fausse ou trompeuse
c. A-8, s. 16(1)(b)	
false pretence	faux semblant
c. C-8, s. 90(1)(a)	
c. C-46, s. 361(1)	

false statement
    c. A-1, s. 36(3)

fausses déclarations

falsehood
  by deceit, falsehood or other
  fraudulent means
    c. C-46, s. 380(1)

par supercherie, mensonge ou autre
  moyen dolosif

falsification
  (of entries)
    c. B-1, s. 157(3)(b)

falsification

  (of records)
    c. C-44, s. 22(2)(b)

falsification

falsify/to
  forge or falsify a credit card/to

falsifier une carte de crédit ou en
  fabriquer une fausse

    c. C-46, s. 342(1)(b)

family allowance recipient

bénéficiaire d'une allocation
  familiale

    c. C-8, s. 42(1)(c)

family provision
    c. 4 (2nd Supp.), s. 2

disposition familiale

fare
  to collect as fare, toll, ticket or
  admission

percevoir un prix de passage, un
  péage, un billet ou un droit
  d'entrée

    c. C-46, s. 392(a)(i)

farm

ferme

    c. B-1, s. 2(1)
    c. N-11, s. 2

exploitation agricole

Farm Credit Corporation
    c. A-1, Schedule I
    c. F-11, Schedule III, Part I

Société du crédit agricole

farmer
    c. B-1, s. 2(1)

agriculteur

    c. B-1, s. 2(1)

cultivateur

fault
    c. A-12, s. 7(1)
    c. C-27, Schedule, Article III,
    8

faute

favourable treatment
    c. C-29, s. 35(3)(c)

traitement privilégié

federal business
    c. L-2, s. 2

entreprises fédérales

  federal work, undertaking or
  business
    c. L-2, s. 2

entreprises fédérales

**Federal Business Development
Bank**
    c. A-1, Schedule I

Banque fédérale de développement

Federal Court Appeal Division
    c. F-7, s. 2

Section d'appel de la Cour fédérale

federal customs laws
    c. C-53, s. 2(1)

législation douanière fédérale

**Federal Mortgage Exchange
Corporation**
    c. A-1, Schedule I

Bourse fédérale d'hypothèques

**federal work, undertaking or
business**
    c. C-32, s. 2

entreprise fédérale

federal works
  associated or related, federal
  works
    c. L-2, s. 255(1)

entreprises fédérales associées ou
  connexes

Federal-Provincial Relations Office
    c. A-1, Schedule I
federation
    c. B-1, s. 2(1)
    c. C-21, s. 2(1)
fee
    c. A-10, s. 6(5)
    c. C-40, s. 44
    c. C-44, s. 85(1)
    fee or other amount
        c. A-1, s. 11(6)
    fee or other amount
        c. A-1, s. 11(6)
    for a fee
        c. A-1, s. 20(2)
    licence fee
        c. C-15, s. 15(2)(b)
    official fee
        c. C-46, s. 347(2)
    prescribe a fee/to
        c. A-1, s. 77(1)(d)
    witness fee
        c. C-39, s. 74(2)
fee simple
    lands granted in
        c. T-7, s. 2
feeble-minded person
    c. C-46, s. 2
feeble-minded, insane, idiot or imbecile
    c. C-46, s. 162(2)(b)(ii)
feed mill
    c. C-24, Schedule
feed warehouse
    c. C-24, Schedule
fees
    (for attendances at meetings)
        c. C-25, s. 7(1)
    fees and allowances
        c. A-1, s. 36(4)
    fees and costs (to be taxed)
        c. S-26, s. 97(1)(d)
    fees and expenses of
    transmission (of a case)
        c. S-26, s. 63
    fees for licenses
        c. A-2, s. 18(1)(h)
    fees or emoluments
        c. C-42, s. 68(3)
    fees or other remuneration
        c. C-42, s. 68(5)
    legal fees and disbursements
        c. C-44, s. 242(2)
    tariff of fees and costs
        c. C-50, s. 35(a)
feigned marriage
    c. C-46, s. 292(1)
Fellow of the Canadian Institute of Actuaries
    c. C-46, s. 347(4)
fellowship
    award a scholarship or
    fellowship/to
        c. A-13, s. 4(g)

Secrétariat des relations fédérales-provinciales

fédération

jeton de présence

cotisation d'affiliation
honoraires
versement

montant

à titre onéreux

droit de permis

taxe officielle

fixer le montant des droits

honoraire des témoins

terres concédées en pleine propriété

personne d'esprit faible

simple d'esprit, aliéné, idiot ou imbécile

fabrique d'aliments pour animaux

entrepôt d'aliments pour animaux

rétribution

frais et indemnités

honoraires et frais

droits et frais de transmission

droits pour les permis

salaire ou émolument

honoraires ou autre rémunération

honoraires légaux et déboursés

tarif d'honoraires

mariage feint

Fellow de l'Institut canadien des actuaires

attribuer une bourse d'études

felony
    c. F-32, s. 3(1)

félonie

fiat
  (of judge)
    c. S-26, s. 66(2)

décision

fictitious person
    c. B-4, s. 20(5)

personne fictive

fidelity and secrecy
  oath of fidelity and secrecy

serment de fidelité et de secret professionnel

    c. C-7, s. 13(2)

fidelity bond
  security or fidelity bond

assurance responsabilité

    c. B-1, s. 294(4)
  to provide a security or fidelity bond

fournir une sûreté ou une assurance-responsabilité

    c. C-44, s. 223(4)

fiduciary
    c. B-1, s. 88(2)

représentant

    c. C-44, s. 48(2)
  act in a fiduciary capacity/to

agir à titre de fiduciaire

    c. B-3, s. 178(1)(f)
  fiduciary activities

activités fiduciaires

    c. B-1, s. 174(1)
  fiduciary duty

obligation de représentant

    c. C-44, s. 75
  fiduciary obligation

obligation fiduciaire

    c. B-3, s. 120(6)
  fiduciary relationship

lien fiduciaire

    c. C-40, s. 77(5)

field representative
    c. C-31, s. 16

représentant ambulant

fieri facias
  writ of fieri facias

bref de saisie-exécution

    c. C-46, s. 771(3.1)

file/to
  (a complaint)

déposer

    c. A-7, s. 8(1)
  (a complaint)

présenter

    c. A-7, s. 8(2)
  (a notice)

enregistrer

    c. C-44, s. 19(4)
  (an assignment)

déposer

    c. B-3, s. 2
  (returns)

déposer

    c. A-2, s. 18(1)(d)
  file a copy/to

enregistrer un exemplaire

    c. C-44, s. 262(2)(b)(iii)
  file a return/to

produire une déclaration

    c. C-8, s. 15(3)
  file with the clerk/to

déposer auprès du greffier

    c. C-46, s. 754(1)(c)

filing
  (of a document)

dépôt

    c. C-44, s. 262(2)(b)(i)
  (of a prospectus)

dépôt

    c. C-44, s. 2(7)(a)

filings or clippings
  (gold)

limailles ou rognures

    c. C-46, s. 451

fill/to
  (a vacancy)

pourvoir (à une vacance)

    c. P-35, s. 82

fill a position/to   pourvoir un poste
    c. B-1, s. 37(e)
fill a vacancy/to   combler une vacance
    c. B-1, s. 40(3)
final
    final and binding/to be (decision)   être final et obligatoire
       c. P-35, s. 96(3)
    final and conclusive (decision)   définitif et sans appel
       c. B-9, s. 16
    final and conclusive judgment   arrêt définitif et sans appel
    (Supreme Court)
       c. S-26, s. 52
    final decision   décision sans appel
       c. L-12, s. 76(6)
    final judgment   jugement définitif
       c. S-26, s. 2(1)
    final judgment   décision non susceptible de recours
       c. B-7, Schedule II, Article
        VII, Section 3
    final or interim (judgment or   définitif ou provisoire
    order)
       c. C-3, s. 21(1)
    final order   ordonnance définitive
       c. C-44, s. 190(22)
       c. N-1, s. 19
    final settlement of differences   règlement définitif des différends
    (disputes)
       c. C-46, s. 422(2)(b)
    highest court of final resort in a   plus haut tribunal de dernier
    province   ressort dans une province
       c. S-26, s. 2(2)
    interim or final order   ordonnance provisoire ou finale
       c. C-44, s. 192(4)
    proposed interim or final   projet de répartition provisoire ou
    distribution (money or property)   définitive
       c. C-44, s. 217(1)
final order
    obtain a final order/to   obtenir une ordonnance définitive
       c. N-1, s. 19
finance a program/to   financer un programme
    c. A-13, s. 4(a)
financial assistance
    subsidy, subvention and other   aide financière, sous forme
    financial assistance   notamment de subvention
       c. C-25, s. 12(1)(a)
financial corporation   société financière
       c. B-1, s. 109(1)
       c. B-1, s. 193(1)   société de crédit
financial institution   institution financière
       c. B-1, s. 254
financial responsibility   solvabilité
       c. A-12, s. 8(1)
financial statement   état financier
       c. A-13, s. 36
    interim financial statement   état financier provisoire
       c. C-44, s. 160(4)
financial statements
    comparative financial   états financiers comparatifs
    statements
       c. C-44, s. 155(1)(a)
financial transaction   opération financière
       c. A-13, s. 35

find/to
(an indictment) — prononcer
  c. C-46, s. 604(1)
(to reach a decision) — juger
  c. A-7, s. 8(4)(a)
finding
(of the Commission) — conclusion
  c. B-9, s. 15(3)
finding an indictment — mise en accusation
  c. C-46, s. 573
finding of delinquency — déclaration de culpabilité pour acte de délinquance
  c. Y-1, s. 14(2)(c)(iii)
finding of the jury — verdict du jury
  c. C-46, s. 166(1)(b)(iv)
fine — amende
  c. A-2, s. 7(13)
fineness
millesimal fineness (gold) — millième de fin
  c. C-26, Schedule I, Article 22(4)
standard millesimal fineness (for gold coins) — titre légal en millièmes
  c. C-52, Schedule
fingerprint
fingerprint examiner — préposé aux empreintes digitales
  c. C-46, s. 667(1)(a)(iii)
fire bomb
incendiary grenade, fire bomb, molotov cocktail — grenade incendiaire, bombe incendiaire, cocktail molotov
  c. C-46, s. 2
fire insurance
policy of fire insurance — police d'assurance-incendie
  c. C-46, s. 435
firearm — arme à feu
  c. C-46, s. 84(1)
firearm acquisition certificate — autorisation d'acquisition d'armes à feu
  c. C-46, s. 84(1)
firearm, air gun or air pistol — arme à feu, fusil à vent ou pistolet à vent
  c. C-46, s. 244
serial number on a firearm — numéro de série sur une arme à feu
  c. C-46, s. 104(3)(a)
firearms officer — préposé aux armes à feu
  c. C-46, s. 84(1)
firing stud cartridge
firing stud cartridge, explosive-driven rivet or similar industrial ammunition — cartouche d'ancrage, rivet explosif ou autre munition industrielle
  c. C-46, s. 84(1)
firm — maison d'affaires
  c. B-1, s. 174(2)(g)
  c. B-1, s. 35(1)(i) — entreprise
  c. L-12, s. 5(4)(a)
  c. C-46, s. 362(1)(c) — maison de commerce
(of auditors) — cabinet
  c. C-7, s. 30(3)
corporation, firm or partnership — personne morale, firme ou société de personnes
  c. C-46, s. 391
firm of accountants — cabinet de comptables
  c. L-12, s. 60(4)

firm or partner thereof c. C-46, s. 384(a)	firme ou un de ses associés
first degree murder c. C-46, s. 231(2)	meurtre au premier degré

first directors
    (of an association)
    c. C-40, s. 129(4)(e)
	premiers administrateurs

first preferred share c. B-1, Schedule I	action privilégiée de premier rang

fiscal agent
    c. B-2, s. 24
    c. F-11, s. 2
	agent financier

fiscal year
    c. A-3, s. 11
    c. F-11, s. 2
	exercice

Fisheries Price Support Board
 	
    c. F-11, Schedule II
	Office des prix des produits de la
	    pêche

fishery officer c. C-33, s. 2	agent des pêches
fishing equipment and supplies c. B-1, s. 2(1)	engins et fournitures de pêche
fishing vessel c. B-1, s. 2(1)	bateau de pêche

fitness
    (of a sentence)
    c. C-46, s. 687(1)
	justesse

fix/to
    (salary)
    c. A-4, s. 3(6)
	fixer

fix, impose and collect/to (levies
    or charges)
    c. A-6, s. 2(2)(a)
	instituer et percevoir

fix by proclamation/to
    (a date)
    c. A-2, s. 28(1)
	fixer par proclamation

fixed
    fixed or ascertainable amount
    c. C-46, s. 347(2)
	somme déterminée ou déterminable

flat rate c. C-8, s. 56(1)	taux uniforme

fleet
    foreign fishing fleet
    c. C-33, s. 2
	flotille de pêche étrangère

flight
    aircraft in flight
    c. C-46, s. 7(1)(b)
	aéronef en vol

escape by flight c. C-46, s. 25(4)	fuite

float
    lumber, timber, log, float, boom,
    dam or slide
 	
    c. C-46, s. 433(1)(i)
	bois de construction, de service ou
	    en grume, radeau, barrage
	    flottant, digue ou glissoir

floating charge c. C-40, s. 93(1)(c)	charge flottante
flour mill c. C-24, Schedule	minoterie

follow/to
    (a vessel)
    c. C-9, s. 43(7)
	poursuivre

follow the event/to (costs) c. A-1, s. 53(1)	suivre le sort du principal

food
  food, lodging or other
  accomodation (at an inn)
    c. C-46, s. 364(1)

aliments, logement ou autres
  commodités

for cause
  (to remove)
    c. A-10, s. 8(1)
  remove for cause/to
    c. C-19, s. 6(3)

pour motif valable

démettre pour motif valable

for value
  (purchaser)
    c. B-1, s. 75(2)
  for value in good faith without
  notice (lender)
    c. C-44, s. 44(3)

contre valeur

à titre onéreux de bonne foi qui n'a
  pas été avisé

forbear/to
    c. B-1, s. 313(1)(a)

s'abstenir

forbid/to
  forbid the doing or continuing of
  any act/to
    c. A-2, s. 14(2)(b)

interdire l'accomplissement ou la
  continuation de tout acte

force
  cease to have force or effect/to (a
  subsection)
    c. B-1, s. 113(2)
  excessive force
    c. C-46, s. 26
  force of law (an agreement)
    c. L-12, s. 102(10)
  force or effect (of an agreement)
    c. A-3, s. 6
  force reasonably necessary
    c. C-46, s. 27
  force reasonably proportioned to
  the danger
    c. C-46, s. 30
  have full force and effect/to (act)

    c. C-36, s. 8
  have no force or effect/to
    c. B-1, s. 263(3)
  of no force or effect/to be (a
  term)
    c. C-24, s. 51(2)
  police force
    c. C-23, s. 13(2)(b)
  regular force
    c. C-17, s. 2(1)
  use force by way of correction/to
  (toward a child)
    c. C-46, s. 43
  use of force
    c. A-1, s. 15(2)(d)
  visiting force
    c. C-12, s. 2

cesser de s'appliquer

force excessive

force de loi

effet

force raisonnablement nécessaire

force raisonnablement
  proportionnée au danger

être pleinement exécutoire et
  effectif

être inopérant

être réputé non écrit

service de police

force régulière

employer la force pour corriger

emploi de la force

force étrangère

force of law
    c. C-8, s. 4(3)

force de loi

forcible
  forcible entry
    c. C-46, s. 72(1)
  forcible entry and detainer

    c. C-46, s. 73

prise de possession par la force

prise de possession et détention par
  la force

forcibly
    forcibly break into or forcibly enter the dwelling-house/to   accomplir une effraction ou s'introduire de force dans une maison d'habitation
        c. C-46, s. 40

foreclosure   forclusion
        c. B-1, s. 185(1)
        c. C-7, s. 28(2)
    foreclosure proceedings   procédures de forclusion
        c. N-11, s. 12(2)(a)

foreign
    foreign animal   animal étranger
        c. A-11, s. 2
    foreign corporation   société étrangère
        c. B-1, s. 193(1)
    foreign cultural property   biens culturels étrangers
        c. C-51, s. 37(1)

Foreign Investment Review Agency   Agence d'examen de l'investissement étranger
        c. A-1, Schedule I

foreman
    foreman of the grand jury   chef du grand jury
        c. C-46, s. 594

forest   forêt
        c. B-1, s. 2(1)

forestry   sylviculture
        c. B-1, s. 2(1)

forestry equipment   matériel sylvicole immobilier
        c. B-1, s. 2(1)

forestry implements   matériel sylvicole mobilier
        c. B-1, s. 2(1)

forestry producer
    forestry producer   sylviculteur
        c. B-1, s. 2(1)

foretell/to
    inducement to bet on, to guess or to foretell the result of a contest   incitation à parier sur le résultat d'une partie ou à conjecturer ce résultat ou à le prédire
        c. C-46, s. 202(1)(h)

forfeit/to   confisquer
        c. C-11, s. 24(1)
    (an animal)   confisquer un animal
        c. A-11, s. 43(2)
    (earned remission)   annuler
        c. P-20, s. 6(4)
    forfeit a claim/to   perdre un droit
        c. A-11, s. 10
    forfeit to Her Majesty/to   confisquer au profit de Sa Majesté
        c. F-27, s. 27(1)

forfeited/to be
    forfeited to Her Majesty/to be   être confisqué au profit de Sa Majesté
        c. C-46, s. 102(3)

forfeited share   action frappée de déchéance
        c. C-41, s. 27(3)(j)

forfeiture   confiscation
        c. A-7, s. 13(f)
        c. A-12, s. 27(2)
    (of pay)   suppression (de solde militaire)
        c. C-17, s. 50(c)
    fine, pecuniary penalty or forfeiture   amende, peine pécuniaire ou confiscation
        c. C-46, s. 724

forfeiture of stock	confiscation des actions
c. L-12, s. 29(1)(a)	
forfeiture or pecuniary penalty	confiscation
c. F-11, s. 23(1)	
order for forfeiture	ordonnance de confiscation
c. C-46, s. 192(2)	
forge/to	
(a passport)	faire un faux
c. C-46, s. 57(1)(a)	
(a signature)	contrefaire
c. B-4, s. 48(1)	
forge or falsify a credit card/to	falsifier une carte de crédit ou en fabriquer une fausse
c. C-46, s. 340(a)	
forged/to be	
(a document)	être contrefait
c. C-46, s. 368(1)	
forgery	faux
c. C-44, s. 48(2)	
c. C-46, s. 366	
form	modèle ou formulaire
c. C-50, s. 35(b)	
classification and form of licences	classification et forme des permis
c. A-2, s. 18(1)(a)	
form and draftmanship (of regulations)	présentation et rédaction
c. S-22, s. 3(2)(d)	
in the form	selon le modèle
c. L-12, s. 5(1)	
form/to	
form an intention/to	former le dessein
c. C-46, s. 46(2)(e)	
incorporate, form or organize a corporation/to	constituer, former ou établir une personne morale
c. B-1, s. 109(1)(b)	
form a marriage	
to go through a form of marriage	passer par une formalité de mariage
c. C-46, s. 290(1)(a)(i)	
formal	
(meeting)	officiel
c. C-4, s. 8(2)	
formal equity	participation ordinaire
c. C-20, s. 2(1)	
formal judgment	jugement formel
c. C-46, s. 677	
former	
former Act	ancienne loi
c. C-17, s. 2(1)	
former spouse	ex-époux
c. 3 (2nd Supp.), s. 15(1)	
formulation	
(of a law)	élaboration
c. C-43, s. 19(3)	
forthwith	immédiatement
c. A-2, s. 14(2)(a)	
advise forthwith/to	mentionner sans retard
c. A-1, s. 33	
forthwith or as soon as practicable	immédiatement ou dès que possible
c. C-46, s. 254(3)	
foster parent	
parent, foster parent, guardian or head of a family	père ou mère, parent nourricier, tuteur ou chef de famille
c. C-46, s. 215(1)(a)	

fraction
  (of a share)   fraction
    c. C-44, s. 39(1)
fractional
  fractional share   fraction d'action
    c. B-1, s. 76(5)
  fractional shares   fractionnement des actions
    c. C-44, s. 35(1)(b)
frame/to
  (a by-law)   rédiger
    c. B-6, s. 31(1)
framing
  (of an instrument)   rédaction
    c. C-42, s. 61
franchise
  granting of franchise   octroi de franchise
  (professional sport)
    c. C-34, s. 48(3)
fraud   fraude
    c. C-44, s. 60(1)
fraudulent
  by deceit, falsehood or other   par supercherie, mensonge ou autre
  fraudulent means   moyen dolosif
    c. C-46, s. 380(1)
  false or fraudulent   représentation fausse ou trompeuse
  representation
    c. C-46, s. 162(2)(b)(i)
  fraudulent conveyance   transporter frauduleusement
    c. B-3, s. 42(1)(b)
  fraudulent intent   intention frauduleuse
    c. C-46, s. 361(1)
  fraudulent misrepresentation of   dénaturation frauduleuse des faits
  fact
    c. C-46, s. 361(2)
  fraudulent or unlawful   frauduleux ou illégal
    c. C-44, s. 229(2)(c)
  make a fraudulent gift/to (of   donner frauduleusement
  property)
    c. B-3, s. 42(1)(b)
fraudulently   frauduleusement
    c. B-1, s. 85(2)
  act fraudulently or   commettre des actes frauduleux ou
  dishonestly/to   malhonnêtes
    c. C-44, s. 229(2)(d)
  fraudulently and without colour   frauduleusement et sans apparence
  of right   de droit
    c. C-46, s. 322(1)
free
  free from any and all   libre de toute charge
  encumbrances
    c. C-25, s. 10(2)
  free or reduced rate   transport gratuit ou à tarif réduit
  transportation
    c. A-2, s. 19
free-board   franc-bord
    c. A-12, s. 12(1)(a)(vi)
freedom
  freedom of peaceful assembly   liberté de réunion pacifique
    Constitutional Act, 1982,
    Schedule B, s. 2(c)
freehold
  freehold real estate   immeuble détenu en propriété libre
                         et perpétuelle
    c. L-12, s. 2

to sever from the freehold any fixture fixed therein or thereto

séparer de la propriété foncière toute chose qui y est fixée à demeure ou incorporée

  c. C-46, s. 441

freely usable currency
  c. B-7, Schedule I, Article XXX, Section 4(f)

monnaie librement utilisable

freight
  c. C-19, s. 28

fret

  c. C-26, Schedule I, Article 8(k)

prix du transport

frequenter
  to be an inmate or frequenter (of a common bawdy-house)
  c. C-46, s. 212(1)(e)

habiter ou fréquenter

freshly
  to be freshly pursued
  c. C-46, s. 494(1)(b)(ii)

être immédiatement poursuivi

Freshwater Fish Marketing Corporation
  c. A-1, Schedule I

Office de commercialisation du poisson d'eau douce

frivolous or vexatious action
  c. B-3, s. 173(1)(g)

action futile ou vexatoire

from time to time
  c. C-42, s. 66(1)

périodiquement

  c. I-23, s. 31(3)

en tant que de besoin

fuel
  fuel and additive
  c. C-32, s. 15(2)

combustible et additif

fugitive
  c. F-32, s. 2

fugitif

fulfil/to
  (a condition)
  c. B-4, s. 65

réaliser

  fulfil a duty/to
  c. B-1, s. 98(1)(b)

satisfaire à une obligation

fulfilment
  fulfilment of a purpose
  c. A-13, s. 4(m)

poursuite d'une mission

  fulfilment of his responsabilities
  c. A-17, s. 13(1)

exercice de ses fonctions

full
  full answer and defence
  c. C-46, s. 802(1)

réponse et défense complètes

  full legal effect
  c. C-27, Schedule, Article VI

plein effet légal

  full share
  c. B-1, s. 76(1)

action entière

  payment in full of compensation or damages
  c. C-46, s. 722(4)

paiement intégral de l'indemnité ou des dommages-intérêts

  private person of full age and capacity
  c. C-50, s. 3

personne physique majeure et capable

  to make full answer and defence

présenter une pleine réponse et défense

  c. C-46, s. 650(3)

full-time
  (member)
  c. B-9, s. 4

à temps plein

fully
  fully secured (by a mortgage)
  c. L-12, s. 61(1)(b)

totalement garanti

fully paid share   action entièrement libérée
    c. C-44, s. 43(1)
function
    (of the Council)   mission
    c. C-4, s. 7
    power, duty and function (of the   responsabilité, pouvoir et fonction
    Auditor General)
    c. A-17, s. 15(3)
functions
    functions and duties (of the   attributions
    Commission)
    c. A-2, s. 15
    powers, duties and functions   compétence
    c. C-4, s. 7
fund   caisse
    c. C-41, s. 10(1)(i)
    bank guarantee fund   fonds bancaire de garantie
    c. B-1, s. 174(2)(c)
    bank pension fund   fonds bancaire de pension
    c. B-1, s. 174(2)(c)
    mortgage based mutual fund   fonds d'investissement à capital
          variable
    c. B-1, s. 173(1)(o)
    pension fund   caisse de retraite
    c. B-9, s. 35(1)(e)
    pension fund   fonds de la caisse de retraite
    c. C-7, s. 8(4)
    purchase fund or sinking fund   fonds d'amortissement
    c. B-1, s. 124(4)
    segregated fund   fonds réservé
    c. C-20, s. 2(1)
    share or interest in a public   action ou intérêt dans un stock ou
    stock or fund   fonds public
    c. C-46, s. 2
    trust fund   fonds en fiducie
    c. C-44, s. 46(3)
fundamental right of Canadians   droit fondamental des Canadiens
    c. C-13, s. 2
funds
    estate funds   fonds de l'actif
    c. B-3, s. 6(2)
    undistributed funds   fonds non distribués
    c. B-3, s. 154(1)
fungible   fongible
    c. C-44, s. 48(2)
    (securities)   fongibles
    c. B-1, s. 75(2)
    fungible bulk   ensemble fongible
    c. B-1, s. 97(3)
    c. C-44, s. 70(3)
furnish/to
    (information)   donner
    c. A-7, s. 16(2)
further
    further contravention   nouvelle infraction
    c. C-32, s. 37
    without further proof   sans autre preuve
    c. A-2, s. 27(2)
future
    future or contingent (obligation)   futur ou éventuel
    c. B-1, s. 289(h)
    unliquidated, future or   créance non liquidée, future ou
    contingent claim   éventuelle
    c. C-44, s. 216(3)(c)

g

gain
  for the purposes of gain   aux fins de lucre
    c. C-46, s. 212(1)(h)
  material financial gain   profit financier appréciable
    c. A-1, s. 20(1)(c)
gain access/to
  (to an information)   prendre connaissance
    c. C-12, s. 33(4)(a)
gambling   jeu
    c. B-3, s. 173(1)(e)
game   jeu
    c. C-46, s. 197(1)
  game of mixed chance and skill   jeu où se mêlent le hasard et l'adresse
    c. C-46, s. 197(1)
game of chance   jeu de hasard
    c. C-46, s. 197(1)
  lottery or game of chance   loterie ou jeu de hasard
    c. C-46, s. 206(1)
gaming
  gaming equipment   matériel de jeu
    c. C-46, s. 197(1)
  gaming house   maison de jeu
    c. C-46, s. 553(c)(i)
garnishable
  garnishable moneys   sommes saisissables
    c. 4 (2nd Supp.), s. 23
garnishee
  garnishee summons   bref de saisie-arrêt
    c. 4 (2nd Supp.), s. 23
garnishment   saisie-arrêt
    c. B-3, s. 70(1)
  attachment and garnishment   saisie et saisie-arrêt
    c. B-3, s. 70(1)
  garnishment proceedings   procédures de saisie-arrêt
    c. L-2, s. 238
gathering
  (of statistics)   rassemblement
    c. C-34, s. 70(2)(a)
general
  general agent   agent général
    c. B-1, s. 173(1)(b)
  general or special Act   loi générale ou spéciale
    c. A-2, s. 19
  general verdict (libel)   verdict général
    c. C-46, s. 317
general counsel
  (of corporation)   chef du contentieux
    c. C-44, s. 126(1)(a)
general manager
  (of corporation)   directeur général
    c. C-44, s. 126(1)a)
generality
  without limiting the generality of (a section of an Act)   sans préjudice de la portée générale
    c. C-22, s. 14(3)
  without limiting the generality of subsection   sans que soit limitée la portée générale du paragraphe
    c. C-10, s. 16(2)

generally
made applicable generally/to be
(regulation)   être d'application générale
    c. L-2, s. 136(2)
generative organs
disease of the generative organs   maladie des organes génitaux
    c. C-46, s. 163(2)(d)
genocide
advocate or promote genocide/to   préconiser ou fomenter le génocide
    c. C-46, s. 318(1)
genuine   authentique
    c. B-1, s. 75(2)
    c. C-44, s. 48(2)
(document)   authentique
    c. C-44, s. 18(e)
(gun collector)   véritable
    c. C-46, s. 109(3)(d)
genuine coin   pièce de bon aloi
    c. C-46, s. 448
genuine paper money   monnaie de papier authentique
    c. C-46, s. 448
genuine series of law reports   série authentique de rapports
                           judiciaires
    c. C-46, s. 166(4)(c)(i)
to alter a genuine document in   altérer, en quelque partie
any material part   matérielle, un document
                           authentique
    c. C-46, s. 366(2)(a)
valid or genuine (document)   valable ou authentique
    c. B-1, s. 21(e)
gift   don
    c. A-13, s. 4(j)
    c. B-1, s. 313(1)(a)   cadeau
acquire by gift, bequest or   acquérir par don, legs ou autre
otherwise/to (securities)   mode de libéralité
    c. A-13, s. 4(j)
gift, conveyance, assignment,   don, transport, cession, vente,
sale, transfer or delivery of   transfert ou remise de biens
property
    c. C-46, s. 392(a)(i)
give/to
make, give or issue/to (a   faire, donner ou émettre
document)
    c. A-2, s. 27(1)(b)
give effect/to
(to a provision)   mettre à effet
    c. P-35, s. 23(1)(b)
give notice/to
(Canada Gazette)   publier un avis
    c. C-44, s. 13(1)
give notice in writing/to   notifier par écrit
    c. C-42, s. 44
give rise/to
(to a right)   donner ouverture (à un droit)
    c. B-4, s. 6(2)(c)
give up/to
(regular judicial duty)   abandonner
    c. J-1, s. 28(1)
give written notice/to   aviser par écrit
    c. A-1, s. (a)
giving
giving of judgement   prononcé du jugement
    c. F-7, s. 45(2)

go to the validity/to
    defect going to the validity   vice mettant en cause la validité
      c. C-44, s. 53(c)
gold value   valeur-or
      c. C-26, Schedule II
good
    for the public good   dans l'intérêt public
      c. F-11, s. 30(1)
good and valuable   bonne et valable contrepartie
consideration
      c. B-1, Schedule VI
good faith   bonne foi
      c. B-1, s. 75(2)
    a person acting in good faith and   un tiers qui ignore qu'une infraction
    without notice has acquired   a été commise a acquis
    lawful title for valuable   légitimement de bonne foi pour
    consideration   une contrepartie valable
      c. C-46, s. 491.1(3)(b)(i)
    act in good faith/to   agir de bonne foi
      c. C-46, s. 32(3)(a)
    exercise good faith and   agir de bonne foi et avec une
    reasonable diligence/to   diligence raisonnable
      c. C-44, s. 81(1)(a)
    in good faith and without ill-will   de bonne foi et sans malveillance
      c. C-46, s. 306(c)
good order
    good order and discipline (on a   bon ordre et discipline (à bord d'un
    vessel)   navire)
      c. C-46, s. 44
goods   effets
      c. B-1, s. 2(1)
      c. A-10, s. 6(1)(b)   marchandises
    (search of)   biens
      c. A-2, s. 7(7)
    dangerous goods   marchandises dangereuses
      c. T-19, s. 2
    goods, wares or merchandise   effets, denrées ou marchandises
      c. C-46, s. 383(1)
    in the lawful execution of a   dans l'exécution légale d'un acte
    process against lands or goods   judiciaire contre des terres ou des
                      effets
      c. C-46, s. 270(1)(b)
    lawful execution of a process   exécution légitime d'un acte
    against lands and goods   judiciaire contre des terres ou des
                      biens meubles
      c. C-46, s. 129(c)
goodwill   achalandage
      c. C-40, s. 93(1)(c)
    goodwill of the business   achalandage
      c. B-3, s. 30(1)(a)
govern/to
    (the Board's proceedings)   régir
      c. A-4, s. 3(5)
governed/to be
    (means of redress)   se régler
      c. C-42, Schedule II Article 4
governing body   organe directeur
      c. C-13, s. 2
    (of a body corporate)   direction
      c. B-1, s. 68(2)
    trustee of the governing body   administrateur du corps dirigeant
      c. B-6, s. 2

government
 c. A-13, s. 4(b)
 c. A-1, s. 2(1)
 (of the Corporation)
  c. B-6, s. 22(h)
 municipal government
  c. A-1, s. 13(1)(d)
 regional government
  c. A-1, s. 13(1)(d)
  c. A-10, s. 5(1)(c)
government change
 c. A-1, s. 15(2)(d)
**Government Film
Commissioner**
 c. C-16, s. 3
government institution
 c. A-1, s. 3
governmental
 administrative, research,
 supervisory, advisory or
 regulatory functions of a
 governmental nature
  c. F-11, s. 3(1)(a)
Governor in Council
 c. A-1, s. 3
Governor of the Bank of Canada

 c. A-1, s. 70(2)
governors
 board of governors, management
 or directors
  c. C-46, s. 287(6)
grade
 (agricultural product standard)
  c. A-7, s. 2
 (of livestock product)
  c. L-9, s. 2
 grade name (agricultural
 product)
  c. A-7, s. 2
 variety, grade or class (of grain)
  c. C-24, s. 48(1)
grade name
 (of wheat)
  c. C-24, s. 43
grader
 (agricultural product)
  c. A-7, s. 2
graduated
 graduated payment mortgage
  c. N-11, s. 12(3)(a)
grain
 c. B-1, s. 2(1)
 c. C-24, s. 2(1)
**Grain Transportation Agency
Administrator**
 c. A-1, Schedule I
**Grand Trunk Railway Company
of Canada**
 c. C-19, s. 3
grant
 c. A-13, s. 33
 c. C-14, s. 11(1)(b)
 c. C-51, s. 35

pouvoir public

pouvoir exécutif
administration

administration municipale

administration régionale

changement de gouvernement

commissaire du gouvernement à la
 cinématographie

institution fédérale

fonctions étatiques
 d'administration, de recherche, de
 contrôle, de conseil ou de
 réglementation

gouverneur en conseil

gouverneur de la Banque du
 Canada

conseil des gouverneurs, conseil de
 direction, conseil d'administration

qualité ou classe

catégorie

dénomination de qualité

variété, grade ou classe

appellation de grade

préposé au classement

prêt à paiements progressifs

grain

grains
Administrateur de l'Office du
 transport du grain

Compagnie du Grand Tronc de
 chemin de fer du Canada

subvention

assignment or grant (of an interest)   cession ou concession
    c. C-42, s. 13(4)
free grant   concession gratuite
    c. T-7, s. 23(d)
grant or extension of credit   ouverture ou extension d'un crédit
    c. C-46, s. 362(1)(c)(iv)
grant or gratuity   don en espèces ou en nature
    c. B-1, s. 250

grant/to
grant a clearance/to   donner congé
    c. A-11, s. 33(1)
grant authority/to   habiliter
    c. A-6, s. 2(2)

granted/to be
(citizenship)   obtenir par attribution
    c. C-29, s. 3(1)(c)

grantee
(of a right)   concessionnaire
    c. C-34, s. 39(5)(c)

granting
(of a lease)   cession
    c. N-14, s. 7(1)(g)
(of a lease or a licence)   octroi
    c. N-14, s. 7(1)(h)
(of a licence)   délivrance
    c. A-2, s. 21(4)
granting and revocation of authority   action et retrait des habilitations
    c. A-6, s. 3

grantor
(of a right)   concédant
    c. C-34, s. 39(5)(c)(i)
assignor, grantor, licensor or mortgagor   cédant, concesseur, octroyeur de licence ou débiteur sur gage
    c. C-42, s. 58(1)

gratuitous   gratuit
    c. C-26, Schedule I, Article 1(1)

gratuity   gratification
    c. B-9, s. 35(1)(d)
grant or gratuity   don en espèces ou en nature
    c. B-1, s. 250
payment, consideration, gratuity or benefit   paiement, contrepartie, gratification ou profit
    c. A-2, s. 12

Great Lakes Pilotage Authority, Ltd   Administration de pilotage des Grands Lacs, Limitée
    c. F-11, Schedule III, Part I

Great Seal   grand sceau
    c. A-9, s. 2(1)

greater
greater punishment   peine plus sévère
    c. C-46, s. 665(1)
    c. Y-1, s. 36(5)

grievance
remedy or redress for a private or public wrong or grievance   réparation ou redressement pour un tort ou grief privé ou public
    c. C-46, s. 315

grievious
grievious bodily harm   lésion corporelle grave
    c. C-46, s. 25(3)

gross indecency
    act of gross indecency   acte de grossière indécence
        c. C-46, s. 161
ground
    ground of appeal   motif d'appel
        c. C-46, s. 675(1)(a)(i)
    ground of mixed law and fact   question mixte de droit et de fait
        c. C-46, s. 759(2)
    on any ground of law, or fact or   sur toute question de droit, de fait
    mixed law and fact   ou mixte
        c. N-1, s. 25(3)
    on the ground of insanity   pour le motif d'aliénation mentale
        c. C-46, s. 16(3)
    on the primary ground   pour le motif principal
        c. C-46, s. 515(10)(a)
ground personnel
    (of aircraft)   personnel non navigant
        c. C-46, s. 7(9)
ground rent   rente foncière
        c. C-41, s. 11(1)(j)
        c. L-12, s. 61(1)(k)
        c. T-7, s. 18(2)   loyer
grounds
    frivolous or vexatious grounds   motifs futiles ou vexatoires
        c. C-44, s. 185(2)(b)(ii)
    grounds of appeal   motifs de l'appel
        c. C-46, s. 112(8)(b) in fine
    grounds of dissent   motifs de dissidence
        c. C-46, s. 677
    on special grounds   pour des motifs particuliers
        c. C-3, s. 21(4)
    on special grounds and by   pour des motifs particuliers et par
    special leave   autorisation spéciale
        c. S-26, s. 62(3)
    reasonable grounds   considérations raisonnables
        c. C-44, s. 32(2)
group
    (of air carriers)   groupe de transporteurs aériens
        c. A-2, s. 18(1)(g)
    related group (of corporations)   groupement lié
        c. F-11, s. 90(5)(d)
group home
    community, residential centre,   centre résidentiel local, foyer
    group home, child care   collectif, établissement d'aide à
    institution, or forest or   l'enfance, camp forestier ou camp
    wilderness camp   de pleine nature
        c. Y-1, s. 20(7)
group of persons   groupement
        c. A-1, s. 3
Groupe d'études de recherche   Groupe d'études de recherche et de
et de formation professionnelles   formation professionnelles
        c. C-18, Schedule
guarantee   garantie
        c. A-14, s. 6(2)
        c. C-44, s. 44(1)   caution
    (for the payment of a debt)   garantie
        c. F-11, s. 29(1)
    bank guarantee fund   fonds bancaire de garantie
        c. B-1, s. 174(2)(c)
    give a guarantee/to   garantir
        c. C-44, s. 189(1)(c)
    guarantee fund   fonds de garantie
        c. B-1, s. 111(6)

guarantee of rights and freedoms
    Constitutional Act, 1982,
      Schedule B, s. 1
garantir des droits et libertés

guarantee of the signature
    c. C-44, s. 77(2)
garantie de la signature

warranty or guarantee
    c. C-34, s. 52(1)(b)
garantie

guarantee the payment or repayment/to
    c. B-1, s. 173(1)(g)
garantir le paiement ou le remboursement

guaranteed
evidence of indebtedness of or guaranteed by the government
    c. C-41, s. 49(1)
titre de créance émis ou garanti par le gouvernement

guaranteed investment certificate
    c. B-1, s. 270(1)
certificat de placement garanti

guaranteed trust money
    c. B-1, s. 270(1)
fonds en fiducie garantie

guaranteed home extension loan
    c. N-11, s. 45(2)
prêt garanti à l'agrandissement

guarantor
    c. B-1, s. 136(6)
caution

    c. C-44, s. 69(4)
garant

surety or guarantor
    c. B-3, s. 85(3)
caution ou répondant

guaranty company
    c. B-3, s. 16(1)
compagnie de garantie

guard
warden, deputy warden, instructor, keeper, jailer, guard, or other officer or permanent employee of a prison (peace officer)
    c. C-46, s. 2
directeur, sous-directeur, instructeur, gardien, geôlier, garde ou tout autre fonctionnaire ou employé permanent d'une prison

guard-room
penitentiary, common jail, public or reformatory prison, lock-up, guard-room

    c. C-46, s. 2
pénitencier, prison commune, prison publique, maison de correction, poste de police ou corps de garde

guardian
    c. C-46, s. 150
tuteur

guardian, curator, committee, executor, administrator or other legal representative

    c. C-8, s. 2(1)
tuteur, curateur à la personne ou aux biens, conseil judiciaire, exécuteur testamentaire ou autre représentant légal

trustee, guardian, committee, curator, tutor, executor, administrator or representative of a deceased person
    c. B-1, s. 75(2)
    c. C-44, s. 48(2)
fiduciaire, tuteur, curateur, exécuteur ou administrateur de succession

tutor, curator, guardian or trustee
    c. L-12, s. 41(3)
tuteur, curateur ou fiduciaire

guardianship
    c. C-30, Schedule, Article II, 2(d)(ii)
tutelle

guess
  inducement to bet on, to guess
  or to foretell the result of a
  contest
    c. C-46, s. 202(1)(h)

incitation à parier sur le résultat
  d'une partie ou à conjecturer ce
  résultat ou à le prédire

guidance
  (of the board of arbitrator)
    c. B-6, s. 22(e)

gouverne

  guidance and assistance
    c. Y-1, s. 3(1)(c)

conseils et assistance

  marriage counselling or
  guidance facilities
    c. C-3, s. 9(1)(b)

services de consultation ou
  d'orientation matrimoniales

guided/to be
  (by recommendations of the
  Board)
    c. A-8, s. 10(2)

se fonder

guidelines
    c. C-32, s. 9

directives

guilty
  plead guilty or not guilty/to (to a
  charge)
    c. Y-1, s. 12(3)(b)

plaider coupable ou non coupable

guilty/to be
  (of an offence)
    c. C-44, s. 20(6)

commettre

h

habeas corpus
    c. C-46, s. 482(3)(c)

habeas corpus

habeas corpus ad subjiciendum
    c. C-46, s. 784(3)

habeas corpus ad subjiciendum

habitual
  habitual drunkenness
    c. C-46, s. 172(1)

ivrognerie habituelle

Halifax Port Corporation
    c. F-11, Schedule III, Part II

Société de port de Halifax

hand
  cash on hand
    c. L-12, s. 72(4)(a)

fonds en caisse

  under his hand and seal
    c. C-39, s. 70

sous ses seing et sceau

  under the hand and seal (of
  someone)
    c. A-8, s. 15(1)

sous les seing et sceau (de qqn)

handle/to
  (agricultural products)
    c. A-7, s. 14

manutentionner

handling
    c. T-19, s. 2

manutention

  handling, secure storage and
  display (of firearms)
    c. C-46, s. 116(b)

manipulation, entreposage et mise
  en montre

harass/to
  (a person)
    c. C-46, s. 372(3)

harasser

harbour/to
  (a person)
    c. C-46, s. 281

héberger

harbour or conceal a deserter or absentee/to
c. C-46, s. 54

Harbourfront Corporation
c. F-11, Schedule III, Part I

hard labour
c. C-39, s. 106
c. C-42, s. 42(1)

hardship
c. C-29, s. 5(4)
economic hardship
c. C-25, s. 17(4)(b)
economic hardship
c. C-3, s. 15(7)(c)
to result in injustice or undue hardship
c. S-22, s. 20(d)(iii)
undue hardship
c. P-20, s. 11(2)
undue hardship
c. C-8, s. 66(3)(c)
unnecessary hardship
c. C-46, s. 679(4)(a)

harm
bodily harm
c. C-46, s. 221

harmless
indemnified and saved harmless/to be
c. C-40, s. 73(1)

hatchery
c. L-9, s. 42(1)

hate propaganda
c. C-46, s. 319(7)

hatred
to expose a person to hatred, contempt or ridicule
c. C-46, s. 298

have authority/to
c. A-7, s. 2

have charge/to
(of a person)
c. A-11, s. 12(3)

have notice/to
c. B-1, s. 104(7)

hazard
(war)
c. C-31, s. 48

hazardous/to be
c. A-2, s. 8(1)(n)

head
c. A-1, s. 3
administrative head
c. 31 (4th Supp.), s. 62(2)
head of a branch of government

c. C-46, s. 121(1)(b)
head of a government
c. C-46, s. 2
head of State
c. C-46, s. 2

head of a family
parent, foster parent, guardian or head of a family
c. C-46, s. 215(1)(a)

receler ou cacher un déserteur ou un absent

Harbourfront Corporation

travaux forcés

détresse

perturbations économiques

difficulté économique

être une cause d'injustice ou de difficultés excessives

préjudice injustifié

préjudice abusif

épreuve non nécessaire

lésion corporelle

être indemnisé et dédommagé

couvoir

propagande haineuse

exposer quelqu'un à la haine, au mépris ou au ridicule

être habilité

avoir la charge

recevoir avis

risque

constituer des dangers

responsable d'institution fédérale

responsable administratif

chef d'une division du gouvernement

chef de gouvernement

chef d'Etat

père ou mère, parent nourricier, tuteur ou chef de famille

head office
  c. A-10, s. 4   siège social

headline
  harbour headline   ligne de démarcation
  c. C-9, s. 35

headquarter
  (of the Service)   administration centrale
  c. P-5, s. 11
  regional headquarter   administration régionale
  c. P-5, s. 15(4)

headquarters
  (of Board)   siège
  c. A-4, s. 3(4)

health care insurance plan   régime d'assurance-santé
  c. C-6, s. 2

health care practitioner   professionnel de la santé
  c. C-6, s. 2

hear/to
  (Commission has jurisdiction)   connaître de
  c. A-2, s. 14(3)
  hear and decide/to (an appeal)   entendre et décider
  c. C-36, s. 13
  hear and determine an   entendre et statuer sur une
  application/to   demande
  c. C-46, s. 754(1)
  hear and determine/to (actions)   instruire et juger
  c. C-42, s. 37
  hear and determine/to (by the   entendre et décider
  court)
  c. C-46, s. 754(2)
  hear and determine/to   connaître de
  (questions of law)
  c. A-7, s. 12
  hear, try and determine a   connaître d'une plainte
  complaint/to
  c. L-2, s. 160
  hear, try and determine/to (by a   instruire et juger
  magistrate)
  c. A-7, s. 23
  hear, try or determine/to (a   connaître de
  complaint)
  c. C-32, s. 40

hear and decide/to
  (an appeal)   entendre et décider
  c. C-36, s. 13

hearing   audition
  c. A-7, s. 8(4)(c)
  c. B-1, s. 32(4)
  c. N-1, s. 17(2)
  c. C-51, s. 27   débats
  (of an appeal)   audition
  c. C-8, s. 86(2)
  new hearing   nouvelle audition
  c. C-46, s. 679(7)
  place of hearing   lieu de l'audition
  c. C-46, s. 537(1)(a)
  public hearing   audience publique
  c. C-11, s. 5(d)
  representations made at a   observations faites au cours d'une
  hearing   audition
  c. C-46, s. 276(4)
  ripe for hearing (appeal)   prêt pour l'audition
  c. S-26, s. 71(1)

heat of passion
    in the heat of passion caused by
    sudden provocation
    (manslaughter)
        c. C-46, s. 232

    dans un accès de colère causé par
    une provocation soudaine

heir
    c. B-1, s. 56(1)

héritier

helper
    c. C-31, s. 16

auxiliaire

Her Majesty in right of Canada
    c. A-12, s. 3(2)

Sa Majesté du chef du Canada

Her Majesty's Forces
    c. A-2, s. 13

forces de Sa Majesté

**Her Majesty's Realms and
Territories**
    c. C-42, s. 2

royaumes et territoires de Sa
Majesté

high
    high judicial office
        c. C-42, s. 68(2)

haute charge judiciaire

    high seas
        c. A-2, s. 8(1)

haute mer

High Contracting Party
    c. C-26, s. 2(3)

haute partie contractante

High Court
    (of Ontario)
        c. J-1, s. 12(c)

Haute Cour

high water mark
    c. T-7, s. 13

laisse de haute mer

highway
    c. C-46, s. 2

voie publique ou grande route

    street, road or highway
        c. C-46, s. 249(1)(a)

rue, chemin ou grande route

hijacking

détournement de moyens de
transport

    c. A-1, s. 15(2)(c)
    (of aircraft)
        c. C-46, s. 76

détournement

hinder/to
    obstruct or hinder/to (an
    inspector)
        c. A-7, s. 17

entraver l'action

    obstruct or hinder/to (an
    inspector)
        c. C-24, s. 58(1)

gêner l'action d'un inspecteur

    obstruct or hinder/to (an
    investigation)
        c. A-2, s. 8(5)

entraver ou gêner

hire
    carriage for hire

transport moyennant un prix de
louage

        c. C-46, s. 159
    for hire or reward
        c. T-19, s. 3(1)

à titre onéreux

    for sale or hire
        c. C-42, s. 27(4)(d)

pour la vente ou la location

    hire or reward
        c. A-2, s. 12

rémunération

    use or hire (of a ship)
        c. F-7, s. 22(2)(i)

usage ou louage

hiring out
    hiring out of labour
        c. P-20, s. 10(2)(b)

louage de service

Historic Sites and Monuments Board of Canada

Commission des lieux et monuments historiques du Canada

    c. A-1, Schedule I

history
    criminal history
        c. Y-1, s. 41(1)
        antécédent criminel
    history and circumstances (of a prisoner)
        c. C-46, s. 761(2)
        antécédents et situation
    personal and family history and present environment
        c. Y-1, s. 2(2)
        antécédents et situation actuelle (de l'adolescent et de sa famille)

hold/to
    (meetings)
        c. A-4, s. 3(4)
        tenir
    hold an office or position/to
        c. B-2, s. 6(4)(c)
        occuper un poste
    hold office/to
        c. C-35, s. 2(2)
        occuper une charge

hold out/to
    represent or hold out to be/to
        c. N-1, s. 4(1)
        prétendre ou estimer être

holder
    (of a certificate)
        c. C-20, s. 10(4)
        titulaire
    (of a share)
        c. B-1, s. 9(3)
        titulaire
    (of a share)
        c. L-12, s. 36(2)
        porteur
    (of securities)
        c. B-1, s. 75(2)
        détenteur
    holder of a permit
        c. C-46, s. 89
        titulaire d'un permis
    holder of an office
        titulaire d'une charge ou d'un emploi
        c. B-4, s. 18(3)
    holder or endorsee (of a receipt)
        c. C-46, s. 390
        détenteur ou endossataire
    joint holder (of a share)
        c. C-44, s. 149(2)
        codétenteur

holder in due course
    (of a bill or note)
        c. B-4, s. 13(2)
        détenteur régulier

holding
    c. B-1, s. 216(2)(a)
    participation
    holding body corporate
        c. C-44, s. 2(4)
        société mère
    holding corporation
        c. B-1, s. 2(2)(h)
        personne morale mère

holdings
    (of securities)
        c. B-1, s. 190(1)
        portefeuille

holiday
    general holiday
        c. L-2, s. 166
        jours fériés

holidays
    legal holidays
        c. B-4, s. 2
        jours de fête légale

home owner
    c. N-11, s. 9(1)(b)(i)
    propriétaire-occupant

home ownership savings plan
    c. B-1, s. 173(1)(m)
    régime d'épargne-logement

home purchaser
    c. N-11, s. 9(1)(b)(ii)

acquéreur-occupant

homicide
    c. C-46, s. 222(1)

homicide

honestly
    c. B-1, s. 54(1)(a)

avec intégrité

    honestly and in good faith with
    a view to the best interests of
    the holders
    c. C-44, s. 91(a)

avec intégrité et de bonne foi, au mieux des intérêts des détenteurs

honorarium
    c. C-16, s. 4(2)

rétribution

    honorarium
    c. P-2, s. 10(3)

honoraires

honorary
    honorary officer
    c. C-2, s. 9

membre honoraire

honour
    acceptor for honour (of a bill)
    c. B-4, s. 151(1)

intervenant

    notarial act of honour
    c. B-4, s. 153(1)

acte notarié d'intervention

    payer for honour (of a bill)
    c. B-4, s. 152(4)

intervenant

    payment for honour
    c. B-4, s. 153(1)

paiement par intervention

honour/to
    (a bill of exchange)
    c. C-46, s. 362(5)

honorer

    (a security)
    c. B-1, s. 92(8)

honorer (une valeur mobilière)

hospital service
    c. C-6, s. 2

services hospitaliers

hostage taking
    kidnapping, hostage taking and
    abduction
    c. C-46, s. 279

enlèvement, prise d'otage et rapt

hostel
    housing accomodation of the
    hostel or dormitory type
    c. N-11, s. 9(3)(a)(ii)

facilités de logement de type foyer ou pension

hostile
    subversive or hostile activities
    c. A-1, s. 15(2)

activités hostiles ou subversives

house
    c. N-11, s. 2

maison

house of assignation
    inveigle or entice a person to a
    house of assignation/to
    c. C-46, s. 212(1)(b)

attirer ou entraîner une personne vers une maison de rendez-vous

housing
    cooperative housing project
    c. N-11, s. 2

ensemble d'habitation coopératif

    family housing unit
    c. N-11, s. 2

logement familial

    housing project
    c. N-11, s. 2

ensemble d'habitation

    limited-dividend housing
    company
    c. N-11, s. 2

société immobilière à dividendes limités

    low-rental housing project

ensemble d'habitation HLM ou HLM

    c. N-11, s. 2

public housing agency — organisme de logement public
c. N-11, s. 78
public housing project — ensemble d'habitation public
c. N-11, s. 78
student housing project — ensemble d'habitation destiné à des
étudiants
c. N-11, s. 87

humanitarian
absence with escort for — sortie sous surveillance pour des
humanitarian and rehabilitative — raisons humanitaires ou en vue de
reasons — la réadaptation
c. C-46, s. 747(2)

hurt
infliction of hurt or mischief — fait d'infliger un mal ou un
dommage
c. C-46, s. 37(2)

hydrocarbons — hydrocarbures
c. B-1, s. 2(1)

hypothec
dispose of a mortgage, an — céder une hypothèque, un privilège,
hypothec, a lien, a charge/to — une sûreté
c. C-25, s. 23(1)(d)
mortgage and hypothec — hypothèque
c. B-1, s. 2(1)

hypothecate/to — grever d'une hypothèque
c. B-1, s. 185(2)
(a share) — nantir (une action)
c. A-14, s. 4(1)(b)
hypothecate or mortgage/to — grever par hypothèque
c. B-1, s. 173(1)(d)(ii)

hypothecation
pledge or hypothecation — nantissement avec ou sans
dépossession de bien
c. B-2, s. 18(h)

i

identifiable group
(genocide) — groupe identifiable
c. C-46, s. 318(4)
identification
(of aircraft) — identification
c. A-2, s. 8(1)(b)
ignorance
ignorance of the law — ignorance de la loi
c. C-46, s. 19
ill-will
in good faith and without ill-will — de bonne foi et sans malveillance
c. C-46, s. 306(c)
produce feelings of hostility or — produire des sentiments d'hostilité
ill-will — ou de malveillance
c. C-46, s. 60(d)
illegal
illegal behaviour — conduite illicite
c. Y-1, s. 3(1)(b)
illegality — acte illégal
c. C-44, s. 60(1)
fraud or illegality — fraude ou acte illégal
c. B-1, s. 87(1)

illegitimate
   illegitimate child   enfant illégitime
     c. C-46, s. 214
   illegitimate person   personne illégitime
     c. C-26, Schedule II
illness
   physical or mental illness or   maladie ou dérèglement d'ordre
   disorder, psychological disorder,   physique ou mental, dérèglement
   emotional disturbance, learning   d'ordre psychologique, troubles
   disability or mental retardation   émotionnels, troubles
                                   d'apprentissage ou déficience
                                   mentale

     c. Y-1, s. 13(1)(e)
imbecility
   mental defectiveness not   déficience mentale n'allant pas
   amounting to imbecility   jusqu'à l'imbécillité
     c. C-46, s. 2
immediate
   immediate family   proche parent
     c. L-2, s. 210(3)(a)
   immediate, contingent or   actuel, éventuel ou autre
   otherwise (interest)
     c. C-34, s. 2
immediately
   mediately or immediately, in   directement ou par intermédiaire,
   possession, or expectancy   pour jouissance immédiate ou ulté
                                     rieure
     c. C-29, s. 38(e)
immediately preceding
   immediately preceding financial   exercice précédent
   year
     c. C-44, s. 155(1)(a)(ii)
Immigration Appeal Board   Commission d'appel de
                                     l'immigration

     c. A-1, Schedule I
immoral
   immoral, indecent or obscene   représentation, spectacle ou
   performance, entertainment or   divertissement immoral, indécent
   representation   ou obscène
     c. C-46, s. 167(2)
immorality
   sexual immorality   immoralité sexuelle
     c. C-46, s. 172(1)
immovable property   immeuble
     c. C-30, Schedule Article III,
      2
immune/to be
   (liability)   être exempté (d'une obligation)
     c. B-7, Schedule I, Article IX,
     Section 9(a)
   (taxation)   être exonéré (d'impôt)
     c. B-7, Schedule I, Article IX,
     Section 9(a)
immunities
   powers, privileges and   droits et immunités
   immunities
     c. B-1, s. 7(1)
immunity   exonération
     c. C-27, Schedule, Article II
   diplomatic immunity   immunité diplomatique
     c. C-29, s. 3(2)(c)
impair
   impair the efficiency or impede   diminuer l'efficacité ou gêner le
   the working (of an aircraft)   fonctionnement
     c. C-46, s. 52(2)(a)

impair/to
  (the right to act)
    c. C-13, s. 9
  impair the paid-in capital/to
    c. B-1, s. 130(1)
  impair, diminish or lighten
  (coin)/to
    c. C-46, s. 455(a)

entraver (le fonctionnement)

entamer le capital versé

affaiblir, diminuer ou alléger

impaired
  ability to operate a vehicle
  impaired by alcohol or a drug
    c. C-46, s. 253(a)

capacité de conduire affaiblie par
l'effet de l'alcool ou une drogue

impairment
  impairment of capital
    c. C-40, s. 76(1)

altération du capital

impartially
  faithfully, impartially and to the
  best of my abilities
    c. C-23, Schedule

avec fidélité, impartialité et dans
toute la mesure de mes moyens

impede
  impair the efficiency or impede
  the working (of an aircraft)
    c. C-46, s. 52(2)(a)

diminuer l'efficacité ou gêner le
fonctionnement

impede/to
  (an inquiry)
    c. C-34, s. 64(1)

entraver

implement/to
    c. A-17, s. 7(2)(e)
    c. B-9, s. 5
  (a judgment)
    c. C-34, s. 40(a)
  implement a program/to
    c. A-13, s. 4(b)

mettre en oeuvre

exécuter

mettre en oeuvre un programme

implementation
  (of a judgment)
    c. C-34, s. 40(b)
  (of an Act)
    c. C-46, s. 534(4)
  (of water policies and programs)
    c. C-11, s. 4(c)
  period for implementation (of
  provisions of collective
  agreement)
    c. P-35, s. 57(1)(b)

exécution

mise en oeuvre

mise en oeuvre

délai de mise en application

implements
  agricultural implements
    c. B-1, s. 2(1)
  agricultural implements
    c. B-1, s. 2(1)
  forestry implements
    c. B-1, s. 2(1)

instruments agricoles

matériel agricole immobilier

matériel sylvicole mobilier

implied
  (provision)
    c. C-40, s. 92(1)(a)
  actual, implied or apparent
  (authority)
    c. B-1, s. 75(2)
  express, implied or constructive
  trust
    c. L-12, s. 89(1)
  implied contract
    c. C-8, s. 2(1)

tacite

autorisation réelle, implicite ou
apparente

fiducie explicite, implicite ou
judiciaire

contrat tacite

Import Control List
    c. C-15, s. 21
impose/to
    (charges)
        c. A-2, s. 5
    fix, impose and collect/to (levies
    or charges)
        c. A-6, s. 2(2)(a)
impost
    tax, impost, duty or toll

        c. F-11, s. 23(1)
impound/to
    (a security)
        c. B-1, s. 99(3)
        c. C-44, s. 72(3)
impractical
    it would be impractical
        c. C-46, s. 487.1(1)
impress/to
    affix or impress/to (an official
    seal onto a document)
        c. C-42, s. 58(1)
impression
    (of an official seal)
        c. C-42, s. 51
imprison/to
    confine, imprison or forcibly
    seize another person/to
        c. C-46, s. 279(2)
    imprison or restrain/to
        c. C-46, s. 46(1)(a)
imprisonment
    c. A-2, s. 7(13)
    undergo imprisonment/to
        c. B-3, s. 160
improper
    improper conduct
        c. C-44, s. 231(2)
improperly
    c. B-1, s. 85(2)
improvement
    economic lifetime of the
    improvement
        c. L-12, s. 114(2)
impugn/to
    c. B-1, s. 95(1)(b)
impugning
    precluded from impugning the
    effectiveness/to be (of an
    endorsement)
        c. C-44, s. 61(1)
impulse
    sexual impulse
        c. C-46, s. 753(b)
in accordance with
    (an Act)
        c. A-10, s. 10(2)
    (regulations)
        c. A-7, s. 4
    in accordance with generally
    accepted actuarial practices and
    principles
        c. C-46, s. 347(2)

liste des marchandises
    d'importation contrôlée

imposer

instituer et percevoir

impôts, taxes, droits ou autres
    contributions

mettre sous séquestre

il serait peu commode

apposer

empreinte

séquestrer, emprisonner ou saisir
    de force une autre personne

emprisonner ou détenir

emprisonnement

subir un emprisonnement

conduite répréhensible

irrégulièrement

durée économique des améliorations

contester

être privé du droit de contester la
    validité

impulsion sexuelle

en conformité avec

selon

conformément aux règles et
    pratiques actuarielles
    généralement admises

in bearer form
    (security)   au porteur
        c. C-44, s. 48(2)
in blank
    (endorsement)   en blanc
        c. B-1, s. 75(2)
    endorsed in blank (security)   endossé en blanc
        c. C-44, s. 48(2)
in camera   à huis clos
        c. C-12, s. 34(1)(b)
        c. C-44, s. 229(5)
    hearing in camera   audience à huis clos
        c. A-1, s. 47(1)
in contravention of   en contravention avec
        c. C-24, s. 66(1)
    (an Act)   en violation de
        c. A-11, s. 41
in force   en vigueur
        c. B-1, s. 173(1)(d)
in forma pauperis
    application for leave to appeal in   demande d'autorisation d'appel avec
    forma pauperis   dispense des frais
        c. S-26, s. 59(4)
in kind   en nature
        c. B-1, s. 287(7)(c)
    to compensate in kind or by way   indemniser soit en nature soit en
    of personal services   services
        c. Y-1, s. 20(1)(f)
in lieu   en remplacement
        c. B-1, s. 177(12)
in lieu of   à la place de
        c. C-24, s. 62(2)
    (any other sentence)   à l'exclusion(de toute autre peine)
        c. N-1, s. 23
    resolution in lieu of meeting   résolution tenant lieu d'assemblée
        c. C-44, s. 119(1)
in order form
    (a security)   à ordre
        c. C-44, s. 48(2)
in personam
    action in personam   action personnelle
        c. F-7, s. 43(4)
    jurisdiction in personam   compétence en matière personnelle
        c. F-7, s. 43(1)
in possession
    (person)   en possession
        c. C-44, s. 48(2)
in private   à huis clos
        c. C-23, s. 27
        c. C-23, s. 48(1)   en secret
    act committed in private   acte commis dans l'intimité
        c. C-46, s. 161
    conduct in private/to   mener secrètement
    (investigation)
        c. A-1, s. 35(1)
in rem
    action in rem   action réelle
        c. F-7, s. 43(7)
    jurisdiction in rem   compétence en matière réelle
        c. F-7, s. 43(2)
    statutory right in rem   droit réel créé par une loi
        c. T-19, s. 16(4)(b)

in the alternative
    c. C-46, s. 590(1)(a)
                    sous forme d'alternative
in the name of
    in the name of or on behalf of   au nom de ou pour le compte de
    c. C-44, s. 14(1)
in the right of
    (to hold)   du chef de
    c. B-1, s. 110(7)
in transit
    (cheque or other item)   en transit
    c. B-1, Schedule X, Section 6
in trust   en fiducie
    c. A-16, s. 11(1)
    hold in trust/to   détenir en trust
    c. C-19, s. 4(2)
in whole or in part
    to publish in whole or in part   publier intégralement ou en partie
    c. C-44, s. 230(1)(j)
in-patient
    in-patient or out-patient   malade hospitalisé ou externe
    c. C-6, s. 2
in-store
    in-store, door-to-door or   opération de vente en magasin, par
    telephone selling   démarchage ou par téléphone
    c. C-34, s. 52(2)(d)
inability   inaptitude
    c. B-1, s. 245(2)
inanimate
    animate or inanimate (thing)   animé ou inanimé
    c. C-46, s. 322(1)
inappropriate   contre-indiqué
    c. Y-1, s. 3(2)
incapable   incapable
    c. C-8, s. 89(1)(d)
incapacitated
    become permanently   être frappé d'incapacité permanente
    incapacitated/to
    c. B-2, s. 10(5)
incapacity   empêchement
    c. A-13, s. 14
incendiary grenade
    incendiary grenade, fire bomb, grenade incendiaire, bombe
    molotov cocktail   incendiaire, cocktail molotov
    c. C-46, s. 2
incentive/to be an   encourager
    c. A-8, s. 13(1)(b)
incest   inceste
    c. C-46, s. 155(1)
inchoate/to be
    (a note)   être incomplet
    c. B-4, s. 178
incident/to be
    (to property)   se rattacher
    c. B-3, s. 2
incidental
    ancillary or incidental power   pouvoir auxiliaire ou accessoire
    c. C-40, s. 16(a)
    disclosure necessarily incidental divulgation nécessairement
                          accessoire
    c. C-46, s. 193(2)(d)
    incidental expenditures   faux frais
    c. J-1, s. 27(1)

proceeding incidental
c. C-46, s. 683(3) — procédure accessoire

incitement
incitement to perjury
c. C-46, s. 137 — incitation au parjure

include/to
(a provision in an agreement)
c. A-5, s. 4(1) — renfermer

included offence
c. C-46, s. 508(1)(b) — infraction incluse
c. C-46, s. 676(2) — infraction comprise

incollectable
incollectable taxes
c. N-14, s. 7(2) — impôts irrécouvrables

income
statement of income
c. L-12, s. 53(2) — état des résultats

incompetent
incompetent or missing person
c. C-44, s. 51(2)(b) — incapable ou absent
incompetent person
c. B-1, s. 78(2)(b) — incapable
incompetent to contract
marriage
c. C-46, s. 290(3) — inhabile à contracter mariage

inconsistency
(laws)
c. C-30, s. 3 — incompatibilité

inconsistent
(with the Act)
c. C-19, s. 16(b) — incompatible

incorporate/to
c. B-3, s. 2 — constituer en personne morale
incorporate a bank/to
c. B-1, s. 7(2) — constituer une banque
incorporate, form or organize a
corporation/to
c. B-1, s. 109(1)(b) — constituer, former ou établir une personne morale

incorporated
company incorporated
c. A-16, s. 2 — personne morale constituée
entry or record of an
incorporated society

c. Y-1, s. 57(2)(b) — inscription ou mention consignée par un organisme doté de la personnalité morale
incorporated company

c. C-41, s. 5(1) — compagnie constituée en personne morale
incorporated society

c. C-46, s. 658 — société constituée en personne morale

incorporation
(of a bank)
c. B-1, s. 25(2) — constitution
articles of incorporation,
amendment, amalgamation,
continuance, reorganization,
dissolution or revival

c. C-44, s. 2(1) — clauses réglementant la constitution ainsi que toute modification, fusion, prorogation, réorganisation, dissolution, reconstitution ou tout arrangement
certificate of incorporation,
continuation, amendment or
amalgamation
c. C-40, s. 5 — certificat de constitution en personne morale, de continuation, de modification ou de fusion

c. C-44, s. 2(1)

instrument of incorporation	acte constitutif
c. B-1, s. 2(1)	
Act of incorporation, articles, letters patent, or memorandum or articles of association	acte constitutif, statuts, lettres patentes ou mémoire de conventions
c. C-44, s. 187(2)	

incorporator   fondateur
   c. C-44, s. 2(1)

incorporeal
   property of any kind, whether real or personal or corporeal or incorporeal   biens de toute nature, meubles ou immeubles, corporels ou incorporels
     c. F-7, s. 2

incorrectness   défaut
   c. C-44, s. 58(1)(b)

increase/to
   increase (the rights)/to   accroître (les droits)
     c. C-44, s. 176(1)(d)

incumbency   mandat
   c. B-1, s. 104(1)(b)
   evidence of appointment or incumbency   preuve de la nomination ou du mandat
     c. B-1, s. 104(4)
     c. C-44, s. 77(4)

incumbent
   incumbent auditor   vérificateur en fonctions
     c. C-44, s. 162(3)

incumbrancer   créancier hypothécaire
   c. B-3, s. 91(3)(b)

incur/to
   (a debt)   contracter
     c. C-9, s. 45(1)
   (expenses)   entraîner
     c. A-7, s. 7(9)(b)
   (expenses)   encourir
     c. A-5, s. 10
   acquire or incur a right or obligation/to   assumer un droit ou une obligation
     c. A-16, s. 3(2)
   incur liability/to   engager sa responsabilité
     c. C-44, s. 110(4)

indebted/to be   être endetté
   c. B-3, s. 165(1)

indebtedness   dette
   c. B-1, s. 2(1)
   c. B-7, Schedule I(j), 7
   c. B-1, s. 277(2)   créance
   c. B-7, Schedule I(j), 7
   evidence of indebtedness   titre de créance
     c. B-1, s. 175(3)
     c. C-7, s. 21(2)
     c. L-12, s. 61(1)(b)

indecent
   immoral, indecent or obscene performance, entertainment or representation   représentation, spectacle ou divertissement immoral, indécent ou obscène
     c. C-46, s. 167(2)
   indecent show   spectable indécent
     c. C-46, s. 163(2)(b)
   indecent telephone call   propos indécents au téléphone
     c. C-46, s. 372(2)

indemnified
    indemnified and saved   être indemnisé et dédommagé
    harmless/to be
        c. C-40, s. 73(1)
indemnify/to
    (against liability)   mettre à couvert
        c. B-1, s. 270(4)(a)
    indemnify against all costs,   indemniser des frais et dépenses
    charges and expenses/to
        c. C-44, s. 124(1)
    indemnify of all costs/to (in   indemniser de tous les frais
    court)
        c. F-11, s. 119(2)
indemnity
    right of indemnity   droit à une indemnité
        c. A-12, s. 7(3)
indenture
    deed or indenture   acte
        c. B-1, s. 133(1)
    trust indenture   acte de fiducie
        c. B-1, s. 133(1)
        c. C-44, s. 39(12)
independently
    vote independently/to   voter séparément
        c. B-3, s. 54(2)
index
    (of the register)   index
        c. C-42, s. 54(4)
    (price)   indice
        c. A-8, s. 10(1)(a)
    consolidated index (of   répertoire général
    regulations)
        c. S-22, s. 14(1)
Index Number of Farm Prices of   indice des prix à la ferme des
Agricultural Products for   produits agricoles pour le Canada
Canada
        c. B-1, s. 178(7)(b)(ii)
indictable
    indictable offence   acte criminel
        c. C-46, s. 47(1)
indictment   mise en accusation
    c. A-11, s. 47(1)(b)
    c. C-46, s. 673   acte d'accusation
    allege in the indictment/to   alléguer dans l'acte d'accusation
        c. C-46, s. 356(2)
    bill of indictment   projet d'acte d'accusation
        c. C-46, s. 576(2)
    offence punishable by   infraction punissable sur acte
    indictment or on summary   d'accusation ou déclaration de
    conviction   culpabilité par procédure
                      sommaire
        c. C-46, s. 12
    on conviction or indictment   par mise en accusation
        c. C-15, s. 20(1)(b)
    separate indictment   acte d'accusation distinct
        c. C-46, s. 591(5)
indifference
    substantial degree of   indifférence marquée
    indifference (by offender)
        c. C-46, s. 753(a)(ii)
indifferent
    (juror)   impartial
        c. C-46, s. 638(1)(b)

individual   particulier
    c. A-13, s. 4(b)
    c. C-20, s. 2(1)
    c. C-44, s. 2(1)
    c. 31 (4th Supp.), s. 64(1)
    c. C-23, s. 2   individu
    (Income Tax Act)   personne physique
    c. C-53, s. 2(1)

inducement   incitation
    c. B-1, s. 313(1)(a)
    inducement to bet on, to guess   incitation à parier sur le résultat
    or to foretell the result of a   d'une partie ou à conjecturer ce
    contest   résultat ou à le prédire
    c. C-46, s. 202(1)(h)

Industrial Composite   indice composite des activités
     économiques
    c. P-1, s. 55(3)(b)(i)

industrial farm   ferme industrielle
    c. P-20, s. 12(1)

industrial peace
    secure industrial peace/to   favoriser la bonne entente dans le
     monde du travail
    c. L-2, s. 107

industrial school
    reformatory school or industrial   école de réforme ou école
    school   industrielle
    c. C-46, s. 618(5)

ineffective   sans effet
    c. B-1, s. 84
    c. C-44, s. 49(11)
    to render data meaningless,   dépouiller des données de leur sens,
    useless or ineffective   les rendre inutiles ou inopérantes
    c. C-46, s. 430(1.1)(b)

ineffective/to be
    (defect)   être inopposable
    c. C-44, s. 53(d)

ineffectiveness
    (of endorsement)   invalidité
    c. B-1, s. 95(1)

infancy
    infancy or minority   minorité
    c. B-1, s. 92(1)(d)
    c. C-44, s. 65(1)(d)

infant   mineur
    c. B-1, s. 78(2)(b)
    c. C-44, s. 51(2)b)
    infant or minor   mineur
    c. F-11, s. 60(1)(b)(ii)

infanticide
    murder, manslaughter or   meurtre, homicide involontaire
    infanticide   coupable ou infanticide
    c. C-46, s. 222(4)

infer/to
    (evidence)   déduire
    c. C-46, s. 658(2)
    (from facts)   conclure
    c. C-46, s. 715(1)

inference
    draw an inference adverse/to (to   tirer une conclusion défavorable
    the accused)
    c. C-46, s. 475(2)
    draw inference/to   déterminer par déduction
    c. Y-1, s. 58(1)

under circumstances that give rise to a reasonable inference

    c. C-46, s. 352

dans des circonstances qui permettent raisonnablement de conclure

unfavourable inference
    c. C-34, s. 61(10)

conclusion défavorable

infliction

infliction of hurt or mischief

    c. C-46, s. 37(2)

fait d'infliger un mal ou un dommage

influence

influence on the mind
    c. C-46, s. 228(a)

influence sur l'esprit

undue influence
    c. C-39, s. 49

influence indue

influence or affect/to

(the result)
    c. C-46, s. 121(1)(a)(ii)

influencer ou affecter

influenced

foreign influenced activities
    c. C-23, s. 2

activités influencées par l'étranger

informal

informal equity
    c. C-20, s. 2(1)

participation non ordinaire

informality
    c. S-26, s. 84

vice de forme

by reason of any irregularity, informality or insufficiency (of a conviction)
    c. C-46, s. 777(1)

pour cause d'irrégularité, vice de forme ou insuffisance

informally

as informally and expeditiously as
    c. C-51, s. 28

avec aussi peu de formalisme et autant de célérité

informant
    c. C-46, s. 507(1)

dénonciateur

    c. L-2, s. 146(4)(a)

informateur
dénonciation

information
    c. A-11, s. 47(3)

false information
    c. A-2, s. 18(1)(o)(ii)

faux renseignements

false or misleading information or misrepresentation
    c. C-51, s. 42

renseignements faux ou fallacieux ou fausse déclaration

information and intelligence
    c. C-23, s. 12

informations et renseignements

information, presentment and count (indictment)

    c. C-46, s. 2

dénonciation, déclaration d'un acte d'accusation émise par le grand jury.et chef d'accusation

lay an information/to
    c. C-46, s. 504

faire une dénonciation

on the information and belief

    c. C-46, s. 196(4)

sur la foi de renseignments tenus pour véridiques

provincial information bank
    c. 4 (2nd Supp.), s. 2

fichier provincial

information bank director
    c. 4 (2nd Supp.), s. 2

directeur de fichier

information circular

(business corporations)
    c. C-44, s. 115(3)(g)

circulaire d'information

Information Commissioner	Commissaire à l'information
c. A-1, s. 3	
infringe/to	
(the rules)	déroger à
c. C-26, Schedule I, Article 32	
infringement	
(of copyright)	violation
c. C-42, s. 4(2)	
infringer	
(of a copyright)	contrefacteur
c. C-42, s. 35(1)	
infringing	
(copyright)	contrefaçon
c. C-42, s. 2	
inheritance	
estate, legacy, succession or inheritance duties or taxes	droits ou impôts sur les successions, legs ou héritages
c. C-17, s. 50(o)	
inhibited/to be	
inhibited by normal standards of behavioural restraint/to be	être inhibé par les normes ordinaires de restriction du comportement
c. C-46, s. 753(a)(iii)	
initial	
initial distribution (of shares)	première émission
c. B-1, s. 148(2)	
initial/to	
(a cheque)	parapher
c. B-4, s. 168(7)	
(an entry)	parapher
c. C-24, s. 24(2)	
initial payment	paiement initial
c. A-5, s. 2	
c. C-48, s. 13(1)	
initiate/to	
(a program)	entreprendre
c. C-11, s. 11(2)(c)	
(criminal proceedings)	intenter
c. B-3, s. 21	
initiate a complaint/to	prendre l'initiative d'une plainte
c. A-1, s. 30(3)	
initiate, recommend or undertake/to (programs)	lancer, recommander ou prendre en main
c. C-37, s. 5(1)(a)	
initiative	
on his own initiative	de sa propre initiative
c. Y-1, s. 28(3)	
injunction	injonction
c. A-7, s. 12	
c. B-1, s. 205(2)(b)	
injure/to	
(a person)	léser
c. C-46, s. 363	
injure any animal or bird/to	estropier un animal ou un oiseau
c. C-46, s. 373(1)(c)	
injure public moral/to	offenser la morale publique
c. C-46, s. 166(1)(a)	
injure the reputation/to (defamatory libel)	nuire à la réputation
c. C-46, s. 298(1)	
injurious	
injurious affection	trouble de jouissance
c. F-7, s. 17(2)(c)	

injurious to health 　　c. F-27, s. 2"unsanitary 　　conditions"	nuisible à la santé
injurious/to be 　　c. A-1, s. 14	porter préjudice
c. A-1, s. 16(1)(c)	nuire
injuriously 　　property injuriously affected 　　c. A-2, s. 8(10)	bien lésé
injury 　　bodily injury 　　c. C-26, Schedule I, Article 　　17	lésion corporelle
employment injury 　　c. L-2, s. 122	dommage professionnel
personal injury 　　c. B-8, s. 18	blessures corporelles
personal injury 　　c. Y-1, s. 20(1)(c)	lésion corporelle
physical injury 　　c. C-46, s. 180(1)(b)	lésion physique
serious personal injury offence 　　c. C-46, s. 752	sévices graves à la personne
injustice 　　to result in injustice or undue 　　hardship 　　c. S-22, s. 20(d)(iii)	être une cause d'injustice ou de difficultés excessives
inland waters 　　c. A-12, s. 3(2)	eaux internes
c. A-12, s. 23(1)	eaux intérieures
inlet 　　(of the sea) 　　c. T-7, s. 13(a)	échancrure
inmate 　　c. N-1, s. 26(2)	détenu
paroled inmate 　　c. N-1, s. 26(2) 　　c. P-2, s. 2	libéré conditionnel
to be an inmate in a 　　penitentiary, jail, reformatory or 　　prison 　　c. C-29, s. 21(c)	être détenu dans un pénitentier, une prison ou une maison de correction
to be an inmate or frequenter (of 　　a common bawdy-house) 　　c. C-46, s. 212(1)(e)	habiter ou fréquenter
innocent 　　innocent of any complicity/to be 　　c. N-1, s. 17(4)(a)	ne pas être coupable de complicité
innocent purchaser 　　c. C-46, s. 726(1)	acheteur de bonne foi
innuendo 　　by innuendo (libel) 　　c. C-46, s. 584(2)	par insinuation
inoperative/to be 　　(a cancellation) 　　c. B-4, s. 143	être sans effet
inquiry 　　c. A-17, s. 15(3)	enquête
board of inquiry 　　c. A-2, s. 10(1)	commission d'enquête
duty of inquiry 　　c. C-44, s. 78(2)	obligation de s'informer

investigation or inquiry   enquête
  c. P-2, s. 26
make an inquiry or   mener une enquête
investigation/to
  c. C-24, s. 29(1)
inquisition
  verdict on coroner's inquisition   verdict sur enquête de coroner
    c. C-46, s. 529(1)
insane   aliéné
    c. C-46, s. 614(1)
insanity   maladie mentale
    c. C-8, s. 89(1)(d)
    c. C-46, s. 16(3)   aliénation mentale
  on account of insanity   pour cause d'aliénation mentale
    c. C-46, s. 614(1)
    c. Y-1, s. 13(1)(b)
  on the ground of insanity   pour le motif d'aliénation mentale
    c. C-46, s. 16(3)
inscription
  inscription or registration (of   inscription
securities)
    c. F-11, s. 60(3)
insider   initié
    c. B-1, s. 168(1)
    c. C-44, s. 126(1)
  insider report   rapport d'initié
    c. C-44, s. 127(5)
  insider trading   transaction d'initiés
    c. C-40, s. 79(1)
insinuation
  expressed directly or by   exprimé directement ou par
insinuation or irony (defamatory   insinuation ou ironie
libel)
    c. C-46, s. 298(2)
insolvency   insolvabilité
    c. A-10, s. 22
    c. B-1, s. 132(2)(b)
inspect/to
  (agricultural product)   examiner
    c. A-7, s. 16(1)(b)
  (books and accounts)   inspecter
    c. A-5, s. 7
  (documents)   examiner
    c. B-9, s. 10(7)
  observe and inspect/to (persons)   surveiller et inspecter
    c. A-2, s. 7(9)
inspection
  (of aircraft)   inspection
    c. A-2, s. 8(1)(b)
  (of books)   consultation
    c. C-40, s. 102(2)
  for inspection (certificate)   pour fins d'examen
    c. C-46, s. 102(2)
  keep open for inspection/to   être accessible à l'inspection
(books)
    c. C-41, s. 35(2)
  open to inspection (a register)   accessible au public
    c. C-42, s. 54(5)
  production and inspection of   production et examen des
documents   documents
    c. A-7, s. 8(4)
inspection or investigation
  (of an estate)   investigation ou enquête
    c. B-3, s. 5(3)(e)

Inspector General   inspecteur général
   c. C-23, s. 2
Inspector General of Bank   Inspecteur général des banques
   c. B-1, s. 2(1)
instalment
   (of a contribution)   versement
      c. C-8, s. 34(2)
   reserve an instalment/to   retenir un versement
      c. C-17, s. 9(2)
instalments
   payments by instalments   paiements échelonnés
      c. C-17, s. 10
instance
   in the first instance   d'abord
      c. C-25, s. 11(3)
institute/to
   (an action)   engager
      c. C-9, s. 28(2)
   (legal proceedings)   intenter
      c. A-7, s. 18(2)
   (proceedings)   engager
      c. C-38, s. 15(4)(ii)
   (security measures)   prendre
      c. A-2, s. 7(9)
   institute and conduct/to (a   entamer et diriger
   prosecution)
      c. C-34, s. 73(1)
institution   institution
      c. A-13, s. 3(b)
      c. B-7, Schedule I, Article   établissement
        XIII, Section 2
      c. C-42, s. 27(2)(h)
      c. C-51, s. 2
      c. A-1, s. 13(1)(a)   organisme
      c. C-32, s. 4(3)
   (of judicial proceedings)   introduction
      c. C-19, s. 17(1)(c)
   educational institution   établissement d'enseignement
      c. C-28, Schedule 2
   financial institution   institution financière
      c. B-1, s. 254
      c. C-52, s. 17(2)(b)
   financial institution   établissement financier
      c. F-11, s. 17(2)(d)
   government institution   institution fédérale
      c. A-1, s. 3
   government institution   administration fédérale
      c. A-1, s. 2(1)
   institution and enforcement (of   établissement et application
   laws, rules)
      c. A-2, s. 8(1)(i)
   institution of higher learning   institution de haut savoir
      c. C-2, s. 15(2)(b)
   institution or body (of the   institution ou organisme
   government)
      c. C-23, s. 2
instruct/to
   instruct the jury/to   informer le jury
      c. C-46, s. 274
   right to retain and instruct   droit d'obtenir les services d'un
   counsel   avocat
      c. Y-1, s. 11(1)

instructed
    counsel instructed under an Act   avocat commis en exécution d'une loi
        c. C-34, s. 26(2)

instructor
    warden, deputy warden, instructor, keeper, jailer, guard, or other officer or permanent employee of a prison (peace officer)   directeur, sous-directeur, instrumenteur, gardien, geôlier, garde ou tout autre fonctionnaire ou employé permanent d'une prison (agent de la paix)
        c. C-46, s. 2

instrument   titre
        c. B-1, s. 2(1)
        c. C-44, s. 48(2)a)
        c. B-1, s. 2(1)(d)   effet
    (share)   titre
        c. C-44, s. 187(10)
    approved instrument   alcootest approuvé
        c. C-46, s. 254(1)
    constating instrument   acte constitutif
        c. C-21, s. 2(1)
    controlling instrument   acte qui habilite
        c. C-44, s. 65(10)
    duplicate instrument, memorial, certificate or document in respect to registration of titles   double de tout instrument, mémoire, certificat concernant l'enregistrement de titres
        c. C-46, s. 2
    instrument creating the trust   acte créant la fiducie
        c. L-12, s. 120(2)
    instrument of incorporation   acte constitutif
        c. L-12, s. 2
    instrument of indebtedness   titre de créance
        c. B-1, s. 190(9)
    instrument or writing   effet ou écrit
        c. B-4, s. 4
    instrument originating the proceedings   acte introductif d'instance
        c. C-50, s. 23(3)
    judicial or official instrument   acte judiciaire ou officiel
        c. L-12, s. 42(1)a)(iii)
    negotiable instrument   effet de commerce
        c. B-1, s. 17
    negotiable instrument   effet négociable
        c. C-44, s. 48(3)
    testamentary instrument   acte testamentaire
        c. C-46, s. 555(2)
    testamentary instrument   titre testamentaire
        c. C-46, s. 334(a)

insubordination
    insubordination, disloyalty, mutiny or refusal of duty   insubordination, déloyauté, mutinerie ou refus de servir
        c. C-46, s. 62(1)(c)

insufficiency   déficit
        c. C-10, s. 32(2)
    by reason of any irregularity, informality or insufficiency (of a conviction)   pour cause d'irrigularité, vice de forme ou insuffisance
        c. C-46, s. 777(1)
    insufficiency of the notice   défaut d'avis
        c. C-50, s. 12(2)(b)

insurance
    group life insurance plan   régime collectif d'assurance-vie
        c. C-24, s. 11(1)(a)

group medical-surgical insurance plan
    c. C-24, s. 11(1)(b)
régime collectif d'assurance médicale-chirurgicale

insurance charge
    c. C-46, s. 347(2)
frais d'assurance

insurance company
    c. C-44, s. 3(2)(b)
compagnie d'assurance

insurance scheme
    c. C-48, s. 2
régime d'assurance

policy of mortgage insurance
    c. L-12, s. 61(1)(l)ii)
police d'assurance hypothécaire

private or public insurance
    c. C-8, s. 11(6)(a)(i)
assurance privée ou publique

insured

insured crop
    c. C-48, s. 2
récolte assurée

insured health services
    c. C-6, s. 2
services de santé assurés

insured person
    c. C-6, s. 2
assuré

intelligence

(of a child)
    c. Y-1, s. 62(2)
degré de maturité

information and intelligence
    c. C-23, s. 12
informations et renseignements

intent

(of a law)
    c. C-29, s. 32(2)
esprit

according to its true spirit, intent and meaning (of enactment)
    c. I-23, s. 10
selon son esprit, son sens et son objet

fraudulent intent
    c. C-46, s. 361(1)
intention frauduleuse

intent and purpose (of an Act)
    c. A-2, s. 18(1)(q)
esprit et objet

spirit and intent of this Act
    c. 31 (4th Supp.), s. 58(1)(c)
esprit de la présente loi et intention du législateur

with intent
    c. C-46, s. 120(a)(iii) in fine
avec l'intention

with intent to defraud
    c. C-44, s. 229(2)(a)
avec une intention de fraude

intention

certificate of intention
    c. B-1, s. 178(4)(b)
préavis

notice of intention
    c. B-1, s. 12(1)
    c. L-12, s. 5(3)
avis d'intention

statement of intention
    c. C-46, s. 610
énoncé d'intention

unless a contrary intention appears
    c. I-23, s. 3(1)
sauf indication contraire

Inter-American Development Bank
    c. L-12, s. 61(1)(a)(ix)
Banque interaméricaine de développement

inter-insurance

(contract)
    c. C-40, s. 27(5)
assurance réciproque

intercept/to
    c. C-23, s. 2
intercepter

interest
 c. B-1, s. 174(2)(g) — participation
(in land) — droits (sur des terres)
 c. T-7, s. 29(1)(1a1)
(in the capital of a partnership) — participation
 c. C-20, s. 2(1)
(real property) — droit
 c. A-13, s. 4(i)
beneficial interest — droit du véritable propriétaire
 c. C-44, s. 2(1)(c)
beneficial interest — propriété effective
 c. C-44, s. 2(1)
claim an interest/to — revendiquer un droit
 c. N-1, s. 17(1)
controlling interest (in the stock) — intérêt prépondérant
 c. C-19, s. 14(1)
criminal interest rate — taux d'interêt criminel
 c. C-46, s. 347(2)
debt or equity interest — droit de créance ou action
 c. A-2, s. 21(3)
declaration of interest — déclaration d'intérêt
 c. C-40, s. 77(3)
estate or interest (in — droit de propriété ou droit de jouissance
hydrocarbons or minerals)
 c. B-1, s. 177(1)(c)
have an interest directly or — avoir un intérêt direct ou indirect dans
indirectly in/to
 c. B-2, s. 10(3)
have an interest in a thing/to — avoir un intérêt dans une chose
 c. C-46, s. 490(15)
have an interest/to — détenir un droit
 c. C-44, s. 48(2)
have title to or an interest/to (in — avoir un droit de propriété ou autre
an object)
 c. P-20, s. 11(3)
in the best interest (of a young — dans l'intérêt
person)
 c. Y-1, s. 10(1)
interest in or charge on property — droit grevant des biens
 c. C-44, s. 2(1)
land or any interest therein — biens-fonds et droits réels immobiliers

 c. C-38, s. 2
lawful interest — intérêts légitime
 c. L-12, s. 65(1)
part interest — droit partiel
 c. B-1, s. 2(1)
pay interest/to — porter intérêt
 c. B-2, s. 18(m)
pecuniary interest (of a person) — intérêts financiers
 c. L-2, s. 81(2)
pecuniary or proprietary — intérêt pécuniaire ou droit de propriété
interest
 c. C-22, s. 5(1)(b)
principal interest — capital et intérêt
 c. N-11, s. 88(3)(e)
reasonable interest return — rendement suffisant
 c. L-12, s. 61(1)(m)(B)(ii)
rights, interests, claims and — droits et créances
demands
 c. C-9, s. 43(5)
security interest — sûreté
 c. C-44, s. 2(1)

share or interest in a public stock or fund
    c. C-46, s. 2 — action ou intérêt dans un stock ou fonds public

simple interest
    c. C-17, s. 7(1)(j) — intérêt simple

title to or interest in a chattel personal
    c. C-46, s. 2 — titre à un bien ou droit mobilier ou à un intérêt dans ce bien ou droit

title to real property or to any interest in real property
    c. C-46, s. 2 — titre à un bien immeuble ou à un intérêt dans un bien immeuble

to be in the best interest of the administration of justice
    c. C-46, s. 186(1)(a) — servir au mieux l'administration de la justice

to have a special property or interest in (a thing)
    c. C-46, s. 322(1)(a) — avoir un droit de propriété spécial ou un intérêt spécial

to have an interest in a mining claim
    c. C-46, s. 395(1) — avoir un intérêt dans un claim minier

interest expense
    c. B-1, Schedule XXI — frais d'intérêts

interest rate
    c. F-11, s. 21(2) — taux d'intérêt

criminal interest rate
    c. C-46, s. 183 — usure

interested

interested party
    c. C-44, s. 248 — partie concernée

interested person
    c. B-1, s. 238(8)
    c. C-44, s. 205(4) — intéressé

interested/to be

(in a contract)
    c. B-1, s. 53(2)(b) — avoir un intérêt

interests

best interests (of the child)
    c. C-3, s. 16(8) — intérêt

honestly and in good faith with a view to the best interests of the holders
    c. C-44, s. 91(a) — avec intégrité et de bonne foi, aux mieux des intérêts des détenteurs

interests of justice
    c. C-46, s. 196(3) — intérêts de la justice

to be in the best interests of justice
    c. C-46, s. 530(4) — être dans les meilleurs intérêts de la justice

to be in the interests of the administration of justice
    c. C-46, s. 193(2)(e) — servir l'administration de la justice

interfere/to

(with the administration of justice)
    c. C-46, s. 515(10)(b) — nuire

alter or interfere/to (with fuel seized)
    c. C-32, s. 27(4) — modifier l'état

interfere with the administration of justice/to
    c. C-46, s. 120a)iv) — entraver l'administration de la justice

obstruct, interrupt or interfere/to (with a person)
    c. C-46, s. 430(1.1)(c) — empêcher, interrompre ou gêner

interference
  least possible interference (with
  freedom)
    c. Y-1, s. 3(1)(f)

minimum d'entraves

interim
  final or interim (judgment or
  order)
    c. C-3, s. 21(1)

définitif ou provisoire

  in interim or definitive form (a
  debenture or a bond)
    c. C-19, s. 41(1)

sous une forme intérimaire ou
  définitive

  interim financial statement
    c. C-44, s. 160(4)

état financier provisoire

  interim injunction
    c. C-34, s. 33(1)(b)(ii)

injonction provisoire

  interim or final order
    c. C-44, s. 192(4)

ordonnance provisoire ou finale

  interim payment
    c. C-24, s. 33(3)

versement intérimaire

  judicial interim release

mise en liberté provisoire par voie
  judiciaire

    c. C-46, s. 515(1)
  judicial interim release

mise en liberté provisoire par voie
  judiciaire

    c. Y-1, s. 36(1)(e)
  proposed, interim or final
  distribution (money or property)
    c. C-44, s. 217(l)

projet de répartition provisoire ou
  définitive

interim distribution
  (a liquidation)
    c. B-1, s. 289(l)

répartition provisoire

interlineation
  erasure, alteration or
  interlineation on election
  document
    c. C-46, s. 377(1)(d)

rature, altération ou interlinéation
  dans un document d'élection

interlocutory
  interlocutory judgment
    c. F-7, s. 27(1)(c)

jugement interlocutoire

intermediary
    c. B-1, s. 88(3)
    c. C-44, s. 2(1)

intermédiaire

  financial intermediary
    c. C-44, s. 174(1)(b)(iii)

intermédiaire financier

intermittent
  intermittent sentence
    c. C-46, s. 735

peine discontinue

  order of committal to
  intermittent custody
    c. Y-1, s. 24(13)

ordonnance de placement sous
  garde discontinue

internal waters
    c. A-12, s. 23(1)

eaux intérieures

**International Bank for
Reconstruction and
Development**
    c. B-2, s. 18(m)

Banque internationale pour la
  reconstruction et le
  développement

International Boundary Line
    c. C-9, Schedule II

frontière internationale

**International Civil Aviation
Organization**
    c. C-26, Schedule III

Organisation de l'Aviation civile
  internationale

**International Development
Research Centre**
    c. F-11, s. 85(1)

Centre de recherches pour le
  développement international

International Monetary Fund
    c. B-2, s. 18(f)
    c. B-7, s. 2
    c. C-52, s. 17(2)(a)
International postal Convention
    c. C-26, Schedule I, Article
      2(2)
internationally protected
person
    c. C-46, s. 2
interposition
    by the interposition of a trustee
      c. P-1, s. 34
interprovincial
    interprovincial and export trade

      c. A-6, s. 2(1)
interprovincially
    operate interprovincially/to
      c. A-2, s. 20
interrupt/to
    obstruct, interrupt or
    interfere/to (with a person)
      c. C-46, s. 430(1.1)(c)
intervene/to
    intervene in an action/to
      c. C-44, s. 239(1)
intervener
    c. T-19, s. 16(4)
interview
    personally interview/to (an
    inmate)
      c. P-2, s. 17
intestate
    c. L-12, s. 41(3)
intimation of policy
    directive, instruction, intimation
    of policy or other communication
      c. C-34, s. 41(1)(a)(ii)
intimidate/to
    c. C-46, s. 423(1)(b)
introduction
    c. A-11, s. 3(a)
    introduction or presentation (of
    a Bill)
      c. C-8, s. 115(2)
Inuit Tapirisat of Canada
    c. C-18, Schedule
invalid
    (an act)
      c. B-1, s. 20(1)
    invalid action
      c. F-11, s. 102(4)
invalidate/to
    c. B-1, s. 35(3)
    (a payment or a transfer of
    property)
      c. B-3, s. 44(3)
    (a share)
      c. C-44, s. 49(11)
    (an amalgamation)
      c. C-44, s. 183(2)(b)

Fonds monétaire international

Fond monétaire international
convention postale internationale

personne jouissant d'une protection
   internationale

par l'intermédiaire d'un mandataire

marchés interprovincial et
   international

exploiter un service interprovincial

empêcher, interrompre ou gêner

intervenir dans une action

intervenant

entendre

intestat

directive, instruction, principe
   indiqué ou autre communication

intimider

introduction

dépôt ou présentation

Inuit Tapirisat of Canada

nul

acte nul

entraîner la nullité

invalider

invalider

rendre nul

invasion
  invasion of privacy   violation de la vie privée
    c. C-23, s. 19(2)(d)
inveigle/to
  inveigle or entice a person to a   attirer ou entraîner une personne
  house of assignation/to   vers une maison de rendez-vous
    c. C-46, s. 212(1)(b)
inventory
  (of personal property)   inventaire
    c. C-25, s. 10(1)(b)
  establish an inventory/to   dresser un inventaire
    c. C-11, s. 7
invest/to
  (assets)   investir
    c. B-1, s. 173(1)(n)(ii)
  invest and deal with/to (moneys)   placer et gérer
    c. A-10, s. 6(1)(h)
invested/to be
  (with a jurisdiction)   posséder
    c. B-3, s. 183(1)
investigate/to   mener une enquête
    c. C-23, s. 19(2)(a)
  (an accident)   examiner
    c. A-2, s. 10(1)
investigation   enquête
    c. A-1, s. 16(4)
    c. A-2, s. 8(1)(o)
  criminal investigation   enquête criminelle
    c. C-46, s. 134(2)
  examination or investigation   examen ou recherches
    c. B-1, s. 139(b)
  examination or investigation   examen et enquêtes
    c. B-1, s. 139(c)
  investigation or inquiry   enquête
    c. P-2, s. 26
  make an inquiry or   mener une enquête
  investigation/to
    c. C-24, s. 29(1)
investigative
  investigative power   pouvoir d'enquête
    c. C-43, s. 23(1)(e)
  investigative procedure   méthode d'enquête
    c. C-23, s. 21(2)(b)
    c. C-46, s. 185(1)(h)
investigator   enquêteur
    c. A-2, s. 8(1)(o)
    c. C-12, s. 2
investigatory
  investigatory power   pouvoir d'enquête
    c. C-44, s. 231(2)
investment   mise de fonds
    c. C-16, s. 10(3)
  (a fund)   placement
    c. B-1, s. 109(1)(a)(ii)
  guaranteed investment   certificat de placement garanti
  certificate
    c. B-1, s. 270(1)
  investment advice   conseil en matière de placements
    c. L-12, s. 116(1)
  investment counselling   conseil de placements
    c. B-1, s. 174(1)
  investment dealer   courtier en placement
    c. B-1, s. 208(7)(e)

mortgage investment company c. L-12, s. 112(2)	société de crédit immobilier
real estate investment trust c. B-1, s. 193(6)(b)	fonds immobilier de placement
Investment Dealers' Association of Canada c. B-1, s. 35(1)(i)	Association des courtiers en valeurs du Canada
investor c. C-20, s. 2(1)	investisseur
Investor's Indemnity Account c. F-11, s. 57	compte d'indemnisation placement
invoice c. B-1, s. 17	facture
Commercial invoice c. C-51, s. 48(1)	facture commerciale
invoke/to invoke a right/to c. C-44, s. 195(c)	se prévaloir d'un droit
involve/to c. C-32, s. 8(3)	mettre en cause
irony expressed directly or by insinuation or irony (defamatory libel) c. C-46, s. 298(2)	exprimé directement ou par insinuation ou ironie
irredeemable (debenture) c. C-40, s. 91	irrachetable
irregularity (of ticket) c. C-26, Schedule I, Article 3(2)	irrégularité
by reason of any irregularity, informality or insufficiency (of a conviction) c. C-46, s. 777(1)	pour cause d'irrégularité, vice de forme ou insuffisance
defect of form or irregularity in procedure c. C-46, s. 189(3)b)	vice de forme ou de procédure
irregularity or defect in the substance or form (of a warrant) c. C-46, s. 546(a)	irrégularité ou défaut dans la substance ou la forme
procedural irregularity c. C-46, s. 686(1)(b)(iv)	irrégularité de procédure
irrevocable become irrevocable/to (an acceptance) c. B-4, s. 38	devenir irrévocable
irrevocable election c. C-17, s. 64(c)	choix irrévocable
isotopic concentration c. C-46, s. 7(3.6)(a)	concentration d'isotope
issue c. A-11, s. 3(q)	délivrance
(letters patent) c. B-1, s. 258(1)(g)	octroi
equipment issue (of securities) c. C-19, s. 32	émission gagée sur le matériel
issue of copies c. C-42, s. 4(1)	édition d'exemplaires
issue out of the court/to (subpoena) c. C-46, s. 699(2)	émaner du tribunal

issue, transfer or ownership (of a share)　　émission, transfert ou appartenance
　　c. C-44, s. 6(1)(d)
try an issue/to　　instruire un procès
　　c. C-46, s. 643(2)

issue/to
　(a certificate)　　délivrer
　　　c. C-44, s. 8
　(a document)　　délivrer
　　　c. A-10, s. 14(1)(b)
　(a process)　　décerner
　　　c. B-3, s. 229
　(a proclamation)　　prendre
　　　c. C-11, s. 10
　(a share)　　émettre
　　　c. C-44, s. 6(1)(c)
　(a warrant)　　décerner
　　　c. C-23, s. 21(3)
　　　c. C-46, s. 512(1)
　(an injunction)　　prononcer
　　　c. C-34, s. 33(b)(ii)
　(licenses)　　délivrer
　　　c. A-2, s. 18(1)(a)
　issue a subpoena/to　　lancer une assignation
　　　c. C-46, s. 698(1)
　issue a subpoena/to　　émettre une assignation
　　　c. C-46, s. 699(2)
　issue a summons/to　　lancer une sommation
　　　c. C-46, s. 164(2)
　issue a warrant/to　　décerner un mandat
　　　c. C-46, s. 698(2)
　make, give or issue/to (a document)　　faire, donner ou émettre
　　　c. A-2, s. 27(1)(b)

issued
　issued shares　　capital souscrit
　　　c. L-12, s. 100(2)

issuer
　(of securities)　　émetteur
　　　c. B-1, s. 75(2)
　　　c. C-44, s. 48(2)
　issuer of a specific security　　émetteur d'une valeur particulière
　　　c. C-34, s. 5(1)

item
　(budget)　　poste
　　　c. F-11, s. 32(1)
　extraordinary item (consolidated statement of income)　　élément extraordinaire
　　　c. B-1, Schedule XV

j
───────────────────────────

jail
　common jail　　prison commune
　　　c. C-39, s. 105(2)
　inmate in a penitentiary, jail, reformatory or prison/to be　　être détenu dans un pénitentier, une prison ou une maison de correction
　　　c. C-29, s. 21(c)

jailer
  warden, deputy warden, instructor, keeper, jailer, guard, or other officer or permanent employee of a prison (peace officer)
    c. C-46, s. 2

directeur, sous-directeur, instrumenteur, gardien, geôlier, garde ou tout autre fonctionnaire ou employé permanent d'une prison (agent de la paix)

Japanese Canadian Citizen's Association
    c. C-18, Schedule

Japanese Canadian Citizen's Association

join/to
  join as a party/to
    c. C-44, s. 190(20)

mettre en cause

joinder
  joinder or severance of counts
    c. C-46, s. 588

réunion ou séparation de chefs

joint
  joint adventure
    c. C-40, s. 27(d)

participation

  joint application (for a permit)
    c. L-2, s. 170(5)

demande conjointe

  joint auditor
    c. F-11, s. 134(3)

covérificateur

  joint financial obligation (of spouses)
    c. C-3, s. 15(8)(a)

obligation financière commune

  joint holder (of securities)
    c. C-44, s. 49(3)

codétenteur

  joint or joint and several
    c. C-44, s. 14(3)

solidairement

  joint owner tenant in common or partner
    c. C-46, s. 328(d)

copropriétaire tenancier en commun ou associé

  joint ownership or joint operation
    c. C-19, s. 23(3)(e)

copropriété ou exploitation commune

  joint shareholders
    c. C-44, s. 140(4)

coactionnaires

  joint stock company
    c. C-41, s. 43

compagnie par actions

  work of joint authorship
    c. C-42, s. 2

oeuvre créée en collaboration

joint and several
    c. C-44, s. 14(3)

solidairement

joint auditor
    c. F-11, s. 134(2)

covérificateur

joint holders
  (of capital stock)
    c. L-12, s. 46(3)

codétenteurs

jointly
    c. A-17, s. 9(b)

conjointement

  hold jointly a security/to
    c. C-44, s. 49(3)

détention conjointe d'une valeur mobilière

  jointly and severally (liability)
    c. C-44, s. 118(1)

solidairement

  jointly or in concert
    c. C-44, s. 194a)

conjointement ou de concert

jointly and severally
    c. B-1, s. 130(4)

solidairement

jointly and severally liable
    c. A-12, s. 6(1)(c)

responsabilité solidaire

    c. C-26, Schedule I, Article 30(3)

solidairement responsable

    c. L-2, s. 255(2)

solidairement responsable

judge
    judge of a superior court or   juge d'une juridiction supérieure
    county court
        c. J-1, s. 3
    provincial judge   juge provincial
        c. C-46, s. 2
    single judge   juge seul
        c. C-36, s. 9(2)
    trial judge   juge instructeur
        c. C-39, s. 2(1)
judge of the sessions of the peace
    magistrate, police magistrate,   magistrat, magistrat de police,
    stipendiary magistrate, district   magistrat stipendiaire, magistrat
    magistrate, provincial   de district, magistrat provincial,
    magistrate, judge of the sessions   juge des sessions de la paix,
    of the peace, recorder   recorder
        c. C-46, s. 2
judgment
    conviction, ruling, order or   décision judiciaire ou quasi-
    judgment   judiciaire
        c. B-1, s. 258(1)(e)
    final and conclusive judgment   arrêt définitif et sans appel
    (Supreme Court)
        c. S-26, s. 52
    formal judgment   jugement formel
        c. C-46, s. 677
    judgment appealed from   jugement attaqué
        c. S-26, s. 65(1)(c)
    judgment creditor   créancier en vertu d'un jugement
        c. C-41, s. 48
    judgment creditor   partie gagnante
        c. C-30, Schedule Article I
    judgment creditor of a   créancier titulaire d'un jugement
    shareholder   contre un actionnaire
        c. L-12, s. 52
    judgment debt   dette entérinée
        c. B-3, s. 70(3)(a)
    judgment debtor   partie perdante
        c. C-30, Schedule Article I
    judgment debtor of the Crown   débiteur, par jugement, de la
        Couronne
        c. Y-1, s. 49(3)
    judgment or order (of the   arrêt ou ordonnance
    Supreme Court)
        c. S-26, s. 2(1)"s. judgment"
    judgment, rule, order, decision,   décision
    decree, decretal order, or
    sentence
        c. S-26, s. 2(1)
judicial
    high judicial office   haute charge judiciaire
        c. C-42, s. 68(2)
    judicial centre or district town   centre ou chef-lieu de la
        circonscription
        c. J-1, s. 35(1)
    judicial division   division judiciaire
        c. A-2, s. 8(6)
    judicial official   fonctionnaire judiciaire
        c. T-15, s. 5(2)
    judicial or official instrument   acte judiciaire ou officiel
        c. L-12, s. 42(1)a)iii)

judicial personality   personnalité juridique
    c. B-7, Schedule I, Article IX,
      Section 2
judicial proceeding   procédure judiciaire
    c. Y-1, s. 2(1)
judicial record   dossier judiciaire
    c. C-47, s. 6(1)
judicial separation   séparation judiciaire
    c. C-46, s. 166(1)(b)
judicially
judicially notice/to   admettre d'office
    c. A-7, s. 8(3)
judicially noticed/to be   être admis d'office
    c. C-42, s. 51
    c. C-46, s. 781(2)
juridical day   jour juridique
    c. B-4, s. 120(2)
jurisdiction   ressort
    c. C-9, s. 22(1)
    c. C-44, s. 187(6)
    c. A-12, s. 6(4)   tribunal
    c. A-12, s. 22(1)   compétence
    c. B-1, s. 146(2)   autorités
    c. C-26, Schedule I, Article   lieu de compétence
      32
    c. C-44, s. 188(1)   autorité législative
    c. C-30, Schedule Article I   compétence judiciaire
(of a peace officer)   ressort
    c. C-46, s. 69
absolute jurisdiction   juridiction absolue
    c. C-46, s. 536(1)
appellate civil jurisdiction   juridiction d'appel en matière civile
    c. S-26, s. 35
appellate criminal jurisdiction   juridiction d'appel en matière
      pénale

    c. S-26, s. 35
competent jurisdiction   tribunal compétent
    c. A-12, s. 6(4)
concurrent jurisdiction (of   juridiction concurrente
courts)
    c. C-42, s. 37
court having jurisdiction   tribunal compétent
    c. A-2, s. 8(6)
court of competent jurisdiction   tribunal compétent
    c. C-17, s. 36(1)
    c. C-19, s. 44(1)
court of criminal jurisdiction   cour de juridiction criminelle
    c. C-46, s. 2
court of original jurisdiction   tribunal de première instance
    c. S-26, s. 47
court of original jurisdiction or   juridiction de première instance ou
court of appeal   d'appel
    c. F-27, s. 2(1)
equivalent jurisdiction (of court)   juridiction équivalente
    c. C-46, s. 739(2)
excess of jurisdiction   excès de compétence
    c. C-46, s. 830(1)(b)
exclusive ultimate appellate   juridiction suprême en matière
civil jurisdiction   d'appel au civil
    c. S-26, s. 52
federal jurisdiction   administration fédérale
    c. C-13, s. 5(b)(i)

have jurisdiction/to c. A-8, s. 4(4)	être compétent
in any jurisdiction outside Canada c. C-44, s. 15(3)	à l'étranger

jurisdiction in bankruptcy/to
have
    c. B-3, s. 2
	avoir juridiction en matière de
	    faillite

jurisdiction in personam c. F-7, s. 43(1)	compétence en matière personnelle
jurisdiction in rem c. F-7, s. 43(2)	compétence en matière réelle
law of a jurisdiction outside Canada c. C-44, s. 2(7)(a)	loi étrangère

law of the jurisdiction governing
the fiduciary relationship
    c. C-44, s. 61(1)a)
	lois régissant le statut de
	    représentant

ordinary jurisdiction c. A-12, s. 22(1)	ressort

original, auxiliary and ancillary
jurisdiction (in bankruptcy)
    c. B-3, s. 183(1)
	juridiction de première instance,
	    auxiliaire et subordonnée

process issued without
jurisdiction or in excess of
jurisdiction
    c. C-46, s. 25(2)
	acte judiciaire délivré sans
	    juridiction ou au-delà de la
	    juridiction

territorial jurisdiction c. B-3, s. 184(d)	compétence territoriale

territorial jurisdiction
    c. C-11, s. 23(1)
    c. Y-1, s. 23(2)(b)
	ressort

to exercise a regulative,
administrative or executive
jurisdiction
    c. S-26, s. 2(1)
	exercer des pouvoirs
	    réglementaires, administratifs ou
	    exécutifs

want of jurisdiction c. C-46, s. 118	manque de juridiction

within the territorial
jurisdiction
    c. C-46, s. 495(1)(c)
	dans les limites de la juridiction
	    territoriale

within the territorial jurisdiction (of a judge) c. C-46, s. 513	dans le ressort
juror's book c. C-46, s. 671	registre des jurés
jury	
empanelling of the jury c. C-46, s. 670(a)	constitution de jury
full jury c. C-46, s. 641(1)	jury complet
grand jury c. C-46, s. 118	grand jury
jury list c. C-46, s. 671	liste des jurys
mixed jury c. C-46, s. 627	jury mixte

justice
    c. C-34, s. 19(5)
    c. C-46, s. 2
	juge de paix
	
	juge de la paix

natural justice c. F-7, s. 28(1)(a)	justice naturelle

senior associate chief justice, associate chief justice, supernumery judge, chief judge, senior judge and junior judge
   c. J-1, s. 2, "judge"

juge en chef associé, juge en chef adjoint, juge surnuméraire, juge principal et juge junior

justice of the peace
   c. A-11, s. 20(1)

juge de paix

justification
justification or excuse for an act
   c. C-46, s. 8(3)

justification ou excuse d'un acte

plea of justification
   c. C-46, s. 612(1)

plaidoyer de justification

without justification or provocation
   c. C-46, s. 38(2)

sans justification ni provocation

juvenile court
officer of a juvenile court

fonctionnaire d'un tribunal pour enfants

   c. C-46, s. 120a)

k

keeper

gardien

   c. B-1, s. 2(1)(b)
   c. C-46, s. 197(1)

tenancier

keeper of a prison
   c. C-46, s. 28(2)b

gardien de prison

keeper of a warehouse, factor, agent or carrier
   c. C-46, s. 389(1)(a)

gardien d'un entrepôt, facteur, agent ou voiturier

warden, deputy warden, instructor, keeper, jailer, guard, or other officer or permanent employee of a prison (peace officer)
   c. C-46, s. 2

directeur, sous-directeur, instrumenteur, gardien, geôlier, garde ou tout autre fonctionnaire ou employé permanent d'une prison (agent de la paix)

key
key, pick, rocker key or other instrument
   c. C-46, s. 353(5)

clef, crochet, clef à levier ou tout autre instrument

kidnapping
kidnapping, hostage taking and abduction
   c. C-46, s. 279

enlèvement, prise d'otage et rapt

kind
degree or kind of punishment
   c. C-46, s. 717(1)

degré ou genre de peine

in money or in kind
   c. C-44, s. 222(2)(a)

en numéraire ou en nature

Knights of Columbus Canadian Army Huts
   c. C-31, s. 16

Knights of Columbus Canadian Army Huts

knowingly
   c. C-10, s. 59(a)
   c. F-27, s. 24(1)
   c. C-20, s. 15(4)
   c. C-46, s. 4(3)(a)
   c. P-1, s. 35(b)

en connaissance de cause

sciemment

knowingly and wilfully
   c. B-1, s. 130(4)

en pleine connaissance de cause
en toute connaissance de cause

knowingly and wilfully   sciemment et volontairement
    c. C-46, s. 389(1)(b)
knowledge
    have notice or knowledge/to   recevoir avis ou avoir connaissance
       c. C-44, s. 17
    matter of fact or knowledge   question de fait ou de connaissance
       c. C-46, s. 136(1)
    to be under a legal duty to have   être légalement tenu d'apporter une
    and to use reasonable   connaissance, une habilité et des
    knowledge, skill and care   soins raisonnables
       c. C-46, s. 216
    to the best of their knowledge   au mieux de leur connaissance et
    and belief   croyance
       c. C-45, s. 5
    with the knowledge and consent   au su et avec le consentement
       c. C-46, s. 4(3)(b)
    without his knowledge or   sans sa connaissance ou son
    consent   consentement
       c. A-2, s. 22(3)
    without the knowledge   à l'insu
       c. A-12, s. 20(1)
knowlingly   sciemment
    c. B-1, s. 115(1)

l

---

label   étiquette
    c. F-27, s. 2
labour
    hard labour   travaux forcés
       c. C-46, s. 732(2)
Lake Shippers Clearance   Lake Shippers Clearance
Association   Association
    c. B-1, s. 2(1)(d)
land   bien-fonds
    c. C-9, s. 37(1)
    c. C-25, s. 11(1)   immeuble
    land affected (by zoning   terrain visé
    regulation)
       c. A-2, s. 8(8)
    land registry   bureau d'enregistrement
       c. B-1, s. 177(8)(b)
    land titles office   bureau des titres fonciers
       c. B-1, s. 177(8)
land territory of Canada   territoire terrestre du Canada
    c. C-53, s. 2(1)
land titles office   bureau des titres de biens-fonds
    c. B-3, s. 20(1)
landing   débarcadère
    c. T-7, s. 23(b)
    landing field   piste d'atterrissage
       c. T-7, s. 23(b)
landlord   propriétaire
    c. C-24, s. 2(1)
    (of a farm)   bailleur
       c. B-1, s. 2(1)
    as owner, landlord, lessor,   en qualité de possesseur,
    tenant, occupier or agent (of   propriétaire, locateur, locataire,
    common gaming house)   occupant ou agent
       c. C-46, s. 201(2)(b)

lands
in the lawful execution of a
process against lands or goods

   c. C-46, s. 270(1)(b)
lawful execution of a process
against lands and goods

   c. C-46, s. 129(c)
public lands
   c. N-14, s. 2

landward
waters on the landward side

   c. A-2, s. 4(k)

language
insulting or obscene language
   c. C-46, s. 175(1)(a)(i)

lapse/to
(a right)
   c. B-1, s. 123(5)
(an offer)
   c. C-44, s. 190(14)
(an option)
   c. B-1, s. 123(5)
(appropriation)
   c. F-11, s. 37(1)

lapse of time
   c. B-1, s. 133(1)

later
until the later of

   c. C-46, s. 7(8)

latest
at his latest or usual place of
abode
   c. C-46, s. 509(2)

Laurentian Pilotage Authority

   c. A-1, Schedule I
   c. F-11, Schedule III, Part I

law

   c. C-12, s. 25(3)
   c. A-12, s. 2
   c. A-13, s. 6
   c. A-16, s. 8(b)
(by law (authorized))
   c. F-11, s. 74(2)
at law
   c. B-1, s. 269(3)(a)
bind in law/to
   c. C-46, s. 366(4)
corporation law
   c. C-44, s. 4
court of law
   c. F-7, s. 3
court of law and equity
   c. S-26, s. 3
foreign law
   c. F-7, s. 22(3)(d)
general and public law (of
Canada)
   c. P-1, s. 5

dans l'exécution légale d'un acte
judiciaire contre des terres ou des
effets

exécution légitime d'un acte
judiciaire contre des terres ou des
biens meubles

terres domaniales

les eaux du côté de la ligne de base
qui fait face à la terre

langage insultant ou obscène

devenir périmé

devenir caduc

devenir périmé

annuler

délai

jusqu'au moment où se réalise le
plus éloigné des évènements
suivants

à sa dernière ou habituelle
résidence

Administration de pilotage des
Laurentides

règles de droit

disposition législative
droit
règle de droit
de droit

juridiquement

lier légalement

droit des sociétés

tribunal de droit

tribunal de droit et d'équité

droit étranger

droit général et public

genuine series of law reports
    c. C-46, s. 166(4)(c)(i)
série authentique de rapports judiciaires

governing law
    c. C-44, s. 51(8)(b)
loi applicable

in law or in fact
    c. Y-1, s. 2(1)
en droit ou en fait

in law or in fact
    c. C-46, s. 150
en droit ou de fait

jurisdiction at law and equity
    c. B-3, s. 183(1)
compétence en droit et en équité

law merchant
    c. B-4, s. 9
droit commercial

law of a jurisdiction outside Canada
    c. C-44, s. 2(7)(a)
loi étrangère

law of a province
    c. A-1, s. 16(1)(a)(ii)
    c. C-44, s. 2(7)(a)
loi provinciale

law of evidence
    c. C-23, s. 39(2)
droit de la preuve

law of nations
    c. C-46, s. 74(1)
droit des gens

law of the place
    c. C-46, s. 214
loi du lieu

law of the place (where the contract was made)
    c. B-4, s. 159(1)
droit du lieu (où le contrat a été passé)

law of the province
    c. C-32, s. 23(4)(b)
loi de la province

law of the Court seized of the case
    c. C-26, Schedule I, Article 22(1)
loi du tribunal saisi

law of Canada
    c. C-44, s. 2(7)(a)
    c. F-7, s. 22(1)
loi fédérale

law of Canada
    c. A-1, s. 16(1)(a)(ii)
loi fédérale

law of Canada
    c. B-4, s. 159(3)
droit canadien

punishment warranted by law
    c. C-46, s. 478(3)(b) in fine
peine autorisée par la loi

question of law
    c. C-46, s. 32(5)
question de droit

revise and reform the law/to
    c. C-44, s. 4
refondre et réformer le droit

statute or law
    c. N-11, s. 24(1)
loi ou autre règle de droit

Law Reform Commission of Canada
    c. A-1, Schedule I
Commission de réforme du droit du Canada

lawful
    c. B-1, s. 56(1)(b)
conforme à la loi

(agreement)
    c. C-44, s. 146(2)
licite

(excuse)
    c. C-12, s. 43
excuse légitime

by lawful means
    c. C-46, s. 60(c)
par des moyens légaux

disobey a lawful order/to
    c. C-46, s. 127(1)
désobéir à une ordonnance légale

lawful authority c. A-11, s. 40	autorisation légitime
lawful authority (of the government) c. C-46, s. 2	autorité légitime
lawful charge c. F-11, s. 33(3)(a)	imputation régulière
lawful conduct c. C-44, s. 124(1)(b)	conduite conforme à la loi
lawful custody c. C-46, s. 145(1)(a)	garde légale
lawful deputy c. C-46, s. 132(2)	suppléant légitime
lawful deputy (of the Attorney General) c. C-46, s. 2	substitut légitime
lawful disbursement c. F-11, s. 47	décaissement régulier
lawful excuse c. A-11, s. 40	excuse légitime

lawful execution of a process
against lands and goods
	exécution légitime d'un acte
	    judiciaire contre des terres ou des
	    biens meubles

c. C-46, s. 129(c)	
lawful interest c. L-12, s. 65(1)	intérêts légitimes
lawful owner c. C-46, s. 490(3)(b)(i)	propriétaire légitime
lawful use c. C-9, s. 40	utilisation légitime
without lawful excuse c. C-46, s. 57(3)	sans excuse légitime

lawfully
    c. C-10, s. 15(1)(c)
    c. L-12, s. 8(2)
	licitement

c. B-1, s. 44(6) c. C-44, s. 114(6)	régulièrement
lawfully dispose/to (of a firearm) c. C-46, s. 90(3)	se défaire légalement
lawfully entitled/to be c. C-6, s. 2	légalement autoriser
lawfully present/to be (in Canada) c. C-29, s. 2(2)(b)	se trouver légalement
laws c. C-10, s. 42(3)	législation
(of a province) c. B-1, s. 236	droit
administration of the laws of Canada c. S-26, s. 3	application du droit canadien

domestic laws
    c. C-42, Schedule III Article
    7
	droit interne

laws of a province c. C-46, s. 626(1)	loi provinciale
laws of the place c. C-29, s. 2(1)	droit du lieu
laws, rules and regulations	principes de droit, règles et règlements
c. A-2, s. 8(1)(i)	

lay/to
(a report before Parliament)
    c. A-4, s. 6
    c. A-5, s. 8
	déposer

lay an appeal/to	interjeter appel
c. F-7, s. 27(1)	
lay an information/to	faire une dénonciation
c. C-46, s. 504	
lay off/to	licencier
c. C-25, s. 18(2)	
lead/to	
lead evidence/to	présenter une preuve
c. C-46, s. 518(1)(c)	
Leader of the Opposition	chef de l'Opposition
c. P-1, s. 62(a)	
league	confédération
c. B-1, s. 2(1)	
(of credit societies)	confédération
c. C-21, s. 2(1)	
learn/to	
receive a notice or otherwise	être informé, notamment par voie
learn/to (of a meeting)	d'avis
c. C-44, s. 168(5)(b)	
lease	location
c. A-2, s. 18(1)(e)	
c. L-12, s. 61(1)f)(ii)	cession à bail
(of property)	bail
c. F-11, s. 7(1)(c)	
lease and option	bail avec option d'achat
c. N-11, s. 30(3)(i)	
lease/to	prendre à bail
c. C-10, s. 16(2)	
c. B-1, s. 173(1)(j)	donner à bail
c. B-1, s. 173(1)(j)	louer
(real property)	louer
c. C-9, s. 36	
lease contract	
financial lease contract	bail financier
c. B-1, s. 193(1)	
leasehold	immeuble loué à bail
c. C-41, s. 11(1)(b)(i)	
c. L-12, s. 61(1)(b)(i)	tenure à bail
leasing	
financial leasing	crédit-bail financier
c. B-1, s. 173(1)(j)	
leasing corporation	société de crédit-bail
c. B-1, s. 193(1)	
leave	permission
c. A-2, s. 14(1)(b)	
application for leave to appeal	demande d'autorisation d'appel
c. C-46, s. 678(2)	
c. F-7, s. 16(1)	
bereavement leave	congé de décès
c. L-2, s. 210(2)	
leave of absence without pay	congé sans traitement
c. P-2, s. 10(2)	
leave of the court	permission du tribunal
c. B-3, s. 6(3)	
leave of the court	autorisation du tribunal
c. A-12, s. 21(2)	
on special grounds and by	pour des motifs particuliers et par
special leave	autorisation spéciale
c. S-26, s. 62(3)	
with leave (of the court)	avec l'autorisation
c. S-26, s. 37	
leave/to	
leave the chair/to (of the Senate)	abandonner la présidence
c. P-1, s. 17	

lecture
    c. C-42, s. 2   conférence
legacy
    c. C-17, s. 50(o)   legs
legal
    bring actions, suits or other   ester en justice
    legal proceedings/to
      c. A-8, s. 4(4)
    company or other legal person   société ou autre personne morale
      c. C-30, Schedule Article II,
        2(d)(v)
    current and legal tender/to be   avoir cours légal et pouvoir
                                      libératoire
      c. C-52, s. 7(1)(b)
    guardian, curator, committee,   tuteur, curateur à la personne ou
    executor, administrator or other   aux biens, conseil judiciaire,
    legal representative   exécuteur testamentaire ou autre
                                    représentant légal
      c. C-8, s. 2(1)
    heir and legal representative   héritier et mandataire
      c. F-11, s. 119(2)
    in the capacity of a legal   en qualité de mandataire
    representative
      c. C-44, s. 32(1)
    individual, partnership,   particulier, société de personnes,
    association, body corporate,   association, personne morale,
    trustee, executor, administrator   fiduciaire, exécuteur
    or legal representative   testamentaire, tuteur, curateur ou
                                    mandataire
      c. C-44, s. 2(1)
    legal and equitable estate   droits de propriété en droit et en
                                    equity
      c. B-3, s. 84
    legal consequences   sanction
      c. C-42, Schedule II, Article 9
    legal cost (of acquisition)   frais légaux
      c. N-11, s. 12(2)(e)
    legal costs   frais légaux
      c. B-3, s. 136(1)(b)(ii)
    legal counsel   conseiller juridique
      c. C-44, s. 87(b)(i)
    legal domicile   domicile légal
      c. B-6, s. 10
    legal effect/to have (order)   être valide
      c. C-3, s. 20(2)
    legal effect/to have (order)   être exécutoire
      c. C-3, s. 18(2)
    legal expense   frais judiciaires
      c. C-8, s. 86(2)
    legal officer   conseiller juridique
      c. P-35, s. 2
    legal or customary right   droit découlant de la loi ou de la
                                    coutume
      c. 31 (4th Supp.), s. 83(1)
    legal process   autorité de justice
      c. B-3, s. 2
    legal representative   représentant
      c. A-14, s. 2
    legal representative   mandataire
      c. B-1, s. 56(1)
    legal representative   ayant cause
      c. C-42, Schedule II, Article
        15

legal representative   représentant légal
    c. C-42, s. 2
    c. S-26, s. 73(1)
legal representative (of the   mandataire
heirs)
    c. B-1, s. 78(2)(a)
legal representative or agent   mandataire
    c. B-1, s. 2(1)
legal right or legal liability   droit légal ou obligation légale
    c. C-46, s. 118
legal suspension or cancellation   suspension ou annulation légale
(of a permit or a licence)
    c. C-46, s. 256(1)
to be under a legal duty to   être légalement tenu de subvenir
provide for   aux besoins
    c. Y-1, Schedule, Form I

legality
(of imprisonnement)   légalité
    c. C-46, s. 775
legality of claim   légimité des prétentions
    c. L-12, s. 43(1)

legally
legally or in fact   de droit ou de fait
    c. C-43, s. 2(3)(c)

legally entitled/to be
(person)   avoir qualité
    c. C-8, s. 104(1)

legible
in legible writing   dans une écriture lisible
    c. C-46, s. 540(1)(b)(i)

legislature   assemblée législative
    c. F-7, s. 19
(of a province)   législature
    c. C-46, s. 306(b)
    c. P-2, s. 14(2)
    c. L-2, s. 2(i)
member of a legislature   membre d'une législature
    c. C-46, s. 748(2)
Parliament or legislature of a   Parlement ou législature d'une
province   province
    c. C-46, s. 60(b)(ii)

legitimation   légitimation
    c. C-29, s. 2(1)

legitimize/to
(a child)   légitimer
    c. C-29, s. 2(1)

lend money/to   consentir un prêt
    c. B-1, s. 174(2)(f)
    c. B-1, s. 2(1)(d)   effectuer des opérations de prêt
      d'argent

lender   prêteur
    c. C-44, s. 44(3)
    c. C-49, s. 2(1)

lending
lending value   valeur d'emprunt
    c. N-11, s. 2

lending institution   institution de prêt
    c. B-1, s. 190(8)
    c. C-7, s. 2   établissement de crédit

lessee   locataire
    c. B-1, s. 173(1)(j)
owner, lessee, occupier or   possesseur, locataire, occupant ou
operator (of a stockyard)   exploitant
    c. L-9, s. 10

lesser
   lesser notice
      c. C-11, s. 12(2)   délai moindre
lessor   bailleur
      c. C-53, s. 2(2)
   as owner, landlord, lessor,   en qualité de possesseur,
   tenant, occupier or agent (of   propriétaire, locateur, locataire,
   common gaming house)   occupant ou agent
      c. C-46, s. 201(2)(b)
letter of credit   lettre de crédit
      c. B-1, s. 202(4)(c)
letters of administration
   grant of letters of   jugement de nomination d'une
   administration   exécution
      c. B-1, s. 78(7)(a)
   grant of letters of   jugement de nomination d'un
   administration   exécuteur testamentaire ou d'un
                     administrateur
      c. C-44, s. 51(7)(a)
letters patent   lettres patentes
      c. B-1, s. 2(1)
   issue letters patent/to   octroyer des lettres patentes
      c. B-1, s. 116(2)(b)
   letters patent under the Great   lettres patentes revêtues du grand
   Seal   sceau
      c. S-26, s. 4(2)
letters patent of land   acte de concession
      c. C-37, s. 7(1)
level
   (of grievance)   palier
      c. P-35, s. 91(1)
levy
   (under an execution)   prélèvement
      c. S-26, s. 66(1)
   levy or charge   droits
      c. C-15, s. 12(1)(f)
levy/to
   (taxes)   lever
      c. N-14, s. 7(2)
   assess or levy/to (municipal   établir ou percevoir
   taxes)
      c. B-3, s. 136(1)(e)
liabilities   passif
      c. B-7, s. 11
      c. C-40, s. 27(b)
      c. C-7, s. 23(b)   dettes
      c. L-12, s. 8(6)   responsabilité
      c. L-12, s. 62(2)a)   éléments du passif
   (of a company)   dettes
      c. L-12, s. 15(3)
   assets and liabilities   actif et passif
      c. A-2, s. 18(1)(d)
   assets and liabilities (of Canada)   ressources et charges
      c. F-11, s. 64(2)(a)(ii)
   direct and contingent liabilities   charges directes ou éventuelles
      c. F-11, s. 63(2)
   extinction of liabilities   extinction de dettes
      c. C-52, s. 20(2)(ii)
   limitations, liabilities and   obligations
   requirements
      c. B-1, s. 7(1)
   statement of assets and   état des ressources et des charges
   liabilities
      c. F-11, s. 25(2)

liability — responsabilité
  c. A-12, s. 6(2)
  c. C-40, s. 8(5)
  c. C-44, s. 38(6)
  c. C-44, s. 2(1) — passif
  absolute liability — responsabilité absolue
    c. A-12, s. 7(1)
  assume a liability/to — assumer une responsabilité
    c. B-1, s. 86(2)
  civil liability — responsabilité civile
    c. C-9, s. 39(1)(e)
  current liability — passif courant
    c. C-41, s. 11(1)(e)(ii)
  current liability — passif à court terme
    c. L-12, s. 61(1)(h)
  deposit liability (of a bank) — dépôt
    c. B-1, s. 132(2)(c)
  incur liability/to — engager sa responsabilité
    c. B-1, s. 41(4)
    c. C-44, s. 110(4)
  legal right or legal liability — droit légal ou obligation légale
    c. C-46, s. 118
  liability in tort — responsabilité civile délictuelle
    c. C-50, s. 3
  obligation and liability (of a corporation) — obligation et responsabilité
    c. L-12, s. 97(1)

liable — responsable
  c. A-12, s. 7(1)
  c. B-1, s. 51(1)
  (to a person) — responsable (envers une personne)
    c. B-1, s. 249
  indirectly liable/to be — être indirectement responsable
    c. B-3, s. 2
  jointly and severally liable — responsabilité solidaire
    c. A-12, s. 6(1)(c)
  liable for any liability, act or default (shareholders) — responsable de ses obligations, actes ou fautes
    c. C-44, s. 45(1)
  liable to execution (property) — saisissable
    c. F-7, s. 56(3)
  personnally liable/to be — engager sa responsabilité personnelle
    c. L-2, s. 137
  secondarily liable/to be — être secondairement responsable
    c. B-3, s. 2

liable/to be — tenir responsable
  c. A-5, s. 4(1)
  (to a fine) — encourir
    c. C-44, s. 20(6)
  (to punishment) — encourir
    c. A-4, s. 5(1)

liable on summary conviction/to be — être passible sur déclaration de culpabilité par procédure sommaire
  c. A-1, s. 67(2)

libel — diffamation écrite
  c. A-1, s. 66(2)
  c. C-46, s. 59(2) — libelle
  blasphemous libel — libelle blasphématoire
    c. C-46, s. 296(1)
  blasphemous, seditious or defamatory libel — libelle blasphématoire, séditieux ou diffamatoire
    c. C-46, s. 584(1)

defamatory libel c. C-46, s. 297	libelle diffamatoire
libel or slander c. 31 (4th Supp.), s. 75(2)	diffamation verbale ou écrite
licence	permis ou licence
c. A-11, s. 3(q)	
c. C-46, s. 191(2)d)	permis
(to carry on business) c. C-44, s. 174(1)b)i)	permis
compulsory licence (copyright) c. C-42, s. 9(1)	licence obligatoire
licence for manufacture (of controlled drugs) c. F-27, s. 45(1)(b)	permis de fabrication
licence for the sale (of controlled drugs) c. F-27, s. 45(1)(b)	permis de vente
licence issued under the regulation c. N-1, s. 6(1)	permis réglementaire
licence to carry on business c. B-1, s. 28(5)	permis d'exploitation
licence to operate (an air service) c. A-2, s. 21	permis d'exploitation
license/to c. A-16, s. 10(d)	attribuer une licence
licensed	
licensed dealer c. A-7, s. 8(1)	marchand titulaire de permis
licensed/to be	être autorisé par permis
c. B-6, s. 31(2)	
c. C-24, s. 48(1)	être agréé
licensee	porteur de licence
c. C-42, s. 18(2)	
licensing	
licensing of pilots c. A-2, s. 8(1)(a)	émission de permis aux pilotes

provincial professional licensing
authority
 	
    c. F-27, s. 45(1)(e)
	autorité provinciale officiellement
	    chargée de la délivrance des
	    permis

licensor	

assignor, grantor, licensor or
mortgagor
    c. C-42, s. 58(1)
	cédant, concesseur, octroyeur de
	    licence ou débiteur sur gage

lien	
(on goods) c. C-46, s. 325	droit de rétention
first and preferential lien c. B-1, s. 178(2)(d)	gage ou privilège de premier rang
lien on shares c. C-44, s. 45(2)	actions grévées d'une charge
mechanic's lien c. B-1, s. 177(7)	privilège de constructeur
lien-giver c. N-1, s. 17(4)(b)	débiteur assujetti au privilège
lieu	

in addition to or in lieu of any
other punishment
    c. C-46, s. 718(1)
	en sus et au lieu de toute autre
	    peine

life	
imprisonment for life c. C-46, s. 47(1)	emprisonnement à perpétuité

light
    supply of light, power, gas or water   approvisionnement de lumière, d'énergie, de gaz ou d'eau
      c. C-46, s. 422(1)(d)

lighten/to
    impair, diminish or lighten (coin)/to   affaiblir, diminuer ou alléger
      c. C-46, s. 455(a)

like
    like offence   même infraction
      c. A-2, s. 22(3)

limit
    limit, boundary or angle of a concession, range, lot or parcel of land   limite ou angle d'une concession, d'un rang, d'un lot ou d'un lopin de terre
      c. C-46, s. 443(1)(b)
    maximum acceptable limit (air quality)   maximum acceptable
      c. C-32, s. 2
    maximum desirable limit (air quality)   maximum souhaitable
      c. C-32, s. 2
    maximum tolerable limit (air quality)   maximum tolérable
      c. C-32, s. 2

limit/to
    (territorial jurisdiction)   restreindre
      c. B-3, s. 184(d)

limitation   prescription
      c. C-46, s. 48(1)
    (maximum amount)   plafond
      c. C-24, s. 53(3)
    (on voting rights)   limites
      c. C-44, s. 174(6)(c)
    devolve by descent, limitation or marriage/to   échoir par voie de transmission ou pour cause de prescription, ou par mariage
      c. P-1, s. 40(b)
    laws relating to prescription and limitation (of actions)   règles de droit en matière de prescription
      c. F-7, s. 39(1)
    limitation of liability   limitation de la responsabilité
      c. C-50, s. 6(1)
    prescribed period of limitation   délai prescrit
      c. C-46, s. 601(4.1)
    prescription and limitation (of actions)   prescription
      c. C-50, s. 32(1)
    statute of limitation or prescription   disposition relative aux délais et à la prescription
      c. B-1, s. 159(4)

limitations
    (prescribed by regulations)   restrictions réglementaires
      c. A-1, s. 4(3)

limited partnership   société en commandite
      c. B-1, s. 174(2)(i)

limits
    (of a province)   limites
      c. L-2, s. 2(b)

liquid fund   liquidité
      c. B-1, s. 173(1)(p)
      c. C-41, s. 98(2)

liquidate/to
  (an obligation)   liquider
    c. B-1, s. 289(h)
liquidation
  (of a corporation)   liquidation
    c. L-12, s. 61(5)
  (of a share)   liquidation
    c. C-44, s. 35(3)(b)(ii)
  liquidation distribution   partage consécutif à la liquidation
    c. C-44, s. 134(1)(b)
  voluntary liquidation   liquidation volontaire
    c. B-1, s. 287(1)
liquidator   liquidateur
    c. B-1, s. 181
list
  basic list   liste principale
    c. C-44, s. 21(3)
  jury list   liste des jurys
    c. C-46, s. 671
listed
  listed for trading (a share)   coté (en bourse)
    c. B-1, s. 62(4)(b)
  listed for trading (shares)   coté
    c. C-44, s. 134(4)(b)
literary
  literary work (copyright)   oeuvre litéraire
    c. C-42, s. 2
  literary, scientific or artistic   domaine littéraire, scientifique et
  domain   artistique
    c. C-42, s. 2
litigation   litige
    c. C-44, s. 72(3)
livestock   bétail
    c. B-1, s. 2(1)
  livestock exchange   halle aux animaux de ferme
    c. L-9, s. 10
  livestock or livestock product   animal de ferme ou produit
                                               d'animal de ferme
    c. L-9, s. 2
living
  travel and living expenses   frais de déplacement et autres
    c. A-7, s. 7(9)(b)
loan
  day loan   prêt au jour le jour
    c. B-1, s. 208(7)(e)
  guaranteed home improvement   prêt garanti à l'amélioration ou prêt
  loan   garanti à l'amélioration de maison
    c. N-11, s. 2
  loan company   société de prêt
    c. B-3, s. 2
  loan of obligation   prêt d'obligation
    c. N-11, s. 2
  loan receivable   fonds de prêt à recevoir
    c. B-1, s. 193(1)
  loan secured by mortgage   prêt hypothécaire
    c. C-7, s. 26(a)
  subordinated shareholder loan   prêt de dernier rang
    c. L-12, s. 2
local
  (of a trade union)   section locale
    c. L-2, s. 3(1)
  local advisory board   comité consultatif local
    c. L-12, s. 27

local authority
    c. A-11, s. 28
local registrar of firearms
    c. C-46, s. 84(1)
lock
    key suited to a lock
        c. C-46, s. 356(1)(a)(iii)
lock-up
    penitentiary, common jail,
    public or reformatory prison,
    lock-up, guard-room

        c. C-46, s. 2
lockout
    c. L-2, s. 3(1)
lodge/to
    (an attachment)
        c. B-3, s. 70(2)
lodging
    food, lodging or other
    accomodation (at an inn)
        c. C-46, s. 364(1)
    lodging, boarding or eating
    house
        c. C-46, s. 364(1)
log
    lumber, timber, log, float, boom,
    dam or slide

        c. C-46, s. 433(1)(i)
loiter/to
    (in a public place)
        c. C-46, s. 175(1)(c)
loose-leaf
    loose-leaf form register
        c. F-11, s. 60(2)
loss
    c. A-12, s. 6(1)(c)
    direct loss
        c. C-44, s. 131(4)(a)
    incur a loss/to
        c. B-1, s. 105(2)(b)
    loan loss
        c. B-1, Schedule XII
    material financial loss
        c. A-1, s. 20(1)(c)
lost security
    c. F-11, s. 60(1)(c)
lot
    limit, boundary or angle of a
    concession, range, lot or parcel
    of land
        c. C-46, s. 443(1)(b)
Loto Canada Inc.
    c. F-11, Schedule III, Part I
lottery
    lottery or game of chance
        c. C-46, s. 206(1)
lottery sheme
    c. C-46, s. 207(1)
low income
    family of low income
        c. N-11, s. 2

autorité locale

registraire local d'armes à feu

clef correspondant à un cadenas

pénitencier, prison commune,
  prison publique, maison de
  correction, poste de police ou corps
  de garde

lock-out

déposer

aliments, logement ou autres
  commodités

hôtel garni, maison de pension ou
  restaurant

bois de construction, de service ou
  en grume, radeau, barrage
  flottant, digue ou glissoir

flâner

registre à feuilles mobiles

perte

dommage direct

subir un préjudice

perte sur prêt

perte financière appréciable

titre perdu

limite ou angle d'une concession,
  d'un rang, d'un lot ou d'un lopin
  de terre

Loto Canada Inc.

loterie ou jeu de hasard

loterie

famille à faible revenu

loyalty
  appraisal of loyalty   évaluation de loyauté
    c. C-23, s. 2
lumber   bois
    c. C-46, s. 339(6)
  lumber found adrift or cast   bois trouvé à la dérive ou jeté sur le
  ashore   rivage
    c. C-46, s. 339(c)
  lumber, timber, log, float, boom,   bois de construction, de service ou
  dam or slide   en grume, radeau, barrage
     flottant, digue ou glissoir
    c. C-46, s. 433(1)(i)
  timber, mast, spar, shingle bolt,   bois d'oeuvre, mâts, espars, bois à
  sawlog or lumber of any   bardeaux et bois en grume
  description
    c. C-46, s. 339(6)
lumbering equipment   matériel d'exploitation forestière
    c. C-46, s. 339(6)
lump
  lump sum   montant global
    c. C-8, s. 57(1)
  lump sum   versement unique
    c. P-1, s. 70(4)
  lump sum   paiement en une somme globale
    c. C-17, s. 6(b)(ii)(j)
  lump sum payment   paiement forfaitaire
    c. N-7, s. 86(2)(a)

m

magistrate
  chief magistrate of a city,   premier magistrat d'une
  borough or town corporate   municipalité, ville ou autre
     agglomération
    c. S-26, s. 82(c)
  magistrate, police magistrate,   magistrat, magistrat de police,
  stipendiary magistrate, district   magistrat stipendiaire, magistrat
  magistrate, provincial   de district, magistrat provincial,
  magistrate, judge of the sessions   juge des sessions de la paix,
  of the peace, recorder   recorder
    c. C-46, s. 2
mail   envoi ou courrier
    c. A-10, s. 2(1)
  registered or certified mail   courrier certifié ou recommandé
    c. C-46, s. 260(4)
mail bag   contenant postal
    c. A-10, s. 2(1)
mail contractor   entrepreneur postal
    c. A-10, s. 2(1)
mail-order sale   vente postale
    c. C-46, s. 97(1)
maintain/to
  (books and records)   tenir
    c. C-32, s. 25(b)(i)
  establish, maintain and carry   prendre et exercer
  out/to (security measures)
    c. A-2, s. 7(4)
  establish, maintain and   constituer et exploiter
  operate/to (facilities)
    c. A-13, s. 4(f)

maintain records/to   tenir des registres
   c. L-2, s. 134(b)

maintenance   obligation alimentaire
   c. C-30, Schedule Article
     II,2(a)

agreement for maintenance and   convention pour l'entretien et le
support (of a spouse or a child)   soutien
   c. B-3, s. 178(1)(c)

establishment, operation,   mise sur pied, exploitation,
maintenance and   entretien et gestion d'ouvrages
administration (of public works)
   c. N-14, s. 7(1)(v)

maintenance of order   maintien de l'ordre
   c. C-46, s. 486(1)

make/to

(a conviction)   prononcer (une condamnation)
   c. L-2, s. 161

(an agreement)   conclure
   c. A-5, s. 4(4)

(payments)   effectuer
   c. A-8, s. 12(1)(c)

(recommendations)   formuler
   c. A-8, s. 7(1)(b)

(rules)   établir
   c. A-4, s. 3(5)

administer, take, swear, make   souscrire
or affirm/to (oath)
   c. S-26, s. 81(2)

make a complaint/to   déposer une plainte
   c. A-1, s. 9(1)(c)

make a disposition/to   rendre une décision
   c. C-46, s. 523(1), (b), (ii)

make a toll/to   réclamer une taxe
   c. A-15, s. 3(2)

make counterfeit money/to   fabriquer de la monnaie contrefaite
   c. C-46, s. 449

make the charges/to   réclamer les frais
   c. A-15, s. 3(2)

make/to (a conviction)   prononcer une (condamnation)
   c. L-2, s. 161

make, execute, draw, sign,   faire, souscrire, rédiger, signer,
accept or endorse a document/to   accepter ou endosser un document
   c. C-46, s. 374(a)

make, give or issue/to (a   faire, donner ou émettre
document)
   c. A-2, s. 27(1)(b)

make fast/to

to make fast a boat to a signal,   amarrer un bateau à un signal, une
buoy or other sea-mark   bouée ou un autre amer
   c. C-46, s. 439(1)

make good/to

(a default)   réparer (une faute)
   c. C-44, s. 100e)

(a loss)   compenser (une perte)
   c. C-19, s. 34(1)

maker

(of a promise)   souscripteur
   c. B-4, s. 176(1)

making

making, accepting, discounting   création, acceptation, escompte ou
or endorsing of a bill of   endossement d'une lettre de
exchange, cheque, draft or   change, d'un chèque, d'une traite
promissory note   ou d'un billet à ordre
   c. C-46, s. 362(1)(c)(vi)

on the making of a summary
application
    c. C-46, s. 490(2)(a)

malfeasance
    c. B-8, s. 14(a)

breach of duty or malfeasance
    c. C-46, s. 723(2)(ii)

by reason of any malfeasance or
negligence
    c. F-11, s. 77

malice
without malice
    c. P-1, s. 9

maliciously
fraudulently, maliciously, or
without colour of right
    c. C-46, s. 326(1)

manage/to
conduct or manage any scheme,
contrivance or operation/to
    c. C-46, s. 206(1)(d)

manage the affairs/to
(Foundation)
    c. A-13, s. 7

management
board of governors, management
or directors

    c. C-46, s. 287(6)
charge, management or
control/to have (person)
    c. C-32, s. 2
control and management (of the
Service)
    c. C-23, s. 6(1)
direction and management (of
business)
    c. C-21, s. 16(2)
entrusted with the receipt,
custody or management/to be (of
revenue funds)
    c. C-46, s. 399
financial management
    c. F-11, s. 7(1)(c)
management and control (of a
penitentiary)
    c. P-5, s. 16(1)
management and direction/to
have (of a department)
    c. C-37, s. 2(3)
perform management
functions/to
    c. L-2, s. 3(1)
under the management of
    c. C-25, s. 8(1)

manager
    c. L-2, s. 167(2)(a)
    c. F-11, s. 60(3)
(Canada Evidence Act)
    c. F-11, s. 60(3)
general manager
    c. L-12, s. 54(2)

à la suite d'une demande sommaire

accomplissement d'un acte interdit

abus de fonction ou prévarication

du fait de leur malversation ou
négligence

sans intention malveillante

frauduleusement, malicieusement
ou sans apparence de droit

conduire ou administrer un plan, un
arrangement ou une opération

assurer la conduite des affaires

conseil des gouverneurs, conseil de
direction ou conseil
d'administration

avoir compétence ou pleine autorité

gestion

conduite

être chargé de la réception, garde
ou gestion

gestion financière

gestion et contrôle

assurer la direction et la gestion

occuper un poste de direction

sous l'autorité de

directeur

administrateur
gérant

directeur général

managing
  managing agent (of an estate)   agent-gérant
    c. B-1, s. 174(1)
  managing director (of   administrateur-gérant
  corporation)
    c. C-44, s. 115(1)
mandamus   mandamus
    c. C-46, s. 482(3)(c)
mandate   mandat
    c. 31 (4th Supp.), s. 39(1)(b)
mandatory supervision   surveillance obligatoire
    c. C-46, s. 100(3)
    c. P-2, s. 2   liberté surveillée
manifestly
  manifestly unlawful   manifestement illégal
    c. C-46, s. 32(3)(b)
manner   modalités
    c. A-7, s. 3(1)(a)
  manner of payment   mode de paiement
    c. B-1, s. 261(1)(e)
  prescribed manner   manière prescrite
    c. C-42, s. 8(1)
manslaughter
  murder, manslaughter or   meurtre, homicide involontaire
  infanticide   coupable ou infanticide
    c. C-46, s. 222(4)
manually
  sign manually/to   revêtir d'une signature manuscrite
    c. B-1, s. 76(4)
manufacture/to
  (narcotic)   fabriquer
    c. N-1, s. 2
manufacturer   fabricant
    c. B-1, s. 2(1)
margin
  buy and carry on margin any   acheter et porter sur une marge des
  shares/to   actions
    c. C-46, s. 384
marginal
  marginal note (of an enactment)   note marginale
    c. I-23, s. 14
marihuana   chanvre indien ou marihuana
    c. N-1, s. 2
marine animals
  shellfish, crustaceans and   mollusques, crustacés et animaux
  marine animals   marins
    c. C-33, s. 2
Maritime Code   Code maritime
    c. B-1, s. 179(5)
mark
  brand or mark (on cattle)   marque ou empreinte
    c. C-46, s. 338(1)(b)(i)
  high water mark   laisse de haute mer
    c. T-7, s. 13
  mark, brand, seal, wrapper or   marque, signe, sceau, enveloppe ou
  design   dessin
    c. C-46, s. 376(3)
  safety mark   indication de danger
    c. T-19, s. 2
mark/to
  stamp and mark/to (with an   timbrer et marquer
  official mark)
    c. C-42, s. 26(3)

market
market restriction   limitation du marché
    c. C-34, s. 39(1)
market value   valeur marchande
    c. A-11, s. 12(2)
market value   valeur de marché
    c. C-52, s. 20(1)(c)
open market   marché libre
    c. C-34, s. 58(3)(c)
    c. N-7, s. 97(2)
securities exchange or market   bourse ou marché de valeurs
       mobilières
    c. C-44, s. 48(2)(b)

market price
public market price of stocks   cote publique des stocks
    c. C-46, s. 380(2)

marketable
(securities)   négociable
    c. B-2, s. 18(i)

marketing   commercialisation
    c. A-11, s. 3(q)
marketing contract   contrat de commercialisation
    c. C-40, s. 77(1)
marketing plan   plan de commercialisation
    c. C-24, s. 48(1)

marriage
connected by blood relationship,   être uni par les liens du sang, du
marriage or adoption/to be   mariage ou de l'adoption
    c. B-3, s. 4(2)(a)
contract marriage/to   contracter mariage
    c. C-46, s. 290(3)
dissolution of marriage   dissolution de mariage
    c. C-46, s. 166(1)(b)
nullity of marriage   annulation de mariage
    c. C-46, s. 166(1)(b)

marshal   prévôt
    c. F-7, s. 13(4)

mass media   média
    c. C-34, s. 25(3)(f)

master
(of the land titles or registry   conservateur
office)
    c. B-3, s. 20(1)
timber, mast, spar, shingle bolt,   bois d'oeuvre, mâts, espars, bois à
sawlog or lumber of any   bardeaux et bois en grume
description
    c. C-46, s. 339(6)

master or officer in command
(of a vessel)   capitaine, patron ou commandant
    c. C-46, s. 44

master plan
master plan of community   plan directeur de développement
development and land   local et d'occupation du sol
utilization
    c. N-11, s. 2

material   appréciable
    c. A-1, s. 20(1)(c)
(evidence)   substantiel
    c. C-46, s. 118
(to an application)   pertinent
    c. B-9, s. 14(2)
at the material time   à l'époque considérée
    c. C-3, s. 2(1)

corroborated in a material particular/to be c. C-46, s. 292(2)	être corroborée sous un rapport essentiel
in a material respect c. C-46, s. 76(d)	considérablement
material alteration (of a bill) c. B-4, s. 145	altération substantielle
material contract c. C-44, s. 120(7) c. F-11, s. 116(1)(a)	contrat important
material evidence c. C-46, s. 698(1)	preuve substantielle
material evidence c. Y-1, s. 59	preuve pertinente
material fact c. C-20, s. 23 c. C-44, s. 154(1)	fait important
material false statement or representation c. C-46, s. 386(a)	fausse énonciation ou représentation essentielle
material financial gain c. A-1, s. 20(1)(c)	profit financier appréciable
material financial loss c. A-1, s. 20(1)(c)	perte financière appréciable
material form (of a work) c. C-42, s. 3(1)	forme matérielle
material information c. C-44, s. 216(3)	renseignements pertinents
material interest (in a person) c. B-1, s. 53(1)(b)	intérêt important
material particular c. B-2, s. 32	point important
nuclear material c. C-46, s. 7(3.6)	matières nucléaires
statement of material facts c. C-44, s. 2(7)(a)	déclaration de faits importants
to alter a genuine document in any material part c. C-46, s. 366(2)(a)	altérer, en quelque partie matérielle, un document authentique
to be not material c. C-46, s. 322(4)	être sans conséquence
Matriculation, Secondary school graduation or equivalent education c. C-28, Schedule 6	stage d'immatriculation, école secondaire ou enseignement équivalent
matter act, matter or thing c. A-2, s. 14(1)(a)	acte ou chose
defamatory matter c. C-46, s. 611(2)	matière diffamatoire
mature/to (a security) c. C-24, s. 8(1)	venir à échéance
maturing debt obligation c. C-41, s. 98(2)	titre de créance venant à échéance
maturity (a bank debenture) c. B-1, s. 132(2)	échéance
on maturity (debentures) c. C-41, s. 11(1)(c)	à leur échéance
term to maturity c. C-8, s. 111(1)(b)	terme d'échéance

term to maturity
  c. C-43, s. 3(1)(b)(ii)   date d'échéance
**maximum contributory
earnings**
  c. C-8, s. 2(1)   maximum des gains cotisables
maximum pensionable earnings   maximum des gains ouvrant droit à
                                              pension
  c. C-8, s. 2(1)
mayor
  mayor, warden, reeve, sheriff,   maire, président de conseil de
  deputy sheriff, sheriff's officer   comté, préfet, shérif, shérif adjoint,
  and justice of the peace   officier de shérif et juge de paix
  c. C-46, s. 2
mean
  lawful mean   moyen légitime
  c. C-45, s. 23
meaning
  (of a word)   sens
  c. C-23, s. 2
  according to its true spirit,   selon son esprit, son sens et son
  intent and meaning (of   objet
  enactment)
  c. I-23, s. 10
  substance, meaning or purport   substance, sens ou objet
  (of private communication)
  c. C-46, s. 191(2)(c)
meaningless
  to render data meaningless,   dépouiller des données de leur sens,
  useless or ineffective   les rendre inutiles ou inopérantes
  c. C-46, s. 430(1.1)(b)
medal
  military medal, ribbon, badge or   médaille, ruban, insigne ou chevron
  chevron   militaire
  c. C-46, s. 419(b)
mediately
  mediately or immediately, in   directement ou par intermédiaire,
  possession, or expectancy   pour jouissance immédiate ou ulté
                                              rieure
  c. C-29, s. 38(e)
medical practioner   médecin
  c. C-6, s. 2
  duly qualified medical   médecin dûment qualifié
  practioner
  c. C-46, s. 537(1)(b)
Medical Research Council   Conseil de recherches médicales
  c. F-11, Schedule II
meet/to
  (the interest)   acquitter
  c. L-12, s. 61(1)(c)
  (the requirements)   répondre
  c. A-7, s. 3(2)
  meet an emergency/to   faire face à un état d'urgence
  c. C-32, s. 22(3)
  meet an obligation/to   s'acquitter d'une obligation
  c. C-15, s. 10(2)
meeting
  (of shareholders)   assemblée d'actionnaires
  c. C-44, s. 132(1)
  notice of meeting   avis de convocation
  c. L-12, s. 55(3)
  special meeting (of   assemblée extraordinaire
  shareholders)
  c. B-1, s. 63(5)

melting down
  (coins)   fonte
    c. C-52, s. 11(1)
member
  (of a committee)   membre
    c. A-3, s. 9(1)
  (of the Senate and the House of   membre
  Commons)
    c. P-1, s. 4
  (of Board)   membre ou conseiller
    c. A-7, s. 7(1)
  member of a force   membre d'une force
    c. C-46, s. 62(2)
  member of a legislature   membre d'une législature
    c. C-46, s. 748(2)
  member of the public   public
    c. 31 (4th Supp.), s. 21
  member of the public service of   fonctionnaire fédéral
  Canada
    c. A-17, s. 13(1)
  member of the Board   membre de la Commission
    c. A-16, s. 2
  member of the Senate   sénateur
    c. P-1, s. 14(1)
  member of Parliament   membre du Parlement
    c. C-46, s. 748(2)
members
  members of the legal profession   gens de loi
    c. C-46, s. 166(4)(c)(ii)
membership   conditions d'appartenance
    c. A-13, s. 26(c)
    c. C-41, s. 54(1)   statut de membre
  (of a cooperative organization)   membres
    c. B-1, s. 2(1)
  application for membership   demande d'adhésion
    c. C-21, s. 4(1)(d)
  deny membership/to (in a trade   refuser l'adhésion
  union)
    c. L-2, s. 25(2)
  membership fee   cotisation d'affiliation
    c. C-40, s. 44
  membership interest (in a   droit des membres
  corporation)
    c. F-11, s. 83(1)
memorandum
  (of a date of receipt of an   mémorandum
  objection)
    c. B-3, s. 221(2)
  memorandum of adjudication   procès-verbal de décision
    c. C-46, s. 570(3)
  memorandum of agreement   mémorandum de convention
    c. B-6, s. 45
  memorandum of association   acte d'association
    c. F-11, s. 83(1)
  memorandum of association (a   acte constitutif
  corporation)
    c. B-1, s. 178(5)(a)
  memorandum of satisfaction   mémoire d'acquittement
    c. C-40, s. 95
  minute or memorandum (of the   minute ou procès-verbal
  conviction)
    c. C-46, s. 806(1)

Act of incorporation, articles, letters patent, or memorandum or articles of association
c. C-44, s. 187(2)

memorial
caution, caveat or memorial

c. B-1, s. 177(8)(b)
duplicate instrument, memorial, certificate or document in respect to registration of titles
c. C-46, s. 2

Mennonite Central Committee Canada
c. C-18, Schedule

mental defectiveness
mental defectiveness not amounting to imbecility
c. C-46, s. 2

mental hospital
provincially operated mental hospital
c. P-5, s. 30(1)

mentally ill
to be mentally ill
c. C-46, s. 537(1)(b)(iii)

mention/to
(in a section of an Act)
c. A-6, s. 2(2)

merchandise
goods, wares and merchandise
c. B-1, s. 2(1)

Merchant Seamen Compensation Board
c. A-1, Schedule I

merchantable
merchantable value
c. C-46, s. 379

mercy
royal mercy
c. C-46, s. 749(1)
royal prerogative of mercy
c. C-46, s. 751

merger
c. A-2, s. 18(1)(e)

merit
selection of personnel according to merit
c. 31 (4th Supp.), s. 39(3)
with due regard to the principle of selection of personnel according to merit
c. 31 (4th Supp.), s. preamble

merits
merits of matters of policy

c. F-11, s. 145
on the merits
c. C-44, s. 124(3)a)
on the merits (defence)
c. B-1, s. 56(3)(a)
to be substantially successful on the merits of the defence
c. F-11, s. 119(2)(a)

acte constitutif, statuts, lettres patentes ou mémoire de conventions

mise en garde, avertissement ou bordereau

double de tout instrument, mémoire, certificat concernant l'enregistrement de titres

Comité central Mennonite du Canada

déficience mentale n'allant pas jusqu'à l'imbécillité

hôpital psychiatrique sous administration provinciale

être atteint de maladie mentale

viser

effets, denrées ou marchandises

Commission d'indemnisation des marins marchands

valeur marchande

clémence royale

prérogative royale de clémence

fusion

mode de sélection fondé sur le mérite

dans le strict respect du principe du mérite en matière de sélection

bien-fondé de questions d'orientation

au fond

défense au fond

obtenir gain de cause sur la plupart des moyens au fond

try the merits/to | juger l'affaire au fond
c. C-46, s. 776(b)

metals
dealer in marine stores or in old metals | commerçant de gréements de marine ou marchand de vieux métaux
c. C-46, s. 421(2)
Metis National Council | Conseil national des Métis
c. C-18, Schedule
Metric Commission | Commission du système métrique
c. A-1, Schedule I
metrology
legal metrology | métrologie légale
c. C-37, s. 4(g)
metropolitan area | communauté urbaine
c. N-11, s. 2
military law | loi militaire
c. C-46, s. 2
mill
(one-tenth of a cent) | mill
c. C-52, s. 3(2)
feed mill | fabrique d'aliments pour animaux
c. C-24, Schedule
flour mill | minoterie
c. C-24, Schedule
seed cleaning mill | station de nettoiement des semences
c. C-24, Schedule
millesimal
millesimal fineness (gold) | millième de fin
c. C-26, Schedule I, Article 22(4)
standard millesimal fineness (for gold coins) | titre légal en millièmes
c. C-52, Schedule
milling
(coin) | cordonnet
c. C-46, s. 448
mineral
ore or mineral | minerai ou minéraux
c. C-46, s. 333
minerals | substances minérales
c. B-1, s. 2(1)
Mingan Associates, Ltd. | Les Associés Mingan, Ltée
c. F-11, Schedule III, Part I
mining
mining of precious metals | extraction de métaux précieux
c. C-46, s. 394(1)(a)(ii)
mining claim
to have an interest in a mining claim | avoir un intérêt dans un claim minier
c. C-46, s. 395(1)
minister
clergyman or minister | membre du clergé ou ministre du culte
c. C-46, s. 176(1)(a)
minister of the Crown in right of a province | ministre provincial
c. B-1, s. 35(1)(n)
minister of the Crown in right of Canada | ministre fédéral
c. B-1, s. 35(1)(n)

ministry of state	département d'État
c. A-1, s. 3	
Ministry of State	département d'État
c. C-23, s. 2	
Ministry of State for Economic	Département d'État au
and Regional Development	Développement économique et
	régional
c. A-1, Schedule I	
Ministry of State for Science	Département d'État des Sciences et
and Technology	de la Technologie
c. A-1, Schedule I	
Ministry of State for Social	Département d'État au
Developement	Développement social
c. A-1, Schedule I	
minor	mineur
c. C-29, s. 2(1)	
(person)	mineur
c. F-11, s. 60(1)(b)(ii)	
infant or minor	mineur
c. F-11, s. 60(1)(b)(ii)	
minority	
infancy or minority	minorité
c. B-1, s. 92(1)(d)	
minority interest	participation minoritaire
c. C-41, s. 11(1)(e)(ii)	
English and French linguistic	minorités francophones et
minority communities	anglophones
c. 31 (4th Supp.), s. 84	
mint	
Her Majesty's mint in Canada	hôtel de la Monnaie de Sa Majesté
	au Canada
c. C-46, s. 459	
minting	
(of coins)	frappe
c. C-52, s. 5(1)(a)	
minutes	procès-verbal
c. B-1, s. 53(1)	
minutes of the proceedings	procès-verbaux des délibérations
c. C-44, s. 117(2)	
minutes of the proceedings (of a	procès-verbal des délibérations
meeting)	
c. C-13, s. 14(2)	
mis-statement	renseignement inexact
c. C-44, s. 171(6)	
misappropriate/to	
conceal, withhold or	dissimuler, retenir ou détourner
misappropriate (property)/to	
c. C-44, s. 222(3)	
misappropriation	
fraud, embezzlement,	fraude, détournement, concussion
misappropriation or defalcation	ou abus de confiance
c. B-3, s. 178(1)(d)	
misappropriation of money held	distraction de fonds détenus en
under direction	vertu d'instructions
c. C-46, s. 332	
misbehaviour	mauvaise conduite
c. B-1, s. 245(2)	
miscarriage	fausse couche
c. C-46, s. 163(2)(c)	
procure a miscarriage/to	procurer un avortement
c. C-46, s. 287(2)	
miscarriage of justice	erreur judiciaire
c. C-46, s. 646(4)	

to correct a substantial wrong or
miscarriage of justice
    c. C-3, s. 21(6)

réparer un dommage important ou
remédier à une erreur judiciaire

mischief
inflicting of hurt or mischief

fait d'infliger un mal ou un
dommage

    c. C-46, s. 37(2)
public mischief
    c. C-46, s. 140

méfait public

misconduct
    c. C-17, s. 50(n)
    c. F-11, s. 11(2)(f)
    c. B-3, s. 175(1)
    c. C-46, s. 128(a)
wilful misconduct
    c. C-26, Schedule I, Article
    25(1)

inconduite

mauvaise conduite
prévarication
dol

misconduct/to
misconduct oneself/to
    c. C-46, s. 758(2)(a)

se conduire mal

misdemeanour
    c. F-32, s. 3(1)

délit

misdescription
    c. B-4, s. 97(2)
misnomer or misdescription
    c. C-46, s. 638(1)(a)

fausse désignation

erreur de nom ou de désignation

misdescriptive
deceptively misdescriptive
(name)
    c. B-1, s. 16(1)(b)
deceptively misdescriptive
(name)
    c. C-44, s. 12(1)(a)

description fausse et trompeuse

trompeur

misfeasance

faute dans l'accomplissement d'un
acte licite

    c. B-8, s. 14(a)
misfortune
(of bankrupt)
    c. B-3, s. 175(1)

malheur

mislead/to
(a person)
    c. B-4, s. 97(2)

induire en erreur

misleading
false or misleading
representation
    c. C-38, s. 7(2)
misleading statement
    c. A-12, s. 17
misleading, false or deceptive
(statement)
    c. B-1, s. 147(4)(a)(ii)

information fausse et trompeuse

déclaration trompeuse

fallacieux, faux ou trompeur

misnomer
misnomer or misdescription
    c. C-46, s. 638(1)(a)

erreur de nom ou de désignation

misrepresentation
    c. B-5, s. 4
    c. C-8, s. 22(3)
    c. C-44, s. 213(1)(c)
false or misleading information
or misrepresentation
    c. C-51, s. 42
fraudulent misrepresentation

fausse déclaration

présentation de faits erronés
renseignements faux ou fallacieux
ou fausse déclaration

présentations erronées et
frauduleuses des faits

    c. B-3, s. 178(1)(e)

fraudulent misrepresentation of fact
    c. C-46, s. 361(2)

dénaturation frauduleuse des faits

wilful misrepresentation

fausse représentation faite de propos délibéré

    c. B-3, s. 125

missing

incompetent or missing person
    c. C-44, s. 51(2)(b)

incapable ou absent

missing person
    c. B-1, s. 78(2)(b)

absent

misstate

knowingly misstate/to

faire sciemment une déclaration fausse

    c. C-27, Schedule, Article IV, 5

mistake
    c. B-1, s. 249(b)

méprise

mitigate/to
    c. C-20, s. 13(1)

mitiger

mitigated

aggravated or mitigated by a plea/to be (guilt)
    c. C-46, s. 612(3)

être aggravé ou atténué par le plaidoyer

mixed

question of mixed law and fact
    c. C-46, s. 164(6)c)

question de droit et de fait

mode

mode of publication
    c. A-2, s. 8(7)

mode de publication

mode of trial
    c. C-46, s. 567

mode de procès

modifications

with such modifications, as the circumstances require
    c. C-46, s. 522(5)

compte tenu des adaptations de circonstance

molotov cocktail

incendiary grenade, fire bomb, molotov cocktail
    c. C-46, s. 2

grenade incendiaire, bombe incendiaire, cocktail molotov

monetary penalty
    c. B-1, s. 56(1)(b)

amende

monetary value

monetary value of remuneration other than money

équivalent en argent de la rémunération versée autrement qu'en espèces

    c. L-2, s. 264(d)

money
    c. A-13, s. 4(j)

argent

    c. A-3, s. 6

crédits

    c. F-11, s. 2

fonds

action for money had and received
    c. S-26, s. 67

action en recouvrement de sommes reçues

in money
    c. B-1, s. 119(2)

en numéraire

in money or in kind
    c. C-44, s. 222(2)(a)

en numéraire ou en nature

to pay in money or in property or in past services
    c. C-44, s. 25(3)

libérer soit en numéraire, soit en biens ou en services rendus

money order
    c. C-21, s. 31(1)

mandat-poste

postal note, money order or postal remittance	titre de versement postal
c. F-11, s. 2	
money value	valeur en argent
c. B-3, s. 97(2)	
moneys	
(appropriated by Parliament)	crédits
c. A-8, s. 15(1)	
appropriate moneys/to	affecter des crédits
c. C-25, s. 32	
moneys appropriated by Parliament therefor	crédits votés à cette fin par le Parlement
c. C-10, s. 22(4)	
moneys on hand	sommes en caisse
c. B-3, s. 27(1)	
monitor/to	
(the establishment and operation of a committee)	surveiller
c. L-2, s. 222(2)(a)	
(water quality levels)	contrôler
c. C-11, s. 15(4)(d)	
monitor the compliance/to (with policies)	suivre l'observation
c. C-23, s. 30(2)(a)	
monitoring	
random monitoring (of communications)	contrôle au hasard
c. C-46, s. 184(2)(c)(ii)	
monopolistic situation	situation de monopole
c. C-34, s. 75(1)(a)	
monopoly	monopole
c. C-34, s. 2	
Montreal Port Corporation	Société du port de Montréal
c. F-11, Schedule III, Part II	
morals	
public morals	moralité publique
c. C-46, s. 486(1)	
public morals	bonnes moeurs
c. Y-1, s. 39(1)(b)	
moratoria	moratoire
c. B-7, Schedule I, Article IX, Section 6	
mortgage	hypothèque
c. C-7, s. 2	
chattel mortgage	hypothèque sur des biens meubles
c. N-11, s. 20(1)(e)	
graduated payment mortgage	prêt à paiements progressifs
c. N-11, s. 12(3)(a)	
mortgage and hypothec	hypothèque
c. B-1, s. 2(1)	
mortgage insurance	assurance-hypothèque
c. B-1, s. 176(1)(e)	
mortgage investment company	société de crédit immobilier
c. B-1, s. 173(1)(o)	
c. L-12, s. 112(2)	
mortgage loan	prêt sur hypothèque
c. B-1, Schedule XI	
mortgage loan corporation	société de prêt hypothécaire
c. B-1, s. 193(1)	
policy of mortgage insurance	police d'assurance hypothécaire
c. L-12, s. 61(1)(l)(ii)	
mortgage/to	grever d'une hypothèque
c. B-1, s. 185(1)	

hypothecate or mortgage/to c. B-1, s. 173(1)(d)(ii)	grever par hypothèque
mortgage loan c. B-1, Schedule XI	prêt sur hypothèque
mortgagee c. C-46, s. 385(1)	créancier hypothécaire
mortgagor vendor or mortgagor c. C-46, s. 385(1)	vendeur ou débiteur hypothécaire
motion by petition or by way of originating summons or notice of motion c. C-36, s. 10	par requête ou par voie d'assignation introductive d'instance ou d'avis de motion
motion to quash (an indictment or a count) c. C-46, s. 601(1)	requête pour faire annuler
notice of motion c. L-12, s. 45(6)	avis de motion
on its own motion c. C-46, s. 625.1(1)	de sa propre initiative
on its own motion or on the application (of a person) c. Y-1, s. 13(1)(e)	d'office ou à la demande de quelqu'un
sign a notice of motion/to c. A-15, s. 5(4)	signer un avis de motion
to be in motion (vehicle) c. C-46, s. 254(2)	être en mouvement
to set in motion (vehicle) c. C-46, s. 258(1)(a)	mettre en marche
motor vehicle c. C-46, s. 2	véhicule à moteur
move/to move the Court for dismissal of the appeal/to c. S-26, s. 71(1)	demander le rejet de l'appel à la Cour
movement (of oil and gas) c. N-7, s. 123	acheminement
preferred movement of traffic c. A-15, s. 4(1)	mouvement préféré du trafic
multifarious double or multifarious (count) c. C-46, s. 590(1)(b)	double ou multiple
municipal corporation c. C-41, s. 10(1)(a)(ii)	municipalité
municipal official c. C-46, s. 123(3)	fonctionnaire municipal
murder first degree murder c. C-46, s. 231(2)	meurtre au premier degré
murder, manslaughter or infanticide c. C-46, s. 222(4)	meurtre, homicide involontaire coupable ou infanticide
non-capital murder c. C-46, s. 522(1)	meurtre non qualifié
planned and deliberate murder c. C-46, s. 231(2)	meurtre commis avec préméditation et de propos délibéré
second degree murder c. C-46, s. 231(7)	meurtre au deuxième degré
murder/to to cause another person to be murdered c. C-46, s. 465(1)(a)	faire assassiner

muscular power
    vehicle drawn, propelled or
    driven by any means other than
    by muscular power
        c. C-46, s. 2

véhicule tiré, mû ou poussé par
quelque moyen que ce soit, autre
que la force musculaire

musical work
    (copyright)
        c. C-42, s. 2

oeuvre musicale

mutilate/to
    destroy, alter, mutilate
    records/to
        c. C-8, s. 41(4)(b)

détruire, altérer, mutiler

mutinous
    traitorous or mutinous act
        c. C-46, s. 53(b)

acte de trahison ou de mutinerie

mutual fund

        c. B-1, s. 2(1)
    mortgage based mutual fund

fonds de placement à capital
variable

fonds d'investissement à capital
variable

        c. B-1, s. 173(1)(o)
    mutual fund corporation
        c. B-1, s. 2(1)
    mutual fund trust
        c. B-1, s. 2(1)

société de fonds mutuels

fiducie de fonds mutuels

n

name
    (of a company)
        c. L-12, s. 5(4)(a)

dénomination

    (of a corporation)
        c. C-44, s. 6(1)(a)

dénomination sociale

    corporate name
        c. C-11, s. 12(3)(a)

dénomination

    in the name or on the account of
    another person
        c. C-46, s. 374(a)

au nom ou pour le compte d'une
autre personne

name/to
        c. C-46, s. 145(5)

désigner nommément

name and style
        c. B-6, s. 8(2)

dénomination et raison

narcotic
        c. N-1, s. 2

stupéfiant

narcotic addict
        c. N-1, s. 2

toxicomane

national
    local national
        c. B-7, Schedule I, Article IV,
            Section 8

ressortissant de l'État

    Canadian national
        c. C-31, s. 6

ressortissant du Canada

**National Action Committee on
Status of Women**
        c. C-18, Schedule

Comité d'Action sur le Statut de la
Femme

**national ambient air quality
objective**
        c. C-32, s. 2

objectif national

**National Arts Centre
Corporation**
        c. F-11, s. 85(1)

Corporation du Centre national des
Arts

National Bank of Canada c. B-1, Schedule I	Banque Nationale du Canada
National Bank of Detroit Canada c. B-1, Schedule II	Banque Nationale de Détroit du Canada
National Bank of Greece (Canada) c. B-1, Schedule II	Banque Nationale de Grèce (Canada)
National Battlefields Commission c. A-1, Schedule I	Commission des champs de bataille nationaux
National Black Coalition c. C-18, Schedule	National Black Coalition
National Capital Commission c. A-1, Schedule I	Commission de la capitale nationale
National Capital Region c. A-1, s. 52(1)(b)	région de la capitale nationale
National Company (railway) c. C-19, s. 2	Compagnie du National
National Council of Women of Canada c. C-18, Schedule	Conseil National des Femmes du Canada
National Design Council c. A-1, Schedule I	Conseil national de l'esthétique industrielle
National Energy Board c. A-1, Schedule I c. C-12, Schedule	Office national de l'énergie
National Farm Products Marketing Council c. A-1, Schedule I	Conseil national de commercialisation des produits de ferme
National Farmers Union c. C-18, Schedule	National Farmers Union
National Film Board c. A-1, Schedule I	Office national du film
National Historic Park c. N-14, s. 9(1)	parc historique national
National Library c. A-1, s. 68(c)	Bibliothèque nationale
National Museums of Canada c. A-1, s. 68(c) c. F-11, Schedule II	Musées nationaux du Canada
National Parole Board c. A-1, Schedule I	Commission nationale des libérations conditionnelles
National Parole Service c. A-1, Schedule I	Service national des libérations conditionnelles
National Railways c. C-19, s. 2	Chemins de fer nationaux
National Research Council of Canada c. C-12, Schedule	Conseil national de recherches du Canada
nationality (of aircraft) c. C-26, s. 2(2)	nationalité
native native author c. C-42, Schedule II, Article 5	auteur national
Native Council of Canada c. C-18, Schedule	Conseil des autochtones du Canada

natural child   enfant naturel
    c. C-8, s. 42(1)
natural person   personne physique
    c. A-10, s. 6(2)
    c. C-44, s. 2(1)
    capacity of a natural person   capacité d'une personne physique
    c. A-13, s. 4
Natural Sciences and   Conseil de recherches en sciences
Engineering Research Council   naturelles et en génie
    c. F-11, Schedule II
naturalization
    certificate of naturalization   certificat de la naturalisation
    c. C-29, s. 2(1)
navigation
    navigation or operation (of   utilisation ou conduite
    vessel or aircraft)
    c. C-46, s. 662(5)
necessaries of life   choses nécessaires à l'existence
    c. C-46, s. 215(1)(b)
necessary
    (endorsement)   obligatoire
    c. B-1, s. 90(1)
    necessary or advisable   souhaitable
    c. A-2, s. 18(1)(q)
necessitous
    to be in destitute or necessitous   se trouver dans le dénuement ou
    circumstances   dans le besoin
    c. C-46, s. 215(2)(a)(i)
necessity
    public convenience and necessity   commodité et besoins du public
    c. A-2, s. 21(10)
negative
    negative amount   solde débiteur
    c. B-7, s. 11(b)
    negative balance   solde négatif
    c. B-7, Schedule I, Article
    XVIII, Section 2(f)
    negative or positive amount   résultat déficitaire ou bénéficiaire
    c. C-52, s. 20(3)
negative/to
    (a liability)   nier
    c. B-4, s. 33(a)
    (an exception)   réfuter
    c. C-46, s. 601(3)(b)(ii)
    set out or negative/to (exception)   énoncer ou nier
    c. N-1, s. 7(1)
neglect   négligence
    c. A-12, s. 20(2)
    wilful neglect   négligence volontaire
    c. C-46, s. 446(b)
negligence   négligence
    c. A-12, s. 7(1)
    c. C-27, Schedule, Article III,
    8.
    criminal negligence   négligence criminelle
    c. C-46, s. 220
    wilful negligence   négligence volontaire
    c. C-31, s. 32
negotiable
    negotiable form (of security)   forme négociable
    c. B-1, s. 98(2)
    negotiable instrument   effet de commerce
    c. B-3, s. 2

negotiate/to
  (an appointment)   négocier
    c. C-46, s. 125(b)
  cash or negotiate/to (a cheque)   encaisser ou négocier (un chèque)
    c. B-2, s. 24(3)
net interest income   revenu net d'intérêts
    c. B-1, Schedule XII
net quantity
  (of a product)   quantité nette
    c. C-38, s. 4(2)
New Year's Day   1er janvier
    c. L-2, s. 193(2)
newly-born child   enfant nouveau-né ou nouveau-né
    c. C-46, s. 2
newspaper   journal
    c. C-46, s. 478(5)
nil   nul
    c. C-20, s. 15(4)(c)
nominal
  nominal consideration   somme symbolique
    c. T-7, s. 23(c)
  without nominal or par value   sans valeur au pair ou nominale
  (share)
    c. C-44, s. 24(1)
nominal value
  (of a share)   valeur nominale
    c. B-1, s. 2(2)(b)(i)
nominate/to
  (a person)   proposer un candidat
    c. P-35, s. 79(2)
  (a psychiatrist)   nommer
    c. C-46, s. 755(3)
  (an officer)   désigner
    c. B-2, s. 5(2)
nominated member   délégué
    c. C-24, s. 8(2)(a)
nominee
  (of an investor)   personne désignée
    c. C-20, s. 16(1)(a)
non culpable homicide   homicide non coupable
    c. C-46, s. 222(3)
non-assessable
  (a share)
    c. B-1, s. 118(3)
non-assignable
  (an agreement)   incessible
    c. C-44, s. 35(1)(c)
non-bank affiliate of a foreign   établissement non bancaire membre
bank   d'un groupe bancaire étranger
    c. B-1, s. 303(1)
non-compliance   inobservation
    c. C-44, s. 168(9)
non-copyright
  non-copyright matter   matière non protégée
    c. C-42, s. 27(2)(d)
non-current loan   prêt en souffrance
    c. B-1, s. 58(1)
non-custodial
  non-custodial disposition   décision ne comportant pas la mise
       sous garde
    c. Y-1, s. 25(1)
non-feasance   faute par abstention
    c. B-8, s. 14(a)

non-interest
    non-interest bearing certificate   certificat ne portant pas intérêt
        c. F-11, s. 2
non-juridical days   jours non ouvrables
        c. B-4, s. 2
non-observance
    (of a by-law)   inobservation
        c. C-9, s. 40
non-payment
    forfeiture for non-payment of   confiscation pour défaut de
    taxes (of lands)   paiement des impôts
        c. N-14, s. 7(1)(w)
non-performance
    (of a condition)   inexécution
        c. F-7, s. 37
non-profit
    non-profit corporation   association personnalisée
        c. N-11, s. 2
non-profit basis   sans but lucratif
        c. C-6, s. 8(1)(a)
non-signatory States   États non signataires
        c. C-26, Schedule III
non-transferable
    (an acknowledgment)   incessible
        c. B-1, s. 76(1)
non-working day   jour chômé
        c. L-2, s. 193(1)
Northern Canada Power   Commission d'énergie du Nord
Commission   canadien
        c. F-11, Schedule III, Part I
Northern Pipeline   pipe-line du Nord
        c. C-32, s. 2
Northern Pipeline Agency   Administration du pipe-line du
         Nord
        c. A-1, Schedule I
Northern Transportation   Société des transports du nord
Company Limited   Limitée
        c. F-11, Schedule III, Part II
Northland Bank   Norbanque
        c. B-1, Schedule I
Northwest Territories Water   Office des eaux des Territoires du
Board   Nord-Ouest
        c. A-1, Schedule I
notarial
    in notarial or authentic form   suivant la forme notariée ou
         authentique
        c. L-12, s. 42(1)(c)
    notarial or registrar's copy (of   copie notariée ou copie émise par un
    title to land)   régistrateur
        c. C-46, s. 2
    perform notarial acts/to   dresser des actes notariés
        c. C-42, s. 58(1)
notarially
    notarially certified (copies of   visé par notaire
    mortgages)
        c. C-19, s. 33
notary   notaire
        c. B-4, s. 10
        c. C-46, s. 183
notary public   notaire public
        c. B-6, s. 7(1)
        c. S-26, s. 82(b)   officier public

note

bank note, bank bill and bank post bill c. C-46, s. 2	billet de banque, papier de banque et effet postal de banque
bond, debenture, note or other evidence of indebtedness c. C-44, s. 2(1)	obligation, débenture, billet ou autre preuve de créance
bought and sold note c. C-46, s. 2	bordereau d'achat et de vente délivré à l'acheteur et au vendeur
budgetary note c. F-11, s. 25(2)	crédit budgétaire
consumer note c. B-4, s. 189(4)	billet de consommation
debenture, deed, bond, bill, note, warrant, order or other security for money c. C-46, s. 2	débenture, titre, obligation, billet, lettre, mandat, ordre ou autre garantie d'argent
note secured c. L-12, s. 61(1)(1)	effet de commerce garanti
subordinated note c. L-12, s. 2	effet de second rang
Bank of Canada note c. B-1, s. 208(1)(b)	billet de la Banque du Canada

notice — avis

c. B-1, s. 13	
c. B-1, s. 28(3)	préavis
c. L-12, s. 33(3)	mise en demeure
(of meeting) c. B-1, s. 44(5)	avis de convocation d'une réunion
acquire notice/to (of a forgery) c. B-4, s. 49(3)	avoir connaissance
appearance notice c. C-46, s. 493	citation à comparaître
contravention notice c. C-24, s. 72(1)	avis de contravention
deemed to have notice/to be (of an adverse claim) c. C-44, s. 53(c)	être réputé avisé (de l'existence d'opposition)
deliver a notice/to c. A-11, s. 25(1)	délivrer un avis
deliver a notice/to c. A-11, s. 6	donner avis
give a notice/to c. A-1, s. 28(1)	donner avis
give notice/to c. C-20, s. 8(1)	aviser
give written notice/to c. A-1, s. (a)	aviser par écrit
have notice or knowledge/to c. C-44, s. 17	recevoir avis ou avoir connaissance
have notice/to c. B-1, s. 104(6)	connaître
have notice/to c. B-1, s. 107(2)(a)	avoir connaissance
judicial notice c. C-36, s. 18(4)	admission d'office
judicial notice c. C-46, s. 781(2)	connaissance d'office
judicially notice/to (statutory instrument) c. S-22, s. 16(1)	admettre d'office

lesser notice   délai moindre
    c. C-11, s. 12(2)
notice deposit liabilities   passif-dépôts à préavis
    c. B-1, s. 208(2)(c)
notice entitled in the Court and   avis portant le sceau de la Cour et
in the cause   l'intitulé de la cause
    c. S-26, s. 69(1)
notice in writing   notification écrite
    c. B-8, s. 12
notice of concern   avis
    c. C-6, s. 14(2)(a)
notice of intention   avis d'intention
    c. L-12, s. 5(3)
notice of intention   préavis
    c. B-1, s. 178(5)
notice of meeting   avis de convocation
    c. L-12, s. 55(3)
notice of the extension   avis de prorogation de délai
    c. A-1, s. 9(1)(c)
notice served personally or sent   avis signifié à personne ou envoyé
by mail   par la poste
    c. Y-1, s. 9(7)
notice to appear   avis de comparaître
    c. Y-1, s. 23(8)
official notice   notice légale
    c. F-11, s. 56(1)
person giving a notice   donneur d'avis
    c. Y-1, s. 9(3)
prescribed notice   notification obligatoire
    c. C-42, s. 8(1)
prior notice   préavis
    c. C-11, s. 23(1)
    c. C-32, s. 28(1)
reasonable notice   préavis suffisant
    c. C-46, s. 347(5)
reasonable notice   publicité suffisante
    c. C-44, s. 185(3)(b)
receive a notice or otherwise   être informé, notamment par voie
learn/to (of a meeting)   d'avis
    c. C-44, s. 168(5)(b)
serve a notice(of the hearing)/to   adresser notification
    c. N-1, s. 17(3)
sign a notice of motion/to   signer un avis de motion
    c. A-15, s. 5(4)
take notice judicially/to   admettre d'office
    c. P-1, s. 5
noticed
    judicially noticed/to be   être admis d'office
    c. B-3, s. 209(4)
notification   notification
    c. C-26, Schedule I, Article
    38(2)
    c. T-7, s. 2   avis
    c. C-44, s. 190(12)b)   notification (d'une décision)
    (of a decision)
    c. A-11, s. 15(2)
    acceptance completed by   acceptation complétée par
    notification   notification
    c. B-4, s. 2
    prior notification   préavis
    c. N-1, s. 15(1)
notify/to   notifier
    c. C-26, Schedule I, Article
    37(1)
    c. C-44, s. 197(f)(ii)   informer

c. C-44, s. 201(2) — aviser
c. S-26, s. 53(5)
c. C-44, s. 206(3)(d) — donner avis
noting
(of a bill) — inscription
   c. B-4, s. 118(2)
notwithstanding — malgré
   c. F-7, s. 7(2)
c. A-11, s. 14 — par dérogation à
c. A-2, s. 19 — nonobstant
noxious
poison or other destructive or — poison ou autre substance
noxious thing — destructive ou délétère
   c. C-46, s. 245
nuclear material — matières nucléaires
   c. C-46, s. 7(3.6)
nude
nude in a public place/to be — être nu dans un endroit public
   c. C-46, s. 174(1)(a)
nugatory
(an agreement) — inopérant
   c. B-1, s. 303(9)(b)
nuisance
common nuisance — nuisance publique
   c. C-46, s. 180(2)
nullity
judgment of nullity of the — jugement en nullité de mariage
marriage
   c. C-8, s. 55(1)
nullity of marriage — annulation de mariage
   c. C-46, s. 166(1)(b)
number
serial number on a firearm — numéro de série sur une arme à feu
   c. C-46, s. 104(3)(a)
nursing aid — aide-infirmière
   c. C-31, s. 48
Nursing Auxiliary Canadian — Corps des infirmières auxiliaires de
Red Cross Corps — la Croix-Rouge canadienne
   c. C-31, s. 43
Nursing Division of the St-John — Division des infirmières de la
Ambulance Brigade of Canada — Brigade ambulancière Saint-Jean
du Canada
   c. C-31, s. 43
nursing service — services infirmiers
   c. C-6, s. 2
nutrient — substance nutritive
   c. C-11, s. 19

O

oath
administer an oath/to — faire prêter un serment
   c. C-12, s. 19(e)
attend under oath/to — comparaître sous la foi du serment
   c. C-12, s. 19(e)
give evidence under oath/to — témoigner sous la foi du serment
   c. C-12, s. 19(e)
information on oath — dénonciation faite sous serment
   c. C-12, s. 20(4)(b)

oath of fidelity and secrecy	serment de fidélité et de secret professionnel
c. A-16, s. 19(1)	
oath of office	serment professionnel
c. B-6, s. 37(1)	
receive evidence on oath/to	accepter sous serment un témoignage
c. L-2, s. 16(c)	
take an oath of fidelity/to	prêter le serment de fidélité
c. B-2, s. 16	
take an oath of secrecy/to	prêter le serment de secret professionnel
c. B-2, s. 16	
take an oath/to	prêter serment
c. S-26, s. 10	
obedience	
in obedience (to an order)	en conformité avec
c. C-34, s. 22(2)	
in obedience to the laws	en exécution des lois
c. C-46, s. 15	
obey/to	
(a judgment)	se conformer
c. S-26, s. 65(1)(a)	
object	mission
c. C-11, s. 15(1)	
objection	opposition
c. B-1, s. 12(3)	
c. S-26, s. 93	
(to an indictment)	objection
c. C-46, s. 601(1)	
objectionable	
(count)	inadmissible
c. C-46, s. 590(1)	
objective	
political objective	objectif politique
c. C-23, s. 2	
objects	
(of a corporation)	mission
c. A-10, s. 5(1)(c)	
(of the Commission)	mission et pouvoirs
c. C-22, s. 14(1)	
obligation	engagement
c. B-1, s. 2(1)	
contractual obligation	obligation contractuelle
c. C-19, s. 31	
debt obligation	titre de créance
c. C-44, s. 2(1)	
debt, obligation or claim	créance
c. F-11, s. 25(1)	
equipment trust obligation	engagement garanti par du matériel
c. B-1, s. 2(1)	
joint financial obligation (of spouces)	obligation financière commune
c. C-3, s. 15(8)(a)	
loan of obligation	prêt d'obligation
c. N-11, s. 2	
obligation and liability (of a corporation)	obligation et responsabilité
c. L-12, s. 97(1)	
obligations	titres
c. C-9, s. 50(1)	

obliterate/to
  (a crossing)   effacer
    c. B-4, s. 170(2)
  (serial number on a firearm)   effacer
    c. C-46, s. 104(4)
obscene
  immoral, indecent or obscene   représentation, spectacle ou
  performance, entertainment or   divertissement immoral, indécent
  representation   ou obscène
    c. C-46, s. 167(2)
observation
  (of the court)   observation
    c. C-46, s. 760
observe/to
  (a provision of an agreement)   respecter
    c. C-20, s. 11(1)(d)
  observe and inspect/to (persons)   surveiller et inspecter
    c. A-2, s. 7(9)
observer status   statut d'observateur
    c. C-12, s. 26(3)
obstruct/to
  (someone)   entraver l'action (de qqn)
    c. A-1, s. 67(1)
  obstruct or hinder/to (an   faire obstacle
  administrator)
    c. C-40, s. 107(1)(a)
  obstruct or hinder/to (an   entraver l'action
  inspector)
    c. A-7, s. 17
  obstruct or hinder/to (an   gêner l'action d'un inspecteur
  inspector)
    c. C-24, s. 58(1)
  obstruct or hinder/to (an   entraver ou gêner
  investigation)
    c. A-2, s. 8(5)
  obstruct, interrupt or   empêcher, interrompre ou gêner
  interfere/to (with a person)
    c. C-46, s. 430(1.1)(c)
  obstruct, pervert or defeat the   entraver, détourner ou contrecarrer
  course of justice/to   le cours de la justice
    c. C-46, s. 139(1)
obstruct or hinder/to
  (an inspector)   entraver l'action
    c. C-11, s. 27(1)
obtain/to
  (evidence)   obtenir
    c. A-7, s. 5(2)(a)
occult
  occult or crafty science   science occulte ou magique
    c. C-46, s. 365(c)
occupation
  occupation rent   loyer d'occupation
    c. B-3, s. 136(1)(f)
  tenancy or right of occupation   location ou droit d'occupation
    c. C-46, s. 210(4)
occupational
  occupational category   catégorie professionnelle
    c. T-7, s. 2
  occupational classification   catégorie professionnelle
    c. L-2, s. 212(3)(b)
occupied/to be
  principally occupied in/to be   avoir comme activité principale
    c. C-49, s. 11(2)(b)

occupier
(of a parcel of land)   occupant
  c. N-7, s. 33(3)
as owner, landlord, lessor,   en qualité de possesseur,
tenant, occupier or agent (of   propriétaire, locateur, locataire,
common gaming house)   occupant ou agent
  c. C-46, s. 201(2)(b)
occupier of the premises   occupant du local
  c. C-46, s. 164(2)
owner, lessee, occupier or   possesseur,locataire, occupant ou
operator (of a stockyard)   exploitant
  c. L-9, s. 10

occurrence
aviation occurrence   fait aéronautique
  c. C-12, s. 2
occurence of an event   production d'un évènement
  c. C-46, s. 429(1)

octroi
formality of custom, octroi or   formalité de douane, d'octroi ou de
police   police
  c. C-26, Schedule I, Article
    16(1)

offence   infraction
  c. A-11, s. 12(3)
disciplinary offence   mauvaise conduite
  c. P-5, s. 26
first offence   première infraction
  c. C-46, s. 85(1)(c)
further offence   récidive
  c. C-38, s. 17(2)(b)
included offence   infraction comprise
  c. C-46, s. 676(2)
indictable offence   acte criminel
  c. C-46, s. 47(1)
offence included in the principal   infraction incluse dans l'infraction
offence   principale
  c. S-26, s. 43(2)(b)
offence of delinquency   infraction de délinquance
  c. Y-1, s. 45(8)
offence punishable on summary   infraction punissable par procédure
conviction   sommaire
  c. A-11, s. 33(3)
second or subsequent offence   infraction subséquente à une
                                                 première infraction
  c. C-46, s. 85(1)(d)
separate offence   infraction distincte
  c. C-32, s. 35(4)
serious personal injury offence   sévices graves à la personne
  c. C-46, s. 752

offend/to
with intent thereby to insult or   avec l'intention d'ainsi insulter ou
offend any person   offenser quelqu'un
  c. C-46, s. 173(b)

offender   contrevenant
  c. A-11, s. 42(2)
  c. Y-1, s. 41(1)   délinquant
dangerous offender   délinquant dangereux
  c. C-46, s. 753(b)
young offender   jeune contrevenant
  c. Y-1, s. 69

offensive
offensive volatile substance   substance volatile malfaisante
  c. C-46, s. 178(a)

offensive weapon   arme offensive ou arme
    c. C-46, s. 2
    offensive weapon or explosive   arme offensive ou substance
    substance   explosive
      c. C-46, s. 78(1)
offer   pollicitation
    c. C-44, s. 194
    offer of shares   offre d'actions
      c. B-1, s. 110(6)
offer/to
    (evidence)   présenter
      c. C-34, s. 13(2)
    offer for sale/to   mettre en vente
      c. A-7, s. 3(2)(a)
offeree   pollicité
    c. C-44, s. 194
    dissenting offeree   pollicité dissident
      c. C-44, s. 206(1)
offerer   pollicitant
    c. C-44, s. 194
offering price   prix offert
    c. B-1, s. 146(4)
offeror
    rival offeror   pollicitant concurrent
      c. C-44, s. 205(4)(d)
office   poste
    c. B-1, s. 46(4)(b)
    c. A-1, s. 3   organisme
    c. B-6, s. 12(2)   fonction
    c. C-8, s. 2(1)
    c. C-46, s. 118   charge ou emploi
    (of a bank)   bureau
      c. B-1, s. 2(1)
    (of judge)   charge
      c. S-26, s. 9(2)
    (of the Information Commission)   commissariat
      c. A-1, s. 38
    (of Chairman)   poste
      c. C-22, s. 6(3)
    branch office   succursale
      c. C-34, s. 68(a)
    by virtue of his office   en raison de ses fonctions
      c. C-46, s. 24(2)
    continue in office/to   poursuivre son mandat
      c. 31 (4th Supp.), s. 108
    head or central office   siège ou administration centrale
      c. S-22, s. 18(b)
    high judicial office   haute charge judiciaire
      c. C-42, s. 68(2)
    hold office of emolument/to   remplir des fonctions rétribuées
      c. S-26, s. 7
    hold office/to   occuper un poste
      c. C-44, s. 121c)
    hold office/to (under Her   occuper une fonction
    Majesty)
      c. C-46, s. 748(3)
    holder of an office   titulaire d'une charge ou d'un
         emploi
      c. B-4, s. 18(3)
    judicial office   charge judiciaire
      c. C-46, s. 119(1)(a)
    judicial office   fonction judiciaire
      c. C-46, s. 469(c)

office of profit   charge publique lucrative
    c. P-1, s. 33(4)
office under the Crown   fonction relevant de la Couronne
    c. C-46, s. 748(1)
principal office   siège
    c. A-1, s. 60
seal of office (of a minister)   sceau officiel
    c. L-12, s. 5(1)
term of office   mandat
    c. C-44, s. 168(7)

Office of the Co-ordinator, Status of Women   Bureau de la coordinatrice de la situation de la femme
    c. A-1, Schedule I

Office of the Comptroller General   Bureau du contrôleur général
    c. A-1, Schedule I

Office of the Correctional Investigator   Bureau de l'enquêteur correctionnel
    c. A-1, Schedule I

Office of the Custodian of Enemy Property   Bureau du séquestre (biens ennemis)
    c. A-1, Schedule I

Office of the International Union for the Protection of Literary and Artistic Works   Bureau de l'Union internationale pour la protection des oeuvres littéraires et artistiques
    c. C-42, Schedule II Article 21

officer   fonctionnaire
    c. A-1, s. 5(1)(d)
    c. B-3, s. 2
    c. A-11, s. 3(t)   agent
    c. A-17, s. 12   cadre
    c. C-44, s. 2(1)   dirigeant
(of a government institution)   cadre
    c. A-1, s. 18(c)
(of a Department)   fonctionnaire
    c. C-9, s. 9(2)(c)
any officer, director or agent (of a corporation)   dirigeant, administrateur ou mandataire
    c. A-4, s. 5(2)
arresting officer or officer in charge   agent qui a procédé à l'arrestation ou fonctionnaire responsable
    c. Y-1, s. 11(2)
chief executive officer   premier dirigeant
    c. C-9, s. 17(4)
clerk, servant or officer   commis, préposé ou dirigeant
    c. B-3, s. 10(3)
conciliation officer   conciliateur
    c. L-2, s. 3(1)
consular officer   agent consulaire
    c. C-29, s. 3(2)(a)
diplomatic officer   agent diplomatique
    c. C-29, s. 3(2)(a)
officer in charge   fonctionnaire responsable
    c. C-46, s. 493
officer of the court   fonctionnaire du tribunal
    c. C-46, s. 482(3)(a)
officer of the Court   fonctionnaire judiciaire
    c. S-26, s. 24
officer of the Court   personnel judiciaire
    c. S-26, s. 21
officer of the Minister   personne désignée par le ministère
    c. A-11, s. 14(b)

probation officer	agent de probation
c. C-46, s. 735(1)	
protection officer (fishery)	garde-pêche
c. C-33, s. 2	
public officer	fonctionnaire public
c. C-46, s. 120(a)	
safety officer	agent de sécurité
c. L-2, s. 122	
senior executive officer	premier dirigeant
c. C-43, s. 13(5)	
warrant officer	sous-officier breveté
c. C-17, s. 60(1)	
officer-director	administrateur-dirigeant
c. F-11, s. 105(10)	
officers	
officers and employees	personnel
c. C-11, s. 16(2)	
officers, clerks and employees	fonctionnaires, commis et préposés
c. A-2, s. 25	
officers, clerks and employees	personnel
c. A-4, s. 3(7)	
official	fonctionnaire
c. C-44, s. 187(6)	
c. C-46, s. 118	
judicial or official instrument	acte judiciaire ou officiel
c. L-12, s. 42(1)(a)(iii)	
municipal official	fonctionnaire municipal
c. C-46, s. 123(3)	
official character (of a person)	caractère officiel
c. A-2, s. 27(2)	
official character (of a person)	qualité officielle
c. C-12, s. 45(1)	
official of a department	fonctionnaire d'un ministère
c. L-2, s. 112(2)	
perform an official act/to	accomplir un acte officiel
c. C-46, s. 123(1)(f)	
official capacity	qualité officielle
c. F-11, s. 2	
officials	
(of the Minister)	personnel
c. L-2, s. 260	
offshore	
offshore area	zone entrecôtière
c. N-7, s. 123	
oil well	
existing or prospective oil well	puits de pétrole existant ou en perspective
c. C-46, s. 396(1)(a)	
omission	
commit an act or omission/to	commettre une action ou omission
c. C-46, s. 7(1)	
commit an act or omission/to	commettre un acte
c. C-46, s. 7(3)(d)	
wilful omission	omission volontaire
c. C-46, s. 214	
on account of	
on account of insanity	pour cause d'aliénation mentale
c. C-46, s. 537(3)	
on behalf of	
(a Minister)	au nom de
c. A-10, s. 13(2)	
act on behalf/to (of the complainants)	par l'intermédiaire d'un représentant
c. A-1, s. 30(2)	

in the name of or on behalf of
c. C-44, s. 14(1)

au nom de ou pour le compte de

on demand
payable on demand
c. B-1, s. 270(4)(c)(i)

payable à vue

on oath
c. A-1, s. 36(1)(a)

sous la foi du serment

on oath or by affidavit

déclaration verbale ou écrite sous serment

c. A-1, s. 36(1)(c)

onus
c. B-3, s. 81(3)

charge

the onus is on the accused to prove
c. C-46, s. 115(1)

c'est à l'inculpé qu'il incombe de prouver

open
open court
c. S-26, s. 27(1)

audience publique

open market
c. N-7, s. 97(2)

marché libre

open to inspection (a register)
c. C-42, s. 54(5)

accessible au public

open court
in open court
c. C-46, s. 486(1)

en audience publique

open custody
c. Y-1, s. 24(1)

garde en milieu ouvert

open-end mutual fund

société d'investissement à capital variable

c. C-44, s. 26(11)

open-market
c. B-2, s. 18(k)

marché libre

open-market operation
c. B-2, s. 18(k)

opération d'open-market

operate/to
(ship)
c. C-31, s. 56(1)(j)

mettre en service

establish, maintain and operate/to (facilities)
c. A-13, s. 4(f)

constituer et exploiter

operate a vessel/to
c. C-46, s. 259(1)

conduire un bateau

operate in favour of the accused/to
c. N-1, s. 7(2)

jouer en faveur de l'accusé

operate in favour of the defendant/to
c. C-46, s. 794(2)

jouer en faveur du défendeur

operated
provincially operated mental hospital
c. P-5, s. 30(1)

hôpital psychiatrique sous administration provinciale

operating
c. N-11, s. 82(4)

exploitation

operating balance
c. C-8, s. 110(1)

solde d'exploitation

operating budget
c. F-11, s. 123

budget de fonctionnement

operating expense
c. C-11, s. 12(1)(c)

dépense de fonctionnement

operating expense (of a corporation)
c. N-11, s. 30(3)(c)

frais d'exploitation

operation
  c. A-10, s. 5(2)(b)
  c. A-13, s. 4(k)
  (of a clause)
  c. A-11, s. 3(k)
  (of a committee)
  c. L-2, s. 136(1)(d)
  (of an Act)
  c. C-24, s. 20(1)
  by operation of law
  c. B-1, s. 75(2)
  by operation of law
  c. C-46, s. 90(3)
  conduct or manage any scheme, contrivance or operation/to
  c. C-46, s. 206(1)(d)
  navigation or operation (of vessel or aircraft)
  c. C-46, s. 662(5)
Operation Dismantle
  c. C-18, Schedule
operational
  general operational policies
  c. C-23, s. 7(1)(a)
  operational activity
  c. C-23, s. 30(2)(b)
  operational policies

  c. C-23, s. 30(2)(a)
operative
  operative to vest/to be
  c. C-42, s. 14(1)
operator
  c. C-32, s. 2
opinion
  (of court)
  c. S-26, s. 36
  (of judge)
  c. S-26, s. 27(1)
  in the opinion (of the Minister)
  c. A-11, s. 12(3)
opium poppy
  c. N-1, s. 2
opportunity
  at the first reasonable opportunity
  c. C-46, s. 486(4)
  reasonable opportunity to be heard
  c. C-32, s. 16(3)
  reasonable opportunity to be heard
  c. C-32, s. 19(4)(a)
opposite
  opposite party
  c. C-39, s. 27
  c. C-46, s. 822(5)(c)
Opposition House Leader
  c. P-1, s. 62(e)
oppressive/to be
  c. C-44, s. 214(a)
option
  c. C-6, s. 12(2)(a)

exploitation

opération
application

fonctionnement

application

par effet de la loi

de par la loi

conduire ou administrer un plan, un arrangement ou une opération

utilisation ou conduite

Operation Dismantle

orientation générale des opérations

activité opérationnelle

règles générales en matière opérationelle

avoir l'effet d'investir

responsable

avis

opinion

d'après

pavot somnifère

à la première occasion raisonnable

possibilité de se faire entendre

occasion de se faire entendre

partie adverse

leader de l'Opposition

abuser des droits

choix

at the option
    c. B-1, s. 111(8)

au gré

lease and option
    c. N-11, s. 30(3)(i)

bail avec option d'achat

order

(of a justice of the peace)
    c. A-11, s. 21(2)

ordonnance

(of the Minister)
    c. A-11, s. 6

arrêté

(of the Senate)
    c. F-11, s. 22

règlement

(of Governor in Council)
    c. A-11, s. 6

décret

by standing or other order (of the Senate or House)
    c. P-1, s. 13(1)(c)

par règlement ou ordre

conviction, ruling, order or judgment
    c. B-1, s. 258(1)(e)

décision judiciaire ou quasi-judiciaire

debenture, deed, bond, bill, note, warrant, order or other security for money
    c. C-46, s. 2

débenture, titre, obligation, billet, lettre, mandat, ordre ou autre garantie d'argent

designate by order/to
    c. A-1, s. 3

désigner par décret

judgment or order (of the Supreme Court)
    c. S-26, s. 2(1)"s. judgment"

arrêt ou ordonnance

judgment, rule, order, decision, decree, decretal order, or sentence
    c. S-26, s. 2(1)

décision

maintenance order
    c. B-3, s. 178(1)(i)

ordonnance de pension alimentaire

make an order/to
    c. A-11, s. 3

prendre un décret

make an order/to
    c. B-1, s. 50(4)(c)

rendre une ordonnance

making of an order
    c. A-12, s. 28(1)

prise d'un décret

order for attendance of parent
    c. Y-1, Schedule, Form 3

ordonnance pour requérir la présence du père ou de la mère

order for compensation
    c. Y-1, Schedule, Form 7

ordonnance accordant une indemnité

order for examination and report
    c. Y-1, Schedule, Form 5

ordonnance en vue d'un examen et d'un rapport

order for forfeiture
    c. C-46, s. 192(2)

ordonnance de confiscation

order for money
    c. C-40, s. 36(4)(c)

mandat de paiement

order in council
    c. B-1, s. 114(8)(b)

décret

order of disposition
    c. Y-1, Schedule, Form 7

ordonnance portant décision

order of general or specific application
    c. P-20, s. 11(4)

mesure d'application générale ou particulière

order or regulation (under an Act)
    c. A-11, s. 7(1)

texte d'application

order, exchequer acquittance or other security
    c. C-46, s. 2 — ordre, quittance de l'échiquier ou autre valeur

probation order
    c. C-46, s. 91(6) — ordonnance de probation

proclamation, order, regulation or appointment
    c. C-46, s. 370(a) — proclamation, décret, arrêté, règlement ou nomination

provisional order (divorce)
    c. 3 (2nd Supp.), s. 18(1) — ordonnance conditionnelle

receiving order
    c. C-21, s. 31(2) — ordonnance de mise sous séquestre

restraining order
    c. B-1, s. 105(2)(a)

order/to
(a person)
    c. C-11, s. 32 — enjoindre

order and require/to
    c. A-2, s. 14(2)(a) — ordonner

order someone to do something/to
    c. C-24, s. 66(1) — enjoindre à qqn de faire qqch

ordered/to be
    c. A-12, s. 24(2) — faire l'objet d'une ordonnance

ordinance
    c. Y-1, s. 2(1) — ordonnance

ordinary
ordinary place of residence
    c. A-7, s. 7(9)(b) — lieu de résidence habituelle

ordinary place of residence
    c. C-8, s. 116(3) — lieu ordinaire de résidence

ordinary procedure
    c. N-1, s. 17(5) — procédure ordinaire

ordinary resolution
    c. B-1, s. 2(1) — résolution ordinaire

ordinary shareholder
    c. L-12, s. 35(4) — actionnaire ordinaire

ordinary course
(of a business)
    c. C-44, s. 31(2) — cours ordinaire (d'une activité commerciale)

ordinary course of business
    c. B-3, s. 2 — cours ordinaire des affaires

ordinary court
    c. Y-1, s. 2(1) — juridiction normalement compétente

ordinary way
(proof)
    c. L-2, s. 253(4) — cours normal

prove in the ordinary way/to
    c. F-11, s. 158 — établir la validité de la façon habituelle

proven in the ordinary way (document)
    c. F-11, s. 74 — au même titre que l'original

ore
ore or mineral
    c. C-46, s. 333 — minerai ou minéraux

organization
    c. A-1, s. 3 — organisation
    c. A-13, s. 3(b)
    c. L-12, s. 46 — groupement

charitable or religious
organization
   c. C-46, s. 207(1)(b)

organisme de charité ou organisme
religieux

employers' organization
   c. L-2, s. 3(1)

organisation patronale

private organization
   c. A-13, s. 4(b)

organisation privée

public organization
   c. A-13, s. 4(b)

organisation publique

organize/to
incorporate, form or organize a
corporation/to
   c. B-1, s. 109(1)(b)

constituer, former ou établir une
personne morale

original
court of original jurisdiction
   c. S-26, s. 47

tribunal de première instance

original article (of incorporation)
   c. F-11, s.
    83(1)(b)(a)"articles"

clause initiale

original cause
   c. S-26, s. 65(1)

cause en première instance

original character (of a work)
   c. C-42, s. 2

caractère original

original court
   c. C-30, Schedule, Article I

tribunal d'origine

original document
   c. A-2, s. 27(1)(a)

pièce originale

original or collateral agreement
or arrangement
   c. C-46, s. 347(2)

convention initiale ou annexe

original or restated (articles)
   c. C-44, s. 2(1)

initial ou mis à jour

original owner
   c. B-5, s. 3(c)

propriétaire primitif

original parties to the suit
   c. S-26, s. 77

parties à l'origine du procès

original purchase price
   c. L-12, s. 78(1)

prix d'achat originaire

original security
   c. B-1, s. 107(3)

valeur initiale

original article
(of incorporation)
   c. F-11, s.
    83(1)(b)(a)"articles"

clause initiale

originate/to
(proceeding)
   c. C-36, s. 14(1)

prendre naissance

originating
by petition or by way of
originating summons or notice
of motion
   c. C-36, s. 10

par requête ou par voie
d'assignation introductive
d'instance ou d' avis de motion

to make an application in a
summary manner by petition or
originating notice of motion

présenter une demande par voie
sommaire sous forme de requête
ou d'avis de motion introductive
d'instance

   c. C-44, s. 248

ostensibly
person ostensibly in control of
the place or premises
   c. C-46, s. 487.1(7)

personne apparemment responsable
des lieux

otherwise
gold in dust, solution or
otherwise
   c. C-46, s. 451

or en poudre, en solution ou sous
d'autres formes

out of the Consolidated Revenue Fund
    c. A-13, s. 31
out-patient
    in-patient or out-patient
    c. C-6, s. 2
outcome
    (of a hearing)
    c. B-3, s. 8(1)(a)(i)
outer edge
    outer edge of the continental margin
    c. C-53, s. 2(1)
output
    (of process)
    c. P-35, s. 2
outstanding
    (amount)
    c. B-1, s. 176(1)
    outstanding debenture

    c. C-43, s. 4(1)(k)
    outstanding share
    c. C-44, s. 26(5)(b)
over-payment
    c. F-11, s. 155(3)
over-the-counter market
    (share)
    c. C-44, s. 194(b)
overage
    overage and shortage
    c. C-24, s. 37(1)(b)
overdue
    overdue payments
    c. N-11, s. 47(f)(ii)
overdue/to be
    (a bill)
    c. B-4, s. 71
overissue
    (of securities)
    c. B-1, s. 75(2)
    c. C-44, s. 48(2)
overpayment
    c. C-8, s. 8(2)(b)
overpowering
    stupefying or overpowering thing
    c. C-46, s. 230(b)
Overseas Welfare Worker

    c. C-31, s. 48
overt
    overt act
    c. C-46, s. 46(2)(d)
overthrow/to
    (the government)
    c. C-46, s. 46(2)(a)
own/to
    (shares)
    c. B-1, s. 119(3)
    own and possess/to (property)
    c. B-1, s. 264(2)

par prélèvement sur le trésor

malade hospitalisé ou externe

résultat (d'une audition)

rebord externe de la marge continentale

rendement

impayé

débenture émise mais non remboursée

action en circulation

paiement en trop

hors bourse

excédant et manquant

arrérages

être échu

émission excédentaire

versement excédentaire

stupéfiant ou soporifique

préposée d'assistance sociale outre-mer

acte manifeste

renverser (le gouvernement)

posséder

être propriétaire

own beneficially/to
    c. C-44, s. 2(1)(a)
own and to hold/to
  (of a share)
    c. B-1, s. 9(7)(b)
owned/to be
  (a corporation)
    c. B-1, s. 35(1)(j)
owner
  as owner, landlord, lessor,
  tenant, occupier or agent (of
  common gaming house)
    c. C-46, s. 201(2)(b)
  every one, person, owner

    c. C-46, s. 2
  home owner
    c. N-11, s. 9(1)(b)(i)
  home owner
    c. N-11, s. 71(1)(a)
  owner, lessee, occupier or
  operator (of a stockyard)
    c. L-9, s. 10
  registered owner (of securities)
    c. F-11, s. 60(1)(b)(i)
ownership
    c. A-2, s. 18(1)(e)
  beneficial ownership
    c. B-1, s. 110(14)(a)
  beneficial ownership
    c. C-44, s. 2(1)
  issue, transfer or ownership (of
  a share)
    c. C-44, s. 6(1)(d)
  stock ownership
    c. C-19, s. 6(7)
  Canadian ownership or control
    c. C-44, s. 174(1)(c)
  Canadian ownership rate
    c. C-20, s. 2(6)
oyster bed
    c. C-46, s. 323(1)

avoir la propriété effective

conserver la possession

appartenir

en qualité de possesseur,
propriétaire, locateur, locataire,
occupant ou agent

quiconque, individu, personne ou
propriétaire

propriétaire-occupant

propriétaire de maison

possesseur, locataire, occupant ou
exploitant

titulaire

propriété

propriété effective

véritable propriétaire

émission, transfert ou appartenance

détention du capital-actions

participation ou contrôle canadien

taux de participation canadienne

huîtrière

p

Pacific Pilotage Authority

    c. A-1, Schedule I
    c. F-11, Schedule III, Part I

pacing
  running, trotting or pacing
  horse-races
    c. C-46, s. 204(1)(c)
package
    c. A-7, s. 2
    c. F-27, s. 2
    c. L-9, s. 31
packer
    c. L-9, s. 10

Administration de pilotage du
Pacifique

Administration du pilotage du
Pacifique

courses de chevaux, courses de
chevaux en trot ou à l'amble

emballage

exploitant de salaison

packer's yard
    c. L-9, s. 10   parc de salaison
packet
    c. C-46, s. 187(1)   paquet
paid
  fully paid share   action entièrement libérée
    c. B-1, s. 118(3)
  paid instrument   acquit
    c. B-1, s. 157(1)
paid-in capital   capital versé
    c. B-1, s. 2(2)(c)
paid-up
  paid-up and unimpaired   capital versé et intact
    c. L-12, s. 72(1)
paid-up capital   capital versé
    c. B-2, s. 27(a)
panel   groupe
    c. C-6, s. 12(2)(b)
  appoint a panel/to   nommer un groupe
    c. P-35, s. 61(1)
  general panel (of jurors)   liste générale
    c. C-46, s. 642(3)
  original panel (of jurors)   première liste
    c. C-46, s. 642(3)
  panel of jurors   liste de jurés
    c. C-46, s. 474
  regional panel   liste régionale
    c. P-2, s. 8(2)
Papaver sommiferum/L   Papaver somniferum/L
    c. N-1, s. 2
paper
  to be on paper   être rédigé par écrit
    c. C-46, s. 580
par value
  (shares)   valeur nominale
    c. B-1, s. 2(2)(b)(i)
  (shares)   valeur au pair
    c. B-1, s. 116(2)
  without nominal or par value   sans valeur au pair ou nominale
  (shares)
    c. C-44, s. 24(1)
paragraph   alinéa
    c. A-1, s. 3
parcel of land
  limit, boundary or angle of a   limite ou angle d'une concession,
  concession, range, lot or parcel   d'un rang, d'un lot ou d'un lopin
  of land   de terre
    c. C-46, s. 443(1)(b)
parcels
  sell in parcels/to   vendre par lots
    c. B-3, s. 30(1)(a)
pardon   pardon
    c. C-46, s. 607(1)(c)
    c. C-46, s. 748(4)   réhabilitation
  (of persons convicted)   réhabilitation
    c. C-47, s. 2(1)
  free or conditional pardon   pardon absolu ou conditionnel
    c. C-46, s. 749(2)
  to be granted a pardon   obtenir la réhabilitation
    c. Y-1, s. 44(2)(b)
pardon/to   accorder un pardon
    c. T-15, s. 18

parent
    c. B-8, s. 14(a)
    c. C-46, s. 110(7)
    c. C-31, s. 36
    c. Y-1, s. 2(1)
  parent, foster parent, guardian
  or head of a family
    c. C-46, s. 215(1)(a)
parent Crown corporation
    c. F-11, s. 2
pari passu
  rank pari passu/to
    c. A-12, s. 6(4)(a)
pari-mutual system
    c. C-46, s. 204(1)(c)
Parliament
  member of Parliament
    c. C-46, s. 748(2)
  Parliament or legislature of a
  province
    c. C-46, s. 60(b)(ii)
Parliament Hill

    c. P-1, s. 80(1)
Parliamentary Librarian
    c. C-10, s. 35(2)(c)
parol
  trustee of an express trust
  created by deed, will or
  instrument in writing, or by
  parol
    c. C-46, s. 2

parole
  day parole
    c. C-46, s. 100(3)
  day parole
    c. C-46, s. 747(2)
    c. P-2, s. 2
  parole certificate

    c. P-2, s. 18
  parole supervisor
    c. P-2, s. 2
paroled inmate
    c. P-2, s. 2
part
  all or part (of the property)
    c. C-44, s. 224(1)(b)
part/to
  alienate or part with the
  property/to
    c. C-46, s. 390
part-time
  (member)
    c. B-9, s. 4
participant
  agent of a participant
    c. C-34, s. 69(1)
participate/to
  (in a pension plan)
    c. C-23, s. 5(2)
particular
  (of an issue of shares)
    c. B-1, s. 77(1)(c)

père ou mère

parent
père ou mère ou père et mère
père ou mère, parent nourricier,
  tuteur ou chef de famille

société d'État mère

venir au même rang

système de pari mutuel

membre du Parlement

Parlement ou législature d'une
  province

Colline parlementaire ou Colline du
  Parlement

bibliothécaire parlementaire

fiduciaire aux termes d'une fiducie
  explicite établie par acte, tes
  tament ou instrument écrit, ou
  verbalement

libération conditionnelle de jour

semi-liberté

certificat de libération
  conditionnelle

surveillant de liberté conditionnelle

libéré conditionnel

tout ou partie

aliéner un bien ou s'en dessaisir

à temps partiel

agent d'un participant

cotiser

condition

parent

particularly
made applicable particularly to a committee/to be (a regulation)
c. L-2, s. 136(2)
être applicable à un comité particulier

particulars
c. B-1, s. 155(1)(c)
c. C-44, s. 129
modalités

c. C-46, s. 587(1)
détails

c. C-44, s. 50(1)(c)
conditions

set out particulars/to
donner des précisions
c. 4 (2nd Supp.), s. 9(d)

parties
(to an agreement)
intéressés
c. A-8, s. 13(1)(a)

partner
associé
c. B-1, s. 35(1)(i)

c. C-20, s. 4(c)
sociétaire

(partnership)
associé
c. C-44, s. 2(1)(b)

business partner
associé
c. C-44, s. 161(2)b)

firm or partner thereof
firme ou un de ses associés
c. C-46, s. 384(a)

general partner
commandité
c. C-20, s. 5(3)(a)

joint owner tenant in common or partner
copropriétaire tenancier en commun ou associé
c. C-46, s. 328(d)

limited partner
commanditaire
c. B-1, s. 193(1)

partnership
société de personnes
c. A-14, s. 2
c. B-1, s. 2(1)
c. C-44, s. 2(1)(b)

c. C-49, s. 11(2)
société

(of auditors)
société
c. F-11, s. 83(1)(b)

corporation, firm or partnership
personne morale, firme ou société de personnes

c. C-46, s. 391

limited partnership
société en commandite
c. C-20, s. 5(3)(a)

partnership agreement
contrat de société de personnes
c. C-44, s. 77(7)

party
partie
c. A-12, s. 21(2)

(to an offence)
coauteur
c. C-8, s. 103(3)
c. C-44, s. 32(4)

accommodation party (to a bill)
partie à un effet de complaisance
c. B-4, s. 54(1)

add as a party/to
mettre en cause
c. C-44, s. 226(5)(a)

opposite party
partie adverse
c. C-39, s. 27

party adverse
partie adverse
c. C-39, s. 20(1)

party to an offense/to be
être des coauteurs de l'infraction
c. A-16, s. 20(2)

remote party
partie qui n'est pas détenteur régulier

c. B-4, s. 39(1)

party/to be
 (an offence)   participer
  c. C-46, s. 21(1)
pass/to
 (a resolution)   adopter
  c. C-44, s. 2(1)
 (a sentence)   prononcer
  c. C-46, s. 676(1)(d)
 (an Act)   adopter
  c. S-26, s. 53(5)
pass off
 to pass off other services as and   passer d'autres services pour et
 for those ordered   contre les services requis
  c. C-46, s. 408(a)
pass through/to   en transit
  c. A-11, s. 3(j)
passage-way
 doorway or passage-way (in   baie de porte ou passage
 dwelling-house)
  c. C-46, s. 2
passenger   voyageur
  c. C-26, s. 2(1)
passing
 passing (of an Act)   adoption
  c. P-2, s. 14(2)
 suspend the passing of   surseoir au prononcé de la sentence
 sentence/to
  c. C-46, s. 737(1)(a)
passing off   substitution
  c. C-46, s. 408
passport   passeport
  c. C-46, s. 57(1)(b)(ii)
past services
 to pay in money or in property   libérer soit en numéraire, soit en
 or in past services   biens ou en services rendus
  c. C-44, s. 25(3)
Patent Office   Bureau des brevets
  c. C-42, s. 46
patent right   brevet d'invention
  c. A-16, s. 10(c)
patron   membre bienfaiteur
  c. A-13, s. 26(f)
  c. C-40, s. 3(1)   client
patronage
 patronage dividend   ristourne
  c. L-9, s. 31.
 patronage return   ristourne à la clientèle
  c. C-40, s. 3(1)
pattern
 pattern of repetitive behaviour   répétition d'actes
  c. C-46, s. 753(a)(i)
pawn   nantissement
  c. B-3, s. 79
 taking in pawn (of firearms)   prise en gage
  c. C-46, s. 105(1)
pay   solde
  c. C-17, s. 2(1)
 holiday with pay   congé payé
  c. L-2, s. 193(1)
 vacation pay   indemnité de congé annuel
  c. L-2, s. 183
pay/to
 (an amount of money)   acquitter
  c. A-5, s. 9

(for the share)   libérer
    c. C-44, s. 25(3)
(to producers)   verser
    c. A-8, s. 12(1)(b)
pay one's liability/to   honorer son engagement
    c. B-1, s. 278(2)

pay into/to
    proceeds to be paid into court (of   consignation en justice du produit
    a sale)
        c. S-26, s. 68

pay out/to
    (of such moneys)   prélever (sur les crédits)
        c. 31 (4th Supp.), s. 109(2)
    (of the moneys)   acquitter (sur les deniers)
        c. A-6, s. 10

pay-day   jour de paye
    c. L-2, s. 247(a)

payable   exigible
    c. B-1, s. 133(1)
    payable after notice (a deposit)   payable à préavis
        c. B-1, Schedule X, Section 2
    payable on a fixed date (a   payable à terme fixe
    deposit)
        c. B-1, Schedule X, Section 3
    payable on demand (a bill of   payable à vue
    exchange)
        c. B-1, s. 188
    payable out of public money/to   être rémunéré avec le fonds public
    be (a salary or remuneration)
        c. B-2, s. 10(4)(b)
    payable to bearer on demand (a   payable sur demande au porteur
    note)
        c. B-2, s. 26(1)
    recovery or collection of any debt   recouvrement d'une créance
    or obligation due or payable
        c. F-11, s. 156(a)
    sum due or payable   somme due
        c. F-11, s. 155(4)

payee
    (of a bill)   preneur
        c. B-4, s. 18(2)
    (of a cheque)   bénéficiaire
        c. C-8, s. 90(1)(b)

paying officer   agent payeur
    c. F-11, s. 66

payment
    initial payment   acompte à la livraison
        c. C-24, s. 48(1)
    payment item   instrument de paiement
        c. C-21, s. 2(1)
    payment out of court (of moneys   remboursement hors cour
    deposited as security for costs)
        c. C-39, s. 81

payment bond   cautionnement
    c. F-11, s. 72

payroll   feuille de paye
    c. L-2, s. 249(2)(a)

peace
    keep the peace/to   ne pas troubler l'ordre public
        c. C-47, s. 2(1)
peace officer   agent de la paix
    c. C-9, s. 22(2)
    c. C-12, s. 36(5)(a)

peaceable
actual and peaceable possession (of real property)
c. C-46, s. 72(1)
     possession effective et paisible

peaceable possession (of personal property)
c. C-46, s. 38(1)
     paisible possession

Pêcheries Canada Inc
c. F-11, Schedule III, Part I
     Pêcheries Canada Inc.

pecuniary
fine, pecuniary penalty or forfeiture
c. C-46, s. 724
     amende, peine pécuniaire ou confiscation

have a pecuniary interest/to
c. C-16, s. 5
     détenir un intérêt pécuniaire

pecuniary interest (of a person)
c. L-2, s. 81(2)
     intérêts financiers

pecuniary or proprietary interest
c. C-22, s. 5(1)(b)
     intérêt pécuniaire ou droit de propriété

pedigree
(title)
c. C-46, s. 385(1)(b)
     généalogie

pen
pen or enclosure (for animals)
c. C-46, s. 348(3)(d)
     parc ou enclos

penal
penal action
c. C-45, s. 27
     action pénale

penalize/to
(a person)
c. C-34, s. 19(3)
     infliger une peine

penalties
imposition of penalties
c. B-6, s. 22(b)
     imposition de pénalités

penalty
c. A-11, s. 47(2)
c. A-12, s. 24(1)
     peine

c. C-44, s. 233
     sanction

drawback or penalty
c. F-7, s. 37
     retenue ou pénalité

financial penalty
c. L-2, s. 154(d)
     sanction pécuniaire

pecuniary penalty
c. C-19, s. 9(1)(b)
     peine pécuniaire

pendency
during the pendency of an appeal
c. S-26, s. 48(1)
     à tout stade de l'appel

pending
(proceeding)
c. C-50, s. 21(3)
     pendant

action or proceeding pending
c. C-9, s. 28(2)
     poursuite ou procédure en cours

case pending in court
c. S-26, s. 90
     instance devant la Cour

pending proceeding
c. C-40, s. 126
     procédure en instance

penitentiary
c. C-46, s. 731(8)
c. P-5, s. 2
     pénitencier

inmate in a penitentiary, jail, reformatory or prison/to be
c. C-29, s. 21(c)
     être détenu dans un pénitentier, une prison ou une maison de correction

penitentiary hospital   hôpital-pénitencier
    c. P-5, s. 22(5)
penitentiary, common jail,   pénitencier, prison commune,
public or reformatory prison,   prison publique, maison de
lock-up, guard-room   correction, poste de police ou corps
    de garde

    c. C-46, s. 2

pension   régime de pension
    c. C-7, s. 13(4)
bank pension fund   fonds bancaire de pension
    c. B-1, s. 174(2)(c)
pension fund   caisse de retraite
    c. B-2, s. 15(2)
provincial pension plan   régime provincial de pensions
    c. C-17, s. 2(1)
retirement pension   pension de retraite ou rente de
    retraite

    c. L-2, s. 235(2)(b)
Pension Appeals Board   Commission d'appel des pensions
    c. A-1, Schedule I
Pension Index   indice de pension
    c. C-8, s. 2(1)
Pension Review Board   Conseil de révision des pensions
    c. A-1, Schedule I
pensionable
pensionable employment   emploi ouvrant droit à pension
    c. C-8, s. 2(1)
pensionable service   service ouvrant droit à pension
    c. C-17, s. 4(1)
percentage
establish a percentage/to   fixer un pourcentage
    c. B-2, s. 19(e)
peremptorily   péremptoirement
    c. C-46, s. 633(1)
perfect/to
perfect a security/to   valider une sûreté
    c. C-46, s. 347(2)
perfect an interest/to   régulariser un droit
    c. B-1, s. 212(1)
perform/to
(duties)   acquitter
    c. A-2, s. 4(m)
perform an official act/to   accomplir un acte officiel
    c. C-46, s. 123(1)(f)
perform notarial acts/to   dresser des actes notariés
    c. C-42, s. 58(1)
performance   représentation, exécution ou
    audition

    c. C-42, s. 2
(of a contract)   exécution
    c. C-26, Schedule I, Article
    18(3)
(of a duty or function)   exercice
    c. A-1, s. 34
(of a person)   comportement
    c. Y-1, s. 4(4)(b)
(of an obligation)   exécution
    c. B-1, s. 83
    c. C-44, s. 2(1)
immoral, indecent or obscene   représentation, spectacle ou
performance, entertainment or   divertissement immoral, indécent
representation   ou obscène
    c. C-46, s. 167(2)

performing right
    c. C-42, Schedule II
period of time
    c. A-1, s. 12(2)(b)
perjury
    c. C-44, s. 233
    c. C-46, s. 132(1)
    prosecution for perjury
    c. B-3, s. 10(5)
permanent
    permanent resident
    c. A-1, s. 4(1)(b)
    permanent staff (of the Militia)
    c. C-17, s. 2(1)
Permanent Active Air Force
    c. C-17, s. 2(1)
Permanent Active Militia
    c. C-17, s. 2(1)
Permanent Militia Corps
    c. C-17, s. 2(1)
Permanent Services Pension Account
    c. C-17, s. 4(2)
permission
    grant a permission/to
    c. B-1, s. 28(9)
permissive
    (provision of section)
    c. C-42, s. 58(4)
permit
    export permit
    c. C-51, s. 2
    permit book
    c. C-24, s. 2(1)
permit/to
    issue a permit/to
    c. L-2, s. 170(1)
persistent
    pattern of persistent aggressive behaviour
    c. C-46, s. 753(a)(ii)
person
    every one, person, owner

    c. C-46, s. 2
    person apprehended
    c. A-11, s. 21(2)
    person in charge
    c. A-7, s. 15(3)
    c. C-24, s. 56(4)
    person liable
    c. B-2, s. 23(c)
    person liable
    c. C-26, Schedule I, Article 27
    young person
    c. Y-1, s. 2(1)
personal
    by personal delivery
    c. C-20, s. 7(1)
    personal estate
    c. C-40, s. 48

droit d'exécution ou de représentation

délai

parjure

poursuite pour parjure

résident permanent

État-major permanent

Aviation active permanente

Milice active permanente

Corps de la milice permanente

compte de pension des services permanents

accorder une permission

facultatif

licence

carnet de livraison

accorder une dérogation

répétition continuelle d'actes d'agression

quiconque, individu, personne ou propriétaire

contrevenant

responsable

obligé

débiteur

adolescent

en main propre

bien personnel

personal estate   bien immeuble
    c. L-12, s. 31
personal property   meuble
    c. A-10, s. 18(c)
personal representative   représentant personnel
    c. C-26, Schedule II
serious personal injury offence   sévice grave à la personne
    c. C-46, s. 179(1)(b)
to have something in one's   avoir une chose en sa possession
personal possession   personnelle
    c. C-46, s. 4(3)(a)
personal services
to compensate in kind or by way   indemniser soit en nature soit en
of personal services   services
    c. Y-1, s. 20(1)(f)
personally
deliver personally/to (order)   remettre en mains propres
    c. Y-1, s. 10(2)
notice served personally or sent   avis signifié à personne ou envoyé
by mail   par la poste
    c. Y-1, s. 9(7)
personate/to   se faire passer pour une autre
    personne

    c. C-29, s. 29(2)(b)
(a person)   se faire passer pour une personne
    c. C-46, s. 403
personation   supposition de personne
    c. C-39, s. 57
personation with intent   supposition intentionnelle de
    personne
    c. C-46, s. 403
pertaining to
(a right)   attaché à
    c. B-1, s. 111(2)(c)
perusal
on perusal of the evidence   après avoir examiné les dépositions
    c. C-46, s. 777(1)
pervert/to
obstruct, pervert or defeat the   entraver, détourner ou contrecarrer
course of justice/to   le cours de la justice
    c. C-46, s. 139(1)
petition
(for letters patent)   requête
    c. L-12, s. 5(1)
(to the Senate or House of   pétition
Commons)
    c. C-46, s. 306(a)
application or petition   demande ou requête
    c. B-1, s. 122(5)(b)
by petition or by way of   par requête ou par voie
originating summons or notice   d'assignation introductive
of motion   d'instance ou d' avis de motion
    c. C-36, s. 10
election petition   requête en contestation d'élection
    c. S-26, s. 59(3)
to make an application in a   présenter une demande par voie
summary manner by petition or   sommaire sous forme de requête
originating notice of motion   ou d'avis de motion introductive
    d'instance

    c. C-44, s. 248
petitioner   pétitionnaire
    c. C-39, s. 8
    c. L-12, s. 5(1)   requérant

petitioning creditor   créancier pétitionnaire
    c. B-3, s. 43(2)
Petro-Canada   Petro-Canada
    c. F-11, Schedule III, Part II
Petroleum Compensation Board   Office des indemnisations
                                    pétrolières
    c. A-1, Schedule I
Petroleum Monitoring Agency   Agence de surveillance du secteur
                                      pétrolier
    c. A-1, Schedule I
philanthropic
    philanthropic corporation   organisme humanitaire doté de la
                                      personnalité morale
    c. L-12, s. 61(1)(d)
photographic
    photographic film form register   registre sous forme de
                                      reproductions photographiques
    c. F-11, s. 60(2)
physical
    actual physical possession   possession matérielle
    c. C-25, s. 13
physician services   services médicaux
    c. C-6, s. 2
Physicians for Social   Professionnels de la Santé pour une
Responsibility   Responsabilité Nucléaire
    c. C-18, Schedule
pick
    key, pick, rocker key, or other   clef, crochet, clef à levier, ou tout
    instrument   autre instrument
    c. C-46, s. 353(5)
pier
    slide, dam, pier or boom   glissoir, digue, jetée ou barrage
                                      flottant
    c. T-7, s. 19(a)
pipeline   pipeline
    c. N-7, s. 2
pirate
    (copyright)   contrefacteur
    c. C-42, Schedule II Article
    15
pirated work   oeuvre contrefaite
    c. C-42, Schedule II Article
    16
piratical act   acte de piraterie
    c. C-46, s. 75
place   lieu
    c. A-7, s. 2
    c. C-46, s. 197(1)   local ou endroit
    at his latest or usual place of   à sa dernière ou habituelle
    abode   résidence
    c. C-46, s. 509(2)
    building or place   lieux
    c. C-38, s. 15(5)
    place of business   établissement commercial
    c. C-42, s. 10
    place of business (of a drawee or   établissement
    an acceptor)
    c. B-4, s. 87(1)
    time and place   date, heure et lieu
    c. C-46, s. 700(1)
place of business   établissement
    (of a drawee or an acceptor)
    c. B-4, s. 87(1)

place of temporary detention
    c. Y-1, s. 7(1)

lieu de détention provisoire

placement
    private placement (of securities)
        c. B-1, s. 190(1)

souscription privée

plain
    full, fair and plain (disclosure)
        c. B-1, s. 148(1)

complet, exact et clair

    full, fair and plain (disclosure)
        c. B-1, s. 149(2)

sincère et complet

plaintiff
    c. C-44, s. 53(d)

demandeur

    c. C-50, s. 22(1)

plaignant

plan
    master plan of community
    development and land
    utilization
        c. N-11, s. 2

plan directeur de développement
local et d'occupation du sol

    official community plan
        c. N-11, s. 2

plan d'urbanisme

    plan of old age pensions and
    supplementary benefits
        c. C-8, s. 3(1)

régime de pension de vieillesse et de
prestations supplémentaires

plan/to
    c. C-21, s. 5

planifier

    (a program)
        c. C-11, s. 11(2)(c)

planifier

planned and deliberate murder

meurtre commis avec préméditation
et de propos délibéré

    c. C-46, s. 231(2)

planning
    local planning authority
        c. N-11, s. 2

service d'urbanisme local

plans and specifications
    c. C-32, s. 12(2)

plans et devis

plant
    c. L-12, s. 61(1)(b)(ii)

usine

    plant or equipment
        c. C-41, s. 11(1)(b)(ii)

usine ou matériel

plate
    (for sound recordings)
        c. C-42, s. 2

planche

plea
    enter a plea/to
        c. C-46, s. 606(2)

inscrire un plaidoyer

    plea of justification
        c. C-46, s. 612(1)

plaidoyer de justification

    plea of not guilty
        c. Y-1, s. 12(4)

plaidoyer de non-culpabilité

    plea, replication or other
    pleading (indictment)
        c. C-46, s. 2

défense, réplique ou autre pièce de
plaidoirie

    special plea
        c. C-46, s. 607

moyen de défense spéciale

plead/to
    (privileges)
        c. P-1, s. 5

démontrer

    plead a tender/to
        c. F-7, s. 40(1)

faire une offre de paiement

    plead guilty or not guilty/to (to a
    charge)
        c. Y-1, s. 12(3)(b)

plaider coupable ou non coupable

pleading
    c. B-1, s. 80(a)
    c. C-46, s. 482(3)(c)
    plea, replication or other
    pleading (indictment)
      c. C-46, s. 2
pleadings
    c. C-44, s. 53(a)
    c. S-26, s. 48(1)
pledge
    pledge or hypothecation

      c. B-2, s. 18(h)
pledge/to
    (a debt obligation)
      c. C-44, s. 39(12)
    (a security)
      c. B-1, s. 102
    pledge or deposit as security/to

      c. C-46, s. 322(b)
    pledge or hypothecate/to (a debt
    obligation)
      c. C-44, s. 39(11)
    secure by mortgage, charge or
    pledge/to

      c. C-40, s. 90(1)(e)
pledgee
    c. B-1, s. 90(4)
    c. C-44, s. 63(4)
Plenipotentiary
    c. C-26, Schedule I
point/to
    point a firearm/to
      c. C-46, s. 86(1)
point of law
    submission on a point of law
      c. C-46, s. 166(1)(b)(iii)
police
    police force
      c. C-23, s. 13(2)(b)
    police magistrate
      c. A-7, s. 23
    police officer or police constable
      c. C-46, s. 84(3)
    police officer, police constable,
    bailiff or constable
      c. C-46, s. 2
police officer
    police officer, police constable,
    bailiff or constable
      c. C-46, s. 2
policies
    general operational policies
      c. C-23, s. 7(1)(a)
    operational policies

      c. C-23, s. 30(2)(a)
    water policies and programs

      c. C-11, s. 4(b)

acte de procédure

plaidoirie
défense, réplique ou autre pièce de
    plaidoirie

actes de procédure

actes de procédures

nantissement avec ou sans
    dépossession de bien

donner en gage (un titre de créance)

donner en gage

mettre en gage ou déposer en
    garantie

donner en garantie (un titre de
    créance)

garantir au moyen d'une
    hypothèque, d'une charge ou d'un
    nantissement

créancier gagiste

Plénipotentiaire

braquer une arme à feu

représentation sur un point de droit

service de police

magistrat de police

officier ou agent de police

officier de police, agent de police ou
    huissier

officier de police, agent de police ou
    huissier

orientation générale des opérations

règles générales en matière
    opérationelle

politique et programmes afférents à
    l'eau

policing
    responsible for policing/to be   être responsable des questions de
        c. C-23, s. 13(2)(b)   police
policy
    determination of policy   fixation d'orientations générales
        c. S-22, s. 2(1)
    merits of matters of policy   bien-fondé de questions
            d'orientation
        c. F-11, s. 145
    national ports policy   politique nationale portuaire
        c. C-9, s. 3(1)
    policy decision   décision administrative
        c. C-9, s. 23(2)
    policy of mortgage insurance   police d'assurance hypothécaire
        c. L-12, s. 61(1)(l)(ii)
    public policy   ordre public
        c. C-27, Schedule, Article VI
political subdivision
    (of a government)   subdivision politique
        c. B-1, s. 8(b)
pollution prevention officer   fonctionnaire compétent
    c. A-12, s. 2
polygamy   polygamie
    c. C-46, s. 293(1)(a)(i)
pool
    (pari-mutuel)   cagnotte
        c. C-46, s. 204(4)
pool period   période de mise en commun
    c. C-24, s. 31
pool-selling
    book-making, pool-selling or   bookmaking, vente d'une mise
    betting   collective ou pari
        c. C-46, s. 201(2)(e)
port
    local port corporation   société portuaire locale
        c. C-9, s. 2
    non-corporate port   port non-autonome
        c. C-9, s. 2
Port of Quebec Corporation   Société de port de Québec
    c. F-11, Schedule III, Part II
portability
    (of health care insurance plan)   tranférabilité
        c. C-6, s. 7(d)
portfolio
    investment portfolio   portefeuille
        c. B-1, s. 190(4)(a)
    investment portfolio   portefeuille de placement
        c. L-12, s. 63(1)(c)
    mortgage portfolio   portefeuille hypothécaire
        c. B-1, s. 191(5)(a)
    portfolio management   gestion de portefeuille
        c. B-1, s. 174(1)
portion
    (of a department)   secteur
        c. C-23, s. 2
    (of the term of imprisonment)   fraction
        c. P-2, s. 27(1)(b)
    portion of the trial   phase de procès
        c. C-46, s. 648(1)
position
    fill a position/to   pourvoir un poste
        c. B-1, s. 37(e)

financial position
    c. A-2, s. 18(1)(h)
    c. B-7, Schedule II, Article V,
      Section 13(a)
official position (of a person)
    c. A-7, s. 22(3)
position or employment in a
public department
    c. C-46, s. 118
positive
  negative or positive amount
    c. C-52, s. 20(3)
possess/to
    c. C-24, s. 28(l)
  own and possess/to (property)
    c. B-1, s. 264(2)
possession
    c. A-12, s. 2
  acquire possession/to (of a
  security)
    c. C-44, s. 70(1)(a)
  actual and peaceable possession
  (of real property)
    c. C-46, s. 72(1)
  actual physical possession
    c. C-25, s. 13
  actual, visible and continued
  possession
    c. B-1, s. 2(1)(a)
  be in possession or control/to (of
  premises or things)
    c. C-34, s. 12(2)
  deliver possession/to
    c. C-25, s. 13
  have in possession for sale/to
    c. A-7, s. 3(2)(a)
  in one's possession or control
  (moneys)
    c. C-24, s. 8(1)
  in the possession of or under the
  control of (a person)
    c. C-51, s. 22(2)
  lawfully in possession
    c. C-26, Schedule I, Article
    12(3)
  mediately or immediately, in
  possession, or expectancy

    c. C-29, s. 38(e)
  peaceable possession (of
  personal property)
    c. C-46, s. 38(1)
  person in lawful possession
    c. C-38, s. 17(1)
  right of possession
    c. C-19, s. 17(1)(b)
  to have possession (of a child)
    c. 4 (2nd Supp.), s. 9(a)(ii)
  to have something in actual
  possession or custody (of
  another person)
    c. C-46, s. 4(3)(a)i)

situation financière

qualité officielle

poste ou emploi dans un ministère
  public

résultat déficitaire ou bénéficiaire

avoir la possession

être propriétaire

possession

prendre possession

possession effective et paisible

possession matérielle

possession réelle, publique et
  continue

être en possession ou avoir le
  contrôle

transmettre la possession

avoir en sa possession pour la vente

en sa possession ou sous sa
  responsabilité

en la possession ou sous l'autorité

régulièrement en possession

directement ou par intermédiaire,
  pour jouissance immédiate ou ulté
  rieure

paisible possession

possesseur légitime

droit de possession

détenir

avoir une chose en la possession ou
  garde réelle (d'une autre
  personne)

to have something in one's
personal possession
   c. C-46, s. 4(3)(a)

avoir une chose en sa possession
personnelle

to have something in possession
   c. C-46, s. 4(3)(a)

être en possession d'une chose

post/to
(mailable matter)
   c. A-10, s. 2(1)

poster

post a bond/to
   c. A-7, s. 13(f)

garantir par un cautionnement

post bill
bank note, bank bill and bank
post bill
   c. C-46, s. 2

billet de banque, papier de banque
et effet postal de banque

post office
   c. A-10, s. 2(1)

bureau de poste

post up/to
post up in a conspicuous part/to
(of an aircraft)
   c. C-46, s. 208(3)

afficher dans quelque partie bien en
vue

post-dated
(a bill)
   c. B-4, s. 26(d)

postdaté

postage
   c. A-10, s. 2(1)

port

postage stamp
   c. A-10, s. 2(1)

timbre-poste

postal note
postal note, money order or
postal remittance
   c. F-11, s. 2

titre de versement postal

postal remittance
   c. A-10, s. 2(1)
   c. F-11, s. 2

titre de versement postal

postal note, money order or
postal remittance
   c. F-11, s. 2

titre de versement postal

posthumous work
   c. C-42, s. 7

oeuvre posthume

posting up
posting up in a conspicuous
place (of a summons)
   c. T-7, s. 20(5)

affichage dans un endroit bien en
vue

postpone/to
(a right)
   c. B-3, s. 69(2)

différer

(the performance)
   c. Y-1, s. 33(8)

reporter

potable
edible and potable (product)
   c. C-38, s. 8

comestible et potable

poultry
   c. L-9, s. 31

volailles

poundage
   c. S-26, s. 66(3)

commission

power
   c. A-12, s. 14(1)

pouvoir

international power line

ligne internationale de transport
d'électricité ou ligne
internationale

   c. N-7, s. 2
power, duty and function (of the
Auditor General)
   c. A-17, s. 15(3)

responsabilité, pouvoir et fonction

supply of light, power, gas or water
   c. C-46, s. 422(1)(d)

Power
   c. C-26, Schedule I, Article 1(2)

power of attorney
   c. B-1, s. 92(1)(f)
   c. C-44, s. 65(1)(f)
   c. C-46, s. 331
   c. B-1, s. 68(4)

power of sale
   c. B-1, s. 184

powers
   capacity, rights, powers and privileges (of a natural person)
      c. C-21, s. 6(2)
   powers, duties and functions
      c. C-4, s. 7
   powers, rights and privileges
      c. A-7, s. 8(4)

practicable
   as soon as practicable
      c. C-29, s. 19(5)
   as soon as practicable
      c. C-23, s. 19(3)
   as soon as practicable
      c. C-46, s. 487(1)(e)
   as soon as practicable

      c. C-46, s. 497(1)
   as soon as practicable
      c. C-38, s. 15(3)
   where practicable
      c. C-38, s. 14(3)

practice
   according to the practice of the Court
      c. S-26, s. 73(2)
   business practice
      c. C-46, s. 362(5)
   corrupt or illegal practice
      c. C-45, s. 3(a)
   practice and procedure
      c. A-7, s. 13(g)
   practice and procedure (of court)
      c. F-7, s. 28(4)
   respecting the practice and procedure
      c. B-1, s. 178(6)(a)

practices
   in accordance with generally accepted actuarial practices and principles
      c. C-46, s. 347(2)
   sound business and financial practices
      c. C-21, s. 30(1)(c)(ii)

practitioner
   qualified medical practitioner
      c. L-2, s. 206(5)

Prairie Farm Assistance Administration
   c. A-1, Schedule I

approvisionnement de lumière, d'énergie, de gaz ou d'eau

Puissance

procuration

procuration écrite
pouvoir de vendre

capacité

compétence

pouvoirs et attributions

dans les meilleurs délais

dans les plus brefs délais

dans les plus brefs délais possible

dès que cela est matériellement possible

dès que possible

si possible

suivant les usages de la Cour

pratique commerciale

manoeuvre frauduleuse ou illégale

procédure

pratique et procédure

relatifs aux règles et à la procédure

conformément aux règles et pratiques actuarielles généralement admises

pratiques éprouvées en affaires et en finance

médecin qualifié

Administration de l'assistance à l'agriculture des Prairies

Prairie Farm Rehabilitation Administration
  c. A-1, Schedule I

Administration du rétablissement agricole des Prairies

Prairy Farm Emergency Fund

Caisse d'urgence des terres des Prairies

  c. C-48, s. 13(4)

pre-disposition report
  c. Y-1, s. 2(1)

rapport prédécisionnel

pre-emptive
  pre-emptive right
    c. C-44, s. 176(1)(c)(iv)

droit de préemption

pre-flight preparation
  c. C-46, s. 7(9)

préparatifs pour un vol

pre-hearing
  pre-hearing conference
    c. C-46, s. 625.1(1)

conférence préparatoire

pre-printed
  pre-printed portion (of a form)
    c. 31 (4th Supp.), s. 19(1)

imprimé (d'un acte judiciaire)

  pre-printed portion (of a form)
  (offences punishable on summary conviction)
    c. 31 (4th Supp.), s. 95(3)

texte (d'un formulaire)

preamble
  (of an Act)
    c. I-23, s. 4(2)

préambule

precept
  c. Y-1, Schedule, Form 5

instruction

precious metals
  mining of precious metals
    c. C-46, s. 394(1)(a)(ii)

extraction de métaux précieux

preclude/to
  c. A-13, s. 33

empêcher

  c. B-1, s. 195

interdire

precluded
  precluded from impugning the effectiveness/to be (of an endorsement)
    c. C-44, s. 61(1)

être privé du droit de contester la validité

predecessor in title
  c. C-36, s. 3(a)

prédécesseur en titre

predisposed
  to be predisposed
    c. Y-1, s. 15(2)

être influencé

prefer/to
  (an indictment)
    c. C-46, s. 566(2)

déposer

  prefer an indictment/to
    c. C-46, s. 478(4)

intenter une accusation

preference
  c. C-21, s. 31(6)

préférence

  dividend preference
    c. B-1, s. 70(2)(a)(iii)
    c. C-44, s. 176(1)(c)(iii)

préférence en matière de dividende

  fraudulent preference
    c. B-3, s. 97(3)

préférence frauduleuse

  liquidation preference
    c. B-1, s. 70(2)(a)(iii)
    c. C-44, s. 176(1)(c)(iii)

préférence en matière de liquidation

  preference stock
    c. L-12, s. 35(1)

action privilégiée

  undue preference
    c. B-3, s. 173(1)(h)

préférence indue

preferential
  first and preferential lien   gage ou privilège de premier rang
      c. B-1, s. 178(2)(d)
preferred
  preferred claim   réclamation privilégiée
      c. B-3, s. 2
  preferred share (of an   part privilégiée
  association)
      c. C-40, s. 3(1)
prejudice   préjudice
      c. B-7, Schedule I, Article V,
      Section 7(h)
  to the prejudice of any one   au préjudice de quelqu'un
      c. C-46, s. 366(1)(a)
  without prejudice   sans préjudice
      c. C-26, Schedule I, Article
      24(2)
      c. L-12, s. 8(2)
  without prejudice to the rights   sans préjudice des droits
      c. C-42, Schedule II, Article
      14
prejudice/to   nuire
      c. A-1, s. 18(b)
      c. B-5, s. 3   porter atteinte
      c. C-44, s. 161(5)   causer préjudice
      c. C-44, s. 2(8)   causer un préjudice
prejudicial
  legal effect prejudicial to the   conséquence juridique préjudiciable
  person   à l'intéressé
      c. F-11, s. 23(8)
  to the interests/to be (of an   porter atteinte aux intérêts
  employee)
      c. L-2, s. 175(1)(a)(i)
prejudicial/to be
  unfairly prejudicial/to be   porter atteinte
      c. C-44, s. 214(1)(a)
prejudicially   de manière préjudiciable
      c. C-44, s. 176(1)(c)(i)
preliminary inquiry   enquête préliminaire
      c. C-46, s. 490(1)
premises
  occupier of the premises   occupant du local
      c. C-46, s. 164(2)
  official premises   locaux officiels
      c. C-46, s. 431
  person ostensibly in control of   personne apparemment responsable
  the place or premises   des lieux
      c. C-46, s. 487.1(7)
premium
  single premium   prime unique
      c. C-17, s. 68(1)(d)
premium ticket   billet de prime
      c. C-46, s. 379
prepackaged product   produit préemballé
      c. C-38, s. 2
prepaid   franco
      c. B-1, s. 178(4)(d)
prepare/to
  (an annual report)   établir
      c. A-4, s. 6
      c. L-2, s. 121(2)
  consider, draft and prepare for   étudier, rédiger et préparer
  approval/to (regulations)
      c. A-2, s. 4(l)

prerogative
   royal prerogative of mercy   prérogative royale de clémence
      c. C-46, s. 751
prescribe/to   préciser
      c. A-7, s. 13(a)
   (a fee)   déterminer
      c. A-7, s. 3(1)(c)
   (a size or specifications)   fixer
      c. A-7, s. 3(1)(d)
   (by regulation)   fixer par règlement
      c. A-1, s. 11(1)(a)
   (by regulation)   prévoir un règlement
      c. A-1, s. 11(1)(b)
   (by regulation)   déterminer par règlement
      c. A-1, s. 11(2)
   (limits)   déterminer
      c. A-11, s. 24(2)
   (measures)   fixer
      c. A-11, s. 3(m)
   (powers)   attribuer
      c. A-8, s. 7(1)(b)
prescribed
   (by regulations)   prescrit
      c. B-1, s. 202(2)
   (by regulations)   prescrit ou réglementaire
      c. C-44, s. 2(1)
   (fee)   réglementaire
      c. C-44, s. 262(2)(b)
   in prescribed form and manner   selon la formule et de la manière
                                            prescrite
      c. C-8, s. 85
   prescribed by the regulation   réglementaire
      c. A-12, s. 12(1)(a)
   prescribed day   jour prescrit
      c. B-1, s. 113(1)
   prescribed day   date de référence
      c. L-12, s. 49(1)
   prescribed manner   manière prescrite
      c. C-42, s. 8(1)
   prescribed notice   notification obligatoire
      c. C-42, s. 8(1)
   prescribed price   prix réglementaire
      c. A-8, s. 2(1)
   prescribed substances   substances réglementées
      c. A-16, s. 2
prescription
   (of a tariff)   établissement
      c. A-2, s. 18(1)(m)(iii)
   laws relating to prescription and   règles de droit en matière de
   limitation (of actions)   prescription
      c. F-7, s. 39(1)
   prescription and limitation (of   prescription
   actions)
      c. C-50, s. 32(1)
   statute of limitation or   disposition relative aux délais et à
   prescription   la prescription
      c. B-1, s. 159(4)
presentation
   evidence of presentation and   preuve de la présentation et du
   dishonour   défaut d'acceptation
      c. B-4, s. 10
   introduction or presentation (of   dépôt ou présentation
   a Bill)
      c. C-8, s. 115(2)

presentation or surrender (of a security)
    c. C-44, s. 56(b)
  présentation ou livraison

presentation or surrender (of a security)
    c. B-1, s. 83(a)
  présentation ou remise (d'une valeur)

presentment
  (for acceptance)
    c. B-4, s. 36(2)
  présentation

  information, presentment and count (indictment)
  dénonciation, déclaration d'un acte d'accusation émise par le grand jury et chef d'accusation

    c. C-46, s. 2
preservation
  preservation and enhancement (of languages)
  maintien et valorisation

    c. 31 (4th Supp.), s. 83(2)
preserve
  game preserve
  réserve de chasse

    c. T-7, s. 23(e)
preserve/to
  secure or preserve an evidence/to
  recueillir ou conserver une preuve

    c. C-46, s. 497(1)(f)(ii)
preserve order/to
  (in court)
  maintenir l'ordre

    c. C-46, s. 484
preside a meeting/to
  (Board)
  diriger une réunion

    c. A-13, s. 13
preside over/to
  (a department)
  être chargé de l'administration

    c. F-11, s. 2
president
  (of corporation)
  président

    c. C-44, s. 126(1)(a)
presiding
  presiding judge
  juge qui préside

    c. C-46, s. 486(1)
presume/to
  présumer

    c. C-26, Schedule I, Article 18(3)
presumed/to be
  être présumé

    c. B-1, s. 80(b)
    c. C-44, s. 53(b)
    c. B-3, s. 95(2)
  être réputé

presumption
  raise beyond reasonable doubt a presumption/to
  créer une présomption hors de tout doute raisonnable

    c. C-17, s. 37
pretence
  false pretence
  fausse représentation

    c. B-3, s. 178(1)(e)
  false pretence
  faux semblant ou faux prétexte

    c. C-46, s. 361(1)
pretended
  under colour of pretended authority
  sous le prétexte d'une prétendue autorisation

    c. C-46, s. 146(c)
prevent/to
  (the Commission of an offence)
  empêcher

    c. A-2, s. 22(3)

preventive detention	détention préventive
c. C-46, s. 690	
c. N-1, s. 23	
previous	
previous conviction	déclaration antérieure de culpabilité
c. C-46, s. 360(2)	
prima facie	
prima facie evidence/to be	valoir présomption
c. C-27, Schedule, Article III, 4.	
prima facie evidence/to be	faire foi, jusqu'à preuve contraire
c. C-26, Schedule I, Article 11(a)	
primary	
on the primary ground	pour le motif principal
c. C-46, s. 515(10)(a)	
primary instrument of indebtedness	titre de créance principale
c. B-1, s. 190(1)	
principal	mandant
c. B-4, s. 50	
c. C-14, s. 10(1)(b)	
c. C-44, s. 75	
(money)	principal
c. C-44, s. 82(1)(b)	
agent and principal	agent et commettant
c. C-46, s. 426(4)	
as principal or agent	en qualité de commettant ou d'agent
c. C-46, s. 386	
as principal or as agent	à titre de commettant ou de mandataire
c. C-40, s. 87(1)	
offence included in the principal offence	infraction incluse dans l'infraction principale
c. S-26, s. 43(2)(b)	
principal amount	principal
c. A-10, s. 14(1)	
c. B-1, s. 132(2)(b)	
principal amount	montant en principal
c. B-1, s. 174(2)(f)(ii)	
principal and interest	principal et intérêt
c. C-19, s. 32	
principal and surety	cautionné et caution
c. Y-1, s. 49(3)	
principal interest	capital et intérêt
c. N-11, s. 88(3)(e)	
principal or surety	cautionné ou caution
c. C-46, s. 770(4)	
principal place of business	principal établissement
c. B-1, s. 178(5)	
repayment of the principal	remboursement du principal
c. L-12, s. 68(3)	
principles	
in accordance with generally accepted actuarial practices and principles	conformément aux règles et pratiques actuarielles généralement admises
c. C-46, s. 347(2)	
prior approval	approbation préalable
c. B-1, s. 114(1)	
prior right	
prior right to possession	droit prioritaire à la possession
c. C-24, s. 26(2)	

priority
    c. B-1, s. 121(3)
    c. C-44, s. 27(3)
    have priority/to (a right or a   primer
    power)
    c. B-1, s. 177(7)
    in priority (ranking)   par préférence
    c. C-44, s. 190(25)(b)
    priority payment instrument   instrument de paiement privilégié
    c. C-21, s. 31(1)

prison   prison
    c. C-46, s. 2
    penitentiary, common jail,   pénitencier, prison commune,
    public or reformatory prison,   prison publique, maison de
    lock-up, guard-room   correction, poste de police ou corps
        de garde
    c. C-46, s. 2
    special prison   prison spéciale
    c. C-46, s. 731(3)

prison authorities   autorités de la prison
    c. C-46, s. 231(4)(c)

privacy
    invasion of privacy   violation de la vie privée
    c. C-23, s. 19(2)(d)

private
    for private profit   dans un but de lucre personnel
    c. C-42, s. 27(5)
    in private   à huis clos
    c. C-46, s. 488.1(10)
    in private (investigation)   secret
    c. 31 (4th Supp.), s. 60(1)
    private act   loi d'intérêt privé
    c. I-23, s. 9
    private communication   communication privée
    c. C-50, s. 16
    private contract (to sell by)   de gré à gré
    c. B-3, s. 30(1)(a)
    private party   simple particulier
    c. C-19, s. 44(3)
    private person   particulier
    c. C-46, s. 25(1)(a)
    c. C-50, s. 5(1)
    private person of full age and   personne physique majeure et
    capacity   capable
    c. C-50, s. 3
    private placement (of securities)   souscription privée
    c. B-1, s. 190(1)
    private sector   secteur privé
    c. A-13, s. 3(c)
    sell by private tender/to   vendre de gré à gré
    c. C-9, s. 48(1)
    sell by public auction or private   vendre aux enchères publiques ou
    sale   de gré à gré
    c. C-44, s. 222(1)(d)

private prosecutor   poursuivant à titre privé
    c. Y-1, s. 13(6)(a)

privately-owned   de propriété privée
    c. A-14, s. 3

privative
    privative conversation   conversation privée
    c. C-46, s. 319(2)

privilege
    (of citizenship)   avantage
    c. C-29, s. 5(1)(e)

(solicitor-client)   secret professionnel
    c. A-1, s. 23
    c. C-44, s. 236
(under the law of evidence)   immunité
    c. A-1, s. 36(2)
    c. C-23, s. 39(2)
absolute privilege   immunité absolue
    c. C-44, s. 234
conversion privilege   privilège de conversion
    c. B-1, s. 70(2)(a)(iv)
qualified privilege   immunité relative
    c. C-44, s. 172
solicitor-client privilege   privilège des communications entre client et avocat

    c. C-46, s. 488.1(2)
privileged
    (communication)   protégé
       c. B-8, s. 19
    privileged communication   communication sous le sceau du secret professionnel
    (between solicitors and clients)
       c. C-46, s. 186(3)
privileges
    capacity, rights, powers and   capacité
    privileges (of a natural person)
       c. C-21, s. 6(2)
    powers, privileges and   droits et immunités
    immunities
       c. B-1, s. 7(1)
    powers, rights and privileges   pouvoirs et attributions
       c. A-7, s. 8(4)
privity
    actual fault or privity (of a   fait ou faute
    carrier)
       c. C-27, Schedule, Article IV, 2(b)
privy
    person being privy   personne ayant intérêt
       c. B-3, s. 100(2)
Privy Council Office   Bureau du Conseil privé
    c. A-1, Schedule I
privy to/to be   contribuer
    c. C-46, s. 386(c)
prize fight   combat concerté
    c. C-46, s. 83(2)
pro rata
    on a pro rata basis   au prorata
       c. A-13, s. 34
pro-consul
    consul, vice-consul, acting   consul ou tout autre agent
    consul, pro-consul or consular   consulaire de Sa Majesté
    agent of Her Majesty
       c. S-26, s. 82(e)
probabilities
    on a balance of probabilities   selon la prépondérance des probabilités

       c. Y-1, s. 4(4)(a)
probate
    grant of probate   jugement d'homologation d'un testament

       c. B-1, s. 78(7)(a)
       c. C-44, s. 51(7)(a)
probation
    period of probation (of persons   période de probation
    convicted)
       c. C-47, s. 2(1)

    privileged

probation officer   agent de probation
    c. Y-1, s. 2(1)
probation order   ordonnance de probation
    c. C-46, s. 91(6)
probative force   valeur probante
    c. B-3, s. 10(7)
    c. C-8, s. 25(3)   force probante
    c. C-34, s. 13(2)
procedendo   procedendo
    c. C-46, s. 774
procedure   procédé
    c. C-11, s. 18(1)(b)
investigative procedure   méthode d'enquête
    c. C-46, s. 185(1)(h)
legal procedure   procédure judiciaire
    c. C-19, s. 15
ordinary procedure   procédure ordinaire
    c. N-1, s. 17(5)
practice and procedure   procédure
    c. A-7, s. 13(g)
practice and procedure (of court)   pratique et procédure
    c. F-7, s. 28(4)
prescribe the procedure   établir les formalités
    c. A-1, s. 77(1)(b)
procedure in all business   conduite des travaux
    c. A-13, s. 26(a)
respecting the practice and   relatifs aux règles et à la procédure
procedure
    c. B-1, s. 178(6)(a)
procedures   modalités
    c. A-1, s. 2(2)
    c. A-1, s. 39(2)   formalités
prescribe the procedures/to   fixer les règles
    c. A-1, s. 77(1)(h)
proceed/to
(against a person)   intenter une action
    c. C-9, s. 44
proceeding
action, suit or other proceeding   action en recouvrement
for the recovery
    c. C-9, s. 46(2)
administrative proceeding   procédure administrative
    c. B-1, s. 23(2)
civil proceeding   procédure civile
    c. B-1, s. 23(2)
    c. B-3, s. 10(5)
civil, criminal or administrative   poursuite civile, pénale ou
action or proceeding   administrative
    c. C-44, s. 124(1)
criminal proceeding   procédure pénale
    c. B-1, s. 23(2)
judicial proceeding   procédure judiciaire
    c. C-46, s. 118
    c. S-26, s. 2(1)
    c. Y-1, s. 2(1)
judicial proceeding   instance
    c. F-27, s. 2(1)
    c. S-26, s. 2(1)
legal proceeding   instance
    c. B-1, s. 212(1)
proceeding in rem   action réelle
    c. C-50, s. 14

proceedings
    c. A-12, s. 6(3)
    c. B-6, s. 19(1)
    (of a Committee)
    c. C-8, s. 116(6)
    (of committee)
    c. B-2, s. 13(3)
    (of the Board)
    c. A-4, s. 3(5)
    (of the Commission)
    c. A-2, s. 15
    adjourn the proceedings/to
    c. Y-1, s. 9(10)(a)
    appear at and be present during
    proceedings/to (accused)
    c. C-46, s. 7(5.1)(a)
    at any stage of the proceedings
    c. C-46, s. 359(1)
    bring or take actions, suits or
    other legal proceedings/to
    c. C-11, s. 14(4)
    bring or take an action, suit or
    other legal proceedings/to
    c. A-16, s. 3(2)
    bring proceedings/to
    c. A-12, s. 6(3)
    civil or criminal proceedings
    c. C-24, s. 20(3)
    conduct of proceedings
    c. P-2, s. 6
    criminal proceedings
    c. C-12, s. 36(6)
    criminal proceedings
    c. C-20, s. 18(1)
    fair report of the proceedings (of
    the Senate)
    c. C-46, s. 307(1)
    final conclusion of the
    proceedings
    c. N-1, s. 15(3)(b)
    for the purpose of any
    proceedings
    c. C-50, s. 6(2)
    foreclosure proceedings
    c. N-11, s. 12(2)(a)
    have the proceedings re-
    opened/to
    c. C-46, s. 552
    in any debates and other
    proceedings (of Parliament)
    c. 31 (4th Supp.), s. 4(1)
    institute proceedings/to
    c. A-12, s. 25(2)
    judicial proceedings
    c. C-19, s. 17(1)(c)
    legal proceedings
    c. C-20, s. 18(1)
    legal, disciplinay or other
    proceedings
    c. C-12, s. 20(3)(b)
    minutes of the proceedings
    c. C-44, s. 117(2)

poursuite

délibérations
débats

travaux

travaux

délibérations

ajourner l'affaire

être présent et demeurer présent
    lors des procédures

à toute étape des procédures

ester en justice

ester en justice

engager une poursuite

procédure civile ou pénale

déroulement des travaux

procédure pénale

poursuites pénales

compte rendu loyal des
    délibérations

issue de la poursuite

dans le cadre d'instances

procédures de forclusion

faire rouvrir les procédures

dans les débats et travaux

intenter une poursuite

procédures judiciaires

instances

procédure judiciaire, disciplinaire
    ou autre

procès-verbaux des délibérations

minutes of the proceedings (of a meeting)
   c. C-13, s. 14(2)

procès-verbal des délibérations

no civil or criminal proceedings lie against (a peace officer)

   c. C-46, s. 33(2)

il ne peut être intenté aucune procédure civile ou pénale contre (un agent de la paix)

pending proceedings
   c. C-36, s. 12(b)

procédures pendantes

proceedings or process (in a court)
   c. A-7, s. 12

recours

recording of proceedings (in court)
   c. F-7, s. 46(1)(viii)

enregistrement des débats

stage of proceedings
   c. Y-1, s. 10(1)

phase de l'instance

stay proceedings/to
   c. C-44, s. 208(2)

suspendre une procédure

take proceedings/to
   c. A-12, s. 6(3)

engager une poursuite

proceeds

net proceeds (of a sale)
   c. B-1, s. 122(6)

produit net

process

   c. C-9, s. 60

actes de procédure

   c. C-46, s. 4(6)

acte judiciaire

(an action)
   c. B-1, s. 205(2)(a)

acte

accept service of process/to
   c. C-9, s. 60

accepter signification

after payment made or enforced by process or execution
   c. F-11, s. 23(3)(b)

après le paiement volontaire ou par voie d'exécution forcée

be served with process/to
   c. C-9, s. 60

recevoir signification

execution of process
   c. C-46, s. 683(4)

exécution d'un acte judiciaire

grievance process
   c. P-35, s. 91(1)

procédure de grief

in the lawful execution of a process against lands or goods

   c. C-46, s. 270(1)(b)

dans l'exécution légale d'un acte judiciaire contre des terres ou des effets

in the process of
   c. A-2, s. 20(3)

en voie de

lawful execution of a process against lands and goods

   c. C-46, s. 129(c)

exécution légitime d'un acte judiciaire contre des terres ou des biens meubles

make a service process/to
   c. B-6, s. 10

signifier un exploit

proceedings or process (in a court)
   c. A-7, s. 12

recours

process for resolution (of a dispute)
   c. C-23, s. 9(1)(a)

mode de règlement

seizure under legal process
   c. C-27, Schedule, Article IV, 2(g)

saisie judiciaire

writ of subpoena or process
   c. C-45, s. 17

bref de subpoena ou sommation

processor
  (of agricultural products)   conditionneur
    c. A-5, s. 2
proclamation
  proclamation, order, regulation   proclamation, décret, arrêté,
  or appointment   règlement ou nomination
    c. C-46, s. 370(a)
procuration
  by procuration or otherwise   par procuration ou autrement
    c. C-46, s. 374(a)
  signature by procuration   signature par procuration
    c. B-4, s. 50
procure/to
  aid, consent, abet or procure the   aider, assister, conseiller ou amener
  commission of an offence/to   quelqu'un à commettre une
                              infraction
    c. C-39, s. 57
  counsel or procure/to (a person   conseiller ou inciter
  to be a party to an offence)
    c. C-46, s. 22(1)
  procure a miscarriage/to   procurer un avortement
    c. C-46, s. 287(2)
procurer   entremetteur
    c. C-46, s. 170(a)
procuring
  (prostitution)   entremetteurs
    c. C-46, s. 212
  (prostitution)   proxénétisme
    c. C-46, s. 212
produce/to
  (a certificate)   présenter
    c. A-7, s. 15(3)
  (evidence)   produire (une preuve)
    c. A-12, s. 21(3)
  (evidence)   fournir
    c. A-7, s. 5(2)(a)
    c. C-42, s. 45(4)
producer   producteur
    c. C-48, s. 10(1), (a)
  (of agricultural products)   producteur
    c. A-4, s. 5(1)(a)
  forestry producer   sylviculteur
    c. B-1, s. 2(1)
production
  (of a copy)   dépôt
    c. A-8, s. 18
  (of copies)   confection
    c. C-42, s. 38
  production and inspection of   production et examen des
  documents   documents
    c. A-7, s. 8(4)
products
  products of agriculture   produits agricoles
    c. B-1, s. 2(1)
  products of the forest   produits de la forêt
    c. B-1, s. 2(1)
  products of the quarry and mine produits des carrières et des mines
    c. B-1, s. 2(1)
  products of the sea, lakes and   produits aquatiques
  rivers
    c. B-1, s. 2(1)
professed
  professed standard   norme reconnue
    c. F-27, s. 10(3)(a)

profession
  lawful profession or calling   profession ou occupation légitime
    c. C-46, s. 179(1)(a)
  members of the legal profession   gens de loi
    c. C-46, s. 166(4)(c)(ii)
professional
  technical, professional or other   personnel technique, professionnel
  officers   ou autre
    c. C-24, s. 6(e)
professionnal
  professionnal employee   membre de profession libérale
    c. L-2, s. 3(1)
  professionnal organization   organisation professionnelle
    c. L-2, s. 3(1)
profit   bénéfice
    c. A-13, s. 30
    c. C-7, s. 29(2)
  for private profit   dans un but de lucre personnel
    c. C-42, s. 27(5)
  net profit or loss   bénéfices ou pertes nets
    c. F-11, s. 18(5)
profit-sharing   participation aux bénéfices
    c. C-31, s. 13(2)
profits and losses   profits et pertes
    c. N-11, s. 79(2)
progress
  progress report   rapport
    c. C-13, s. 14(2)
progress report   rapport d'évaluation
    c. Y-1, s. 2(1)
prohibit/to   interdire
    c. A-11, s. 3(d)
    c. C-34, s. 34(1)(b)
prohibited
  prohibited act   acte prohibé
    c. C-46, s. 52(2)
  prohibited weapon   arme prohibé
    c. C-46, s. 84(1)
prohibition
  (procedure)   prohibition
    c. C-46, s. 482(3)(c)
  order of prohibition or   ordonnance d'interdiction ou de
  dissolution (against a monopoly)   dissolution
    c. C-34, s. 34(3)
prohibitory
  interim prohibitory order   arrêté provisoire d'interdiction
    c. C-10, s. 43(1)
Project Ploughshares   Project Ploughshares
    c. C-18, Schedule
prolongation
  natural prolongation of the land   prolongement naturel du territoire
  territory   terrestre
    c. C-53, s. 2(1)
prominence
  equal prominence   égale importance
    c. 31 (4th Supp.), s. 11(2)
prominent
  in a prominent place   dans un endroit bien en vue
    c. C-46, s. 487.1(8)
promise   engagement
    c. B-1, s. 180(1)(b)
  promise to appear   promesse de comparaître
    c. C-46, s. 493

promise to pay   promesse de paiement
    c. C-44, s. 25(5)
promissory note   billet à ordre
    c. B-1, s. 173(1)(c)
    c. C-44, s. 25(5)
    c. B-1, s. 202(4)(d)(ii)   billet à arrêté
the making, accepting,   création, acceptation, escompte ou
discounting or endorsing of a bill   endossement d'une lettre de
of exchange, cheque, draft or   change, d'un chèque, d'une traite
promissory note   ou d'un billet à ordre
    c. C-46, s. 362(1)(c)(vi)
promote/to
(a prize fight)   être le promoteur
    c. C-46, s. 83(1)(b)
(development of aeronautics)   favoriser
    c. A-2, s. 4(b)
(the election of a candidate)   favoriser
    c. C-46, s. 121(2)(a)
advocate or promote genocide/to   préconiser ou fomenter le génocide
    c. C-46, s. 318(1)
promote and encourage/to   faciliter et encourager
(practices)
    c. C-37, s. 5(1)(c)
promote the objects/to   réaliser les objets
    c. B-6, s. 14
promoter
(of incorporations)   fondateur
    c. B-1, s. 145
promotion   avancement
    c. C-23, s. 42(1)
promotional contest   concours publicitaire
    c. C-34, s. 59(1)
pronounce/to
(a judgment)   prononcer
    c. C-39, s. 67(2)
pronouncement
pronouncement of an order   prononcé de l'ordonnance
    c. C-44, s. 190(24)
proof   preuve
    c. A-11, s. 3(j)
burden of proof   charge de la preuve
    c. C-34, s. 43(2)
on proof orally or by affidavit   sur preuve orale ou par affidavit
    c. C-34, s. 13(2)
require proof/to   exiger la preuve
    c. A-11, s. 3(j)
the proof of which lies on him   dont la preuve lui incombe
    c. C-46, s. 417(2)
without proof of the signature or   sans qu'il soit nécessaire de prouver
official character of the person   l'authenticité de la signature ni la
(by whom the certificate   qualité officielle du signataire
purports to be signed)
    c. C-46, s. 136(2.1)
proof/to be   faire foi
    c. A-12, s. 21(1)
proof of the signature   authenticité de la signature
    c. C-12, s. 45(1)
propaganda
hate propaganda   propagande haineuse
    c. C-46, s. 319(7)
proper
proper administration (of an   application régulière
Act)
    c. A-2, s. 25

proper conduct (of business) c. C-21, s. 6(1)4	bonne marche
properly c. B-1, s. 66(2)(b)(i)	régulièrement
properly attributable (sum) c. F-11, s. 20(2)	régulièrement imputable
to be properly convicted c. C-46, s. 777(2)	être régulièrement déclaré coupable
property c. C-46, s. 2	biens de propriété
adjacent property c. N-7, s. 113	biens-fonds adjacents
animal or bird that is the property of any person c. C-46, s. 264.1	animal ou oiseau qui est la propriété de quelqu'un
have a special property or interest in/to (a thing) c. C-46, s. 322(1)(a)	avoir un droit de propriété spécial ou un intérêt spécial
in property (distribution) c. B-1, s. 289(l)	en nature
property tax c. C-46, s. 347(2)	impôt foncier
proportion (of the revenues) c. A-3, s. 5(c)	part
proportion of the cost (of a project) c. A-3, s. 5(b)	contribution
proportioned force reasonably proportioned to the danger c. C-46, s. 30	force raisonnablement proportionnée au danger
proposal c. B-1, s. 161(3)	proposition
c. B-1, s. 307(1)(c)	offre
c. C-32, s. 23(3)(a)	projet
(at meeting of shareholders) c. C-44, s. 137(1)(a)	proposition
(by a bankrupt) c. B-3, s. 50	proposition concordataire
(of order) c. A-12, s. 11(2)	projet
proposed existing or proposed (proceeding) c. C-46, s. 137	existant ou projeté
proposed contract c. A-2, s. 18(1)(f) c. C-44, s. 120(1)(a) c. F-11, s. 116(1)(a)	projet de contrat
proposed regulation c. C-10, s. 20(2)	projet de règlement
proposed tariff of tolls c. A-2, s. 18(1)(h)	tarifs de taxes projetés
proposed, interim or final distribution (money or property) c. C-44, s. 217(l)	projet de répartition provisoire ou définitive
proprietary pecuniary or proprietary interest c. C-22, s. 5(1)(b)	intérêt pécuniaire ou droit de propriété
proprietary interest c. B-9, s. 26(1)(b)	droit de propriété

proprietary name c. C-34, s. 37(2)	nom de propriétaire

proprietor
  (of a newspaper)
   c. C-46, s. 303(1)
  (of a stockyard)
   c. L-9, s. 10
	propriétaire
	
	propriétaire

Proprietor's Equity Account c. B-9, s. 36(4)	compte d'avoir propre

prorogue/to
  (Parliament)
   c. P-1, s. 3
	proroger

prosecute/to
   c. A-1, s. 36(3)
   c. A-7, s. 20(2)
   c. A-11, s. 46
	poursuivre

prosecution c. A-4, s. 5(3)	poursuite

prosecutor
   c. C-46, s. 486(2)
  private prosecutor
   c. Y-1, s. 13(6)(a)
  private prosecutor
   c. C-46, s. 750(2)
	poursuivant
	
	poursuivant à titre privé
	
	poursuivant privé

prospective
  (purchaser)
   c. B-1, s. 150(1)
  existing or prospective oil well
 	
   c. C-46, s. 396(1)(a)
  prospective warrantor
   c. N-11, s. 99(b)
	éventuel
	
	puits de pétrole existant ou en
	  perspective
	
	garant éventuel

prospectively or retroactively c. C-3, s. 17(1)	rétroactivement ou pour l'avenir

prospectus
   c. C-34, s. 5(2)(a)
   c. C-44, s. 2(7)(a)
   c. F-11, s. 56(1)
  (of corporation)
   c. C-44, s. 193
  circulate a prospectus/to
   c. C-46, s. 400(1)
  preliminary prospectus
   c. B-1, s. 146(1)
	prospectus
	
	prospectus
	
	mettre en circulation un prospectus
	
	prospectus provisoire

prostitute c. C-46, s. 197(1)	prostitué

protected
  internationally protected person
 	
   c. C-46, s. 2
	personne jouissant d'une protection
	  internationale

protected loan c. N-11, s. 64	prêt protégé

protection
  provincial child welfare or youth
  protection legislation
 	
   c. Y-1, s. 40(3)(f)
	loi provinciale sur le bien-être de
	  l'enfance ou la protection de la
	  jeunesse

protest
  (a bill or note)
   c. B-4, s. 10
  advocacy, protest or dissent
 	
   c. C-23, s. 2
	protêt
	
	défense d'une cause, protestation ou
	  manifestation d'un désaccord

note for protest/to (a bill) c. B-4, s. 117	faire une notation de protêt
protest/to (a bill) c. B-4, s. 108	protester
prothonotary c. B-3, s. 90 c. C-39, s. 2(1) c. C-46, s. 771(3.1)	protonotaire
Protocol c. C-26, s. 2(2)	protocole
protract/to (the administration) c. B-3, s. 151	prolonger la durée
provable liability provable c. B-3, s. 2	créance pouvant être prouvée
prove/to c. B-1, s. 51(2)(c) prove on the trial/to c. C-46, s. 356(2)	établir prouver lors de l'instruction
provide/to (facilities) c. C-11, s. 15(4)(d) (for payment of money) c. A-3, s. 6 (in regulation) c. A-7, s. 4 provide evidence/to c. A-12, s. 8(1) provide for the discharge of its oblibations/to c. C-44, s. 217 to be under a legal duty to provide for c. Y-1, Schedule, Form I	pourvoir stipuler prévoir fournir la preuve constituer une provision pour honorer ses obligations être légalement tenu de subvenir aux besoins
provision c. A-1, s. 3 (for payment) c. B-1, s. 289(h) (in agreement) c. A-5, s. 4(1) (in agreement) c. C-44, s. 183(4) (letters patent) c. B-1, s. 9(4) (of an Act) c. C-19, s. 15 (of an Act) c. B-1, s. 9(4) making of an adequate provision c. A-13, s. 34	disposition provision stipulation clause clause prescription disposition constitution d'une réserve suffisante
provisional provisional director c. C-41, s. 6(1) provisional judicial district c. C-46, s. 480(1) provisional order (divorce) c. 3 (2nd Supp.), s. 18(1)	administrateur provisoire district judiciaire provisoire ordonnance conditionnelle
proviso c. C-27, s. 5	réserve

exception, exemption, proviso, excuse or qualification prescribed by law
c. C-46, s. 794(1)

exception, exemption, limitation, excuse ou réserve prévue par le droit

provocation
in the heat of passion caused by sudden provocation (manslaughter)
c. C-46, s. 232

dans un accès de colère causé par une provocation soudaine

provocation by blows, words or gestures
c. C-46, s. 36

provocation faite par des coups, des paroles ou des gestes

without justification or provocation
c. C-46, s. 38(2)

sans justification ni provocation

prowl/to
prowl at night/to
c. C-46, s. 177

rôder la nuit

proxy
c. B-1, s. 160
c. C-44, s. 137(2)
c. B-1, s. 9(5)
c. C-44, s. 137(5)(c)

procuration

fondé de pouvoir

dissident's proxy circular

circulaire dissidente sollicitant des procurations

c. B-1, s. 65(5)(d)
c. C-44, s. 137(5)(d)
form of proxy
c. C-44, s. 147

formulaire de procuration

management proxy circular

circulaire de sollicitation de procurations envoyée par la direction

c. B-1, s. 41(3)
management proxy circular
c. C-44, s. 137(2)

circulaire de la direction

present in person or represented by proxy (shareholder)
c. C-44, s. 139(1)

présent ou représenté

proxy in blank
c. B-3, s. 51(1)(e)

formule de procuration en blanc

proxyholder
c. B-1, s. 69(1)
c. C-44, s. 141(1)

fondé de pouvoir

alternate proxyholder
c. C-44, s. 148(1)

fondé de pouvoir suppléant

prudent
care, diligence and skill of a reasonably prudent trustee
c. C-44, s. 91(b)

soin, diligence et compétence d'un bon fiduciaire

exercise the care, diligence and skill of a reasonably prudent person/to
c. C-44, s. 122(1)(b)

agir avec le soin, la diligence et la compétence d'un bon père de famille

reasonably prudent person
c. B-1, s. 54(1)(b)

bon père de famille

reasonably prudent person
c. F-11, s. 115(1)(b)

personne prudente et avisée

reasonably prudent trustee
c. B-1, s. 142(b)

bon fiduciaire

public
travelling public
c. 31 (4th Supp.), s. 23

voyageurs

Public Archives
    c. A-1, s. 68(c)   Archives publiques

public auction
    sell by public auction or private   vendre aux enchères publiques ou
    sale   de gré à gré
       c. C-44, s. 222(1)(d)

public authority   administration
    c. C-51, s. 2

public benefit   intérêt public
    c. C-46, s. 319(3)(c)

public body   administration
    c. C-44, s. 187(6)
    legally constituted public body   personne juridique de droit public
       c. C-26, Schedule I, Article
         2(1)

public debt
    management of the public debt   gestion de la dette publique
       c. B-2, s. 24(2)

public department   ministère public
    c. C-46, s. 2
    position or employment in a   poste ou emploi dans un ministère
    public department   public
       c. C-46, s. 118

public good
    defence of public good   défense portant sur le bien public
       c. C-46, s. 163(3)

public interest   intérêt public
    c. A-1, s. 12(2)(b)
    c. A-2, s. 14(1)(b)
    subject of public interest   question d'intérêt public
       c. C-46, s. 319(3)

public lands   terres domaniales
    c. N-14, s. 2

public money   fonds public
    c. F-11, s. 2

public moneys   fonds publics
    c. C-7, s. 8(1)(d)

public moral
    injure public moral/to   offenser la morale publique
       c. C-46, s. 166(1)(a)

public officer   fonctionnaire public
    c. C-46, s. 2
    c. F-11, s. 2

public peace
    break the public peace/to   violer la paix publique
       c. C-46, s. 49(a)

public place   endroit public
    c. C-46, s. 150

public property   domaine public
    c. B-9, s. 3(a)
    c. F-11, s. 2   biens publics

public purposes   intérêt public
    c. A-7, s. 2

public sector   secteur public
    c. A-13, s. 3(c)

public service   administration publique
    c. A-10, s. 24

Public Service   fonction publique
    c. C-22, s. 9(1)

Public Service Commission   Commission de la fonction publique
    c. A-1, Schedule I

public service of Canada   administration publique fédérale
    c. A-10, s. 6(5)
    c. C-22, s. 9(2)

Public Service Staff Relations Board
 c. A-1, Schedule I
public stores
 c. C-46, s. 2
Public Works Lands Company Limited
 c. A-1, Schedule I
publicize/to
 c. C-32, s. 4(1)(d)
puisne
 puisne judge
  c. S-26, s. 4(1)
 senior puisne judge
  c. S-26, s. 30(1)
puisne judge
 c. A-17, s. 4(1)
pullorum test
 (poultry)
  c. L-9, s. 42(1)
punishment
 c. A-11, s. 45
 c. C-46, s. 6(1)
 c. C-46, s. 120(a)(iv)
 corporal punishment
  c. P-20, s. 10(2)(a)
 degree or kind of punishment
  c. C-46, s. 717(1)
 greater punishment
  c. C-46, s. 665(1)
  c. Y-1, s. 36(5)
 minimum punishment
  c. C-46, s. 717(2)
punitive damages
 c. C-46, s. 194(1)
purchase/to
 (an insurance)
  c. B-1, s. 56(4)
purchase money security agreement
 c. B-1, s. 173(1)(e)
purchaser
 c. B-1, s. 75(2)
 c. C-44, s. 48(2)
 innocent purchaser
  c. C-46, s. 726(1)
 purchaser for value in good faith and without notice of an adverse claim
  c. B-1, s. 75(2)
purchaser for value without notice
 c. B-1, s. 86(1)
purchasing
 purchasing company
  c. L-12, s. 101(1)(b)(ii)
purchasing bank
 c. B-1, s. 273(4)
purport
 (of the regulations)
  c. S-22, s. 11(2)(b)
 nature and purport (of indictment)
  c. C-46, s. 621(2)

Commission des relations de travail dans la fonction publique

approvisionnements publics

Société immobilière des travaux publics limitée

rendre public

juge puîné

doyen des juges puînés

juge puîné

épreuve de la pullorose

peine

châtiment
châtiment corporel

degré ou genre de peine

peine plus sévère

peine minimale

dommages-intérêts punitifs

souscrire (une assurance)

contrat garantissant un prix d'achat

acquéreur

acheteur de bonne foi

acquéreur contre valeur et non avisé de l'existence d'oppositions

acquéreur contre valeur non avisé (d'irrégularités)

société acquéreur

banque acheteuse

teneur

nature et teneur

substance, meaning or purport (of private communication)
    c. C-46, s. 191(2)(c)
substance, sens ou objet

purport/to
    c. A-7, s. 21
censé être

purport to sell an appointment/to
    c. C-46, s. 124(a)
prétendre vendre une nomination

purport to be/to
    c. C-46, s. 138(a)
donner comme étant

purported
    c. C-44, s. 73(2)
(purported warranty)
    c. C-34, s. 52(1)(c)(ii)
prétendu

exercise or purported exercise (of a duty)
    c. A-1, s. 66(1)
exercice effectif ou censé tel

in the course of the exercice or performance or purported exercice or performance of any power, duty or function
    c. 31 (4th Supp.), s. 75(1)
dans l'exercice effectif ou censé tel de ses attributions

purported sale
    c. L-9, s. 29(g)
prétendue vente

purporting
authorizing or purporting to authorize (document)
    c. C-46, s. 2
autorisant ou étant donné comme autorisant

copy purporting to be certified
    c. A-4, s. 5(3)
copie censée certifiée conforme

purporting to be
    c. C-42, s. 34(4)(a)
paraissant être

purporting to be (document)
    c. F-11, s. 158
censé être

purpose
    c. A-13, s. 3
mission

carrying out of a purpose
    c. A-16, s. 7
réalisation d'une mission

common purpose
    c. C-46, s. 63(1)
but commun

for a fraudulent purpose
    c. C-46, s. 58(1)
pour une fin frauduleuse

for that purpose
    c. A-7, s. 6
à cet effet

for that purpose
    c. A-6, s. 2(2)(a)
à cette fin

fulfilment of the purpose
    c. A-13, s. 4(m)
poursuite de sa mission

the intent and purpose (of an Act)
    c. A-2, s. 18(1)(q)
esprit et objet

purposes
for the purposes of this section
    c. A-2, s. 7(11)
aux fins du présent article

for the purposes of this Act
    c. A-10, s. 2(2)
    c. C-46, s. 4(1)
pour l'application de la présente loi

public purposes
    c. A-7, s. 2
intérêt public

pursuant to
    c. A-11, s. 12(1)(c)
conformément à

    c. C-19, s. 42
selon

    c. C-24, s. 37(1)(a)
aux termes de

(a paragraph) c. A-11, s. 10	au titre de
(a paragraph) c. A-10, s. 12(1)(b)	sous le régime de
(a program) c. A-11, s. 12(2)(b)	en exécution de
(a regulation) c. A-11, s. 12(2)(b)	réglementaire
(a section) c. A-12, s. 6(4)	en application de
(a section) c. A-12, s. 6(5)	sous l'autorité de
(a section) c. A-12, s. 7(1)	aux termes de
(a section) c. A-10, s. 12(1)(a)	au titre de
(a section) c. A-11, s. 5	visé à
(a subsection) c. A-14, s. 2	au sens de
(an Act) c. A-11, s. 12(1)(d)	sous le régime de
(an Act) c. A-11, s. 3(t)	en application de

put
(sale of shares) c. B-1, s. 168(1)	option de vente
call or put (in respect of a share) c. C-44, s. 131(1)	option d'achat ou de vente

pyramid selling
  c. C-34, s. 55(1) — vente pyramidale

q

qualification
(of a trustee) c. C-44, s. 84	qualités requises

exception, exemption, proviso,
excuse or qualification
prescribed by law
  c. C-46, s. 794(1)
	exception, exemption, limitation,
	  excuse ou réserve prévue par le
	  droit

qualifications
(of delegates) c. C-41, s. 27(3)(a)	qualités requises

qualified
(person) c. C-44, s. 168(8)	compétent
(regulation) c. C-8, s. 7(3)	restreint
qualified medical practitioner c. C-46, s. 287(6)	médecin qualifié
qualified person c. Y-1, s. 13(11)	personne compétente
qualified privilege c. C-44, s. 172	immunité relative
qualified technician c. C-46, s. 258(1)(c)	technicien qualifié

qualified/to be
(as a candidate) c. C-24, s. 17(4)(c)	éligible

(to vote)
 c. C-24, s. 17(4)(c)   habile à voter

qualify/to
 (a director)   habiliter un administrateur
  c. C-19, s. 6(5)
 (as security officers)   avoir les qualités requises
  c. A-2, s. 7(11)

qualifying
 competitive or qualifying   examen de concours ou d'aptitudes
 examination
  c. C-46, s. 404
 director's qualifying shares   actions d'éligibilité des
     administrateurs
  c. N-11, s. 28
 minimum qualifying period   période minimale d'admissibilité
  c. C-8, s. 44(1)(c)

quantitative
 quantitative information (in   renseignements chiffrés
 auditor's report)
  c. F-11, s. 132(1)(b)

quarantine restriction   restriction de quarantaine
  c. C-27, Schedule, Article IV,
  2

quarter sessions
 court of general or quarter   Cour de sessions générales ou
 sessions of the peace   trimestrielles de la paix
  c. C-46, s. 2

quarter-year   trimestre
  c. C-41, s. 52(3)(d)

quash/to
 (a conviction)   annuler
  c. S-26, s. 42(2)(a)
 (proceedings)   casser
  c. S-26, s. 44
 motion to quash (an indictment   requête pour faire annuler
 or a count)
  c. C-46, s. 601(1)
 quash the indictment/to   casser l'acte d'accusation
  c. C-46, s. 575(1)

quasi-delict
 delict and quasi-delict   délit et quasi-délit
  c. C-50, s. 2

Quebec Deposit Insurance   Régie de l'assurance-dépôts du
Board   Québec
  c. C-44, s. 206(7)

Queen's Printer   imprimeur de la Reine
  c. B-3, s. 210(3)
 Queen's Printer and Controller   imprimeur de la Reine et contrôleur
 of Stationnary   de la papeterie
  c. I-23, s. 25(2)

Queen's Printer and Controller   imprimeur de la Reine et contrôleur
of Stationnary   de la papeterie
  c. I-23, s. 25(2)

Queen's Printer for a province   imprimeur de la Reine pour une
     province
  c. C-46, s. 370(a)

Queen's Printer for Canada   imprimeur de la Reine pour le
     Canada
  c. C-46, s. 370(a)

Queen's Privy Council for   Conseil privé de la Reine pour le
Canada   Canada
  c. A-1, s. 3
  c. A-12, s. 28(1)

question
    question of fact   question de fait
        c. B-1, s. 238(6)(a)
    question of law   question de droit
        c. C-46, s. 32(5)
    question of mixed law and fact   question de droit et de fait
        c. C-46, s. 164(6)c)
    question of mixed law and fact   question mixte de droit et de fait
        c. C-46, s. 320(6)(c)
question/to
    (the establishment of a   contester
    conciliation board)
        c. P-35, s. 83(2)
questions of fact or law   litiges
    c. A-7, s. 12
quiet
    disturb the peace and quiet (of   troubler la paix et la tranquillité
    occupants)/to
        c. C-46, s. 175(1)(d)
quit claim
    notice of quit claim   avis de renonciation
        c. B-3, s. 20(1)
quo warranto   quo warranto
    c. A-7, s. 12
quorum   quorum
    c. A-7, s. 7(8)
quota   contingent
    c. C-24, s. 2(1)

r

radiation
    radiation safety level   niveau de rayonnement permis
        c. L-2, s. 126(1)(c)
radio communication   transmission radiophonique
    c. C-42, s. 2
radiocommunication   radiocommunication
    c. C-22, s. 2
railway company   compagnie de chemin de fer
    c. B-3, s. 2
raise/to
    raise money/to   réunir des sommes
        c. C-41, s. 10(1)(c)
random
    random monitoring (of   contrôle au hasard
    communications)
        c. C-46, s. 184(2)(c)(ii)
range
    limit, boundary or angle of a   limite ou angle d'une concession,
    concession, range, lot or parcel   d'un rang, d'un lot ou d'un lopin
    of land   de terre
        c. C-46, s. 443(1)(b)
rank   grade
    c. C-17, s. 2(1)
    rank with respect to capital   rang quant au capital
        c. L-12, s. 35(2)
rank/to
    (creditors)   colloquer
        c. C-44, s. 40(3)

rank equally/to	occuper le même rang
c. B-1, s. 132(2)(c)	
rank on the estate/to (of assets)	prendre rang sur l'actif
c. B-1, s. 281(2)	
rapeseed	graine de colza
c. C-24, s. 48(1)	
rate	
(for health services)	taux
c. C-6, s. 11(1)(b)(i)	
rate of bank interest	taux d'intérêt bancaire
c. A-1, s. 18(d)(ii)	
tariff rate	barème
c. C-24, s. 32(3)	
rateably	au prorata
c. B-1, s. 121(2)	
c. C-44, s. 27(2)	
ratification	
(of a signature)	ratification
c. B-4, s. 48(2)	
ratify/to	
(a convention)	ratifier
c. C-26, Schedule I, Article 37(1)	
(an endorsement)	ratifier
c. B-1, s. 95(1)(a)	
c. C-44, s. 68(1)(a)	
ratio	rapport
c. B-1, s. 114(7)	
c. C-8, s. 18(1)(a)(ii)	
c. B-1, s. 32(5)	prorata
re-appoint/to	renouveler un mandat
c. F-11, s. 102(3)	
(for a further term)	renouveler (le mandat)
c. A-1, s. 54(3)	
re-appointed	
eligible to be re-appointed/to be	pouvoir recevoir un nouveau mandat
c. A-7, s. 7(3)	
re-appointment	reconduction de mandat
c. C-7, s. 7(5)	
re-assess/to	réévaluer
c. C-8, s. 22(1)	
re-enact/to	
(a provision)	édicter de nouveau
c. C-24, s. 47(2)	
re-examination	nouvel interrogatoire
c. C-39, s. 22(2)	
re-examine/to	interroger de nouveau
c. C-39, s. 44(2)	
(a decision)	revoir
c. P-2, s. 27(1)(l)	
re-integrating	
for the purpose of rehabilitating or re-integrating the person into the community	en vue de sa réhabilitation ou de sa réinsertion sociale
c. Y-1, s. 35(1)(a)	
re-opened	
have the proceedings re-opened/to	faire rouvrir les procédures
c. C-46, s. 552	
reach/to	
(an agreement)	arriver à un accord
c. C-11, s. 6(2)	

read/to
    read in evidence/to   lire en preuve
        c. C-46, s. 712(2)
real estate investment trust   fonds de placement immobilier
        c. B-1, s. 173(1)(o)
real estate or land   immeuble
        c. L-12, s. 2
real property   bien immobilier
        c. A-13, s. 4(i)
        c. A-10, s. 18(c)   immeuble
    delivery of possession of real   livraison de biens-fonds ou de biens
    property or chattels real   personnels immobiliers
        c. S-26, s. 65(1)(c)
realizable
    realizable value of the assets   valeur de réalisation de l'actif
        c. C-44, s. 241(6)(b)
realization
    (of security)   réalisation
        c. B-1, s. 174(12)(b)
    disposal or realization (of a   aliénation ou réalisation
    security)
        c. N-11, s. 47(f)(i)
    enforcement or realization (of   recouvrement ou réalisation
    security)
        c. C-24, s. 52(3)
realize/to
    (a security)   réaliser (une garantie)
        c. B-1, s. 58(2)(b)
    realize a security interest/to   réaliser (une sûreté)
        c. C-44, s. 94
realized
    moneys realized (from the sale)   sommes rapportées
        c. A-6, s. 2(2)(b)
reasonable
    act on reasonable grounds/to   agir en s'appuyant sur des motifs
                       raisonnables
        c. C-46, s. 25
    all reasonable assistance   toute l'assistance possible
        c. C-11, s. 26(2)
    at the first reasonable   à la première occasion raisonnable
    opportunity
        c. C-46, s. 486(4)
    be under a legal duty to have   être légalement tenu d'apporter une
    and to use reasonable   connaissance, une habilité et des
    knowledge, skill and care/to   soins raisonnables
        c. C-46, s. 216
    believe on reasonable grounds/to   avoir des motifs raisonnables de
                       croire
        c. A-1, s. 26
        c. C-12, s. 19(a)
    beyond a reasonable doubt   hors de tout doute raisonnable
        c. C-46, s. 136(1)
    raise beyond reasonable doubt a   créer une présomption hors de tout
    presomption/to   doute raisonnable
        c. C-17, s. 37
    reasonable and fair (contract)   équitable
        c. B-1, s. 53(7)
    reasonable and fair (contract)   équitable
        c. C-44, s. 120(7)
    reasonable assistance   assistance raisonnable
        c. C-20, s. 15(3)
    reasonable assistance   aide nécessaire
        c. C-20, s. 16(1)

reasonable assurance
c. C-44, s. 76(1)(d)

garanties suffisantes

reasonable care
c. A-1, s. 74

diligence nécessaire

reasonable cause
c. C-44, s. 20(6)

motif raisonnable

reasonable diligence
c. L-2, s. 40(2)(a)

diligence normale

reasonable diligence
c. C-46, s. 188(2)

diligence raisonnable

reasonable doubts
c. L-12, s. 43(1)

doute sérieux

reasonable excuse
c. C-50, s. 12(2)(b)

excuse valable

reasonable force
c. C-9, s. 40

force raisonnable

reasonable grounds
c. C-44, s. 32(2)

considérations raisonnables

reasonable grounds
c. 12 (2nd Supp.), s. 13(1)

motifs raisonnables

reasonable interest return
c. L-12, s. 61(1)(m)B)(ii)

rendement suffisant

reasonable notice
c. C-32, s. 42(3)
c. C-46, s. 347(5)

préavis suffisant

reasonable notice
c. C-44, s. 185(3)(b)

publicité suffisante

reasonable period of time
c. A-1, s. 12(2)(b)

délai convenable

reasonable period of time

c. A-1, s. 9(1)

période que justifient les
circonstances

reasonable precautions
c. B-1, s. 157(3)

mesures adéquates

reasonable standard
c. B-1, s. 104(3)

norme raisonnable

reasonable time
c. C-44, s. 14(2)

délai raisonnable

reasonable time
c. C-11, s. 26(1)

heure convenable

reasonable time (for inspection)
c. F-27, s. 23(1)

heure convenable

reasonable times
c. C-20, s. 15(2)

temps convenable

take all reasonable steps/to

c. C-46, s. 69

prendre toutes les mesures
raisonnables

under circumstances that give
rise to a reasonable inference

c. C-46, s. 352

dans des circonstances qui
permettent raisonnablement de
conclure

without reasonable cause
c. C-20, s. 15(4)

sans raison valable

without reasonable excuse
c. C-46, s. 69

sans excuse valable

reasonableness
c. C-44, s. 169(3)

bien-fondé

reasonably

force reasonably proportioned to
the danger
c. C-46, s. 30

force raisonnablement
proportionnée au danger

reasonably prudent person
c. F-11, s. 115(1)(b)

personne prudente et avisée

reasonably require/to   valablement exiger
    c. A-7, s. 16(2)
reasoned judgment   jugement éclairé
    c. B-1, s. 63(6)(a)
reasons
    (for a decision)   motifs
      c. A-7, s. 11(1)
    give reasons/to (for a decision)   motiver
      c. A-7, s. 8(6)
rebut/to
    rebut evidence/to   repousser une preuve
      c. C-46, s. 276(1)(a)
rebuttal
    by way of rebuttal   à titre de réfutation
      c. C-46, s. 794(2)
      c. F-27, s. 41(2)
      c. N-1, s. 7(2)
recall/to   révoquer
    c. C-21, s. 9(4)
receipt   quittance
    c. C-10, s. 39(4)
    c. L-12, s. 89(2)
    c. B-1, s. 2(1)(a)   récépissé
    c. B-1, s. 2(1)(a)   reçu
    be entrusted with the receipt,   être chargé de la réception, garde
    custody or management (of   ou gestion
    revenue funds)/to
      c. C-46, s. 399
    receipt for or acknowledgement   reçu ou récépissé de biens
    of property
      c. C-46, s. 388(a)
    release, receipt, discharge or   décharge, reçu, quittance ou autre
    other instrument evidencing   instrument constatant le
    payment of money   paiement de deniers
      c. C-46, s. 2
    warehouse receipt   récépissé ou warrant
      c. B-2, s. 20(a)
receipts
    accounts of receipts and   comptes de recettes et de débours et
    disbursements and final   états définitifs
    statements
      c. B-3, s. 5(3)(g)
    examine all receipts and   vérifier les recettes et dépenses
    expenditures/to
      c. A-16, s. 17
    receipts and disbursements   recettes et déboursés
      c. A-17, s. 21(1)
    record of receipts   état des recettes
      c. F-11, s. 17(3)
receive/to
    take or receive affidavit/to   recevoir des affidavits
      c. P-5, s. 9(2)
receive, comfort or assist/to
    (a person to escape)   recevoir, aider ou assister
      c. C-46, s. 23(1)
receiver
    receiver of wreck   receveur des épaves
      c. C-46, s. 415(b)
receiver and manager   séquestre-gérant
    c. B-1, s. 181
Receiver General   receveur général
    c. A-12, s. 23(2)

receiver-manager	séquestre-gérant
c. C-44, s. 95	
c. F-11, s. 135(2)(b)(iii)	
receiving	
receiving order	ordonnance de mise sous séquestre
c. C-21, s. 31(2)	
receiving order	ordonnance de séquestre
c. B-1, s. 178(7)	
c. B-3, s. 2	
recent complaint	plainte spontanée
c. C-46, s. 275	
receptacle	contenant
c. B-3, s. 10(2)	
c. C-38, s. 2	récipient
reception	
(of inmates)	écrou
c. P-5, s. 18(1)	
recipient	prestataire
c. C-17, s. 10	
c. B-1, s. 50(4)(a)	bénéficiaire
c. C-44, s. 38(4)	
eligible contribution recipient	bénéficiaire admissible
c. N-11, s. 95(1)	
named recipient	bénéficiaire inscrit
c. F-11, s. 2	
reciprocal agreement	accord réciproque
c. C-8, s. 6(2)(h)	
reciprocating State	État contractant
c. C-51, s. 37(1)	
reckless	
wanton or reckless disregard	insouciance déréglée ou téméraire
c. C-46, s. 219(1)	
reclaim possession/to	
(of a security)	réclamer la possession
c. B-1, s. 99(1)	
recognition of judgment	reconnaissance de jugement
c. C-30, Schedule, Article VIII	
recognizance	engagement
c. C-46, s. 493	
recognizance of bail	
aknowledge a recognizance of bail, a confession of judgment, a consent to judgment/to	reconnaître un engagement de caution, une confession de jugement, un consentement à jugement
c. C-46, s. 405	
recommitment	
apprehension and recommitment(of the inmate)	arrestation et réincarcération
c. P-2, s. 16(2)	
reconciliation	
(of spouses)	réconciliation
c. C-3, s. 8(3)(b)(ii)	
statement of reconciliation	rapport de conciliation
c. C-20, s. 7(5)	
reconsider its findings/to	procéder au réexamen
c. C-12, s. 31(2)	
reconstruction	
amalgation or reconstruction	fusion ou reconstitution
c. C-40, s. 125(5)	
record	document
c. A-1, s. 3	
c. C-42, s. 27(2)(i)	
c. A-17, s. 9(a)	registre

(for evidence)   pièce
    c. F-11, s. 60(3)
(indictment)   procès-verbal ou dossier
    c. C-46, s. 2
(of public property)   inventaire
    c. F-11, s. 10(d)
accounting record   registre de comptabilité
    c. C-40, s. 108(1)
address of record   adresse d'enregistrement
    c. C-43, s. 4(1)(e)(ii)(A)
book, record or account   document comptable
    c. F-11, s. 9(1)
court of record   cour d'archives
    c. C-46, s. 559(1)
court record   dossier judiciaire
    c. C-44, s. 78(3)(c)
criminal record   dossier ou relevé relatif à des affaires pénales

    c. C-47, s. 6(2)
entry or record of an incorporated society   inscription ou mention consignée par un organisme doté de la personnalité morale

    c. Y-1, s. 57(2)(b)
judicial record   dossier judiciaire
    c. C-47, s. 6(1)
record of a trial   dossier d'un procès
    c. C-46, s. 559(2)
school attendance and performance record and the employment record   assiduité et résultats scolaires, et antécédents professionnels
    c. Y-1, s. 14(2)(c)(vii)

record/to
(a certificate)   enregistrer un certificat
    c. B-6, s. 6(2)(b)
(revenues)   inscrire
    c. F-11, s. 7(1)(c)
record or register a fishing vessel/to   inscrire, enregistrer ou immatriculer un bateau de pêche
    c. B-1, s. 179(5)
record or register bets/to   inscrire ou enregistrer des paris
    c. C-46, s. 201(2)(a)
record verbatim/to   consigner mot à mot
    c. C-46, s. 487.1(2)
take or record/to (evidence)   recueillir ou enregistrer
    c. C-46, s. 549(1)

record date   date de référence
    c. B-1, s. 62(1)
(for determination of shareholders)   date de référence
    c. C-44, s. 134(1)

record in a register/to   consigner dans un registre
    c. B-6, s. 7(1)

record of earnings   registre des gains
    c. C-8, s. 2(1)

recorded
recorded address   adresse inscrite
    c. B-1, s. 2(1)
recorded vessel   navire enregistré
    c. B-1, Schedule VII

recorder
magistrate, police magistrate, stipendiary magistrate, district magistrate, provincial magistrate, judge of the sessions of the peace, recorder   magistrat, magistrat de police, magistrat stipendiaire, magistrat de district, magistrat provincial, juge des sessions de la paix, recorder

c. C-46, s. 2

recording
  recording of proceedings (in   enregistrement des débats
  court)
    c. F-7, s. 46(1)(viii)
records   livre
    c. B-1, s. 155(5)
    c. A-2, s. 18(1)(c)   registres
    c. A-7, s. 13(e)   dossiers
  (of a corporation)   livre
    c. C-44, s. 20(3)
  tax records   archives d'impôt
    c. B-3, s. 158(b)
recoup/to   rembourser
    c. B-1, s. 247(2)
recourse   recours
    c. A-12, s. 7(3)
    c. B-3, s. 86(4)
  right of recourse   recours
    c. A-12, s. 7(3)
  right of recourse   droit de recours
    c. B-4, s. 94(2)
recover/to
  (compensation)   recouvrer
    c. A-2, s. 8(10)
  action to recover (damages)   action en recouvrement
    c. N-7, s. 87(3)
recoverable
  recoverable or enforceable (in   recouvrable ou exécutoire
  civil proceedings)
    c. C-46, s. 724(1)
recovery
  (of property)   restitution
    c. C-51, s. 37(3)
  right of recovery   recours
    c. C-26, Schedule I, Article
    12(3)
  to provide for the repayment of   prévoir le remboursement, la
  accounting for and recovery of   justification et le recouvrement
  (accountable advances)
    c. F-11, s. 38(1)(b)
recredit/to   réattribuer à l'actif
    c. P-2, s. 25(3)
rectification
  (of the register)   rectification
    c. F-11, s. 60(1)(c)
recurrence
  (of an offence)   renouvellement
    c. C-46, s. 210(4)
redeem/to
  (securities)   racheter
    c. A-17, s. 9(b)
redeemable
  (security)   rachetable
    c. C-8, s. 111(1)(c)
  redeemable security   titre rachetable à échéance
    c. L-12, s. 78(1)
redemption   remboursement
    c. F-11, s. 46
  (of a security)   rachat
    c. C-8, s. 109(2)
  equity of redemption   droit de réméré
    c. B-1, s. 185(1)

redemption of a security c. F-11, s. 58	rachat d'un titre
redemption right c. C-44, s. 176(1)(b)(ii)	droit de rachat
right of redemption c. B-3, s. 79	droit de rachat
redetermination c. C-20, s. 2(6)	nouvelle détermination
redress	
procedure for redress c. L-2, s. 240(3)(b)	recours
remedy or redress for a private or public wrong or grievance c. C-46, s. 315	réparation ou redressement pour un tort ou grief privé ou public
reduce/to	
(a loan) c. A-10, s. 19(4)	rembourser partiellement
reduced rate c. A-15, s. 4(1)	taux abaissé
free or reduced rate transportation c. A-2, s. 19	transport gratuit ou à tarif réduit
reduction	
reduction in tariff c. A-15, s. 4(1)	abaissement de tarif
reduction of sentence c. C-46, s. 722(2)	réduction de sentence
redundant	
redundant employee c. L-2, s. 211	surnuméraire
reeve c. A-11, s. 20(1)	préfet
mayor, warden, reeve, sheriff, deputy sheriff, sheriff's officer and justice of the peace c. C-46, s. 2	maire, président de conseil de comté, préfet, shérif,shérif adjoint, officier de shérif et juge de paix
refer/to	
(the hearing) c. B-9, s. 10(5)	déférer
(to in a provision) c. A-3, s. 4	viser
refer the matter/to (court) c. Y-1, s. 11(6)(a)(ii)	soumettre le cas
refer to an arbitration board/to (a complaint) c. L-2, s. 152(4)	soumettre à un conseil d'arbitrage
referee	recommandataire
c. B-4, s. 32(1)	
c. B-1, s. 289(c) c. C-44, s. 217(c) c. F-7, s. 46(1)(vi)	arbitre
reference	
(of a question of fact) c. F-7, s. 46(1)(vi)	renvoi
(to an enactment) c. C-17, s. 2(3)	renvoi
book of reference c. A-2, s. 27(1)	livre de renvoi
for convenience of reference only c. C-46, s. 3	pour la seule commodité de la consultation
give a direction or make a reference/to (Minister of Justice) c. C-46, s. 679(7)	prendre une ordonnance ou faire un renvoi

referral
  (of a question)   renvoi
    c. L-2, s. 65(2)
  (to employment)   placement
    c. L-2, s. 69(1)
  (to Governor in Council)   renvoi
    c. C-6, s. 14
  referral selling   vente par recommandation
    c. C-34, s. 56(1)
refinancing   refinancement
    c. N-11, s. 65(4)(d)(ii)
reflect/to   représenter
    c. C-20, s. 21(1)(a)
reform
  reform and rehabilitation(of an   amendement et réadaptation
  inmate)
    c. P-2, s. 16(1)(a)(ii)
reform/to
  revise and reform the law/to   refondre et réformer le droit
    c. C-44, s. 4
reformation
  (of a young person)   amélioration de conduite
    c. C-46, s. 733(2)
reformatory   maison de correction
    c. P-5, s. 17(1)
reformatory prison
  penitentiary, common jail,   pénitencier, prison commune,
  public or reformatory prison,   prison publique, maison de
  lock-up, guard-room   correction, poste de police ou corps
                        de garde
    c. C-46, s. 2
reformatory school
  reformatory school or industrial école de réforme ou école
  school   industrielle
    c. C-46, s. 618(5)
reforming right   droit d'exécution ou de
                        représentation
    c. C-42, Schedule II
refusal
  (to work)   refus de travailler
    c. L-2, s. 3(1)
refusal of duty
  insubordination, disloyalty,   insubordination, déloyauté,
  mutiny or refusal of duty   mutinerie ou refus de servir
    c. C-46, s. 62(1)(c)
refuse/to
  refuse to grant exemption/to   refuser la dispense
    c. C-44, s. 246(c)
regard
  with due regard to the principle   dans le strict respect du principe du
  of selection of personnel   mérite en matière de sélection
  according to merit
    c. 31 (4th Supp.), s. preamble
  without regard (to ethnic origin) sans distinction
    c. 31 (4th Supp.), s. 39(1)
regional
  regional headquarter   administration régionale
    c. P-5, s. 15(4)
Regional Development   Conseil des subventions au
Incentives Board   développement régional
    c. A-1, Schedule I
register   registre
    c. F-11, s. 60(1)(d)

bound form register c. F-11, s. 60(2)	registre en volumes reliés
central securities register c. C-44, s. 50(2)	registre central des valeurs mobilières
loose-leaf form register c. F-11, s. 60(2)	registre à feuilles mobiles
photographic film form register c. F-11, s. 60(2)	registre sous forme de reproductions photographiques
securities register c. B-1, s. 75(4)(a) c. C-44, s. 20(1)(d)	registre des valeurs mobilières

register/to

(a association) c. C-40, s. 27(p)	enregistrer
(a share) c. A-10, s. 13(3)	inscrire
(aircraft) c. A-2, s. 4(e)	immatriculer
(ship) c. C-31, s. 11	immatriculer
record or register a fishing vessel/to c. B-1, s. 179(5)	inscrire, enregistrer ou immatriculer un bateau de pêche
record or register bets/to c. C-46, s. 201(2)(a)	inscrire ou enregistrer des paris

Register of Copyrights
  c. C-42, s. 25(4)

registre des droits d'auteur

registered

registered charity c. A-13, s. 28	organisme de charité enregistré
registered debenture c. L-12, s. 44(1)(i)	débenture enregistrée
registered holder c. B-1, s. 78(4)	détenteur inscrit
registered office c. C-30, Schedule, part VI, Article IX, c. C-44, s. 6(1)(b)	siège social
registered owner (of a security) c. B-1, s. 78(4)	propriétaire inscrit
registered owner (of shares) c. L-12, s. 45(4)	propriétaire immatriculé
registered owner or holder (of shares) c. C-44, s. 46(3)	propriétaire ou détenteur inscrit
share in registered form c. C-44, s. 24(1)	action nominative

registering court
  c. C-30, Schedule Article I

tribunal d'enregistrement

registrable

(copyright) c. C-42, s. 54(7)	enregistrable

registrant

(broker or dealer in securities) c. C-44, s. 147	courtier attitré

registrar

c. F-11, s. 2	agent comptable
(land) c. T-7, s. 9(1)	registrateur
(land titles or registry office) c. B-3, s. 20(1)	registrateur

(of a corporation)
    c. C-44, s. 49(4)
(of land titles)
    c. A-2, s. 8(8)
judge or registrar
    c. C-46, s. 386(b)
registrar of deeds

    c. P-1, s. 32(1)(b)
registrar of deeds
    c. N-7, s. 2
registrar of motor vehicles

    c. C-46, s. 260(7)
registrar or clerk (of the Court of appeal)
    c. C-46, s. 673
Registrar
    c. A-17, s. 2
(Supreme Court)
    c. S-26, s. 2(1)
Registrar General of Canada
    c. C-25, s. 10(1)(b)
Registrar of Copyrights
    c. C-42, s. 48
registrar of deeds
(Nova Scotia)
    c. C-25, s. 10(1)(a)
registrar of motor vehicles
    c. C-46, s. 256(4)
registration
(of a security)
    c. C-44, s. 50(4)
(of aircraft)
    c. A-2, s. 8(1)(b)
(of savings plan)
    c. B-1, s. 173(1)(m)
duplicate instrument, memorial, certificate or document in respect to registration of titles
    c. C-46, s. 2
inscription or registration (of securities)
    c. F-11, s. 60(3)
registration certificate (of a restricted weapon)
    c. C-46, s. 84(1)
registration district
    c. C-25, s. 10(1)(a)
registration division
    c. A-2, s. 8(8)
registration statement (securities)
    c. C-44, s. 2(7)(a)
transmission and registration (of regulations)
    c. S-22, s. 5(1)
registry
port of registry (of vessel)
    c. B-1, Schedule VI
registry office
    c. B-3, s. 20(1)

agent d'inscription

registrateur des titres

juge ou registrateur

conservateur des titres et hypothèques

directeur de l'Enregistrement

directeur du bureau des véhicules automobiles

registraire ou greffier

registraire

registraire

registraire général du Canada

registraire des droits d'auteurs

registrateur des titres

registrateur des véhicules à moteur

inscription

immatriculation

enregistrement

double de tout instrument, mémoire, certificat concernant l'enregistrement de titres

inscription

certificat d'enregistrement

circonscription d'enregistrement

division d'enregistrement

déclaration d'enregistrement

transmission et enregistrement

port d'immatriculation

bureau d'enregistrement

Registry
    Registry of the Court   greffe de la cour
        c. F-7, s. 14(1)
regular basis prescribed   périodicité réglementaire
        c. C-32, s. 36(1)(a)
Regular Force Death Benefit   compte des prestations de décès de
Account   la force régulière
        c. C-17, s. 68(1)
regularity
    (of a signature)   régularité
        c. B-4, s. 132(b)
regulate/to   régir
        c. A-11, s. 3(a)
        c. A-11, s. 3(d)   réglementer
    control and regulate/to (air   contrôler et régler
    navigation)
        c. A-2, s. 8(1)
regulated product   produit réglementé
        c. C-15, s. 2
regulation
    (of proceeding)   réglementation des travaux
        c. A-10, s. 11(b)
    (under an Act)   règlement d'application
        c. A-11, s. 18
    contravene a regulation/to   enfreindre un règlement
        c. A-12, s. 23(1)
    make a regulation/to   prendre un règlement
        c. A-11, s. 3
    order, rule or regulation (made   textes d'application
    under an Act)
        c. C-50, s. 22(3)(a)
    regulation of wages   réglementation des salaires
        c. C-46, s. 425(a)
regulation-making
    regulation-making authority   autorité réglementante
        c. S-22, s. 2(1)
regulative
    to exercise a regulative,   exercer des pouvoirs
    administrative or executive   réglementaires, administratifs ou
    jurisdiction   exécutifs
        c. S-26, s. 2(1)
regulatory
    administration or regulatory   attributions administratives ou de
    responsability   réglementation
        c. C-12, s. 16(4)
    administrative, research,   fonctions étatiques
    supervisory, advisory or   d'administration, de recherche, de
    regulatory functions of a   contrôle, de conseil ou de
    governmental nature   réglementation
        c. F-11, s. 3(1)(a)
rehabilitating
    for the purpose of rehabilitating   en vue de sa réhabilitation ou de sa
    or re-integrating the person into   réinsertion sociale
    the community
        c. Y-1, s. 35(1)(a)
rehabilitation   réinsertion sociale
        c. C-46, s. 733(2)
    (of accused)   réhabilitation
        c. C-46, s. 617(2)
    reform and rehabilitation(of an   amendement et réadaptation
    inmate)
        c. P-2, s. 16(1)(a)(ii)

rehabilitative
    absence with escort for humanitarian and rehabilitative reason
      c. C-46, s. 747(2)

sortie sous surveillance pour des raisons humanitaires ou en vue de la réadaptation

rehear/to
    (an application)
      c. P-35, s. 27(1)

réentendre

    (an application)
      c. L-2, s. 18

réinstruire

reinsurance
    reinsurance agreement
      c. C-48, s. 2

accord de réassurance

reissue
    (of a security)
      c. B-1, s. 75(2)

réémission

reissue/to
    (debt obligation)
      c. C-21, s. 17(2)(a)

émettre de nouveau

reject/to
    reject a by-law/to
      c. B-1, s. 43(3)

rejeter un règlement administratif

    reject or rescind a transfer/to
      c. B-1, s. 100(2)

refuser un transfert ou en demander la rescision

relate/to
    (to an agricultural product)
      c. A-5, s. 2

viser

related
    associated or related, federal works
      c. L-2, s. 255(1)

entreprises fédérales associées ou connexes

    related amendment (to Acts)
      c. 31 (4th Supp.)

modification connexe

    related creditor
      c. B-3, s. 54(3)

créancier lié

    related group
      c. B-3, s. 4(1)

groupe lié

    related group (of corporations)
      c. F-11, s. 90(5)(d)

groupement lié

    related matters
      c. C-21, s. 18(1)(d)

questions connexes

relation back to/to have
    c. B-3, s. 71(1)

rétroagir

relationship
    c. C-26, Schedule II

parenté

    by blood relationship
      c. C-46, s. 155(1)

par les liens du sang

    fair relationship
      c. A-8, s. 7(1)(b)

juste rapport

    legal relationship
      c. B-1, s. 215(6)(d)

lien juridique

relative
    c. C-41, s. 10(2)(d)

membre de la famille

    c. C-44, s. 2(1)(e)

parent

release
    c. C-37, s. 7(1)

quittance

    application for release from custody
      c. Y-1, s. 8(3)

demande de mise en liberté

    certificate of release
      c. B-1, s. 178(4)(b)

certificat de dégagement

judicial interim release	mise en liberté provisoire par voie judiciaire
c. Y-1, s. 36(1)(e)	
release of information	communication de renseignements
c. 4 (2nd Supp.), s. 13	
release, receipt, discharge or other instrument evidencing payment of money	décharge, reçu, quittance ou autre instrument constatant le paiement de deniers
c. C-46, s. 2	
temporary release	mise en liberté provisoire
c. Y-1, s. 35(1)	
release/to	
(information)	communiquer
c. C-12, s. 2	
(seized article)	donner mainlevée (de la saisie)
c. F-27, s. 26	
release and discharge a security/to	donner quittance et mainlevée d'une garantie
c. F-11, s. 81(a)(ii)	
released/to be	
(on parole)	être relâché
c. P-2, s. 19(1)	
relevant	
relevant change	changement pertinent
c. C-20, s. 11(4)(a)	
relevant site	lieu approprié
c. C-20, s. 15(3)	
reliability	
(of an individual)	fiabilité
c. C-23, s. 2	
relic	antiquité ou souvenir
c. C-46, s. 109(3)(e)	
relief	réparation
c. C-50, s. 22(1)	
claim for relief	demande de réparation
c. F-7, s. 2	
relieve/to	
(from a duty)	libérer (d'une obligation)
c. B-1, s. 54(3)	
(of liability)	exonérer
c. C-26, Schedule I, Article 23	
relieve from default/to	décharger d'une faute
c. C-44, s. 217(k)	
relieve of an obligation/to	dégager d'une obligation
c. C-46, s. 767.1(1)	
relieved/to be	
(of an obligation)	relever
c. C-21, s. 4(7)(c)	
religious	
religious, educational or charitable object	entreprise religieuse, éducative ou charitable
c. C-42, s. 27(3)	
relinquish/to	
(rights)	abandonner
c. B-3, s. 81(2)	
rely/to	
(on evidence)	invoquer
c. C-32, s. 28(2)(d)	
remain/to	
(property)	subsister
c. A-13, s. 34	

remainder
  (of a sum)   solde
    c. A-13, s. 31
  (of a term)   reste
    c. C-21, s. 11(1)
  (of an amount)   reliquat
    c. C-31, s. 14
remaining property   reliquat des biens
    c. B-3, s. 29(1)
    c. C-44, s. 24(3)(c)
remand
  adjournment or remand   ajournement ou renvoi
    c. C-46, s. 485(1)
  remand for observation (of an   renvoi pour observation
  accused)
    c. C-46, s. 537(2)
  remand to custody/to   ordonner l'envoi en détention
    c. N-1, s. 24
remedial treatment   traitement curatif
    c. C-31, s. 42(h)
remedy
  (under an Act)   recours
    c. F-7, s. 23
  civil remedy   recours civil
    c. C-11, s. 36(2)
    c. C-46, s. 11
  exercise a remedy/to   exercer un recours
    c. B-2, s. 20(b)
  remedy or redress for a private réparation ou redressement pour un
  or public wrong or grievance   tort ou grief privé ou public
    c. C-46, s. 315
  remedy the default/to   remédier à la situation
    c. C-6, s. 14(1)(b)
  right or remedy available at law recours ouvert en droit
    c. C-9, s. 44
remedy allowance
  (for gold coins)   marge de tolérance
    c. C-52, Schedule
Remembrance Day   jour du Souvenir
    c. L-2, s. 193(2)
remission
  (of a fee)   remise
    c. C-9, s. 16(2)
  (of fees)   exemption
    c. C-29, s. 27(c)
  period of statutory remission   période de réduction légale de peine
    c. C-47, s. 4(4)
  remission in whole or in part (of remise intégrale ou partielle
  a fine)
    c. C-46, s. 750(1)
  statutory and earned remission réduction de peine légale ou méritée
    c. P-2, s. 25(2)
  total, partial, conditional or   remise totale, partielle,
  unconditional remission   conditionnelle ou absolu
    c. F-11, s. 23(3)
remit/to
  (a tax)   faire remise
    c. F-11, s. 23(2)
remitted
  remitted to a party's former   être réintégré dans les droits
  rights/to be   antérieurs d'une partie
    c. B-4, s. 139(b)

remote service unit
    c. C-46, s. 321

terminal d'un système décentralisé

removal
    (of a director)
        c. C-44, s. 109(3)

révocation

    (of a thing)
        c. C-23, s. 22(a)

enlèvement

    removal of tariff
        c. A-15, s. 5(1)

suppression de tarif

    summary removal (of a person)
        c. N-14, s. 7(1)(q)

expulsion sans formalité

    summary removal (warrant)
        c. T-7, s. 20(2)

expulsion sommaire

    warrant for removal of prisoners
        c. C-37, s. 7(1)

mandat de transfèrement

remove/to
    (a decision)
        c. F-7, s. 29

évoquer

    (a director)
        c. C-44, s. 109(1)

révoquer

    (a person)
        c. A-10, s. 20(1)

démettre de ses fonctions

    (out of court)
        c. C-46, s. 758(2)(a)

expulser

    (seized property)
        c. F-27, s. 24(2)

déplacer

    (seized property)
        c. F-27, s. 25

transférer

    alter, deface or remove/to (a
    serial number on a firearm)
        c. C-46, s. 104(3)(a)

modifier, maquiller ou effacer

    remove any disqualification/to
        c. C-47, s. 5(b)

faire cesser toute incapacité

    remove from parental
    supervision/to
        c. Y-1, s. 4(1)(a)

soustraire à l'autorité parentale

remuneration
    c. A-5, s. 6

rémunération

    without remuneration
        c. Y-1, s. 69

à titre bénévole

render/to
    (a judgment)
        c. C-44, s. 118(3)

rendre un jugement

rendition
    oral rendition or delivery (of
    judgment)
        c. 31 (4th Supp.), s. 20(3)

prononcé

renewal
    (of a licence)
        c. B-3, s. 5(3)(a)

renouvellement

    (of lease)
        c. C-53, s. 2(1)

reconduction

renounce/to
    (a liability)
        c. B-4, s. 141(2)

libérer (d'une obligation)

    (a right)
        c. B-4, s. 141(1)

renoncer (à un droit)

    (citizenship)
        c. C-29, s. 9(1)

répudier

rent
    accelerated rent
        c. B-3, s. 136(1)(f)

loyer perçu par anticipation

arrear of rent
   c. B-3, s. 136(1)(f)
                              arriéré de loyer
ground rent
   c. L-12, s. 61(1)(k)
                              rente foncière
occupation rent
   c. B-3, s. 136(1)(f)
                              loyer d'occupation
rent reduction fund
   c. N-11, s. 2
                              caisse d'assistance locative

rental
   (of a property)
   c. F-11, s. 7(1)(c)
                              location
   rental housing project
   c. N-11, s. 2
                              ensemble d'habitation locatif

renunciation
   certificate of renunciation
   c. C-29, s. 2(1)
                              certificat de répudiation

reopen/to
   (a crossed cheque)
   c. B-4, s. 169(7)
                              débarrer (un chèque)

reorganization
   (of the corporation)
   c. L-12, s. 61(5)
                              réorganisation

repay/to
   (a loan)
   c. A-10, s. 19(4)
                              rembourser intégralement

repayable
   (a loan)
   c. A-10, s. 19(1)
                              remboursable

repayment
   c. A-10, s. 19(3)
                              remboursement
   repayment of the principal
   c. L-12, s. 68(3)
                              remboursement du principal
   to provide for the repayment of
   accounting for and recovery of
   (accountable advances)
   c. F-11, s. 38(1)(b)
                              prévoir le remboursement, la justification et le recouvrement

repeal
   (of a by-law)
   c. B-1, s. 43(3)
                              révocation

repeal/to
   repeal a by-law/to
                              révoquer un règlement administratif
   c. B-1, s. 45(1)

repetition
   continuation or repetition of
   offence
                              continuation ou répétition d'une infraction
   c. C-34, s. 34(1)(b)

repetitive
   pattern of repetitive behaviour
                              répétition d'actes
   c. C-46, s. 753(a)(i)

replication
   plea, replication or other
   pleading (indictment)
                              défense, réplique ou autre pièce de plaidoirie
   c. C-46, s. 2

reply
   by way of reply
   c. C-46, s. 537(1)(f)
                              par voie de réplique

report
   (of a warrant)
   c. F-32, s. 9
                              rapport
   official report
   c. F-7, s. 58(2)
                              recueil (de décisions judiciaires)

report/to
 c. B-2, s. 28(5)
 c. F-11, s. 38(3)
 report the seizure/to

 c. A-11, s. 20(1)
reportable disease
 c. A-11, s. 2
reported/to be
 c. A-11, s. 12(1)(c)
reporter
 (of the Court)
  c. S-26, s. 27(1)
 to be present as an aid, second,
 surgeon, umpire, backer or
 reporter
  c. C-46, s. 83(1)(c)
reporting period
 (for a corporation)
  c. C-43, s. 2(1)
repository
 central repository
  c. Y-1, s. 41(1)
repossession
 c. B-3, s. 232(5)(a)
represent/to
 falsely represent himself to be a
 peace officer/to
  c. C-46, s. 130(a)
 represent or hold out to be/to
  c. N-1, s. 4(1)
representation
 c. C-23, s. 48(2)
 contention or representation (at
 hearing)
  c. C-42, s. 23(1)
 false or fraudulent
 representation
  c. C-46, s. 162(2)(b)(i)
 false or misleading
 representation
  c. C-38, s. 7(2)
 false representation
  c. C-34, s. 52(4)
 immoral, indecent or obscene
 performance, entertainment or
 representation
  c. C-46, s. 167(2)
 make representation/to
  c. C-32, s. 23(3)(a)
 material false statement or
 representation
  c. C-46, s. 386(a)
 representation or testimonial
  c. C-34, s. 52(4)
representational
 representational allowance
  c. J-1, s. 27(6)
representations
 c. A-7, s. 10(2)
 (before court)
  c. A-1, s. 47(1)

faire rapport

signaler
transmettre un procès-verbal de la
 saisie

maladie déclarable

faire l'objet d'un procès-verbal

arrêtiste

assister en qualité d'aide, second,
 médecin, arbitre, soutien ou
 reporter

période de rapport

répertoire central

rentrée en possession

se présenter faussement comme
 agent de la paix

prétendre ou estimer être

observation

représentation

représentation fausse ou trompeuse

information fausse ou trompeuse

indications fausses

représentation, spectacle ou
 divertissement immoral, indécent
 ou obscène

présenter une observation

fausse énonciation ou
 représentation essentielle

indication ou attestation

frais de représentation

observations

arguments

make representations/to
   c. A-1, s. 27(3)(c)
   c. C-12, s. 34(1)(c)
	présenter des observations

representations made at a
hearing
   c. C-46, s. 276(4)
	observations faites au cours d'une
	  audition

representative
   c. C-26, Schedule I, Article
   30(2)
	ayant droit

trustee, guardian, committee,
curator, tutor, executor,
administrator or representative
of a deceased person
   c. B-1, s. 75(2)
	fiduciaire, tuteur, curateur,
	  exécuteur ou administrateur de
	  succession

trustee, guardian, committee,
curator, tutor, executor,
administrator or representative
of a deceased person
   c. B-1, s. 75(2)
	fiduciaire, tuteur, curateur,
	  exécuteur ou administrateur de
	  succession

representative action c. C-44, s. 226(5)	action en justice collective

representative office
  (of a foreign bank)
   c. B-1, s. 302(4)
	bureau de représentation

republication c. C-42, s. 15	nouvelle publication

repudiation
  repudiation or avoidance
   c. B-1, s. 78(5)
   c. C-44, s. 51(5)
	désaveu

repurchase/to
  (shares)
   c. C-44, s. 194(e)
	racheter

reputation
  evidence of sexual reputation
   c. C-46, s. 277
	preuve de réputation sexuelle

repute
  evidence of character and repute
   c. C-46, s. 757
	preuve de moralité ou de réputation

reputed father c. C-26, Schedule II	prétendu père

request
  at the request of (a peace officer)
   c. C-46, s. 353(3)(b)
  request for access
   c. A-1, s. 3
	à la demande de
	
	demande de communication

require
  require the accused to attend
court/to
   c. C-46, s. 509(1)(c)
	enjoindre au prévenu d'être présent

require/to
  (a person)
   c. C-34, s. 11(1)
  order and require/to
   c. A-2, s. 14(2)(a)
	enjoindre
	
	ordonner

require payment/to c. A-1, s. 11(2)	exiger le versement
required c. C-44, s. 174(6)(a)	obligatoire

requirement
   c. B-1, s. 124(4)
   c. B-1, s. 123(1)
   c. C-21, s. 4(2)
	obligation
	
	exigence

(of a regulation) c. A-11, s. 33(1)	prescription
requirements	
limitations, liabilities and requirements c. B-1, s. 7(1)	obligations
requisition	requête
c. B-1, s. 72(1)	
c. C-44, s. 143(1)	
c. S-26, s. 30(3)	demande
requisition for payment c. F-11, s. 33(2)	demande de paiement
requisition/to	exiger
c. B-1, s. 72(1)	
requisition a property/to c. A-16, s. 14	réquisitionner un bien
resale	revente
c. B-4, s. 188	
c. C-34, s. 38	
c. L-12, s. 68(2)	
rescind/to	
(a decision) c. C-8, s. 84(2)	annuler
(issue of licence) c. B-9, s. 14(3)(a)	annuler
reject or rescind a transfer/to c. B-1, s. 100(2)	refuser un transfert ou en demander la rescision
rescind a transaction/to c. C-44, s. 205(3)(f)	annuler une opération
rescind or vary/to (an order) c. C-24, s. 20(2)	annuler ou modifier
rescue	
(of a prisoner) c. P-5, s. 3(4)	délivrance illégale
rescue/to	
(a person from legal custody) c. C-46, s. 147(a)	délivrer
reservable day	jour où une banque peut faire des opérations au compte de réserve
c. B-1, s. 208(11)	
reservation	réserve
c. A-17, s. 6	
(in the application of the Convention) c. C-42, Schedule II Article 13	réserve
stipulation, condition, reservation or exemption c. C-27, Schedule, Article VII	stipulation, condition, réserve ou exonération
reserve	réserve
c. F-11, s. 63(2)	
primary reserve (of a bank) c. B-1, s. 208(1)	réserve primaire
statement of general reserve c. L-12, s. 53(2)(d)	état de la réserve générale
reserve/to	attribuer
c. C-21, s. 21	
reserves	
creation of reserves c. A-6, s. 2(2)(b)	création de réserves
residence	
ordinary place of residence c. C-16, s. 6	lieu ordinaire de résidence

ordinary place of residence
    c. A-7, s. 7(9)(b)
                    lieu de résidence habituelle
ordinary residence
    c. B-1, s. 174(2)(f)(i)
                    résidence principale
place of residence
    c. C-41, s. 6(1)
                    lieu de résidence
residence or usual place of residence
    c. L-9, s. 5
                    résidence ou lieu de résidence habituel

resident
    c. C-6, s. 2
                    habitant
permanent resident
    c. A-1, s. 4(1)(b)
                    résident permanent

residential
community, residential centre, group home, child care institution, or forest or wilderness camp
    c. Y-1, s. 20(7)
                    centre résidentiel local, foyer collectif, établissement d'aide à l'enfance, camp forestier ou camp de pleine nature

residue
(of fund)
    c. B-2, s. 27(a)
                    reliquat

resign/to
    c. C-44, s. 161(2)(b)(iii)
                    se démettre
    c. B-1, s. 41(2)(a)
                    démissionner
resign the seat/to
    c. P-1, s. 23(2)
                    se démettre de son mandat

resignation
    c. B-1, s. 39(2)
    c. C-44, s. 108(2)
                    démission

resist or wilfully obstruct a member/to
    c. C-12, s. 43
                    s'opposer délibérément à l'action d'un membre

resolution
negative resolution (of Parliament)
    c. C-32, s. 8(4)
                    résolution de rejet
ordinary resolution
    c. C-44, s. 2(1)
                    résolution ordinaire
process for resolution (of a dispute)
    c. P-35, s. 37(2)
                    mode de règlement
special resolution
    c. B-1, s. 2(1)
    c. C-44, s. 2(1)
                    résolution spéciale

resort
highest court of final resort
    c. C-36, s. 14(1)
                    tribunal de dernier ressort
highest court of final resort in a province
    c. S-26, s. 2(2)
                    plus haut tribunal de dernier ressort dans une province
public resort
    c. T-7, s. 23(e)
                    lieu de villégiature

respect
with respect to
    c. A-6, s. 2(2)
                    relativement à
with respect to (any agreement)
    c. A-5, s. 5(1)
                    à l'égard de

respondentia
bottomry or respondentia
    c. F-7, s. 22(2)(c)
                    prêt à la grosse

responsibilities
    c. A-10, s. 7(2)
                    attributions

responsibility
  criminal responsibility   responsabilité pénale
    c. C-46, s. 14
  to bear responsability for their   assumer la responsabilité de leur
  contravention   délit
    c. Y-1, s. 3(1)(a)
responsible   digne de confiance
    c. B-1, s. 104(2)
responsible/to be   rendre compte à
    c. C-25, s. 8(2)
  (for an undertaking)   être chargé
    c. A-3, s. 5(a)
responsible person   personne digne de confiance
    c. C-44, s. 77(3)
ressources
  treatment or correctional   moyens de traitement ou de
  ressources   réadaptation
    c. Y-1, s. 16(4)(d)
rest fund   fonds de réserve
    c. B-2, s. 27
restate/to
  restate the articles of   mettre à jour les statuts
  incorporation/to
    c. C-44, s. 180(1)
restated
  original or restated (articles)   initial ou mis à jour
    c. C-44, s. 2(1)
  original or restated articles (of   clauses initiales ou mises à jour
  incorporation)
    c. F-11, s. 83(1)
restitution
  (of a incorporeal right)   restitution
    c. F-7, s. 2
  order for compensation or for   ordonnance d'indemnisation ou de
  the restitution (of property)   restitution
    c. C-46, s. 689(1)
restoration
  order of restoration   ordonnance de restitution
    c. C-11, s. 23(1)
restore/to
  (property)   restituer
    c. C-44, s. 217(n)(iii)
  restore to a person entitled to   restituer au possesseur légitime
  possession/to
    c. C-32, s. 28(3)
  restore to the person from whom   restituer au saisi
  it was seized/to
    c. C-32, s. 28(3)
restrain/to
  (holding of a meeting)   empêcher
    c. B-1, s. 65(8)
  imprison or restrain/to   emprisonner ou détenir
    c. C-46, s. 46(1)(a)
restraining order
  restraining order or other order   ordonnance d'un tribunal
  of a court
    c. C-44, s. 78(2)(a)
restraint
  arrest or restraint of princes,   arrêt ou contrainte de prince,
  rulers or people   autorité ou peuple
    c. C-27, Schedule, Article IV, 2

restraint of trade   restriction du commerce
     c. C-34, s. 75(1)(a)
restraint of trade   pratique commerciale restrictive
     c. C-37, s. 4(c)
secure containment or restraint   placement ou internement
         sécuritaires
     c. Y-1, s. 24(11)
to be inhibited by normal   être inhibé par les normes
standards of behavioural   ordinaires de restriction du
restraint   comportement
     c. C-46, s. 753(a)(iii)

restricted
     (regulation)   limité
     c. C-8, s. 7(3)
     restricted drug   drogue d'usage restreint
     c. F-27, s. 46
     restricted weapon   arme à autorisation restreinte
     c. C-46, s. 84(1)

restriction
     (for licences)   restriction
     c. A-2, s. 18(1)(a)
     right, privilege, restriction and   droit, privilège, restriction et
     condition (attaching to shares)   condition
     c. C-44, s. 6(1)(c)(i)

Restrictive Trade Practices   Commission sur les pratiques
Commission   restrictives du commerce
     c. A-1, Schedule I
     c. C-34, s. 2

resume/to
     (citizenship)   réintégrer
     c. C-29, s. 10(1)

resumption
     resumption of citizenship   réintégration dans la citoyenneté
     c. C-29, s. 11(1)(9)

retain/to
     (information)   conserver
     c. C-23, s. 12
     retain a person/to   retenir les services d'une personne
     c. C-44, s. 131(1)(e)
     right to retain and instruct   droit d'obtenir les services d'un
     counsel   avocat
     c. Y-1, s. 11(1)

retained
     retained earnings   bénéfices non répartis
     c. C-43, s. 5(2)(d)
     c. C-44, s. 26(6)
     retained in the custody of/to be   retenir
     c. A-12, s. 23(2)

retardation
     physical or mental illness or   maladie ou dérèglement d'ordre
     disorder, psychological disorder,   physique ou mental, dérèglement
     emotional disturbance, learning   d'ordre psychologique, troubles
     disability or mental retardation   émotionnels, troubles
         d'apprentissage ou déficience
         mentale
     c. Y-1, s. 13(1)(e)

retention
     (of assets)   rétention
     c. B-1, s. 289(h)
     retention of assets   rétention d'éléments d'actif
     c. C-44, s. 217(h)

retirement
     age of retirement   mise à la retraite d'office
     c. J-1, s. 2

retirement income fund   fonds de revenu de retraite
   c. B-1, s. 173(1)(m)
retirement savings plan   régime d'épargne-retraite
   c. B-1, s. 173(1)(m)
retiring director   administrateur sortant
   c. C-41, s. 21(2)
retransfer/to
   (goods)   rétrocéder
   c. B-1, s. 187(1)
retrieval
   data processing, storage or   traitement des données,
   retrieval of data   mémorisation, recouvrement ou
               relevé des données
   c. C-46, s. 342.1(2)
retroactive
   be retroactive/to (a provision)   avoir un effet rétroactif
   c. P-35, s. 71(2)
retrospective effect   rétroactivement
   c. B-1, s. 164(1)
   c. C-44, s. 127(8)
return   déclaration
   c. B-3, s. 22
   (of a bank)   relevé
   c. B-1, s. 235(2)
   (of contributions)   remboursement
   c. C-17, s. 6(b)(ii)(j)
   (of proceeds of the sale)   remise
   c. A-5, s. 2
   (of sheriff)   rapport
   c. C-46, s. 773
   patronage return   ristourne à la clientèle
   c. C-40, s. 3(1)
   reasonable interest return   rendement suffisant
   c. L-12, s. 61(1)(m)(B)(ii)
   return of capital   remboursement du capital
   c. C-44, s. 27(2)
   return of evidence   rapport des dépositions
   c. C-46, s. 713(2)
   return of income   déclaration du revenu
   c. B-3, s. 149(3)
   tax return   déclaration d'impôt
   c. B-3, s. 158(b)
   written return   état écrit
   c. C-34, s. 11(1)
return/to
   (a share)   rétrocéder
   c. C-44, s. 118(5)(b)
returnable
   to be made returnable/to   fixer le rapport
   (warrant)
   c. C-46, s. 511(2)
returned
   duly returned or elected/to be   être dument élu
   c. P-1, s. 30(2)
   returned as a juror/to be   être mis au nombre des jurés
   c. C-46, s. 670(b)
revenue   revenu public
   c. C-46, s. 321
   revenue law   loi fiscale
   c. F-11, s. 80(c)
   revenue paper   papier de revenu
   c. C-46, s. 321

revenues　　　　　　　　　　　　revenus
　　c. A-2, s. 18(1)(d)
　　c. A-3, s. 5(c)
reversal
　　(of judgment)　　　　　　　　cessation
　　　c. S-26, s. 70
reverse/to
　　(an assessment)　　　　　　　infirmer
　　　c. C-8, s. 28(2)
　　confirm or reverse/to (an act or a　　confirmer ou infirmer
　　decision)
　　　c. B-3, s. 37
reversionary interest　　　　　droit de réversibilité
　　c. C-42, s. 14(1)
reversioner　　　　　　　　　droit de réversion
　　c. C-46, s. 328(c)
revert/to
　　(lands)　　　　　　　　　　　retourner
　　　c. N-14, s. 6(3)
revest/to
　　(right, title and interest of a　　　réattribuer
　　trustee)
　　　c. B-3, s. 61(1)
review
　　(by court)　　　　　　　　　contrôle judiciaire
　　　c. B-1, s. 147(5)
　　(of a case)　　　　　　　　　examen
　　　c. C-46, s. 619(5)
　　(of a disposition)　　　　　　examen
　　　c. Y-1, s. 11(3)(d)
　　(of an order)　　　　　　　　révision
　　　c. Y-1, s. 8(7)
　　(of order)　　　　　　　　　révision
　　　c. C-46, s. 521(1)
　　apply for a review/to　　　　　exercer un recours en révision
　　　c. A-7, s. 10(1)
　　request a review/to (of a　　　　exercer un recours en révision
　　decision)
　　　c. A-1, s. 28(3)(a)
　　review of application　　　　　révision de la demande
　　　c. C-51, s. 29(1)
review/to
　　(a case)　　　　　　　　　　réexaminer
　　　c. P-2, s. 22(3)
review board
　　(young offenders)　　　　　　commission d'examen
　　　c. Y-1, s. 2(1)
Review Committee　　　　　　comité de surveillance
　　c. C-23, s. 2
　　c. C-8, s. 2(1)　　　　　　　comité de révision
Review Tribunal　　　　　　　commission de révision
　　c. A-7, s. 9(1)
reviewable transaction　　　　transaction révisable
　　c. B-3, s. 3(1)
revise/to
　　revise and reform the law/to　　refondre et réformer le droit
　　　c. C-44, s. 4
Revised Berne Convention　　　Convention de Berne revisée
　　c. C-42, Schedule II
revival
　　(of a body corporate)　　　　reconstitution
　　　c. C-44, s. 209(2)

(of an association)
    c. C-40, s. 121(3)

rétablissement

articles of incorporation, amendment, amalgamation, continuance, reorganization, arrangement, dissolution or revival
    c. C-44, s. 2(1)

clauses réglementant la constitution ainsi que toute modification, fusion, prorogation, réorganisation, dissolution, reconstitution ou tout arrangement

articles of revival (of a corporation)
    c. F-11, s. 83(1)

clauses régissant la reconstitution

revocation

(of a certificate)
    c. C-46, s. 112(5)

révocation

(of a proxy)
    c. C-44, s. 147c)

révocation

(of licence)
    c. B-9, s. 10(1)(b)

annulation

(of licenses)
    c. A-2, s. 8(1)(a)

révocation

granting and revocation of authority
    c. A-6, s. 3

action et retrait des habilitations

revoke/to

(a name of a corporation)
    c. C-44, s. 12(5)

annuler

(a permit)
    c. C-46, s. 112(2)

révoquer

(an action of the Board)
    c. F-11, s. 8

annuler

(authority)
    c. A-6, s. 2(3)

retirer

reward
    c. B-1, s. 313(1)(a)

récompense

for hire or reward
    c. T-19, s. 3(1)

à titre onéreux

for reward
    c. C-26, Schedule I, Article 1(1)

contre rémunération

hire or reward
    c. A-2, s. 12

rémunération

loan, reward, advantage or benefit (to an official)
    c. C-46, s. 121(1)(c)(ii)

prêt, récompense, avantage ou bénéfice

reward or immunity

(for something lost or stolen)
    c. C-46, s. 143

récompense ou immunité

ribbon

military medal, ribbon, badge or chevron
    c. C-46, s. 419(b)

médaille, ruban, insigne ou chevron militaire

ridicule

to expose a person to hatred, contempt or ridicule
    c. C-46, s. 298

exposer quelqu'un à la haine, au mépris ou au ridicule

rigging

fish, tackle, rigging, apparel, furniture, stores and cargo
    c. C-33, s. 2

poissons, agrès, apparaux, garnitures, équipement, matériel, approvisionnements et cargaison

right
    c. A-12, s. 2

droit

exercise of the right (to access)   exercice du droit
    c. A-1, s. 5(1)(b)
legal right or legal liability   droit légal ou obligation légale
    c. C-46, s. 118
right of action   droit d'action
    c. B-5, s. 2
right to act   droit d'agir
    c. C-19, s. 10(4)
right to dispose (of the cargo)   droit de disposer
    c. C-26, Schedule I, Article
      12(1)
sole right   droit exclusif
    c. C-42, s. 3(1)

right-of-way
(for a road bed)   emprise
    c. T-7, s. 23(f)
(of a railway)   emprise
    c. N-14, s. 6(2)(a)

rightfulness   régularité
    c. B-1, s. 88(2)
(of a transfer)   régularité
    c. C-44, s. 61(2)

rights
capacity, rights, powers and   capacité
privileges (of a natural person)
    c. C-21, s. 6(2)
offences against rights of   infractions contre les droits de
property   propriété
    c. C-46, s. 321
powers, rights and privileges   pouvoirs et attributions
    c. A-7, s. 8(4)
rights of any person   droits subjectifs
    c. I-23, s. 9
rights, privileges and   droits
immunities (holder of a security)
    c. C-44, s. 81(1)(b)

rim-fire
rim-fire or center-fire   munition à percussion annulaire ou
ammunition   centrale
    c. C-46, s. 84(1)

riot
riot and civil commotion   émeute ou trouble civil
    c. C-27, Schedule, Article IV,
      2
suppress a riot/to   réprimer une émeute
    c. C-46, s. 32(1)(a)

rioter   émeutier
    c. C-46, s. 33(1)

ripe
ripe for hearing (appeal)   prêt pour l'audition
    c. S-26, s. 71(1)

rise
give rise/to (to a complaint)   donner lieu
    c. L-2, s. 97(5)(a)
rise or fall in price of stocks   hausse ou baisse des actions
    c. C-46, s. 383(1)

risk
undue risk to society   risque trop grand pour la société
    c. P-2, s. 16(1)(a)(iii)

road
street, road or highway   rue, chemin ou grande route
    c. C-46, s. 249(1)(a)

rob/to
    c. C-46, s. 345
voler

robbery
    c. C-46, s. 343
vol qualifié

rocker key
    key, pick, rocker key, or other
    instrument
        c. C-46, s. 353(5)
clef, crochet, clef à levier ou tout autre instrument

role and duties
    c. A-13, s. 26(c)
attributions

rotation
    (of the trials)
        c. C-39, s. 4
roulement

Royal Air Force Ferry Command
    c. C-31, s. 52
Royal Air Force Ferry Command

Royal Air Force Transport Command
    c. C-31, s. 52
Royal Air Force Transport Command

Royal Assent
    c. B-1, s. 11
sanction royale

Royal Canadian Air Force
    c. C-17, s. 2(1)
Corps d'aviation royal canadien

Royal Canadian Legion
    c. C-18, Schedule
Légion Royale Canadienne

Royal Canadian Mint
    c. A-1, Schedule I
    c. F-11, Schedule III, Part I
Monnaie royale canadienne

Royal Canadian Mounted Police
    c. A-1, s. 16(3)
    c. F-11, s. 85(2)(a)
Gendarmerie royale du Canada

Royal Canadian Navy
    c. C-17, s. 2(1)
Marine royale du Canada

royalties
    (copyright)
        c. C-42, s. 8(1)
tantièmes

royalty
    c. B-3, s. 83(2)(a)
    c. T-7, s. 12
redevance

rule
    judgment, rule, order, decision,
    decree, decretal order, or
    sentence
        c. S-26, s. 2(1)
décision

    order, rule or regulation (made
    under an Act)
        c. C-50, s. 22(3)(a)
textes d'application

rule of law
primauté du droit

rulers
    arrest or restraint of princes,
    rulers or people
        c. C-27, Schedule, Article IV,
        2
arrêt ou contrainte de prince, autorité ou peuple

ruling
    c. Y-1, s. 58(1)
décision

    conviction, ruling, order or
    judgment
        c. B-1, s. 258(1)(e)
décision judiciaire ou quasi-judiciaire

run/to
    begin to run/to (time)
        c. B-4, s. 44
commencer à courir

running
    running, trotting or pacing
    horse-races
        c. C-46, s. 204(1)(c)
courses de chevaux, courses de chevaux en trot ou à l'amble

running right
    c. C-19, s. 23(3)(c)

droit de circulation

S

sabotage
    c. A-1, s. 15(2)(b)
    c. C-23, s. 2
    c. C-46, s. 52

sabotage

sack
    bag, sack or other container or covering (for mail)
      c. C-46, s. 356(1)(a)(ii)

sac ou autre contenant ou couverture

safety
    safety mark
      c. T-19, s. 2

indication de danger

    safety officer
      c. L-2, s. 122

agent de sécurité

    safety or security of Canada
      c. C-47, s. 6(3)

sûreté ou sécurité du Canada

    safety requirements
      c. T-19, s. 2

règle de sécurité

    safety standards
      c. T-19, s. 2

normes de sécurité

salaried officer
    salaried officer of the Crown
      c. C-50, s. 29(1)

fonctionnaire salarié de l'État

salary
    c. A-5, s. 6
    c. C-17, s. 2(1)

traitement

    c. A-16, s. 12

rémunération

    salary and expenses
      c. C-13, s. 18(1)

traitement et indemnités

sale
    for sale or hire
      c. C-42, s. 27(4)(d)

pour la vente ou la location

    sale or disposal
      c. L-12, s. 100(2)

cession

    sale under execution
      c. N-7, s. 114(1)(a)

vente en justice

    sale under execution or under the decree, order or judgment of a court of competent jurisdiction
      c. L-12, s. 45(1)

vente en justice

    sheriff's sale
      c. B-1, s. 184

vente par le shérif

salvage
    civil salvage
      c. C-50, s. 5

sauvetage civil

Salvation Army Canadian War Services
    c. C-31, s. 16

Salvation Army Canadian War Services

sample
    sample of blood
      c. C-46, s. 254(1)

échantillon de sang

    sample of the breath
      c. C-46, s. 254(1)

échantillon d'haleine

    submit sample/to
      c. C-32, s. 25(b)(ii)

transmettre un échantillon

take a sample/to — prélever un échantillon
    c. C-32, s. 31(1)(b)
sanction — sanction
    c. A-2, s. 14(1)(b)
    (of a compromise) — homologation
    c. C-36, s. 20
    approval, sanction or — approbation, sanction ou
    confirmation (by shareholders) — confirmation
    c. C-19, s. 12(1)
sanction/to — sanctionner
    c. A-2, s. 14(1)(b)
sanctioned
    (by shareholders) — ratifié
    c. L-12, s. 35(3)(b)
Sanctuary
    bird Sanctuary — refuge d'oiseaux
    c. T-7, s. 23(e)
    game Sanctuary — refuge de gibier
    c. T-7, s. 23(e)
satisfaction — acquittement
    c. B-1, s. 179(13)
    (of a claim) — règlement
    c. B-1, s. 289(h)
    by way of satisfaction or — comme réparation ou
    compensation — dédommagement
    c. C-46, s. 725(1)
    entry of satisfaction on a — constat judiciaire d'acquittement de
    judgment — l'obligation
    c. F-11, s. 23(4)(d)
    establish to the satisfaction of — démontrer au tribunal
    the court/to
    c. C-38, s. 23(2)
    establish to the satisfaction of — prouver à la satisfaction du
    the magistrate/to — magistrat
    c. C-46, s. 112(12)
    memorandum of satisfaction — mémoire d'acquittement
    c. C-40, s. 95
    payment, satisfaction or — paiement, règlement ou transaction
    compromise (of claims)
    c. C-44, s. 217h)
    prove to the satisfaction/to (of a — convaincre un tribunal
    court)
    c. F-27, s. 34(1)
    to the satisfaction of (a Minister) — à la satisfaction de
    c. B-1, s. 114(8)(a)
    to the satisfaction of the court — à la satisfaction du tribunal
    c. C-46, s. 400(2)
satisfactory evidence — preuve établissant d'une manière
    satisfaisante
    c. B-1, s. 263(1)(a)
satisfied/to be — être convaincu
    c. C-8, s. 11(3)
    (judge) — être convaincu
    c. C-46, s. 777(2)
satisfy/to — convaincre
    c. N-1, s. 15(2)
    (a judgment) — exécuter (un jugement)
    c. B-1, s. 56(1)
    (its liabilities) — acquitter
    c. C-21, s. 4(5)(b)
    (the Minister) — convaincre
    c. C-20, s. 7(1)

if the court is satisfied
   c. C-44, s. 217
satisfay the judgment/to
   c. C-30, Schedule, part V,
     Article VIII
satisfy a claim/to
   c. C-44, s. 119(6)
satisfy a condition/to
   c. B-1, s. 133(1)
satisfy a judgment/to
   c. C-44, s. 226(2)(c)
settle an action or satisfy a
judgment/to
   c. C-44, s. 124(1)

saving
   saving all just exceptions

   c. S-26, s. 91(2)
savings bank
   c. B-3, s. 2
sawlog
   timber, mast, spar, shingle bolt,
   sawlog or lumber of any
   description
   c. C-46, s. 339(6)
scheduled
   commercial air service
   c. A-2, s. 21(7)
scheme
   conduct or manage any scheme,
   contrivance or operation/to
   c. C-46, s. 206(1)(d)
scholarship
   award a scholarship or
   fellowship/to
   c. A-13, s. 4(g)
scholarships
   establish scholarships and
   grants/to
   c. A-16, s. 8(e)
school corporation
   c. C-41, s. 11(1)(a)(iv)
Science Council of Canada
   c. A-1, Schedule I
   c. F-11, Schedule II
Science for Peace
   c. C-18, Schedule
scire facias
   (proceeding)
   c. C-40, s. 137
screening device
   approved screening device
   c. C-46, s. 254(1)
scrip certificate
   (share)
   c. B-1, s. 76(5)
   c. C-44, s. 49(5)(b)
scurrilous
   (matter)
   c. C-46, s. 168
sea
   territorial sea of Canada
   c. C-12, s. 3(a)

si le tribunal constate

éteindre les obligations du jugement

acquitter une créance

remplir une condition

satisfaire un jugement

transiger sur un procès ou exécuter
   un jugement

sous réserve de toute objection
   valable

caisse d'épargne

bois d'oeuvre, mâts, espars, bois à
   bardeaux et bois en grume

service aérien commercial à horaire

conduire ou administrer un plan, un
   arrangement ou une opération

attribuer une bourse d'études

offrir des bourses d'études et des
   subventions

administration scolaire

Conseil des sciences du Canada

Science for Peace

scire facias

appareil de détection approuvé

scrip

injurieux et grossier

mer territoriale du Canada

sea-mark
    to make fast a boat to a signal,   amarrer un bateau à un signal, une
    buoy or other sea-mark   bouée ou un autre amer
        c. C-46, s. 439(1)
seabed   fond de la mer
        c. C-53, s. 2(1)
seal
    certified under his hand and   authentifié, signé et revêtu de son
    official seal   cachet officiel
        c. S-26, s. 82(b)
    corporate seal   sceau de la société
        c. C-44, s. 23
    seal of office (of a minister)   sceau officiel
        c. L-12, s. 5(1)
    under his hand and seal   sous ses seing et sceau
        c. C-39, s. 70
    under the hand and seal (of   sous les seing et sceau (de qqn)
    someone)
        c. A-8, s. 15(1)
seal of office   sceau
        c. B-1, Schedule V
        c. C-9, s. 25(1)
        c. C-40, s. 6(4)(b)   sceau officiel
sealed/to be   porter le sceau
        c. P-2, s. 29
sealing
    (of ballot boxes)   scellage
        c. P-35, s. 36(3)(b)
search
    (of a person)   fouille
        c. N-1, s. 11
search/to   perquisitionner
        c. B-3, s. 10(2)
    (a person or a vehicle)   fouiller
        c. C-46, s. 101(1)
search for/to
    (a vessel)   rechercher
        c. C-9, s. 43(7)
    (firearm)   perquisitionner
        c. C-46, s. 103(2)
seasonal
    seasonal or temporary employee   employé saisonnier ou temporaire
        c. L-2, s. 190(f)
Seaway International Bridge   Corporation du Pont international
Corporation, Ltd.   de la voie maritime, Ltée.
        c. A-1, Schedule I
second
    be present as an aid, second,   assister en qualité d'aide, second,
    surgeon, umpire, backer or   médecin, arbitre, soutien ou
    reporter/to   reporter
        c. C-46, s. 83(1)(c)
second degree murder   meurtre au deuxième degré
        c. C-46, s. 231(7)
second preferred share   action privilégiée de deuxième rang
        c. B-1, Schedule I
second-hand
    dealer in second-hand goods   commerçant d'articles d'occasion
                            (fripiers et revendeurs)
        c. C-46, s. 339(2)
secrecy
    without secrecy or attempt at   ouvertement ou sans tentative de
    concealment   dissimulation
        c. C-46, s. 322(3)

secretary
   (of corporation)   secrétaire
      c. C-44, s. 126(1)(a)
secrete/to
   assign, remove, secrete or   céder, enlever, cacher ou aliéner
   dispose/to (property)
      c. B-3, s. 42(1)(g)
   secrete a wreck/to   cacher une épave
      c. C-46, s. 415(a)
   secrete records/to   cacher les registres
      c. C-8, s. 41(4)(b)
sect
   religious sect   secte religieuse
      c. C-8, s. 11(2)(b)(ii)
section   article
      c. A-1, s. 3
secure/to   grever d'une sûreté
      c. B-2, s. 23(c)
   (a loan)   garantir
      c. B-1, s. 174(2)(f)(i)
   (an obligation)   garantir
      c. C-21, s. 17(2)(c)
   (an obligation)   garantir l'exécution d'une obligation
      c. C-44, s. 39(12)
   secure on real property/to   gager sur un bien immeuble
      c. B-1, s. 2(1)
   secure or preserve an   recueillir ou conserver une preuve
   evidence/to
      c. C-46, s. 497(1)(f)(ii)
   secure payment/to   garantir le paiement
      c. C-44, s. 2(1)
   secure the attendance/to (of a garantir la comparution
   witness)
      c. C-46, s. 550(1)
   secure the due performance/to garantir la bonne exécution
   (of contracts)
      c. F-11, s. 41(1)(b)
secure containment or restraint placement ou internement
                     sécuritaires
      c. Y-1, s. 24(11)
secure custody   garde en milieu fermé
      c. Y-1, s. 24(1)
secured
   (a debt obligation)   garanti
      c. A-10, s. 18(b)
   note secured   effet de commerce garanti
      c. L-12, s. 61(1)(1)
   secured claim   réclamation garantie
      c. B-3, s. 2
   secured creditor   créancier titulaire d'une sûreté
      c. C-21, s. 31(2)
   secured creditor   créancier garanti
      c. C-44, s. 94
   secured or unsecured   avec ou sans sûreté
   (guarantee)
      c. C-21, s. 17(3)
   secured or unsecured guarantee garantie donnée avec ou sans sûreté
      c. C-44, s. 2(1)
   sully secured (by a mortgage) totalement garanti
      c. L-12, s. 61(1)(b)
securities   valeurs mobilières
      c. A-1, s. 18(d)(v)
      c. B-2, s. 18(c)   valeurs ou titres
      c. F-11, s. 2   valeur

government securities 　　c. C-41, s. 49(1)	titres de gouvernement
municipal securities 　　c. C-41, s. 49(1)	titres municipaux
school securities 　　c. C-41, s. 49(1)	titres d'administration scolaire
securities to bearer 　　c. C-40, s. 96(1)	valeurs payables au porteur
security	garantie
c. A-12, s. 25(1)	
c. F-11, s. 83(2)	
c. B-1, s. 75(2)	valeur mobilière
c. C-44, s. 2(1)	
c. A-7, s. 13(f)	sûreté
collateral security	sûreté
c. B-4, s. 176(3)	
collateral security	garantie subsidiaire
c. C-40, s. 93(2)	
continuing security	garantie continue
c. B-1, Schedule VI	
create a security interest/to (property)	grever d'une sûreté
c. C-44, s. 189(1)(d)	
debt security	titre non garanti
c. B-1, s. 193(1)	
deposit of security for costs	dépôt d'un cautionnement
c. S-26, s. 64	
give security/to	fournir une caution
c. C-44, s. 190(18)	
give security/to (by insurance)	couvrir
c. C-24, s. 52(4)	
pay or discharge a valuable security/to	payer ou rembourser des valeurs
c. C-46, s. 491.1(3)(b)(ii)	
perfect a security/to	valider des sûretés
c. C-46, s. 347(2)	
redeemable security	titre rachetable à échéance
c. L-12, s. 78(1)	
safety or security of Canada	sûreté ou sécurité du Canada
c. C-47, s. 6(3)	
security as collateral	sureté supplémentaire
c. L-12, s. 61(9)	
security certificate	certificat de valeur mobilière
c. B-1, s. 75(2)	
security clearance	habilitation de sécurité
c. C-23, s. 42(1)	
security clearance	habilitation sécuritaire
c. Y-1, s. 40(3)(j)	
security for costs	caution pour frais
c. C-44, s. 206(13)	
security interest	sûreté
c. A-10, s. 18(c)	
c. C-10, s. 27	
c. C-44, s. 2(1)	
valuable security	valeur
c. C-46, s. 363(a)	
value of valuable security	valeur d'un effet appréciable
c. C-46, s. 4(2)	
Security Intelligence Review Committee	comté de surveillance des activités de renseignement de sécurité
c. F-11, s. 13(2)	
security officer	agent de sécurité
c. A-2, s. 7(5)	

seditious
  seditious conspiracy   conspiration séditieuse
    c. C-46, s. 59(3)
  seditious word   parole séditieuse
    c. C-46, s. 59(1)
seduce/to
  seduce a person from his duties   détourner une personne de son
  and allegiance (to Her   devoir et de son allégeance
  Majesty)/to
    c. C-46, s. 53(a)
  seduce under promise of   séduire sous promesse de mariage
  marriage/to
    c. C-46, s. 157
seed cleaning mill   station de nettoiement des
                            semences
    c. C-24, Schedule
segregated
  segretated fund   fonds réservé
    c. C-20, s. 2(1)
seize/to   saisir
    c. A-11, s. 33(3)
  (an agricultural product)   saisir
    c. A-7, s. 18(1)
  confine, imprison or forcibly   séquestrer, emprisonner ou saisir
  seize another person/to   de force une autre personne
    c. C-46, s. 279(2)
seizure   saisie
    c. A-12, s. 25(2)
    c. C-44, s. 74
  (of an agricultural product)   saisie
    c. A-7, s. 18(2)(b)
  bailee of things under seizure   dépositaire de choses frappées de
                            saisie
    c. C-46, s. 324
  distress or seizure   saisie
    c. C-46, s. 271(1)(c)(i)
  lawfull distress or seizure   saisie légale
    c. C-46, s. 129(c)
  make a seizure/to   opérer une saisie
    c. A-12, s. 23(2)
  report the seizure/to   transmettre un procès-verbal de la
                           saisie
    c. A-11, s. 20(1)
  seizure and detention (of fuel)   saisie et rétention
    c. C-32, s. 27(1)
  seizure under legal process   saisie judiciaire
    c. C-27, Schedule, Article IV,
    2(g)
select territory   territoire choisi
    c. A-15, s. 2
self-balancing
  self-balancing financial   état financier autonome
  statement
    c. C-43, s. 12(4)
self-control
  power of self-control   pouvoir de se maîtriser
    c. C-46, s. 232(2)
self-defence
  self-defence against unprovoked   légitime défense contre une attaque
  assault   sous provocation
    c. C-46, s. 34(1)
self-employed   travailleur autonome
    c. C-8, s. 2(1)

self-sufficiency
    economic self-sufficiency   indépendance économique
        c. C-3, s. 15(7)(d)
self-sufficient
    be financially self-sufficient/to   être viable sur le plan financier
        c. C-9, s. 3(2)(a)
self-sustaining
    self-sustaining operations (of a   autofinancement de l'exploitation
    corporation)
        c. A-10, s. 5(2)(b)
sell/to
    sell a pool/to (betting)   vendre une mise collective
        c. C-46, s. 201(2)(a)
sell or deal with/to
    (shares or debt obligations)   vendre ou aliéner
        c. A-10, s. 6(1)(g)
selling
    selling agency   organisme de vente
        c. A-5, s. 7
    selling bank   banque vendeuse
        c. B-1, s. 273(4)
    selling group   syndicat de placement
        c. B-1, s. 190(1)
semi-annual   semestriel
        c. C-41, s. 60
semi-detached dwelling   maison jumelée
        c. N-11, s. 2
seminar   colloque
        c. J-1, s. 41(1)
Senate
    member of the Senate   sénateur
        c. C-10, s. 35(2)(b)
send/to
    (narcotic)   expédier
        c. N-1, s. 2
    send or convey/to   expédier
        c. A-7, s. 4
    send or deliver/to (securities)   envoyer ou remettre
        c. C-44, s. 2(1)
sending
    sending or conveying (of   transport
    agricultural products)
        c. A-7, s. 5(1)
senior
    senior associate chief justice,   juge en chef associé, juge en chef
    associate chief justice,   adjoint, juge surnuméraire, juge
    supernumery judge, chief judge,   principal et juge junior
    senior judge and junior judge
        c. J-1, s. 2
    senior executive officer   premier dirigeant
        c. C-43, s. 13(5)
    senior judge   juge principal
        c. J-1, s. 22(3)
    senior puisne judge   doyen des juges puînés
        c. S-26, s. 30(1)
    senior Divisional Head   chef divisionnaire principal
        c. P-5, s. 11
seniority   ancienneté
        c. L-2, s. 45(4)
sentence   sentence, peine ou condamnation
        c. C-46, s. 785(1)
    by sentence of law   par sentence de la loi
        c. C-46, s. 222(6)

intermittent sentence c. C-46, s. 735	peine discontinue
judgment, rule, order, decision, decree, decretal order, or sentence c. S-26, s. 2(1)	décision
sentence/to c. N-1, s. 25(2)	condamner
sentenced/to be c. C-46, s. 47(1)	être condamné
convicted and sentenced/to be c. C-34, s. 35(1)	être déclaré coupable et condamné

separable
  (rights)
  c. C-44, s. 29(2)
	pouvant être séparé

separate c. C-46, s. 611(2)	chef d'accusation séparé
separate employer c. F-11, s. 11(1)	employeur distinct
separate indictment c. C-46, s. 591(5)	acte d'accusation distinct
separate trial c. C-46, s. 591(4)(b)	procès séparé

separate and apart
  live separate and apart/to
  (spouses)
  c. C-3, s. 8(2)
	vivre séparément

Sergeant-at-Arms
  (House of Commons)
  c. P-1, s. 51(2)
	sergent d'armes

serial c. C-42, s. 24	feuilleton

series
  (of shares)
  c. B-1, s. 2(1)
	série

seriousness
  (of the offence)
  c. Y-1, s. 24(6)
	gravité

servant
  (of Her Majesty)
  c. B-1, s. 109(1)(a)(iii)
	employé

(of Her Majesty) c. C-7, s. 13(1)	préposé
clerk, servant or officer c. B-3, s. 10(3)	commis, préposé ou dirigeant
officer or servant of Her Majesty c. C-25, s. 30(1)	préposé de Sa Majesté

officer or servant of Her Majesty
 	
  c. C-46, s. 184(2)(d)
	fonctionnaire ou préposé de Sa
	  Majesté

servant of the Crown c. C-50, s. 17(2)(c)	préposé de l'État
servant of the Crown c. F-7, s. 38	préposé de la Couronne

serve/to
  (a term of office)
  c. C-22, s. 3(3)
	remplir un mandat

serve a notice/to (of the hearing) c. N-1, s. 17(3)	adresser notification
serve by personal service/to c. C-32, s. 28(2)	signifier à personne

serve concurrently or
consecutively a term of
imprisonment/to
  c. C-46, s. 149(1)
	purger concurremment ou
	  consécutivement une peine
	  d'emprisonnement

serve his disposition and sentence/to
   c. Y-1, s. 24(15)

purger son temps de garde et son temps de peine

serve personally on the person/to (subpoena)
   c. C-46, s. 701(2)

signifier personnellement à la personne

service
   c. A-12, s. 22(2)

signification

address for service
   c. C-44, s. 82(1)

adresse aux fins de signification

bank service corporation
   c. B-1, s. 35(2)(b)

société de service bancaire

contract of service or apprenticeship
   c. C-42, s. 13(3)

contrat de louage de service ou d'apprentissage

in service/to be (aircraft)
   c. C-46, s. 9

être en service

make service of a notice or process/to
   c. B-6, s. 10

signifier un avis ou un exploit

method of service
   c. C-46, s. 4(6)

mode de signification

non-profit public service
   c. B-1, s. 173(1)(l)(i)

service public non lucratif

telecommunication facility or service
   c. C-46, s. 327(1)

installations ou service en matière de télécommunication

Service Pension Board
   c. C-17, s. 49(1)

Conseil des pensions militaires

sessional

sessional allowance
   c. P-1, s. 55(1)

indemnité annuelle de session

set apart/to
(a judicial district)
   c. B-6, s. 2

délimiter

set aside/to
(a contract)
   c. F-11, s. 118(1)

annuler

(issue of licence)
   c. B-9, s. 14(1)

annuler

set fire/to
   c. C-46, s. 433(1)

mettre le feu

set off/to
(a debt)
   c. F-11, s. 9(3)(b)

compenser (une créance)

set out/to

set out or negative/to (exception)
   c. N-1, s. 7(1)

énoncer ou nier

set out particulars/to
   c. 4 (2nd Supp.), s. 9(d)

donner des précisions

set out the facts of the case/to
   c. C-46, s. 527(1)(d)

exposer les faits de l'espèce

set-off
   c. B-4, s. 2

défense de compensation

law of set-off
   c. B-3, s. 97(3)

règles de la compensation

to recover by deduction or set-off against garnishable moneys

recouvrer, par déduction ou compensation de sommes saisissables

   c. 4 (2nd Supp.), s. 59

set-out/to
clearly set-out/to (information)
   c. F-11, s. 123(3)

mettre en évidence

settle/to
  (a debt) — régler
    c. B-3, s. 30(1)(h)
  (an action) — transiger (sur un procès)
    c. B-1, s. 56(1)
  (particulars of amounts, times of payment) — arrêter
    c. B-3, s. 220(1)(b)(ii)
  settle an action or satisfy a judgment/to — transiger sur un procès ou exécuter un jugement
    c. C-44, s. 124(1)
  settle and dispose of/to (of an appeal, an objection, an application) — régler et disposer
    c. B-3, s. 41(4)
  settle and to determine/to (by a judge) — statuer
    c. B-1, s. 32(4)

settlement — disposition de biens en fiducie
    c. B-3, s. 177(a)
    c. C-21, s. 18(1)(e) — paiement
    c. C-46, s. 385(1) — contrat de constitution
  compromise, adjustment or settlement (of a charge or complaint) — compromis, transaction ou règlement
    c. F-11, s. 80(f)
  dispose by gift or settlement/to — aliéner par donation ou disposition en fiducie
    c. B-3, s. 158(g)
  settlement of disputes — règlement des différends
    c. C-6, s. 12(2)(b)
  settlement of industrial disputes — règlement de conflits industriels
    c. C-46, s. 422(2)(b)
  submit for final settlement/to (a difference) — soumettre pour règlement définitif
    c. L-2, s. 57(2)

settlor — disposant
    c. B-3, s. 91(3)(c)

sever/to
  sever from the freehold any fixture fixed therein or thereto/to — séparer de la propriété foncière toute chose qui y est fixée à demeure ou incorporée
    c. C-46, s. 441

severally
  jointly and severally (liability) — solidairement
    c. C-44, s. 118(1)
  lay severally/to (estimates) — déposer séparément
    c. P-1, s. 52

severance
  joinder or severance of counts — réunion ou séparation de chefs
    c. C-46, s. 588
  severance pay — indemnité de départ
    c. L-2, s. 213(2)

severe
  (disability) — grave
    c. C-8, s. 42(2)(a)
  severe psychological damage — dommages psychologiques graves
    c. C-46, s. 752

sexual intercourse — rapports sexuels
    c. C-46, s. 4(5)
  have sexual intercourse/to — avoir des rapports sexuels
    c. C-46, s. 153(1)

sexual services
obtain sexual services/to
    c. C-46, s. 213(1)   retenir les services sexuels
shackle
boomchain, chain, line and   chaîne d'estacade, chaîne, ligne et
shackle   lien
    c. C-46, s. 339(6)
share   part
    c. B-1, s. 2(1)
constrained share   action faisant l'objet de restrictions
    c. C-44, s. 46(2)
convertible share   action convertible
    c. C-44, s. 26(5)
equity share   action assortie du droit de vote
    c. L-12, s. 64(4)
fractional share   fraction d'action
    c. C-44, s. 49(5)(a)(ii)
full share   action entière
    c. C-44, s. 49(15)
fully paid share   action entièrement libérée
    c. B-1, s. 130(2)
preferred share   action privilégiée
    c. B-1, s. 124(4)
preferred share or common   action privilégiée ou action
share   ordinaire
    c. C-41, s. 11(1)(e)(i)
share of stock   action
    c. L-12, s. 44(1)c)
unissued share   action non émise
    c. C-44, s. 39(10)
share capital   capital social
    c. C-40, s. 2(b)
share of the capital stock of a   action de compagnie
company
    c. A-16, s. 11(1)
share, debenture or other   action, obligation ou autre valeur
securities
    c. A-14, s. 4(1)(a)
shareholder   actionnaire
    c. B-1, s. 109(4)
    c. C-44, s. 2(1)
(of an association)   détenteur de parts
    c. C-40, s. 3(1)
subordinated shareholder loan prêt de dernier rang
    c. L-12, s. 2
sharing
deferred profit sharing plan   régime de participation différée aux
                          bénéfices
    c. L-12, s. 114(1)
sheep
horses, cattle, sheep, swine   chevaux, bovins, ovins, porcins
    c. L-9, s. 10
sheriff   shérif
    c. B-3, s. 2
mayor, warden, reeve, sheriff, maire, président de conseil de
deputy sheriff, sheriff's officer comté, préfet, shérif, shérif adjoint,
and justice of the peace   officier de shérif et juge de paix
    c. C-46, s. 2
shingle bolt
timber, mast, spar, shingle bolt, bois d'oeuvre, mâts, espars, bois à
sawlog or lumber of any   bardeaux et bois en grume
    c. C-46, s. 339(6)

ship stores	provisions de bord
c. C-53, s. 5(2)(b)	
shipper	expéditeur
c. B-5, s. 3(c)	
c. C-27, Schedule, Article IV, 3	chargeur
shipping	
bill of lading, cargo manifest, shipping order, way-bill and switching order	connaissement, manifeste, ordre d'expédition, feuille de route et bulletin de manoeuvre
c. T-19, s. 2	
shipping bill	bordereau d'expédition
c. A-7, s. 16(1)(c)	
shipping document	document d'expédition
c. C-51, s. 48(1)	
c. T-19, s. 2	
short	
day, call and short (loan)	au jour le jour, à vue ou à court terme
c. B-1, Schedule X, Section 12(a)	
shortage	
overage and shortage	excédant et manquant
c. C-24, s. 37(1)(b)	
shot, bullet or other missile (firearm)	plomb, balle ou autre projectile
c. C-46, s. 84(1)	
show/to	démontrer
c. B-3, s. 46(1)	
show cause	
summons to vacate or show cause	sommation de déguerpir ou d'exposer ses raisons
c. T-7, s. 20(1)	
show cause/to	faire valoir les motifs
c. B-6, s. 6(2)(a)	
c. C-46, s. 517(1)	faire valoir des motifs justificatifs
c. C-46, s. 522(2)	démontrer
show of hands	
by show of hands (vote)	à main levée
c. C-44, s. 141(1)	
sight	
bill payable after sight	lettre payable à un certain délai de vue
c. B-4, s. 149	
payable at sight/to be	être payable à vue
c. B-4, s. 23(a)	
sign/to	
sign judgment for costs/to	demander la taxation
c. S-26, s. 69(2)	
sign, certify, attest or execute/to	signer, certifier, attester ou établir
c. A-2, s. 27(1)(c)	
signal	
make fast a boat to a signal, buoy or other sea-mark/to	amarrer un bateau à un signal, une bouée ou un autre amer
c. C-46, s. 439(1)	
signatory	
signatory government	gouvernement signataire
c. B-7, Schedule I, Article XXXI, Section 2(h)	
signatory States	États signataires
c. C-26, Schedule III	
signature	
manual signature	signature manuscrite
c. C-44, s. 49(1)	

significant
  (danger)

    c. C-32, s. 23(4)(b) — appréciable

  (risk)

    c. C-32, s. 21(1) — appréciable

  significant demand

    c. 31 (4th Supp.), s. 22(b) — demande importante

  significant interest

    c. B-1, s. 174(2)(g) — participation importante

signify one's approval/to
  (the Minister)

    c. B-1, s. 287(5) — notifier son approbation

signing authority

  c. B-1, s. 157(1) — procuration de signature

  c. B-1, s. 211(1)(a) — délégation de signature

similar
  similar offence

    c. A-2, s. 8(6) — infraction semblable

sine die
  adjournment sine die

    c. F-11, s. 30(5) — ajournement sine die

single
  single judge

    c. C-39, s. 62 — juge seul

sinking fund

  c. C-44, s. 176(1)(c)(iv) — fonds d'amortissement

  purchase fund or sinking fund

    c. B-1, s. 124(4) — fonds d'amortissement

sit/to

  c. A-7, s. 7(7) — siéger

site
  relevant site

    c. C-20, s. 15(3) — lieu approprié

sitting

  c. C-8, s. 83(4) — séance

  sitting day (of Parliament)

    c. C-13, s. 26(3) — jour de séance

  subsequent sitting (of a court)

    c. C-34, s. 67(1) — session postérieure

sittings
  opening of the term or sittings (of a court)

    c. C-46, s. 474 — ouverture de la session

skill
  care, diligence and skill

    c. B-1, s. 54(1)(b) — soin, diligence et compétence

  care, diligence and skill of a reasonably prudent trustee

    c. C-44, s. 91(b) — soin, diligence et compétence d'un bon fiduciaire

  game of chance or skill

    c. C-34, s. 59(1) — jeu de hasard ou d'adresse

  game of mixed chance and skill

    c. C-46, s. 197(1) — jeu où se mêlent le hasard et l'adresse

  reasonable care and skill

    c. C-46, s. 45(a) — soins et habileté raisonnable

  to be under a legal duty to have and to use reasonable knowledge, skill and care

    c. C-46, s. 216 — être légalement tenu d'apporter une connaissance, une habilité et des soins raisonnables

slander

  c. A-1, s. 66(2) — diffamation verbale

libel or slander
    c. 31 (4th Supp.), s. 75(2)

slaughter
  (livestock)
    c. L-9, s. 10

slide
  lumber, timber, log, float, boom,
  dam or slide

    c. C-46, s. 433(1)(i)
  slide, dam, pier or boom

    c. T-7, s. 2 19(a)

slip
  (for boats)
    c. C-19, s. 29
  deposit slip
    c. B-3, s. 6(2)

slot machine
    c. C-46, s. 198(3)

slow-down
  slow-down of work
    c. P-35, s. 2

slug
  slug or token (slot machine)
    c. C-46, s. 198(3)(iii)

smoke screen
  apparatus making a smoke
  screen
    c. C-46, s. 257

So help me God
    c. S-26, s. 10

Social Insurance Number
    c. C-24, s. 67(1)

Social Insurance Number Card
    c. C-8, s. 98(4)

**Social Sciences and Humanities
Research Council**
    c. A-1, Schedule I
    c. F-11, Schedule II

Société Générale (Canada)
    c. B-1, Schedule II

society
  building society
    c. B-3, s. 2
  building society
    c. N-11, s. 2
  company, body corporate,
  unincorporated body or society

    c. C-46, s. 328(e)
  cooperative credit society
    c. C-34, s. 50(3)
  entry or record of an
  incorporated society

    c. Y-1, s. 57(2)(b)
  incorporated society

    c. C-46, s. 658
  society or company
    c. B-6, s. 45(a)

diffamation verbale ou écrite

abattage

bois de construction, de service ou
en grume, radeau, barrage
flottant, digue ou glissoir

glissoir, digue, jetée ou barrage
flottant

cale

bordereau de dépôt

appareil à sous

ralentissement du travail

piécette ou jeton

appareil produisant un écran de
fumée

Ainsi Dieu me soit en aide

numéro d'assurance sociale

carte matricule d'assurance sociale

Conseil de recherches en sciences
humaines

Société Générale (Canada)

société de construction

société de prêt à la construction

compagnie, personne morale,
organisme non constitué en
personne morale ou société

société coopérative de crédit

inscription ou mention consignée
par un organisme doté de la
personnalité morale

société constituée en personne
morale

société ou compagnie

sole
    sole and exclusive jurisdiction   compétence exclusive
      c. A-7, s. 12
    sole and exclusive privilege   privilège exclusif
      c. C-10, s. 14(1)
    sole arbitrator   arbitre unique
      c. L-2, s. 3(1)
    sole proprietorship   entreprise unipersonnelle
      c. C-34, s. 39(4)(c)
    sole right   droit exclusif
      c. C-42, s. 3(1)

solemn
    administer a solemn   recevoir une affirmation solennelle
    affirmation/to
      c. L-2, s. 16(6)

solemnize/to
    (a marriage)   célébrer
      c. C-8, s. 55(2)

solicit/to
    (proxies)   briguer
      c. B-3, s. 202(1)(g)

solicitation
    (of request for proxy)   sollicitation
      c. C-44, s. 147

solicitor   solicitor
    c. C-46, s. 183
    c. C-46, s. 183   avocat
    attorney or solicitor   procureurs
      c. S-26, s. 23
    attorney or solicitor   avocat
      c. S-26, s. 69(1)
    attorney-at-law or solicitor   avocat ou procureur
      c. C-39, s. 88
    counsel, barrister or solicitor   avocat ou procureur
      c. C-46, s. 2
    solicitor or agent   procureur ou agent
      c. C-46, s. 385(1)
    solicitor or counsel   conseil
      c. C-50, s. 29(1)

solution
    gold in dust, solution or   or en poudre, en solution ou sous
    otherwise   d'autres formes
      c. C-46, s. 451

soon
    as soon as possible   dans les meilleurs délais
      c. Y-1, s. 9(2)

sorcery
    witchcraft, sorcery,   magie, sorcellerie, enchantement ou
    enchantment or conjuration   conjuration
      c. C-46, s. 365(a)

sovereign
    sovereign power   pouvoir souverain
      c. C-46, s. 15
    sovereign power   État souverain
      c. A-12, s. 12(2)

sovereignty
    sovereignty, suzerainty,   souveraineté, suzeraineté, mandat
    mandate or authority   ou autorité
      c. C-26, s. 2(4)

spar
    timber, mast, spar, shingle bolt,   bois d'oeuvre, mâts, espars, bois à
    sawlog or lumber of any   bardeaux et bois en grume
    description
      c. C-46, s. 339(6)

speak/to
    speak to sentence/to   prendre la parole avant la sentence
        c. C-46, s. 668
speaker
    (of the Senate or House of   président
    Common)
        c. C-46, s. 316(3)
special
    general or special Act   loi générale ou spéciale
        c. A-2, s. 19
    special business   question spéciale
        c. B-1, s. 63(5)
    special examiner   commissaire-enquêteur spécial
        c. C-39, s. 22(1)
    special meeting (shareholders)   assemblée extraordinaire
        c. B-1, s. 63(5)
Special Drawing Rights   Département des droits de tirage
Department   spéciaux
        c. B-7, Schedule I,
          introductory article (ii)
special examination   examen spécial
        c. F-11, s. 120
species
    class or species (of business)   catégorie ou espèce
        c. C-34, s. 2
specific
    specific case or particular   cas bien précis, ou spécifiques
    matter
        c. A-4, s. 4(2)
specific performance   exécution intégrale
        c. F-7, s. 44
specification   devis descriptif
        c. B-8, s. 10
specify/to
    (in an agreement)   viser
        c. A-3, s. 3(b)
    (in an agreement)   indiquer
        c. A-3, s. 5
    (terms and conditions)   spécifier
        c. A-2, s. 6
    (territorial jurisdiction)   spécifier
        c. B-3, s. 184(d)
    specify in the regulation/to   déterminer par règlement
        c. A-1, s. 16(1)(a)
    specify in the regulation/to   préciser dans le règlement
        c. A-1, s. 16(4)(c)
speculation
    rash and hazardous speculation   spéculation téméraire et
           hasardeuse
        c. B-3, s. 173(1)(e)
speech
    open and considered speech   propos publics et réfléchis
        c. C-46, s. 48(2)
spirit
    according to its true spirit,   selon son esprit, son sens et son
    intent and meaning (of   objet
    enactment)
        c. I-23, s. 10
    spirit and intent of this Act   esprit de la présente loi et intention
           du législateur
        c. 31 (4th Supp.), s. 58(1)(c)
split
    split or consolidation (of shares)   fonctionnement ou regroupement
        c. B-1, s. 123(6)

spokesman	représentant
c. C-8, s. 11(3)(b)	
sponsor	commanditaire
c. B-9, s. 19(2)	
sponsor/to	financer
c. C-32, s. 4(3)	
sponsor or support/to (conferences)	appuyer ou prendre en charge
c. A-13, s. 4(c)	
spot exchange transaction	transaction de change au comptant
c. B-7, Schedule I-C, 5	
St.Lawrence Seaway Authority	Administration de la voie maritime du Saint-Laurent
c. A-1, Schedule I	
St-John Ambulance Brigade of Canada	Brigade ambulancière Saint-Jean du Canada
c. C-31, s. 48	
staff	personnel
c. A-7, s. 7(5)	
c. A-4, s. 3(7)	effectifs
stage	
at any stage (of the hearing)	à tout stade
c. B-9, s. 10(5)	
at any stage (of the proceedings)	à tout stade
c. P-1, s. 8(1)	
at any stage of preliminary inquiry	à tout stade d'une enquête préliminaire
c. C-46, s. 549(1)	
at any stage of the proceedings	à toute étape des procédures
c. C-46, s. 359(1)	
stage of proceedings	phase de l'instance
c. Y-1, s. 10(1)	
stake	enjeu
c. C-46, s. 197(4)(b)	
stamp	
impressed or adhesive stamp	timbre imprimé ou gommé
c. C-46, s. 376(c)	
trading stamp	bon-prime
c. C-46, s. 427(1)	
stamp/to	
stamp and mark/to (with an official mark)	timbrer et marquer
c. C-42, s. 26(3)	
stamped signature	
written or stamped signature of an official to the endorsement of the duplicate summary	signature manuscrite ou griffe d'un fonctionnaire, apposée sous la mention faite sur ce double
c. C-40, s. 118(4)	
stand/to	
stand permanently referred to/to (a committee)	saisir d'office
c. S-22, s. 19	
stand trial/to	
committed to stand trial (an accused)	renvoyé pour subir son procès
c. C-46, s. 478(4)	
to be ordered to stand trial/to	être astreint à passer en jugement
c. C-46, s. 536(4)	
standard	
standard weight (of coins)	poids légal
c. C-52, s. 6(3)	
standardization	
voluntary standardization	normalisation volontaire
c. F-11, s. 89(7)(a)	

standards
    reasonable commercial
    standards   normes commerciales raisonnables
        c. B-1, s. 102
        c. C-44, s. 75
Standards Council of Canada   Conseil canadien des normes
        c. A-1, Schedule I
standing
    by standing or other order (of   par règlement ou ordre
    the Senate or House)
        c. P-1, s. 13(1)(c)
standing committee   comité permanent
        c. B-9, s. 35(1)(b)
state   État
        c. A-1, s. 3
    foreign state   État étranger
        c. A-1, s. 3
    state of an account   situation de compte
        c. C-17, s. 56
stated
    pay by stated instalments/to   faire un paiement par versements
                                  spécifiés
        c. B-4, s. 27(1)(b)
    stated capital account   compte capital déclaré
        c. C-44, s. 26(1)
    stated term   mandat pour une durée déterminée
        c. C-44, s. 106(5)
stated case
    appeal on a stated case   appel sur le dossier
        c. S-26, s. 62(1)
statement   déclaration
        c. A-12, s. 17
    (in a waybill)   énonciation
        c. C-26, Schedule I, Article
        11(2)
    (in the House)   déclaration
        c. P-1, s. 70(3)
    (of a transaction)   relevé
        c. B-4, s. 16(3)(b)
    (of the evidence)   exposé
        c. C-34, s. 20(1)(b)
    acknowledge a statement of   approuver un relevé de compte
    account/to
        c. B-1, s. 209(1)(a)
    annual statement   rapport annuel
        c. B-1, s. 215(2)(a)
    false or deceptive statement   déclaration fausse ou trompeuse
        c. A-8, s. 16(1)(b)
    false or deceptive statement   déclaration inexacte ou trompeuse
        c. C-47, s. 7(b)(ii)
    false statement   déclaration fausse
        c. A-12, s. 17
    false statement   fausse assertion
        c. C-46, s. 585(b)
    false statement   fausse déclaration
        c. A-2, s. 18(1)(o)(ii)
    financial statement   état financier
        c. A-13, s. 36
    profit and loss statement   compte profits et pertes
        c. B-7, Schedule II, Article V,
        Section 13(a)
    proposal or statement   proposition ou exposé
        c. B-1, s. 65(6)

registration statement (securities) c. C-44, s. 2(7)a)	déclaration d'enregistrement
statement by affidavit c. C-46, s. 133	énonciation par affidavit
statement of account c. B-3, s. 124(4)	état de compte
statement of adjudication c. C-46, s. 778(a)	énonciation de la décision
statement of affairs c. B-3, s. 19(3)	bilan
statement of claim (in the Federal Court) c. C-50, s. 24(b)	demande introductive
statement of income c. L-12, s. 53(2)	état des résultats
statement of intention c. C-46, s. 610	énoncé d'intention
statement of material facts c. C-44, s. 193	déclaration de faits importants
sworn statement c. B-1, s. 30(2)	relevé sous serment
sworn statement c. B-1, s. 31(1)	déclaration sous serment
wilfully false statement c. B-3, s. 125	déclaration délibérément fausse
statements	
accounts of receipts and disbursements and final statements c. B-3, s. 5(3)(g)	comptes de recettes et de débours et les états définitifs
stationary source (of contaminant) c. C-32, s. 2	source fixe
Statistics Canada c. A-1, Schedule I	Statistique Canada
status c. B-1, s. 35(1)(d)	statut
(as a claimant) c. C-44, s. 190(25)(b)	qualité
control status c. C-20, s. 2(1)	état de contrôle
equality of status (of official languages) c. 31 (4th Supp.), s. 38(1)(e)	égalité de statut
have equality of status/to c. C-31, s. 5	avoir un statut égal
legal status c. B-3, s. 2	situation juridique
to have equality of status and equal rights and privileges (of official languages) c. 31 (4th Supp.), s. preamble	avoir un statut et des droits et privilèges égaux
statute	
statute or law c. N-11, s. 24(1)	loi ou autre règle de droit
Statute Revision Commission c. A-1, Schedule I	Commission de révision des lois
statutory	
statutory and earned remission c. P-2, s. 25(2)	réduction de peine légale ou méritée
statutory charge c. L-12, s. 61(1)(e)	sûreté prévue par des textes législatifs

statutory declaration   déclaration solennelle
    c. B-3, s. 2
    c. C-12, s. 19(e)
statutory instrument   texte réglementaire
    c. S-22, s. 2(1)
statutory law   loi
    c. B-1, s. 173(1)(d)
statutory preference   privilège prévu par une loi
    c. B-3, s. 136(1)(j)
statutory right in rem   droit réel créé par une loi
    c. T-19, s. 16(4)(b)

stay
    stay of execution   sursis d'exécution
       c. C-30, Schedule, Article I
    stay of proceedings   arrêt des procédures
       c. C-46, s. 579(2)

stay/to
    (a liquidation)   surseoir à
       c. C-44, s. 217(n)(i)
    (proceedings)   surseoir à
       c. B-3, s. 43(10)
    stay an action/to   suspendre une action
       c. C-44, s. 242(1)
    stay proceedings/to   suspendre une procédure
       c. C-44, s. 208(2)
    stay the filing/to   empêcher le dépôt
       c. A-7, s. 13(h)

steal/to   voler
    c. C-46, s. 2

stench
    stink or stench bomb   bombe ou dispositif fétide ou
                  méphitique
    c. C-46, s. 178(b)

stenographer
    Court stenographer   sténographe judiciaire
    c. C-46, s. 540(4)

step-child   beau-fils ou belle-fille par
                  remariage
    c. C-17, s. 2(2)

stink
    stink or stench bomb   bombe ou dispositif fétide ou
                  méphitique
    c. C-46, s. 178(b)

stipendiary
    magistrate, police magistrate,   magistrat, magistrat de police,
    stipendiary magistrate, district   magistrat stipendiaire, magistrat
    magistrate, provincial   de district, magistrat provincial,
    magistrate, judge of the sessions   juge des sessions de la paix,
    of the peace, recorder   recorder
    c. C-46, s. 2

stipendiary magistrate   magistrat stipendiaire
    c. A-7, s. 23

stipulate/to
    stipulate terms/to   stipuler des modalités
    c. C-44, s. 197(b)

stipulation
    express stipulation (on a bill)   clause expresse
    c. B-4, s. 33

stock   capital-actions
    c. B-2, s. 35(1)(e)
    (of coal)   stock
       c. C-25, s. 12 (1)

debenture stock c. C-36, s. 2 c. C-46, s. 206(8)(c)	stock-obligation
debenture stock c. L-12, s. 44(1)(j)	débentures-actions
preference stock c. L-12, s. 35(1)	action privilégiée
share of stock c. L-12, s. 44(1)(c)	action
share or interest in a public stock or fund c. C-46, s. 2	action ou intérêt dans un stock ou fonds public
stock book c. L-12, s. 11(1)	registre des actions
stock exchange c. B-1, s. 98(3)	bourse de valeurs mobilières
c. B-1, s. 35(1)(i) c. C-44, s. 134(4)(b)	bourse bourse de valeurs
stock exchange, curb market or other market c. C-46, s. 382	bourse de valeurs, curb market ou autre bourse
stock-in-trade c. C-40, s. 27(j)	fonds de commerce
stocks public market price of stocks c. C-46, s. 380(2)	cote publique des stocks
stockyard c. L-9, s. 10	parc à bestiaux
stoppage right of stoppage c. B-5, s. 3(a)	droit d'arrêt
stoppage of work c. C-46, s. 422(2)(b)	cessation de travail
storage data processing, storage or retrieval of data c. C-46, s. 342.1(2)	traitement des données, mémorisation, recouvrement ou relevé des données
handling, secure storage and display (of firearms) c. C-46, s. 116(b)	manipulation, entreposage et mise en montre
stores cargo, stores and tackle of a vessel wrecked, stranded or in distress c. C-46, s. 2	cargaison, approvisionnement, agrès et apparaux d'un navire naufragé, échoué ou en détresse
dealer in marine stores or in old metals c. C-46, s. 421(2)	commerçant de gréements de marine ou marchand de vieux métaux
defective stores c. C-46, s. 418(1)	approvisionnements défectueux
military stores c. C-46, s. 420(1)	approvisionnements militaires
ship stores c. C-53, s. 5(2)(b)	provisions de bord
stranded cargo, stores and tackle of a vessel wrecked, stranded or in distress c. C-46, s. 2	cargaison, approvisionnement, agrès et apparaux d'un navire naufragé, échoué ou en détresse
strangle/to choke, suffocate or strangle another person/to c. C-46, s. 246(a)	étouffer, suffoquer ou étrangler une autre personne

street
    street, road or highway   rue, chemin ou grande route
        c. C-46, s. 249(1)(a)
strike/to
    (a coin)   frapper
        c. C-52, s. 4(3)
stringent
    render more stringent/to   renforcer
    (provisions of an Act)
        c. P-1, s. 59
structure
    building or structure   bâtiment ou construction
        c. C-46, s. 2
stupefying
    stupefying or overpowering   stupéfiant ou soporifique
    thing
        c. C-46, s. 230(b)
sub-lease   sous-location
        c. C-41, s. 11(1)(i)
subdivision
    (of lands)   lotissement
        c. N-14, s. 7(1)(y)
    (of shares)   fractionnement
        c. B-1, s. 45(1)(a)
    political subdivision (of a foreign   subdivision politique
    country)
        c. B-1, s. 2(1)
subject
    subject to appeal or review/to be   être susceptible d'appel ou faire
                                   l'objet d'une révision
        c. P-2, s. 28
subject/to
    (an individual to a penalty or   exposer
    proceedings)
        c. C-34, s. 22(2)
subject to
    property subject to a security   biens grevés de toute sûreté
    interest
        c. C-44, s. 86(1)(b)
    subject to and in accordance   en conformité avec
    with (terms and conditions)
        c. A-2, s. 6
    subject to the regulations   sous réserve des règlements
        c. A-1, s. 12(1)
subject-matter
    subject-matter of the charge   actes à l'origine de l'accusation
        c. C-46, s. 271(2)
subjects
    claim between subjects   action relevant du droit privé
        c. C-9, s. 59(1)
submission
    submission on a point of law   représentation sur un point de droit
        c. C-46, s. 166(1)(b)(iii)
submit/to
    (a report)   présenter
        c. A-3, s. 11
    (a sample)   soumettre
        c. C-11, s. 21(c)(ii)
    (an annual report to the   remettre
    Minister)
        c. A-8, s. 19
    (information)   communiquer
        c. C-32, s. 25(b)(iii)

(report)
c. A-5, s. 7

soumettre

submit for the approval/to (a plan)
c. C-25, s. 17(1)

soumettre pour approbation

subordinated
subordinated note
c. L-12, s. 2

effet de second rang

subordinated shareholder loan
c. L-12, s. 2

prêt de dernier rang

subpoena
(witness)
c. Y-1, s. 54(2)

assignation

issue a subpoena/to
c. C-46, s. 698(1)

lancer une assignation

subpoena ad testificandum or duces tecum
c. C-39, s. 25

bref d'assignation à témoigner ou à produire des pièces

writ of subpoena or process
c. C-45, s. 17

bref de subpoena ou sommation

subrogated/to be
(the payer)
c. B-4, s. 154

être subrogé

subscriber
(of securities)
c. F-11, s. 56(1)

souscripteur

subscriber to or holder of (stock)
c. L-12, s. 2

souscripteur ou détenteur

subsection
c. A-1, s. 4(2)

paragraphe

subsequent
for a subsequent offence
c. N-1, s. 3(2)(a)

en cas de récidive

for each subsequent offence
c. C-46, s. 202(2)(c)

pour chaque récidive

subsequent offence
c. C-42, s. 42(1)

récidive

subsidiary
(corporation)
c. C-44, s. 2(2)(a)

filiale

foreign bank subsidiary
c. B-1, s. 2(1)

filiale d'une banque étrangère

subsidiary body corporate

c. C-44, s. 30(1)(b)

filiale dotée de la personnalité morale

subsidiary coin
c. C-52, s. 2

pièce de monnaie divisionnaire

wholly-owned subsidiary
c. F-11, s. 83(1)(b)

filiale à cent pour cent

wholly-owned subsidiary of a holding body corporate
c. C-44, s. 163(4)

filiale appartenant en propriété exclusive à la société mère

subsidiary coin
c. C-52, s. 2

pièce de monnaie divisionnaire

subsidy
c. C-41, s. 11(1)(c)

subvention

subsidy, subvention and other financial assistance
c. C-25, s. 12(1)(a)

aide financière, sous forme notamment de subvention

subsisting
valid and subsisting certificate
c. A-2, s. 21(8)

certificat valide

valid and subsisting licence
    c. A-2, s. 22

permis valide

subsoil
    subsoil of submarine areas
        c. C-53, s. 2(1)

sous-sol des zones sous-marines

substance
    (of the complaint)
        c. A-1, s. 32

objet

    bodily substance
        c. C-46, s. 258(1)(e)

substance corporelle

    irregularity or defect in the
    substance or form (of a warrant)
        c. C-46, s. 546(a)

irrégularité ou défaut dans la
    substance ou la forme

    substance of the offence
        c. C-46, s. 501(1)(b)

l'essentiel de l'infraction

    substance, meaning or purport
    (of private communication)
        c. C-46, s. 191(2)(c)

substance, sens ou objet

substantial
    (summary)
        c. C-12, s. 37(a)

résumé appréciable

    in substantial compliance

d'une façon qui respecte les
    conditions essentielles

        c. C-20, s. 10(4)
    substantial connection (with
    Canada)

liens manifestes (avec le Canada)

        c. C-29, s. 8(b)
    substantial degree of
    indifference (by offender)

indifférence marquée

        c. C-46, s. 753(a)(ii)
    substantial part (of a work)

partie importante

        c. C-42, s. 3(1)
    substantial shareholder
        c. L-12, s. 64(1)(a)(ii)

actionnaire important

substantially
    all or substantially all (property)
        c. C-44, s. 224(1)(a)

totalité ou quasi-totalité

    control substantially or
    completely/to (business)
        c. C-34, s. 2

contrôler pour une grande part ou
    complètement

    most substantially connected/to
    be (in a province)
        c. C-3, s. 6(1)

avoir ses principales attaches

    sell or otherwise dispose of all or
    substantially all of the assets/to

vendre ou d'une façon générale,
    céder la totalité ou la quasi-
    totalité des actifs

        c. F-11, s. 90(2)
    substantially the same
        c. C-46, s. 382(b)

sensiblement le même

    substantially the same
    (proposal)
        c. C-44, s. 137(6)

à peu près identique

    to be substantially successful on
    the merits of the defence
        c. F-11, s. 119(2)(a)

obtenir gain de cause sur la plupart
    des moyens au fond

    wholly or substantially

entièrement ou dans une large
    mesure

        c. C-8, s. 42(1)(c)
substantiate/to
    (a proof of claim)
        c. B-3, s. 124(4)

établir le bien-fondé

substantive
    determine a substantive right/to
        c. S-26, s. 2(1)

statuer au fond sur un droit

material substantive change c. C-44, s. 261(3)(d)	modification de fond important
substantive provision c. B-3, s. 72(1)	droit substantif
substantive provisions c. F-7, s. 36	dispositions de fond
substitute	
temporary substitute (of a board) c. A-8, s. 3(5)	remplaçant
temporary substitute member (of the Board) c. P-2, s. 4(1)	suppléant
substituted	
substituted right c. C-42, s. 60(1)	droit substitué
substituted trustee c. B-3, s. 36(1)	syndic substitué
substitution	
(of a tariff) c. A-2, s. 18(1)(m)(ii)	substitution
subvention	
subsidy, subvention and other financial assistance c. C-25, s. 12(1)(a)	aide financière, sous forme notamment de subvention
subversive	
subversive or hostile activities c. A-1, s. 15(2)	activités hostiles ou subversives
subvert/to	
(the administration of justice) c. C-3, s. 11(4)	déjouer
succeed/to	
(to the rights and duties of a person) c. B-4, s. 154	succéder
successful/to be	
(in an action) c. B-1, s. 56(3)(a)	obtenir gain de cause
succession	
estate, legacy, succession or inheritance duties or taxes c. C-17, s. 50(o)	droits ou impôts sur les successions, legs ou héritages
successor	remplaçant
c. B-1, s. 133(1)	
c. B-6, s. 8(2)	successeur
successor in ownership c. L-9, s. 16(2)	successeur en propriété
successor in title to goods c. C-53, s. 6(4)	successeur aux biens
successors	
successors and assigns c. C-30, Schedule Article I(e)	héritiers et ayants cause
sue/to	intenter une action
c. B-4, s. 73(a)	
(a party) c. B-4, s. 67(3)	poursuivre
capacity to sue and be sued in its own name c. C-49, s. 5(c)(d)	capacité d'ester en justice
sue a claim/to c. A-12, s. 6(4)	porter en justice une réclamation
sue for a debt/to c. B-1, s. 51(2)(a)	intenter une action en recouvrement de créance

suffer/to
    (damages)   subir
      c. C-42, s. 35(1)
suffering
    suffering of anything to be done   tolérance de tout acte à accomplir
      c. A-2, s. 8(1)(j)
sufficient
    (notice)   adéquat
      c. Y-1, s. 9(5)
suffocate/to
    choke, suffocate or strangle   étouffer, suffoquer ou étrangler une
    another person/to   autre personne
      c. C-46, s. 246(a)
suffrage
    right of suffrage   droit de suffrage
      c. C-46, s. 748(2)
suggested retail price   prix de détail proposé
      c. C-34, s. 61(3)
suggestion
    suggestion of the death   déclaration de décès
      c. S-26, s. 72
suit
    action, suit or other proceeding   action en recouvrement
    for the recovery
      c. C-9, s. 46(2)
    bring or take an action, suit or   ester en justice
    other legal proceedings/to
      c. A-16, s. 3(2)
    original parties to the suit   parties à l'origine du procès
      c. S-26, s. 77
suited to
    key suited to a lock   clef correspondant à un cadenas
      c. C-46, s. 356(1)(a)(iii)
summarily
    convict summarily/to   déclarer coupable par procédure
                        sommaire
      c. C-46, s. 10(1)
summary
    in a summary manner   en procédure sommaire
      c. 31 (4th Supp.), s. 80
    make an application in a   présenter une demande par voie
    summary manner by petition or   sommaire sous forme de requête
    originating notice of motion/to   ou d'avis de motion introductive
                        d'instance
      c. C-44, s. 248
    offences punishable on summary infractions punissables par
    conviction   procédure sommaire
      c. 31 (4th Supp.), s. 94(2)
    on summary application   sur demande sommaire
      c. C-46, s. 490(15)
    on the making of a summary   à la suite d'une demande sommaire
    application
      c. C-46, s. 490(2)(a)
    summary conviction court   cour des poursuites sommaires
      c. C-46, s. 432(3)
    summary determination   décision sommaire
      c. C-46, s. 685
    summary manner   procédure sommaire
      c. L-12, s. 85(4)
    summary removal (of a person) expulsion sans formalité
      c. N-14, s. 7(1)(q)
    summary trial (of indictable   instruction sommaire
    offences)
      c. N-14, s. 5(5)

summary conviction
    c. A-11, s. 47(2)
    c. A-12, s. 19(3)
    liable on summary conviction

    c. A-12, s. 18(1)
    offence punishable by
    indictment or on summary
    conviction

    c. C-46, s. 12
    offence punishable on summary
    conviction

    c. C-44, s. 251
    c. C-46, s. 787(1)
    summary conviction court
    c. C-46, s. 785
summary trial court
    c. C-39, s. 2(1)
summer-fallowing
    (of the land)
    c. C-48, s. 9(3)(b)(ii)(A)
summing up
    address of the prosecutor by way
    of summing up
    c. C-46, s. 646
    summing up of the judge
    c. C-46, s. 166(1)(b)(iv)
summon/to
    (jurors)
    c. C-46, s. 642(1)
summons
    c. B-3, s. 166
    c. C-46, s. 493
    garnisher summons
    c. C-4, s. 23
    instrument of summons
    c. C-37, s. 7(1)
    issue a summons/to
    c. C-46, s. 164(2)
    originating summons
    c. L-12, s. 45(6)
    summons to vacate or show
    cause
    c. T-7, s. 20(1)
    writ of summons
    c. C-50, s. 23(3)
superintend/to
    (employees)
    c. S-26, s. 15
superintendent
    c. L-2, s. 167(2)(a)
Superintendent of Bankruptcy
    c. B-3, s. 2
Superintendent of Insurance
    c. C-41, s. 2
superior court
    (of a province)
    c. A-2, s. 10(4)(b)
    judge of a superior court or
    county court
    c. J-1, s. 3

déclaration de culpabilité par
    procédure sommaire

sur déclaration de culpabilité par
    procédure sommaire

infraction punissable sur acte
    d'accusation ou déclaration de
    culpabilité par procédure
    sommaire

infraction punissable sur
    déclaration de culpabilité par
    procédure sommaire

cour des poursuites sommaires

tribunal d'instruction sommaire

mise en jachère

exposé du poursuivant par voie de
    résumé

résumé du juge

assigner

assignation

sommation
bref de saisie-arrêt

acte de convocation

lancer une sommation

bref d'assignation

sommation de déguerpir ou
    d'exposer ses raisons

bref d'assignation

diriger

chef

surintendant des faillites

surintendant des assurances

cour supérieure

juge d'une juridiction supérieur

superior court of criminal
jurisdiction
    c. C-46, s. 468

cour supérieure de juridiction
criminelle

superior court of record
    c. A-7, s. 8(4)

cour supérieure d'archives

supernumerary
supernumerary judge
    c. F-7, s. 5(2)

juge surnuméraire

supersede/to
(substantive provision)
    c. B-3, s. 72(1)

remplacer

superseded/to be
    c. C-26, s. 2(3)

être remplacé

supervise/to
    c. A-2, s. 4(a)

diriger

direct, supervise and
coordinate/to (a program)
    c. C-11, s. 5 in fine

diriger, contrôler et coordonner

supervision
    c. C-26, Schedule I, Article
      30(1)

contrôle

care and supervision (of
children)
    c. Y-1, s. 3(1)(h)

entretien et surveillance

care, supervision and control (of
a person)
    c. C-46, s. 2

soins, surveillance et contrôle

have supervision over and
direction of/to (activities and
staff)
    c. A-13, s. 17

assurer la direction et contrôler la
gestion

have supervision over/to (the
staff)
    c. A-7, s. 7(5)

contrôler la gestion

mandatory supervision
    c. P-2, s. 2

liberté surveillée

remove from parental
supervision/to
    c. Y-1, s. 4(1)(a)

soustraire à l'autorité parentale

under the supervision of
    c. S-26, s. 16

sous l'autorité générale

supervisor
    c. C-31, s. 16

surveillant

supervisory
administrative, research,
supervisory, advisory or
regulatory functions of a
governmental nature
    c. F-11, s. 3(1)(a)

fonctions étatiques
d'administration, de recherche, de
contrôle, de conseil ou de
réglementation

supplement
deed, indenture or other
instrument, including any
supplement or amendment
thereto
    c. C-44, s. 82(1)

instrument, ainsi que tout acte
additif ou modificatif

**Supplementary Retirement
Benefits Account**
    c. C-17, s. 74

compte de prestations de retraite
supplémentaires

supply
supply of light, power, gas or
water
    c. C-46, s. 422(1)(d)

approvisionnement de lumière,
d'énergie,de gaz ou d'eau

supply/to
    c. C-34, s. 2   fournir ou approvisionner

support
    agreement for maintenance and   convention pour l'entretien et le
    support (of a spouse or a child)   soutien
        c. B-3, s. 178(1)(c)
    financial support order   ordonnance de soutien financier
        c. C-17, s. 36(1)
    support order   ordonnance alimentaire
        c. C-3, s. 2(1)

support/to
    sponsor or support/to   appuyer ou prendre en charge
    (conferences)
        c. A-13, s. 4(c)

suppress/to
    suppress a riot/to   réprimer une émeute
        c. C-46, s. 32(1)(a)

suppression
    suppression of the truth   suppression de la vérité
        c. C-46, s. 123(2)(a)

Supreme Court of Ontario   Cour suprême de l'Ontario
    c. J-1, s. 12

surcharge
    charge or surcharge   taxe ou surtaxe
        c. A-10, s. 2(1)

surety   caution
    c. A-12, s. 25(1)
    c. C-46, s. 139(1)(b)
    principal and surety   cautionné et caution
        c. Y-1, s. 49(3)
    surety or guarantor   caution ou répondant
        c. B-3, s. 85(3)

surf-board
    water skis, surf-board, water   skis nautiques, planche de surf,
    sled   aquaplane
        c. C-46, s. 250(1)

surface right   droit de surface
    c. T-7, s. 12

surgeon
    be present as an aid, second,   assister en qualité d'aide, second,
    surgeon, umpire, backer or   médecin, arbitre, soutien ou
    reporter/to   reporter
        c. C-46, s. 83(1)(c)

surgical-dental services   services de chirurgie dentaire
    c. C-6, s. 2

surplus   exédant
    c. L-12, s. 53(2)
    (of a company)   surplus
        c. L-12, s. 61(6)(c)(i)
    contributed surplus   surplus d'apport
        c. B-1, s. 58(1)
    contributed surplus account   compte surplus d'apport
        c. B-1, s. 120(2)
    surplus account   compte de surplus
        c. C-44, s. 26(6)
    surplus dividends   surplus de dividendes
        c. B-3, s. 132(3)(a)
    surplus earnings   surplus de bénéfices
        c. N-11, s. 30(3)(e)
    surplus fund   excédent
        c. C-11, s. 17(4)
    surplus funds   surplus de fonds
        c. C-41, s. 101(2)

surrender
  (of a security)   livraison
    c. B-1, s. 83(b)
  for collection or for surrender   pour recouvrement ou pour remise
    c. B-1, s. 88(1)(a)
  for collection, for surrender   pour recouvrement, pour remise
  (endorsement)
    c. C-44, s. 61(1)(a)
  presentation or surrender (of a   présentation ou livraison
  security)
    c. C-44, s. 56(b)
  presentation or surrender (of a   présentation ou remise (d'une
  security)   valeur)
    c. B-1, s. 83(a)

surrender/to
  (a document)   restituer
    c. C-27, Schedule, Article III,
    7.
  (a lease)   abandonner
    c. B-3, s. 30(1)(k)
  (a right)   renoncer
    c. C-17, s. 9(3)
  (a security)   remettre
    c. B-3, s. 127(2)
  (security)   renoncer
    c. B-3, s. 112
  surrender oneself into custody/to   se livrer
    c. C-46, s. 679(4)(b)

surreptitious
  surreptitious interception of   interception clandestine de
  private communications   communications privées
    c. C-46, s. 191(1)

surveyor
  land surveyor   arpenteur
    c. C-46, s. 443(1)(b)

surviving spouse   conjoint survivant
    c. C-31, s. 34(1)

survivorship
  right of survivorship   gain de survie
    c. B-1, s. 92(1)(e)
    c. C-44, s. 65(1)(e)

suspected
  suspected offence   infraction dont on soupçonne la
                     perpétration
    c. C-34, s. 20(1)(b)

suspend/to
  suspend the passing of   surseoir au prononcé de la sentence
  sentence/to
    c. C-46, s. 737(1)(a)

suspension
  (of work)   suspension du travail
    c. L-2, s. 3(1)

suspicion   soupçon
    c. C-46, s. 140(b)

suzerainty   souveraineté
    c. B-7, Schedule I, Article
      XXXI, Section 2(g)
  sovereignty, suzerainty,   souveraineté, suzeraineté, mandat
  mandate or authority   ou autorité
    c. C-26, s. 2(4)

swear/to
  administer, take, swear, make   souscrire
  or affirm/to (oath)
    c. S-26, s. 81(2)

swine
    horses, cattle, sheep, swine   chevaux, bovins, ovins, porcins
         c. L-9, s. 10
switching order
    bill of lading, cargo manifest,   connaissement, manifeste, ordre
    shipping order, way-bill and   d'expédition, feuille de route et
    switching order   bulletin de manoeuvre
         c. T-19, s. 2
sworn statement   relevé sous serment
         c. B-1, s. 30(2)
         c. B-1, s. 31(1)
         c. B-3, s. 49(2)   déclaration sous serment
symbol
    depiction or symbol (on product)   description ou symbole
         c. C-38, s. 7(2)(a)
syndicate
    (company)   syndicat
         c. C-46, s. 400(2)
    consortium or syndicate of   consortium ou syndicat de
    financing   financement
         c. B-1, s. 190(8)
system of registration   archives
         c. B-1, s. 178(5)

t

tackle
    cargo, stores and tackle of a   cargaison, approvisionnement,
    vessel wrecked, stranded or in   agrès et apparaux d'un navire
    distress   naufragé, échoué ou en détresse
         c. C-46, s. 2
    fish, tackle, rigging, apparel,   poissons, agrès, apparaux,
    furniture, stores and cargo   garnitures, équipement, matériel,
                                approvisionnements et cargaison
         c. C-33, s. 2
take/to
    (an action)   intenter une action
         c. C-19, s. 44(2)
    administer, take, swear, make   souscrire
    or affirm/to (oath)
         c. S-26, s. 81(2)
    bring, defend or take part (in an   ester en justice
    action)
         c. B-1, s. 293(1)(b)
    bring, defend or take part in any   ester en justice, lors de toute
    action or proceeding/to   procédure
         c. C-44, s. 222(1)(b)
    take and receive affidavits,   recevoir les affidavits, déclarations
    declarations and affirmations/to   et affirmations solennelles
         c. A-2, s. 10(3)
    take before/to (a justice of the   faire comparaître
    peace)
         c. A-11, s. 21(1)
    take down a deposition in   prendre une déposition par écrit
    writing/to
         c. C-46, s. 540(2)(a)
    take land/to   exproprier un terrain
         c. C-19, s. 17(1)(b)
    take or receive affidavit/to   recevoir des affidavits
         c. P-5, s. 9(2)

take or record/to (evidence) c. C-46, s. 549(1)	recueillir ou enregistrer
take over/to (ship) c. C-31, s. 56(1)(j)(b)	prendre en charge
take up a share/to c. C-44, s. 195(a)	prendre livraison d'une action
take-over bid c. C-44, s. 194	offre d'achat visant à la mainmise
securities exchange take-over bid circular c. C-44, s. 193	circulaire d'offre d'achat en bourse visant à la mainmise
taking	
expropriation or taking c. C-19, s. 17(1)(c)	expropriation ou prise de possession
taking or abandonment (of property) c. C-25, s. 11(1)	prise de possession ou cession
taking or conversion of anything (fraudulent) c. C-46, s. 322(3)	prise ou détournement d'une chose
tangible	
tangible personal property c. C-25, s. 13	bien meuble corporel
tariff	
proposed tariff of tolls c. A-2, s. 18(1)(h)	tarifs de taxes projetés
tariff of fees c. C-40, s. 147(1)	tarif des droits
tariff of fees c. C-12, s. 42(1)(f)	tarif des frais
tariff of fees (of witness) c. A-2, s. 10(4)(b)	tarif d'honoraires
tariff of fees and costs c. C-50, s. 35(a)	tarif d'honoraires
tariff rates c. A-1, s. 18(b)(iii)	taux tarifaires
Tariff Board c. A-1, Schedule I	Commission du tarif
tax	
property tax c. C-46, s. 347(2)	impôt foncier
tax/to	
(an account) c. B-3, s. 41(4)	taxer
Tax Court of Canada c. J-1, s. 11(1)	Cour canadienne de l'impôt
tax-paid	
(appropriations) c. B-1, Schedule XIII	libéré d'impôt
taxable	
evidence taxable c. C-39, s. 74(2)	témoignage taxable
taxation	
(of costs) c. C-50, s. 28	taxation
taxation of costs c. C-39, s. 73(2)	taxe des frais
taxed	
costs and charges to be taxed c. C-46, s. 779(1)	frais et dépens à taxer
taxes	
duties and taxes (paid under federal customs) c. C-53, s. 3(2)	droits et taxes

taxing authority
    c. B-3, s. 149(2)   autorité taxatrice
    c. C-7, s. 28(2)(a)   autorité fiscale
taxing officer   fonctionnaire taxateur
    c. B-3, s. 152(4)
teach/to
    teach or advocate (the use of   enseigner ou préconiser
    force)/to
        c. C-46, s. 59(4)(a)
technical
    technical error   erreur de procédure
        c. P-35, s. 32
    technical, professional or other   personnel technique, professionnel
    officers   ou autre
        c. C-24, s. 6(e)
technological change   changement technologique
    c. L-2, s. 51(1)
telecommunication   télécommunication
    c. C-22, s. 2
    c. C-46, s. 326(2)
Teleglobe Canada   Téléblobe Canada
    c. F-11, Schedule III, Part II
telephone selling
    in-store, door-to-door or   opération de vente en magasin, par
    telephone selling   démarchage ou par téléphone
        c. C-34, s. 52(2)(d)
tell fortune/to   dire la bonne aventure
    c. C-46, s. 365(b)
teller
    (of a bank)   caissier
        c. B-4, s. 12
temporary
    seasonal or temporary employee   saisonnier ou employé temporaire
        c. L-2, s. 190(f)
    temporary interest (in a   intérêt provisoire
    property)
        c. B-3, s. 30(1)(k)
    temporary release   mise en liberté provisoire
        c. Y-1, s. 35(1)
    temporary substitute (of a   remplaçant
    board)
        c. A-8, s. 3(5)
    temporary substitute member   suppléant
    (of a Board)
        c. A-4, s. 3(3)
tenancy
    tenancy or right of occupation   location ou droit d'occupation
        c. C-46, s. 210(4)
tenant
    (of a farm)   locataire
        c. B-1, s. 2(1)
    as owner, landlord, lessor,   en qualité de possesseur,
    tenant, occupier or agent (of   propriétaire, locateur, locataire,
    common gaming house)   occupant ou agent
        c. C-46, s. 201(2)(b)
    joint owner tenant in common or   copropriétaire tenancier en commun
    partner   ou associé
        c. C-46, s. 328(d)
tender   soumission
    c. C-46, s. 121f)
    (railway)   tender
        c. C-46, s. 422(1)(e)

(to sell by)   soumission
    c. B-3, s. 30(1)(a)
current and legal tender/to be   avoir cours légal et pouvoir
           libératoire
    c. C-52, s. 7(1)(b)
legal tender   pouvoir libératoire
    c. A-1, s. 18(d)(i)
legal tender/to be (note)   avoir cours légal
    c. B-2, s. 26(1)
plead a tender/to   faire une offre de paiement
    c. F-7, s. 40(1)
tender in evidence/to   présenter en preuve
    c. C-46, s. 256(3)

tender/to
    (shares)   offrir
    c. C-44, s. 204(1)
tender in evidence/to   présenter en preuve
    c. C-46, s. 256(3)
tender money into court/to   consigner au tribunal une somme
           d'argent
    c. F-7, s. 48(3)

tenderer   soumissionnaire d'offres
    c. C-9, s. 38(2)
bidder or tenderer   enchérisseur ou soumissionnaire
    c. C-34, s. 47(2)

tenders
call or request for bids or   appel ou demande d'offres ou de
tenders   soumissions
    c. C-34, s. 47(1)(a)
call tenders/to   faire des appels d'offres
    c. C-9, s. 38(1)

tenements
goods and chattels, lands and   biens, effets, terrains et bâtiments
tenements
    c. C-46, s. 773(1)

tenets and teachings
    (of religious organization)   doctrine et enseignements
    c. C-8, s. 11(6)(a)(i)

tenor
original tenor (of a bill)   termes originaux
    c. B-4, s. 144(2)

tenure   mandat
    c. C-9, s. 19(2)(b)
    (of office)   occupation (de poste)
    c. A-1, s. 55(3)
tenure of an office   période d'occupation d'une fonction
    c. C-8, s. 2(1)
tenure of office   occupation de poste
    c. C-23, s. 5(2)

tenure of appointment   durée du mandat
    c. A-16, s. 8(c)

term
    (of director)   mandat
    c. C-44, s. 106(4)
in term time (court)   lors d'une session régulière
    c. C-46, s. 834(2)
opening of the term or sittings   ouverture de la session
(of a court)
    c. C-46, s. 474
short or long term conditions   conditions de durée variable
    c. C-32, s. 5(1)
stated term   mandat pour une durée déterminée
    c. C-44, s. 106(5)

term of imprisonment	période d'emprisonnement
c. C-46, s. 721(5)	
term of office	mandat
c. A-13, s. 12	
term to maturity (for	date d'échéance
subordinated note)	
c. L-12, s. 71(2)(e)	
terminate/to	
(a collective agreement)	mettre fin
c. L-2, s. 67(1)	
(an agreement)	mettre fin
c. C-11, s. 12(2)	
(an agreement)	résilier
c. N-11, s. 25(2)(d)	
(an agreement)	résilier
c. C-44, s. 183(6)	
terminate an authority/to	mettre fin à un mandat
c. L-2, s. 113	
termination	
(of a function)	cessation
c. C-19, s. 19(2)	
(of dispositions)	cessation des effets
c. Y-1, s. 36(2)	
(of the bid)	expiration
c. C-44, s. 206(3)	
termination date (of a collective	date d'expiration
agreement)	
c. L-2, s. 67(3)	
termination of employment	licenciement
c. L-2, s. 221(1)(a)	
termination of pregnancy	arrêt de grossesse
c. C-46, s. 287(6)	
terms	conditions
c. A-13, s. 4(j)	
c. C-44, s. 48(5)	libellé
at such time and on such terms	aux dates et selon les modalités
c. Y-1, s. 20(1)(g)	
terms of acquisition	conditions d'achat
c. N-11, s. 30(2)(f)	
terms of the contract	stipulations du contrat
c. N-11, s. 30(2)(g)	
terms and conditions	modalités
c. A-2, s. 6	
territorial	
territorial division	circonscription territoriale
c. C-46, s. 2	
c. Y-1, s. 49(4)	
territorial division	district judiciaire
c. Y-1, s. 25(1)	
territorial jurisdiction	ressort
c. A-7, s. 23	
c. Y-1, s. 23(2)(b)	
territorial lands	terres territoriales
c. T-7, s. 2	
territorial sea	mer territoriale
c. A-2, s. 4(k)	
c. A-12, s. 23(1)	
territory	
law of the territory	loi du territoire
c. C-30, Schedule Article I(e)	
terrorist acts	
commission of terrorist acts	perpétration d'actes de terrorisme
c. A-1, s. 15(2)(c)	

test
    assay, test or valuation   essai, épreuve ou évaluation
        c. C-46, s. 396(1)(a)
testamentary
    testamentary instrument   instrument testamentaire
        c. B-1, s. 207(1)(b)(i)
    testamentary instrument   titre testamentaire
        c. C-46, s. 334(a)
    will, codicil or other   testament, codicille ou autre écrit
    testamentary writing or   ou disposition testamentaire
    appointement
        c. C-46, s. 2
testimonial
    representation or testimonial   indication ou attestation
        c. C-34, s. 52(4)
Textile and Clothing Board   Commission du textile et du
                                      vêtement
    c. A-1, Schedule I
théâtre   théâtre
    c. C-46, s. 150
    theatre of war   théâtre de guerre
        c. C-31, s. 56(2)(b)(i)
theft
    commit theft/to   commettre un vol
        c. C-46, s. 2
    theft of cattle   vol de bétail
        c. C-46, s. 553(a)(i)
then and there   sur-le-champ
        c. C-46, s. 102(1)(a)
therapeutic abortion committee   comité de l'avortement
                                        thérapeutique
    c. C-46, s. 287(6)
thing   objet
    c. C-23, s. 21(2)(d)
    act, matter or thing   acte ou chose
        c. A-2, s. 14(1)(a)
    deposit to ensure the doing of   cautionnement en garantie
    any act or thing   d'exécution d'un acte ou d'une
                                        chose
    c. F-11, s. 20(1)
things in action   droits incorporels
    c. B-3, s. 2
third party   tiers
    c. A-1, s. 3
    c. C-44, s. 189(9)
    c. C-46, s. 7(3)   tierce personne
third person   tiers
    c. B-1, s. 88(2)
third State   Etat tiers
    c. C-30, Schedule, Article IX,
    1
threat
    by a threat or an artifice or by   au moyen d'une menace ou d'un
    collusion with a person   artifice ou de collusion avec une
                                          personne
    c. C-46, s. 350(b)(i)
threaten/to
    (safety of a person)   menacer
        c. A-1, s. 15(2)(f)
    (the safety of property)   mettre en danger
        c. A-1, s. 15(2)(f)
three-card monte   bonneteau
    c. C-46, s. 206(2)

through
  (a member)   par l'intermédiaire
    c. C-46, s. 121(1)(c)
ticket
  collect as fare, toll, ticket or   percevoir un prix de passage, un
  admission/to   péage, un billet ou un droit
                                 d'entrée
    c. C-46, s. 392(a)(i)
  passenger ticket   billet de passage
    c. C-26, Schedule I, Article
      3(1)
tie
  closer commercial tie   rapprochement commercial
    c. A-13, s. 3(d)
  closer economic tie   rapprochement économique
    c. A-13, s. 3(d)
tied selling   ventes liées
    c. C-34, s. 39(1)
ties
  develop closer ties/to   resserrer les liens
    c. A-13, s. 3
timber   bois
    c. T-7, s. 2
  lumber, timber, log, float, boom,   bois de construction, de service ou
  dam or slide   en grume, radeau, barrage
                                 flottant, digue ou glissoir
    c. C-46, s. 433(1)(i)
  timber mark or boom chain   marque de bois ou marque de
  brand   chaîne d'estacade
    c. C-46, s. 339(4)
  timber, mast, spar, shingle bolt,   bois d'oeuvre, mâts, espars, bois à
  sawlog or lumber of any   bardeaux et bois en grume
  description
    c. C-46, s. 339(6)
time
  at any time   à tout moment
    c. C-46, s. 487(1)(c)
  at such time and on such terms   aux dates et selon les modalités
    c. Y-1, s. 20(1)(g)
  extend the time limit/to   proroger le délai
    c. A-1, s. 9(1)
  extension of time   prorogation de délai
    c. S-26, s. 59(2)
  from time to time   en tant que de besoin
    c. I-23, s. 31(3)
  in force at any time   en vigueur à un moment donné
    c. S-22, s. 14(1)
  place and time   date, heure et lieu
    c. C-38, s. 16(2)(b)
  reasonable time   délai raisonnable
    c. C-44, s. 14(2)
  reckoning time   calcul des échéances
    c. B-4, s. 6(1)
  sufficient time   délai convenable
    c. C-6, s. 14(3)
  time and place   date, heure et lieu
    c. C-46, s. 700(1)
  time limit   délai
    c. A-1, s. 9(1)
  within the time specified   délai imparti
    c. A-1, s. 37(3)
title
  (of real property)   titre
    c. C-29, s. 34(b)

a person acting in good faith and without notice has acquired lawful title for valuable consideration
  c. C-46, s. 491.1(3)(b)(i)

un tiers qui ignore qu'une infraction a été commise a acquis légitimement de bonne foi pour une contrepartie valable

abstract of title
  c. C-46, s. 385(1)

extrait de titre

clear title
  c. C-24, s. 62(2)

titre incontestable

clear title (to lands)
  c. N-14, s. 3(2)(a)

titre incontestable

document of title to goods
  c. C-46, s. 325

titre de marchandises

document of title to goods or lands
  c. C-46, s. 340(a)

titre de marchandises ou de biens-fonds

give a title/to (to a cheque)
  c. B-4, s. 174

conférer un titre

good title
  c. B-3, s. 73(1)

titre valable

have title to or an interest/to (in an object)
  c. P-20, s. 11(3)

avoir un droit de propriété ou autre

title to or interest in a chattel personal
  c. C-46, s. 2

titre à un bien ou droit mobilier ou à un intérêt dans ce bien ou droit

title to real property or to any interest in real property
  c. C-46, s. 2

titre à un bien immeuble ou à un intérêt dans un bien immeuble

token

coin or token-operated device

appareil automatique fonctionnant au moyen d'une pièce de monnaie ou d'un jeton

  c. C-46, s. 454(b)

counterfeit token of value
  c. C-46, s. 448

symbole de valeur contrefait

slug or token (slot machine)
  c. C-46, s. 198(3)(iii)

piécette ou jeton

toll

charge a toll/to
  c. A-15, s. 3(2)

facturer une taxe

collect as fare, toll, ticket or admission/to

percevoir un prix de passage, un péage, un billet ou un droit d'entrée

  c. C-46, s. 392(a)(i)

make a toll/to
  c. A-15, s. 3(2)

réclamer une taxe

tax, impost, duty or toll

impôts, taxes, droits ou autres contributions

  c. F-11, s. 23(1)

tolls

duties or tolls
  c. C-10, s. 42(1)

droits ou taxes

proposed tariff of tolls
  c. A-2, s. 18(1)(h)

tarifs de taxes projetés

tort

liability in tort
  c. C-50, s. 3

responsabilité civile délictuelle

total pensionable earnings

total des gains ouvrant droit à pension

  c. C-8, s. 2(1)

town corporate

chief magistrate of a city, borough or town corporate

premier magistrat d'une municipalité, ville ou autre agglomération

c. S-26, s. 82(c)

town hall   hôtel de ville
    c. T-7, s. 23(b)

tract
    (of land)   parcelle
    c. T-7, s. 23(a)
    unorganized tract of country   étendue de pays non organisée
    c. C-46, s. 480(1)

trade
    (in securities)   transaction
    c. B-1, s. 145(a)
    for purpose of trade   dans un but commercial
    c. C-42, s. 27(4)(b)
    international trade   commerce international
    c. B-7, Schedule II, Article
      I(ii)
    international trade   échanges internationaux
    c. B-7, Schedule II, Article
      I(ii)
    interprovincial and export trade   marchés interprovincial et
                                   international
    c. A-6, s. 2(1)
    trade combination   entente industrielle ou coalition
                                       industrielle
    c. C-46, s. 467(2)
    trade in securities   commerce des valeurs
    c. C-34, s. 5(2)(a)
    trade or commerce   commerce
    c. C-46, s. 379
    trade terms   conditions de commerce
    c. C-34, s. 37(3)
    trade union   syndicat ouvrier
    c. C-46, s. 425(a)
    trade union   syndicat
    c. L-2, s. 3(1)

trade-mark   marque de commerce
    c. C-46, s. 406
    trade-mark, trade-name or   marque de commerce, nom
    corporate name   commercial ou dénomination
                                     sociale
    c. B-1, s. 16(1)(c)

trade-name   nom commercial
    c. C-46, s. 411
    trade-mark, trade-name or   marque de commerce, nom
    corporate name   commercial ou dénomination
                                     sociale
    c. B-1, s. 16(1)(c)
    trade-name, mark or   nom commercial, marque de
    designation   commerce ou désignation
    c. A-10, s. 5

trader   commerçant
    c. C-46, s. 400(1)

trading
    active public trading (in a   négociation publique active
    security)
    c. C-46, s. 382
    insider trading   transaction d'initiés
    c. C-40, s. 79(1)

trading stamps   bons-primes
    c. C-46, s. 379

traffic
    (drugs)   faire le trafic
    c. N-1, s. 2

amount of traffic	intensité de la circulation
c. C-46, s. 249(1)(a)	
illicit international traffic (in	commerce international illicite
cultural property)	
c. C-51, s. 37(1)	
traffic/to	
(a certificate)	faire le trafic
c. C-29, s. 29(2)(d)	
(drugs)	faire le trafic
c. F-27, s. 38	
traitorous	
offence involving traitorous or	infraction pour conduite assimilable
treasonable behaviour	à la trahison
c. C-17, s. 18(4)(d)	
traitorous or mutinous act	acte de trahison ou de mutinerie
c. C-46, s. 53(b)	
transact/to	
transact (business)/to (at a	délibérer
meeting)	
c. C-44, s. 143(3)	
transact a business/to	exercer les opérations
c. B-6, s. 5	
transaction	opération
c. B-1, s. 190(1)	
c. C-46, s. 581(1)	affaire
(relating to real property)	opération
c. C-46, s. 386	
gold transaction	opération sur l'or
c. B-7, Schedule VIII, Section	
5(a)(vi)	
investment transaction	opération de placement
c. C-24, s. 8(2)	
transaction of business	conclusion d'affaires
c. C-46, s. 121(1)(a)(iii)	
transaction of business (of a	conduite des opérations
bank)	
c. B-2, s. 9(3)	
transcript	transcription
c. C-46, s. 482(3)(d)(ii)	
transfer	transfert
c. A-2, s. 18(1)(e)	
c. B-1, s. 75(2)	
(of a bill)	transfert
c. B-4, s. 137(1)	
(of funds)	virement
c. B-1, Schedule XIV	
(of securities)	transfert (de titres)
c. F-11, s. 60(1)(b)	
gift, conveyance, assignment,	don, transport, cession, vente,
sale, transfer or delivery of	transfert ou remise de biens
property	
c. C-46, s. 392(a)(i)	
issue, transfer or ownership (of	émission, transfert ou appartenance
a share)	
c. C-44, s. 6(1)d)	
receipt and transfer certificate	récipissé, reçu et warrant de transit
c. B-1, s. 2(1)(d)	
take or receive by transfer or	transférer
delivery/to (a negotiable	
instrument)	
c. C-46, s. 491.1(3)(b)(iii)	
transfer agent (securities)	agent de transfert
c. C-44, s. 49(4)	

transfer or transmission (of a security)
    c. B-1, s. 75(2)
    c. C-44, s. 48(1)
transfer right
    c. C-44, s. 176(1)c)iv)

transfer/to
(a sum to an account)
    c. C-24, s. 39(1)(a)(ii)
(proceedings)
    c. C-50, s. 22(2)
(wheat)
    c. C-24, s. 44(2)

transferable
    c. B-1, s. 2(1)(d)
(a deposit liability)
    c. B-1, s. 303(5)(a)
(a share)
    c. A-10, s. 13(3)
(endorsement)
    c. B-1, s. 92(9)
(privileges)
    c. B-1, s. 123(2)
(rights)
    c. C-44, s. 29(2)
transferable by delivery (securities)
    c. C-44, s. 2(1)
transferable instrument
    c. C-41, s. 10(1)(h)

transferance
(of companies)
    c. C-44, s. 4

transferee
(of a security)
    c. C-44, s. 49(8)

transferor
(of a security)
    c. B-1, s. 87(1)
    c. C-44, s. 60(1)
(of a security)
    c. C-44, s. 61(1)(b)

transferred
option or right transferred or transmitted
    c. B-1, s. 123(4)

transient
transient or trifling in nature (injury)
    c. C-46, s. 267(1)(a)

transitional
transitional arrangement
    c. B-7, Schedule I, Article XIV, Section 1

transmission
(of a security)
    c. B-1, s. 78(7)(b)
(of securities)
    c. F-11, s. 60(1)(b)
document of transmission
    c. L-12, s. 42(1)
fees and expenses of transmission (of a case)
    c. S-26, s. 63

transfert

droit de transfert

virer

déférer

transférer

cessible

cessible

transférable

transférable

négociable

négociable

négociable par tradition ou transfert

effet transférable

passage

cessionnaire

cédant

auteur du transfert

option ou droit transmissible à titre onéreux ou à titre gratuit

de nature passagère ou sans importance

disposition transitoire

transmission

transmission (de titres)

acte de transmission

droits et frais de transmission

transfer or transmission (of a
security)   transfert
    c. B-1, s. 75(2)
    c. C-44, s. 48(1)
transmission and registration   transmission et enregistrement
(of regulations)
    c. S-22, s. 5(1)
transmitted
   option or right transferred or   option ou droit transmissible à titre
   transmitted   onéreux ou à titre gratuit
    c. B-1, s. 123(4)
trap   trappe
    c. C-46, s. 247(1)
travel
   travel and living expenses   frais de déplacement et autres
    c. A-7, s. 7(9)(b)
   travel and living expenses   dépenses de déplacement et de
       séjour
    c. A-10, s. 6(6)
traveller's cheque   chèque de voyage
    c. F-11, s. 2
travelling
   travelling public   voyageurs
    c. 31 (4th Supp.), s. 23
treason
   high treason   haute trahison
    c. C-46, s. 46(1)
treasonable behaviour
   offence involving traitorous or   infraction pour conduite assimilable
   treasonable behaviour   à la trahison
    c. C-17, s. 18(4)(d)
treasurer
   (of a corporation)   trésorier
    c. C-44, s. 126(1)(a)
treasury   trésor
    c. B-7, Schedule I, Article V,
      Section 1
   treasury bill   bon du Trésor
    c. F-11, s. 2
   treasury bill   bon du trésor
    c. B-1, s. 208(7)(d)
   treasury note   billet du Trésor
    c. F-11, s. 2
Treasury Board   Conseil du Trésor
    c. C-4, s. 12
Treasury Board Secretariat   Secrétariat du Conseil du Trésor
    c. A-1, Schedule I
treatment order   ordonnance pour traitement
    c. Y-1, Schedule, Form 7
treaty
   treaty rights   droits issus des traités
    Constitutional Act, 1982,
      Schedule B, s. 35(3)
trespasser   intrus
    c. C-46, s. 38(1)(a)
trespassing   intrusion
    c. C-46, s. 41(1)
triable at law   justiciable des tribunaux
    c. C-29, s. 39
trial   procès
    c. A-12, s. 22(2)
    c. C-46, s. 785   procès ou instruction

hold the trial/to c. A-12, s. 22(2)	instruire le procès
mode of trial c. C-46, s. 739(1)(b)	forme de procès
prove on the trial/to c. C-46, s. 356(2)	prouver lors de l'instruction
separate trial c. C-46, s. 591(4)(b)	procès séparé
summary trial (of indictable offences) c. N-14, s. 5(5)	instruction sommaire
trial court c. C-46, s. 673	tribunal de première instance
trial de novo c. C-46, s. 569(3)	procès de novo
trial judge c. C-39, s. 2(1)	juge instructeur
trial of the charge c. C-46, s. 525(3)	procès sur l'inculpation
trial of the charge c. C-46, s. 556(2)(a)	audition du procès
Trial Division (Federal Court) c. F-7, s. 2	Section de première instance
tried and punished/to be c. C-46, s. 7(5)	être jugé et condamné
trier c. C-46, s. 640(4)	vérificateur
trifling transient or trifling in nature (injury) c. C-46, s. 267(1)(a)	de nature passagère ou sans importance
trivial (designation) c. C-46, s. 448	vulgaire
trivial, frivolous, vexatious or made in bad faith (a complaint) c. C-23, s. 41(1)(b)	frivole, vexatoire, sans objet ou entaché de mauvaise foi
trotting running, trotting or pacing horse-races c. C-46, s. 204(1)(c)	courses de chevaux, courses de chevaux en trot ou à l'amble
trucker c. A-15, s. 2	camionneur
true copy c. C-34, s. 13(2)	copie conforme
true owner (of a bill) c. B-4, s. 158(2)	véritable propriétaire
trust c. A-14, s. 2	fiducie
breach of trust c. C-46, s. 122	abus de confiance
breach of trust or confidence c. C-42, s. 63	abus de confiance
constructive trust c. B-1, s. 206(1) c. C-10, s. 39(3)	fiducie judiciaire
deed of trust c. C-19, s. 34(1)	acte de fiducie
equipment trust obligation c. B-1, s. 2(1)	engagement garanti par du matériel

express trust
    c. B-1, s. 206(1)
    c. C-10, s. 39(3)
	fiducie expresse

express trust c. F-11, s. 59	fiducie explicite

express, implied or constructive
trust
    c. L-12, s. 89(1)
	fiducie explicite, implicite ou
	  judiciaire

express, implied or constructive
trust
    c. C-40, s. 51(1)
	fiducie formelle, implicite ou
	  judiciaire

guaranteed trust money c. B-1, s. 270(1)	fonds en fiducie garantie
hold in trust/to c. C-44, s. 206(7)	détenir en fiducie

implied trust
    c. B-1, s. 206(1)
    c. C-10, s. 39(3)
    c. F-11, s. 59
	fiducie implicite

instrument creating the trust c. L-12, s. 120(2)	acte créant la fiducie
real estate investment trust c. B-1, s. 2(1)	fonds de placement immobilier
real estate investment trust c. B-1, s. 193(6)(b)	fonds immobilier de placement
trust account c. B-3, s. 25(1)	compte de fiducie
trust account c. L-9, s. 11(h)	compte fiduciaire
trust agreement c. C-44, s. 77(7)	contrat de fiducie

trust company
    c. B-1, s. 9(1)
    c. B-3, s. 2
	société de fiducie

trust company c. C-44, s. 3(2)(c)	société fiduciaire
trust corporation c. C-41, s. 11(1)(c)	compagnie de fiducie
trust deed c. N-7, s. 29(3)(b)	acte de fiducie
trust fund c. C-44, s. 46(3)	fonds en fiducie
trust indenture c. C-44, s. 39(12)	acte de fiducie
trust instrument c. C-20, s. 2(3)	contrat de fiducie
trust or estate c. C-44, s. 2(1)(c)	fiducie ou succession
trust or loan corporation c. B-1, s. 193(1)	société de fiducie ou de prêt
trustee of trust funds c. N-11, s. 2	dépositaire de fonds de fiducie

trustee or an express trust
created by deed, will or
instrument in writing, or by
parol
    c. C-46, s. 2
	fiduciaire aux termes d'une fiducie
	  explicite établie par acte,
	  testament ou instrument écrit, ou
	  verbalement

voting trust c. L-12, s. 46(2)(e)	convention de vote fiduciaire
welfare trust fund c. L-2, s. 94(2)(b)	fonds de prévoyance géré en fiducie

trust certificate
    equipment trust certificate
        c. B-1, s. 2(1)
	certificat garanti par du matériel

trustee	fiduciaire
c. A-14, s. 2	
c. F-11, s. 135(2)(ii)	
c. B-3, s. 2	syndic
by the interposition of a trustee	par l'intermédiaire d'un mandataire
c. P-1, s. 34	
licensed trustee	syndic autorisé
c. B-3, s. 2	
trustee in bankruptcy	syndic de faillite
c. C-44, s. 51(2)(c)	
trustee of the governing body	administrateur du corps dirigeant
c. B-6, s. 2	
trustee of trust funds	dépositaire de fonds de fiducie
c. C-7, s. 2	
trustee or an express trust created by deed, will or instrument in writing, or by parol	fiduciaire aux termes d'une fiducie explicite établie par acte, testament ou instrument écrit, ou verbalement
c. C-46, s. 2	
trustee, guardian, committee, curator, tutor, executor, administrator or representative of a deceased person	fiduciaire, tuteur, curateur, exécuteur ou administrateur de succession
c. B-1, s. 75(2)	
c. C-44, s. 48(2)	
trustees	
board of governors, management or directors, or the trustees, commission or other person	conseil des gouverneurs, conseil de direction, conseil d'administra d'administration ou fiduciaire, commisiion ou autre personne
c. C-46, s. 287(6)	
trusteeship	mise en tutelle
c. C-43, s. 12(1)(a)(vii)	
trusts	
powers and trusts	pouvoirs et attributions
c. C-45, s. 9	
powers and trusts	fonctions et attributions
c. C-34, s. 7(2)	
powers and trusts	attributions
c. S-26, s. 10	
trustworthy	
credible or trustworthy (evidence)	plausible ou digne de foi
c. C-46, s. 518(1)(e)	
try/to	juger
c. C-29, s. 30(2)	
hear, try and determine a complaint/to	connaître d'une plainte
c. L-2, s. 160	
hear, try and determine/to (by a magistrate)	instruire et juger
c. A-7, s. 23	
hear, try or determine/to (a complaint)	connaître de
c. C-32, s. 40	
try an indictable offence/to	juger un acte criminel
c. C-46, s. 469	
try an issue/to	instruire un procès
c. C-46, s. 643(2)	
tutor	tuteur
c. B-8, s. 14(a)	
trustee, guardian, committee, curator, tutor, executor, administrator or representative of a deceased person	fiduciaire, tuteur, curateur, exécuteur ou administrateur de succession

c. B-1, s. 75(2)
c. C-44, s. 48(2)
tutor, curator, guardian or
trustee
    c. L-12, s. 41(3)   tuteur, curateur ou fiduciaire

tying product   produit clef
    c. C-34, s. 39(1)

u

ultimate
   exclusive ultimate appellate   juridiction suprême en matière
   civil jurisdiction   d'appel au civil
    c. S-26, s. 52
ultimately
   to be ultimately accountable to   être responsable en dernier ressort
   Parliament   devant le Parlement
    c. F-11, s. 88
   ultimately accountable/to be (to   responsable en fin de compte
   Parliament)
    c. S-22, s. 2(1)
umpire   surarbitre
    c. B-7, Schedule I, Article
    XXIX(c)
   arbitrator or umpire   arbitre ou tiers-arbitre
    c. C-46, s. 118
   be present as an aid, second,   assister en qualité d'aide, second,
   surgeon, umpire, backer or   médecin, arbitre, soutien ou
   reporter/to   reporter
    c. C-46, s. 83(1)(c)
unadministered property   biens non liquidés
    c. B-3, s. 29(1)
    c. B-3, s. 202(1)(e)   biens non administrés
unanimous shareholder   convention unanime des
agreement   actionnaires
    c. C-44, s. 2(1)
unappropriated moneys   montant non affecté
    c. C-14, s. 11(1)(a)
unavoidable
   unavoidable absence   cas d'absence forcée
    c. L-2, s. 190(h)
   unavoidable absence   absence forcée
    c. P-1, s. 43(1)
unconditional
   (regulation)   inconditionnel
    c. C-8, s. 7(3)
unconverted share   action non convertie
    c. B-1, s. 123(7)
uncross/to
   (a crossed cheque)   débarrer (un chèque)
    c. B-4, s. 169(7)
uncrossed cheque   chèque non barré
    c. B-4, s. 168(b)
undeliverable letter   lettre non distribuable
    c. A-10, s. 2(1)
under
   (a paragraph)   au titre de
    c. C-16, s. 19(3)(b)
   (a paragraph)   prévu à
    c. A-12, s. 24(1)

(a subsection) c. A-12, s. 9(2)	visé à
(a subsection) c. A-10, s. 16	en application de
(an Act) c. A-11, s. 12(b)	prévu par
(an Act) c. A-11, s. 13(2)	sous le régime de
(subsection) c. A-7, s. 3(2)(a)	dans le cadre de
delinquency under (the Act) c. Y-1, s. 24(4)(b)	délit tombant sous le coup de (la loi)
under restraint, duress or fear c. C-46, s. 155(3)	sous l'effet de la contraite, de la violence ou de la crainte
under the terms of c. C-26, Schedule I, Article 2(2)	sous l'empire de
undergo/to undergo/to (a sentence of imprisonment) c. P-20, s. 9(1)	purger
undermine/to (system of government) c. C-23, s. 2	saper
undertake/to c. A-5, s. 3(1)	prendre l'engagement
(a program) c. C-11, s. 6(1)	entreprendre
(projects) c. A-2, s. 4(b)	entreprendre
undertake an obligation/to c. B-1, s. 53(5)(a)	souscrire une obligation
undertaking c. B-1, s. 2(1)	engagement
c. C-49, s. 5(b)(i) c. B-1, s. 265(4) c. C-46, s. 493	garantie promesse
(of a program) c. C-11, s. 6(2)	lancement
absolute undertaking c. C-27, s. 3	engagement absolu
federal work, undertaking or business c. L-2, s. 2	entreprises fédérales
telecommunications undertaking c. C-22, s. 2	entreprise de télécommunications
undertaking, operation and maintenance (of a project) c. A-3, s. 5A	réalisation
undertakings works and undertakings c. A-16, s. 18	ouvrages et entreprises
underwriter (of shares) c. L-12, s. 64(3)(b)	souscripteur à forfait
underwriting c. B-1, s. 190(1)	souscription à forfait
(of securities) c. C-34, s. 5(2)	souscription
undistributed balance c. C-24, s. 39(1)	solde non distribué

undue
    undue benefit — avantage injustifié
        c. A-1, s. 18(d)
    undue exploitation of sex — exploitation indue des choses sexuelles
        c. C-46, s. 163(8)
    undue hardship — préjudice abusif
        c. C-8, s. 66(3)(c)
    undue preference — préférence indue
        c. B-3, s. 173(1)(h)
    undue risk to society — risque trop grand pour la société
        c. P-2, s. 16(1)(a)(iii)

unencumbered
    unencumbered balance — solde non grevé
        c. F-11, s. 32(1)
    unencumbered debenture — débenture non grevée de sûretés
        c. L-12, s. 72(4)

unescorted
    unescorted temporary absence — permission de sortir sans surveillance
        c. P-2, s. 8(2)

unexpired
    (term) — non expiré
        c. B-1, s. 42(6)

unfit
    (to stand trial) — incapable
        c. C-46, s. 615(1)
    unfit to stand trial — incapable de subir son procès
        c. Y-1, s. 13(1)(b)

uniform bills of lading — uniformité des connaissements
    c. A-2, s. 18(1)(i)

unimpaired
    paid-up and unimpaired capital stock — capital versé et intact
        c. L-12, s. 72(1)

unincorporated
    (business) — dépourvu de personnalité morale
        c. C-44, s. 169(2)
    company, body corporate, unincorporated body or society — compagnie, personne morale, organisme non constitué en personne morale ou société
        c. C-46, s. 328(e)
    unincorporated association — association non constituée en personne morale
        c. B-3, s. 2
    unincorporated body — corps non doté de la personnalité morale
        c. B-1, s. 2(1)

unit
    (of a mutual fund) — part
        c. B-1, s. 191(5)(b)
    (of a security) — unité
        c. C-44, s. 65(9)
    bargaining unit — unité de négociation
        c. L-2, s. 3(1)
    condominium unit — unité en copropriété
        c. N-11, s. 2
    monetary unit — unité monétaire
        c. C-52, s. 3(1)

United Nations Association in Canada — Association Canadienne pour les Nations Unies
    c. C-18, Schedule

United Nations Educational, Scientific and Cultural Organization
  c. C-2, s. 8(2)

Organisation des Nations Unies pour l'Education, la Science et la Culture

United Nations Monetary and Financial Conference
  c. B-7, Schedule I, Article II, Section 1

Conférence monétaire et financière des Nations Unies

universality
  (of health care insurance plan)
  c. C-6, s. 7(c)

universalité

University Capital Grants Funds
  c. C-2, s. 15(1)

Fonds d'assistance financière aux universités

unlawful
  (act)
  c. B-1, s. 50(2)

illégal

  unlawful act
  c. N-1, s. 17(4)(b)

acte illégal

unlawfully
  c. C-10, s. 49

illégalement

unliquidated
  (obligation)
  c. B-1, s. 289(h)

non liquidé

  unliquidated claim
  c. B-3, s. 121(2)

réclamation non liquidée

  unliquidated, future or contingent claim
  c. C-44, s. 216(3)c)

créance non liquidée, future ou éventuelle

unmarried
  c. C-46, s. 290(3)

célibataire

unnecessary
  unreasonable or unnecessary (exercice of powers)
  c. C-23, s. 33(2)(b)

abusif ou inutile

unorganized
  unorganized tract of country
  c. C-46, s. 480(1)

étendue de pays non organisée

unpaid
  due and unpaid (amount)
  c. C-41, s. 46

exigible et impayé

unprovoked
  self-defence against unprovoked assault
  c. C-46, s. 34(1)

légitime défense contre une attaque sans provocation

unqualified
  (regulation)
  c. C-8, s. 7(3)

absolu

unreasonable
  c. A-11, s. 15(1)(a)

injustifié

  (amount)
  c. A-1, s. 30(1)(b)

excessif

  (amount)
  c. A-11, s. 15(1)(b)

insuffisant

  (delay)
  c. B-1, s. 103(2)

indu

  search and seizure

fouille, perquisition ou saisie abusive

  Constitutional Act, 1982, Schedule B, s. 8
  unreasonable delay
  c. C-46, s. 525(3)

délai anormal

unreasonable extension (time limits) c. A-1, s. 30(1)(c)	prorogation abusive
unreasonable or unnecessary (exercice of powers) c. C-23, s. 33(2)(b)	abusif ou inutile
unsanitary conditions c. F-27, s. 2	conditions non hygiéniques
unseaworthy vessel c. C-46, s. 251(1)	bateau innavigable
unsecured (bond, debenture, obligation) c. B-1, s. 2(1)	non gagé
(debt obligation) c. A-10, s. 18(b)	non garanti
secured or unsecured (guarantee) c. C-21, s. 17(3)	avec ou sans sûreté
secured or unsecured guarantee c. C-44, s. 2(1)	garantie donnée avec ou sans sûreté
unsolicited unsolicited request c. C-44, s. 147(e)	demande faite spontanément
unsound mind c. B-1, s. 35(1)(b)	faible d'esprit
untrue untrue statement c. C-44, s. 154(1)	faux renseignment
untrue statement c. L-9, s. 41(d)	déclaration inexacte
untrue suggestion of death c. S-26, s. 75	fausse déclaration de décès
unwarranted to result in serious and unwarranted detriment c. S-22, s. 20(d)(iii)	être la cause de préjudice grave et injustifié
upbringing (of a child) c. C-3, s. 2(1)	éducation
Uranium Canada Limited c. A-1, Schedule I	Uranium Canada Limitée
usable freely usable currencies c. C-52, s. 17(2)(d)	devises ayant libre cours
usage of trade c. B-1, s. 75(2)	usages du commerce
use c. A-12, s. 2	usage
for the use or benefit of c. B-1, s. 110(7)	à l'usage ou au profit de
use or hire (of a ship) c. F-7, s. 22(2)(i)	usage ou louage
use/to c. B-8, s. 12	avoir l'usage
(in evidence) c. B-3, s. 10(5)	invoquer
(levies) c. A-6, s. 2(2)(b)	employer
use of the surface (of land) c. T-7, s. 23(j)	usage en surface
user (of a device) c. F-27, s. 19	usager

proof of user
    c. C-40, s. 121(2)
                preuve d'utilisation

user charge
    c. C-6, s. 2
                frais modérateurs

usurious
  usurious contract
    c. B-4, s. 58
                contrat usuraire

utility
    c. N-7, s. 108(1)(c)
                installation de service public

utilization
  master plan of community
  development and land
  utilization
    c. N-11, s. 2
                plan directeur de développement
                  local et d'occupation du sol

utter/to
  (a document)
    c. C-46, s. 148(a)
                mettre en circulation

V

vacancy
  fill a vacancy/to
    c. B-1, s. 40(3)
                combler une vacance

  fill a vacancy/to
    c. B-1, s. 43(2)
                pourvoir à un poste vacant

vacant position
    c. A-13, s. 9
                poste vacant

vacate/to
  (an order)
    c. C-46, s. 523(2)
                annuler

  summons to vacate or show
  cause
    c. T-7, s. 20(1)
                sommation de déguerpir ou
                  d'exposer ses raisons

  vacate a conviction/to
    c. C-47, s. 5(b)
                effacer une condamnation

vacation
  (of court)
    c. B-3, s. 183(1)
                vacance judiciaire

  in vacation (court)
    c. C-46, s. 834(2)
                lors des vacances judiciaires

vagrancy
    c. C-46, s. 179(1)
                vagabondage

valid
  valid and subsisting licence
    c. A-2, s. 22
                permis valide

  valid or genuine (document)
    c. B-1, s. 21(e)
                valable ou authentique

validate/to
  (a security)
    c. C-44, s. 52(1)
                valider

valuable
  for valuable consideration
    c. C-42, s. 13(2)
                contre rémunération

  pay or discharge a valuable
  security/to
    c. C-46, s. 491.1(3)(b)(ii)
                payer ou rembourser des valeurs

  valuable consideration
    c. B-5, s. 4
                considération valable

  valuable security
    c. C-46, s. 363(a)
                valeur

valuable security
c. C-46, s. 2

valeur ou effet appréciable

valuation
c. C-17, s. 55(1)(a)

évaluation

assay, test or valuation
c. C-46, s. 396(1)(a)

essai, épreuve ou évaluation

value
amortized value (of a
redeemable security)
c. L-12, s. 78(1)

valeur amortie d'un titre rachetable

fair market value
c. B-3, s. 100(1)

juste valeur du marché

give value/to
c. B-1, s. 126(1)(a)(ii)

verser un montant en nature

holder for value
c. B-4, s. 53(2)

détenteur à titre onéreux

merchantable value
c. C-46, s. 379

valeur marchande

monetary value
c. C-46, s. 347(2)

valeur pécuniaire

monetary value
c. C-52, s. 12

valeur en argent

realizable value
c. C-44, s. 34(2)(b)

valeur de réalisation

realizable value (of a property)
c. B-3, s. 32

valeur réalisable (de biens)

value/to
(stocks)
c. C-25, s. 12(2)

évaluer

Vancouver Port Corporation
c. F-11, Schedule III, Part II

Société du port de Vancouver

variance
(between charges)
c. C-46, s. 546(b)

divergence

variation
(of a budget)
c. C-21, s. 22(3)

modification

(of payment)
c. A-5, s. 5(1)(a)

variation

variation order
c. C-3, s. 2(1)

ordonnance modificative

variation proceeding (divorce)
c. 3 (2nd Supp.), s. 2

action en modification

vary/to
c. C-26, Schedule I, Article
15(2)

déroger

(a decision)
c. A-7, s. 10(2)

modifier

vault-breaking
c. C-46, s. 351(1)

effraction de voûtes de sûreté

vehicle
vehicle drawn, propelled or
driven by any means other than
by muscular power
c. C-46, s. 2

véhicule tiré, mû ou poussé par
quelque moyen que ce soit, autre
que la force musculaire

vehicle identification number
c. C-46, s. 354(3)

numéro d'identification

vendor
c. C-24, s. 2(1)

vendeur

vendor or mortgagor
c. C-46, s. 385(1)

vendeur ou débiteur hypothécaire

venture
c. C-31, s. 13(2)

entreprise

venture capital corporation
c. B-1, s. 193(1) — société de capitaux à risque

venue
c. C-44, s. 190(17) — compétence territoriale
change of venue
c. C-46, s. 531 — renvoi devant un autre tribunal

verbatim
record verbatim/to
c. C-46, s. 487.1(2) — consigner mot à mot

verdict
special verdict (libel)
c. C-46, s. 317 — verdict spécial
verdict on coroner's inquisition
c. C-46, s. 529(1) — verdict sur enquête de coroner

verify/to
verify by affidavit/to
c. S-26, s. 38 — certifier par affidavit

vessel
c. C-9, s. 2 — navire
c. C-46, s. 258(10) — bateau
fishing vessel
c. C-33, s. 2 — bateau de pêche
foreign fishing vessel
c. C-33, s. 2 — bateau de pêche étranger
government vessel
c. C-33, s. 2 — bateau de l'État

vest/to
(a power in an officer)
c. A-12, s. 14(2) — conférer (un pouvoir à un agent)
(an estate)
c. B-3, s. 84 — saisir
(by will)
c. B-9, s. 26(2) — être dévolu
operative to vest/to be
c. C-42, s. 14(1) — avoir l'effet d'investir

vest in/to
c. B-1, s. 179(9) — attribuer
(a right)
c. B-1, s. 123(5) — être dévolu à

vested/to be
(an interest)
c. C-19, s. 14(1) — être attribué
to be vested in the name of the Crown (property)
c. F-11, s. 99(1) — appartenir à Sa majesté

vesting
vesting in Crown
c. C-44, s. 47(5) — dévolution à sa majesté

vexatious
vexatious conduct
c. C-39, s. 73(1)(a) — conduite vexatoire

Via Rail Canada Inc.
c. F-11, Schedule III, Part I — Via Rail Canada Inc.

viable
economically viable
c. C-25, s. 17(1) — économiquement viable

vice-consul
consul, vice-consul, acting consul, pro-consul or consular agent of Her Majesty
c. S-26, s. 82(e) — consul ou tout autre agent consulaire de Sa Majesté

video device
c. C-46, s. 207(4) — dispositif électronique de visualisation

view
(by jurors)
c. C-46, s. 652(2)
seize on view/to
c. N-14, s. 8(2)(c)

visite des lieux

saisir à vue

violence
acts of serious violence
c. C-23, s. 2
use of violence
c. A-1, s. 15(2)(d)

usage de la violence grave

emploi de la violence

visible
actual, visible and continued
possession
c. B-1, s. 2(1)(a)

possession réelle, publique et
continue

visitation
right of access to or visitation (of
a child)
c. 4 (2nd Supp.), s. 2

droit d'accès ou de visite

visiting force
c. C-12, s. 2

force étrangère

vitiate/to
(an act)
c. B-3, s. 14(7)

vicier

viva voce
(evidence)
c. C-46, s. 189(5)(a)

de vive voix

Voice of Women
c. C-18, Schedule

La Voix des Femmes

void
(regulation)
c. P-2, s. 27(4)
become void/to (certificate)
c. B-1, s. 76(12)(a)
render void/to
c. C-44, s. 153(6)
void as against (rights and
powers)
c. B-1, s. 178(4)(a)
void or voidable (transfer of
shares)
c. C-44, s. 32(6)
void or voidable contract
c. F-11, s. 117

invalide

être frappé de nullité

annuler

inopposable

entaché de nullité

contrat nul ou annulable

void/to
c. B-1, s. 35(3)

annuler

voidable
c. B-1, s. 111(8)
void or voidable contract
c. F-11, s. 117

annulable

contrat nul ou annulable

voir dire
c. C-46, s. 640(1)

voir dire

voluntary
voluntary transaction
c. C-44, s. 48(2)

opération consensuelle

Voluntary Aid Detachment
member of the Voluntary Aid
Detachment
c. C-31, s. 43

membre du détachement des
auxiliaires volontaires

volunteer worker
c. C-31, s. 30

engagé volontaire

vote
additional vote
c. C-7, s. 10(2)

voix prépondérante

affirmative vote (of shareholder) c. L-12, s. 35(3)(a)	vote positif
second or casting vote c. B-3, s. 105(3)	voix prépondérante
second vote c. C-21, s. 15(3)	voix prépondérante
tie vote c. C-21, s. 15(3)	partage des voix
voting	
cumulative voting c. C-44, s. 107	vote cumulatif
voting letter c. B-3, s. 51(1)(f)	formule de votation
voting right c. C-44, s. 2(1)	droit de vote
voting share c. B-1, s. 2(2)(d)	action à droit de vote
voting trust c. L-12, s. 46(2)(e)	convention de vote fiduciaire
voucher c. A-17, s. 14(3) c. B-3, s. 124(4) c. C-8, s. 24(2) c. C-39, s. 7	pièce justificative

W

wage c. B-3, s. 136(1)(d)	gage
minimum hourly wage c. L-2, s. 178(2)	salaire horaire minimum
wages	
claims for wages c. C-9, s. 43(5)	créances salariales
regulation of wages c. C-46, s. 425(a)	réglementation des salaires
waive/to c. A-1, s. 11(6)	dispenser
(a notice) c. C-44, s. 114(6)	renoncer
(a requirement) c. A-1, s. 27(2)	renoncer
(a right of appeal) c. C-46, s. 820(1)	se désister
waiver c. C-31, s. 9	désistement
(of notice) c. B-1, s. 44(6)	renonciation
wall	
common or party wall c. N-11, s. 2	mur commun ou mitoyen
want	
for want of prosecution c. C-46, s. 340	faute de poursuite
for want of prosecution c. C-44, s. 242(2)	pour cause de défaut de procédure utile
want of authority c. B-4, s. 48(1)	absence d'autorisation

want of jurisdiction c. C-46, s. 118	manque de juridiction
wanton wanton or reckless disregard c. C-46, s. 219(1)	insouciance déréglée ou téméraire
war service injury c. C-31, s. 43	blessure de service de guerre
War Veterans Allowance board c. A-1, Schedule I	Commission des allocations aux anciens combattants
warden mayor, warden, reeve, sheriff, deputy sheriff, sheriff's officer and justice of the peace c. C-46, s. 2	maire, président de conseil de comté, préfet, shérif, shérif adjoint, officier du shérif et juge de paix
park warden c. N-14, s. 2	gardien de parc
warden, deputy warden, instructor, keeper, jailer, guard, or other officer or permanent employee of a prison (peace officer) c. C-46, s. 2	directeur, sous-directeur, instructeur, gardien, geôlier, garde ou tout autre fonctionnaire ou employé permanent d'une prison
warehouse warehouse receipt c. B-2, s. 20(a)	récépissé ou warrant
warehouse receipt c. B-1, s. 2(1)	récépissé d'entrepôt
wares c. B-1, s. 2(1)	denrées
goods, wares or merchandise c. C-46, s. 383(1)	effets, denrées ou marchandises
warrant c. C-46, s. 493	mandat
c. C-41, s. 10(1)(h)	warrant
(for payment of dividend) c. B-4, s. 7	mandat
debenture, deed, bond, bill, note, warrant, order or other security for money c. C-46, s. 2	débenture, titre, obligation, billet, lettre, mandat, ordre ou autre garantie d'argent
outstanding share warrant c. L-12, s. 44(1)(f)	option d'achat d'actions en circulation
royal warrant c. C-46, s. 413	brevet royal (de fournisseur de Sa Majesté)
search warrant c. C-46, s. 487(3)	mandat de perquisition
share warrant c. C-44, s. 187(10)	option d'achat d'actions
sufficient warrant c. Y-1, Schedule, Form 5	mandat suffisant
warrant for removal of prisoners c. C-37, s. 7(1)	mandat de transfèrement
warrant for the arrest c. C-46, s. 485(1)	mandat d'arrestation
warrant of extradition c. C-37, s. 7(1)	mandat d'extradition
warrant officer c. C-17, s. 60(1)	sous-officier breveté
warrant to arrest c. C-46, s. 28(2)	mandat d'arrêt

warrant/to
    c. B-1, s. 86(1)   garantir
    c. C-44, s. 63(1)
    (the settling of an amount)   justifier
    c. B-3, s. 220(1)(b)(ii)
warranted
    punishment warranted by law   peine autorisée par la loi
    c. C-46, s. 478(3)(b) in fine
warrantor
    prospective warrantor   garant éventuel
    c. N-11, s. 99(b)
warranty
    warranty or guarantee   garantie
    c. C-34, s. 52(1)(b)
waste   déchet
    c. C-11, s. 2(1)
watch/to
    beset and watch/to (a place)   cerner et surveiller
    c. C-46, s. 423(1)(f)
water
    water quality management   gestion qualitative des eaux
    c. C-11, s. 2(1)
    water quality management   organisme de gestion qualitative
    agency   des eaux
    c. C-11, s. 2(1)
    water resource management   gestion des ressources en eau
    c. C-11, s. 2(1)
    water skis, surf-board, water   skis nautiques, planche de surf,
    sled   aquaplane
    c. C-46, s. 250(1)
waters
    boundary waters   eaux limitrophes
    c. C-11, s. 2(1)
    federal waters   eaux fédérales
    c. C-11, s. 2(1)
    inland waters   eaux intérieures
    c. A-12, s. 23(1)
    inter-jurisdictional waters   eaux relevant de plusieurs
                             juridictions
    c. C-11, s. 2(1)
    internal waters of Canada   eaux intérieures
    c. C-12, s. 3(a)
    international waters   eaux internationales
    c. C-11, s. 2(1)
way-bill
    bill of lading, cargo manifest,   connaissement, manifeste, ordre
    shipping order, way-bill and   d'expédition, feuille de route et
    switching order   bulletin de manoeuvre
    c. T-19, s. 2
waybill
    air waybill   lettre de transport aérien
    c. C-26, Schedule I, Article
    5(1)
weapon
    offensive weapon   arme offensive ou arme
    c. C-46, s. 2
weight
    least current weight   poids faible
    c. C-52, Schedule
welfare
    provincial child welfare or youth   loi provinciale sur le bien-être de
    protection legislation   l'enfance ou la protection de la
                            jeunesse
    c. Y-1, s. 40(3)(f)

welfare trust fund c. L-2, s. 94(2)(b)	fonds de prévoyance géré en fiducie
wharfinger c. C-19, s. 29	propriétaire de quais
wheat product c. C-24, s. 2(1)	produit du blé
wheel of fortune c. C-46, s. 206(1)(g)	roue de fortune
whole in whole or in part c. C-46, s. 718.1(1) remission in whole or in part (of a fine) c. C-46, s. 750(1)	en totalité ou en partie remise intégrale ou partielle
wholly wholly or partially c. C-42, s. 13(4) wholly or substantially c. C-8, s. 42(1)(c)	en totalité ou en partie entièrement ou dans une large mesure
wholly-owned c. B-1, s. 193(1) wholly-owned subsidiary of a holding body corporate c. C-44, s. 163(4)	en toute propriété filiale appartenant en propriété exclusive à la société mère
wild living creature c. C-46, s. 322(5)	créature sauvage vivante
wilderness camp community, residential centre, group home, child care institution, or forest or wilderness camp c. Y-1, s. 20(7)	centre résidentiel local, foyer collectif, établissement d'aide à l'enfance, camp forestier ou camp de pleine nature
wilful wilful omission c. C-46, s. 214	omission volontaire
wilfully c. A-7, s. 19(1)(a) c. C-46, s. 56 knowingly and wilfully c. B-1, s. 130(4) knowingly and wilfully c. C-46, s. 389(1)(b)	volontairement de propos délibéré en toute connaissance de cause sciemment et volontairement
will c. B-9, s. 26(2) notarial will c. B-1, s. 78(7)(b) c. C-44, s. 51(7)(a)(b) will, codicil or other testamentary writing or appointement c. C-46, s. 2	testament testament notarié testament, codicille ou autre écrit ou disposition testamentaire
willingness willingness to make amends c. Y-1, s. 14(2)(c)(i)	désir de réparer le tort
winding-up c. A-10, s. 22 final winding-up c. B-1, s. 283(1) winding-up order c. B-1, s. 51(2)(c) winding-up order c. L-12, s. 84(12)	liquidation clôture de la liquidation ordonnance de mise en liquidation ordonnance de liquidation

witchcraft
    witchcraft, sorcery,   magie, sorcellerie, enchantement ou
    enchantment or conjuration   conjuration
        c. C-46, s. 365(a)
withhold/to
    conceal, withhold or   dissimuler, retenir ou détourner
    misappropriate (property)/to
        c. C-44, s. 222(3)
    withhold a discharge/to   suspendre une libération
        c. B-3, s. 41(6)
withold/to
    (information)   refuser
        c. C-23, s. 31(2)
without
    a person acting in good faith and   un tiers qui ignore qu'une infraction
    without notice has acquired   a été commise a acquis
    lawful title for valuable   légitimement de bonne foi pour
    consideration   une contrepartie valable
        c. C-46, s. 491.1(3)(b)(i)
    for value in good faith without   à titre onéreux de bonne foi qui n'a
    notice (lender)   pas été avisé
        c. C-44, s. 44(3)
    without delay   à bref délai
        c. F-7, s. 28(5)
    without good cause   sans raison valable
        c. C-8, s. 89(1)(f)
    without his knowledge or   à son insue ou sans son
    consent   consentement
        c. C-32, s. 38
    without limiting the generality   notamment
    of the foregoing
        c. A-7, s. 3(1)
    without prejudice   sans préjudice
        c. C-9, s. 40
        c. C-17, s. 9(4)
    without prejudice (to any   sous réserve
    copyright)
        c. C-42, s. 12
witness
    witness for the accused   témoin à décharge
        c. C-46, s. 541(3)
witnessed
    witnessed/to be (election)   être attesté
        c. C-17, s. 8(1)
words and expressions
    (in an act)   termes
        c. C-24, s. 2(2)
work
    (copyright)   oeuvre
        c. C-42, s. 2
    federal work, undertaking or   entreprises fédérales
    business
        c. L-2, s. 2
    work for the general advantage   ouvrage à l'avantage général du
    of Canada   Canada
        c. C-24, s. 2(1)
work of sculpture   oeuvre de sculpture
        c. C-42, s. 2
work-force
    composition of the work-force   effectifs
        c. 31 (4th Supp.), s. 39(1)(b)
worker
    youth worker   délégué à la jeunesse
        c. Y-1, s. 2(1)

working capital c. C-25, s. 19(3)	fonds de roulement
working day c. C-26, Schedule I, Article 35	jour ouvrable
works	
literary and artistic works c. C-42, Schedule II Article 1	oeuvres littéraires et artistiques
works and undertakings c. A-16, s. 18	ouvrages et entreprises
World Bank Group c. B-1, s. 190(5)(a)(iii)	Groupe de la Banque mondiale
World Federalists of Canada c. C-18, Schedule	Mouvement Canadien pour une Fédération Mondiale
World War I c. C-31, s. 56(1)(a)(i)	Première Guerre mondiale
World War II c. C-31, s. 56(1)(a)(i)	Seconde Guerre mondiale
worship	
public worship c. C-42, s. 27(2)(e)	culte public
religious worship c. C-46, s. 176(2)	office religieux
wrapper	
mark, brand, seal, wrapper or design c. C-46, s. 376(3)	marque, signe, sceau, enveloppe ou dessin
wreck c. C-46, s. 2	épave
receiver of wreck c. C-46, s. 415(b)	receveur des épaves
secrete a wreck/to c. C-46, s. 415(a)	cacher une épave
wrecked	
cargo, stores and tackle of a vessel wrecked, stranded or in distress c. C-46, s. 2	cargaison, approvisionnement, agrès et apparaux d'un navire naufragé, échoué ou en détresse
writ c. B-1, s. 205(2)(a)	bref
writ of assistance c. F-27, s. 42(1) c. N-1, s. 10	mandat de main-forte
writ of execution c. B-1, s. 173(1)(d)(i)	bref d'exécution
writ of fieri facias c. C-46, s. 771(3.1)	bref de saisie-exécution
writ of summons c. C-50, s. 23(3)	bref d'assignation
write-down	
(of value) c. B-1, s. 308(1)	réduction
writing	
duly authorized in writing (as legal representative) c. C-42, s. 2	régulièrement constitués par mandat écrit
in legible writing c. C-46, s. 540(1)(b)(i)	dans une écriture lisible
reduced to writing c. C-42, s. 2	manuscrit
writing off	
(of a debt) c. F-11, s. 25(1)	radiation

writing off of a debt
c. F-11, s. 24(2)

radiation d'une créance

wrong
decision
c. C-46, s. 686(1)(a)(ii)

décision erronée

remedy or redress for a private
or public wrong or grievance
c. C-46, s. 315

réparation ou redressement pour un
tort ou grief privé ou public

to correct a substantial wrong or
miscarriage of justice
c. C-3, s. 21(6)

réparer un dommage important ou
remédier à une erreur judiciaire

wrongful
(transfer)
c. C-44, s. 48(2)

illégal

wrongful act
c. C-46, s. 232(2)

action injuste

wrongful omission
c. A-12, s. 7(2)

omission dommageable

wrongful act
c. B-8, s. 14(a)

acte illégal

c. A-12, s. 7(2)

acte dommageable

wrongly
c. C-44, s. 243(1)

à tort

Y ━━━━━━━━━━━━━━━━━━━

year
calendar year
c. B-2, s. 30(1)

année civile

financial year
c. B-2, s. 30(2)

exercice

**Year's Maximum Pensionable
Earnings**
c. C-17, s. 15(3)

maximum des gains annuels
ouvrant droit à pension

yield
(of security)
c. C-41, s. 57(4)

rapport

**Young Men's Christian
Association of Canada**
c. C-31, s. 16

Young Men's Christian Association
of Canada

young person
c. C-46, s. 733(3)
c. Y-1, s. 2(1)

adolescent

youth court
c. Y-1, s. 2(1)

tribunal pour adolescents

youth court judge
c. Y-1, s. 2(1)

juge du tribunal pour adolescents

youth justice committee
c. Y-1, s. 69

comité de la justice pour la jeunesse

youth worker
c. Y-1, s. 2(1)

délégué à la jeunesse

Yukon Territory Water Board

c. A-1, Schedule I

Office des eaux du territoite du
Yukon

Z

zone
   shipping safety control zone

     c. A-12, s. 2

zone de contrôle de la sécurité de la navigation

a

abandonner
abandon/to

abandonner une action
discontinue/to

abroger
abrogate/to

absent
missing

absolu
unqualified

abus de confiance
breach

acceptant
acceptor

acceptation
acceptance

accepter signification
process

accepteur
accepting

accès
access

accessoire
incidental

accommodement
arrangement

accord
agreement

accord de compensation
clearing

accord de fusion
agreement

accord de réassurance
reinsurance

accorder les frais et dépens
award costs/to

accréditation
certification

accréditer
authorize/to

acheteur de bonne foi
bona fide

acquéreur
purchaser

acquéreur contre valeur
purchaser

acquéreur contre valeur non avisé
purchaser for value without notice

acquéreur-occupant
home purchaser

acquittement
acquittal

acquitter
acquit/to

acte
act

acte constitutif
incorporation

acte criminel
indictable

acte d'accusation
indictment

acte d'accusation distinct
separate

acte d'association
memorandum

acte de cession
assignment

acte de concession
letters patent of land

acte de Dieu
act of God

acte de faillite
bankruptcy

acte de fiducie
deed

acte de procédure
pleadings

Index

acte de transfert
conveyance

acte de vente
bill of sale

acte dommageable
wrongful act

acte illégal
wrongful act

acte judiciaire
process

acte notarié
notarial

acte prohibé
prohibited

acte testamentaire
instrument

actif
estate

action
equity

action au civil
civil

action convertible
convertible

action en divorce
divorce

action en justice collective
action

action en recouvrement
action

action en responsabilité
action

action indirecte
action

action injuste
wrongful

action nominative
registered

action oblique
action

action ordinaire
equity

action pénale
action

action personnelle
action

action pour collision
collision

action privilégiée
preference

action réelle
action

actionnaire
shareholder

adéquat
sufficient

adhésion
accession

adjudication définitive
disposition

adjudication publique
competition

adjuger
award/to

adjuger des frais
costs

admettre d'office
judicially

admettre en franchise
duty

admettre l'appel
allow/to

administrateur
administrator

administrateur séquestre
administrator

administrateur suppléant
alternate

administrateur-dirigeant
officer-director

administration
administration

administration centrale
headquarter

Index

administration publique
authority

administration publique fédérale
public service of Canada

administration scolaire
corporation

administrer
administer/to

admissible
admissible

admissible en justice
evidence

admission d'office
notice

adolescent
person

adopter
pass/to

adoption
passing

adresse aux fins de signification
address for service

adresse du Sénat
address

adresser notification
serve/to

adulte
adult

aéronef
aircraft

affaires
affairs

affaires internes
affairs

affaires publiques
affairs

affectation
disposition

affecter
appropriate/to

affidavit
affidavit

affirmation préliminaire
assertion

affirmation solennelle
declaration

affréteur
charterer

agence
agency

agence de logement public
agency

agent agréé
authorized agent

agent comptable
registrar

agent d'inscription
registrar

agent de nettoyage
agent

agent de placement
agent

agent de recouvrement
agent

agent financier
fiscal agent

agent négociateur
agent

agent payeur
paying officer

agrément
approval

agressions sexuelles graves
assault

ajournement
adjournment

ajourner
adjourn/to

alcoolémie
alcohol

aliénation
disposal

Index

aliénation de biens
disposition

aliénation mentale
insanity

aliéné
insane

aliéner
alienate/to

alinéa
paragraph

alléguer
allege/to

allocation
allowance

allocation de détention
allowance

amende
monetary penalty

ancienneté
seniority

année civile
calendar year

année de rajustement
adjustment

annuité
annuity

annuité différée
annuity

annuité immédiate
annuity

annuité originaire
annuity

annulation
abatement

annulation de mariage
nullity

annuler
forfeit/to

antécédent criminel
history

apparence fausse
appearance

appartenance
ownership

appel
appeal

appel d'une sentence
against

application
administration

appliquer
apply/to

apport
consideration

apposer
attach/to

appréciable
material

appréhender
apprehend/to

approbation
acquiescence

arbitrage
adjudication

arbitrage obligatoire
binding

arbitre
adjudicator

Archives publiques
Public Archives

arguments
representations

arme à autorisation restreinte
restricted

arme à feu historique
antique firearm

arme prohibé
prohibited

arpenteur
surveyor

arrangement
arrangement

arrestation
arrest

Index

arrêt
judgment

arrêt des procédures
stay

arrêté
order

arrêter
apprehend/to

arrêtiste
editor

article
section

assemblée d'actionnaires
meeting

Assemblée des premières nations
Assembly of First Nations

assemblée extraordinaire
meeting

assemblée législative
legislature

assentiment
approval

assertion
assertion

assesseur
assessor

assignation
subpoena

assigner
summon/to

assigner à comparaître
attend/to

assistance raisonnable
assistance

association
association

association coopérative
cooperative

association de bienfaisance
charitable

association mandataire .
agency

association personnalisée
corporation

associé
partner

assurance réciproque
inter-insurance

assurance responsabilité
fidelity bond

attaquer
assault/to

attestation
acknowledgement

attester
certify/to

attribuer
prescribe/to

audience à huis clos
in camera

audience publique
open

audition
hearing

auteur d'un affidavit
affiant

authentiqué
authenticated

authentiquer
authenticate/to

autorisation
approval

autorisation du tribunal
leave

autorisation légitime
lawful

autoriser
authorize/to

autorité
authority

autorité fiscale
authority

Index

autorité législative
  authority

autorité légitime
  authority

autorité provinciale
  enforcement

autorité réglementante
  regulation-making

autorités
  jurisdiction

autorités fédérales
  agencies

autrefois acquit
  autrefois acquit

autrefois convict
  autrefois convict

avance
  advance

avance comptable
  advance

avance de fonds
  advance

avance opportune
  advisable

avant-projet de loi
  draft/to

avantage
  privilege

avantage injustifié
  undue

avarie
  damage

avarie commune
  average

avertissement
  acknowledgement

aveu
  admission

aveu par écrit
  admission

aveux écrits
  acknowledgement

avis
  notice

avis d'évaluation
  assessment

avis d'intention
  intention

avis d'opposition
  claim

avis de comparaître
  appear/to

avis de contravention
  notice

avis de convocation
  meeting

avis de dissidence
  dissent

avis de motion
  motion

avis de renonciation
  quit claim

aviser
  notice

avocat
  advocate

avortement
  abortion

ayant cause
  legal

ayant droit
  assign

b

bail
lease

bail avec option d'achat
lease

bail financier
lease contract

bailleur
landlord

banque
bank

barrement
crossing

bâtiments
tenements

bénéfices non répartis
earnings

bénéficiaire
beneficiary

bertillonnage
Bertillon Signaletic System

bestialité
bestiality

bien corporel
corporeal

bien immobilier
real property

bien lésé
affected

bien meuble
chattel

bien meuble corporel
tangible

bien personnel
personal

bien-fondé
reasonableness

bien-fonds
land

bien-fonds adjacent
adjacent

biens
estate

biens de propriété
property

biens désignés
designated

biens publics
public property

bigammie
bigamy

billet
note

billet à arrêté
promissory note

billet à ordre
promissory note

billet de banque
note

billet de consommation
note

billet de la Banque du Canada
note

billet du Trésor
treasury

blanc de billet de banque
bank note

blessures corporelles
injury

bon
bond

bon du Trésor
exchequer bill

bon père de famille
prudent

bonne conduite
behaviour

bonne et valable contrepartie
good and valuable consideration

bonne foi
good faith

Index

bonnes moeurs
morals

bordereau
memorial

borne
boundary

bref
writ

bref d'assignation
summons

bref d'assignation à témoigner
ad testificandum

bref d'exécution
writ

bref de saisie-arrêt
garnishee

bref de saisie-exécution
fieri facias

bref de subpoena
subpoena

brevet d'invention
patent right

brevet royal
warrant

budget d'investissement
capital

budget de fonctionnement
operating

bulletin de manoeuvre
switching order

bulletin de vote
ballot

Bureau canadien de la sécurité aérienne
Canadian Aviation Safety Board

bureau d'enregistrement
land

bureau des titres de biens-fonds
land titles office

bureau des titres fonciers
land

Bureau du Conseil privé
Privy Council Office

Bureau du droit d'auteur
Copyright Office

C

cabinet
firm

cachet officiel
seal

caduc
lapse/to

caisse d'assitance locative
rent

caisse de crédit
credit union

caisse de réassurance-récolte
Crop Reinsurance Fund

caisse populaire
caisse populaire

capacité
powers

capacité juridique
capacity

capital social
capital

capital social autorisé
authorized

capital souscrit
capital

capital versé
paid-in capital

capital-actions
capital

Index

capitalisation
capitalization

carence
failure

carte de crédit
charge card

cas de force majeure
act of God

casser
quash/to

catégorie d'actions
class

catégorie professionnelle
classification

cause
case

cause d'action
cause of action

causer préjudice
prejudice/to

caution
guarantee

caution pour frais
security

cautionné
principal

cautionnement
bail

cautionnement à fournir
bonding

cédant
assignor

céder
assign/to

certificat d'action
certificate

certificat d'assurance
certificate

certificat de citoyenneté
certificate

certificat de constitution en personne morale
amendment

certificat de jugement
certificate

certificat de libération conditionnelle
certificate

certificat de prorogation
certificate

certificat de valeur mobilière
certificate

certificat modificateur
amendment

certification
certification

certifié authentique
authenticated

certifier
certify/to

certifier authentique
authenticate/to

certiorari
certiorari

cessation
reversal

cessible
assignable

cession
assignment

cession à bail
lease

cession en garantie
assignment

cessionnaire
transferee

charge
encumbrance

charge de la preuve
proof

charge de premier rang
charge

charge flottante
floating charge

Index

charge judiciaire
  office

charges directes
  direct

charte
  charter

charte-partie
  charterparty

châtiment
  punishment

châtiment corporel
  punishment

chef d'accusation séparé
  separate

chef-lieu du comté
  county town

chèque annulé
  cheque

chèque barré
  cheque

chèque non barré
  uncrossed cheque

circonscription électorale
  district

circonscription judiciaire
  division

circonscription territoriale
  division

circonstances aggravantes
  aggravation

circuit
  circuit

citation à comparaître
  appearance

claim minier
  mining claim

clause
  provision

clauses de prorogation
  articles

clémence royale
  mercy

clôture
  close

coalition
  combine

coauteur
  party

Code canadien du travail
  Canada Labour Code

Code criminel
  Criminal Code

Code maritime
  Maritime Code

codétenteur
  joint

collusion
  collusion

comité consultatif
  advisory

comité d'administration
  committee

comité de révision
  Review Committee

comité de surveillance
  Review Committee

comité exécutif
  committee

comité permanent
  standing committee

commanditaire
  partner

commandité
  partner

commercialisation
  marketing

commettant
  principal

comminatoire
  comminatory

commissaire aux brevets
  commissioner

commissaire aux serments
  affidavits

Index

commissaire-conciliateur
commissioner

commission
commission

Commission d'appel du droit d'auteur
Copyright Appeal Board

commission d'enquête
board

commission d'examen
review board

commission de conciliation
board

Commission de la fonction publique
Public Service Commission

commission de révision
Review Tribunal

commission mixte
commission

commission rogatoire
commission

commission sous le sceau
commission

commissionnaire
commission merchant

common law d'Angleterre
common law

commuer
commute/to

communauté urbaine
metropolitan area

communication
disclosure

communiquer
disclose/to

compagnie
company

compagnie constituée en personne morale
company

compagnie de fiducie
trust

compagnie par actions
company

compagnie privée
company

comparaître
appear/to

comparution
appearance

compensation
clearance

compétence
authority

compétence en matière personnelle
in personam

compétence en matière réelle
in rem

compétence exclusive
sole

compétence territoriale
jurisdiction

compétent
appropriate

complice après le fait
accessory

complot
conspiracy

comportement sexuel
activity

comptabiliser
account/to

comptabilité
accounting

comptable
accountable

compte
account

compte d'indemnisation placement
Investor's Indemnity Account

compte de capital
capital

Index

concédant
grantor

concesseur
grantor

concession
concession

concessionnaire
grantee

conciliateur
conciliation

conciliation
conciliation

conclure
conclude/to

conclure un accord
agreement

conclure un contrat
contract

conclusion
finding

conclusion du contrat
conclusion

concussion
misappropriation

condamner
sentence/to

condition préalable
condition precedent

conditions
terms

conditions d'appartenance
membership

conduite criminelle
conduct

conduite illicite
behaviour

conduite publique
conduct

conduite vexatoire
vexatious

conférence préparatoire
conference

conférer
vest/to

confirmation
affirmance

confirmer
affirm/to

confiscation
forfeiture

confisquer
forfeit/to

conflit d'intérêts
conflict of interest

conformité
correctness

congédiement justifié
cause

congédier
discharge/to

conjointement
jointly

connaissance d'office
notice

connaissement
bill

connaître d'une plainte
determine/to

connaître de
determine/to

conseil
solicitor

Conseil canadien de la
magistrature
Canadian Judicial Council

conseil d'administration
board

Conseil des Arts du Canada
Canada Council

Conseil privé de la Reine pour
le Canada
Queen's Privy Council for Canada

conseiller juridique
counsel

Index

consentement
consent

consentir
consent/to

conservateur
master

conservateur des titres et hypothèques
registrar

considération raisonnable
reasonable

considération valable
valuable

consignataire
consignee

consignateur
consignor

consignation
consignment

consigner
enter/to

consolider
consolidate/to

constituer en personne morale
incorporate/to

constituer une fin de non-recevoir
bar/to

constitution
incorporation

constitution de charges
encumbered

constitution de jury
jury

contaminant
air contaminant

contaminant atmosphérique
air contaminant

contester
defend/to

contingence
contingency

contracter
enter into/to

contraindre à comparaître
appearance

contrainte par corps
attachment

contrat
contract

contrat annulable
voidable

contrat d'acquisition
contract

contrat d'affrètement coque nue
bareboat charter

contrat de fiducie
agreement

contrat de location
agreement

contrat de service
contract

contrat de société de personnes
agreement

contrat de souscription
agreement

contrat exprès
express

contrat important
material

contrat tacite
implied

contravention
contravention

contre rémunération
valuable

contre valeur
for value

contre-accusation
countercharge

contre-interrogatoire
cross-examination

contre-interroger
cross-examine/to

Index

contrefaçon
infringing

contrefacteur
infringer

contrepartie
consideration

contrepartie valable
consideration

contresigner
back/to

contrevenant
offender

contributeur
contributor

contrôle
control

contrôle d'application
administration

contrôle judiciaire
review

contrôler
monitor/to

contrôleur général du Canada
Comptroller General of Canada

convaincre
satisfy/to

convention
agreement

convention collective
collective agreement

convention d'assurer
covenant

convention de fusion
amalgamation

convention de vente
agreement

convention de vote fiduciaire
voting trust

convention unanime des actionnaires
unanimous shareholder agreement

conversion
conversion

convertir
convert/to

convocation
appointment

coopérative
cooperative

copie certifiée
certified

copie certifiée conforme
copy

copie conforme
copy

copie notariée
notarial

Corporation commerciale canadienne
Canadian Commercial Corporation

Corporation de disposition des biens de la Couronne
Crown Assets Disposal Corporation

corps dirigeant
governing body

corps non doté de la personnalité morale
unincorporated

corroboration
corroboration

cotisant
contributor

cotisation d'affiliation
membership

cotiser
contribute/to

coupon d'intérêt
coupon

cour
court

Cour canadienne de l'impôt
Tax Court of Canada

Index

cour d'archives
court

cour de district
court

cour de district de l'Ontario
District Court of Ontario

cour de juridiction criminelle
jurisdiction

cour des poursuites sommaires
court

cour générale d'appel
court

cour supérieure
superior court

cour supérieure d'archives
court

Cour suprême de l'Ontario
Supreme Court of Ontario

covérificateur
joint

créance
claim

créance comptable
book debt

créance conditionnelle
claim

créance douteuse
doubtful debt

créance éventuelle
claim

créance irrécouvrable
bad debt

créancier
claimant

créancier chirographaire
creditor

créancier gagiste
pledgee

créancier garanti
creditor

créancier hypothécaire
incumbrancer

créancier lié
related

créancier pétitionnaire
petitioning creditor

crédit
appropriation

crédit budgétaire
note

crédit-bail financier
leasing

crime d'incendie
arson

curateur
committee

d

date d'entrée en vigueur
effective

date de référence
record date

débarcadère
landing

débarrer
reopen/to

débats
hearing

débenture
debenture

débenture bancaire
debenture

débenture perpétuelle
debenture

débentures-actions
debenture

débiteur hypothécaire
mortgagor

Index

débiteur par jugement
debtor

débours
disbursement

déboursés
disbursements

décerner
issue/to

décharge
discharge

décider
determine/to

décision
adjudication

décision arbitrale
award

décision finale
disposition

décision judiciaire
judgment

décision sans appel
final

décision sommaire
determination

déclarant
declarant

déclaration
presentment

déclaration d'intérêt
interest

déclaration de culpabilité
conviction

déclaration de culpabilité par procédure sommaire
summary conviction

déclaration de faits importants
material

déclaration fausse
statement

déclaration solennelle
declaration

déclaration sous serment
sworn statement

déclaration trompeuse
misleading

déclarer
disclose/to

déclarer coupable
convict/to

déclarer coupable par procédure sommaire
summarily

décret
order

dédommagement
satisfaction

défaut
defect

défense au fond
merits

défense d'une cause
advocacy

déférer
transfer/to

déficience mentale
mental defectiveness

dégagement
release

dégrader
commit waste/to

délai convenable
reasonable

délai de grâce
days of grace

délai ferme
definite

délai raisonnable
time

délégation
assignment

délégué à la jeunesse
worker

Index

déléguer
authorize to perform/to

délibérations
proceedings

délinquant
offender

délit
delict

délivrance
granting

délivrer
issue/to

délivrer un avis
deliver/to

demande
application

demande d'adhésion
membership

demande d'autorisation d'appel
application

demande ex parte
application

demande formelle
demand

demande introductive
statement

demande reconventionnelle
counter-claim

demande sommaire
application

demander la taxation
costs

demandeur
applicant

demandeur reconventionnel
counterclaimant

démission
resignation

démontrer
show cause/to

dénomination
name

dénomination sociale
name

dénonciateur
informant

dénonciation
information

département d'État
Ministry of State

dépenses d'exploitation
expenses

déposant
deponent

déposer
file/to

déposer en justice
evidence

déposer sous serment
evidence

déposer une plainte
complaint

dépositaire
bailee

déposition
deposition

dépôt
deposit

dépôt à vue
demand

dépouiller
count/to

dépourvu de personnalité morale
unincorporated

désavantager
discriminate/to

désaveu
avoidance

désignation
trade-name

désigner
appoint/to

Index

désigner un avocat
appoint counsel/to

désistement
discontinuance

destituer
dismiss/to

détenir en fiducie
trust

détenteur
holder

détenteur à titre onéreux
value

détenteur inscrit
registered

détenteur régulier
holder in due course

détention
custody

détenu
inmate

déterminer
prescribe/to

détournement
conversion

dette
debt

dettes
liabilities

devoir
duty

dévolution
vesting

dévolution de la Couronne
demise

dévolution légale
devolution

diffamation
libel

diffamation écrite
libel

diffamation verbale
slander

différend
controversy

diffusion
distribution

diligence
diligence

diligence nécessaire
care

diligence normale
diligence

diligence raisonnable
diligence

directeur de l'enregistrement
deeds

direction
governing body

diriger
direct/to

discrimination
discriminate/to

dispenser
waive/to

disposant
settlor

disposer de
deal with/to

disposition
clause

disposition contractuelle
contract

disposition de fond
substantive

disposition législative
law

disposition testamentaire
appointment

disposition transitoire
transitional

dissidence
dissent

dissoudre
dissolve/to

Index

district judiciaire
district

diviser un chef d'accusation
divide/to

division judiciaire
division

divulgation
declaration

divulguer
communicate/to

document
record

document comptable
record

document d'autorisation
authorization

dol
misconduct

dolosif
fraudulent

domaine public
public property

domicile
domicile

domicile légal
legal

dommage
damage

dommage certain
damage

dommage direct
loss

dommage professionnel
injury

dommages-intérêts
damages

dommages-intérêts punitifs
damages

don
gift

donner à bail
lease/to

donner avis
notice

donner en gage
pledge/to

donner en garantie
pledge/to

donner mainlevée
release/to

donner quittance
discharge/to

dossier judiciaire
judicial

doté de la personnalité morale
incorporated

doute raisonnable
reasonable

doute sérieux
reasonable

drogue contrôlée
drug

drogue d'usage restreint
drug

droit
estate

droit à la dissidence
dissent

droit d'action
cause of action

droit d'action au civil
civil right of action

droit d'auteur
copyright

droit de jouissance
interest

droit de la preuve
evidence

droit de permis
fee

droit de possession
possession

droit de préemption
pre-emptive

Index

droit de propriété
estate

droit de rachat
redemption

droit de réméré
redemption

droit de rétention
lien

droit de réversibilité
reversionary interest

droit de réversion
reversioner

droit de suffrage
suffrage

droit de tirage
drawing

droit des sociétés
law

droit du lieu
laws

droit du véritable propriétaire
beneficial

droit exclusif
right

droit incorporel
chose in action

droit interne
laws

droit réel immobilier
interest

droit subjectif
rights

droit substantif
substantive

droits conjugaux
conjugal rights

e

eaux fédérales
waters

eaux intérieures
waters

eaux internationales
waters

eaux limitrophes
waters

échéance
maturity

échec du mariage
breakdown

écrou
reception

édicter
enact/to

effacer une condamnation
vacate/to

effectifs
employee

effet
effect

effet de commerce
instrument

effet de commerce garanti
note

effet de second rang
note

effet négociable
instrument

effet transférable
transferable

effets
goods

efficace
effectual

effraction
break

élargissement définitif
discharge

Index

élément de preuve
evidence

émetteur
issuer

émettre
issue/to

émission
issue

émission publique
distribution

emploi
appointment

employé
employee

emprise
right-of-way

enceinte
curtilage

enchères publiques
auction

enchérir
bid/to

enchérisseur
bidder

encourager
abet/to

endossataire
endorsee

endossé en blanc
in blank

endossement
endorsement

endossement en blanc
blank

endossement nominatif
endorsement

endossement obligatoire
endorsement

endossement restrictif
endorsement

endossement spécial
endorsement

endosser
endorse/to

endosseur
endorser

enfant à charge
child

enfant naturel
natural child

engagement
covenant

engagement d'achat
agreement

engagement de revente
agreement

engagement financier
commitment

engager
institute/to

engager une action
bring/to

engager une poursuite
proceedings

enjoindre
direct/to

enlèvement
abduction

énoncé d'intention
intention

énonciation
statement

enquête
inquiry

enquête préliminaire
preliminary inquiry

enregistrement
registration

enregistrer
enter/to

ensemble d'habitation
housing

ensemble d'habitation public
housing

Index

entendre
hear/to

entente
agreement

entité
entity

entreprise
business

entreprise commerciale
business

entreprise unipersonnelle
sole

entreprises fédérales
federal business

entrer en vigueur
come into force/to

épreuve de sang
blood test

équitable
fair

équité
fairness

equity
equitable

erreur de procédure
technical

erreur judiciaire
miscarriage of justice

esprit
intent

ester en justice
action

estimateur
appraiser

estimateur-expert
appraiser

estimer
deem/to

établir
make/to

établir une cotisation
assess/to

établissement
business

établissement commercial
business

établissement financier
institution

établissement principal
business

établissement public
corporation

État
Crown

éteindre
discharge/to

étranger
alien

être affilié
affiliated/to be

être dévolu
devolve/to

être dévolu à
vest in/to

être en faillite
bankrupt/to be

être présumé
presumed/to be

être réputé
presumed/to be

être traduit en justice
amenable/to be

évaluateur
assessor

évaluation de sécurité
assessment

éventualité
contingency

évoquer
remove/to

ex-époux
former spouse

exact
fair

Index

examen
discovery

examinateur
examiner

excès de compétence
jurisdiction

excuse légitime
lawful

exécuter
enforce/to

exécuter un jugement
satisfy/to

exécuteur
executor

exécution
completion

exécution d'un acte judiciaire
execution

exécution intégrale
specific performance

exécutoire
effect

exemption
remission

exemption de base
basic

expectative
expectant on

expert
adviser

expiration
expiration

exploitation agricole
farm

exploitation commerciale
business

exposé
statement

exposé du juge au jury
charge

exposé du poursuivant
address

exposer
allege/to

exproprier un terrain
take/to

extrait
extract

extrait de titre
abstract

f

fabrique
fabrique

facteur
factor

faible d'esprit
unsound mind

failli
bankrupt

faire droit à un appel
allow/to

faire foi
evidence

faire obstacle
bar/to

faire prêter serment
administer/to

faire une dénonciation
lay/to

fait générateur
cause of action

fait important
material

falsifier
adulterate/to

Index

fausse assertion
  statement

fausse déclaration
  misrepresentation

faute
  default

faux frais
  incidental

fête du Canada
  Canada Day

fiduciaire
  fiduciary

fiducie
  in trust

fiducie de fonds mutuels
  mutual fund

fiducie explicite
  trust

fiducie expresse
  express

fiducie implicite
  trust

fiducie judiciaire
  constructive trust

filiale
  subsidiary

firme
  firm

fixer
  prescribe/to

fol enchérisseur
  bidder

folle enchère
  bidding

fonction
  appointment

fonction judiciaire
  adjudicative

fonction publique
  duty

fonctionnaire
  employee

fonctionnaire du tribunal
  officer

fonctionnaire judiciaire
  officer

fonctionnaire public
  public officer

fonctionnaire public ès qualités
  capacity

fonctionnement
  operation

fonctionnement interne
  affairs

fondateur
  incorporator

fondé de pouvoir
  attorney

fonds d'amortissement
  fund

fonds d'investissement à capital variable
  fund

fonds de commerce
  stock-in-trade

fonds de garantie
  guarantee

fonds de roulement
  capital

fonds en fiducie
  fund

fonds public
  public money

fonds réservé
  fund

force probante
  probative force

force raisonnable
  reasonable

forclusion
  foreclosure

formule d'édiction
  enacting

Index

fouille autorisée
authorized

fouiller
search/to

fractionnement
division

frais
charge

frais de constitution
expenses

frais de représentation
allowance

frais et charges
costs

frais et dépens
costs

frais judiciaires
legal

frais modérateurs
user

franchise
franchise

frauder
defraud/to

frauduleusement
fraudulently

frauduleux
fraudulent

frustrer
defraud/to

fusion
amalgamation

fusion horizontale simplifiée
amalgamation

fusion verticale simplifiée
amalgamation

fusionner
amalgamate/to

g

gage
bailment

gager
secure/to

gain de survie
survivorship

garant
guarantor

garanti
secured

garantie
guarantee

garantie subsidiaire
collateral

garanties suffisantes
assurance

garantir
secure/to

garantir par un cautionnement
bond

garde
control

garde en milieu fermé
secure custody

garde en milieu ouvert
custody

garde légale
custody

gardien
custodian

Gazette du Canada
Canada Gazette

gens de loi
members

gérer
deal with/to

Index

gestion financière
management

gestion publique
administration

gouverneur de la Banque du Canada
Governor of the Bank of Canada

gouverneur en conseil
Governor in Council

grand jury
jury

grand sceau
Great Seal

greffe de la cour
Registry

greffier
Clerk

greffier de la Couronne
clerk

greffier du Conseil privé
Clerk of the Privy Council

grever
charge/to

grever d'une hypothèque
hypothecate/to

grever d'une sûreté
secure/to

groupement lié
group

h

habeas corpus ad subjiciendum
habeas corpus ad subjiciendum

habilitation
authority

habiliter
authorize/to

habitation multifamiliale
dwelling

harasser
harass/to

harcèlement
baiting

Haute Cour
High Court

haute partie contractante
High Contracting Party

héritier
heir

héritiers
successors

homicide coupable
culpable

homicide involontaire coupable
manslaughter

homicide non coupable
non culpable homicide

homologation
sanction

honoraires
fee

honoraires et frais
costs

honoraires légaux
fees

honorer une obligation
discharge/to

hôpital accrédité
accredited hospital

huis clos
in camera

huissier
bailiff

hypothèque
hypothec

Index

hypothèque subsidiaire
collateral

hypothèque sur des biens

meubles
chattel

i

illégal
unlawful

immatriculation
registration

immatriculer
register/to

immeuble
immovable property

immeuble détenu en propriété libre et perpétuelle
estate

immeuble loué à bail
leasehold

immunité
privilege

immunité absolue
absolute

immunité relative
privilege

impôt foncier
tax

imprimé
pre-printed

imprimeur de la Reine
Queen's Printer

imputation
application

imputé
alleged

imputer
allege/to

inadmissible
objectionable

incapable
incompetent

incarcération
commitment

incorporel
incorporeal

inculper
charge/to

indemnisation
compensation

indemnité
allowance

indemnité annuelle de session
allowance

indemnité compensatoire
compensation

indemnité de départ
severance

indemnité de vie chère
compensation

indication
representation

indications fausses
representation

indice des prix à la consommation
Consumer Price Index

inexécution
breach

infirmer
reverse/to

informateur
informant

informer
notify/to

informer le jury
instruct/to

Index

infraction
contravention

infraction comprise
offence

infraction de délinquance
delinquency

infraction distincte
offence

infraction présumée
alleged

infraction principale
principal

initié
insider

injonction
injunction

injonction provisoire
interim

inobservation
default

inopérant
effect

inscription
endorsement

inscrire
endorse/to

inscrire un plaidoyer
enter/to

instance
proceeding

instituer
appoint/to

institution financière
financial institution

instruction
direction

instruction sommaire
summary

instruire
determine/to

instruire le procès
trial

instrument
deed

instrument d'adhésion
adherence

instrument testamentaire
testamentary

intenter
bring/to

intenter une accusation
prefer/to

intenter une action
proceed/to

intenter une poursuite
proceedings

intention
intent

interdire
bar/to

intérêt
best interests

intérêt prépondérant
interest

intérêt public
benefit

intérimaire
interim

interjeter appel
appeal

interpréter
construe/to

interrogatoire
examination

interrogatoire au préalable
discovery

interrogatoire explicatif
examination

intervenant
honour

intervenir
intervene/to

intervention
honour

Index

intestat
intestate

introduction
commencement

introduction par effraction
breaking and entering

intrus
trespasser

intrusion
trespassing

invalider
invalidate/to

invalidité mentale
disability

invalidité physique
disability

inventaire
record

invoquer un droit
claim/to

irrégularité
defect

j

joindre
attach/to

jouissance
beneficial

jour chômé
non-working day

jour franc
clear

jour juridique
juridical day

jour ouvrable
day

juge
court

juge de paix
justice

juge en chef
Chief Justice

juge en chef suppléant
acting

juge instructeur
judge

juge puîné
puisne

juge siégeant en chambre
chambers

juge suppléant
ad hoc

juge surnuméraire
supernumerary

jugement
adjudication

jugement d'homologation
probate

jugement déclaratoire
declaratory

jugement définitif
final

jugement formel
judgment

jugement interlocutoire
interlocutory

jugement irrévocable de divorce
decree absolute of divorce

jugement sur appel
disposition

juger
deem/to

juger l'affaire au fond
merits

juridiction concurrente
jurisdiction

Index

juridiction d'appel en matière civile
appellate

juridiction d'appel en matière pénale
appellate

juridiction inférieure
court

juridiction normalement compétente
ordinary court

juridiction suprême en matière d'appel au civil
appellate

jury mixte
jury

juste
fair

juste valeur
fair value

juste valeur du marché
value

juste valeur marchande
fair market value

justice naturelle
justice

l

lancer une assignation
issue/to

lancer une sommation
issue/to

légalité
legality

législation
laws

législature
legislature

légitime défense
self-defence

legs
bequest

léser
aggrieve/to

lésion corporelle
harm

lésion corporelle grave
bodily harm

lésion physique
injury

lettre
note

lettre de change
bill

lettre de complaisance
bill

lettre de consommation
bill

lettre de crédit
letter of credit

lettre de transport aérien
air waybill

lettre de voiture
bill

lettre intérieure
bill

lettres patentes
letters patent

libelle
libel

libelle blasphématoire
blasphemous libel

libelle diffamatoire
defamatory libel

libération
discharge

Index

libération conditionnelle
parole

libération conditionnelle de jour
parole

libération inconditionnelle
discharge

libéré conditionnel
inmate

libérer
discharge/to

liberté surveillée
mandatory supervision

licence
licence

licence obligatoire
compulsory

licenciement
termination

licencier
discharge/to

lien fiduciaire
fiduciary

liens
associate

liens de sang
blood relationship

lier
bind/to

lieu de compétence
jurisdiction

lieux
premises

ligne de démarcation de terrains
boundary

liquidateur
liquidator

liquidation
liquidation

liste des jurys
jury

litige
controversy

livraison
delivery

livraison de biens-fonds
delivery

livrer
deliver/to

local d'habitation
dwelling-place

locataire
lessee

locateur
lessor

location
hire

lock-out
lockout

logement familial
housing

loi
statute

loi d'intérêt privé
private

loi de crédits
appropriation

loi du lieu
law

loi fédérale
Act of Parliament

lopin de terre
parcel of land

lotissement
subdivision

lots
parcels

louage
hire

louage de service
hiring out

louer
lease/to

Index

m

magistrat stipendiaire
stipendiary magistrate

maison d'affaires
firm

maison d'habitation
dwelling house

maison de commerce
firm

maison de correction
reformatory

maison unifamiliale
dwelling

maladie mentale
insanity

malversation
malfeasance

mandant
principal

mandat
incumbency

mandat d'arrestation
warrant

mandat d'exécution
execution

mandat d'extradition
warrant

mandat d'incarcération
committal

mandat de dépôt
committal

mandat de main-forte
writ

mandat de perquisition
warrant

mandat de transfèrement
warrant

mandataire
agent

mandater
authorize/to

manquement
breach

manutention
handling

marchandises
goods

marché
contract

marché libre
market

marque
mark

marque de commerce
trade-mark

marque distinctive
brand-mark

masse des biens
assets

matière non protégée
non-copyright

mauvaise conduite
misbehaviour

médecin qualifié
practitioner

méfait public
mischief

membre du Parlement
member

mémoire
memorial

mémoire d'acquittement
memorandum

Index

mémoire d'honoraires
bill

mémoire de conventions
memorandum

mémorandum
memorandum

mémorandum de convention
memorandum

mention
endorsement

mesure
action

mesure conservatoire
conservatory measure

mesure de rechange
alternative measures

mettre à couvert
indemnify/to

mettre à exécution
act on/to

mettre en cause
add/to

mettre en demeure
demand/to

mettre en gage
pledge/to

mettre sous séquestre
impound/to

meuble
personal

meurtre au deuxième degré
murder

meurtre au premier degré
first degree murder

meurtre non qualifié
murder

mineur
infant

ministre
Crown

ministre de tutelle
appropriate

ministre fédéral
minister

ministre provincial
minister

minorité
minority

mise au rôle
entry

mise en accusation
conviction

mise en demeure
notice

mise en détention
custody

mise en liberté
release

mise en oeuvre
administration

mise en tutelle
trusteeship

mission
objects

mission de constatation
authority

modalités
terms

mode de dépouillement
ballots

mode de scrutin
ballots

modification connexe
amendment

modification corrélative
amendment

monopole
monopoly

moralité publique
morals

moratoire
moratoria

motif de dissidence
dissent

motif raisonnable
reasonable

motifs
reasons

motion
motion

motiver
reasons

moyen de défense
défence

moyen de défense péremptoire
défence

municipalité
corporation

n

nantir
hypothecate/to

nantissement
chattel mortgage

négligence
neglect

négligence coupable
culpable

négligence criminelle
negligence

négligence volontaire
neglect

négociable
transferable

noliser
charter/to

nom commercial
trade-name

nom commercial ou dénomination sociale
corporate

nomination
appointment

nommer
appoint/to

notaire
notary

notaire public
notary public

notation de protêt
protest

note marginale
marginal

notice légale
notice

notice modificative
amendment

notification
notification

notification écrite
notice

notifier
notify/to

nouvelle société
amalgamated

nuire
injure/to

nuisance publique
common nuisance

numéraire
cash

Index

O _____

objection
  objection

obligation
  duty

obligation alimentaire
  maintenance

obligation contractuelle
  obligation

obligation de représentant
  fiduciary

obligation fiduciaire
  fiduciary

obligation légale
  duty

obligé
  person

observation
  representation

occupant
  occupier

octroi
  granting

octroyeur de licence
  licensor

oeuvre
  work

oeuvre artistique
  artistic work

oeuvre cinématographique
  cinematograph

oeuvre d'art architecturale
  architectural work of art

oeuvre de charité
  charitable

oeuvre dramatique
  dramatic work

oeuvre litéraire
  literary

oeuvre musicale
  musical work

offenser
  injure/to

office mixte
  board

officier public
  notary public

offre
  bid

offre d'achat
  application

offre d'achat avec échange
d'actions
  bid

offre d'achat visant à la
mainmise
  take-over bid

offre franche
  exempt offer

omission
  default

omission dommageable
  wrongful

omission volontaire
  wilful

opérant
  effect

opération
  transaction

opérations bancaires
  banking

opinion
  opinion

opportunité
  advisability

opposant
  adverse

opposition
  objection

option d'achat
  call

Index

option d'achat d'actions
warrant

ordonnance
order

ordonnance alimentaire
support

ordonnance conditionnelle
order

**ordonnance d'attribution de
paternité**
affiliation order

ordonnance d'interdiction
prohibition

ordonnance de confiscation
order

ordonnance de garde
custody

**ordonnance de libération
absolue**
discharge

**ordonnance de mise sous
séquestre**
order

**ordonnance de pension
alimentaire**
order

ordonnance de placement
committal

ordonnance de probation
order

ordonnance de restitution
restoration

ordonnance de séquestre
receiving

**ordonnance de soutien
financier**
support

ordonnance déclaratoire
declaratory

ordonnance définitive
final

ordonnance pour traitement
treatment order

ordonner
direct/to

organe collégial
body

organe directeur
governing body

organisme
agency

organisme consultatif
advisory

organisme de bienfaisance
charitable

organisme de charité enregistré
charity

organisme de logement public
agency

organisme de vente
agency

organisme fédéral
board

**organisme non constitué en
personne morale**
unincorporated

organisme privé
agency

organisme public
agency

outrage au tribunal
contempt

Index

Index

personne fictive
fictitious person

personne juridique de droit public
public body

personne lésée
aggrieved

personne morale
body corporate

personne morale absorbée
amalgamating

personne morale constituée
company

personne morale de régime fédéral
company

personne morale fusionnante
amalgamating

personne morale issue de la fusion
amalgamated

personne morale mère
holding

personne physique
natural person

personne prudente et avisée
prudent

perte
loss

pertinent
material

pétition
petition

pétitionnaire
petitioner

pièce
record

pièce à conviction
evidence

plaidoirie
pleading

plaidoyer
plea

plaidoyer de justification
justification

plaidoyer de non-culpabilité
plea

plaignant
complainant

plainte
complaint

plan d'entreprise
corporate

plan d'urbanisme
plan

pleine propriété
fee simple

plus-value
accretion to the value

pollicitant
offerer

pollicitation
offer

pollicité
offeree

pollution atmosphérique
air pollution

portefeuille
holdings

porter atteinte
prejudice/to

porter en justice
sue/to

porter préjudice
injurious/to be

porteur
holder

porteur de licence
licensee

possesseur
owner

possesseur légitime
possession

possession
in possession

personne fictive

Index

possession effective
  possession

possession matérielle
  actual

possession réelle
  actual

pot-de-vin
  bribe

poursuite
  proceedings

poursuite administrative
  action

poursuite civile
  civil action

poursuite pénale
  action

poursuivant
  prosecutor

poursuivant à titre privé
  private prosecutor

poursuivre
  prosecute/to

pouvoir
  power

pouvoir auxiliaire ou accessoire
  ancillary

pouvoir de nomination
  appointment

pouvoir de vendre
  power of sale

pouvoir discrétionnaire
  discretion

pouvoir exécutif
  government

pouvoir judiciaire
  authority

pouvoir judiciaire
discrétionnaire
  discretion

pouvoir libératoire
  tender

pouvoir public
  government

pouvoir réglementaire
  regulative

pratique
  practice

pratique commerciale
  business

pratique commerciale
restrictive
  restraint

préambule
  preamble

préavis
  intention

préavis suffisant
  reasonable

préciser
  prescribe/to

prédécesseur en titre
  predecessor in title

préjudice
  loss

préjudice abusif
  hardship

préjudice injustifié
  hardship

prélèvement
  assessment

premier dirigeant
  chief executive officer

prendre
  institute/to

prendre à bail
  lease/to

prendre effet
  effective

prendre possession
  acquire/to

prendre un décret
  order

Index

prendre un règlement
enact/to

prendre une mesure
deal with/to

prendre une ordonnance
direction

preneur
payee

prépondérance des probabilités
balance

préposé
servant

prérogative
prerogative

prescription
direction

prescrire
direct/to

présence
attendance

présentation
presentation

présenter
file/to

présenter une observation
representation

présenter une preuve
lead/to

président intérimaire
acting

président suppléant
acting

présomption
presumption

presse parlée
broadcast

prestation
benefit

prestation de base
basic

présumer
deem/to

prêt à la grosse
bottomry

prêt à paiements progressifs
mortgage

prêt au jour le jour
day loan

prêt de base
base loan

prêt garanti à l'agrandissement
guaranteed home extension loan

prêt sur hypothèque
mortgage loan

prétendre
claim/to

prétendu
alleged

prétendue violation
alleged

prêter serment
oath

preuve
proof

preuve concluante
conclusive

preuve nouvelle
evidence

preuve péremptoire
conclusive

preuve pertinente
evidence

preuve substantielle
evidence

prévarication
malfeasance

prévenu
accused

prévoir
prescribe/to

prévôt
marshal

principal
principal

Index

principal établissement
business

principal lieu d'affaires
business

prise d'un décret
order

prise de possession
entry

prise en charge
assumption

prise en gage
pawn

prison spéciale
prison

privilège de constructeur
lien

privilège de conversion
privilege

prix
consideration

prix de base
base price

probation
probation

procédé
procedure

procédure
practice

procédure administrative
proceeding

procédure civile
proceeding

procédure en équité
equity

procédure judiciaire
procedure

procédure ordinaire
ordinary

procédure pénale
proceeding

procédure sommaire
conviction

procédures de forclusion
proceedings

procès
action

procès de novo
de novo

procès séparé
separate

procès-verbal
declaration

procès-verbal de décision
memorandum

proclamation
proclamation

procuration
power of attorney

procuration écrite
power of attorney

procureur
attorney

procureur général du Canada
Attorney General of Canada

producteur-exploitant
actual

produire une preuve
adduce/to

programme d'adaptation
adjustment

projet d'acte d'accusation
bill

promesse de cession
agreement

promesse de comparaître
appear/to

prononcé
delivery

prononcé du jugement
giving

prononcer
find/to

propriétaire
landlord

Index

propriétaire immatriculé
registered

propriétaire inscrit
registered

propriétaire légitime
lawful

propriétaire primitif
original

propriétaire-occupant
home owner

propriété
ownership

propriété bénéficiaire
beneficial ownership

propriété effective
beneficial

propriété foncière
freehold

prorogation
extension

prorogation de délai
time

prospectus
prospectus

protestation
protest

protester
protest/to

protêt
protest

protonotaire
prothonotary

provision
appropriation

provisoire
interim

publicité suffisante
reasonable

purger
serve/to

q

qualité
authority

quasi-délit
quasi-delict

question de droit
law

quittance
discharge

quittance de l'échiquier
exchequer acquittance

quo warranto
quo warranto

r

rachat
redemption

rapport d'évaluation
progress report

rapport prédécisionnel
pre-disposition report

ratification
ratification

ratifier
ratify/to

réalisable
enforceable

réalisation
disposition

réaliser
realize/to

Index

récépissé
receipt

recettes
receipts

receveur général
Receiver General

recevoir en preuve
admit/to

recevoir signification
process

recevoir un affidavit
receive/to

**recevoir une affirmation
solennelle**
affirmation

recevoir une déclaration
administer/to

recevoir une plainte
complaint

récidive
subsequent

réclamant
claimant

réclamation
claim

réclamation garantie
secured

réclamation privilégiée
preferred

récoltes sur pied
crops growing or produced on the
farm

recommandataire
referee

récompense
reward

réconciliation
reconciliation

reconduction
renewal

reconnaissance
acknowledgement

reconstitution
revival

recorder
recorder

recours
proceedings

recours civil
remedy

recours en grâce
clemency

recours en révision
review

recouvrement
enforcement

rectification
rectification

reçu
receipt

recueillir des témoignages
evidence

récuser le tableau des jurés
array

redevable
accountable

redevance
charge

redressement
redress

refondre
revise/to

réfutation
rebuttal

régie
control

région désignée
area

régir
regulate/to

registraire
Registrar

registraire adjoint
Deputy Registrar

Index

registraire général du Canada
Registrar General of Canada

registrateur
registrar

registrateur des titres
registrar

registre
record

registre des droits d'auteur
Register of Copyrights

registre des jurés
juror's book

règle de droit
law

règlement
determination

règlement administratif
by-law

règlement administratif homologué
charter by-law

règlement d'application
regulation

réglementation
regulation

réglementer
regulate/to

régler
regulate/to

règles de cour
court

regroupement
consolidation

regroupement d'entreprises
business

réhabilitation
pardon

réinsertion sociale
rehabilitation

réinstruire
rehear/to

rejet de l'appel
dismissal

rejeter
dismiss/to

rejeter l'appel
dismiss/to

rejeter une action
dismiss/to

remettre
surrender/to

remise
allowance

remise de biens
delivery

remplir une condition
satisfy/to

rémunération
reward

rendre compte
account for/to

rendre exécutoire
enforce/to

rendre un jugement
render/to

rendre une décision
disposition

rendre une ordonnance
order

renoncer
surrender/to

renonciation
waiver

rente foncière
ground rent

rentrée en possession
repossession

renvoi
remand

renvoyer
discharge/to

réparation
benefit

Index

répartition provisoire
interim distribution

réplique
answer

répondant
guarantor

reporter
postpone/to

repousser une preuve
rebut/to

représentant
fiduciary

représentant légal
legal

représentant personnel
personal

représentation
representation

réputation
character

réputer
deem/to

requérant
applicant

requête
motion

requête pour faire annuler
quash/to

réquisitionner un bien
requisition/to

rescision
rescind/to

réserve
reservation

réserve secondaire moyenne
average secondary reserve

résidence
latest

résidence habituelle
residence

résidence principale
residence

résident permanent
permanent

résilier
terminate/to

résolution de rejet
resolution

résolution ordinaire
resolution

résolution spéciale
resolution

responsabilité
liability

responsabilité civile
liability

responsabilité civile délictuelle
liability

responsabilité pénale
responsibility

responsabilité solidaire
jointly and severally liable

responsable
accountable

ressort
competence

restituer
surrender/to

restitution
restitution

restriction du commerce
restraint

résumé
summing up

rétablissement
revival

rétention
retention

retourner
revert/to

rétribution
compensation

révélation
disclosure

Index

Index

séparation judiciaire
judicial

série
series

serment professionnel
oath

Service canadien du
renseignement de sécurité
Canadian Security Intelligence
Service

servitude
charge

servitude foncière
charge

sévices graves à la personne
injury

shérif
sheriff

siège social
head office

signer
endorse/to

signification
service

signifier à
serve/to

signifier un exploit
process

situation juridique
status

sociétaire
partner

société
body corporate

société acquéreur
purchasing

société canadienne
corporation

société constituée en personne
morale
society

société coopérative
cooperative

société d'affacturage
factoring

société d'État
corporation

société d'État mère
parent Crown corporation

société d'investissement à
capital variable
open-end mutual fund

société de capitaux à risque
venture

société de crédit
corporation

société de crédit-bail
leasing

société de fiducie
company

société de fonds mutuels
mutual fund

société de personnes
partnership

société de service bancaire
bank service corporation

société en commandite
limited partnership

société fiduciaire
company

société financière
body corporate

société immobilière à
dividendes limités
housing

société mandataire
agent

société mère
holding

société par actions
corporation

société par actions de régime
fédéral
Corporation

société pollicitée
corporation

Index

sodomie
buggery

solde créditeur
balance

solde d'opérations courantes
balance

solde débiteur
negative

solde négatif
negative

solidairement
joint

solidairement responsable
jointly and severally liable

sommation
summons

somme symbolique
consideration

souhaitable
advisable

soumission
bid

soumissionnaire
tenderer

soumissionnaire d'offres
tenderer

sous-location
sub-lease

sous-sol
subsoil

souscripteur
maker

souscripteur à forfait
underwriter

souscription à forfait
underwriting

souscrire
acquire/to

soutien
support

spéculation
adventure

statuer
deal/to

statuer sur une demande
determine/to

statuts
articles

statuts constitutifs
articles

statuts de fusion
amalgamation

sténographe judiciaire
stenographer

stipulation
agreement

stipulations
terms

stock-obligation
debenture

stupéfiant
narcotic

subdéléguer
authorize/to

subdivision
branch

subir son procès
stand trial/to

subir un préjudice
aggrieved/to be

substance
substance

substantiel
material

subvention
grant

successeur
successor

successeur aux biens
successor

successeur en propriété
successor

succession
estate

Index

succursale
branch

suppression
forfeiture

surarbitre
umpire

sûreté
interest

sûreté accessoire
collateral security

surintendant des assurances
Superintendent of Insurance

surintendant des faillites
Superintendent of Bankruptcy

surnuméraire
employee

surplus de bénéfices
earnings

sursis d'exécution
stay

surveillance
control

syndic
trustee

syndic de faillite
bankruptcy

syndicat
syndicate

syndicat de financement
syndicate

t

tantièmes
royalties

tarif d'honoraires
fees

tarif des droits
tariff

tarif des frais
tariff

taxation
taxation

taxe des frais
taxation

témoignage
evidence

témoignage contradictoire
evidence

témoignage contraire
evidence

témoignage oral
evidence

témoignage taxable
taxable

témoigner
evidence

témoin à décharge
witness

temps diurne
daylight

tenancier
keeper

tenancier en commun
tenant

teneur
purport

tentative
attempt

tenure à bail
leasehold

termes
words and expressions

terres
lands

terres domaniales
lands

Index

terres territoriales
territorial

testament
will

testament notarié
will

texte
enactment

texte réglementaire
statutory

textes d'application
regulation

tierce personne
third party

tiers
third party

tiers-arbitre
umpire

tiré
drawee

tirer
draw/to

tireur
drawer

titre
deed

titre de créance
debt

titre détérioré
damaged

titre incontestable
clear

titre testamentaire
instrument

titre valable
title

titres
obligations

titulaire
holder

toxicomane
narcotic addict

trafic
traffic

traite
draft

traite à vue
draft

traitement
salary

transaction
adjustment

transaction à distance
arm's length

transaction d'initiés
insider

transaction de change au
comptant
spot exchange transaction

transaction révisable
reviewable transaction

transférable
transferable

transfèrement
conveyance

transférer
transfer

transfert
transfer

transfert de possession
présumée
constructive possession

transiger
settle/to

transmettre la possession
possession

transmission
transmission

transport
conveyance

transporteur aérien
air

trésor
treasury

Trésor
Consolidated Revenue Fund

tribunal
court

tribunal compétent
jurisdiction

tribunal d'amirauté
admiralty

tribunal d'enregistrement
registering court

tribunal d'équité
equity

tribunal d'instruction sommaire
summary trial court

tribunal de droit
law

tribunal de droit et d'équité
equity

tribunal de première instance
jurisdiction

tribunal disciplinaire
disciplinary court

tribunal judiciaire
court

tribunal pour adolescents
youth court

troquer
barter/to

trouble de jouissance
affection

truquage des offres
bid-rigging

tutelle
guardianship

tuteur
guardian

u

unification
consolidation

unité de négociation
bargaining

unité en copropriété
condominium

urne
ballot

usage
custom

usager
user

usages de la Cour
practice

usure
criminal interest rate

usurpation
conversion

v

vacance judiciaire
vacation

valable
effective

valeur amortie
amortized value

valeur au pair
par value

valeur comptable
book value

valeur de réalisation
value

Index

valeur marchande
market

valeur mobilière
securities

valeur nominale
face value

valeur payable au porteur
bearer

valeur probante
probative force

valide
effect

vente
disposal

vente aux enchères
auction

vente en justice
execution

vente liée
tied selling

vente par le shérif
sale

vente pyramidale
pyramid selling

vente sur exécution
execution

vérificateur
auditor

vérificateur général du Canada
Auditor General of Canada

véritable propriétaire
ownership

vice
defect

vice caché
defect

vice de construction
defect

vice de forme
defect

violation
contravention

violation de la paix
breach

violation de la vie privée
invasion

violer un contrat
break/to

virement
transfer

virer
transfer/to

visa
endorsement

visé par notaire
notarially

viser
certify/to

voies de fait
assault

voir dire
voir dire

voiturier public
carrier

voix prépondérante
casting vote

vote positif
affirmative

W

warrant
warrant

warrant de transit
transfer

whip en chef du gouvernement
Chief Government Whip

whip suppléant du gouvernement
Deputy Government Whip

Z

zone entrecôtière
offshore

Autres publications du Bureau de la traduction

Bulletins de terminologie

- Administration municipale
- Archéologie
- Astronautique
- Bancaire
- Barrages
- Biotechnologie végétale
- Bourse et placement
- Budgétaire, comptable et financier
- Conditionnement d'air
- Cuivre et ses alliages
- Déchets solides
- Dépoussiérage industriel
- Divisions stratigraphiques, géomorphologiques et orogéniques du Canada
- Élections
- Fiscalité
- Génériques en usage dans les noms géographiques du Canada
- Guerre spatiale
- Hélicoptères
- Ichtyologie
- Intelligence artificielle
- Le langage parlementaire
- Logement et sol urbain
- Loisirs et parcs
- Micrographie
- Muséologie
- Précipitations acides et pollution atmosphérique
- Protection civile
- Recueil des définitions des lois fédérales
- Serrurerie
- Services sociaux et services de santé
- Sports d'hiver
- Titres de lois fédérales
- Transport des marchandises dangereuses
- Transports urbains

Other Translation Bureau Publications

Terminology Bulletins

- Acid Precipation and Air Pollution
- Air-Conditioning
- Archaeology
- Artificial Intelligence
- Astronautics
- Banking
- Budgetary, Accounting and Financial
- Copper and its Alloys
- Dams
- Door Locks and Fastenings
- Elections
- Emergency Preparedness
- Generic Terms in Canada's Geographical Names
- Health and Social Services
- Helicopters
- Housing and Urban Land
- Ichthyology
- Industrial Dust Control
- List of Definitions in Federal Statutes
- Micrography
- Municipal Administration
- Museology
- Parks and Recreation
- Plant Biotechnology
- Solid Waste
- Space War
- Stock Market and Investment
- Stratigraphical, Geomorphological and Orogenic Divisions of Canada
- Taxation
- The Language of Parliament
- Titles of Federal Acts
- Transportation of Dangerous Goods
- Urban Transportation
- Winter Sports

Collection Lexique

- Bureautique
- Classification et rémunération
- Comptabilité
- Diplomatie
- Dotation en personnel
- Droits de la personne
- Économie
- Éditique
- Emballage
- Enseignement postsecondaire
- Expressions usuelles des formulaires
- Finance
- Fournitures de bureau
- Gestion
- Gestion des documents
- Gestion financière
- Industries graphiques
- Informatique
- Pensions
- Planification de gestion
- Pluies acides
- Procédure parlementaire
- Régimes de travail
- Relations du travail
- Reprographie
- Réunions
- Services sociaux

Glossary Series

- Accounting
- Acid Rain
- Classification and Pay
- Common Phrases on Forms
- Desktop Publishing
- Diplomacy
- Economics
- Electronic Data Processing
- Finance
- Financial Management
- Graphic Arts
- Human Rights
- Labour Relations
- Management
- Management Planning
- Meetings
- Office Automation
- Office Supplies
- Packaging
- Parliamentary Procedure
- Pensions
- Postsecondary Education
- Records Management
- Reprography
- Social Services
- Staffing
- Work Systems

Langue et traduction

- Aide-mémoire d'autoperfectionnement à l'intention des traducteurs et des rédacteurs
- Guide du rédacteur de l'administration fédérale
- Guide du réviseur
- The Canadian Style: A Guide to Writing and Editing
- Vade-mecum linguistique

Language and Translation

Autre publication

- Bibliographie sélective : Terminologie et disciplines connexes

Other Publication

- Selective Bibliography: Terminology and Related Fields

L'Actualité terminologique

Bulletin d'information portant sur la recherche terminologique et la linguistique en général. (Abonnement annuel, 6 numéros)

On peut se procurer toutes les publications en écrivant à l'adresse suivante :

Centre d'édition du
  gouvernement du Canada
Approvisionnements et Services
  Canada
Ottawa (Ontario)
K1A 0S9
tél. : (819) 997-2560

ou par l'entremise des agents agréés ou de votre libraire.

Terminology Update

Information bulletin on terminological research and linguistics in general. (Annual subscription, 6 issues)

All publications may be obtained at the following address:

Canadian Government
  Publishing Centre
Supply and Services Canada
Ottawa, Ontario
K1A 0S9
tel.: (819) 997-2560

or through authorized bookstore agents or your local bookseller.